Programmed Learning Approach to
MEDICAL TERMINOLOGY

THIRD EDITION

Judi L. Nath, Ph.D.
Professor
Biology & Health Sciences
Lourdes University
Sylvania, Ohio

JONES & BARTLETT
LEARNING

World Headquarters
Jones & Bartlett Learning
5 Wall Street
Burlington, MA 01803
978-443-5000
info@jblearning.com
www.jblearning.com

Jones & Bartlett Learning books and products are available through most bookstores and online booksellers. To contact Jones & Bartlett Learning directly, call 800-832-0034, fax 978-443-8000, or visit our website, www.jblearning.com.

Substantial discounts on bulk quantities of Jones & Bartlett Learning publications are available to corporations, professional associations, and other qualified organizations. For details and specific discount information, contact the special sales department at Jones & Bartlett Learning via the above contact information or send an email to specialsales@jblearning.com.

Copyright © 2019 by Jones & Bartlett Learning, LLC, an Ascend Learning Company

All rights reserved. No part of the material protected by this copyright may be reproduced or utilized in any form, electronic or mechanical, including photocopying, recording, or by any information storage and retrieval system, without written permission from the copyright owner.

The content, statements, views, and opinions herein are the sole expression of the respective authors and not that of Jones & Bartlett Learning, LLC. Reference herein to any specific commercial product, process, or service by trade name, trademark, manufacturer, or otherwise does not constitute or imply its endorsement or recommendation by Jones & Bartlett Learning, LLC and such reference shall not be used for advertising or product endorsement purposes. All trademarks displayed are the trademarks of the parties noted herein. *Programmed Learning Approach to Medical Terminology, Third Edition* is an independent publication and has not been authorized, sponsored, or otherwise approved by the owners of the trademarks or service marks referenced in this product.

There may be images in this book that feature models; these models do not necessarily endorse, represent, or participate in the activities represented in the images. Any screenshots in this product are for educational and instructive purposes only. Any individuals and scenarios featured in the case studies throughout this product may be real or fictitious but are used for instructional purposes only.

This publication is designed to provide accurate and authoritative information in regard to the Subject Matter covered. It is sold with the understanding that the publisher is not engaged in rendering legal, accounting, or other professional service. If legal advice or other expert assistance is required, the service of a competent professional person should be sought.

20913-6

Production Credits
VP, Product Management: Amanda Martin
Director of Product Management: Cathy L. Esperti
Product Specialist: Ashley Malone
Product Coordinator: Elena Sorrentino
Digital Project Specialist: Angela Dooley
Director of Marketing: Andrea DeFronzo
Marketing Manager: Suzy Balk
Production Services Manager: Colleen Lamy
VP, Manufacturing and Inventory Control: Therese Connell
Product Fulfillment Manager: Wendy Kilborn
Composition: S4Carlisle Publishing Services
Project Management: S4Carlisle Publishing Services
Cover & Text Design: Scott Moden
Senior Media Development Editor: Troy Liston
Rights Specialist: Rebecca Damon
Printing and Binding: LSC Communications

Library of Congress Cataloging-in-Publication Data
Library of Congress Cataloging-in-Publication Data unavailable at time of printing.

LCCN: 2020933371

6048

Printed in the United States of America
24 23 22 21 20   10 9 8 7 6 5 4 3 2 1

To Mike, Gabbi, and Quincy,
who have been with me throughout every day and every page

Preface to the Student

SUMMARY OF TEXTBOOK OBJECTIVES

Upon completion of this text, you will be able to:
- Describe the origin of medical terminology.
- Analyze the parts of medical terms and use basic prefixes, suffixes, roots, and combining forms to build medical terms.
- Explain common rules for the proper formation, pronunciation, and spelling of medical terms.
- Identify common pharmaceutical terms and abbreviations used in documenting medical records.
- Identify common anatomical terms related to the major body systems.
- Identify common terms related to signs, symptoms, diagnoses, surgeries, therapies, and diagnostic tests related to the major body systems.
- Explain common terms and abbreviations used in documenting medical records related to the major body systems.

GETTING STARTED
Study Tips

To reach the goal of learning medical terminology, you'll need a reasonable plan for completion. Follow the study path that this text and/or your instructor provides, and work the necessary study time into your personal schedule.

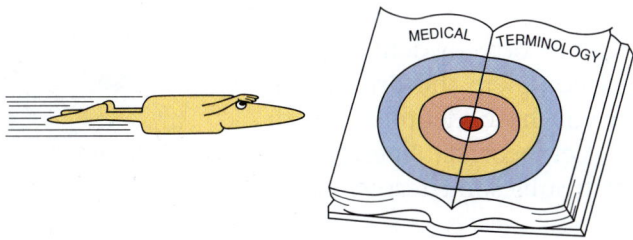

An effective memory depends on intricate processes that recall mental images of sights, sounds, feelings, tastes, and smells. For this reason, try to include as many senses as possible in the process of reinforcing learning. My students use the "see it, hear it, say it, read it, write it, learn it" approach for learning material.

SEE IT	Employ your visual sense (sight) by making and repeatedly reviewing any flash cards or notes you take.
HEAR IT	Listen to your instructor as the terms are pronounced.
SAY IT	Pronounce word parts and terms out loud to reinforce your auditory sense (hearing).
READ IT	Read your textbook carefully and re-read sections until you feel comfortable that you know the material.
WRITE IT	Write and rewrite responses to programmed review sections before highlighting the correct answers. Make flash cards by hand using pleasant colored paper and ink to satisfy your kinesthetic sense (feeling).
LEARN IT	Study at different times of the day and in different places, making sure that you take frequent breaks. Marathon study sessions are counterproductive. Remember that your goal is life-long learning, not just learning for a test.

Mnemonics Can Help

Mnemonics refer to letter patterns, ideas, or associations that help you remember something. The term is derived from the word *Mnemosyne*, the name of the Greek mythological goddess of memory. Mnemonic techniques link terms you want to remember with some other stimulus such as an image, a sound, or a smell. Consider the following applications:

- Make up rhymes or stories that help to differentiate between meanings. For example: *peri-*, the prefix meaning "around," is often confused with *para-*, the prefix meaning "alongside of." Use the two parts in a sentence to compare their meanings. For example, I sat *para* (**alongside of**) Sarah on the merry-*peri*-go-**around**. Often the most absurd associations can help you to remember. It doesn't matter if they don't make sense to anyone but you!
- Make up songs and rhymes to help remember facts. Take a song you are familiar with like "Row, row, row, your boat …" and insert words with definitions that are in tune with the song.
- Draw pictures depicting term parts for reinforcement.

Memory Drill

Give yourself a memory drill by listing word parts, symbols, or terms on one side of a paper and then filling in the definitions from memory. Write corrections in red ink. Make a list of the incorrectly defined parts on a separate paper, and complete the drill again. Repeat this process until you have identified which terms you most frequently get incorrect. Spend additional time studying those troublesome terms.

Slow

ADDITIONAL RESOURCES

Take advantage of the many fun and interactive learning activities provided in the book and on the text's online site. You'll find a variety of exercises to help you remember medical terminology and to reinforce what you've learned including:

- **Programmed Review Exercises**—After every Self-Instruction, you should complete the Programmed Review of that section. Repeat as often as necessary until you know the terms.

- **Practice Exercises and Medical Record Analyses**—Each chapter concludes with Practice Exercises and a Medical Record Analysis so that you can test your knowledge. Here you will find:
  - *Multiple choice* and *fill-in-the-blank* questions to support learning
  - *Figure-labeling* exercises to reinforce your knowledge of both medical terms and basic anatomy
  - *Matching exercises* in which you match combining forms or terms with definitions
  - *Spelling exercises* to help you recognize and correctly spell medical terms
  - *Medical records* that use actual reports so you can apply your learning to real-world examples
- **Review or Test Mode**—Study a single chapter or multiple chapters in a Review or Test environment to test your knowledge. Get comfortable taking tests in a variety of settings.

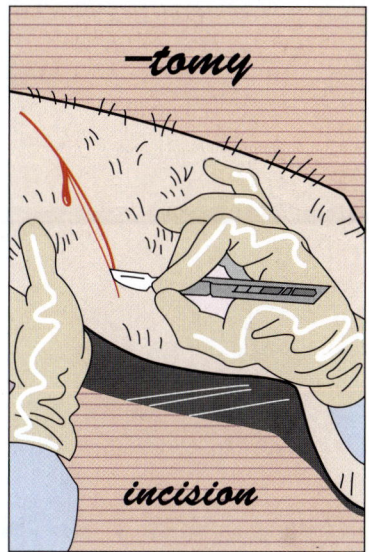

Ready, Set, Go!

Everything is laid out for you to proceed with your study. The techniques used here have proven beneficial in learning and are geared toward efficient memorization. Be creative and enjoy the learning process!

Preface to the Instructor

The third edition of *Programmed Learning Approach to Medical Terminology* provides a sequential, programmed process for learning medical language that is intended to meet the needs of students working independently or within a classroom. The approach is self-directed. Learning segments are presented in self-study increments followed by programmed review frames for immediate feedback and reinforcement. Diagrams, illustrations, and term tips support learning segments, and practice exercises at the end of each chapter provide additional reinforcement. Learning builds from an understanding of the origin of medical terms and basic term construction, to the comprehension of more difficult terms and concepts encountered in relation to the body systems and medical specialty areas. The process culminates in applying the knowledge to understanding selected medical records.

TEXT OVERVIEW

The first chapter delivers the basics for understanding the language of health care. Chapter 1 introduces basic term parts (prefixes, suffixes, and a selected number of combining forms) and shows how these structures are combined to form medical terms. Rules of pronunciation, spelling, and formation of singular and plural forms are included. Medical word parts introduced in this chapter are used repeatedly throughout the text. This chapter also explains how medical terms will be learned and reinforced throughout the text using health records. Common forms, formats, abbreviations, symbols, and methods of documenting patient care are introduced. This helps students understand basic communication between professionals, including physician/provider orders and prescriptions. This chapter prepares students for medical record analyses in succeeding chapters.

Chapters 2 through 14 cover terms related to body systems. Additional combining forms are introduced along with terms related to signs, symptoms, diagnoses, tests, procedures, surgeries, and therapies. After mastering the programmed portions and review exercises, completion of medical record analyses provides further reinforcement of learning through application of knowledge.

At the back of the text, you will find three valuable appendices, including:

- A glossary of medical term parts (prefixes, suffixes, and combining forms) listed both from term part to English meaning and from English meaning to term part
- A glossary of medical abbreviations and symbols
- The top 100 commonly prescribed drugs, including the brand name, generic name, class, and major therapeutic uses

Please contact your Jones & Bartlett Learning Account Representative for additional information on the Instructor Resources available with this text.

- A *Test Bank* to test students' knowledge of key concepts in the text
- *PowerPoint slides* for each chapter organized by learning objectives
- *Lesson plans* for each chapter
- *Image bank*

A solid understanding of medical terminology provides an essential foundation for any career in health care. The *Programmed Learning Approach to Medical Terminology, 3rd Edition*, product suite makes learning and teaching medical terminology a rewarding and exciting process.

User's Guide

Programmed Learning Approach to Medical Terminology, Third Edition, **is not just a textbook**—it is a complete learning resource that will help you understand and master medical terminology. To achieve this, numerous tools are included throughout the text to help you work through the material presented. Please take a few moments to look through this User's Guide to familiarize yourself with the features that will enhance your learning experience.

INTRODUCTORY CHAPTER

The first chapter sets the stage for learning throughout the text. Chapter 1 provides analysis of basic term parts and rules for forming, spelling, and pronouncing medical terms.

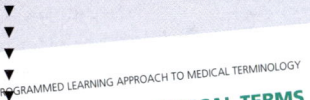

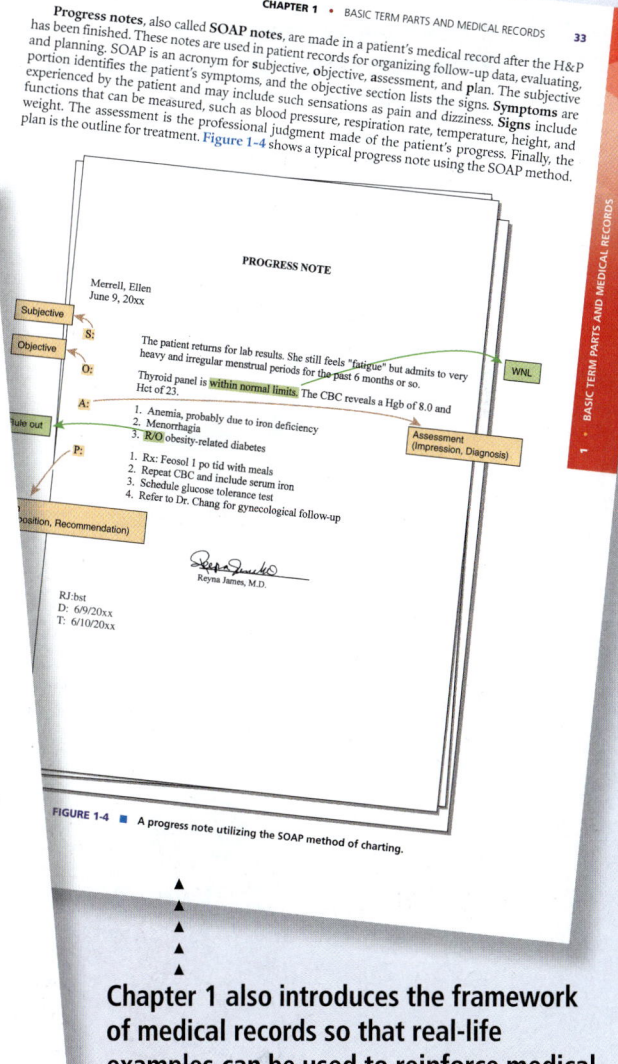

Chapter 1 also introduces the framework of medical records so that real-life examples can be used to reinforce medical terminology understanding. Subsequent chapters contain medical records using terms relevant to each body system.

LEARNING OUTCOMES

Use the learning outcomes at the beginning ▸▸▸▸ of each chapter to orient you to the section topics and to indicate what you should be able to do after completing the chapter.

BODY SYSTEM OVERVIEW

Chapters 2 through 14 open with a **body system overview**. The overview ▸▸▸▸ establishes a basis for each chapter, introducing the body system and laying the foundation for your work.

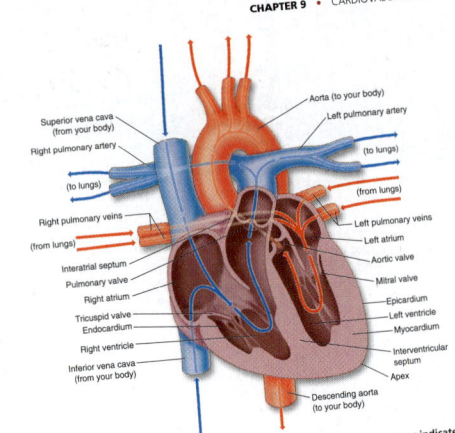

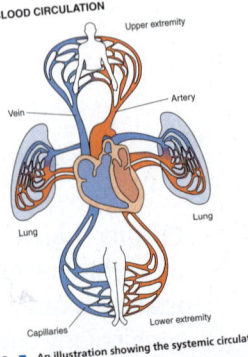

◂◂◂◂◂ Detailed illustrations present a visual overview of each body system being presented.

USER'S GUIDE xiii

FRAMES

This book is broken into learning frames. Two types of frames are used: Self-Instruction and Programmed Review.

The **Self-Instruction frames** help you memorize key terms and their word parts.

The **Programmed Review frames** feature fill-in-the-blank exercises to help you apply what you've memorized.

Use the **Reveal Card** to hide material in the left column while you complete the exercises in the right column.

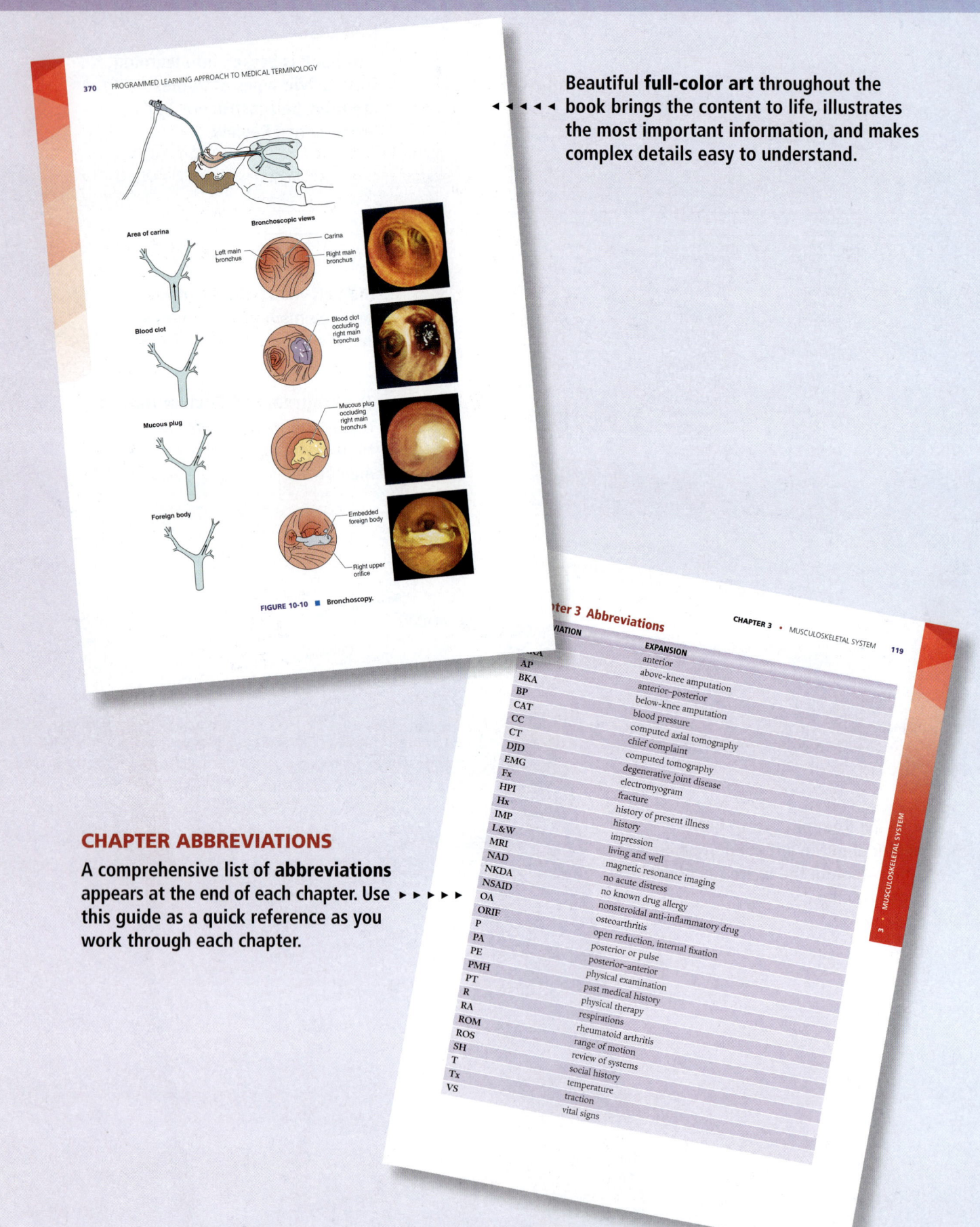

PRACTICE EXERCISES

Practice Exercises are included at the end of every chapter to help you completely understand the content, assess your progress, and review and prepare for quizzes and tests. Put your knowledge to the test with word building, figure-labeling, fill-in-the-blank, matching, spelling, and medical record exercises found throughout the book.

Acknowledgments

Writing textbooks that enhance the student learning experience is quite gratifying. Moreover, working with a team dedicated to the mission of education makes writing textbooks particularly satisfying.

To that end, I want to acknowledge the hard work and dedication of the people who were involved with this revision. The first round of thanks goes to my editor, Jonathan Joyce, for believing in me and bringing this project to my attention. He has two skills that are beyond critical in the publishing industry today: vision and perspective. Both are necessary for textbooks and authors. Another round of thanks goes to Amy Millholen and John Larkin. Their professional skills are of the highest level and greatly appreciated. They provide the necessary services, essential guidance, and positive attitude that get this project from Word documents to printed textbook. Jennifer Clements is fabulous to work with. She understands medical illustrating, and even more impressive is her ability to understand my notes on PDFs! I am deeply appreciative of my team: You make textbook writing more than a most pleasant avocation. To all, I extend my heartfelt thanks!

I am especially thankful for the work of Marjorie Canfield Willis. The programmed learning approach is an ingenious textbook that fulfills a need in today's classroom. Relinquishing the reins was likely tough, and I thank you for making my job as uncomplicated as possible.

As always, comments from reviewers shape the final product. Continuing editions are made possible through the work of those willing to share thoughts, advice, feedback, and comments. My thanks go out to each of them.

Reviewers

The author and publisher acknowledge the contributions of the following reviewers for their valuable comments and suggestions.

Valerie Coppenrath, PharmD, BCPS
Assistant Professor of Pharmacy Practice
School of Pharmacy
Massachusetts College of Pharmacy and Health Sciences
Worcester, Massachusetts

Kelly L. Coreas, MSHS, RRT-NPS
Program Director
Department of Respiratory Therapy
Mt. San Antonio College
Walnut, California

Stephanie J. Counts, PharmD, MEd
Course Coordinator
Department of Pharmacy Practice
Midwestern University
Glendale, Arizona

Patricia M. Crawford, BS
Assistant to Director of Nursing
Nursing/Medical Assisting (Adjunct Faculty)
Allegany College of Maryland
Cumberland, Maryland

Ron Gaines, BS, MS
Assistant Professor
Department of Biological Sciences
Cameron University
Lawton, Oklahoma

Robin Gardenhire, MA, ATC, CSCS
Clinical Instructor
Department of Respiratory Therapy
Byrdine F. Lewis School of Nursing and Health Professions
Georgia State University
Atlanta, Georgia

Gretchen Geller, BA, BSN, RN
Program Coordinator and Instructor
Department of Health Programs
Montana Tech
Butte, Montana

Lisa Ritchie, EdD, RDN, LD
Associate Professor/Director
Didactic Program in Nutrition and Dietetics
Department of Family and Consumer Sciences
Harding University
Searcy, Arkansas

Rodney M. Rutland, PhD
Associate Dean
Department of Arts and Sciences
Chair
Department of Kinesiology
Anderson University
Anderson, South Carolina

Donna Walsworth, RN, BSN
Instructor
Department of Adult Education
State University of New York at Genesco
Genesco, New York

Tamer Youssef, MD
Adjunct Professor
Department of Business and Technology
Northampton Community College
Bethlehem, Pennsylvania

Contents

CHAPTER 1   BASIC TERM PARTS AND MEDICAL RECORDS   1
CHAPTER 2   INTEGUMENTARY SYSTEM   44
CHAPTER 3   MUSCULOSKELETAL SYSTEM   80
CHAPTER 4   NERVOUS SYSTEM AND PSYCHIATRY   127
CHAPTER 5   THE EYE   180
CHAPTER 6   THE EAR   211
CHAPTER 7   ENDOCRINE SYSTEM   236
CHAPTER 8   BLOOD AND LYMPHATIC SYSTEM   267
CHAPTER 9   CARDIOVASCULAR SYSTEM   301
CHAPTER 10   RESPIRATORY SYSTEM   349
CHAPTER 11   DIGESTIVE SYSTEM   389
CHAPTER 12   URINARY SYSTEM   434
CHAPTER 13   MALE REPRODUCTIVE SYSTEM   468
CHAPTER 14   FEMALE REPRODUCTIVE SYSTEM AND OBSTETRICS   494
APPENDIX A   GLOSSARY OF PREFIXES, SUFFIXES, AND COMBINING FORMS   549
APPENDIX B   ABBREVIATIONS AND SYMBOLS   559
APPENDIX C   TOP 100 COMMONLY PRESCRIBED DRUGS   565

Index   571

BASIC TERM PARTS AND MEDICAL RECORDS

Learning Outcomes

After completing this chapter, you should be able to:

- Explain word prefixes, suffixes, roots, and combining forms.
- Know how to connect word parts to construct medical terms.
- Define medical terms through word construction analysis.
- Describe how to form medical terms.
- Cite the rules of pronunciation.
- Apply the rules for forming plural medical terms from singular medical terms.
- Describe the common types of medical records used in health care.
- Build a medical terminology vocabulary from the chapter contents.
- Cite common abbreviations and give the expansion of each.
- Explain terms used in medical records.

INTRODUCTION

Most medical terms have Greek or Latin origins. These terms date back to the founding of modern medicine by the Greeks and to the influence of Latin when it was the universal language in the Western world. Other languages, such as German and French, have also influenced medical terms. Many new terms are derived from English, which is considered the universal language today.

Most of the terms related to diagnosis and surgery have Greek origins, and most anatomic terms come from Latin.

Once you understand the basic medical term structure and know the commonly used prefixes, suffixes, word roots, and combining forms, you can learn the meaning of most medical terms by analyzing their components. Those mysterious words, which are almost frightening at first glance, will soon seem commonplace. You will learn to analyze each term you encounter with your new-found knowledge and the help of a good medical dictionary.

This chapter includes the most common prefixes and suffixes and a selection of common word roots and combining forms. More combining forms and other pertinent prefixes and suffixes are added in the following chapters as you learn terms related to specific body systems. This chapter also gives basic rules for proper medical term formation, pronunciation, and spelling.

START NOW

Make the most of each moment of study time available to you. The key to success in building a medical vocabulary is memorizing key prefixes, suffixes, root words, and combining forms.

How to Use Programmed Learning Sections

Take time to study the material in each self-instruction frame before starting a review section.

Remove the Reveal Card from the back cover of the text. Place the card over the left column of the page to hide the responses to the questions in the learning material in the right column. Slide the card down the page to reveal the answer only after you have written your response in the fill-in space on the right. Use a pencil so that you can quickly erase any wrong response and replace it with the correct one. Go over all the correct responses with a highlighter for additional reinforcement.

You can move at your own pace. Between study periods, use the Reveal Card as a bookmark. If you lose your Reveal Card, you can make your own by using a piece of paper measuring 10 in long and 2 in wide.

TERM PARTS

Most medical terms have several basic parts: root, prefix, suffix, and combining form. The **root** is the foundation or subject of the term. Medical terms have one or more roots. **Prefixes** are term beginnings that modify the term root. **Suffixes** are term endings that give essential meaning to the root. A **combining form** is a word root plus a combining vowel. Combining forms make it easier to form, spell, and pronounce medical terms (see **Figure 1-1**). Many terms can be defined by determining the meaning of the suffix first, then the prefix (if present), then the root(s). Study these tables to prepare for the programmed review that follows.

Self-Instruction: Term Parts

TERM PART	CATEGORY	MEANING
lip	root	fat
lip/o	combining form	fat
-emia	suffix	blood condition
hyper-	prefix	excessive
protein	root	protein

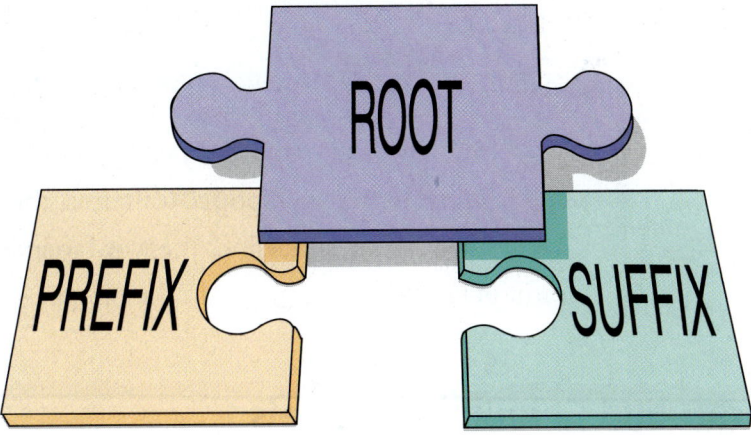

FIGURE 1-1 ■ Basic parts of medical terms. Each term is formed by combining at least one root and a suffix. A prefix is placed at the beginning of a term when needed to further modify the root or roots.

Programmed Review: Three Basic Parts

THE ROOT AND SUFFIX

ANSWERS	REVIEW
fat foundation or subject blood condition	**1.1** In the word lipemia, *lip* (meaning _____) is the root and _____ of the term. It is modified and given essential meaning by the suffix *-emia*, meaning _____ _____.
root, fat suffix, blood condition fat blood	**1.2** Breaking down and defining the key parts in a term often defines the term or gives clues to its meaning. In the term lipemia, *lip* is the _____ that means _____, and *-emia* is the _____ that means _____ _____. Memorizing key medical term parts makes it possible to decipher that the term refers to the condition of _____ in the _____. Note that lipemia is synonymous with lipidemia (formed from *lipid* and *-emia*).

THE PREFIX

ANSWERS	REVIEW
prefix beginning, modify excessive	**1.3** The prefix is a term part placed at the beginning of a term when needed to further modify the root or roots. For example, in the term hyperlipemia, *hyper-* is a _____ placed at the _____ of the term to further _____ the meaning of the term to denote _____ fat in the blood.

ADDITIONAL ROOTS

ANSWERS	REVIEW
root protein	1.4 Often, a medical term is formed from two or more roots. For example, in the term hyperlipo**protein**emia, the addition of the _____ *protein* further defines the word to indicate an excessive amount of fat and _____ in the blood.

Combining Forms and Combining Vowels

When a medical term has more than one root, the roots are joined together by a vowel, usually an "o." As shown in hyper/lip/o/protein/emia, the "o" is used to link the two roots, and it provides easier pronunciation. This vowel is known as a **combining vowel**. The letter "o" is the most common combining vowel ("i" is the second most common) and is used so frequently to join root to root or root to suffix that it is routinely attached to the root and presented as a **combining form**.

Programmed Review: Combining Forms and Combining Vowels

ANSWERS	REVIEW
root combining form o, combining vowel, i	1.5 In *lip/o*, *lip* is the _____ and *lip/o* is the _____ (a root with a combining vowel attached). The vowel ___ is the most common _____, and ___ is the second most common combining vowel.

This text uses combining forms rather than roots for easier term analysis. Each is presented with a slash between the root and the combining vowel. Hyphens are placed after prefixes to indicate their placement at the beginning of a medical term, and hyphens are placed before suffixes to indicate their link at the end of a term.

Programmed Review: Overview of Term Parts

ANSWERS	REVIEW
prefix root, suffix	1.6 Most medical terms have three basic parts: the _____, _____, and _____.
foundation or subject	1.7 The root is the _____ of the term.
suffix	1.8 The _____ is the word ending that modifies and gives essential meaning to the root.

CHAPTER 1 • BASIC TERM PARTS AND MEDICAL RECORDS

ANSWERS	REVIEW
prefix	1.9 The _____ is the part at the beginning of a term that is used when needed to further modify the root.
one	1.10 Often, a medical term is formed by _____ or more roots.
combining vowel, o	1.11 When a medical term has more than one root, it is joined together by a _____ _____, usually an ____.
root, vowel	1.12 A combining form is a _____ with a _____ attached.

Note that each part depends upon the other to express the meaning of the term. Few word parts can stand alone.

CONNECTING WORD PARTS TO CONSTRUCT MEDICAL TERMS

Study these tables to prepare for the programmed reviews that follow.

Self-Instruction: Rules for Constructing Terms

COMBINING FORM	MEANING
angi/o, vas/o, vascul/o	vessel
cardi/o	heart
enter/o	small intestine
esophag/o	esophagus
gastr/o	stomach
hem/o, hemat/o	blood
hepat/o	liver
oste/o	bone
ur/o, urin/o	urine

SUFFIX	MEANING
-al, -eal	pertaining to
-ectasis	expansion or dilation
-ectomy	excision (removal)
-ia	condition of
-itis	inflammation
-logy	study of
-megaly	enlargement
-stomy	creation of an opening
-tomy	incision

PREFIX	MEANING
oligo-	few or deficient
para-	alongside of, abnormal
peri-	around

Once you understand the basics of constructing medical terms, the next steps are to memorize common term parts and to learn the rules for joining medical term parts correctly. Study the Five Basic Rules for Constructing Terms in the box below. Apply these rules to form terms in the Programmed Reviews that follow.

Programmed Review: Five Basic Rules for Constructing Terms

ANSWERS	REVIEW
enlargement of the liver	**1.13** A combining vowel is used to join root to root as well as root to any suffix beginning with a consonant (any letter *except* a, e, i, o, or u): *hepat/o* + *-megaly* is spelled hepatomegaly and is defined as _____.
excision (removal) of a vessel	**1.14** A combining vowel is *not* used before a suffix that begins with a vowel: *vas/o* + *-ectomy* is spelled vasectomy and is defined as _____.
inflammation of the heart	**1.15** If the root ends in a vowel and the suffix begins with the same vowel, drop the final vowel from the root and do *not* use a combining vowel: *cardi/o* + *-itis* is spelled carditis and is defined as _____.
pertaining to the heart and esophagus	**1.16** Most often, a combining vowel is inserted between two roots even when the second root begins with a vowel: *cardi/o* + *esophag/o* + *-eal* is spelled cardioesophageal and is defined as _____.
pertaining to alongside of the small intestine	**1.17** Occasionally, when a prefix ends in a vowel and the root begins with a vowel, the final vowel is dropped from the prefix: *para-* + *enter/o* + *-al* is spelled parenteral and is defined as _____.

Note that all these rules have exceptions. Follow the basic guidelines set forth in this text, but be prepared to accept the exceptions as you encounter them. Rely upon your medical dictionary for additional guidance.

CHAPTER 1 • BASIC TERM PARTS AND MEDICAL RECORDS

In the following review, construct words using the rules previously given and give the meaning for each term.

Programmed Review: Putting the Rules into Practice

ANSWERS	REVIEW
angiectasis expansion or dilation of a vessel	**1.18** *angi/o* + *-ectasis* is spelled _____ and means _____.
gastrotomy incision in the stomach	**1.19** *gastr/o* + *-tomy* is spelled _____ and means _____.
hematology study of blood	**1.20** *hemat/o* + *-logy* is spelled _____ and means _____.
gastroenterostomy creation of an opening (between) the stomach and small intestine	**1.21** *gastr/o* + *enter/o* + *-stomy* is spelled _____ and means _____.
oliguria condition of deficient urine	**1.22** *oligo-* + *ur/o* + *-ia* is spelled _____ and means _____.
ostectomy excision (removal) of bone	**1.23** *oste/o* + *-ectomy* is spelled _____ and means _____.
pericarditis inflammation around the heart	**1.24** *peri-* + *cardi/o* + *-itis* is spelled _____ and means _____.

DEFINING MEDICAL TERMS THROUGH WORD STRUCTURE ANALYSIS

You can usually define a term by interpreting the suffix first, then the prefix (if one is present), and then the root or roots.

EXAMPLE:

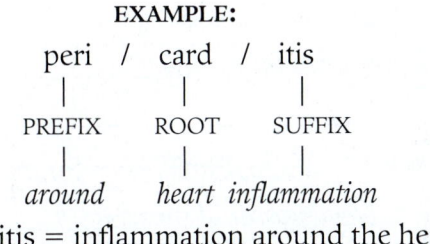

pericarditis = inflammation around the heart

You sense the basic meaning of the term pericarditis by understanding its parts; however, the dictionary clarifies that the term refers to inflammation of the pericardium, which is the sac enclosing the heart.

Beginning students often have difficulty differentiating between prefixes and roots (or combining forms) because the root appears first in a medical term when a prefix is not used. It is important to memorize the most common prefixes so that you can tell the difference. Also, keep in mind that a prefix is used only as needed to further modify the root or roots.

THE FORMATION OF MEDICAL TERMS

Study these tables to prepare for the programmed review that follows.

Self-Instruction: Patterns of Term Formation

COMBINING FORM	MEANING
cardi/o	heart
vascul/o	vessel

SUFFIX	MEANING
-ac, -al, -ar	pertaining to
-dynia	pain
-ium	structure or tissue
-logy	study of
-rrhaphy	suture
-rrhexis	rupture

PREFIX	MEANING
endo-	within
epi-	upon
sub-	below or under

Medical terms are built from the root. Prefixes and suffixes are attached to the root to modify its meaning. Two or more roots are often linked together before being modified. The following examples show the common patterns of medical term formation using the root *cardi* (heart) as a base. Using the term parts listed earlier, define the term as you examine each pattern.

Programmed Review: Patterns of Term Formation

ANSWERS	REVIEW
pertaining to the heart	**1.25** Root/Suffix *cardi/ac* means _____.
structure or tissue upon the heart	**1.26** Prefix/Root/Suffix *epi/card/ium* means _____.
pertaining to below or under and within the heart	**1.27** Prefix/Prefix/Root/Suffix *sub/endo/cardi/al* means _____.
pertaining to the heart and vessels	**1.28** Root/Combining Vowel/Root/Suffix *cardi/o/vascul/ar* means _____.

ANSWERS	REVIEW
study of the heart	**1.29** Root/Combining Vowel/Suffix *cardi/o/logy* means _____.
pain in the heart	**1.30** Root/Combining Vowel/Suffix (Symptomatic) [page 18] *cardi/o/dynia* means _____.
rupture of the heart	**1.31** Root/Combining Vowel/Suffix (Diagnostic) [page 18] *cardi/o/rrhexis* means _____.
suture of the heart	**1.32** Root/Combining Vowel/Suffix (Surgical/Operative) [page 19] *cardi/o/rrhaphy* means _____.

Acceptable Term Formations

As you learn medical terms, you can have fun experimenting with creating words, such as *glyco* (sweet) + *cardio* (heart) = sweetheart! However, in the real medical world, a term must be accepted by the medical community for it to be considered a legitimate word. Often, there seems to be no reason why a word became acceptable. If in doubt, always check your medical dictionary for the correct spelling, formation, or precise meaning of a term.

A FEW EXCEPTIONS

Most medical terms are formed by the combination of a root or roots that are modified by suffixes and prefixes, as shown earlier in this section. Occasionally, terms are formed by a root alone or by a combination of roots.

EXAMPLES:

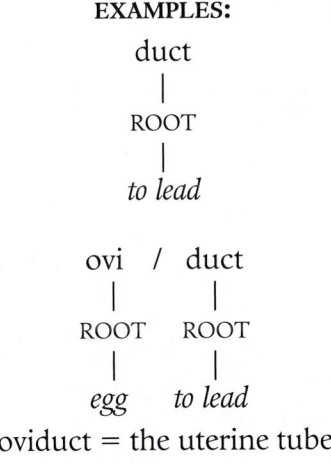

oviduct = the uterine tube

Sometimes, a term is formed by the combination of a prefix and suffix.

EXAMPLE:

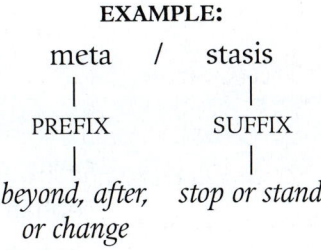

metastasis = the spread of a disease, such as cancer, from one location to another

SPELLING MEDICAL TERMS

Correct spelling of medical terms is crucial for communication among healthcare professionals. Careless spelling causes misunderstandings that can have serious consequences. The following list shows some of the pitfalls to avoid.

1. Some words sound the same but are spelled differently and have different meanings. Context is the clue to spelling. For example:

    ileum (part of the intestine)   ilium (part of the hip bone)
    sitology (study of food)   cytology (study of cells)

2. Other words sound similar but are spelled differently and have different meanings. For example:

    abduction (to draw away from)   adduction (to draw toward)
    hepatoma (liver tumor)   hematoma (blood tumor)
    aphagia (inability to swallow)   aphasia (inability to speak)

3. When letters are silent in a term, they risk being omitted when spelling the word. For example:

    "pt" has a "t" sound if found at the beginning of a term (e.g., pterygium), but both the "p" and "t" are pronounced when found within a term (e.g., nephroptosis [něf-rop-tō′sis])

    "ph" has an "f" sound (e.g., diaphragm)

    "ps" has an "s" sound (e.g., psychology)

4. Some words have more than one accepted spelling. For example:

    orthopedic   orthopaedic
    leukocyte   leucocyte

5. Some combining forms have the same meaning but different origins that compete for usage. For example, there are three combining forms that mean uterus:

    hyster/o (Greek)
    metr/o (Greek)
    uter/o (Latin)

RULES OF PRONUNCIATION

When you are beginning to learn how to pronounce medical terms, the task can seem too great to some. Saying a term out loud for the first time can be a tense moment! The best way to make sure you get it right is through preparation: study the basic rules of pronunciation found in this chapter; repeat the words after your instructor has said them; and try to keep the company of others who use medical language. You will soon discover that there is nothing quite like the validation you feel when you correctly say something "medical" and no one flinches! Your confidence will build with every word you use.

Use these helpful shortcuts to master the pronunciation of medical terminology.

SHORTCUTS TO PRONUNCIATION

CONSONANT	EXAMPLE
c (before a, o, u) = k	cavity, colon, cure
c (before e, i) = s	cephalic, cirrhosis
ch = k	cholesterol

CONSONANT	EXAMPLE
g (before a, o, u) = g	gallstone, gonad, gurney
g (before e, i) = j	generic, giant
ph = f	phase
pn = n	pneumonia
ps = s	psychology
pt = t	ptosis, pterygium
rh, rrh = r	rhythm, hemorrhoid
x (as first letter in a word) = z	xerosis

Phonetic spelling for the pronunciation of most medical terms in this text is provided in parentheses below the term. The phonetic system used here is basic and has only a few standard rules. Diacritical marks are symbols that indicate different pronunciations of a letter. The macron (mā'-krăn) and breve (brĕv) are two common diacritical marks. The macron (¯) is a straight line placed over vowels that have a long sound:

ā in day

ē in bee

ī in pie

ō in no

ū in unit

The breve (˘) is a u-shaped symbol placed over vowels that have a short sound:

ă in alone

ĕ in ever

ĭ in pit

ŏ in ton

ŭ in sun

Vowels that are not accented have a flat sound:

a in mat

e in bed

i in hip

o in got

u in put

The primary accent (') is placed after the syllable that is stressed when saying the word. Monosyllables do not have a stress mark. Other syllables are separated by hyphens.

SINGULAR AND PLURAL FORMS

Plurals are usually formed by adding "s" or "es" to the end of a singular form. The following are common exceptions for forming plurals of Latin and Greek derivatives.

Self-Instruction: Singular and Plural Forms

Study this table to prepare for the programmed review that follows.

SINGULAR ENDING	EXAMPLE	PLURAL ENDING	EXAMPLE
-a	vertebra *věr′tĕ-bră*	-ae	vertebrae *věr′tĕ-brā*
-is	diagnosis *dī-ag-nō′sis*	-es	diagnoses *dī-ag-nō′sēz*
-ma	condyloma *kon-di-lō′mă*	-mata	condylomata *kon′di-lō-mah′tă*
-on	phenomenon *fĕ-nom′ĕ-non*	-a	phenomena *fĕ-nom′ĕ-nă*
-um	bacterium *bak-tēr′ē-ym*	-a	bacteria *bak-tēr′ē-ă*
-us[a]	fungus *fŭng′gŭs*	-i	fungi *fn′jī*
-ax	thorax *thō′raks*	-aces	thoraces *thō-rā′sēz*
-ex	apex *ā′peks*	-ices	apices *ap′i-sēs*
-ix	appendix *ă-pen′diks*	-ices	appendices *ă-pen′di-sēz*
-y	myopathy *mī-op′ă-thē*	-ies	myopathies *mī-op′ă-thēz*

[a]The words *virus* and *sinus* follow the usual rule of adding "s" or "es" to form the plural (viruses and sinuses) instead of using the Latin plural ending *-i*.

Programmed Review: Singular and Plural Forms

ANSWERS	REVIEW
t	**1.33** The *pt* in *pterygium* has a/an ____ sound.
ova	**1.34** An ovum is a fertilized egg. Two fertilized eggs are called _____.
k	**1.35** The *ch* in *chronic* has a/an ____ sound.
metastases	**1.36** The spread of cancer to a distant organ is called metastasis. The spread of cancer to more than one organ is _____.
s	**1.37** The *c* in *cirrhosis* has a/an ____ sound.
verrucae	**1.38** A verruca is a wart. The term for several warts is _____.
z	**1.39** The *x* in *xerosis* has a/an ____ sound.
condyloma	**1.40** Condylomata are genital warts. One genital wart is a _____.
j	**1.41** The *g* in *genital* has a/an ____ sound.

ANSWERS	REVIEW
index	1.42 Indices is a plural form of _____.
thrombi	1.43 A thrombus is a clot. Several clots are termed _____.
n	1.44 The *pn* in *pneumatic* has a/an ____ sound.

BUILDING A VOCABULARY

The key to building a medical vocabulary is to know and understand the basic term parts. To start you on your way, study and memorize the following lists of common prefixes, suffixes, and combining forms used in medical language. Refer to Appendix A for a summary list of prefixes, suffixes, and combining forms.

Common Prefixes

Prefixes are term parts found at the beginning of a word when needed to further modify the root or roots. A list of commonly used prefixes organized into categories follows. Study these tables to prepare for the programmed review that follows.

Self-Instruction: Common Prefixes

PREFIX	MEANING
NEGATION	
a-	without
an-	without
anti-	against or opposed to
contra-	against or opposed to
de-	from, down, or not
POSITION/DIRECTION	
ab-	away from
ad-	to, toward, or near
circum-	around
dia-, trans-	across or through
e-	out or away
ec-	out or away
ecto-	outside
exo-	outside
extra-	outside
en-	within
endo-	within
epi-	upon
ex-	out or away

PREFIX	MEANING
infra-	below or under
inter-	between
intra-	within
meso-	middle
meta-	beyond, after, or change
para-	alongside of or abnormal
peri-	around
retro-	backward or behind
sub-	below or under

QUANTITY OR MEASUREMENT

bi-	two or both
hemi-	half
hyper-	above or excessive
hypo-	below or deficient
macro-	large or long
micro-	small
mono-	one
multi-	many
oligo-	few or deficient
pan-	all
poly-	many
semi-	half
quadri-	four
super-	above or excessive
supra-	above or excessive
tri-	three
uni-	one
ultra-	beyond or excessive

TIME

ante-	before
brady-	slow
tachy-	fast
post-	after or behind
pre-	before
pro-	before
re-	again or back

PREFIX	MEANING
GENERAL PREFIXES	
con-	together or with
dys-	painful, difficult, or faulty
eu-	good or normal
neo-	new
sym-	together or with
syn-	together or with

Programmed Review: Common Prefixes

ANSWERS	REVIEW
away to, toward, or near around across or through out or away one, bi	**1.45** Several prefixes modify position or direction when used in a term. **Ab**duction is used to describe movement _____ from the body, and **ad**duction describes movement _____ the body. **Circum**duction is movement that is _____. A diagonal is an angle that moves _____. **In**version refers to turning in, and **e**version means to turn _____. **Uni**lateral refers to _____ side, whereas _____**lateral** means both sides.
below or under upon across or through within, intra outside between inter, out away, below or under infra	**1.46** **Sub**cutaneous pertains to _____ the skin. **Epi**dermal refers to something _____ the skin, whereas **trans**dermal pertains to _____ the skin. **Intra**dermal pertains to _____ the skin. That which is within a cell is _____cellular. **Extra**cellular pertains to _____ a cell. *Inter-*, a prefix meaning _____, is used in the term describing that which is between cells: _____cellular. **Ec**centric is situated _____ or _____ from center. *Infra-*, a prefix meaning _____, is used to indicate a position below the part to which it is joined. For example, _____umbilical refers to a position below or under the umbilicus (navel).
within endo, middle meso outside, ecto	**1.47** Layers of embryonic tissue are named for their position. *Endo-*, meaning _____, is used to describe the innermost layer, or _____derm. *Meso-*, meaning _____, is used to name the middle layer, or _____derm. *Ecto-*, meaning _____, is used to identify the outer layer, or _____derm.

ANSWERS	REVIEW
exo endo within	**1.48** Glands that secrete within the body are the endocrine glands, and those that secrete outside are the _____crine glands. An instrument to examine within the body is an _____scope. When something is encapsulated, it is held _____.
deficient excessive hypo hyper below above above, excessive above excessive beyond ultra	**1.49** *Hypo-* means below or _____, and *hyper-* means above or _____. A patient with a deficient level of blood glucose (sugar) has a condition of _____glycemia. A condition of excessive blood glucose is _____glycemia. **Hypo**thermia is a condition in which the body temperature is _____ normal, whereas **hyper**thermia is a condition of body temperature well _____ normal. Like *hyper-*, *super-* and *supra-* are prefixes meaning _____ or _____. **Supra**renal pertains to a location _____ the kidney. **Super**numerary pertains to numbers that are above or _____ (too many to count). *Ultra-* is a prefix meaning _____ or excessive. The term describing high-frequency sound beyond that which can be heard by humans is known as _____sound.
large small macro, micro	**1.50** *Macro-* refers to something _____ or long, and *micro-* refers to something _____. A large cell is called a _____cyte. A small cell is called a _____cyte.
mono-, one bi-, tri- quadri-, many one many three four	**1.51** *Uni-* and _____ are prefixes meaning _____. The prefix for two is _____, three is _____, and four is _____. *Multi-* and *poly-* mean _____. **Mono**neuropathy describes the disease of _____ nerve, whereas polyneuropathy involves _____ nerves. A triangle has _____ sides. **Quadri**plegia is a condition of paralysis of all _____ limbs.
all Pan	**1.52** *Pan-* is a prefix meaning _____. A panacea is a cure-all. _____sinusitis refers to an inflammation of all of the sinuses.
semi- one-half	**1.53** The two prefixes meaning one-half are *hemi-* and _____. **Semi**lunar pertains to a half-moon shape. **Hemi**cephalic pertains to _____-_____ of the head.

ANSWERS	REVIEW
without an a, painful difficult, or faulty dys a	**1.54** *A-* and *an-* are prefixes meaning _____. *An-* is used before a vowel. For example, aerobic pertains to air, and ____aerobic pertains to without air. A patient without the ability to speak has a condition called ___phasia. *Dys-* is a prefix meaning _____ _____. **Dys**phasia is a condition of difficult speech. A condition of difficulty swallowing is termed _____phagia. The patient without the ability to swallow has _____phagia.
contra-, against or opposed to anti-	**1.55** Two prefixes meaning against or opposed to are *anti-* and _____. A **contra**ceptive is _____ conception. An _____inflammatory drug acts against or opposed to inflammation by reducing it.
from, down, or not again before backward or behind	**1.56** **De**activated refers to something that is _____ active. When something is reactivated, it is made active _____. **Pro**active refers to an action made _____. **Retro**position refers to a structure that is _____.
fast slow, tachy brady slow fast	**1.57** *Tachy-* is a prefix meaning _____, and *brady-* means _____. A condition of fast heart is _____cardia. A condition of slow heart is _____cardia. **Brady**pnea refers to _____ breathing, whereas **tachy**pnea refers to _____ breathing.
before pre around, after Neo	**1.58** Natal pertains to birth. **Ante**natal is the time _____ birth, also known as the _____natal period. **Peri**natal is the time _____ birth, and **post**natal is the time _____ birth. _____natal pertains to newborn.
good or normal painful, difficult, or faulty	**1.59** *Toc/o* is a combining form meaning labor. Eutocia is a condition of _____ labor, and **dys**tocia is a condition of _____ labor.
together with with together sym	**1.60** *Con-*, *syn-*, and *sym-* are prefixes meaning _____ or _____. A **con**genital disorder is one that an infant is born _____. *Dactyl/o* is a combining form meaning finger or toe. **Syn**dactylism is a condition of fingers or toes that are fused _____. *Syn-* appears as *sym-* before b, p, ph, or m. For example, the term describing the condition in which different species can live together is _____biosis.

Common Suffixes

Suffixes are endings that modify the root. These endings give the root essential meaning by forming a noun, verb, or adjective. The two basic types of suffixes are simple and compound. Simple suffixes form basic terms. For example, the simple suffix *-ic* (pertaining to) combined with the root *gastr* (stomach) forms the term gastric (pertaining to the stomach). Compound suffixes are formed by a combination of basic word parts. For example, the root *tom* (to cut) combined with the simple suffix *-y* (a process of) forms the compound suffix *-tomy* (incision); the compound suffix *-ectomy* (excision or removal) is formed by a combination of the prefix *ec-* (out) with the root *tom* (to cut) and the simple suffix *-y* (a process of).

Compound suffixes are added to roots to provide a specific meaning. For example, combining the root *hyster* (uterus) with *-ectomy* forms hysterectomy (excision of the uterus). Noting the differences between simple and compound suffixes will help you to analyze medical terms.

Suffixes in this text are divided into four categories:

1. Symptomatic suffixes, which describe the evidence of illness
2. Diagnostic suffixes, which provide the name of a medical condition
3. Surgical (operative) suffixes, which describe a surgical treatment
4. General suffixes, which have general application

A listing of commonly used suffixes follows. Study these tables to prepare for the programmed review that follows.

Self-Instruction: Common Suffixes

SUFFIX	MEANING
SYMPTOMATIC SUFFIXES (Word Endings That Describe Evidence of Illness)	
-algia	pain
-dynia	pain
-genesis	origin or production
-lysis	breaking down or dissolution
-megaly	enlargement
-oid	resembling
-penia	abnormal reduction
-rrhea	discharge
-spasm	involuntary contraction
DIAGNOSTIC SUFFIXES (Word Endings That Describe a Condition or Disease)	
-cele	pouching or hernia
-ectasis	expansion or dilation
-emia	blood condition
-iasis	formation or presence of
-itis	inflammation
-malacia	softening

SUFFIX	MEANING
-oma	tumor
-osis	condition or increase
-phil	attraction for
-philia	attraction for
-ptosis	falling or downward displacement
-rrhage	excessive discharge (usually blood)
-rrhagia	excessive discharge (usually blood)
-rrhexis	rupture

SURGICAL (OPERATIVE) SUFFIXES
(Word Endings That Describe a Surgical [Operative] Treatment)

Suffix	Meaning
-centesis	puncture for aspiration
-desis	binding
-ectomy	excision (removal)
-pexy	suspension or fixation
-plasty	surgical repair or reconstruction
-rrhaphy	suture
-tomy	incision
-stomy	creation of an opening

GENERAL SUFFIXES
(Simple or Compound Suffixes That Have General Application)

Suffix	Meaning
-ation	process
-e	general indicator that a word is a person, place, or thing
-ia	condition of
-ism	condition of
-ium	structure or tissue
-y	condition or process of

Adjective Endings (suffixes that form an adjective when combined with a root)

Suffix	Meaning
-ac, -al, -ar, -ary, -eal, -ic, -ous, -tic	pertaining to

Diminutive Endings (suffixes meaning small)

Suffix	Meaning
-icle, -ole, -ula, -ule	small

Other General Suffixes

Suffix	Meaning
-gram	record
-graph	instrument for recording
-graphy	process of recording

SUFFIX	MEANING
-iatric	pertaining to medicine, a physician, or healer
-iatry	treatment
-logy	study
-logist	one who specializes in the study or treatment of
-ist	one who specializes in
-meter	instrument for measuring
-metry	process of measuring
-poiesis	formation
-scope	instrument for examination
-scopy	process of examination
-stasis	stop or stand

We have the Greeks to thank for the suffixes with double rr's. Take a careful look at each so that you will spell them correctly in a term! Each component also has an *h*, and *-rrhaphy* has two! Study these tables to prepare for the programmed review that follows.

Suffix	Meaning	Example
-rrhea	discharge	pyorrhea (a discharge of pus)
-rrhage or -rrhagia	excessive discharge (usually blood)	hemorrhage (an excessive discharge of blood) menorrhagia (an excessive discharge of blood during menstruation)
-rrhexis	rupture	angiorrhexis (a rupture of a vessel)
-rrhaphy	suture	nephrorrhaphy (a suture of the kidney)

Programmed Review: Common Suffixes

ANSWERS	REVIEW
stomach	**1.61** *Gastr/o* is a combining form meaning _____.
prefix, upon	In epigastrium, *epi-* is the _____ meaning _____, and
-ium, suffix	_____ is the _____, a noun ending meaning
structure, tissue	_____ or _____. The noun endings *-ia* and

ANSWERS	REVIEW
condition of process of process, noun	-ism, as seen in the terms pneumonia and hypothyroidism, refer to a _____. The -y ending in atrophy indicates a condition or _____. The suffix in extravasation denotes a _____. The -e in erythrocyte is a _____ marker.
-ic pertaining to upon, epigastrium -eal pertaining to esophagus pertaining to	1.62 In epigastric, use of the suffix _____ forms an adjective that means _____ the stomach—specifically referring to the tissue region _____ the stomach known as the _____. In gastroesophageal, _____ is the adjective ending that modifies the term to mean _____ the stomach and _____. Several other suffixes form adjectives, as noted in the terms cardiac, pedal, glandular, pulmonary, esophageal, hypnotic, and fibrous, and also mean _____.
ending pain enlargement discharge involuntary contraction symptomatic illness	1.63 A symptomatic suffix is a term _____ used to describe evidence of illness. The suffixes -algia or -dynia (meaning _____), -megaly (meaning _____), -rrhea (meaning _____), and -spasm (meaning _____) are examples of suffixes used to form _____ terms that describe evidence of _____.
gastralgia or gastrodynia epigastralgia gastrospasm rrhea gastromegaly	1.64 The symptomatic term that describes stomach pain is _____. Pain located in the tissue upon the stomach is termed _____. Involuntary contraction of the stomach is called _____, and the discharge of gastric juice from the stomach is termed gastro_____. Enlargement of the stomach is termed _____.
pain examination stomach within gastroscope	1.65 Physical examination and test procedures are key to identifying the cause of symptoms to make a diagnosis. A diagnosis is the name of a condition or disease. In evaluating the cause of a symptom such as gastrodynia, or _____ in the stomach, a gastroscopy or _____ of the _____ may be performed. The specific endoscope (instrument to examine _____) used in gastroscopy is called a _____.

ANSWERS	REVIEW
endings diagnosis gastritis iasis gastromalacia pouching, hernia gastrocele blood burst forth gastrorrhagia stasis	**1.66** Diagnostic suffixes are word _____ used to describe a condition or name of a disease, called a _____. If, on gastroscopic examination, the physician notes an inflammation of the stomach, a diagnosis of _____ is made. The presence of a stone in the stomach is termed gastrolith_____. A finding of softening of the stomach wall is referred to as _____. The suffix *-cele*, meaning _____ or _____, is used in the term describing a pouching or hernia of the stomach: _____. Hemorrhage, a term referring to bleeding, was formed by the link of *hem/o*, a combining form meaning _____, with *-rrhage*, a suffix meaning to _____, usually about blood. Using the suffix *-rrhagia*, the condition of bursting forth of blood from the stomach is called _____. The suffix meaning stop or stand is used in the term describing efforts to stop hemorrhaging blood: hemo_____.
stomach suffix, study of gastroenterologist	**1.67** Gastroenterology, a term formed by a link of *gastr/o* (meaning _____), *enter/o* (meaning small intestine), and *-logy* (a _____ meaning _____ _____), is the name of the medical specialty involved with the study of gastrointestinal conditions. Using the suffix referring to one who specializes in the study or treatment of, the physician who specializes in the treatment of the stomach and intestines is called a _____.
condition, increase stenosis gastrostenosis	**1.68** Many symptomatic and diagnostic terms use the suffix *-osis* to indicate a _____ or _____. For example, when combined with *sten/o*, a combining form meaning narrow, the term for a condition or increase of narrowing is _____. A narrowed condition of the stomach is therefore called _____.
endings operative -tomy, gastrotomy gastrectomy downward displacement, stomach	**1.69** Once a diagnosis is made, treatment follows. Some treatments require surgery. Surgical/operative suffixes are term _____ that describe a surgical or _____ treatment. The first step in a surgical procedure is to make an incision, the suffix for which is _____. An incision in the stomach is called a _____. Given a diagnosis of stomach tumor, a surgical remedy might involve a partial or complete removal of the stomach, called a _____. Gastroptosis, defined as a falling or _____ _____ of the _____, may necessitate a surgical suspension

ANSWERS	REVIEW
pexy gastroplasty	or fixation, called a gastro_____. The operative term describing a surgical repair of the stomach is _____. In some cases, the creation of an opening is required, such as to bypass a diseased part. The creation of a new opening in the stomach
gastrostomy gastrorrhaphy	is called _____. Perforation of the stomach requires gastrorrhaphy suturing, the operative term for which is _____. When fluid builds up within the abdominal cavity because of illness or injury, a puncture for aspiration is required. The suffix meaning
-centesis -desis	puncture for aspiration is _____. The surgical suffix specifically referring to binding of tissue is _____.
-icle -iole, -ula, -ule	**1.70** Other general suffixes are commonly seen in health records. Those referring to diminutives (something small) are _____, _____, _____, and _____, as seen in the terms vent**ricle**, bronch**iole**, mac**ula**, and ven**ule**.
record graph electrocardiography measuring instrument	**1.71** You will find several general suffixes describing diagnostic testing. For example, *-gram* is a suffix meaning _____. An electrocardiogram (ECG) is a record of the electrical conduction of the heart. The instrument for recording an ECG is called an electrocardio_____ machine. This process of recording is referred to as _____. The suffix *-metry* is a suffix referring to the process of _____. A thermometer is an _____ for measuring temperature.

Common Combining Forms

The following table shows selected combining forms (roots with vowels attached) to give you a start toward building medical terms. Study these tables to prepare for the programmed review that follows. Appendix A contains a summary list of combining forms.

Self-Instruction: Common Combining Forms

COMBINING FORM	MEANING
COLORS	
cyan/o	blue
erythr/o	red
leuk/o	white
melan/o	black

COMBINING FORM	MEANING
SUBSTANCES	
aer/o	air, gas
hem/o	blood
hemat/o	blood
hydr/o	water
lip/o	fat
py/o	pus
ur/o	urine
urin/o	urine
ORGANS AND STRUCTURES	
abdomin/o	abdomen
acr/o	extremity or topmost
aden/o	gland
angi/o	vessel
arthr/o	joint
cardi/o	heart
cephal/o	head
col/o	colon
colon/o	colon
cutane/o	skin
cyt/o	cell
derm/o	skin
dermat/o	skin
enter/o	small intestine
esophag/o	esophagus
gastr/o	stomach
hepat/o	liver
hist/o	tissue
lapar/o	abdomen
muscul/o	muscle
my/o	muscle
nas/o	nose
nephr/o	kidney
neur/o	nerve
or/o	mouth
oste/o	bone
pneum/o	air or lung
pneumon/o	air or lung

COMBINING FORM	MEANING
ren/o	kidney
rhin/o	nose
vas/o	vessel
vascul/o	vessel

GENERAL COMBINING FORMS

carcin/o	cancer
crin/o	to secrete
esthesi/o	sensation
fibr/o	fiber
gen/o	origin or production
gynec/o	woman
lith/o	stone
morph/o	form
necr/o	death
onc/o	tumor or mass
orth/o	straight, normal, or correct
path/o	disease
ped/o	child or foot
phag/o	eat or swallow
phas/o	speech
phob/o	exaggerated fear or sensitivity
plas/o	formation
psych/o	mind
scler/o	hard
son/o	sound
sten/o	narrow
therm/o	heat
tox/o	poison
toxic/o	poison
troph/o	nourishment or development

Programmed Review: Common Combining Forms

ANSWERS	REVIEW
kidney combining, form suffix	**1.72** *Nephr* is a Greek root meaning _____. Combined with an "*o*", it becomes *nephr/o*, a _____ _____. *Nephr/o* cannot stand alone as a term. At the least, it needs a _____ to

ANSWERS	REVIEW
study kidney	give it essential meaning. In the term nephrology, the addition of the suffix -logy forms a term with a specific meaning: _____ of the _____.
stone, -iasis presence or formation of kidney stones, o suffix ren/o	1.73 In nephrolithiasis, the link of *nephr/o* to *lith*, a root meaning _____, and the suffix _____ forms the term referring to the _____ _____. The combining vowel for *lith* is ___. Notice that the vowel was not used when linked to *-iasis*, because the _____ began with a vowel. Nephrolithiasis is a renal disease. Renal is a term formed using _____, the Latin combining form meaning kidney.
combining form abdomen lapar/o abdomen	1.74 *Abdomin/o* is a _____ _____ meaning _____, the central part of the body trunk. Note that the spelling of *abdomin/o* is different from the anatomic part it represents. Another combining form meaning abdomen is _____. A laparoscope is an instrument used to examine the _____.
water head	1.75 *Hydr/o* is a combining form meaning _____. A person with hydrocephaly has a condition of water (fluid) within the _____.
acro topmost, acro	1.76 An enlarged extremity is called _____megaly. *Acr/o* also means _____. A person with _____phobia has a fear of high places.
gen/o origin or production cancer	1.77 The suffix meaning origin or production is *-genesis*. The combining form meaning origin or production is _____. The suffix *-genic* pertains to _____. Carcinogenic pertains to the origin or production of _____.
melan/o, leuk/o erythr/o, cyan/o black, skin white red cyan	1.78 Several combining forms are listed in the starter set related to color: black is _____, white is _____, red is _____, and blue is _____. Melanoma, referring to a _____ tumor, is a common cutaneous cancer, or _____ cancer. A leukocyte is a _____ blood cell. Erythroderma refers to _____ skin. When the skin turns blue from lack of oxygen, it is termed _____osis.

LEVELS OF ORGANIZATION IN THE BODY

The body has multiple levels of organization, beginning with the chemical level composed of atoms and molecules. Each level becomes more complex, resulting in the human organism (see Figure 1-2).

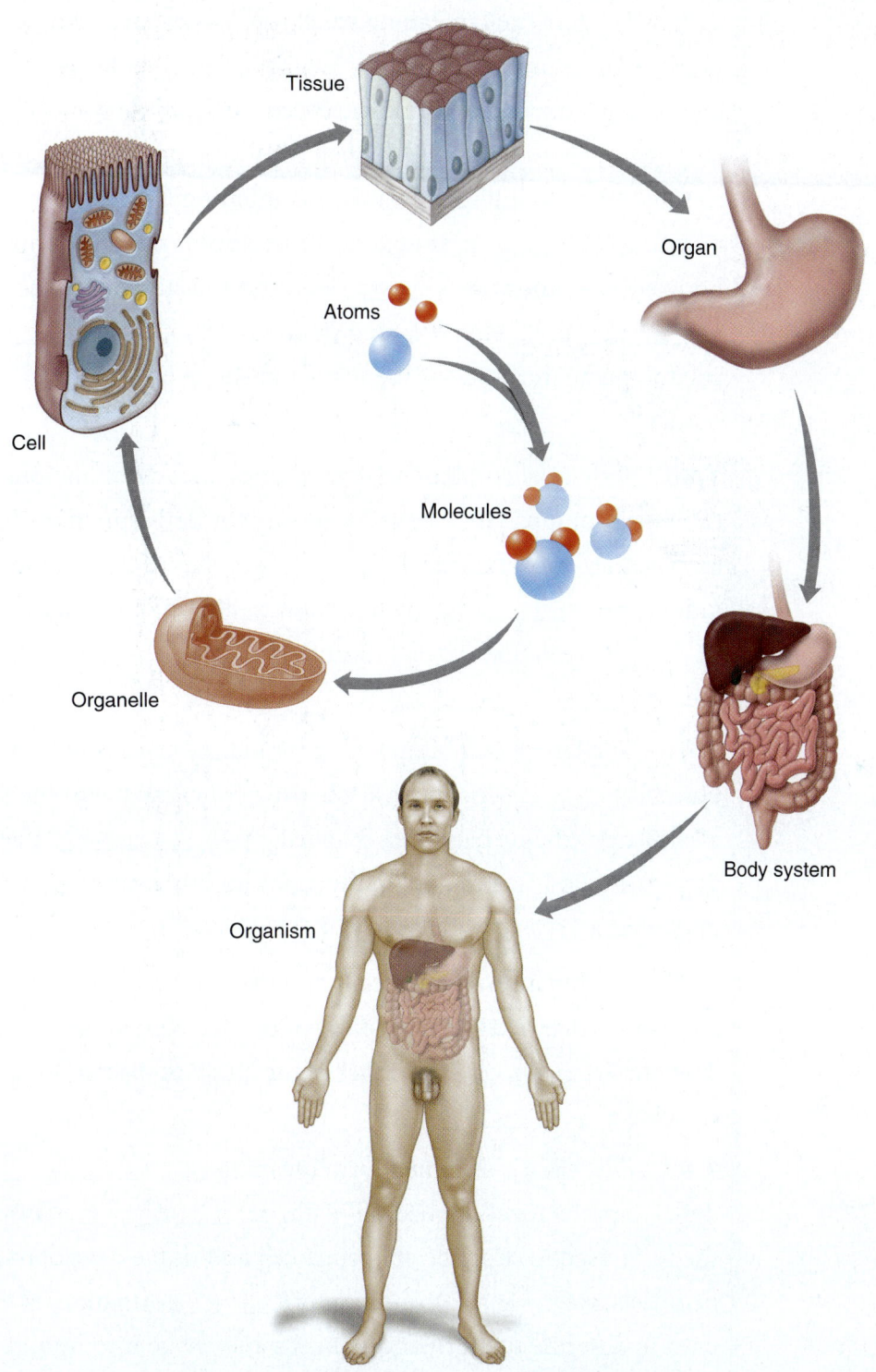

FIGURE 1-2 ■ The levels of body organization.

Programmed Review: Cells/Tissues/Organs/Systems

ANSWERS	REVIEW
small cell cyto histology, form morphology	**1.79** The term cell, meaning small room, was used to describe the structures first observed in 1665 by Robert Hooke as he examined cork using a microscope, an instrument to examine something _____. He noted that the small cells were part of a larger web of woven tissue. Using *cyt/o*, a combining form meaning _____, the study of cells that comprise the human body became known as _____logy and the study of tissue as _____. *Morph/o*, a combining form meaning _____, is used to name the study of the form and shape of cells and tissue: _____.
body organs urine pertaining to	**1.80** Body cells combine to form tissues, and combinations of tissues compose the organs necessary for body functions. Organs act together as part of the _____ systems. For example, the kidneys are _____ that function to filter blood as part of the urinary system (*urin/o* means _____ and *-ary* means _____ _____).
ren/o urology nephro	**1.81** The Greek combining form for kidney is *nephr/o*, and the Latin is _____. The medical specialty concerned with the study and treatment of the urinary tract is called _____. The physician who particularly specializes in the study and treatment of the kidneys is known as a _____logist.
patho pathologist	**1.82** Examination of body cells and tissues is part of the medical specialty concerned with the study of disease, known as _____logy. The physician who is a specialist in the study of disease is called a _____.
formation faulty new -oma, carcinoma oncology	**1.83** *Plas/o* is a combining form meaning _____, and *dys-* is a prefix meaning bad, difficult, or _____. Dysplasia is the term used to describe abnormal cell and tissue development, and neoplasia, referring to a condition of _____ formation, is the term used to describe the formation of cells and tissue into tumor. The suffix for tumor is _____. A cancerous tumor is called a _____. The specialty concerned with the study of tumors and cancers is _____.

Study Appendix A to prepare for the programmed review that follows.

ANSWERS	REVIEW
dermat/o skin study dermatologist	**1.84** The largest organ of the body is the skin. *Cutane/o* is the Latin combining form, and *derm/o* and _____ are the Greek combining forms, that mean _____. Dermatology is the specialty involved with the _____ and treatment of skin diseases. The specialist is called a _____.
Oste/o joint muscle correct foot	**1.85** The musculoskeletal system provides support and gives shape to the body. Bones, which form the skeleton, are covered with muscle to supply the forces that make movement possible. _____ is the combining form for bone, and *arthr/o* is the combining form meaning _____, the connection between bones. *My/o* and *muscul/o* are the combining forms for _____. *Orth/o*, meaning straight, normal, or _____, and *ped/o*, meaning child or _____, were combined to form the term orthopedic (pertaining to the specialty related to the musculoskeletal system).
heart, vessels blood hematology cell red, leukocytes blood, suffix poison py/o formation, pus	**1.86** The cardiovascular system consists of the _____ and _____ that transport blood throughout the body. Blood provides transport for oxygen, nutrients, wastes, etc. *Hem/o* and *hemat/o* are combining forms meaning _____. The study of blood is called _____. It includes analysis of blood and its cellular components. *Cyt/o* means _____. Cells of the blood include erythrocytes, or _____ blood cells, and _____, or white blood cells. Hemopoiesis is a term referring to the formation of _____, and *-emia* is the _____ that means blood. Toxemia is a condition of blood _____. Leukocytes are blood cells that fight infection. They are present in pus, the fluid produced by inflammation of tissue. The combining form for pus is _____. Pyopoiesis describes the _____ of _____.
air or lung nose nas/o	**1.87** *Pneum/o*, meaning _____, is the key combining form of the respiratory system, the body system responsible for the exchange of gases (oxygen and carbon dioxide) within the body. The nose is the first structure to receive oxygen. *Rhin/o* is the Greek combining form meaning _____. The Latin combining form with the same meaning is _____.

ANSWERS	REVIEW
Neur/o	**1.88** The nervous system is a complicated network of nerves and fibers that control all functions of the body. _____ is the combining form for nerve.
within to secrete	**1.89** The ductless glands of the endocrine system affect the function of organs by the secreting hormones. *Endo* means _____, and *crin/o* means _____.
mouth esophagus, stomach small, large liver	**1.90** The gastrointestinal system provides for digestion and elimination. Combining forms related to key structures of the tubular digestive tract are *or/o* (meaning _____), *esophag/o* (meaning _____), *gastr/o* (meaning _____), *enter/o* (meaning _____ intestine), and *col/o* or *colon/o* (meaning _____ intestine). *Hepat/o* is the combining form for _____, the organ that produces bile necessary for digestion.
logist gynecology	**1.91** The male and female reproductive systems produce the sex cells and maintain the organs necessary for production of human offspring. The physician who specializes in the treatment of the male and female urinary system, as well as the male reproductive system, is called a uro_____. Treatment of the female reproductive system involves two medical specialties: obstetrics and _____ (study of woman).

THE MEDICAL RECORD

In healthcare settings, medical terminology is used in both spoken and written communication. The primary form of written communication is the patient's medical record. Because you will likely encounter different types of medical records in your work, later chapters in this text frequently include medical records so that you can become familiar with the different formats and experience real-life uses of medical terminology.

A patient's **medical record** provides the person's physical, emotional, nutritional, and social history. Medical records are collections of all written documents related to a patient's examination, diagnosis, and care. This form identifies individual information along with current and past medical conditions. It also lists prescription and nonprescription drug use, drug sensitivities, and allergies. Patient medical records are also referred to as *hospital records* and *clinic records*.

Patient medical record information is important because it is used to assess previous treatment, to enhance the continuity of care, and to avoid unnecessary tests and/or procedures. Because it is an invaluable tool for healthcare providers, it is a working document that needs to be as complete as possible. So, knowledge of medical terminology is essential. The person documenting the information must be skilled in recording the data accurately, making sure the terms are spelled correctly, and ensuring that the facts supplied by the patient make sense within the context of the conversation. As a primary means of communication, this collection of facts and data is read and scrutinized by all clinicians treating the patient or office personnel servicing the person. A thorough understanding of medical terminology is necessary for adequately documenting, describing, and relaying pertinent health information.

History and physical (H&P) examinations are a record of the patient's medical history, which may include forms the patient fills out, and the healthcare provider's examination of the patient. This is usually a standardized report because the examination is performed in a standard, systematic manner. The aim of the questions on a typical H&P is to obtain a complete representation of the patient. The history (Hx) portion is generally categorized into the following headings:

- chief complaint (CC)
- past history (PH) or past medical history (PMH)
- history of present illness (HPI) or present illness (PI)
- family history (FH)
- social history (SH)
- occupational history (OH)
- diet/exercise history
- review of systems (ROS) or systems review (SR)

Females also answer questions pertaining to menstrual, gynecologic, pregnancy, contraceptive, and sexual history. Males answer questions of contraception, sexual history, and sexual performance.

Once the personal medical history has been obtained, practitioners typically evaluate the patient through a physical examination (PE or Px). The physical examination includes assessment of the following:

- general appearance
- vital signs
- head, eyes, ears, nose, and throat (HEENT)
- neck, lungs, heart, rectopelvis, extremities, and neurologic condition
- laboratory data

The report ends with the general impression (IMP), or general view of patient's condition, and plan (P). An example history and physical is shown in **Figure 1-3**.

Through conversation, written documentation, and a quick examination, more information is obtained for the H&P form. Commonly used terms and phrases (with their abbreviations) to document findings include:

- complains of (c/o)
- diagnosis (Dx)
- family members living and well (L&W)
- no acute distress (NAD)
- no known allergies (NKA)
- no known drug allergies (NKDA)
- pupils equal, round, and reactive to light and accommodation (PERRLA)
- rule out (R/O)
- symptom (Sx)
- usual childhood diseases (UCHD)
- within normal limits (WNL)

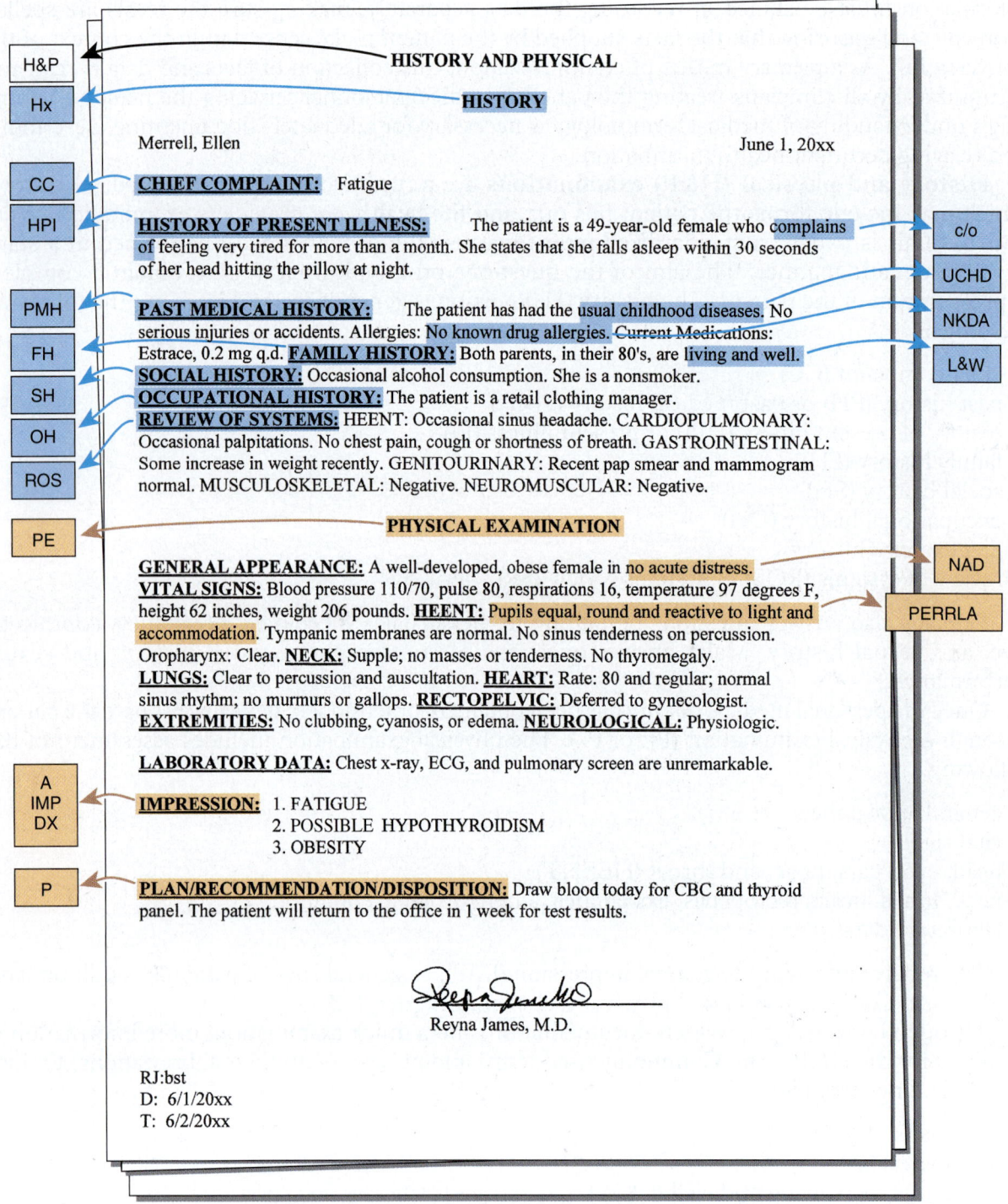

FIGURE 1-3 ■ A typical history and physical (H&P) form.

Progress notes, also called **SOAP notes**, are made in a patient's medical record after the H&P has been finished. These notes are used in patient records for organizing follow-up data, evaluating, and planning. SOAP is an acronym for **s**ubjective, **o**bjective, **a**ssessment, and **p**lan. The subjective portion identifies the patient's symptoms, and the objective section lists the signs. **Symptoms** are experienced by the patient and may include such sensations as pain and dizziness. **Signs** include functions that can be measured, such as blood pressure, respiration rate, temperature, height, and weight. The assessment is the professional judgment made of the patient's progress. Finally, the plan is the outline for treatment. Figure 1-4 shows a typical progress note using the SOAP method.

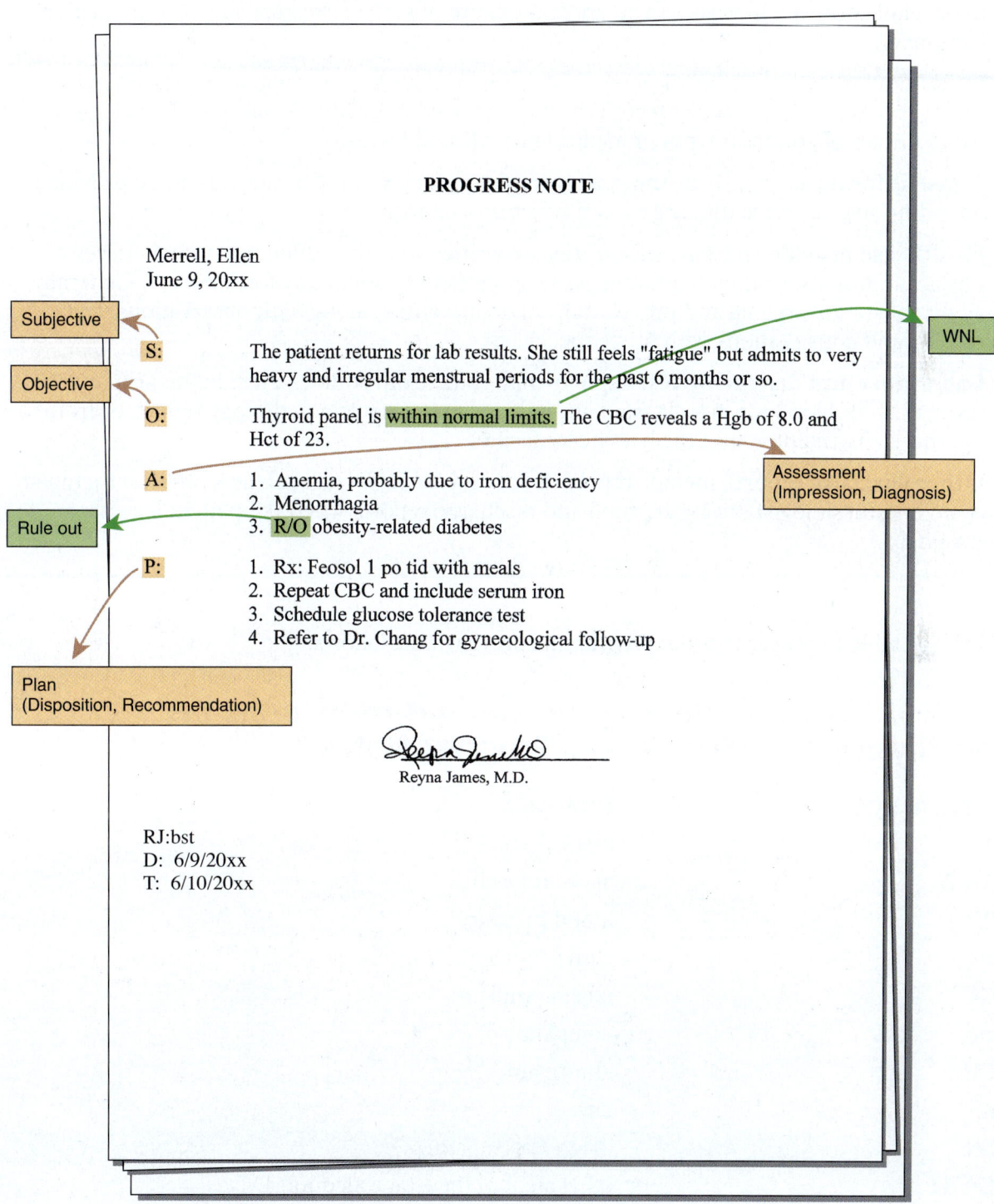

FIGURE 1-4 ■ A progress note utilizing the SOAP method of charting.

Following is a section of a consultation note for a patient who has undergone treatment for lung cancer. As you read this record, underline all medical terms that you do not understand.

> When reading a medical record the first time, do not stop to puzzle out every new term you encounter. Instead, read the record all the way through to gain a general sense of its meaning. You will find it easier to understand specific terms once you are familiar with the overall context. However, if you are still unsure of some terms consult your medical dictionary.
>
> In addition to the patient medical record, history and physical examination, and SOAP notes, there are other types of records and forms used in healthcare setting. The following are examples of common types of medical records and forms.
>
> **Consent forms** are signed by the patient to give permission for health care to be provided, including special forms for surgery and other procedures.
>
> **Healthcare provider patient care notes** are written into the patient record whenever a physician, nurse, or other healthcare provider gives the patient any form of care. Generally, all diagnostic treatments and procedures are documented, along with observations, test results, and consultations with other specialists.
>
> **Laboratory and diagnostic test reports** may come from sources outside the primary care team, such as blood test results from an outside laboratory or a pathology report, or from another department within the healthcare facility.
>
> **Other specialty reports** include reports from other caregivers (such as a physical therapist or an anesthesiologist during surgery) and discharge reports when the patient leaves a hospital.

Study this table to prepare for the programmed review that follows.

Self-Instruction: Common Abbreviations Used in the History and Physical Examination and Progress Notes

ABBREVIATION	EXPANSION
A	assessment
A&W	alive and well
BP	blood pressure
c̄	with
CC	chief complaint
c/o	complains of
CP	chest pain
d	day
Dx	diagnosis
EtOH	ethyl alcohol (beverage alcohol)
FH	family history

ABBREVIATION	EXPANSION
HEENT	head, eyes, ears, nose, and throat
H&P	history and physical
HPI, PI	history of present illness, present illness
Hx	history
IMP	impression
Ⓛ	left
L&W	living and well
NAD	no acute distress
NKA, NKDA	no known allergies, no known drug allergies
O	objective information
OH	occupational history
P	plan (recommendation, disposition); pulse
PE, Px	physical examination
PERRLA	pupils equal, round, and reactive to light and accommodation
PH, PMH	past history, past medical history
Pt	patient
R	respiration
Ⓡ	right
RTC	return to clinic
R/O	rule out
ROS, SR	review of systems, systems review
S	subjective information
š	without
SH	social history
SOAP	subjective, objective, assessment, plan
SOB	shortness of breath
STAT, stat	referring to something that should be done immediately
Sx	symptom
t.i.d.	three times a day
UCHD	usual childhood diseases
WNL	within normal limits
y.o.	year old
yr	year
↑	increased
↓	decreased

Programmed Review: Common Abbreviations Used in the History and Physical and Progress Notes

ANSWERS	REVIEW
history and physical history subjective physical physical examination objective	1.92 The H&P, or _____ _____ _____, is the first document generated in the care of a patient. It is divided into two categories: the Hx, or _____, which provides all _____ information obtained from the patient, including his physical or her own perceptions; and the Px, or _____, or PE, or _____ _____, which records all _____ information that can be seen or verified by the examiner.
chief complaint complains of present illness, history present illness symptoms	1.93 The first thing that is noted in the history is the CC, or _____ _____, or what the patient c/o, or _____ _____. It is a brief explanation of why the patient is seeking medical care. Further details about the complaint are noted in the PI, or _____ _____, or HPI, or _____ of _____ _____, to report how long the patient has had the complaint and how bad it is. All subjective evidence of disease that the patient reports is noted as Sx, or _____.
past history past medical history usual childhood diseases no known allergies, no known drug allergies	1.94 The history continues by gathering information regarding past injuries, illnesses, operations, physical defects, medications, and allergies in the PH, or _____ _____, or PMH, or _____ _____ _____. UCHD notes that the patient had the _____ _____ _____, or commonly contracted illnesses during childhood. NKA, or _____ _____ _____, and NKDA, or _____ _____ _____ _____, indicate that the patient has had no known allergic reaction to a previously administered drug.
family history social history occupational history review of systems systems review	1.95 "Father, age 58, mother, age 54, brother, age 32, all L&W" is an example of an FH, or _____ _____. Notes about recreational interests, hobbies, and use of tobacco and drugs, such as alcohol, are noted in the SH, or _____ _____. Work habits that may involve health risks are included in the OH, or _____ _____. The history is complete after the patient answers questions related to a review of the functions of the body systems in the ROS, or _____ _____ _____, or SR, _____ _____.

ANSWERS	REVIEW
physical physical examination signs head, eyes, ears nose, throat, pupils equal round, reactive light, accommodation within normal limits no acute distress	**1.96** The second portion of the H&P is the Px, or _____, or PE, or _____ _____. Objective evidence of disease, called _____, are documented, and selected tests are ordered and the findings recorded. Common abbreviations include HEENT, which means _____, _____, _____, _____, and _____; PERRLA, which means _____ _____, _____, and _____ to _____ and _____; WNL, which means _____ _____ _____; and NAD, which indicates _____ _____ _____.
impression, diagnosis assessment rule out	**1.97** The identification of a disease or condition is recorded in the IMP, or _____; the Dx, or _____; or the A, or _____. This is made after all subjective and objective data are evaluated. When one or more diagnoses are in question, a differential diagnosis is made using the abbreviation R/O, or _____ _____.
plan recommendation disposition	**1.98** An outline of strategies designed to remedy the patient's condition is noted in the provider's P, or _____, which is also called a _____ or _____. This section includes the provider's instructions to the patient and orders for medications, diagnostic tests, or therapies.
progress subjective objective assessment plan	**1.99** After the initial history and physical is recorded, _____ notes are used for further documentation of the patient's care. The letters "SOAP" represent the order in which progress is noted: **S:** _____; that which the patient describes **O:** _____; observable information (e.g., test results or blood pressure readings) **A:** _____; patient's progress and evaluation of the effectiveness of the plan **P:** _____; decision to proceed or alter the plan strategy

PRACTICE EXERCISES

For each of the following words, write out the term parts (prefixes [P], combining forms [CF], roots [R], and suffixes [S]) on the lines below the word. Then define the term according to the meaning of its parts.

EXAMPLE
hyperlipemia
hyper / lip / emia
P   R   S
DEFINITION: above or excessive/fat/blood condition

1. sympathy
   _____ / _____ / _____
   P   R   S
   DEFINITION: _____

2. pancytopenia
   _____ / _____ / _____
   P   CF   S
   DEFINITION: _____

3. tachycardia
   _____ / _____ / _____
   P   R   S
   DEFINITION: _____

4. macrocephalous
   _____ / _____ / _____
   P   R   S
   DEFINITION: _____

5. orthopedic
   _____ / _____ / _____
   CF   R   S
   DEFINITION: _____

6. carcinophobia
   _____ / _____ / _____
   CF   R   S
   DEFINITION: _____

7. aerophagia
   _____ / _____ / _____
   CF   R   S
   DEFINITION: _____

8. sclerosis
   _____ / _____
   R   S
   DEFINITION: _____

9. hydrocephaly

   _____ / _____ / _____
       CF   R   S

   DEFINITION: _____

10. hypertrophy

    _____ / _____ / _____
        P   R   S

    DEFINITION: _____

Circle the correct meaning for the following word parts.

11. inter-
    a. difficult   b. between   c. within   d. out, away   e. behind

12. anti-
    a. beside   b. outside   c. against   d. around   e. away from

13. poly-
    a. many   b. few   c. above   d. before   e. after

14. hyper-
    a. below   b. after   c. beyond   d. excessive   e. deficient

15. -rrhagia
    a. discharge   b. suture   c. rupture   d. burst forth   e. repair

16. toxic/o
    a. development   b. poison   c. pus   d. swallow   e. black

17. melan/o
    a. death   b. disease   c. black   d. dissolution   e. large

Circle the correct term part for the following meanings.

18. kidney
    a. enter/o   b. gastr/o   c. ren/o   d. hepat/o   e. necr/o

19. large
    a. poly-   b. -malacia   c. -oma   d. hyper-   e. macro-

20. record
    a. -meter   b. -metry   c. -gram   d. -graph   e. -graphy

21. surgical fixation
    a. -ptosis   b. -plasia   c. -penia   d. -pexy   e. -plasty

22. condition or increase
    a. -itis   b. -iasis   c. -osis   d. -ium   e. -ous

Circle the correct plural form for the following words.

23. vertebra
    a. vertebray b. vertebras c. vertebrae d. vertebrus e. vertebraes
24. bulla
    a. bulli b. bullia c. bullae d. bullas e. bullata
25. speculum
    a. speculata b. speculumes c. specula d. speculae e. speculuma
26. fungus
    a. fungi b. fungae c. funges d. funguses e. fungea
27. stoma
    a. stomata b. stomatae c. stomes d. stomatus e. stomatum

Circle the surgical/operative term in each of the following.

28. a. nephroptosis b. hemolysis c. angiectasis d. colostomy e. necrosis
29. a. vasorrhaphy b. hematoma c. gastrocele d. endoscope e. cardiorrhexis
30. a. morphologic b. adenolysis c. abdominocentesis d. osteomalacia e. polyrrhea

Circle the correct spelling.

31. a. nephroraphy b. nephrorrapy c. nephrorrhaphy d. nephrorrhapy
32. a. abdominoscopy b. abdemenoscopi c. abdomenscopy d. abdominoschope
33. a. perrycardium b. pericardium c. periocardium d. paracardium

Circle the prefix that will complete the following terms.

34. _____ nasal = <u>above</u> the nose
    a. para- b. peri- c. supra- d. infra- e. sub-
35. _____ partum = <u>after</u> labor
    a. ante- b. anti- c. post- d. pro- e. retro-
36. _____ morphic = pertaining to <u>one</u> form
    a. bi- b. micro- c. mono- d. tri- e. meta-
37. _____ acute = <u>excessively</u> severe
    a. sub- b. hypo- c. super- d. oligo- e. pan-
38. _____ phonia = <u>difficult</u> speech
    a. ab- b. dys- c. a- d. eu- e. para-
39. _____ phylaxis = to guard <u>before</u>
    a. retro- b. pro- c. post- d. peri- e. anti-
40. _____ cardia = <u>slow</u> heart
    a. hypo- b. tachy- c. brady- d. hyper- e. dys-
41. _____ aerobic = pertaining to life <u>without</u> air
    a. an- b. a- c. hypo- d. hyper- e. dys-

Write the letter of the matching term part in the space after the meaning.

42. black _____
43. three _____
44. red _____
45. four _____
46. white _____
47. one _____
48. blue _____
49. two _____
50. few _____

a. tri-
b. leuk/o
c. cyan/o
d. bi-
e. uni-
f. melan/o
g. quadri-
h. erythr/o
i. oligo-

MEDICAL RECORD ANALYSIS

Medical Record 1-1

CC:	37 y.o. male c̄ diabetes c/o swelling of the ® foot and calf × 3d
S:	There is no Hx of trauma, pain, SOB, or cardiac Sx, smoker × 12 yr, ½ pack every day; denies ETOH consumption
Meds:	subcutaneous insulin every day; NKDA
O:	Pt is afebrile, BP 140/84, P 72, R 16, lungs are clear; abdomen is benign s̄ organomegaly; muscle tone and strength are WNL; there is swelling of the ® calf but s̄ erythema or tenderness
A:	Edema of ® calf of unknown etiology
P:	Schedule STAT vascular sonogram of lower extremities; pt is to keep the leg elevated 2 days, then RTC for follow-up and test results on Thursday (or sooner if ↑ edema, SOB, or CP)

Questions About Medical Record 1-1

1. How old is the patient?
   a. 37
   b. 12
   c. 72
   d. 16

2. Where was the patient seen?
   a. emergency room
   b. outpatient office or clinic
   c. inpatient hospital
   d. not stated

3. What is the condition of the patient's abdomen?
   a. shows signs of cancer
   b. internal organs are enlarged
   c. internal organs are not enlarged
   d. muscle tone and strength are weak

4. How much does the patient smoke per day?
   a. one pack
   b. two pack
   c. half a pack
   d. none; patient quit smoking 12 years ago

5. How is the patient's insulin administered?
   a. orally
   b. transdermally
   c. infusion through implant
   d. by injection

6. What is the cause of the patient's complaint?
   a. unknown
   b. fever
   c. shortness of breath
   d. trauma

7. When should the sonogram be performed?
   a. immediately
   b. within 2 days
   c. at the time of follow-up
   d. only if symptoms persist

8. How long should the patient's leg be kept elevated?
   a. 1 week
   b. 2 weeks
   c. 1 day
   d. 2 days

ANSWERS TO PRACTICE EXERCISES

1. P: sym
   R: path
   S: y
   DEFINITION: together or with/disease/condition or process of
2. P: pan
   CF: cyto
   S: penia
   DEFINITION: all/cell/abnormal reduction
3. P: tachy
   R: card
   S: ia
   DEFINITION: fast/heart/condition of
4. P: macro
   R: cephal
   S: ous
   DEFINITION: large or long/head/pertaining to
5. CF: ortho
   R: ped
   S: ic
   DEFINITION: straight, normal, or correct/foot/pertaining to
6. CF: carcino
   R: phob
   S: ia
   DEFINITION: cancer/fear or sensitivity/condition of
7. CF: aero
   R: phag
   S: ia
   DEFINITION: air or gas/eat or swallow/condition of
8. R: scler
   S: osis
   DEFINITION: hard/condition or increase
9. CF: hydro
   R: cephal
   S: y
   DEFINITION: water/head/condition or process of
10. P: hyper
    R: troph
    S: y
    DEFINITION: above or excessive/nourishment or development/condition or process of
11. b. between
12. c. against
13. a. many
14. d. excessive
15. d. burst forth
16. b. poison
17. c. black
18. c. ren/o
19. e. macro-
20. c. -gram
21. d. -pexy
22. c. -osis
23. c. vertebrae
24. c. bullae
25. c. specula
26. a. fungi
27. a. stomata
28. d. colostomy
29. a. vasorrhaphy
30. c. abdominocentesis
31. c. nephrorrhaphy
32. a. abdominoscopy
33. b. pericardium
34. c. supra-
35. c. post-
36. c. mono-
37. c. super-
38. b. dys-
39. b. pro-
40. c. brady-
41. a. an-
42. f. melan/o
43. a. tri-
44. h. erythr/o
45. g. quadri-
46. b. leuk/o
47. e. uni-
48. c. cyan/o
49. d. bi-
50. i. oligo-

ANSWERS TO MEDICAL RECORD 1-1

1. a
2. d
3. c
4. c
5. d
6. a
7. a
8. d

INTEGUMENTARY SYSTEM

Learning Outcomes

After completing this chapter, you should be able to:

- Identify key structures and functions of the integumentary system.
- Define term parts related to the integumentary system.
- Define symptomatic terms and describe them as primary, secondary, vascular, purpuric lesions, scar formations, or epidermal growths.
- Define general symptomatic and diagnostic terms related to the integumentary system.
- Cite various diagnostic tests and procedures related to the integumentary system and explain their importance.
- Explain operative and therapeutic terms related to the integumentary system.
- Cite common abbreviations related to the integumentary system and give the expansion of each.
- Explain terms used in medical records involving the integumentary system.

INTEGUMENTARY SYSTEM OVERVIEW

The integumentary system (see **Figure 2-1**) consists of the following structures:

- Skin (also called the **integument**)
- Hair
- Nails
- Sweat glands
- Sebaceous (oil) glands

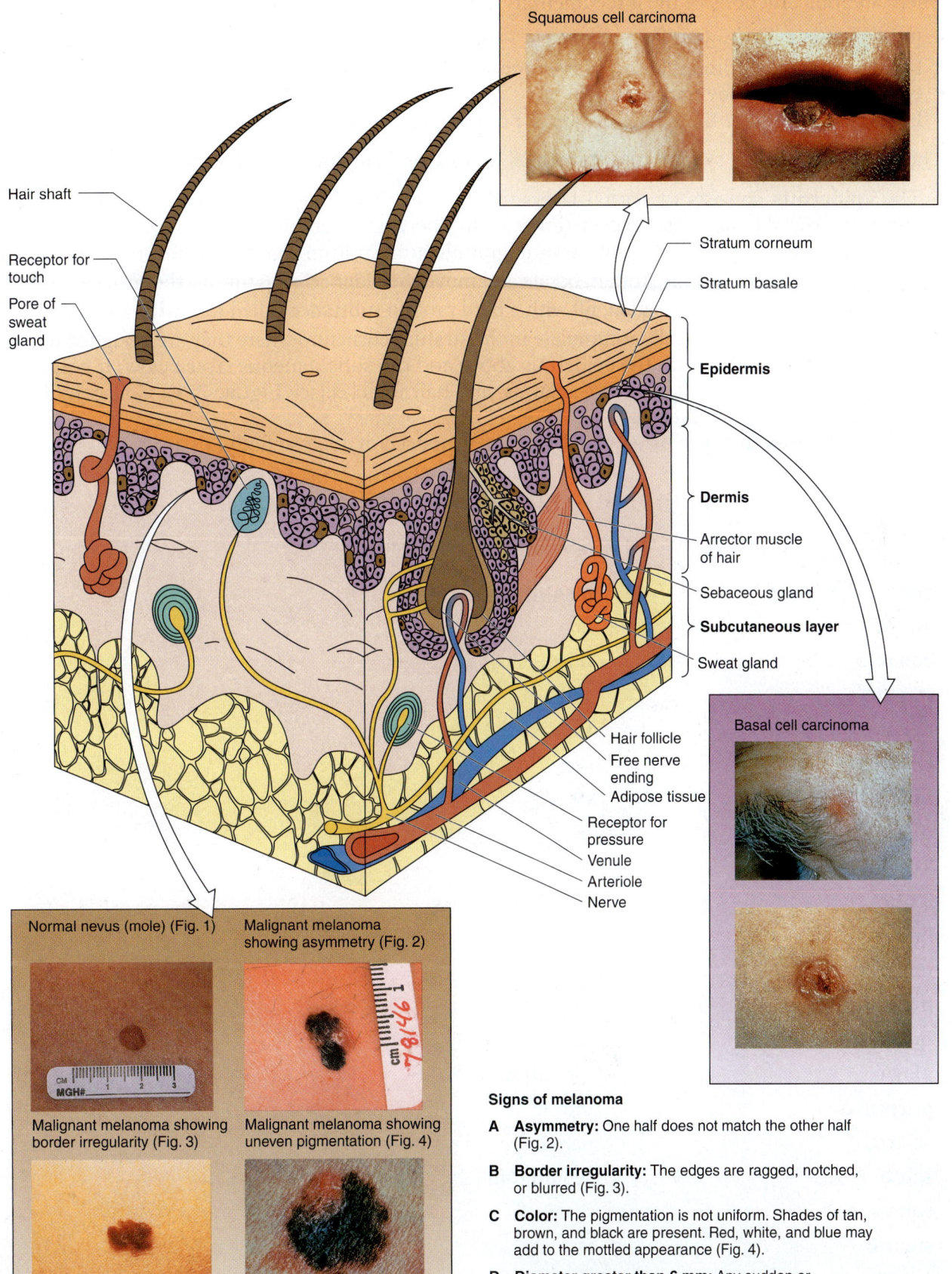

FIGURE 2-1 ■ Anatomy of the skin.

There are four functions of the integumentary system:

- Protects the body from injury
- Protects the body from intrusion of microorganisms
- Helps to regulate body temperature
- Houses receptors for the senses of touch, pressure, and pain

The three layers of the skin are the epidermis, dermis, and subcutaneous layer.

- The **epidermis** consists of several layers called *strata*. The singular form of strata is *stratum*. From superficial (outermost) to deep (innermost), these layers are the stratum corneum, stratum lucidum (found only in thick skin), stratum granulosum, stratum spinosum, and stratum basale.
  1. Cells are produced in the stratum basale and move the older cells up toward the surface.
  2. Cells that are pushed up flatten, fill with a hard protein substance called **keratin**, and die.
  3. Layers of packed dead cells accumulate in the stratum corneum, where they are sloughed off.
- The **dermis** interlocks with the epidermis above and the subcutaneous layer below. It contains blood vessels, nerves, nerve endings, glands, and hair follicles (see **Figure 2-1**). Collagen fibers make the skin tough and elastic.
- The **subcutaneous layer** below the dermis is composed of adipose (fatty) tissue.

Self-Instruction: Combining Forms

Study this table to prepare for the programmed review that follows.

COMBINING FORM	MEANING
adip/o	fat
corne/o	horn, hard
cutane/o	skin
derm/o, dermat/o	skin
erythr/o	red
hidr/o	sweat
hist/o, histi/o	tissue
kerat/o	hard
leuk/o	white
lip/o	fat
melan/o	black
myc/o	fungus
onych/o	nail
plas/o	formation
purpur/o	purple
scler/o	hard
seb/o	sebum (oil)
squam/o	scale
steat/o	fat
trich/o	hair
xanth/o	yellow
xer/o	dry

Programmed Review: Combining Forms

ANSWERS	REVIEW
skin dermatology dermatologist skin under	2.1 *Derm/o* and *dermat/o* are Greek combining forms meaning _____. The medical field specializing in the study of the skin is _____. The physician who specializes in the study and treatment of the skin is called a _____. *Cutane/o* is a Latin combining form meaning _____. Subcutaneous therefore pertains to _____ the skin.
cell tissue histology production, tissue	2.2 Recall that *cyt/o* means _____. Cells with specialized functions combine to form varying types of tissue. *Hist/o* is a combining form meaning _____. The study of tissues is called _____. Histiogenic pertains to the origin or _____ of _____.
plas/o faulty condition of dysplasia	2.3 The combining form meaning formation is _____. *Dys-* is a prefix meaning painful, difficult, or _____, and *-ia* refers to a _____ _____. Therefore, the term used to describe a condition of (faulty) abnormal development of tissue is _____.
upon epi scale pertaining to squamous	2.4 The prefix *epi-*, meaning _____, is used in naming the outer tissue layer of the skin, called the _____dermis. The combining form *squam/o* means _____. The suffix *-ous* means _____ _____. The flat, scale-like cells of the epidermis are aptly called _____ cells.
black darker cells	2.5 The pigment called melanin is found in the stratum basale of the epidermis. The combining form *melan/o* means _____, and people with more melanin have _____ skin. Melanocytes are the _____ in the stratum basale that produce melanin.
Kerat/o epidermis keratin	2.6 _____ is the combining form that means hard. Keratin is the hard protein substance found in the stratum basale of the _____. Keratosis is a condition characterized by an overgrowth of cells having a large amount of _____.
trich/o hair	2.7 Hair follicles are found in the dermis layer of the skin. The combining form for hair is _____. Combined with the suffix meaning rupture, trichorrhexis is the term describing _____ that is broken or split.

ANSWERS	REVIEW
sebum seb/o sebum	**2.8** Sebaceous glands, which open to the hair follicles in the skin, produce _____ (oil). The combining form of this term is _____. Seborrhea refers to an overproduction of _____ by these glands.
water sweat hidro	**2.9** *Hydr/o,* a combining form meaning _____, stems from the Greek word *hydros*. A similar word part, *hidr/o,* stemming from the Greek word *hidros,* means _____. The formation of sweat is termed _____poiesis.
fungus myc/o	**2.10** Mycosis refers to any condition caused by a _____. The term was derived from the combining form _____.
nail softening onycho, fungus or fungal	**2.11** The combining form *onycho* refers to the fingernail or toe_____. Recall that *-malacia* is a suffix meaning _____. An abnormal softening of the nails is therefore called _____malacia. Onychomycosis refers to a _____ infection (condition) of the nails.
lip/o fat adip/o sub fat inflammation, fat	**2.12** Several combining forms refer to body fat. The term lipid is from the combining form _____. Liposuction therefore refers to the procedure for suctioning _____ from body tissues. The adjective adipose, meaning fatty, is from the combining form _____. Adipose tissue is found deep to (below) the dermis in the _____cutaneous layer of the skin. A third combining form, *steat/o,* also refers to _____. Steatitis refers to an _____ of _____.
white leuko	**2.13** The combining form *leuk/o* means _____. It is used to form the term for a partial or total absence of pigment in the skin, known as _____derma.
erythr/o red red skin	**2.14** The combining form _____ means red. Erythema therefore refers to skin that is _____. Erythroderma is another term referring to _____ _____.
purple purple blood	**2.15** The meaning of the combining form *purpur/o* is easy to remember, because it sounds like the color _____. Purpuric lesions are colored_____ because they result from hemorrhages, or the bursting forth of _____ into the skin.

ANSWERS	REVIEW
xanth/o yellow	**2.16** The combining form _____ refers to the color yellow. A xanthoma is a _____ skin tumor.
skin xer/o dry	**2.17** Xeroderma is a term meaning dry _____. The combining form for dry is _____. Xerosis is a condition of pathologically _____ skin.

Self-Instruction: Anatomic Terms

Study this table to prepare for the programmed review that follows.

TERM	MEANING
epithelium ep-i-thē′lē-ŭm	cellular avascular layer covering external and internal surfaces of the body
epidermis ep-i-derm′is	outer layer of the skin
stratum corneum strat′ŭm kōr′nē-ŭm	the outer layer of the epidermis, made up of several layers of flat keratinized (hard, proteinaceous) cells
stratum basale strat′ŭm bā′sā-lē	deepest layer of epidermis, also called the *basal layer*
melanocyte mel′ă-nō-sīt	cell in the stratum basale that gives color to the skin
melanin mel′ă-nin	dark brown to black pigment contained in melanocytes
dermis děr′mis	dense, fibrous connective tissue layer of the skin, also known as corium
sebaceous glands sē-bā′shŭs glanz	oil glands in the skin
sebum sē′bŭm	oily substance secreted by the sebaceous glands
sudoriferous glands sŭ-dō-rif′ĕr-ŭs glanz	sweat glands (*sudor* = sweat; *ferre* = to bear)
subcutaneous layer sŭb-kyū-tā′nē-ŭs lā′er	connective and adipose tissue layer just deep to (under) the dermis
collagen kol′ă-jen	protein substance in skin and connective tissue (*koila* = glue; *gen* = producing)
hair hār	outgrowth of the skin composed of keratin
nail nāl	outgrowth of the skin, composed of keratin, at the end of each finger and toe
keratin ker′ă-tin	hard protein material found in the epidermis, hair, and nails

Programmed Review: Anatomic Terms

ANSWERS	REVIEW
epithelium, upon -ium	2.18 The name for the cellular avascular layer covering the external and internal surfaces of the body is the _____. Recall that the prefix *epi-* means _____, and that the suffix _____ means structure or tissue.
epidermis, epi- skin dermis	2.19 The thin, outer cellular layer of the skin is called the _____, which is formed from the prefix _____ and the combining form *derm/o,* meaning _____. The layer of skin deep to the epidermis is called the _____ and is where nerves and blood vessels are located.
corneum horn, hard	2.20 The stratum _____ is the outermost layer of the epidermis. The combining form *corne/o* means _____, and this layer is so named because the dead skin cells in the outermost layer consist of flat, keratinized (hard) cells.
basale pertaining to epidermis	2.21 Below the stratum corneum is the stratum _____. Recall that the suffix *-al* means _____ ____. This layer is therefore the deepest (or base) layer of the _____.
cyt/o melanin black	2.22 Recall that the combining form for cell is _____. A melanocyte therefore is a cell containing _____, the dark pigment of the skin. *Melan/o* means _____.
sebum adjective dermis	2.23 The sebaceous glands produce _____, an oily substance. The suffix *-ous* is added to a combining form to create an _____. These glands are in the skin layer called the _____.
sudoriferous dermis	2.24 The sweat glands are called the _____ glands, from *sudor* (sweat) and *ferre* (to bear). They are in the skin layer called the _____.
subcutaneous sub- skin	2.25 Beneath the dermis is the _____ layer. The prefix _____ means below or under, and the combining form *cutane/o* means _____.
collagen	2.26 Formed from the roots *koila* (glue) and *gen* (producing), _____ is a protein substance found in skin and connective tissue.
keratin nails hard	2.27 Hair is an outgrowth of the skin composed of _____. The _____ on the fingers and toes also are composed of keratin. The combining form *kerat/o* means _____.

Self Instruction: Symptomatic Terms (Primary and Secondary Lesions)

Study these tables to prepare for the programmed review that follows.

TERM	MEANING
lesion (see Figure 2-2) lē′zhŭn	an area of pathologically altered tissue; types of lesions are primary, secondary, vascular, and purpuric

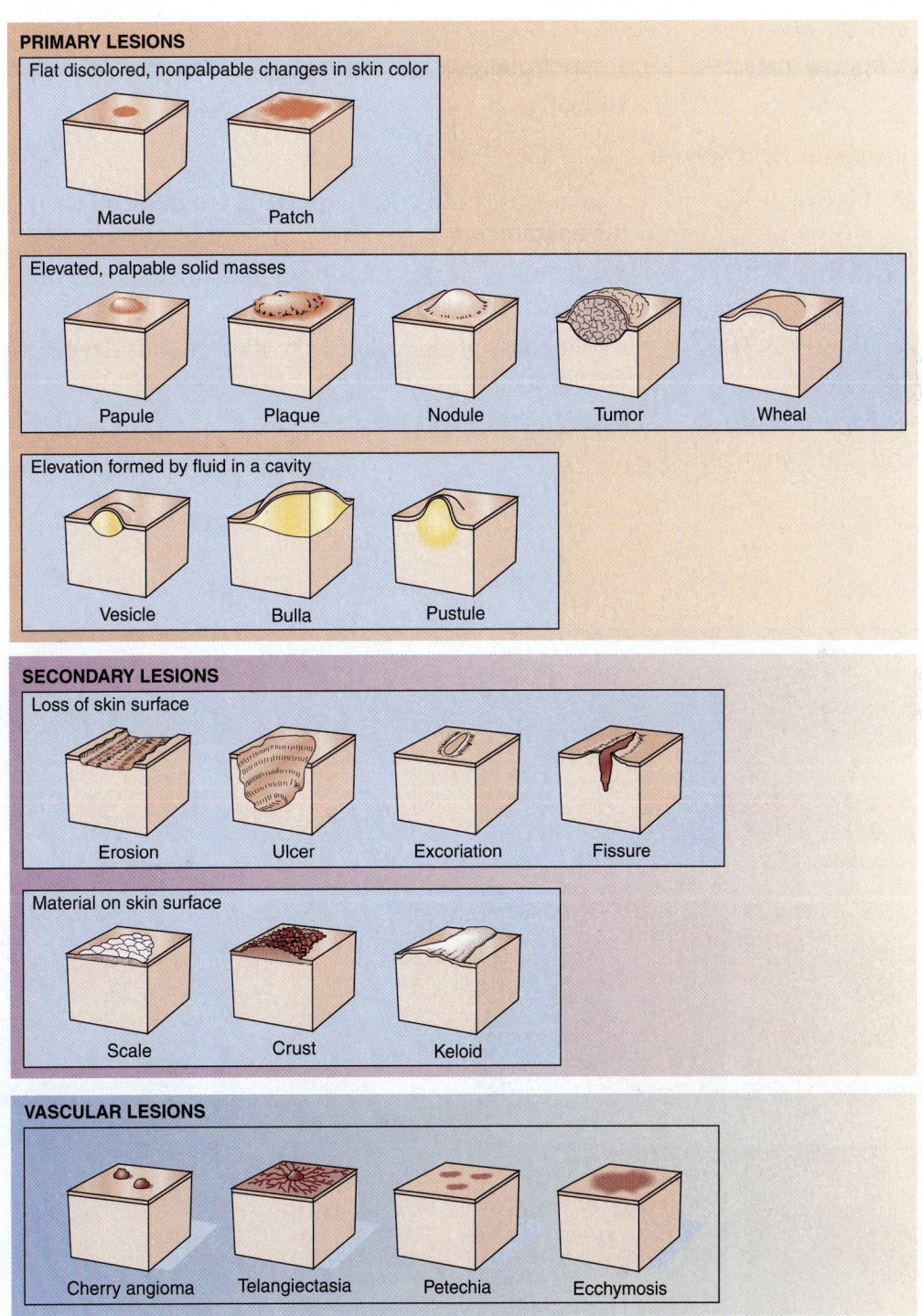

FIGURE 2-2 ■ Types of primary, secondary, and vascular lesions.

TERM	MEANING
PRIMARY LESIONS	
primary lesions prī′mār-ē lē′zhŭnz	lesions arising from previously normal skin
Flat, Nonpalpable Changes in Skin Color	
macule or **macula** (see Figure 2-3A) mak′yūl, mak′yū-lă	a flat, discolored spot on the skin up to 1 cm across (e.g., a freckle)
patch (see Figure 2-3B) patch	a flat, discolored area on the skin larger than 1 cm (e.g., vitiligo)
Elevated, Palpable Solid Masses	
papule (see Figure 2-3C) pap′yūl	a solid mass on the skin up to 0.5 cm in diameter (e.g., a nevus [mole])
plaque (see Figure 2-3D) plak	a solid mass greater than 1 cm in diameter and limited to the surface of the skin
nodule (see Figure 2-3E) nod′yūl	a solid mass greater than 1 cm that extends deeper into the epidermis
tumor (see Figure 2-3F) tū′mŏr	a solid mass larger than 1–2 cm

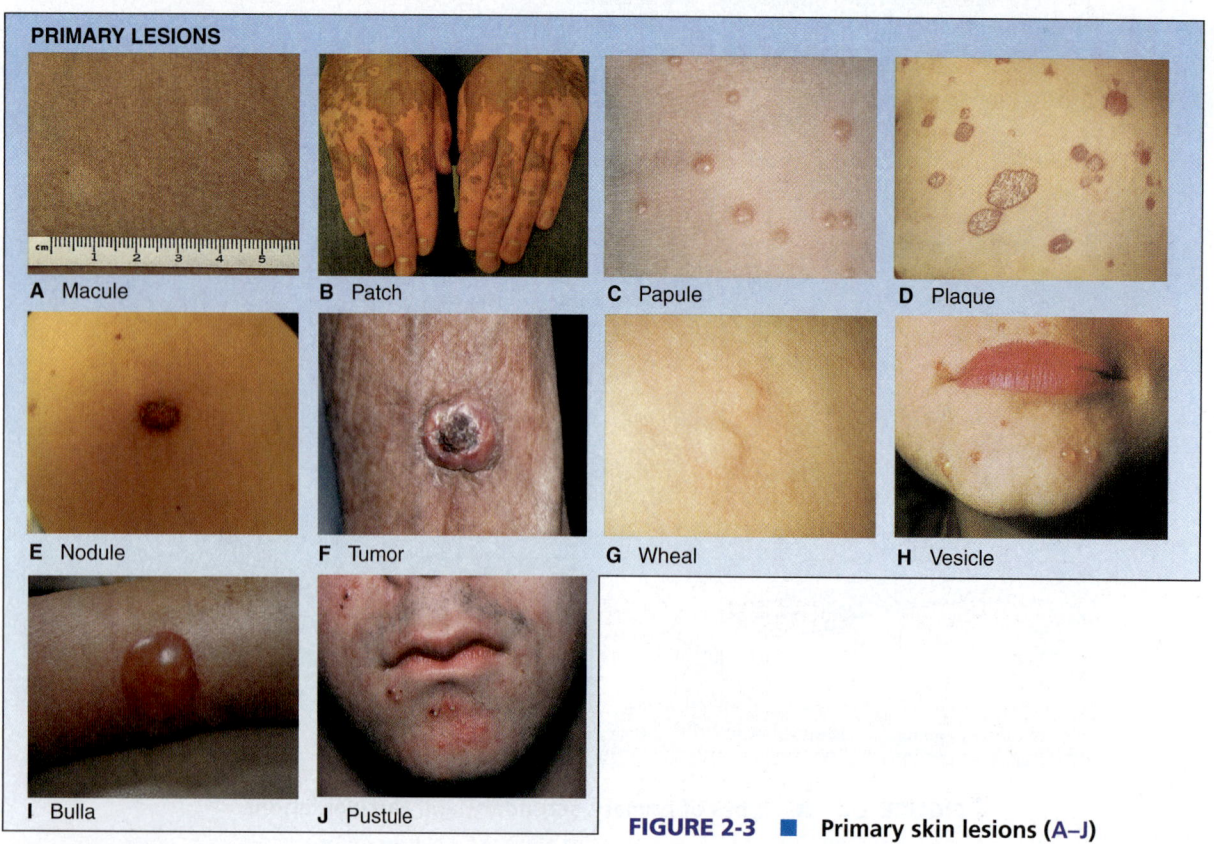

FIGURE 2-3 ■ Primary skin lesions (A–J)

TERM	MEANING
wheal (see Figure 2-3G) wēl	an area of localized skin edema (swelling) (e.g., a hive)
Elevations Formed by Fluid Within a Cavity	
vesicle (see Figure 2-3H) ves′i-kĕl	little bladder; an elevated, fluid-filled sac (blister) within or under the epidermis up to 0.5 cm in diameter (e.g., a fever blister)
bulla (see Figure 2-3I) bul′ă	a blister larger than 0.5 cm (e.g., a second-degree burn) (*bulla* = bubble)
pustule (see Figure 2-3J) pŭs′tyūl	a pus-filled sac (e.g., a pimple)

SECONDARY LESIONS

secondary lesions sek′n-dār-ē lē′zhŭnz	lesions that result in changes to primary lesions
Loss of Skin Surface	
erosion (see Figure 2-4A) ē-rō′zhŭn	gnawed away; loss of superficial epidermis, leaving an area of moisture but no bleeding (e.g., area of moisture after rupture of a vesicle)
ulcer (see Figure 2-4B) ŭl′sĕr	an open sore on the skin or mucous membrane that can bleed and scar; sometimes accompanied by infection (e.g., decubitus ulcer)
excoriation (see Figure 2-4C) eks-kō′rē-ā′shŭn	a scratch mark
fissure (see Figure 2-4D) fish′ŭr	a linear crack in the skin

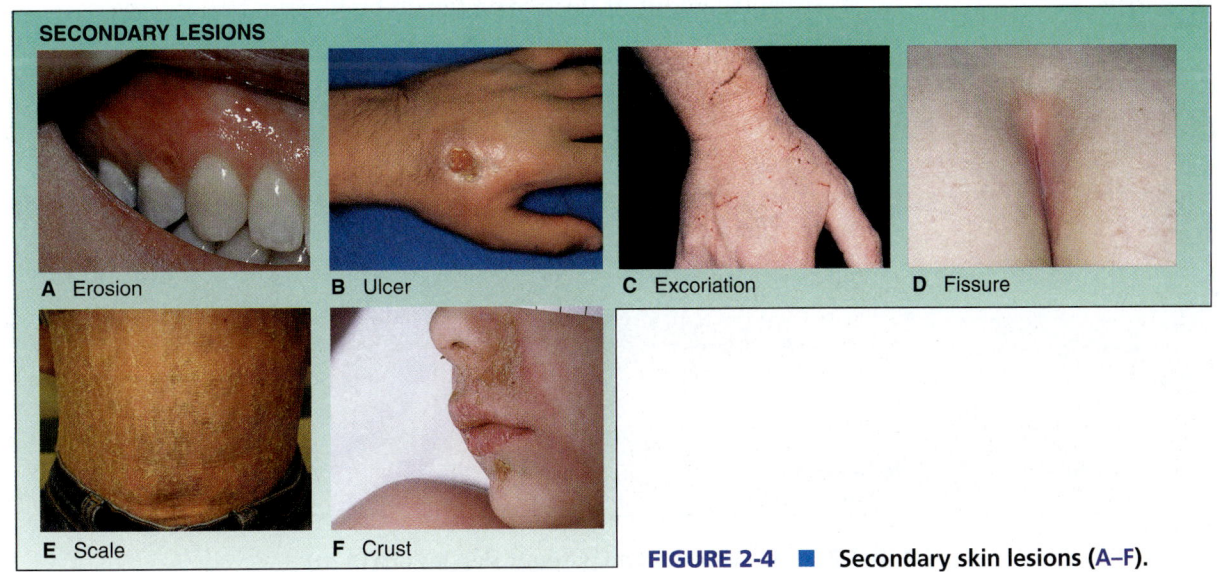

FIGURE 2-4 ■ Secondary skin lesions (A–F).

TERM	MEANING
Material on Skin Surface	
scale (see Figure 2-4E) *skāl*	a thin flake of exfoliated epidermis (e.g., dandruff)
crust (see Figure 2-4F) *krŭst*	a dried residue of serum (body liquid), pus, or blood on the skin (e.g., as seen in impetigo)
VASCULAR LESIONS	
vascular lesions *vas′kyū-lăr lē′zhŭnz*	lesions of a blood vessel
cherry angioma (see Figure 2-5A) *chār′ē an-jē-ō′mă*	a small, round, bright red blood vessel tumor on the skin, seen mostly in people over age 30
telangiectasia (see Figure 2-5B) *tel-an′jē-ek-tā′zē-ă*	a tiny, red blood vessel lesion formed by the dilation of a group of blood vessels radiating from a central arteriole, most commonly on the face, neck, or chest (*telos* = end); also called *spider angioma*
spider angioma *spī′dĕr an-jē-ō′mă*	a tiny, red blood vessel lesion formed by the dilation of a group of blood vessels radiating from a central arteriole, most commonly on the face, neck, or chest; also called *telangiectasia*
PURPURIC LESIONS	
purpuric lesions *pŭr-pū′rik lē′zhŭnz*	purpura; lesions resulting from hemorrhages into the skin
petechia (see Figure 2-5C) *pe-tē′kē-ă*	spot; reddish-brown, minute hemorrhagic spots on the skin that indicate a bleeding tendency; a small purpura
ecchymosis (see Figure 2-5D) *ek-i-mō′sis*	bruise; a black and blue mark; a large purpura (*chymo* = juice)
SCAR FORMATIONS	
cicatrix of the skin *sik′ă-triks*	a mark left by the healing of a sore or wound, showing the replacement of destroyed tissue by fibrous tissue (*cicatrix* = scar)
keloid (see Figure 2-6) *kē′loyd*	an abnormal overgrowth of scar tissue that is thick and irregular (*kele* = tumor)

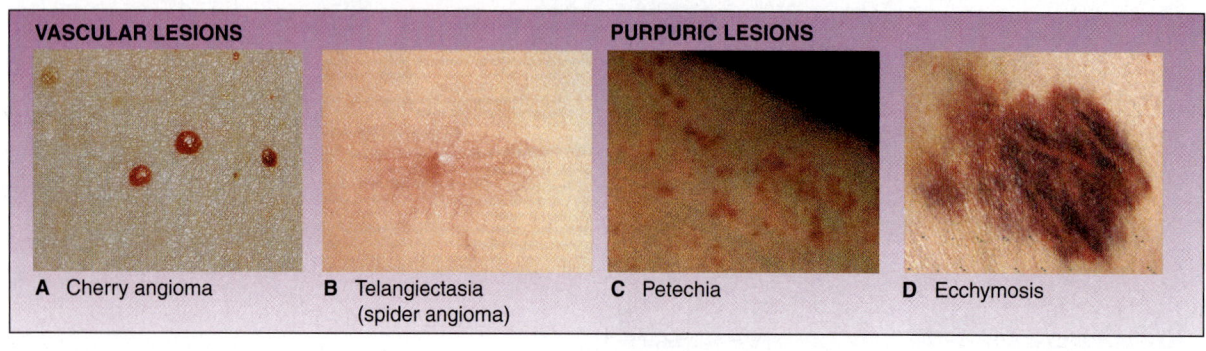

FIGURE 2-5 ■ Vascular and purpuric skin lesions (A–D).

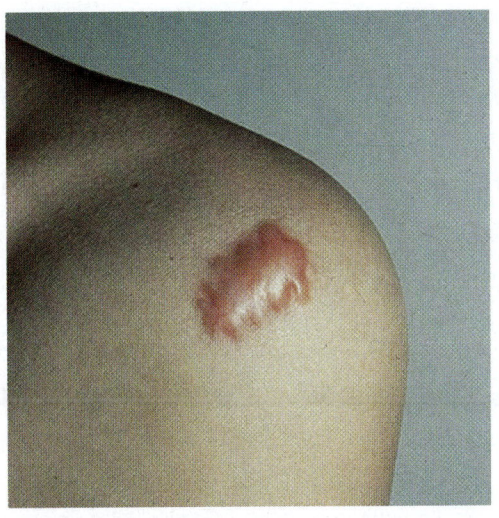

FIGURE 2-6 ■ Keloid.

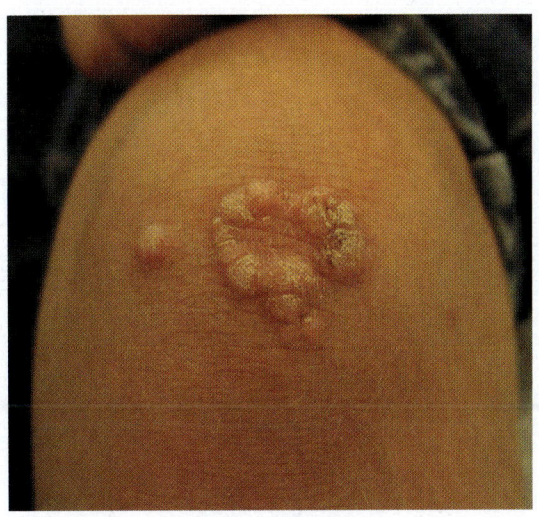

FIGURE 2-7 ■ Verrucae on a knee.

TERM	MEANING
EPIDERMAL GROWTHS	
neoplasm nē′ō-plazm	abnormal tissue that grows by more rapid than normal cellular proliferation
nevus (see Figure 2-1) nē′vŭs	a benign localized overgrowth of melanin-forming cells on the skin present at birth or appearing early in life that can be epidermal or vascular; also called a *mole*
dysplastic nevus dis-plas′tik nē′vŭs	a mole with precancerous changes
verruca (see Figure 2-7) vĕ-rū′kă	an epidermal growth caused by a papilloma virus, also called a *wart*

Programmed Review: Symptomatic Terms (Primary and Secondary Lesions)

ANSWERS	REVIEW
lesion secondary primary secondary	2.28 A _____ is an area of pathologically altered tissue. There are primary and _____ types. Lesions that arise from previously normal skin are called _____ lesions, whereas those that result in changes to primary lesions are called _____ lesions.
macule or macula patch maculae	2.29 A freckle is an example of a _____, which is a flat, discolored spot on the skin up to 1 cm across. A larger, flat, discolored spot is called a _____. The plural of macula is _____.

ANSWERS	REVIEW
solid plaque nodule small	**2.30** A papule is a _____ mass on the skin up to 0.5 cm in diameter, such as a mole. A _____ is like a papule but is greater than 1 cm in diameter and is limited to the surface of the skin. A _____, like a papule, is greater than 1 cm in diameter but extends deeper into the epidermis. Recall that the suffix -*ule* is a diminutive that means _____.
tumor edema	**2.31** Another type of solid mass is a _____, which is larger than 1 to 2 cm. A wheal is an area of localized skin _____ (swelling).
vesicle, bulla -ae, pustule	**2.32** There are three types of elevated skin lesions containing fluid within a cavity. A small, elevated blister up to 0.5 cm, such as a fever blister, is a _____. A larger blister (more than 0.5 cm) is a _____, such as may occur with a second-degree burn. The plural form ends in _____. A pus-filled sac, like a pimple, is called a _____.
erosion, sore excoriation. out or away -ation fissure	**2.33** Some secondary lesions result in a loss of skin surface. If skin is lost, leaving an area of moisture but no bleeding, it is called an _____. An ulcer is an open _____ on the skin or mucous membrane that can bleed. A scratch mark is called an _____. Recall that the prefix *ex-* means _____, and that the suffix _____ refers to a process. A crack in the skin is called a _____.
scale crust blood	**2.34** A thin flake of dead epidermis is called a _____. On the other hand, a _____ on the skin is a dried residue of serum, pus, or _____.
cicatrix keloid tumor	**2.35** A healed sore or wound leaves a scar, which is called a _____ of the skin. An abnormal overgrowth of scar tissue, from the root *kele* (tumor), is a _____. Recall that the suffix *-oid* means resembling, which in this case implies that a keloid resembles but is not actually a _____.
vascular cherry spider tumor telangiectasia	**2.36** Lesions of a blood vessel are called _____ lesions. A _____ angioma is a small, bright red blood vessel tumor on the skin. A _____ angioma is a tiny, red blood vessel lesion in a group of vessels radiating from a central arteriole. The suffix *-oma* means _____. Another term for a spider angioma is _____.

ANSWERS	REVIEW
Purpuric purple petechia, iae ecchymosis es	2.37 _____ lesions look purple because of hemorrhages into the skin. The combining form *purpur/o* means _____. A small purpura appearing as a tiny, reddish-brown spot on the skin is called a _____. The plural form is petech_____. A bruise is called an _____; the plural form is ecchymos_____.
nevus mole painful, difficult, or faulty wart verrucae	2.38 A mole is called a _____. A dysplastic nevus is a _____ with precancerous changes. The prefix *dys-* means _____. A verruca is an epidermal growth caused by a papilloma virus and is also called a _____. The plural of verruca is _____.

Self Instruction: General Symptomatic Terms

Study this table to prepare for the programmed review that follows.

TERM	MEANING
alopecia al-ō-pē′shē-ă	baldness; natural or unnatural deficiency of hair
comedo (*pl.* **comedos, comedones**) (see Figure 2-8) kom′ē-dō	a plug of sebum (oil) within the opening of a hair follicle
closed comedo klōsd kom′ē-dō	a comedo below the skin surface, with a white center (whitehead)
open comedo ō′pĕn kom′ē-dō	a comedo open to the skin surface, with a black center caused by the presence of melanin exposed to air (blackhead)
eruption ē-rŭp′shŭn	appearance of a skin lesion
erythema er-i-thē′mă	redness of skin

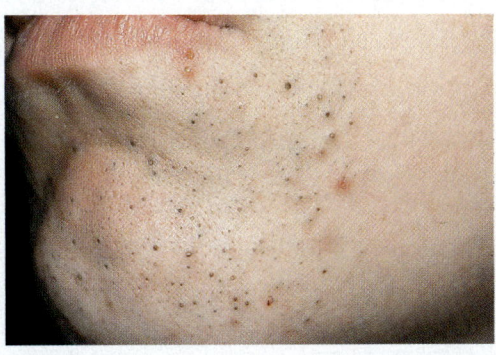

FIGURE 2-8 ■ Closed and open comedones.

TERM	MEANING
pruritus *prū-rī′tŭs*	severe itching
rash *rash*	a general term for skin eruption
skin pigmentation *skin pig-men-tā′shŭn*	skin color resulting from the presence of melanin
depigmentation *dē-pig-men-tā′shŭn*	loss of melanin pigment in the skin
hypopigmentation *hī′pō-pig-men-tā′shŭn*	areas of skin lacking color because of deficient amounts of melanin
hyperpigmentation *hī′pĕr-pig-men-tā′shŭn*	darkened areas of skin caused by excessive amounts of melanin
suppuration *sŭp′yŭ-rā′shŭn*	production of purulent matter (pus)
urticaria *ŭr′ti-kar′i-ă*	hives; an eruption of wheals (see **Figure 2-3G**) on the skin accompanied by itching (*urtica* = stinging nettle)
xeroderma *zēr′ō-dĕr′mă*	dry skin

Programmed Review: General Symptomatic Terms

ANSWERS	REVIEW
alopecia	2.39 Baldness, or a deficiency of hair, is called _____.
comedo comedones whitehead blackhead	2.40 A plug of sebum (oil) within the opening of a hair follicle is called a _____. The plural form is comedos or _____. A comedo below the skin surface with a white center is called a closed comedo or _____. A comedo open to the skin surface with center caused by the presence of melanin exposed to air is called a _____.
lesion rash urticaria condition of	2.41 An eruption is the appearance of a skin _____. A _____ is a general term for a skin eruption. An eruption of wheals on the skin (hives) accompanied by itching is called _____. Remember that the suffix *-ia* means a _____ _____.
pruritus itching	2.42 Any severe itching is called _____. Using the adjective form of pruritus, a pruritic eruption is one that is marked by severe _____.

ANSWERS	REVIEW
erthry/o erythema pertaining to	**2.43** The combining form for red is _____. Redness of the skin is called _____. The adjective erythematous means _____ ____ redness of the skin.
black color not deficient, excessive de hypo hyper	**2.44** *Melan/o* is the combining form meaning _____. Melanin is the pigment that gives _____ to the skin. Pigmentation describes the process of skin coloration. Recall the meaning of the following prefixes: *de-* means from, down, or _____; *hypo-* means below or _____; and *hyper-* means above or _____. Each is used to describe a different pigmentation of the skin. Using the prefix meaning from, down, or not, the total loss or absence of melanin is called ____pigmentation. Too little or deficient melanin causes _____pigmentation, and too much or excessive deposits of melanin cause _____pigmentation.
xer/o skin xeroderma	**2.45** The combining form meaning dry is _____. The Greek word derma means _____. Therefore, the term for dry skin is _____.

Self-Instruction: Diagnostic Terms

Study this table to prepare for the programmed review that follows.

TERM	MEANING
acne (see **Figure 2-9**) *ak'nē*	inflammation of the sebaceous glands and hair follicles of the skin, evidenced by comedones (blackheads), pustules, or nodules on the skin
albinism *al'bi-nizm*	a hereditary condition characterized by a partial or total lack of melanin pigment (particularly in the eyes, skin, and hair)

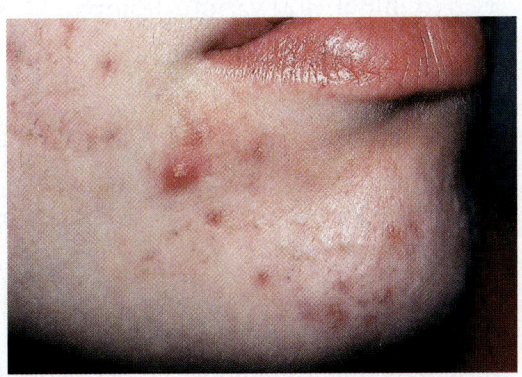

FIGURE 2-9 ■ Acne. Inflammatory papules, pustules, and closed comedones are present on the face.

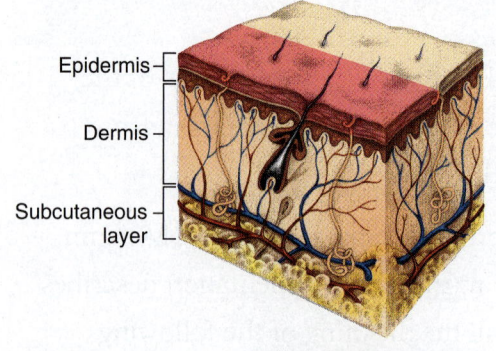
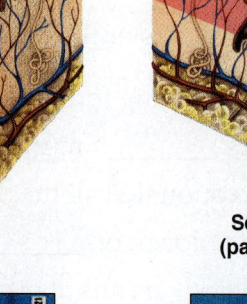
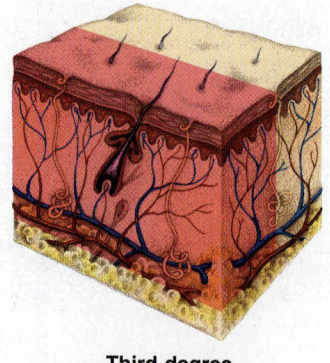

Epidermis
Dermis
Subcutaneous layer

First-degree (superficial) burn

Second-degree (partial-thickness) burn

Third-degree (full-thickness) burn (after skin graft)

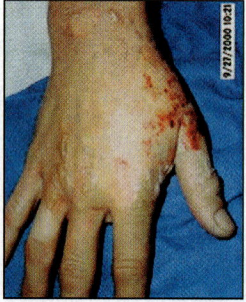
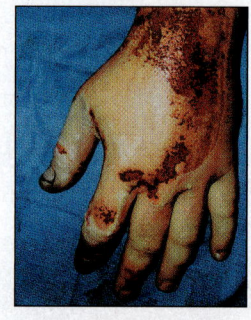
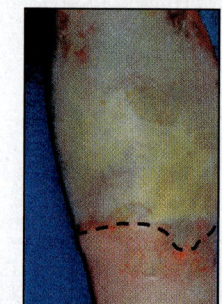

FIGURE 2-10 ■ The three degrees of burns.

TERM	MEANING
burn (see **Figure 2-10**) *běrn*	injury to body tissue caused by heat, chemicals, electricity, radiation, or gases
first-degree (or 1st-degree) burn *first-dĕ-grē' běrn*	a burn involving only the epidermis; characterized by erythema (redness) and hyperesthesia (excessive sensation); also called *superficial burn*
second-degree (or 2nd-degree) burn *sek' ŭnd-dĕ-grē' běrn*	a burn involving the epidermis and the dermis; characterized by erythema, hyperesthesia, and vesications (blisters); also called *partial-thickness burn*
third-degree (or 3rd-degree) burn *third-dĕ-grē' běrn*	a burn involving destruction of the entire skin that extends into the subcutaneous layer; also called *full-thickness burn*
dermatitis *dr-mă-tī' tis*	inflammation of the skin characterized by erythema, pruritus (itching), and various lesions
dermatosis *děr-mă-tō' sis*	any disorder of the skin
exanthematous viral disease *ek-zan-them' ă-t ŭs vī' răl di-zēz*	an eruption of the skin caused by a viral disease (*exanthema* = eruption)
rubella *rū-bel' ă*	an acute but mild disease caused by rubella virus; also called *German measles*
rubeola *rū-bē' ō-lă*	a term used for measles
varicella *var-i-sel' ă*	an acute contagious disease caused by Varicella Zoster; also called *chickenpox*

TERM	MEANING
eczema *ek′zĕ-mă*	generic term for inflammatory conditions of the skin characterized by inflamed, swollen papules and vesicles that crust and scale, often with sensations of itching and burning
furuncle *fū′rŭng-kel*	a painful nodule originating deep in a hair follicle often caused by *Staphylococcus aureus;* also called a *boil*
carbuncle *kar′bŭng-kel*	a skin infection consisting of clusters of furuncles
abscess *ab′ses*	a localized collection of pus in a cavity formed by the inflammation of surrounding tissues, which heals when drained or excised (*abscessus* = a going away)
gangrene *gang′grēn*	tissue death associated with loss of blood supply
herpes simplex virus type 1 (HSV-1) *hĕr′pēz sim′pleks vī′rŭs*	infection caused by herpes virus marked by the eruption of vesicles (cold sores or fever blisters) around the mouth and nose
herpes simplex virus type 2 (HSV-2) (see Figure 14-9) *hĕr′pēz sim′pleks vī′rŭs*	sexually transmitted, ulcer-like lesions of the genital and anorectal skin and mucosa; after initial infection, the virus lies dormant in the nervous system and may recur at times of illness or stress
herpes zoster *hĕr′pēz zos′tĕr*	a viral disease affecting the peripheral nerves characterized by painful blisters that spread over the skin following affected nerves, usually unilateral; also called *shingles* (*zoster* = girdle)
impetigo *im-pe-tī′gō*	a highly contagious, bacterial skin inflammation marked by pustules that rupture and become crusted, most often around the mouth and nostrils
keratosis *ker-ă-tō′sis*	thickened areas of epidermis
actinic keratosis (see Figure 2-11) *ak-tin′ik ker-ă-tō′sis*	localized thickening of the skin caused by excessive exposure to sunlight, a known precursor to cancer (*actinic* = ray; *solar* = sun); also called *solar keratosis*
seborrheic keratosis (see Figure 2-12) *seb-ō-rē′ik ker-ă-tō′sis*	superficial, benign, pigmented, wart-like lesions; more common after the third decade

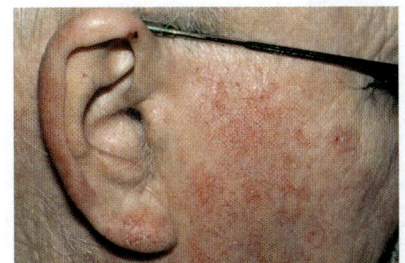

FIGURE 2-11 ■ Actinic (solar) keratosis.

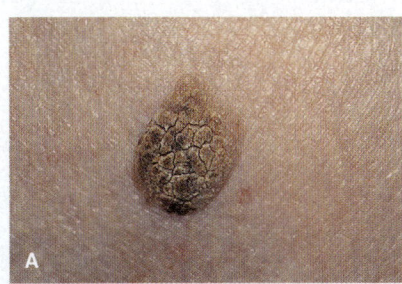 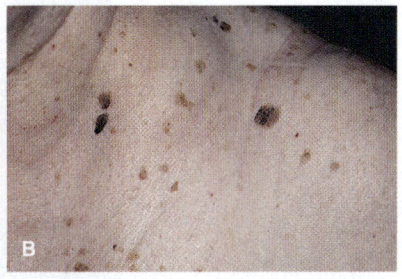

FIGURE 2-12 ■ Seborrheic keratosis. **A.** Lesion with a warty, "stuck-on" appearance. **B.** Multiple lesions showing various colors and sizes.

TERM	MEANING
lupus *lū'pŭs*	any of various chronic autoimmune disease characterized by inflammation of the skin and other tissues (*lupus* = wolf)
cutaneous lupus erythematosus *kyū-tā'nē-ŭs lū'pŭs ĕr-i-thĕ'mă-tō'sŭs*	various skin lesions evidenced by a characteristic rash, especially on the face, neck, and scalp
systemic lupus erythematosus (SLE) *sis-tem'ik lū'pŭs ĕr-i-thĕ'mă-tō'sŭs*	a more severe form of lupus involving the skin, joints, and often vital organs (e.g., lungs or kidneys)
malignant cutaneous neoplasm *mĕ-lig'nănt kyū-tā'nē-ŭs nē'ō-plazm*	skin cancer
squamous cell carcinoma (SCC) (see Figure 2-1) *skwā'mŭs sel kar-si-nō'mă*	malignant neoplasm of the stratified squamous epithelium
basal cell carcinoma (BCC) (see Figure 2-1) *bā'săl sel kar-si-nō'mă*	malignant neoplasm of the stratum basale of the epidermis; the most common type of skin cancer
melanoma (see Figure 2-1) *mel'ă-nō'mă*	malignant neoplasm composed of melanocytes
Kaposi sarcoma (see Figure 2-13) *kă-pō'sē sar-cō'mă*	malignant tumor of the walls of blood vessels, appearing as painless, dark bluish-purple plaques on the skin; often spreads to the lymph nodes and internal organs; commonly seen in patients with HIV/AIDS (human immunodeficiency virus/acquired immunodeficiency syndrome)
onychia *ō-nik'ē-ă*	inflammation of the fingernail or toenail

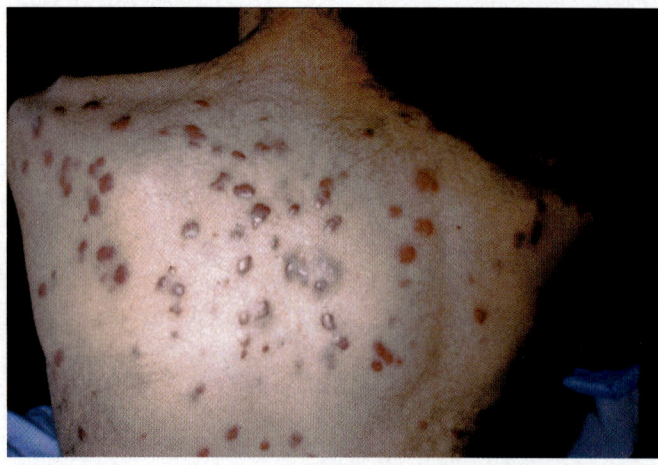

FIGURE 2-13 ■ Lesions of the AIDS-related Kaposi sarcoma.

TERM	MEANING
paronychia (see Figure 2-14) *par-ō-nik′ē-ă*	inflammation of the nail fold
pediculosis (see Figure 2-15) *pĕ-dik′yū-lō′sis*	infestation with lice that causes itching and dermatitis (*pediculo* = louse)
pediculosis capitis *pĕ-dik′yū-lō′sis kap′i-tis*	presence of lice on the scalp, seen especially in children, with nits attached to hairs (*capitis* = head)
pediculosis pubis *pĕ-dik′yū-lō′sis pyū′bis*	infestation with the pubic or crab louse, especially in pubic hair (*pubis* = groin)

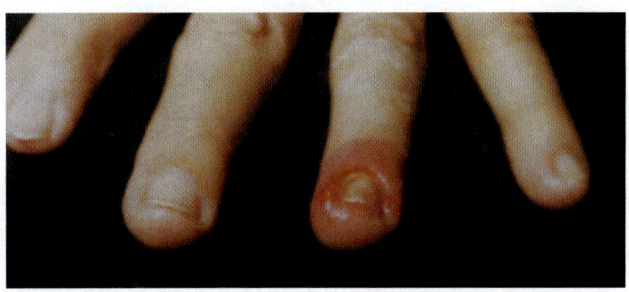

FIGURE 2-14 ■ Paronychia.

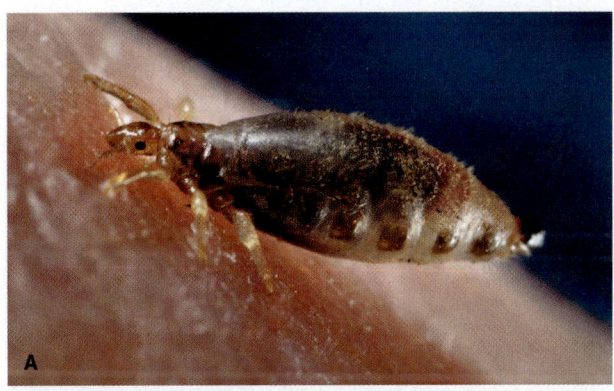

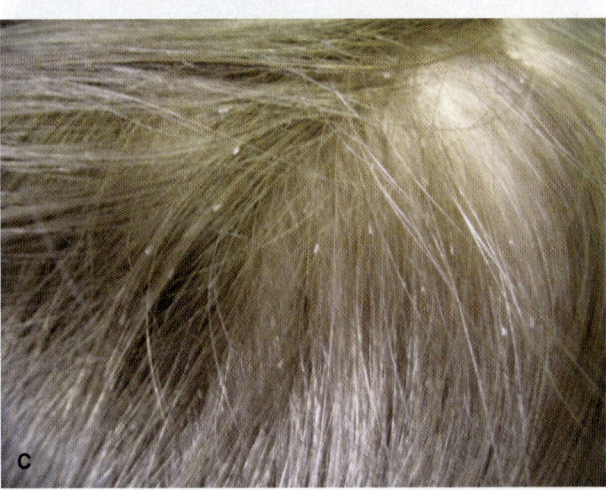

FIGURE 2-15 ■ Pediculosis. **A.** Female body louse obtaining a blood meal from a human host. **B.** Unhatched nit of the head louse attached to a human hair. **C.** Pediculosis capitis (head lice) infestation. Note the unhatched nits visible on the hair shafts.

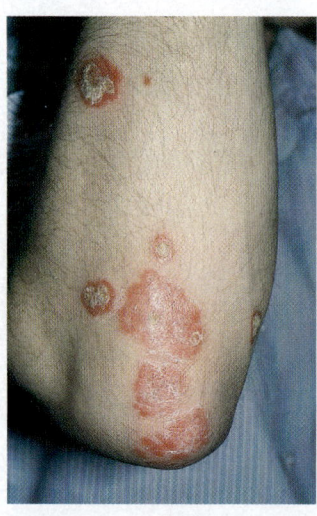

FIGURE 2-16 ■ Psoriasis lesions on the arm and elbow.

TERM	MEANING
psoriasis (see Figure 2-16) *sō-rī′ă-sis*	inherited skin disease marked by red, itchy, scaly patches
scabies *skā′bēz*	a contagious skin disease marked by itching and small raised red spots caused by the itch mite; intense pruritus between the fingers, genitalia, trunk, and extremities is common (*scabo* = to scratch)
seborrhea *seb-ō-rē′ă*	a skin condition marked by the hypersecretion of sebum from the sebaceous glands
tinea *tin′ē-ă*	a group of fungal skin diseases identified by the body part affected, including tinea corporis (body), commonly called ringworm, and tinea pedis (foot), also called *athlete's foot*
vitiligo (see Figure 2-3B) *vit-i-lī′gō*	a condition in which the pigment is lost due to melanin destruction, creating areas of white patches on the skin or hair

Programmed Review: Diagnostic Terms

ANSWERS	REVIEW
condition skin dermatosis -itis dermatitis inflammation, skin eczema	**2.46** The suffix *-osis* refers to an increase or _____. *Dermat/o* means _____. Therefore, the general term meaning skin condition is _____. The suffix meaning inflammation is _____. An inflammation of the skin is therefore called _____. There are many forms of dermatitis or _____ of the _____. A term that is interchangeable with dermatitis, characterized by inflamed skin with various lesions accompanied by itching and burning is _____. Eczematous is the adjective form of the term.

ANSWERS	REVIEW
comedos or comedones acne	**2.47** An inflammation of the sebaceous glands and hair follicles, often evidenced by _____ (blackheads or whiteheads), pustules, or nodules on the skin, is called _____.
condition of melanin vitiligo	**2.48** The suffix *-ism* refers to a _____ ____. Albinism is a hereditary condition characterized by a partial or total lack of _____ pigment in the body. The condition caused by the destruction of melanin that results in the appearance of white patches on the skin is called _____.
first-degree (1st-degree) dermis subcutaneous	**2.49** A _____-_____ burn involves only the epidermis. A 2nd-degree burn involves both the epidermis and the _____. A 3rd-degree burn involves damage to the _____ layer.
viral rubella rubeola chickenpox	**2.50** Exanthematous _____ disease is an eruption of the skin caused by a viral infection. One such viral disease, also called German measles, is _____. A similar-sounding but different form of measles is _____. Varicella, another viral disease, is commonly called _____.
furuncle carbuncle	**2.51** A painful nodule from inflammation in a hair follicle caused by *Staphylococcus aureus* is called a boil, or a _____. A skin infection consisting of clusters of furuncles is a _____.
abscess	**2.52** Pus that collects in a cavity formed by the inflammation of surrounding tissues is called an _____. It usually heals when drained or excised.
blood	**2.53** Gangrene is tissue death because of a loss of _____ supply.
virus vesicles genital or anorectal Herpes vesicles or blisters	**2.54** There are several forms of herpes disease, which are caused by a _____. Herpes simplex virus type 1 causes an eruption of _____, such as cold sores or fever blisters. Type 2 is sexually transmitted and causes lesions in _____ skin. _____ zoster affects the peripheral nerves and is characterized by painful _____ that spread over the skin.

ANSWERS	REVIEW
Impetigo scabies fungus pediculosis capitis pubis	2.55 _____ is a highly contagious, bacterial skin inflammation usually occurring around the mouth and nose. Another contagious skin disease, called _____, is caused by a mite that invades the skin and causes intense itching. Tinea is a different group of contagious skin diseases caused by a _____. Lice also can cause an infestation on the skin, called _____. Head lice are called pediculosis _____, and lice infesting the pubic region are called pediculosis _____.
hard condition of keratosis keratoses actinic sun seborrheic	2.56 Putting the combining form *kerat/o*, meaning _____, with the suffix *-osis*, meaning a _____ ____, makes the word _____, a condition of thickened epidermis. The plural form of this term is _____. Solar keratoses, or _____ keratoses, are caused by excessive exposure to the _____. Benign, wart-like tumors are called _____ keratoses.
   lupus, skin systemic erythematosus	2.57 An autoimmune disease involving inflammation of various parts of the body was named after the Latin word for wolf, _____. Cutaneous lupus is limited to the _____ and causes a characteristic rash. A more serious form, called _____ lupus _____ (SLE), affects many body organs.
condition of fingernail or toenail alongside of paronychia	2.58 In the term onychia, the suffix *-ia* (meaning _____ _____ inflammation), is joined with *onych/o* (meaning a _____). The suffix *para-*, meaning _____ _____, combined with *onych/o* and the suffix *-ia* form the term denoting a condition of inflammation of the nail fold, or _____. (Remember the rules of spelling: drop the final vowel from the prefix before joining it to a combining form that begins with a vowel.)
discharge seborrhea	2.59 Recall that the suffix *-rrhea* means _____. A skin condition marked by the hypersecretion and discharge of sebum is called _____.
psoriasis	2.60 A condition in which the skin has silvery scales covering red patches, papules, and/or plaques is _____.

ANSWERS	REVIEW
new	**2.61** Neoplasia is a term describing a condition of _____
malignant	formation of tissue that is either cancerous (_____) or
benign	noncancerous (_____). Several different forms of malignant
squamous cell	neoplasia can involve the skin. A _____ _____
	carcinoma is a tumor of the squamous epithelium. A malignant
basal cell	tumor of the stratum basale of the epidermis is a _____ _____
carcinoma	_____. A tumor composed of melanocytes is a
melanoma	_____. Remember that the suffix *-oma*
tumor, sarcoma	means _____. Kaposi _____ is a tumor of the walls of
	blood vessels, commonly seen in patients with HIV/AIDS.

Self-Instruction: Diagnostic Tests and Procedures

Study this table to prepare for the programmed review that follows.

TEST OR PROCEDURE	EXPLANATION
biopsy (Bx) (see Figure 2-17) bī′op-sē	removal of a small piece of tissue for microscopic pathologic examination
excisional biopsy ek-sizh′ŭn-ul bī′op-sē	removal of an entire lesion
incisional biopsy in-sizh′ŭn-ul bī′op-sē	removal of a selected portion of a lesion
shave biopsy shāv bī′op-sē	a technique using a surgical blade to "shave" tissue from the epidermis and upper dermis
culture and sensitivity (C&S) kŭl′chŭr and sen-si-tiv′i-tē	a technique of isolating and growing colonies of microorganisms to identify a pathogen and to determine which drugs might be effective for combating the infection it has caused

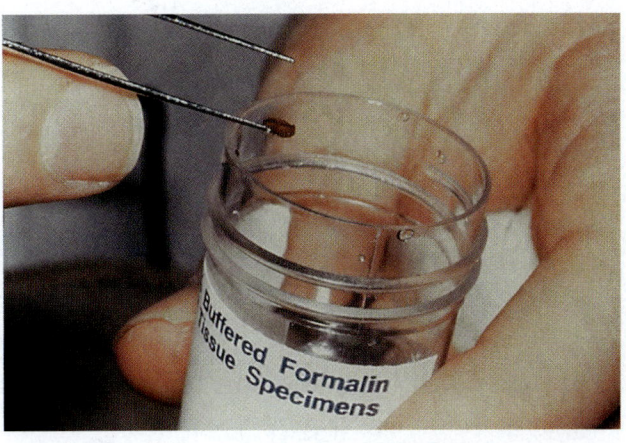

FIGURE 2-17 ■ Collection of biopsy specimen.

TEST OR PROCEDURE	EXPLANATION
frozen section (FS) *frō′zen sek′shŭn*	a surgical technique that involves cutting a thin piece of tissue from a frozen specimen for immediate pathologic examination
skin tests *skin testz*	methods for determining the reaction of the body to a given substance by applying it to, or injecting it into, the skin; commonly used in treating allergies
scratch test *skratch test*	a test in which a substance is applied to the skin through a scratch
patch test *patch test*	a test in which a substance is applied topically to the skin on a small piece of blotting paper or wet cloth

Programmed Review: Diagnostic Tests and Procedures

ANSWERS	REVIEW
biopsy lesion out or away incisional portion, shave	**2.62** In many different body systems, small samples of tissue are removed for a diagnostic test involving microscopic examination. This is called a _____ (Bx). An excisional biopsy involves removal of the entire _____. Remember that the prefix *ex-* means _____. An _____ biopsy, in contrast removes only a _____ of the lesion. Another type, called a _____ biopsy, uses a surgical blade to "shave" tissue from the epidermis and upper dermis.
culture sensitivity	**2.63** A technique for isolating and growing a colony of microorganisms to identify a pathogen is called _____ and _____ (C&S). This helps to determine which drugs may be effective in fighting the infection.
frozen section FS	**2.64** A tissue specimen may be frozen and cut thin for examination. This is called a _____ _____ and is abbreviated _____.
scratch patch	**2.65** Skin tests are commonly used to identify substances to which a person may be allergic. In the _____ test, a small amount of the substance is applied to the skin through a scratch. Applying the substance topically to the skin with a small piece of paper or cloth is called a _____ test.

Self-Instruction: Operative Terms

Study table on following page to prepare for the programmed review that follows (see **Figure 2-18**).

CENTRAL MEDICAL SURGICENTER

211 Medical Center Drive • Central City, US 90000-1234 • PHONE: (012) 125-6784 • FAX: (012) 125-9999

OPERATIVE REPORT

PREOPERATIVE DIAGNOSIS: Complex lacerations of the nose and upper lip due to a dog bite.

POSTOPERATIVE DIAGNOSIS: Complex lacerations of the nose and upper lip due to a dog bite.

OPERATION: Revision and closure of complex lacerations of the nose and upper lip.

ANESTHESIOLOGIST: H. Vaughn, M.D.

INDICATIONS:
This 33-year-old female sustained a dog bite to her face while she was handling a dog at a veterinary clinic. Because of the complexity of her injuries, a plastic surgery consultation was requested.

PROCEDURE:
The patient's face was prepped and draped in the usual sterile fashion. A copious amount of dilute Betadine and saline were used to irrigate out all the lacerations. Subcutaneous tissues in the vicinity of the lacerations were infiltrated with 0.5% Xylocaine with 1:200,000 concentration epinephrine. Attention was directed to the patient's upper lip. There was a laceration approximately 1.5 cm oriented parallel to the mucocutaneous junction. There was another diagonal laceration measuring approximately 1.0 cm. The devitalized tissues were debrided sharply. The laceration was closed in layers with 5-0 Vicryl sutures and then with 6-0 and 7-0 Prolene on the skin. Attention was directed to the patient's nose. There are two major lacerations. There is a 2 cm laceration to the left ala. This was a full thickness laceration through the entire alar cartilage into the nose as well as the entire alar rim. First, the devitalized cartilage was debrided sharply. The intranasal incision was closed with 4-0 chromic catgut suture. The alar rim was meticulously reapproximated with a few tacking sutures to produce perfect anatomic continuity. The remainder of the laceration was closed with 6-0 and 7-0 Prolene sutures in interrrupted and running fashion. At this time, attention was directed to another laceration measuring approximately 2.5 cm located in the right nasal sill area extending to the columella and lip junction. The columella was detached. Again, all devitalized tissues were debrided sharply. Deep subcutaneous tissues were approximated with 5-0 chromic catgut sutures in such a fashion as to meticulously reapproximate the columella into its normal anatomic position. The nasal sill was reapproximated with 6-0 Prolene sutures meticulously reapproximating the detailed anatomy of this area. The remainder of the wounds were closed with 6-0 and 7-0 Prolene sutures in a running and interrupted fashion. A few smaller lacerations were closed with Prolene sutures on the bridge of the nose. All the wounds were covered with Neosporin ointment, Adaptic, and appropriate bandages.

The patient was given intravenous antibiotics; and she will be started on Keflex 250 mg p.o. t.i.d. The patient will be seen in my office in 24 hours for follow-up.

T. Romero, M.D.

TR:kf
D: 10/19/20xx
T: 10/20/20xx

OPERATIVE REPORT

PT. NAME: SMITH, WILMA
ID NO: OPS-167480621
SURGEON: T. ROMERO, M.D.

A: Removing suture from sterile package with needle holder

B: Continuous sutures are several stitches from a single length of suture material, knotted at each end

C: Interrupted sutures are groups of individual stitches, each of which is knotted

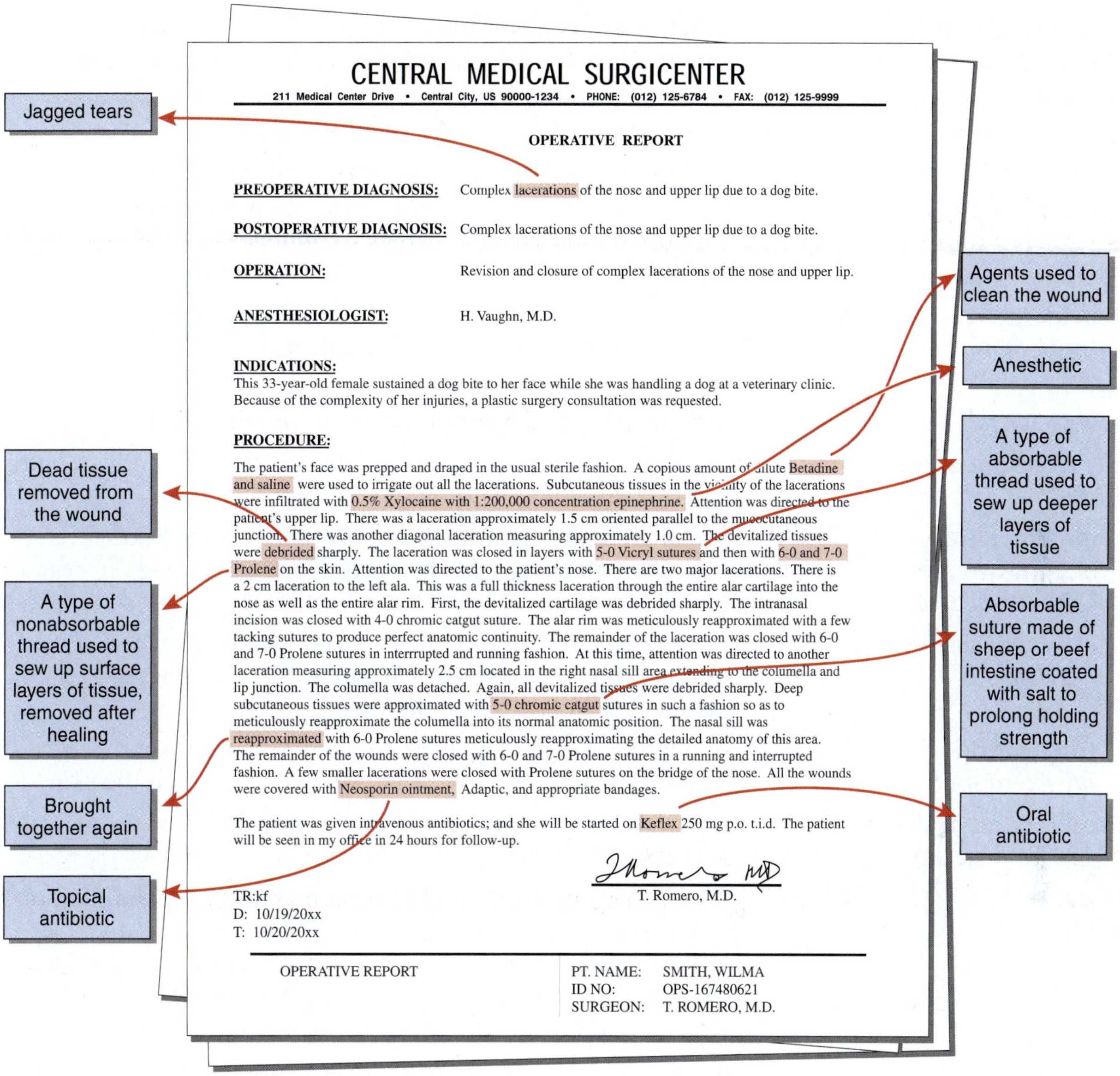

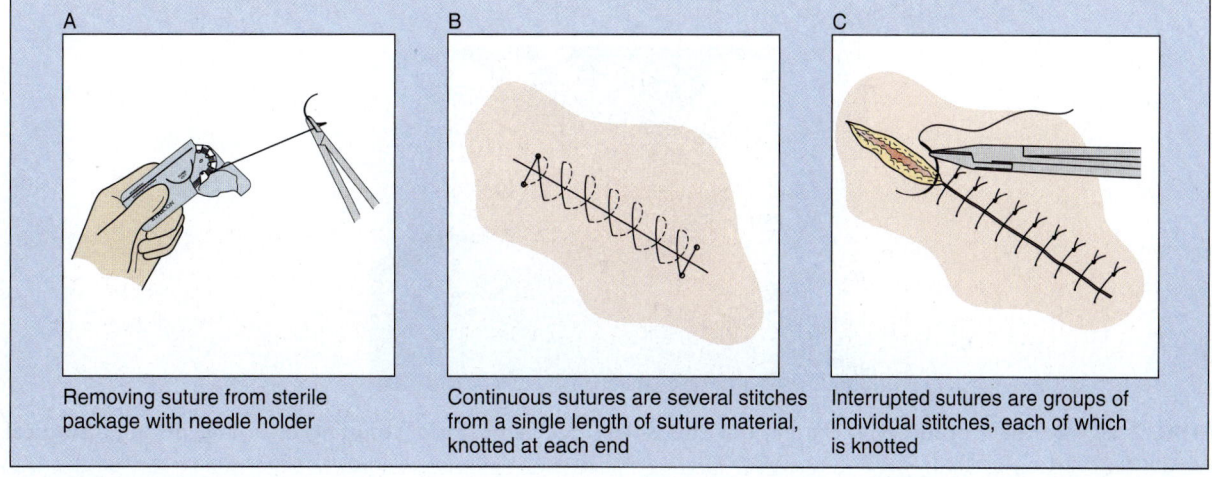

FIGURE 2-18 ■ **Typical documentation of a surgical procedure. Types of sutures (A–C) are also shown.**

TERM	MEANING
chemosurgery kem'ō-sŭr-jĕr-ē	removal of tissue after it has been destroyed by chemical means
chemical peel kĕm'i-kl pēl	a technique for restoring wrinkled, scarred, or blemished skin by applying an acid solution to "peel" away the top layers of the skin
cryosurgery krī-ō-sŭr'jĕr-ē	destruction of tissue by freezing with application of an extremely cold chemical (e.g., liquid nitrogen)
dermabrasion dĕr-mă-brā'zhŭn	surgical removal of epidermis frozen by aerosol spray using wire brushes and emery papers to remove scars, tattoos, and/or wrinkles
debridement dā-brēd-mon'	removal of dead tissue from a wound or burn site to promote healing and to prevent infection
curettage kyū-rĕ-tahzh'	cleaning; scraping a wound using a spoon-like cutting instrument called a curette; used for debridement
electrosurgical procedures ē-lek-trō-sŭr'ji-căl prō-cē'jŭrz	use of electric current to destroy tissue; the type and strength of the current and method of application vary

electrocautery
    (see Figure 2-19)
    ē-lek'trō-kaw'tĕr-ē
	use of an instrument heated by electric current (cautery) to coagulate bleeding areas by burning the tissue (e.g., to sear a blood vessel)

electrodesiccation ē-lek'trō-des-i-kā'shŭn	use of high-frequency electric currents to destroy tissue by drying it; the active electrode makes direct contact with the skin lesion (*desiccate* = to dry up)
fulguration ful-gŭ-rā'shŭn	to lighten; use of long, high-frequency, electric sparks to destroy tissue; the active electrode does *not* touch the skin
incision and drainage (I&D) in-sizh'ŭn and drān'ăj	incision and drainage of an infected skin lesion (e.g., an abscess)
laser lā'zĕr	an acronym for *l*ight *a*mplification by *s*timulated *e*mission of *r*adiation; an instrument that concentrates high frequencies of light into a small, extremely intense beam that is precise in depth and diameter; applied to body tissues to destroy lesions or for dissection (cutting of parts for study)
laser surgery lā'zĕr sŭr'jĕr-ē	surgery using a laser in various dermatologic procedures to remove lesions, scars, or tattoos

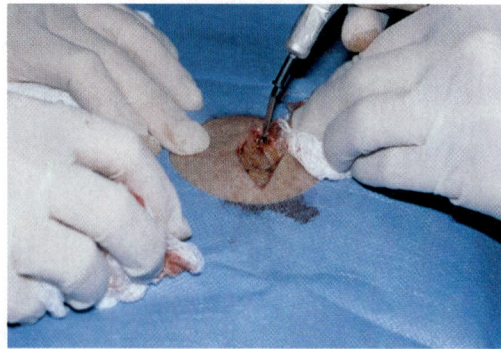

FIGURE 2-19 ■ Electrocautery. A cautery devised is used for hemostasis (stopping bleeding) during a surgical procedure.

TERM	MEANING
Mohs surgery *mōz sŭr′jĕr-ē*	a technique used to excise tumors of the skin by removing fresh tissue, layer by layer, until a tumor-free plane is reached
skin grafting *skin graft′ing*	transfer of skin from one body site to another to replace skin that has been lost through a burn or injury
autograft *aw′tō-graft*	graft transfer to a new position in the body of the same person (*auto* = self)
heterograft or **xenograft** *het′er-ō-graft, zen′ō-graft*	graft transfer between different species, such as from animal to human (*hetero* = different; *xeno* = strange)
homograft or **allograft** *hō′mō-graft, al′ō-graft*	graft transfer between persons of the same species, such as human to human (*homo* = same)

Programmed Review: Operative Terms

ANSWERS	REVIEW
chemical peel	**2.66** A special form of chemosurgery, called a _____ _____, uses an acid to peel away the top layers of skin.
freezing	**2.67** Cryosurgery destroys tissue by _____ it, usually with an extremely cold chemical, such as liquid nitrogen.
dermabrasion	**2.68** Another way to remove skin tissue, particularly scars, tattoos, or wrinkles, is to surgically scrape off the skin using a wire brush or emery paper. This is called _____.
from, down, or not debridement curettage	**2.69** Recall that the prefix *de-* means _____. When dead tissue is removed from a wound or burn site, this is called _____. This is often done with a cutting instrument called a curette, and the technique is thus called _____.
electrosurgery electrocautery drying fulguration process	**2.70** Electricity is used in many dermatologic procedures to destroy unwanted tissue. The general term for such operative procedures is _____. The use of an electrically heated instrument to coagulate a bleeding area by burning the tissue is called _____. Electrodesiccation, in contrast, applies an electrical current directly to a skin lesion to destroy the tissue by _____ it. A process using electrical sparks to destroy tissue is called _____. In both terms, the suffix *-ation* means a _____.
incision, drainage	**2.71** An infected lesion, such as an abscess, may undergo the surgical procedure called _____ and _____ (I&D).

ANSWERS	REVIEW
laser laser	**2.72** An amplified, intense light beam, called a _____, is used to remove various kinds of lesions during an operative procedure called _____ surgery.
layer	**2.73** Mohs surgery is a technique for removing a tumor one _____ at a time until a tumor-free layer is reached.
graft autograft, self human allograft species different, xenograft strange	**2.74** A skin _____ is used to replace skin at a burn or injury site by transferring it from another site. If the graft is transferred from elsewhere on the same person, this is called an _____ (*auto* = _____). A homograft is a graft transferred to one human from another _____ (*homo* = same). This is also called an _____. A heterograft, in contrast, is transferred from a different _____ (*hetero* means _____). The synonym for heterograft is _____ (*xeno* = _____).

Self-Instruction: Therapeutic Terms

Study this table to prepare for the programmed review that follows.

TERM	MEANING
chemotherapy kēm′ō-thār′ă-pē	treatment of malignancies, infections, and other diseases with chemical agents that destroy selected cells or impair their ability to reproduce
radiation therapy rā′dē-ā′shŭn thār′ă-pē	treatment of neoplastic disease using ionizing radiation to deter the proliferation of malignant cells
sclerotherapy sklēr′ō-thār′ă-pē	use of sclerosing agents in treating diseases (e.g., injection of a saline solution into a dilated blood vessel tumor in the skin, resulting in hardening of the tissue within and eventual sloughing away of the lesion)
ultraviolet therapy ŭl-tră-vī′ō-let thār′ă-pē	use of ultraviolet light to promote healing of a skin lesion (e.g., an ulcer)
COMMON THERAPEUTIC DRUG CLASSIFICATIONS	
anesthetic an-es-thet′ik	a drug that temporarily blocks transmission of nerve conduction to produce loss of sensations (e.g., pain)
antibiotic an′tē-bī-ot′ik	a drug that kills or inhibits the growth of microorganisms
antifungal an′tē-fŭng′găl	a drug that kills or prevents the growth of fungi

TERM	MEANING
antihistamine an-tē-his′tă-mēn	a drug that blocks the effects of histamine in the body
histamine his′tă-mēn	a regulating body substance released in excess during allergic reactions, causing swelling and inflammation of tissues (e.g., in urticaria [hives] and hay fever)
anti-inflammatory an′tē-in-flam′ă-tō′rē	a drug that reduces inflammation (swelling)
antipruritic an′tē-prū-rit′ik	a drug that relieves itching
antiseptic an-ti-sep′tik	an agent that inhibits the growth of infectious microorganisms

Programmed Review: Therapeutic Terms

ANSWERS	REVIEW
chemotherapy radiation therapy sclerotherapy light	**2.75** Several different types of therapy are used to treat tumors and other skin lesions. The use of chemical agents as a treatment is called _____. Ionizing _____ is also used on tumors, and this is called radiation _____. In another form of therapy, sclerosing agents are injected into a lesion to harden the tissue within; this is called _____. Finally, ultraviolet therapy is the use of ultraviolet _____ to promote healing of a skin lesion (e.g., an ulcer).
anesthetic	**2.76** An _____ agent (using the suffix *-tic*, which means pertaining to) produces a loss of sensation so that the person undergoing a procedure does not feel pain.
fungus antifungal against or opposed to	**2.77** Recall that tinea is a group of skin diseases caused by a _____. A drug that kills or prevents the growth of such infections is called an _____, using the prefix *anti-*, which means _____.
antibiotic	**2.78** A different sort of drug kills or inhibits the growth of bacteria. A drug of this class is known as an _____.
antihistamine	**2.79** Histamine is a body substance that is released in excess during an allergic reaction. A drug that blocks the effects of this substance is called an _____. This type of drug is used to combat allergic reactions (e.g., hives or hay fever).

ANSWERS	REVIEW
antipruritic antiseptic anti-inflammatory	**2.80** Many drug classifications are named according to what they work against, using the prefix *anti-*, meaning against or opposed to. The term for itching is pruritus, and a drug that relieves itching is called an _____. Sepsis is an infection by microorganisms; a drug that inhibits the growth of such microorganisms is called an _____. Similarly, a drug that reduces inflammation is called an _____.

Chapter 2 Abbreviations

ABBREVIATION	EXPANSION
AIDS	acquired immunodeficiency syndrome
BCC	basal cell carcinoma
Bx	biopsy
C&S	culture and sensitivity
FS	frozen section
HIV	human immunodeficiency virus
HSV-1	herpes simplex virus type 1
HSV-2	herpes simplex virus type 2
I&D	incision and drainage
Rx	medical prescription
SCC	squamous cell carcinoma
Sig	label; instruction to the patient
SLE	systemic lupus erythematosus
t.i.d.	three times a day

PRACTICE EXERCISES

For each of the following words, write out the term parts (prefixes [P], combining forms [CF], roots [R], and suffixes [S]) on the lines below the word. Then define the term according to the meaning of its parts.

EXAMPLE

hypodermic

hypo / derm / ic
P   R   S

DEFINITION: below or deficient/skin/pertaining to

1. onychomalacia

   _____ / _____
       CF   S

   DEFINITION: _____

2. hyperkeratosis

   _____ / _____ / _____
       P   R   S

   DEFINITION: _____

3. subcutaneous

   _____ / _____ / _____
       P   R   S

   DEFINITION: _____

4. erythrodermatitis

   _____ / _____ / _____
       CF   R   S

   DEFINITION: _____

5. melanocyte

   _____ / _____ / _____
       CF   R   S

   DEFINITION: _____

Write the correct medical term for each of the following definitions.

6. _____ severe itching

7. _____ a boil

8. _____ baldness

9. _____ excision of tissue for microscopic study

Complete each medical term by writing the missing word or word part.

10. sebo_____ = discharge of oil
11. _____ section = type of microscopic study of fresh tissue
12. _____ oma = fat tumor
13. _____ dermic = pertaining to below the skin
14. _____ derma = dry skin

Give the medical term for the following viral diseases.

15. German measles _____
16. chickenpox _____
17. 4-day measles _____

Write the letter of the matching definition for each of the primary lesions described.

18. papule _____
19. nodule _____
20. macule _____
21. patch _____
22. plaque _____

a. a tiny, flat discolored spot on the skin up to 1 cm in diameter
b. a large, flat discolored area on the skin larger than 1 cm in diameter
c. a raised spot on the skin less than 0.5 cm in diameter
d. a solid mass greater than 1 cm that extends into the epidermis
e. a solid mass greater than 1 cm limited to the skin's surface

Write out the expanded term for each abbreviation.

23. HSV-2 _____
24. Bx _____
25. I&D _____

Write the plural for each of the following terms.

26. keratosis _____
27. macula _____
28. nevus _____

Match the following terms with their meanings.

29. scabies _____
30. cryosurgery _____
31. chemosurgery _____
32. pediculosis _____
33. laser _____

a. chemical peel
b. crabs
c. mites
d. freezing treatment
e. intense light

Circle the correct spelling.

34. cicatrix　　　　　　scicatrix　　　　　　cicatrex
35. veruca　　　　　　　verucca　　　　　　　verruca
36. soriasis　　　　　　psoreyeasis　　　　　psoriasis
37. eggszema　　　　　 eczema　　　　　　　ecczema
38. debridemant　　　　debridement　　　　　debreedment

Give the noun that is used to form each adjective.

39. keratotic _____
40. bullous _____
41. nodular _____
42. seborrheic _____
43. petechial _____

Identify the parts of the skin's anatomy by writing the missing words in the spaces provided.

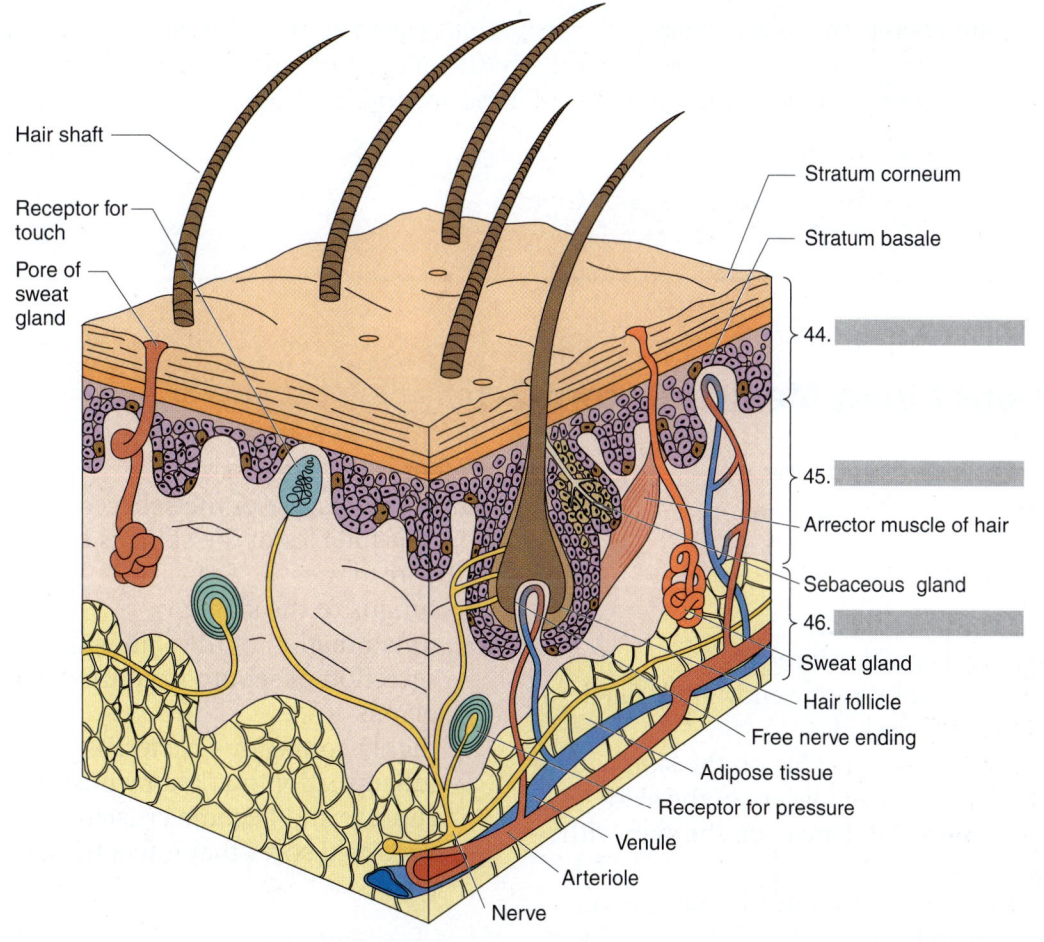

44. _____
45. _____
46. _____

Circle the combining form that corresponds to the meaning given.

47. black	necr/o	trich/o	melan/o
48. nail	onych/o	trich/o	squam/o
49. red	xanth/o	purpur/o	erythr/o
50. oil	py/o	hidr/o	seb/o

MEDICAL RECORD ANALYSIS

Medical Record 2-1

PROGRESS NOTE

S: This is a 30 y.o. ♀ presenting with an erythematous and scaly eruption on the face and ears × 6 mo. Stress and emotional tensions aggravate the rash. Over-the-counter remedies provide no relief.

O: Patchy erythema with greasy, yellowish scaling appears over the nose and along the eyebrows. The external ears are similarly affected. Erythematous papules are scattered across the face, and there is ↑ oiliness around the nose.

A: Seborrheic dermatitis.

P: Rx: hydrocortisone cream, 1/2 oz tube
Sig: apply to affected areas t.i.d.

Questions About Medical Record 2-1

1. What is the sex of the patient?
   a. male
   b. female
   c. not stated

2. What is the patient's CC?
   a. stress and emotional tension
   b. appearance of raised, yellow, pus-filled lesions on the skin
   c. appearance of red areas on the skin with flaking of the outer layers of the skin
   d. appearance of red areas on the skin with open sores
   e. appearance of a communicable rash on the face and ear

3. What is the diagnosis?
   a. inflammation of the sebaceous glands and hair follicles of the skin, as evidenced by comedones
   b. fungus of the skin
   c. inflammation of the skin with excessive secretion of sebum from the sebaceous glands
   d. highly contagious bacterial skin inflammation marked by pustules that rupture and become crusted
   e. viral cold sores that infect the facial area

4. How much hydrocortisone cream was prescribed?
   a. one ounce
   b. two ounces
   c. one-half dram
   d. one dram
   e. one-half ounce

5. What is the Sig: on the prescription?
   a. apply to affected areas twice a day
   b. apply to affected areas three times a day
   c. apply to affected areas four times a day
   d. apply to affected areas every 2 hours
   e. apply to affected areas every 3 hours

ANSWERS TO PRACTICE EXERCISES

1. CF: nail
   S: softening
   DEFINITION: nail/softening
2. P: above or excessive
   R: hard
   S: condition or increase
   DEFINITION: above or excessive/hard/condition or increase
3. P: below or under
   R: skin
   S: pertaining to
   DEFINITION: below or under/skin/pertaining to
4. CF: red
   R: skin
   S: inflammation
   DEFINITION: red/skin/inflammation
5. CF: black
   R: cell
   S: noun marker
   DEFINITION: black/cell/noun marker
6. pruritus
7. furuncle
8. alopecia
9. biopsy
10. seborrhea
11. frozen section
12. lipoma or steatoma
13. hypodermic
14. xeroderma
15. rubella
16. varicella
17. rubeola
18. c
19. d
20. a
21. b
22. e
23. herpes simplex virus type 2
24. biopsy
25. incision and drainage
26. keratoses
27. maculae
28. nevi
29. c
30. d
31. a
32. b
33. e
34. cicatrix
35. verruca
36. psoriasis
37. eczema
38. debridement
39. keratosis
40. bulla
41. nodule
42. seborrhea
43. petechia
44. epidermis
45. dermis
46. subcutaneous layer
47. melan/o
48. onych/o
49. erythr/o
50. seb/o

ANSWERS TO MEDICAL RECORD 2-1

1. b
2. c
3. c
4. e
5. b

MUSCULOSKELETAL SYSTEM

Learning Outcomes

After completing this chapter, you should be able to:

- List structures and functions of the skeleton and skeletal muscles.
- Define term parts related to the musculoskeletal system.
- Identify major bones and muscles.
- Define anatomic terms related to bones, joints, and muscles.
- Describe anatomic position and terms of reference.
- Define symptomatic terms related to the musculoskeletal system.
- Explain diagnostic terms, tests, and procedures related to the musculoskeletal system.
- Explain operative and therapeutic terms related to the musculoskeletal system.
- Cite common abbreviations related to the musculoskeletal system and give the expansion of each.
- Explain terms used in medical records involving the musculoskeletal system.

MUSCULOSKELETAL SYSTEM OVERVIEW

The skeletal system includes the bones, ligaments, and cartilages that make up the framework of the body. It is divided into the appendicular skeleton (bones of the limbs, pectoral girdles, and pelvic girdles) and the axial skeleton (bones of the skull, thorax [chest], hyoid bone, and vertebral column). The muscular system includes all the muscles in the body and is made up of three types of muscle tissue: skeletal, smooth, and cardiac. We will focus on skeletal muscles, which are attached to the skeleton.

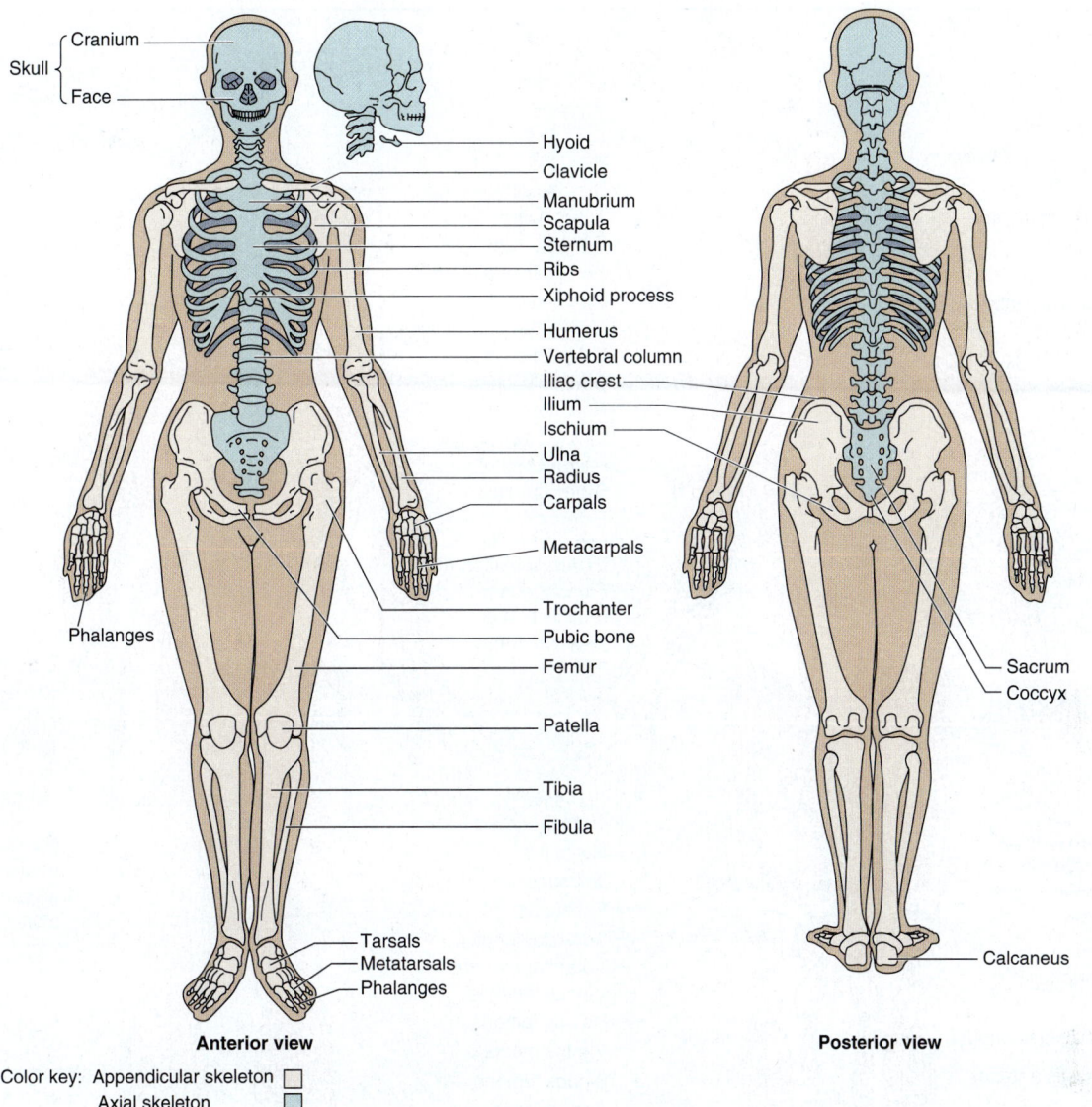

FIGURE 3-1 ■ The skeleton.

The skeleton (see **Figure 3-1**):

- Supports and shapes the body
- Protects tissues and organs
- Stores calcium, phosphorus, and lipids
- Produces certain blood cells within the red bone marrow

The skeletal muscles (see **Figure 3-2**):

- Produce body movement
- Maintain posture and body position
- Support soft tissues
- Maintain body heat

Orthopedics is the specialty most involved with the study and treatment of the musculoskeletal system. The spelling *orthopaedic* (the British form of the term) is frequently used, as in the name of the American Board of Orthopaedic Surgery.

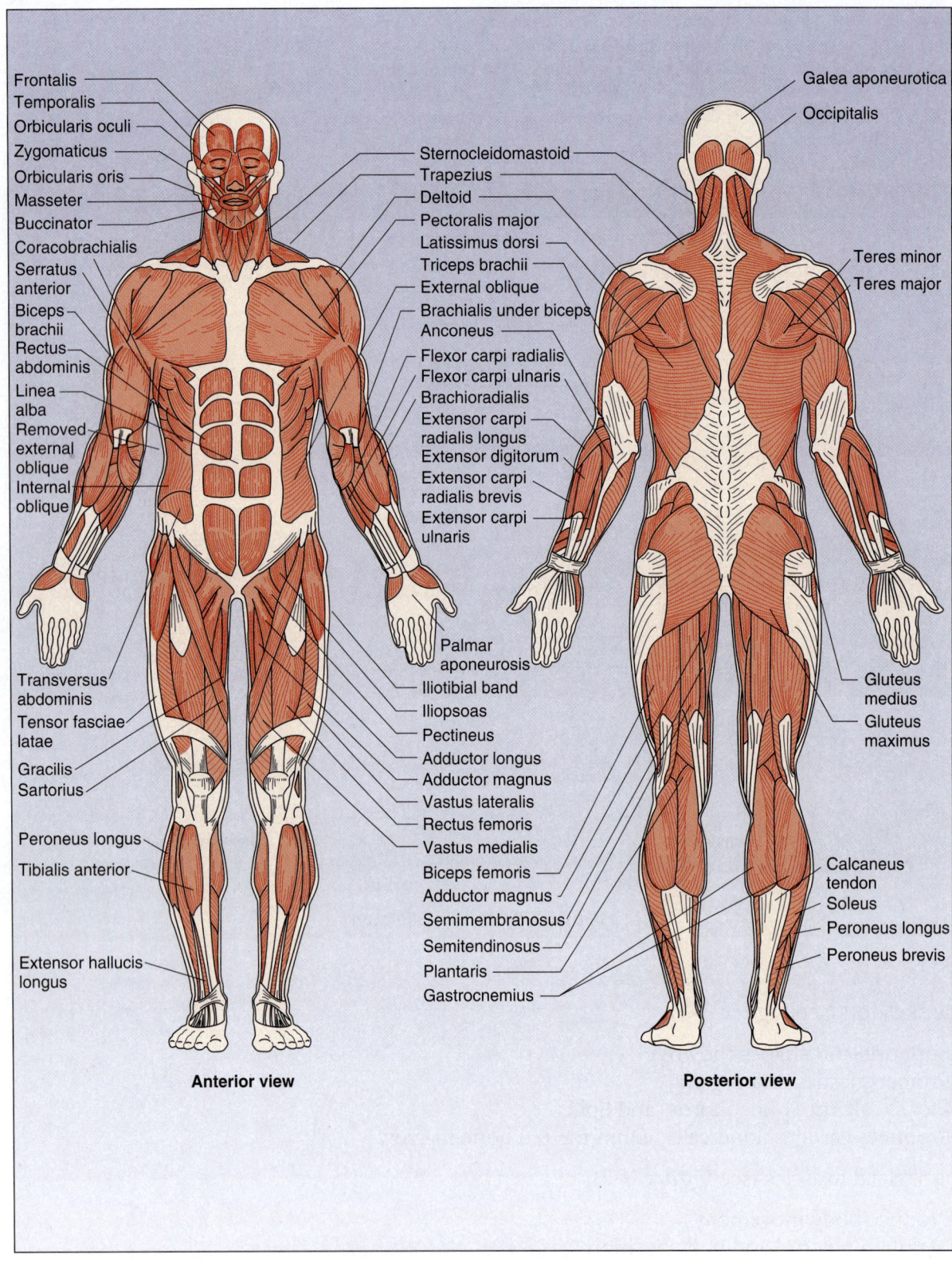

FIGURE 3-2 ■ Skeletal muscles.

Self-Instruction: Combining Forms

Study this table to prepare for the programmed review that follows.

COMBINING FORM	MEANING
ankyl/o	crooked or stiff
arthr/o	joint
articul/o	joint
brachi/o	arm
cervic/o	neck
chondr/o	cartilage (gristle)
cost/o	rib
crani/o	skull
dactyl/o	digit (finger or toe)
fasci/o	fascia (a band)
femor/o	femur
fibr/o	fiber
kyph/o	humped-back
lei/o	smooth
lord/o	bent
lumb/o	loin (lower back)
muscul/o	muscle
my/o	muscle
myel/o	bone marrow or spinal cord
myos/o	muscle
oste/o	bone
patell/o	knee cap
pelv/i	pelvis (basin) or hip bone
radi/o	radius
rhabd/o	rod-shaped or striated (skeletal)
sarc/o	flesh
scoli/o	twisted
spondyl/o	vertebra
stern/o	sternum (breastbone)
ten/o	tendon (to stretch)
tend/o	tendon (to stretch)
tendin/o	tendon (to stretch)
thorac/o	chest
ton/o	tone or tension
uln/o	ulna
vertebr/o	vertebra

Programmed Review: Combining Forms

ANSWERS	REVIEW
straight, normal, or correct foot orthopaedic	3.1 Orth/o, meaning _____, and ped/o, meaning _____, are combined to form the term orthopedic, meaning pertaining to the medical specialty related to the musculoskeletal system. The British spelling for this specialty is _____.
oste/o -itis myel/o	3.2 The combining form meaning bone is _____. The suffix _____ means inflammation. Osteitis therefore refers to inflammation of bone. Inside most bones is bone marrow; the combining form meaning bone marrow is _____, as in the adjective myeloid.
myos/o muscle inflammation	3.3 The three combining forms for muscle are muscul/o, my/o, and _____. The musculoskeletal system involves both muscles and bones. Recalling that the suffix -algia means pain, myalgia must mean _____ pain. Myositis is an _____ of muscle.
skull crani/o cervical neck	3.4 The cranial bones comprise the _____. The combining form that means skull is _____. Neck bones are referred to as the _____ vertebrae, from the combining form cervic/o, meaning _____.
spondyl/o vertebrae twisted condition or increase lord/o kyph/o lumb/o pain, lower	3.5 The two combining forms for vertebrae, the bones of the spine, are vertebr/o and _____. Spondylitis is inflammation of the _____. Scoli/o means _____, and when combined with the suffix -osis, which means _____, it forms the word scoliosis, which refers to a condition of having a twisted spine. The combining form meaning bent is _____, and a spine that is bent forward is called lordosis. The condition of a humped back is called kyphosis, from the combining form _____, meaning humped-back. The lower back is the lumbar spine, from the combining form _____. Lumbodynia refers to _____ in the _____ back.

ANSWERS	REVIEW
sternum sternum or breastbone ribs	**3.6** The breastbone is also called the _____, from the combining form *stern/o*. Most of the ribs connect to the breastbone in the front of the body. The combining form *cost/o* means rib. The sternocostal area, therefore, is where the _____ is connected to the _____.
chest thorac/o -ic	**3.7** Thoracic is the adjective referring to the _____, formed from the combining form _____, which means chest, and the adjective-forming suffix _____.
pelvis pelvis measurement	**3.8** Below the ribs and spine are the bones of the _____, from the combining form *pelv/i*. A pelviscope is used to examine the interior of the _____. Pelvimetry is the _____ of the diameters of the pelvis.
femor/o patell/o	**3.9** Below the pelvis is the longest bone in the body, the femur. The combining form for this term is _____. The femur joins the tibia at the knee joint, where a small bone called the kneecap covers the joint. The medical term for the kneecap is patella, from the combining form _____.
ulna, radi/o radius	**3.10** The two bones of the forearm are the radius and the _____, from the combining forms _____ and *uln/o*. Radioulnar is an adjective referring to both the _____ and the ulna.
digit pain	**3.11** The combining form *dactyl/o* refers to _____ (either a finger or a toe). Dactylalgia therefore means _____ of the fingers or toes.
brachi/o arm	**3.12** The combining form for arm is _____. The brachial artery, for example, runs through the _____.
articul/o arthr/o inflammation	**3.13** A joint is where two or more bones join. This is also called an articulation, from the combining form _____. Another combining term for joint is _____, which is used to form the term arthritis, meaning _____ of a joint.

ANSWERS	REVIEW
stiff	**3.14** *Ankyl/o* is a combining form meaning crooked or _____. Ankylosis therefore is a stiffened joint.
chondr/o	**3.15** Cartilage is a gristle-like substance that covers bones where they articulate at joints. Chondroma is a tumor that arises from cartilage, the combining form for which is _____.
fibr/o smooth tumor, striated	**3.16** Muscle fibers can contract, allowing them to move bones and, thus, body parts. The combining form for fiber is _____, and a common adjective form is fibrous. Muscles are composed of either smooth (*lei/o*) or striated (*rhabd/o*) muscle tissues. A leiomyoma is a tumor of _____ muscle. A rhabdomyoma is a _____ of _____ (skeletal) muscle.
ton/o muscle tone	**3.17** The combining form for tone is _____. Therefore, myotonia refers to a condition of _____ _____.
tend/o inflammation	**3.18** A tendon connects muscle to bone. Three combining forms for tendon are *ten/o*, _____, and *tendin/o*. Tendinitis is _____ of a tendon.
fasci/o	**3.19** Fascia is a band or sheet of fibrous tissue that encloses muscles or groups of muscles. It comes from the combining form _____.
flesh tumor	**3.20** *Sarc/o* means _____ or a muscular substance. A sarcoma, for example, is a fleshy _____.

Self-Instruction: Anatomic Terms Related to Bones

Study this table to prepare for the programmed review that follows.

TERM	MEANING
appendicular skeleton ap′en-dik′yū-lăr skel′ĕ-tŏn	bones of the shoulder girdle, pelvis, and limbs (arms and legs)
axial skeleton ak′sē-ăl skel′ĕ-tŏn	bones of the skull, vertebral column (see **Figure 3-3**), chest (thorax), and hyoid bone (U-shaped bone at the base of the tongue)
bone bōn	specialized connective tissue composed of osteocytes (bone cells); forms the skeleton

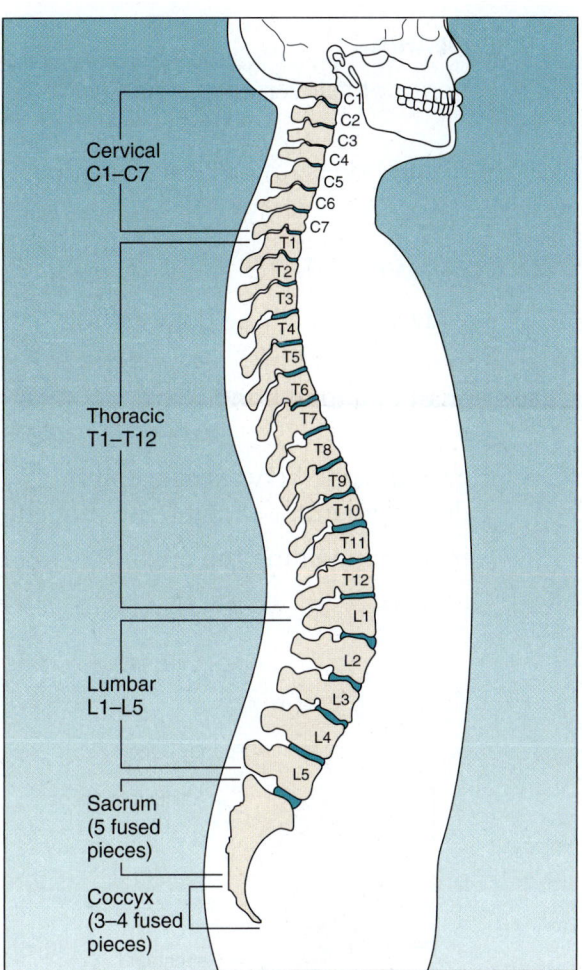

FIGURE 3-3 ■ The vertebral column showing the location of the vertebrae.

TERM	MEANING
TYPES OF BONE TISSUE	
compact bone kom′pakt bōn	tightly solid bone tissue that forms the exterior of bones
spongy bone spŭn′jē bōn	mesh-like bone tissue found in the interior of bones, and surrounding the medullary cavity; also called *cancellous bone*
cancellous bone kan′sĕ-lŭs bōn	mesh-like bone tissue found in the interior of bones, and surrounding the medullary cavity; also called *spongy bone*
CLASSIFICATION OF BONES	
long bones long bōnz	elongated bones of the arms and legs
short bones short bōnz	square-shaped bones of the wrists and ankles
flat bones flat bōnz	thin, flattened bones of the ribs, shoulder blades (scapulae), pelvis, and skull

TERM	MEANING
irregular bones ir-reg′yū-lăr bōnz	bones of the vertebrae and face
sesamoid bones ses′ă-moyd bōnz	round bones found near joints (e.g., the patella)
PARTS OF A LONG BONE (see Figure 3-4)	
epiphysis e-pif′i-sis	wide ends of a long bone (*physis* = growth)
diaphysis dī-af′i-sis	shaft of a long bone
metaphysis mĕ-taf′i-sis	growth zone between the epiphysis and the diaphysis during development of a long bone (not shown in figure)
endosteum en-dos′tē-ŭm	membrane lining the medullary cavity of a bone

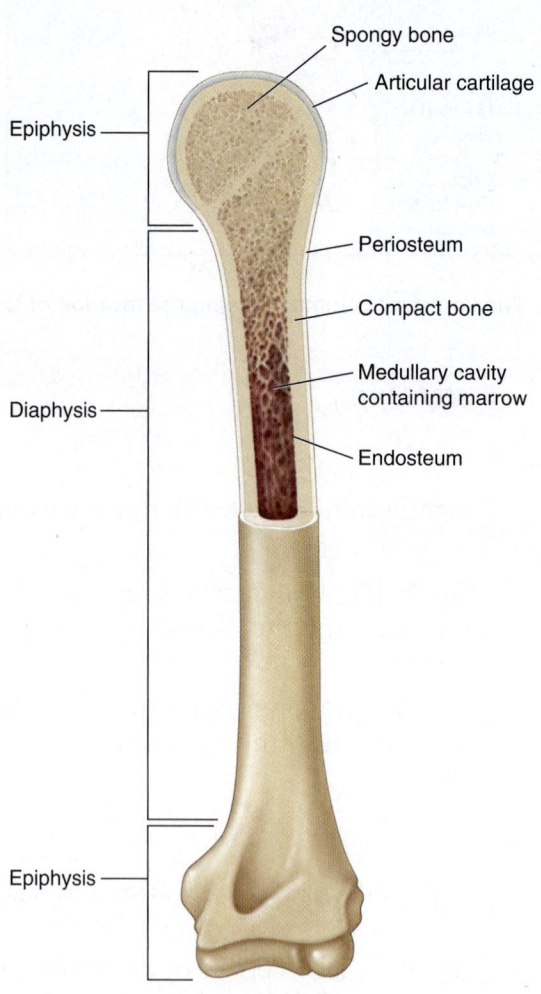

FIGURE 3-4 ■ Major parts of a long bone.

TERM	MEANING
medullary cavity med′ŭl-ār-ē kav′i-tē	cavity within the shaft of the long bones; filled with bone marrow
bone marrow bōn ma′rō	soft connective tissue within the medullary cavity of bones
red bone marrow rĕd bōn ma′rō	functions to form red blood cells, some white blood cells, and platelets; found in the cavities of most bones in infants and in the flat bones in adults
yellow bone marrow yel′ō bōn ma′rō	gradually replaces red bone marrow in adult bones; functions as storage for lipids (fat tissue) and is inactive in the formation of blood cells (not shown in figure)
periosteum per-ē-os′tē-ŭm	a fibrous, vascular membrane that covers the bone
articular cartilage ar-tik′yu-lăr kar′ti-lij	a gristle-like substance on bones where they articulate (join)

Programmed Review: Anatomic Terms Related to Bones

ANSWERS	REVIEW
axial, appendicular skull	**3.21** The skeleton is divided into the appendicular skeleton and the _____ skeleton. The _____ skeleton includes the shoulders, arms, pelvis, and legs. The axial skeleton includes the hyoid bone, spine, chest, and _____.
osteo compact Cancellous	**3.22** Bone cells, or _____cytes, form the skeleton. The tightly solid bone tissue that forms the exterior of bones is called _____ bone. _____ bone is the spongy, mesh-like bone tissue found in the interior of bones, and surrounding the medullary cavity.
arms, legs Short flat round	**3.23** Long bones are found in the _____ and _____. _____ bones are found in the wrists and ankles. The ribs, shoulder blades, and pelvis are _____ bones. Bones of the vertebrae and face are called irregular bones. Sesamoid bones are _____ bones (e.g., the patella) near joints.
end dia, physis	**3.24** Long bones have several parts. Several of these parts are named with terms from the root *physis* (growth), referring to how the bones grow. The epiphysis is the wide _____ of a long bone. The _____ physis is the shaft. The meta_____ is the growth zone between the epiphysis and the diaphysis.

ANSWERS	REVIEW
within bone marrow, Red marrow fat periosteum around	**3.25** The prefix *endo-* means _____. The endosteum is a membrane lining the medullary cavity within a _____. Inside the medullary cavity is bone _____. _____ bone marrow makes red blood cells, whereas yellow bone _____ stores _____ tissue. The membrane that covers a bone is called the _____, from the combining term for bone (*oste/o*) and the prefix *peri-*, meaning _____.
articular	**3.26** The kind of cartilage that is found where bones articulate is called _____ cartilage.

Self-Instruction: Anatomic Terms Related to Joints and Muscles

Study this table to prepare for the programmed review that follows.

TERM	MEANING
articulation (see Figure 3-5) *ar′tik-yū-lā′shŭn*	the point where two bones come together; also called *joint*
joint (*joynt*)	the point where two bones come together; also called *articulation*
bursa *bŭr′să*	a fibrous sac between certain tendons and bones that is lined with a synovial membrane that secretes synovial fluid (not shown in the figure)

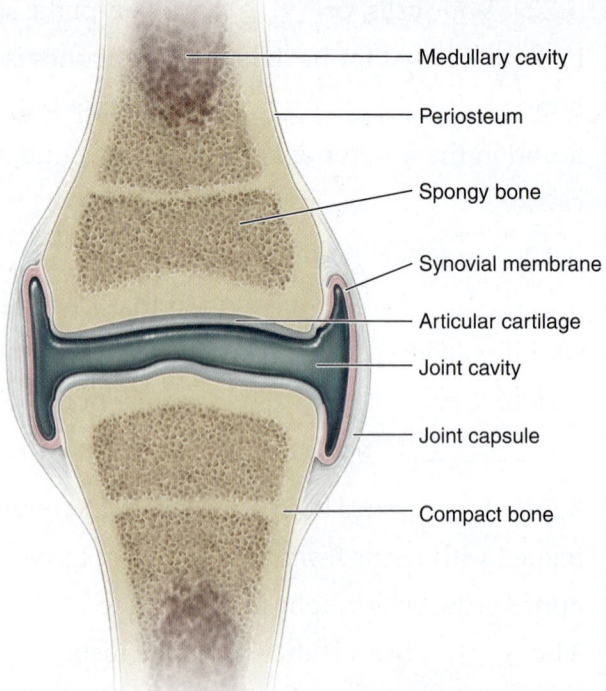

FIGURE 3-5 ■ Structure of a synovial joint.

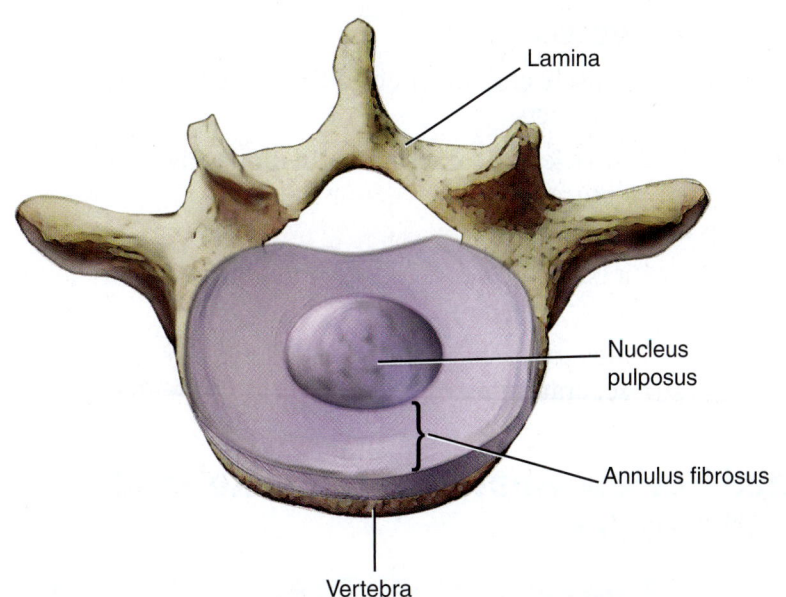

FIGURE 3-6 ■ Cross-sectional view of an intervertebral disk.

TERM	MEANING
intervertebral disk (see **Figure 3-6**) *in'tĕr-ver'tĕ-brăl disk*	a flat, plate-like structure composed of an outer fibrous part (annulus fibrosus) that surrounds a central gelatinous mass (nucleus pulposus) between the vertebrae that reduces friction
annulus fibrosus *an'yū-lŭs fī-brō'sus*	ring of fibrocartilage and fibrous tissue forming the circumference of the intervertebral disk; surrounds the nucleus pulposus
nucleus pulposus *nū'klē-ŭs pōl-pō'sŭs*	the soft, fibrocartilaginous, central portion of intervertebral disk
ligament *lig'ă-mĕnt*	a flexible band of fibrous tissue that connects bone to bone
joint capsule *joynt kap'sūl*	sac enclosing the articulating ends of bones forming a synovial joint
synovial membrane *si-nō'vē-ăl mem'brān*	membrane lining the capsule of a joint
synovial fluid *si-nō'vē-ăl flū'id*	joint-lubricating fluid secreted by the synovial membrane
muscle *mŭs'ĕl*	tissue composed of fibers that can contract, causing movement of an organ or part of the body
striated muscle *strī'āt-ĕd mŭs'ĕl*	voluntary muscle attached to the skeleton; also called *skeletal muscle*
skeletal muscle *skel'e-tăl mŭs'ĕl*	voluntary muscle attached to the skeleton; also called *striated muscle*
smooth muscle *smūth mŭs'ĕl*	involuntary muscle found in internal organs
cardiac muscle *kar'dē-ak mŭs'ĕl*	muscle of the heart

TERM	MEANING
origin of a muscle ōr′i-jin of a mŭs′ĕl	muscle end attached to the bone that does not move when the muscle contracts
insertion of a muscle in-sĕr′shŭn of a mŭs′ĕl	muscle end attached to the bone that moves when the muscle contracts
tendon ten′dŏn	a band of fibrous tissue that connects muscle to bone
fascia fash′ē-ă	a band or sheet of fibrous connective tissue that covers, supports, and separates muscle

Programmed Review: Anatomic Terms Related to Joints and Muscles

ANSWERS	REVIEW
Muscle Smooth muscle, heart striated	**3.27** _____ tissue can contract, causing movement of an organ or body part. There are three types of muscle tissue. _____ muscle is found in internal organs and is also called involuntary muscle, because you cannot will it to contract. Cardiac _____ is an involuntary muscle found only in the _____. Skeletal muscle, or _____ muscle, is under voluntary control.
origin insertion tendons fascia	**3.28** Skeletal muscle is attached to bone at both ends of the muscle. The end attached to the bone that does not move when the muscle contracts is called the _____ of the muscle. The other end, which is attached to the bone and that moves with contraction, is called the _____ of the muscle. Muscles are connected to bones by _____. The band or sheet of fibrous tissue that covers muscles is called _____.
articulation ligament, synovial fluid	**3.29** The point where two muscles come together is called a joint or an _____. A fibrous band that connects bone to bone is a _____. The joint capsule is lined with a _____ membrane, which secretes a lubricating fluid called synovial _____.
bursa inflammation	**3.30** The fibrous sac between certain tendons and bones is a _____; an inflammation of this tissue is called bursitis. The suffix -itis means _____.
disks, discs pulposus	**3.31** The flat, plate-like structures between the vertebrae are called _____, which sometimes is also spelled _____. The nucleus _____ is a soft fibrocartilaginous tissue in the center of intervertebral disks.

Self-Instruction: Anatomic Position and Terms of Reference

Study this table to prepare for the programmed review that follows.

TERM	MEANING
anatomic position (see Figure 3-7) *an-ah-tom′ik pō-zish′ŭn*	a term of reference that health professionals use when noting body planes, positions, or directions: the person is assumed to be standing upright (erect), facing forward, feet pointed forward (anteriorly) and slightly apart, with arms at the sides and palms facing forward; the patient is visualized in this pose when applying any other term of reference; also called *anatomical position*
anatomical position (see Figure 3-7) *an-ah-tom′ik-ăl pō-zish′ŭn*	a term of reference that health professionals use when noting body planes, positions, or directions: the person is assumed to be standing upright (erect), facing forward, feet pointed forward (anteriorly) and slightly apart, with arms at the sides and palms facing forward; the patient is visualized in this pose when applying any other term of reference; also called *anatomic position*
body planes (see Figure 3-7) *bod′ē plānz*	reference planes (imaginary flat surfaces) for indicating the location or direction of body parts
BODY PLANES	
frontal plane *frŏn′tăl plān*	vertical division of the body into front (anterior) and back (posterior) portions; also called *coronal plane*
coronal plane *kōr′ŏ-năl plān*	vertical division of the body into front (anterior) and back (posterior) portions; also called *frontal plane*

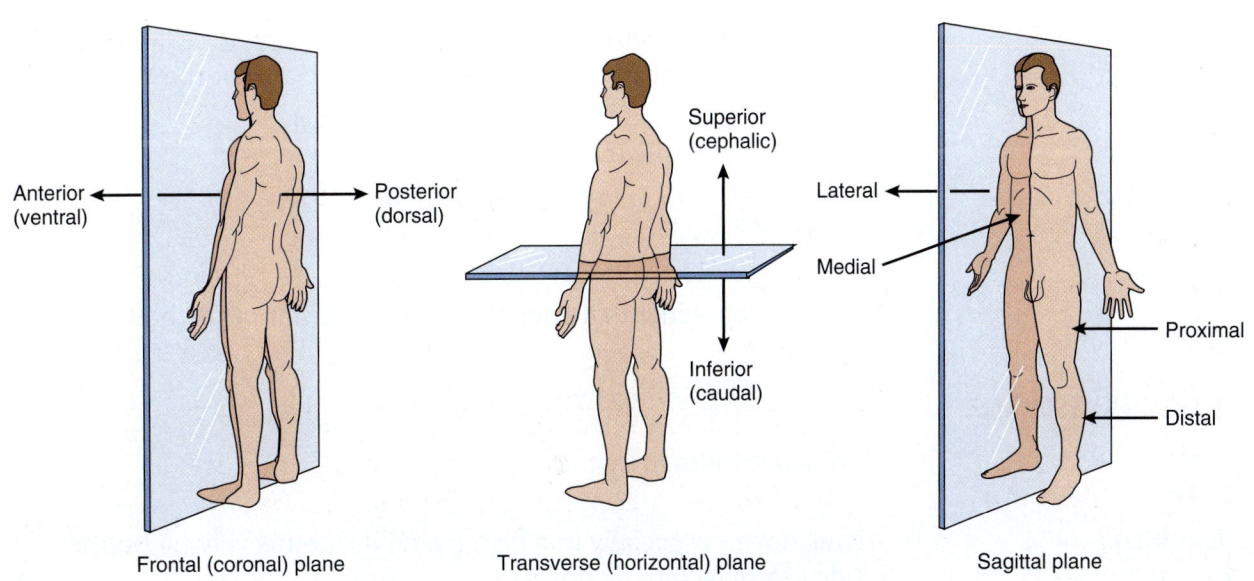

FIGURE 3-7 ■ Anatomic position with body planes.

TERM	MEANING
sagittal plane *saj'i-tăl plān*	vertical division of the body into right and left portions
transverse plane *trans-vĕrs' plān*	horizontal division of the body into upper and lower portions; also called *horizontal plane*

DIRECTIONAL TERMS (see Figure 3-7)

anterior (A) *an-tēr'ē-ōr*	front of the body; also called *ventral*
ventral *ven'trăl*	front of the body; also called *anterior*
posterior (P) *pos-tēr'ē-ōr*	back of the body; also called *dorsal*
dorsal *dōr'săl*	back of the body; also called *posterior*
anterior–posterior (AP)	from front to back, as in reference to the direction of an x-ray beam
posterior–anterior (PA)	from back to front, as in reference to the direction of an x-ray beam
superior *sū-pēr'ē-ōr*	situated above another structure, toward the head; also called *cephalic*
cephalic *se-fal'ik*	situated above another structure, toward the head; also called *superior*
inferior *in-fēr'ē-ōr*	situated below another structure, away from the head; also called *caudal*
caudal *kaw'dăl*	situated below another structure, away from the head; also called *inferior*
proximal *prok'si-măl*	toward the beginning or origin of a structure; for example, the proximal aspect of the femur (thigh bone) is the area closest to where it attaches to the hip
distal *dis'tăl*	away from the beginning or origin of a structure; for example, the distal aspect of the femur (thigh bone) is the area at the end of the bone near the knee
medial *mē'dē-ăl*	toward the middle (midline)
lateral *lat'er-ăl*	toward the side
axis *ak'sis*	the imaginary line that runs through the center of the body or a body part

BODY POSITIONS

erect *ē-rĕkt'*	normal standing position
decubitus *dē-kyū'bi-tŭs*	lying down, especially in a bed; lateral decubitus is lying on the side (*decumbo* = to lie down)

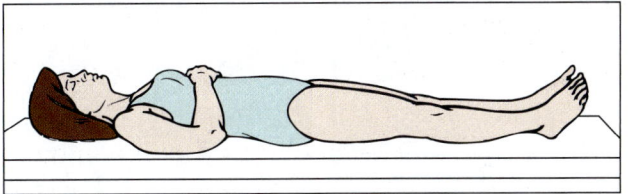

FIGURE 3-8 ■ Supine (horizontal recumbent) position. Patient lies on back with the legs extended.

TERM	MEANING
prone prōn	lying face down and flat
recumbent rē-kŭm′bĕnt	lying down
supine (see Figure 3-8) sū-pīn′	horizontal recumbent; lying flat on the back ("on the spine")
BODY MOVEMENTS (see Figure 3-9)	
flexion flek′shŭn	bending at the joint so that the angle between the bones is decreased
extension eks-ten′shŭn	straightening at the joint so that the angle between the bones is increased
abduction ab-dŭk′shŭn	movement away from the body
adduction ă-dŭk′shŭn	movement toward the body
rotation rō-tā′shŭn	circular movement around an axis
eversion ē-ver′zhŭn	turning outward, that is, of a foot
inversion in-vĕr′zhŭn	turning inward, that is, of a foot
pronation prō-nā′shŭn	turning of the palmar surface (palm of the hand) or plantar surface (sole of the foot) downward or backward
supination sū′pi-nā′shŭn	turning of the palmar surface (palm of the hand) or plantar surface (sole of the foot) upward or forward
dorsiflexion dōr-si-flek′shŭn	bending of the foot or the toes upward
plantar flexion plan′tăr flek′shŭn	bending of the sole of the foot by curling the toes toward the ground
range of motion (ROM) rānj of mō′shŭn	total motion possible at a joint, described by the terms related to body movements (i.e., ability to flex, extend, abduct, or adduct); measured in degrees

goniometer
    (see Figure 3-10)
    gō-nē-om′ĕ-tĕr
	instrument used to measure joint angles (*gonio* = angle)

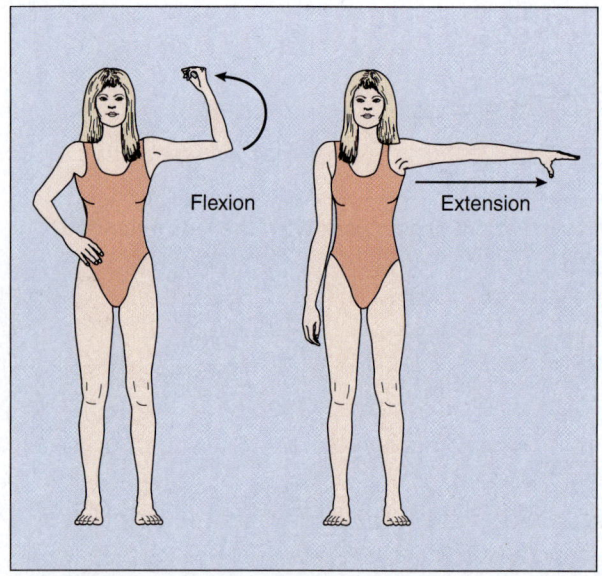
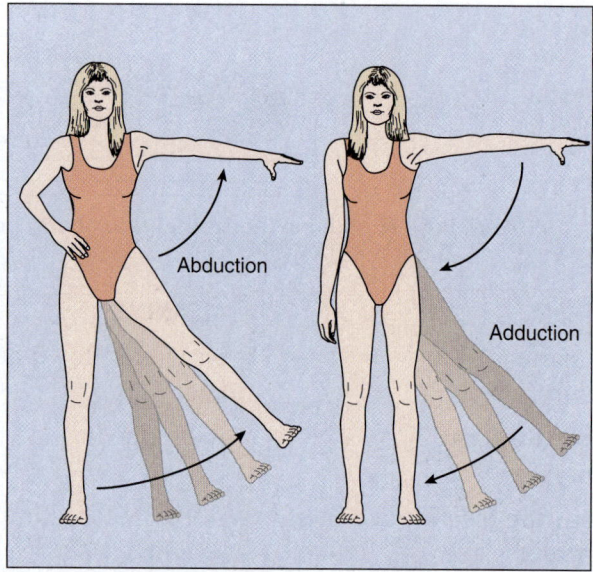
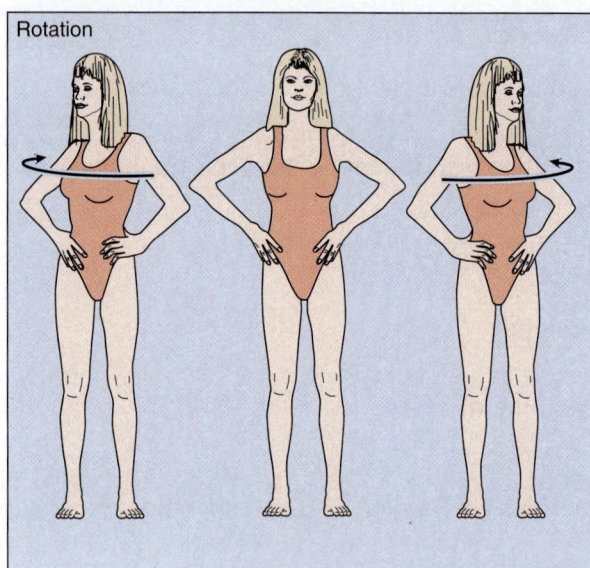
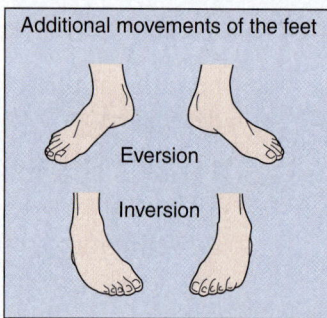
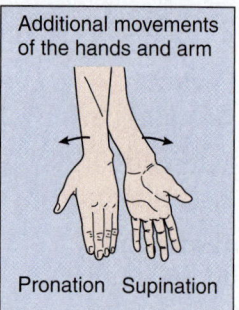
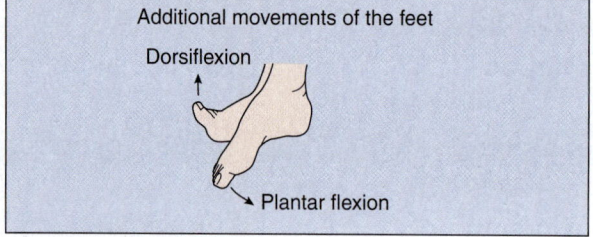

FIGURE 3-9 ■ Body movements.

FIGURE 3-10 ■ Posterior placement of goniometer used when measuring digital motion.

Programmed Review: Anatomic Position and Terms of Reference

ANSWERS	REVIEW
anatomic erect, forward sides forward	**3.32** Health professionals describe body part locations relative to the _____ position, in which one is standing upright, or _____, and is facing _____, with the feet pointed forward and slightly apart, the arms at the _____, and the palms facing _____.
planes coronal sagittal horizontally	**3.33** Body _____ help one to understand directional and positional terms. The body is vertically divided into front (anterior) and back (posterior) portions by the _____, or frontal, plane. The _____ plane divides the body vertically into right and left portions. The transverse plane divides the body _____ into upper and lower portions.
before after anterior posterior	**3.34** Recall that the prefix *ante-* means _____ and the prefix *post-* means _____. Using these word parts, the front of the body is _____ (also called ventral), and the back of the body is _____ (also called dorsal).
anterior–posterior posterior–anterior	**3.35** The direction of an x-ray beam from front to back is designated _____, whereas the direction from back to front is designated _____.
superior inferior	**3.36** The head is _____ to, or above, the shoulders whereas the feet are _____ to, or below, the knees.
closest distal proximal end	**3.37** The proximal aspect of a structure is the area _____ to its origin or attachment. The _____ aspect of a structure is the area away from its origin or attachment. The _____ aspect of the femur (thigh bone) is the area closest to where it attaches to the hip. The distal aspect of the femur (thigh bone) is the area at the _____ of the bone near the knee.
medial side	**3.38** Toward the middle or midline is called _____, whereas lateral means toward the _____.
axis	**3.39** An imaginary line that runs through the center of the body or a body part is called an _____. For example, you can rotate your wrist on its axis.

ANSWERS	REVIEW
erect	**3.40** The normal standing position is _____ (as in the anatomic position). Several terms describe different ways the body lies down. The general term for lying down is _____. Lying down, especially in bed, is called _____. A patient lying on one side in bed is in a _____ decubitus position. Prone means lying _____ down and flat, and _____ means lying face up, flat on the back.
recumbent	
decubitus	
lateral	
face, supine	
decreases	**3.41** Many different terms are used to describe body movements at joints. Flexing a joint (flexion) _____ the angle between the bones; the opposite movement (increasing the angle) is _____. Movement _____ from the body is called abduction (the prefix *ab-* means _____ _____); the opposite movement is called _____ (the prefix *ad-* means _____).
extension, away	
away from	
adduction	
toward	
rotation	**3.42** A circular movement around an axis is called _____. For example, you can rotate your feet inward and outward. The term for inward rotation is inversion; the term for outward rotation begins with the prefix *e-* (out or away): _____.
eversion	
supination, pronation	**3.43** Turning the palm of the hand upward or forward is called _____; the opposite movement is called _____. Note the relationship of these terms to the terms for the body lying supine or prone.
dorsiflexion	**3.44** The foot and toes bend upward in _____ and downward in _____ _____.
plantar flexion	
range	**3.45** The total amount of motion in a joint is called its _____ of motion. In certain musculoskeletal conditions, the range of motion may decrease. The instrument used to measure a joint angle is a _____.
goniometer	

Self-Instruction: Symptomatic Terms

Study this table to prepare for the programmed review that follows.

TERM	MEANING
arthralgia ar-thral′jē-ă	joint pain
atrophy at′rō-fē	shrinking of muscle size

TERM	MEANING
crepitation krep-i-tā′shŭn	grating sound sometimes made by the movement of a joint or by broken bones; also called *crepitus*
crepitus krep′i-tŭs	grating sound sometimes made by the movement of a joint or by broken bones; also called *crepitation*
exostosis eks-os-tō′sis	a projection arising from a bone that develops from cartilage
flaccid flak′sid	flabby, relaxed, or having defective or absent muscle tone
hypertrophy hī-pĕr′trō-fē	increase in the size of tissue, such as muscle
hypotonia hī′pō-tō′nē-ă	reduced muscle tone or tension
myalgia mī-al′jē-ă	muscle pain; also called *myodynia*
myodynia mī′ō-din′ē-ă	muscle pain; also called *myalgia*
ostealgia os-tē-al′jē-ă	bone pain; also called *osteodynia*
osteodynia os-tē-ō-din′ē-ă	bone pain; also called *ostealgia*
rigor rig′ŏr	stiffness; stiff muscle; also called *rigidity*
rigidity ri-jid′i-tē	stiffness; stiff muscle; also called *rigor*
spasm spazm	drawing in; involuntary contraction of muscle
spastic spas′tik	uncontrolled contractions of skeletal muscles, causing stiff and awkward movements (resembles spasm)
tetany tet′ă-nē	tension; prolonged, continuous muscle contraction
tremor trem′ŏr	shaking; rhythmic muscular movement

Programmed Review: Symptomatic Terms

ANSWERS	REVIEW
crepitation	**3.46** Broken bones rubbing together may produce a grating sound, which is called crepitus or _____. This sound may also occur in a joint.
outside exostosis	**3.47** Recall that the prefix *exo-* means _____. A term for a cartilage projection growing outside a bone is _____.

ANSWERS	REVIEW
-algia	**3.48** Two suffixes for pain are -*dynia* and _____. Using the combining form for bone, two terms for bone pain are
osteodynia, ostealgia	_____ and _____. Two similarly formed terms
myodynia, myalgia	for muscle pain are _____ and _____. Using the
arthralgia	combining form *arthr/o*, the term for joint pain is _____.
above or excessive	**3.49** The prefix *hyper-* means _____. Hypertrophy refers
increased	to _____ muscle size. Shrinking muscle size is called
atrophy	_____.
deficient	**3.50** The prefix *hypo-* means below or _____. A condition
hypotonia	of reduced muscle tension or tone is called _____. In such
flaccid	a case, the muscle can be said to be flabby or _____.
rhythmic	**3.51** Tremor, from the Latin word for shaking, is a _____ muscular movement. This may result from certain neurologic conditions.
rigor	**3.52** A stiff muscle is called _____ or rigidity.
spasm tetany condition	**3.53** An involuntary contraction of a muscle is called a _____. A prolonged, continuous muscle contraction is a condition called _____. Recall that the suffix *-y* means a _____ or process.

Self-Instruction: Diagnostic Terms

Study this table to prepare for the programmed review that follows.

TERM	MEANING
ankylosis ang′ki-lō′sis	stiff joint condition
arthritis ar-thrī′tis	inflammation of the joints characterized by pain, swelling, redness, warmth, and limitation of motion; there are more than 100 different types of arthritis
osteoarthritis (OA) (see Figure 3-11) os′tē-ō-ar-thrī′tis	most common form of arthritis, especially affecting the weight-bearing joints (e.g., knee or hip), characterized by the erosion of articular cartilage; also called *degenerative arthritis* and *degenerative joint disease (DJD)*
degenerative arthritis dē-jen′ĕr-ă-tiv ar-thrī′tis	most common form of arthritis, especially affecting the weight-bearing joints (e.g., knee or hip), characterized by the erosion of articular cartilage; also called *osteoarthritis* and *degenerative joint disease (DJD)*

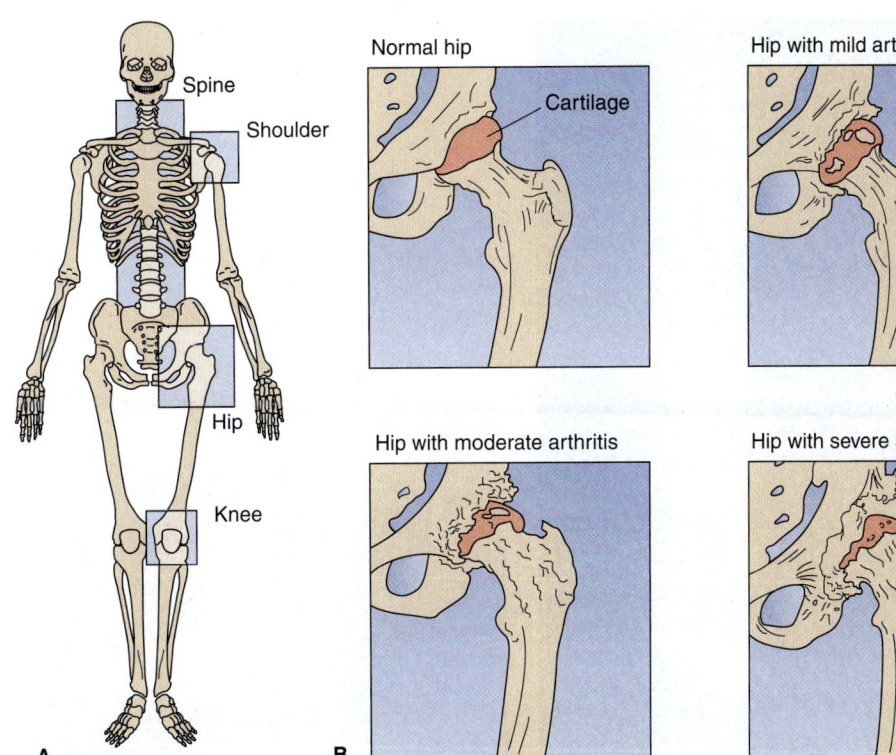

FIGURE 3-11 ■ Osteoarthritis. **A.** Common sites of osteoarthritis. **B.** How osteoarthritis affects the hip joint.

TERM	MEANING
degenerative joint disease (DJD) dē-jen′ĕr-ă-tiv joynt di-zēz′	most common form of arthritis, especially affecting the weight-bearing joints (e.g., knee or hip), characterized by the erosion of articular cartilage; also called *osteoarthritis* and *degenerative arthritis*
rheumatoid arthritis (RA) (see Figure 3-12) rū′mă-toyd ar-thrī′tis	most crippling form of arthritis; characterized by chronic, systemic inflammation, most often affecting joints and synovial membranes (especially in the hands and feet) and causing ankylosis (stiffening of a joint) and deformity
gouty arthritis gow′tē ar-thrī′tis	acute attacks of arthritis, usually in a single joint (especially the great toe), caused by hyperuricemia (an excessive level of uric acid in the blood)
bony necrosis bōn′ē nĕ-krō′sis	bone tissue that has died from loss of blood supply, such as can occur after a fracture (*sequestrum* = something laid aside); also called *sequestrum*
sequestrum sē-kwes′trŭm	bone tissue that has died from loss of blood supply, such as can occur after a fracture (*sequestrum* = something laid aside); also called *bony necrosis*
bunion bŭn′yŭn	swelling of the joint at the base of the great toe caused by inflammation of the bursa
bursitis ber-sī′tis	inflammation of a bursa
chondromalacia kon′drō-mă-lā′shē-ă	softening of cartilage

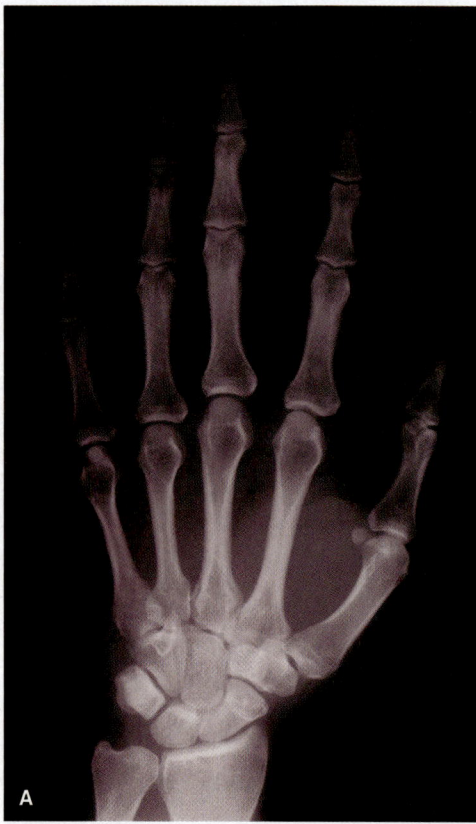
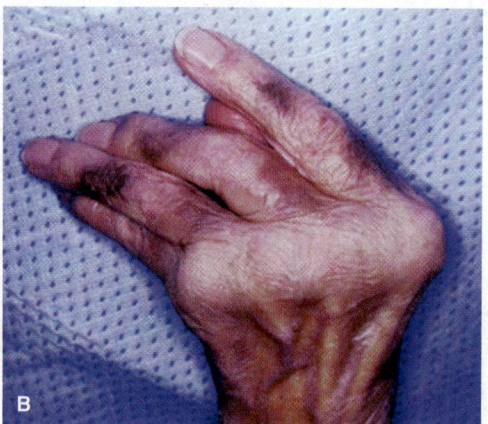

FIGURE 3-12 ■ The changes of severe rheumatoid arthritis. **A.** An x-ray of a normal hand. **B.** A hand that is severely deformed from rheumatoid arthritis.

TERM	MEANING
epiphysitis *e-pif-i-sī′tis*	inflammation of the epiphyseal regions of the long bone
fracture (Fx) (see Figure 3-13) *frak′chūr*	broken or cracked bone
closed fracture *klōsd frak′chūr*	broken bone with no open wound; also called *simple fracture*
open fracture *ō′pen frak′chūr*	compound fracture; broken bone with an open wound; also called *compound fracture*
complex fracture *kom′pleks frak′chūr*	displaced fracture that requires manipulation or surgery to repair
fracture line *frak′chūr līn*	the line of the break in a broken bone (e.g., oblique, spiral, or transverse)
comminuted fracture *kom′i-nyū-těd frak′chūr*	bone is shattered into many small pieces
spiral fracture *spī′răl frak′chūr*	bone break in which the fracture line is helical, usually resulting from a twisting injury
transverse fracture *trans-vers′ frak′chūr*	bone break in which the fracture line forms a right angle with the longitudinal axis of the bone
greenstick fracture *grēn′stik frak′chūr*	bending and incomplete break of a bone; most often seen in children

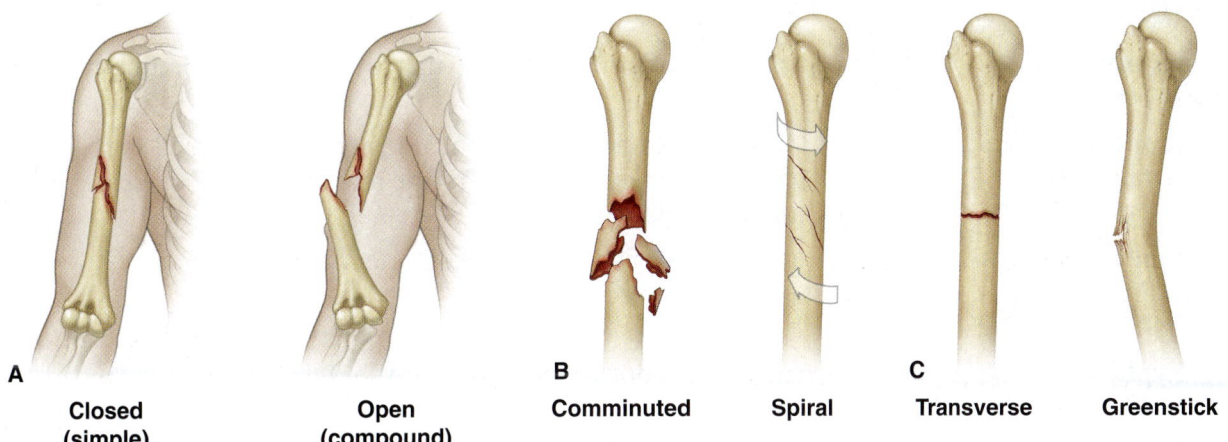

FIGURE 3-13 ■ Fractures. **A.** Types of common fractures. **B.** Anterior-posterior x-ray of a leg showing open fractures of the tibia and fibula at the arrows. **C.** Lateral-view x-ray showing a close spiral fracture of the tibia at the *arrows*.

TERM	MEANING
herniated disk hĕr′nē-ā-tĕd disk	protrusion of a degenerated or fragmented intervertebral disk so that the nucleus pulposus protrudes, causing compression on the nerve root (see **Chapter 4, Figure 4-10**)
myeloma mī-ĕ-lō′mă	bone marrow tumor
myositis mī-ō-sī′tis	inflammation of muscle
myoma mī-ō′mă	muscle tumor
leiomyoma lī′ō-mī-ō′mă	smooth muscle tumor
leiomyosarcoma lī′ō-mī′ō-sar-kō′mă	malignant smooth muscle tumor
rhabdomyoma rab′dō-mī-ō′mă	skeletal muscle tumor
rhabdomyosarcoma rab′dō-mī′ō-sar-kō′mă	malignant skeletal muscle tumor
muscular dystrophy mŭs′kyū-lăr dis′trō-fē	a category of genetically transmitted diseases characterized by progressive atrophy of skeletal muscles; Duchenne type is most common
osteoma os-tē-ō′mă	bone tumor
osteosarcoma os′tē-ō-sar-kō′mă	type of malignant bone tumor
osteomalacia os′tē-ō-mă-lā′shē-ă	disease marked by softening of the bone caused by calcium and vitamin D deficiency
rickets rik′ets	osteomalacia in children; causes bone deformity

TERM	MEANING
osteomyelitis *os′tē-ō-mī-ĕ-lī′tis*	infection of bone and bone marrow, causing inflammation
osteoporosis (see Figure 3-14) *os′tē-ō-pō-rō′sis*	condition of decreased bone density and increased porosity, causing bones to become brittle and to fracture more easily (*porosis* = passage)
spinal curvatures (see Figure 3-15) *spī′năl ker′vă-chŭrz*	curvatures of the spine (backbone) or spinal column (vertebral column)
kyphosis *kī-fō′sis*	anteriorly concave curvature of the thoracic spine (humped-back condition)
lordosis *lōr-dō′sis*	anteriorly convex curvature of the lumbar spine (sway-back condition)
scoliosis (see Figure 3-16) *skō-lē-ō′sis*	abnormal lateral curvature of the spine (S-shaped curve)
spondylolisthesis (see Figure 3-17) *spon′di-lō-lis-thē′sis*	forward slipping of a lumbar vertebra (*listhesis* = slipping)
spondylosis *spon-di-lō′sis*	stiff, immobile condition of vertebrae caused by joint degeneration
sprain *sprān*	injury to a ligament caused by joint trauma but without joint dislocation or fracture
subluxation *sŭb-lŭk-sā′shŭn*	partial dislocation (*luxation* = dislocation)
tendinitis *ten-di-nī′tis*	inflammation of a tendon; also called *tendonitis*
tendonitis *ten′dŏn-ī′tis*	inflammation of a tendon; also called *tendinitis*

Normal bone

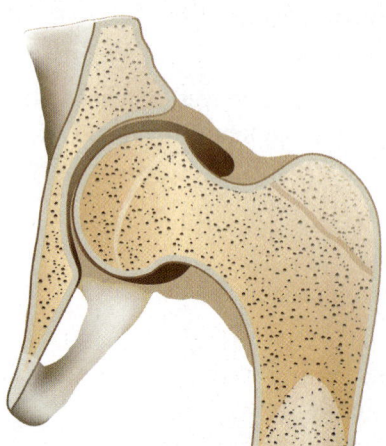

A

Osteoporosis

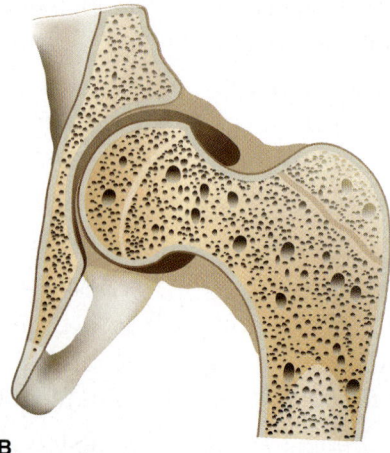

B

FIGURE 3-14 ■ The hip joint showing normal, healthy bone (A) and osteoporotic bone (B).

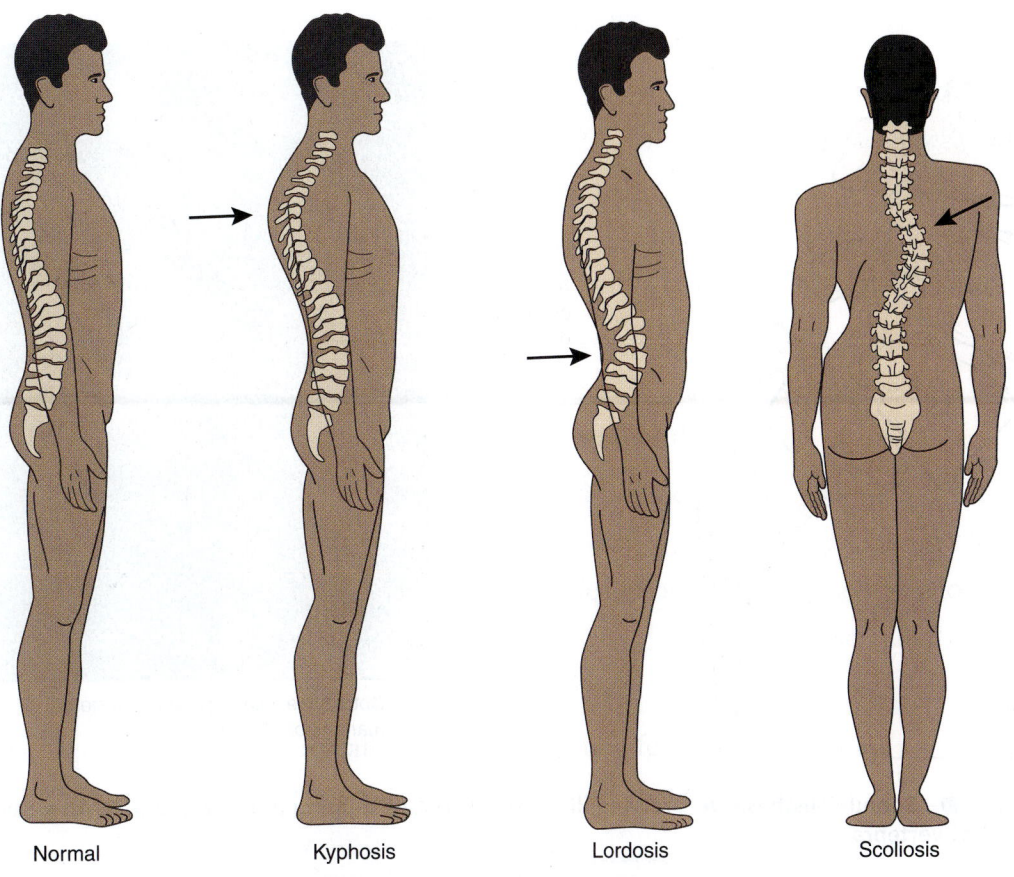

Normal Kyphosis Lordosis Scoliosis

FIGURE 3-15 ■ Spinal curvatures.

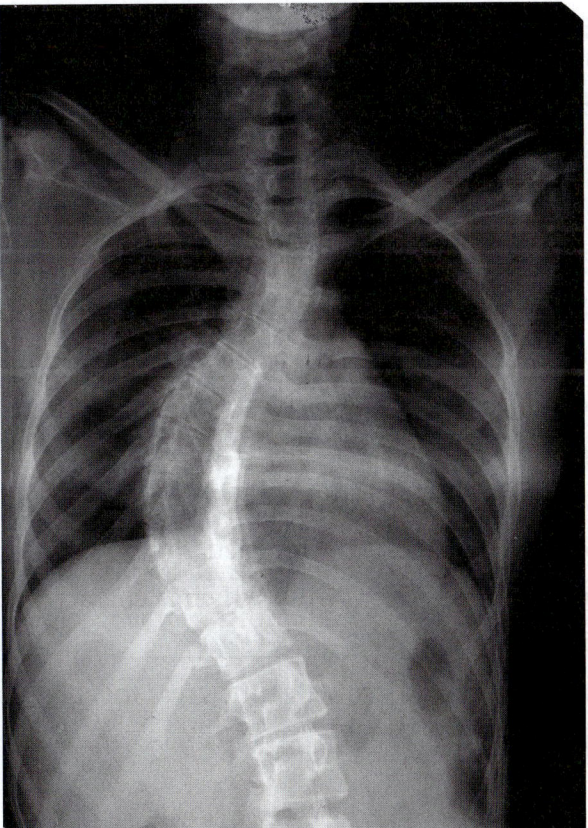

FIGURE 3-16 ■ Anterior–posterior thoracic spine x-ray showing scoliosis.

ANSWERS	REVIEW
leiomyoma rhabdomyoma rhabdomyosarcoma	**3.64** There are several types of muscle tumors. The suffix *-oma* refers to any tumor, but a sarcoma is a malignant tumor. Recall the meanings of the combining forms *lei/o* and *rhabd/o*. A smooth muscle tumor is a _____, whereas a skeletal muscle tumor is a _____. A malignant smooth muscle tumor is a leiomyosarcoma, and a malignant skeletal muscle tumor is a _____.
dystrophy shrinking painful or faulty	**3.65** Muscular _____ is a group of diseases that are characterized by progressive atrophy of skeletal muscles. Recall that atrophy means _____ of muscle size, and the prefix *dys-* means _____.
osteomalacia rickets	**3.66** Recall that chondromalacia means softening of cartilage. The term for softening of bone is _____. This is caused by a deficiency of calcium and vitamin D. In children, this is called _____.
condition or increase osteoporosis	**3.67** The suffix *-osis* means _____. The condition in which bones become less dense and more porous is called _____.
subluxation sprain	**3.68** Joints can be injured by trauma in various ways. If the bones are partially dislocated from their usual position in a joint, this is called _____. An injury to a ligament without a dislocation or fracture is called a _____.
concave lordosis scoliosis	**3.69** Several spinal curvatures are common. Kyphosis is an anteriorly _____ curvature of the thoracic region. From the combining form meaning bent, an anteriorly convex curvature of the lumbar region is called _____. From the combining form meaning twisted, an abnormal lateral curvature is called _____.
vertebra spondylosis spondylolisthesis	**3.70** Recall that *spondyl/o* is the combining form for _____. The term for a stiff, immobile condition of the vertebrae is _____. The term for forward slipping of lumbar vertebra is _____.

Self-Instruction: Diagnostic Tests and Procedures

Study this table to prepare for the programmed review that follows.

TEST OR PROCEDURE	EXPLANATION
electromyogram (EMG) ē-lek-trō-mī′ō-gram	a neurodiagnostic, graphic record of the electrical activity of muscle both at rest and during contraction; used to diagnose neuromusculoskeletal disorders (e.g., muscular dystrophy); usually performed by a neurologist
magnetic resonance imaging (MRI) mag-net′ik rez′ō-nănts im′ăj-ing	a nonionizing (no x-ray) imaging technique using magnetic fields and radiofrequency waves to visualize anatomic structures; useful in orthopedic studies to detect joint, tendon, and vertebral disk disorders
nuclear medicine imaging nū′klē-ăr med′i-sin im′ăj-ing **radionuclide organ imaging** rā′dē-ō-nū′klīd ōr′găn im′ăj-ing	an ionizing imaging technique using radioactive isotopes
bone scan bōn skan	a nuclear scan (radionuclide image) of bone tissue to detect a tumor or malignancy
radiography rā′dē-og′ră-fē	an imaging modality using x-rays (ionizing radiation); commonly used in orthopedics to visualize the extremities, ribs, back, shoulders, and joints
arthrogram ar′thrō-gram	a radiograph of a joint taken after the injection of a contrast medium
computed tomography (CT) (see Figure 3-18) kom-pyū′tĕd tō-mog′ră-fē	a specialized x-ray procedure producing a series of cross-sectional images that are processed by a computer into a two-dimensional or three-dimensional image; also called *computed axial tomography* (CAT)

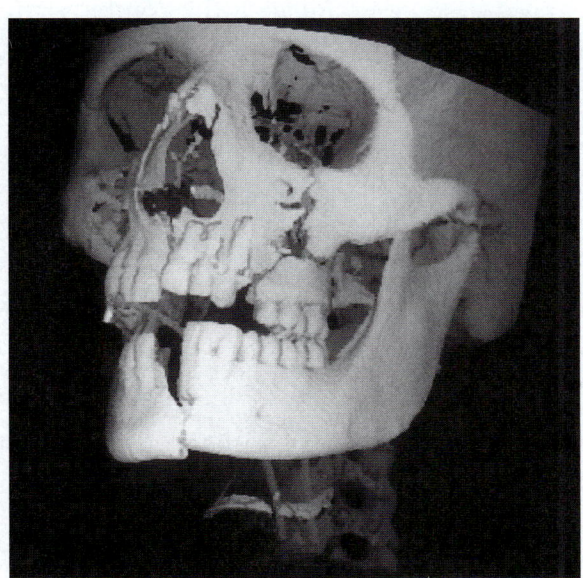

FIGURE 3-18 ■ A three-dimensional computed tomographic reconstruction of a skull showing traumatic injury to facial bones suffered as the result of a motor vehicle accident.

TEST OR PROCEDURE	EXPLANATION
computed axial tomography (CAT) kom-pyū′těd ak′sē-ăl tō-mog′ră-fē	a specialized x-ray procedure producing a series of cross-sectional images that are processed by a computer into a two-dimensional or three-dimensional image; also called *computed tomography* (CT)
sonography sŏ-nog′ră-fē	ultrasound imaging; a nonionizing technique that is useful in orthopedics to visualize muscles, ligaments, displacements, and dislocations or to guide a therapeutic intervention, such as that performed during arthroscopy

Programmed Review: Diagnostic Tests and Procedures

ANSWERS	REVIEW
record electromyogram	3.71 The combining form *electr/o* refers to electricity, and the suffix *-gram* means a _____. Join these word parts with the combining form for muscle to create the word for the diagnostic record of the electrical activity of a muscle: _____.
magnetic resonance imaging	3.72 The imaging technique using magnetic fields and radiofrequency waves to visualize bone and joint structures is called _____ _____ _____ (MRI).
process recording radiography record arthrogram	3.73 The suffix *-graphy* refers to the _____ of _____. *Radi/o* is the combining term for radiation, from the Latin word for ray. The general imaging modality that records images produced by x-rays is called _____. Recall that the suffix *-gram* means a _____. Using the combining form for joint, an x-ray of a joint, usually taken using a contrast medium, is an _____.
computed tomography, axial	3.74 A special imaging modality using an x-ray scanner and a computer to produce cross-sectional images is called _____ _____ (CT). This is also called computed _____ tomography (CAT), because the scanner rotates around the axis of the body to make the image.

ANSWERS	REVIEW
radionuclide bone scan	**3.75** The Latin word nucleus refers to a little nut, or the inside of a thing. In modern physics, nucleus refers to the inside of an atom and radiation using subatomic particles. Nuclear medicine imaging, also called _____ organ imaging, is a diagnostic technique using radioactive isotopes instead of x-rays. A _____ _____ is a nuclear scan of bone tissue to detect abnormalities.
sonography	**3.76** The combining form meaning sound is *son/o*. The imaging modality using high-frequency sound (ultrasound) is called _____.

Self-Instruction: Operative Terms

Study this table to prepare for the programmed review that follows.

TERM	MEANING
amputation am-pyū-tā′shŭn	partial or complete removal of a limb (AKA, above-knee amputation; BKA, below-knee amputation)
arthrocentesis ar′thrō-sen-tē′sis	puncture for aspiration of a joint
arthrodesis ăr-thrō-dē′sis	binding or fusing of joint surfaces
arthroplasty ar′thrō-plas-tē	repair or reconstruction of a joint
arthroscopy (see **Figure 3-19**) ar-thros′kŏ-pē	procedure using an arthroscope to examine, diagnose, and repair a joint from within
bone grafting bōn graft′ing	transplantation of a piece of bone from one site to another to repair a skeletal defect
bursectomy ber-sek′tō-mē	excision of a bursa
myoplasty mī′ō-plas-tē	repair of muscle
open reduction, internal fixation (ORIF) of a fracture (see **Figure 3-20**) ō′pen rē-duk′shŭn, in-tĕr′năl fik-sā′shŭn of a frak′chūr	internal surgical repair of a fracture by bringing bones back into alignment and fixing them in place with devices such as plates, screws, and pins
osteoplasty os′tē-ō-plas-tē	repair of bone

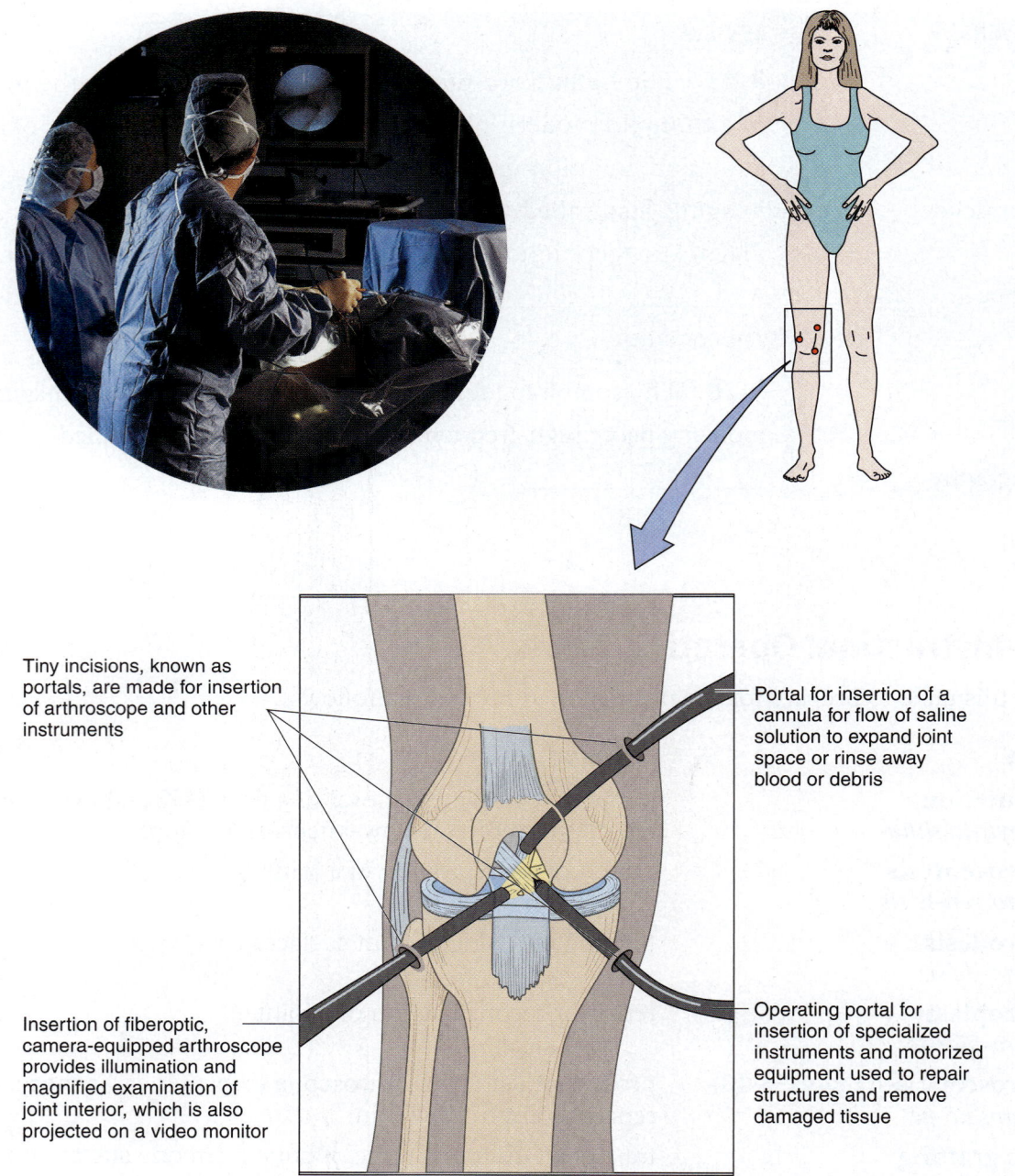

FIGURE 3-19 ■ Arthroscopic knee surgery showing projection of surgeon's view on the video monitor.

TERM	MEANING
osteotomy *os′tē-ot′ŏ-mē*	an incision into bone
spondylosyndesis *spon′di-lō-sin-dē′sis*	spinal fusion
tenotomy *te-not′ŏ-mē*	division of a tendon by incision to repair a deformity caused by shortening of a muscle

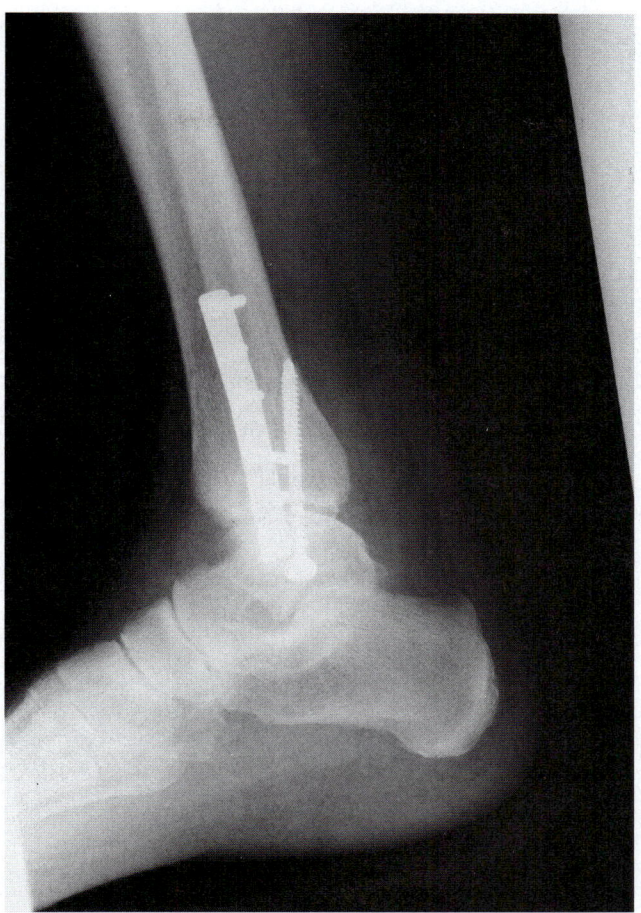

FIGURE 3-20 ■ An x-ray taken after open reduction, internal fixation (ORIF) of right ankle.

Programmed Review: Operative Terms

ANSWERS	REVIEW
joint arthrodesis -centesis arthrocentesis arthroscopy repair arthroplasty	3.77 Several different operative procedures are performed on joints. Often, the term for these procedures is formed using the combining form *arthr/o*, meaning _____. Recall that the suffix *-desis* means binding; the term for binding or fusing of joint surfaces is therefore _____. The suffix meaning a puncture for aspiration is _____; the term for puncture of a joint for aspiration is therefore _____. The procedure using an instrument to examine a joint from within is called _____. The suffix *-plasty* means surgical _____ or reconstruction, and the repair or reconstruction of a joint is called _____.
amputation	3.78 A partial or complete removal of a limb is an _____.

ANSWERS	REVIEW
excision or removal bursectomy	**3.79** Recall that the suffix *-ectomy* means a surgical _____. The excision of a bursa is therefore called a _____.
grafting	**3.80** Transplantation of a piece of bone from one site to another is called bone _____. This is done, for example, to repair a skeletal defect.
-plasty myoplasty osteoplasty	**3.81** The suffix for surgical repair or reconstruction is _____. The repair of a muscle is therefore called _____. The repair of a bone is called _____.
incision osteotomy tenotomy	**3.82** The suffix *-tomy* refers to a surgical _____. An incision into bone is therefore called _____, and an incision into a tendon is called _____.
binding spondylosyndesis	**3.83** The suffix *-desis* means _____ or fusing. From the combining form for vertebrae, the term for surgical spinal fusion is _____.
open reduction, internal fixation	**3.84** Some fractures, particularly comminuted fractures, must be surgically repaired by internal (open) surgery using devices such as screws and pins to hold the bone fragments in place. This procedure is called _____ _____, _____ _____ (ORIF).

Self-Instruction: Therapeutic Terms

Study this table to prepare for the programmed review that follows.

TERM	MEANING
closed reduction, external fixation of a fracture *klōsd rē-dŭk′shŭn, eks-tĕr′năl fik-sā′shŭn of a frak′chūr*	external manipulation of a fracture to regain alignment along with application of an external device to protect and hold the bone in place while healing
casting (see Figure 3-21) *kast′ing*	use of a stiff, solid dressing around a limb or other body part to immobilize it during healing

splinting
   (see Figure 3-22)
   splint′ing
	use of a rigid device to immobilize or restrain a broken bone or injured body part; provides less support than a cast, but can be adjusted more easily to accommodate swelling from an injury

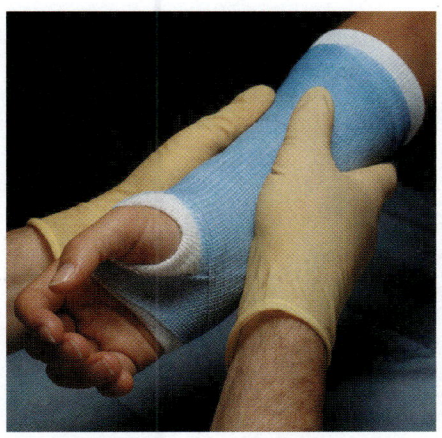

FIGURE 3-21 ■ Short arm cast.

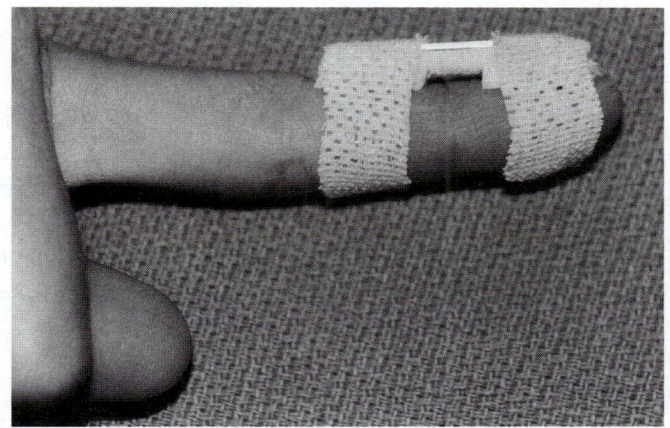

FIGURE 3-22 ■ Finger splint.

TERM	MEANING
traction (Tx) (see Figure 3-23) *trak'shŭn*	application of a pulling force to a fractured bone or dislocated joint to maintain proper position during healing
closed reduction, percutaneous fixation of a fracture (see Figure 3-24) *klōsd rē-dŭk'shŭn, pĕr-kyū-tā'nē-ŭs fik-sā'shŭn of a frak'chūr*	external manipulation of a fracture to regain alignment, followed by insertion of one or more pins through the skin to maintain position; often includes use of an external device called a fixator to keep the fracture immobilized during healing

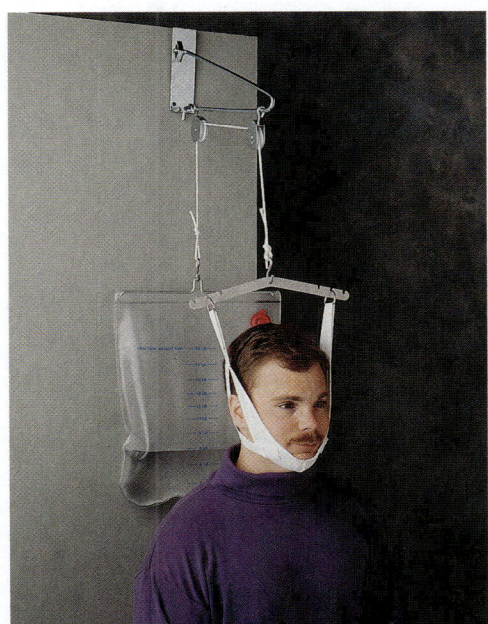

FIGURE 3-23 ■ Cervical traction.

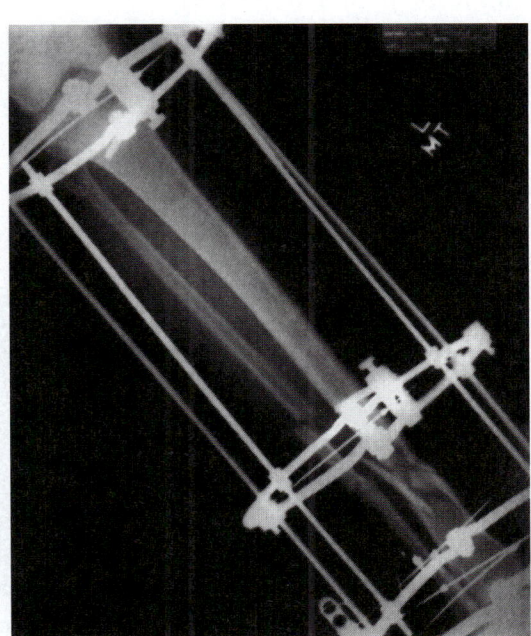

FIGURE 3-24 ■ An x-ray taken after closed reduction, percutaneous fixation of an open comminuted distal tibia/fibula fracture, showing placement of an external fixator to maintain pin placement during the healing process. The injury was the result of a gunshot to the lower extremity.

TERM	MEANING
orthosis (see Figure 3-25) ōr-thō′sis	use of an orthopedic appliance to maintain a bone's position or to provide limb support (e.g., back, knee, or wrist brace)
physical therapy (PT) fiz′i-kăl thār′ă-pē	treatment to rehabilitate patients disabled by illness or injury; involves many different modalities (methods), such as exercise, hydrotherapy, diathermy, and ultrasound
prosthesis (see Figure 3-26) pros′thē-sis	an artificial replacement for a missing body part or a device used to improve a body function, such as an artificial limb, hip, or joint

COMMON THERAPEUTIC DRUG CLASSIFICATIONS

analgesic an-ăl-jē′zik	a drug that relieves pain
narcotic nar-kot′ik	a potent analgesic with addictive properties
anti-inflammatory an′tē-in-flam′ă-tō-rē	a drug that reduces inflammation
antipyretic an′tē-pī-ret′ik	a drug that relieves fever
nonsteroidal anti-inflammatory drug (NSAID) non-stēr-oy′dăl an′tē-in-flam′ă-tōr-ē drŭg	a group of drugs with analgesic, anti-inflammatory, and antipyretic properties (e.g., ibuprofen and aspirin) commonly used to treat arthritis

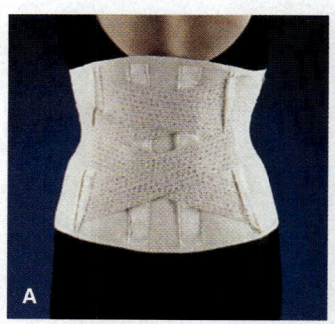 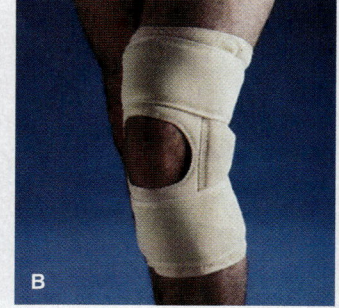 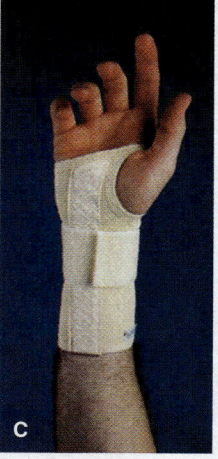

FIGURE 3-25 ■ Examples of orthoses. **A.** Back. **B.** Knee. **C.** Wrist.

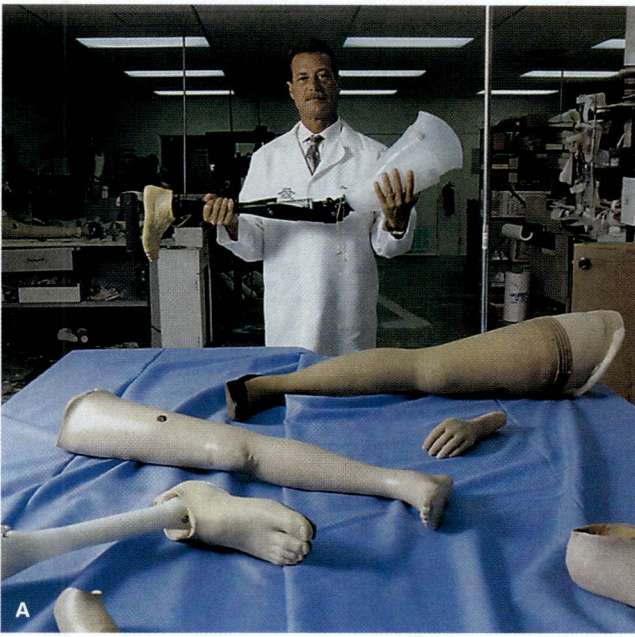 

FIGURE 3-26 ■ **A.** Prosthetist holding an above-the-knee prosthesis, with an array of prostheses on table in foreground. **B.** A prosthetic leg makes it possible for a person with an above-the-knee amputation to lead an active life.

Programmed Review: Therapeutic Terms

ANSWERS	REVIEW
closed reduction external, fixation percutaneous fixation	**3.85** Recall that some fractures require open reduction, internal fixation (ORIF). Other fractures can be reduced (the bone pieces brought into alignment) without surgery and held in place externally. This procedure is called _____ _____, _____ _____. If the fracture is reduced and one or more pins are inserted through the skin (*cutane/o*) to maintain the bone position, this is called closed reduction, _____ _____.
casting splinting traction	**3.86** With closed reduction, external fixation, the fractured bone must be held immobile. The use of a stiff, solid dressing around a limb to immobilize it during healing is called _____. The use of a rigid device to immobilize a limb with a fracture or injury that can be adjusted to accommodate swelling is called _____. Sometimes, it is necessary to maintain a pulling force on a fractured bone or dislocated joint for proper positioning during healing; this is called _____.

ANSWERS	REVIEW
orthosis	**3.87** The combining form *orth/o* means straight. An orthopedic device used to maintain limb support or the position of bones is called an _____.
physical	**3.88** Patients with musculoskeletal injuries or illnesses often receive rehabilitative therapy, called _____ therapy (PT), that combines exercise and other modalities.
prosthesis	**3.89** An artificial limb is an example of a _____.
without analgesic narcotic	**3.90** The prefix *an-* means _____. The Greek word algesis means sensation of pain. A drug that relieves pain is an _____. The combining form *narc/o* means to benumb or deaden; a type of potent, addictive analgesic drug is called a _____.
against antipyretic anti-inflammatory	**3.91** Many drugs are named according to their action against a condition or symptom. The prefix *anti-* means _____. The Greek word pyr means heat or fire, and a drug that relieves fever is an _____. A drug that reduces inflammation is an _____.
nonsteroidal anti-inflammatory	**3.92** There are several types of analgesic and anti-inflammatory drugs. The group that includes aspirin and ibuprofen is called _____ _____ drugs (NSAIDs).

Chapter 3 Abbreviations

ABBREVIATION	EXPANSION
A	anterior
AKA	above-knee amputation
AP	anterior–posterior
BKA	below-knee amputation
BP	blood pressure
CAT	computed axial tomography
CC	chief complaint
CT	computed tomography
DJD	degenerative joint disease
EMG	electromyogram
Fx	fracture
HPI	history of present illness
Hx	history
IMP	impression
L&W	living and well
MRI	magnetic resonance imaging
NAD	no acute distress
NKDA	no known drug allergy
NSAID	nonsteroidal anti-inflammatory drug
OA	osteoarthritis
ORIF	open reduction, internal fixation
P	posterior or pulse
PA	posterior–anterior
PE	physical examination
PMH	past medical history
PT	physical therapy
R	respirations
RA	rheumatoid arthritis
ROM	range of motion
ROS	review of systems
SH	social history
T	temperature
Tx	traction
VS	vital signs

PRACTICE EXERCISES

For each of the following words, write out the term parts (prefixes [P], combining forms [CF], roots [R], and suffixes [S]) on the lines below the word. Then define the term according to the meaning of its parts.

EXAMPLE

Hypertrophy

hyper / tropy / y
P   R   S

DEFINITION: above or excessive/fat/blood condition

1. thoracic

   _____ / _____
       R   S

   DEFINITION: _____

2. spondylolysis

   _____ / _____
       CF   S

   DEFINITION: _____

3. ostealgia

   _____ / _____
       R   S

   DEFINITION: _____

4. spondylomalacia

   _____ / _____
       CF   S

   DEFINITION: _____

5. intercostal

   _____ / _____ / _____
       P   R   S

   DEFINITION: _____

6. craniectomy

   _____ / _____
       R   S

   DEFINITION: _____

7. fibromyalgia

   _____ / _____ / _____
       CF   R   S

   DEFINITION: _____

8. sternocostal

   _____ / _____ / _____
       CF   R   S

   DEFINITION: _____

9. lumbodynia

    _____ / _____
         CF   S
    DEFINITION: _____

10. arthroscopy

    _____ / _____
         CF   S
    DEFINITION: _____

Write the correct medical term for each of the following definitions.

11. _____ lateral curvature of the spine
12. _____ x-ray of a joint
13. _____ plane that divides the body into front and back portions
14. _____ bone marrow tumor
15. _____ physician specializing in x-ray technology

Complete each medical term by writing the missing word or word part.

16. inter_____al = pertaining to between the ribs
17. myo_____ = suture of a muscle
18. osteo_____ = softening of bone
19. _____tomy = incision into bone
20. bony _____osis = dead bone tissue

Write the letter of the matching definition for each body movement.

21. flexion   _____   a. movement toward the body
22. inversion _____   b. straightening
23. adduction _____   c. bending
24. extension _____   d. to turn inward
25. abduction _____   e. to turn outward
26. eversion   _____   f. movement away from the body

Write out the expanded term or meaning for each abbreviation.

27. CT _____
28. PT _____
29. Tx _____
30. ROM _____
31. Fx _____

Circle the correct spelling.

32. scholiosis   scoliosis   scoleosis
33. arthrodynia   arthradynia   arthrodenia
34. sagttal   saggittal   sagittal
35. sekquestrum   sequestrom   sequestrum
36. osteoparosis   osteoporosis   osteophorosis

Identify the directional term and plane of the body by writing the missing words in the spaces provided.

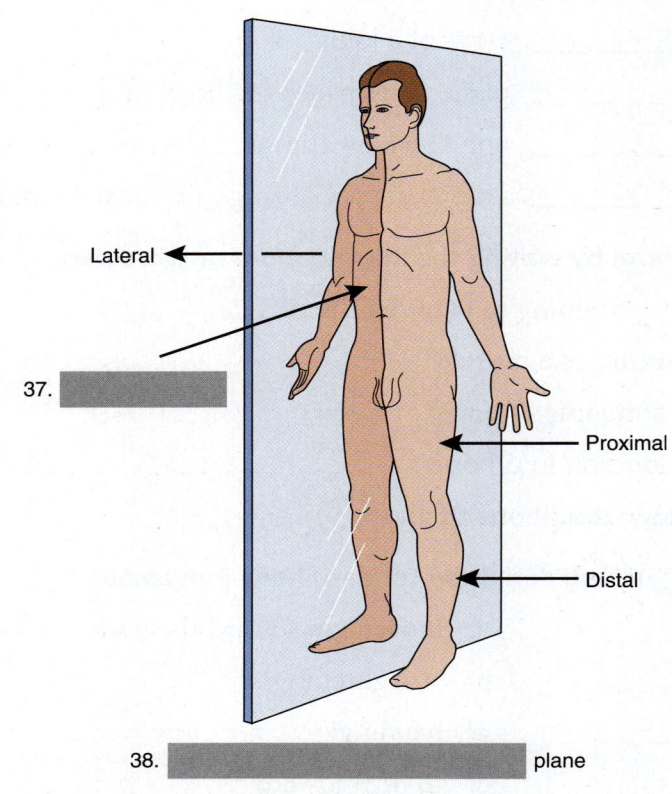

37. _____ 38. _____

Identify the movements of the body by writing the missing words in the spaces provided.

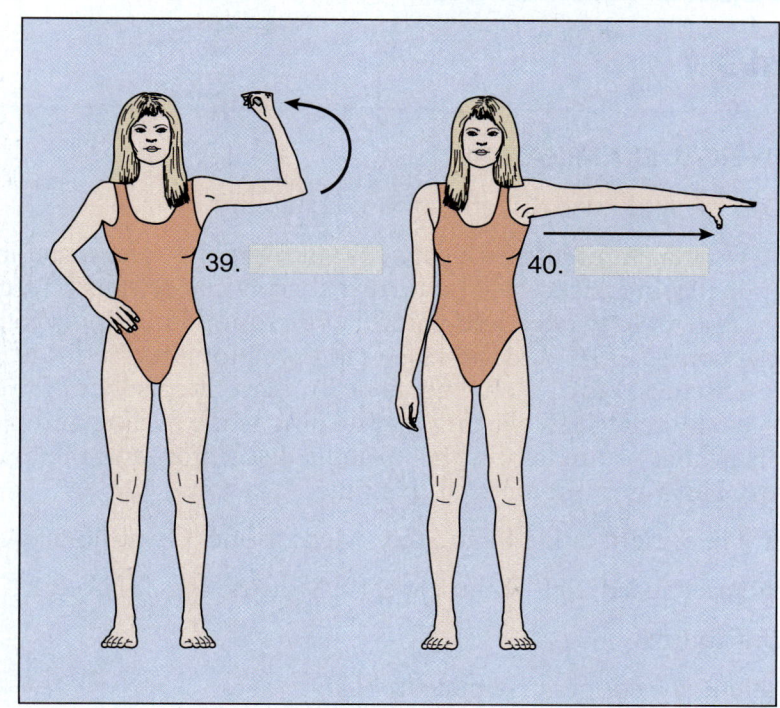

39. _____   40. _____

Circle the combining form that corresponds to the meaning given.

41. cartilage	crani/o	cost/o	chondr/o
42. vertebra	myel/o	spondyl/o	lumb/o
43. bone marrow	my/o	myel/o	muscul/o
44. neck	thorac/o	crani/o	cervic/o
45. joint	oste/o	arthr/o	ankyl/o

Give the noun that is used to form each adjective.

46. osteoporotic _____
47. lordotic _____
48. ulnar _____
49. scoliotic _____
50. prosthetic _____

MEDICAL RECORD ANALYSIS

Medical Record 3-1

HISTORY AND PHYSICAL EXAMINATION

CC: "Attacks" of right knee discomfort and instability

HPI: This 19 y/o male presents with "attacks" of right knee and instability. Three years ago, while playing basketball, he turned sharply and felt his kneecap pop in and out. It was acutely swollen and painful and required manipulation to reduce it. He had a course of PT and did reasonably well for a few months until resuming athletic activities. Since then, he has had recurrent episodes of the knee slipping in and out, all related to twisting and turning while surfing and playing basketball. His primary complaint is the episodic discomfort and the inability to trust the knee. He is asymptomatic at this time.

PMH: NKDA. Hx of right ankle Fx in 20xx. Meds: none. Operations: none.

SH: Alcohol rarely used. FH: Father, age 49; Mother, age 43, both L&W.

ROS: Noncontributory.

PE: The patient is a cooperative male in NAD.

VS: T 97.2°F, P 64, R 14, BP 118/66

HEENT: WNL. Neck: supple, no tenderness, full ROM, no adenopathy.

Lungs, heart, abdomen: WNL. Back: no tenderness or deformity.

Extremities: unremarkable except for involved knee. Knee ROM is 0 to 45 degrees equally. There is no parapatellar tenderness.

Neurologic: Negative.

Radiographs show subluxation of the right knee.

IMP: RECURRENT RIGHT KNEE PATELLAR INSTABILITY

RECOMMENDATION: Patelloplasty is being discussed, and the risks and benefits of the procedure have been explained. The patient will return with his parents for further consultation before deciding whether to proceed with treatment.

Questions About Medical Record 3-1

1. Which describes the patient's symptoms at the time of the initial injury?
   a. severe pain over a short course
   b. pain that comes and goes
   c. pain that progressively gets worse
   d. pain that develops slowly over time
   e. no pain

2. What treatment was provided 3 years ago?
   a. puncture for aspiration of a joint
   b. transplantation of a piece of bone from one site to another
   c. examination of a joint from within
   d. physical rehabilitation including exercise
   e. binding or fusing joint surfaces

3. Which best describes the patient's symptoms at the time of this visit?
   a. severe pain
   b. moderate pain
   c. progressive pain
   d. mild pain
   e. no pain

4. Describe the orthopedic condition noted in the past history.
   a. forward slipping of a vertebra
   b. broken bone
   c. arthritis
   d. bone pain
   e. dislocation

5. What does full ROM indicate?
   a. swelling
   b. spasm
   c. inflammation
   d. bruising
   e. mobility

6. What did the radiographs indicate?
   a. no radiographs were mentioned
   b. patellar instability
   c. partial dislocation
   d. inflammation
   e. joint stiffness

7. What treatment did the physician recommend?
   a. surgical reconstruction of the kneecap
   b. physical therapy
   c. surgical repair of bone
   d. excision of the patella
   e. examination and repair of a joint from within using an endoscope

ANSWERS TO PRACTICE EXERCISES

1. R: thorac
   S: ic
   DEFINITION: chest/pertaining to
2. CF: spondylo
   S: lysis
   DEFINITION: vertebra/breaking down or dissolution
3. R: bone
   S: algia
   DEFINITION: bone/pain
4. CF: spondylo
   S: malacia
   DEFINITION: vertebra/softening
5. P: inter
   R: cost
   S: al
   DEFINITION: between/rib/pertaining to
6. R: crani
   S: extomy
   DEFINITION: skull/excision (removal)
7. CF: fibro
   R: my
   S: algia
   DEFINITION: fiber/muscle/pain
8. CF: sterno
   R: cost
   S: al
   DEFINITION: sternum (breastbone)/rib/pertaining to
9. CF: lumbo
   S: dynia
   DEFINITION: loin (lower back)/pain
10. CF: arthro
    S: scopy
    DEFINITION: joint/process of examination
11. scoliosis
12. arthrogram
13. coronal or frontal
14. myeloma
15. radiologist
16. intercostal
17. myorrhaphy
18. osteomalacia
19. osteotomy
20. bony necrosis
21. c
22. d
23. a
24. b
25. f
26. e
27. computed tomography
28. physical therapy
29. traction or treatment
30. range of motion
31. fracture (broken bone)
32. scoliosis
33. arthrodynia
34. sagittal
35. sequestrum
36. osteoporosis
37. medial
38. sagittal
39. flexion
40. extension
41. chondr/o
42. spondyl/o
43. myel/o
44. cervic/o
45. arthr/o
46. osteoporosis
47. lordosis
48. ulna
49. scoliosis
50. prosthesis

ANSWERS TO MEDICAL RECORD 3-1

1. a
2. d
3. e
4. d
5. e
6. c
7. a

NERVOUS SYSTEM AND PSYCHIATRY

Learning Outcomes

After completing this chapter, you should be able to:

- Name the divisions of the nervous system and cite structures and functions of each.
- Define terms parts related to the nervous system and psychiatry.
- Identify key nervous system anatomic structures and their functions.
- Define symptomatic and diagnostic terms related to the nervous system and psychiatry.
- Explain diagnostic tests, procedures, operative terms, and therapeutic terms related to the nervous system and psychiatry.
- Cite common abbreviations related to the nervous system and psychiatry and give the expansion of each.
- Explain terms used in medical records involving the nervous system and psychiatry.

NERVOUS SYSTEM OVERVIEW

The nervous system is an intricate communication network of neurons (nerve cells), fibers, and other structures that activates and controls all functions of the body and receives all input from the environment. **Neurons** are the functional units of the nervous system, consisting of the cell body that contains the nucleus, branching processes known as dendrites, and the axon, which conducts impulses away from the cell body. Myelin is a mixture of fat and protein that forms a sheath around the axon (see Figure 4-1).

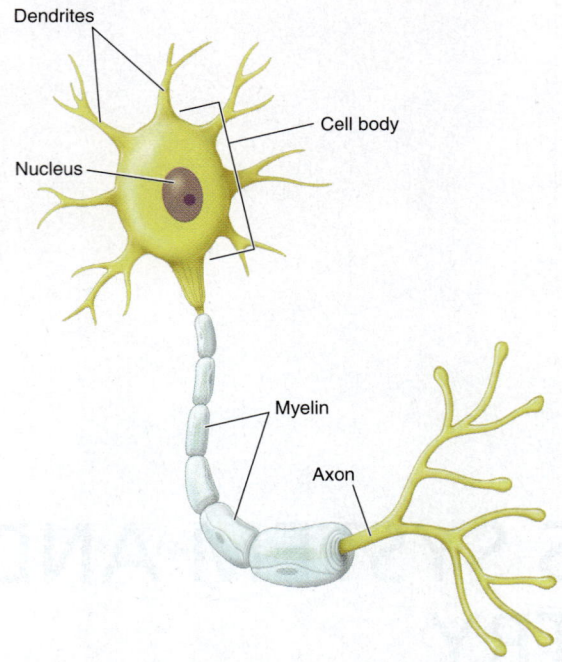

FIGURE 4-1 ■ Basic anatomy of a typical neuron.

The nervous system is divided into the central nervous system (CNS) and peripheral nervous system (PNS) (see **Figure 4-2**).

- The **central nervous system** consists of the brain and spinal cord.
- The **peripheral nervous system** consists of nerves branching from the central nervous system to all parts of the body. These nerves are the cranial nerves and spinal nerves.

The motor division of the PNS includes the somatic nervous system and the autonomic nervous system.

- The **somatic nervous system** is the voluntary component that allows us to consciously control movement, thus it is associated with skeletal muscles.
- The **autonomic nervous system** is the involuntary component that regulates activities automatically. Its two divisions, the parasympathetic division and sympathetic division, are associated with smooth muscle, cardiac muscle, various glands, and adipose tissue.

Self-Instruction: Term Parts

Study this table to prepare for the programmed review that follows.

TERM PART	MEANING
COMBINING FORMS	
cerebell/o	cerebellum (little brain)
cerebr/o	cerebrum (largest part of the brain)
crani/o	skull
encephal/o	entire brain
esthesi/o	sensation
gangli/o	ganglion (knot)
gli/o	glue

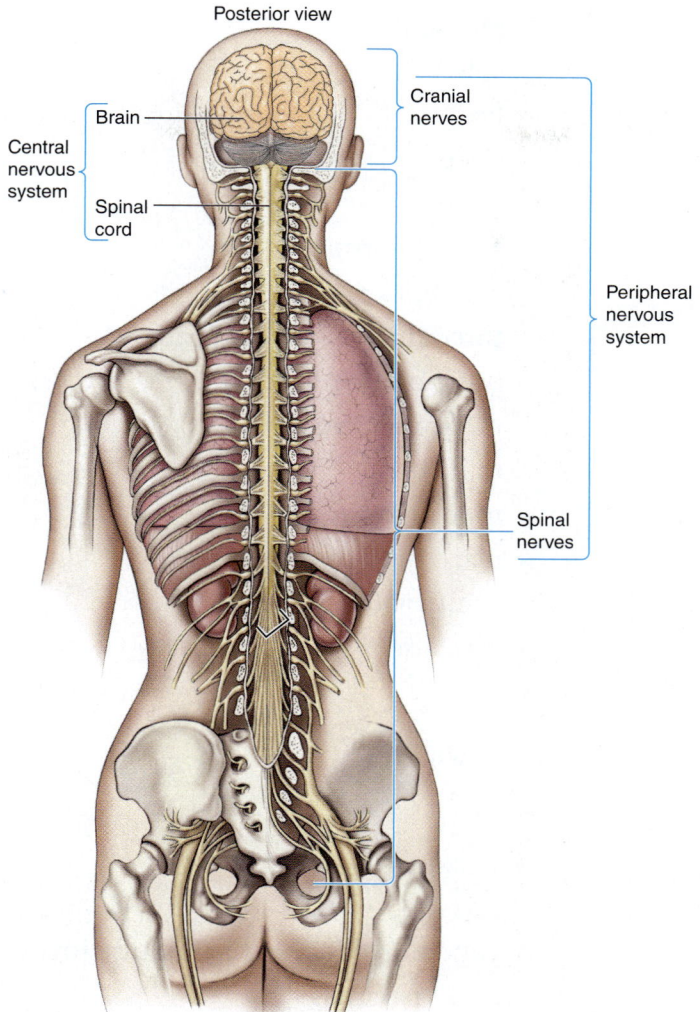

FIGURE 4-2 ■ The two divisions of the nervous system.

TERM PART	MEANING
gnos/o	knowing
hypn/o	sleep
kinesi/o	movement
lex/o	word or phrase
mening/o	meninges (membrane)
meningi/o	meninges (membrane)
myel/o	spinal cord or bone marrow
narc/o	stupor or sleep
neur/o	nerve
phas/o	speech
phob/o	exaggerated fear or sensitivity
phor/o	carry or bear
phren/o	mind
psych/o	mind

TERM PART	MEANING
schiz/o	split
somat/o	body
somn/i	sleep
somn/o	sleep
spin/o	spine (thorn)
spondyl/o	vertebra
stere/o	three-dimensional or solid
tax/o	order or coordination
thalam/o	thalamus (a room)
thym/o	mind
ton/o	tone or tension
top/o	place
ventricul/o	ventricle (belly or pouch)
vertebr/o	vertebra
PREFIX	
cata-	down
SUFFIXES	
-asthenia	weakness
-lepsy	seizure
-mania	condition of abnormal impulse toward
-paresis	slight paralysis
-plegia	paralysis

Programmed Review: Term Parts

ANSWERS	REVIEW
cerebrum cerebrum spine encephal/o recording	4.1 The combining form *cerebr/o* means _____ (largest part of the brain). Thus, the adjective cerebrospinal refers to something involving both the _____ and the _____. The combining form referring to the entire brain is _____, as in the term encephalography. Recall that the suffix *-graphy* means the process of _____.
crani/o	4.2 The brain is housed inside the skull, the combining form for which is _____. The cranium, for example, is the term for the bones of the skull.
cerebell/o	4.3 Another part of the brain is the cerebellum, the combining form for which is _____ (meaning "little brain").

ANSWERS	REVIEW
adjective cerebellar	The suffix *-ar* is an _____ ending. A common adjective referring to the cerebellum is _____.
ventricul/o -stomy ventricle	4.4 Within the brain are interconnected cavities called ventricles. The combining form meaning ventricle is _____. Recall that the surgical suffix for the creation of an opening is _____. Thus, a ventriculostomy is the creation of an opening in a _____.
thalam/o incision	4.5 The thalamus is a part of the brain. The combining form meaning thalamus is _____. A thalamotomy is an _____ into the thalamus.
meningi/o pouching meninges inflammation	4.6 The brain and spinal cord are covered with a membrane called the meninges. The two combining forms for meninges are *mening/o* and _____. Recall that the suffix *-cele* means a hernia or _____. Therefore, a meningocele is a pouching of the _____. Meningitis is _____ of the meninges.
spin/o spinal	4.7 The combining form meaning the spine is _____. The common adjective form is _____.
myel/o spinal cord	4.8 Inside the spine is the spinal cord, a bundle of nerves coming down from the brain and, ultimately, connecting to all areas of the body. The combining form for the spinal cord (and also for bone marrow) is _____, as in the term myelitis, meaning inflammation of the _____ _____.
vertebra spondyl/o vertebral binding or joining vertebra	4.9 The bones of the spine are vertebrae, the plural form of the term _____. The two combining forms meaning vertebra are *vertebr/o* and _____. A common adjective form made with the first combining form is _____. Spondylosyndesis, meaning spinal fusion, is an example of a term using the second combining form. Syndesis is a surgical technique of _____ together, and *spondyl/o* means _____.
neur/o neurology	4.10 Nerve cells exist in the brain, spinal cord, and throughout the nervous system. The combining form meaning nerve is _____. The medical specialty studying the nervous system therefore is called _____.

ANSWERS	REVIEW
gangli/o ganglia	**4.11** A ganglion is a structure of nerves in the peripheral nervous system. The combining form for ganglion is _____, as in the term ganglioneuroma, a neoplasm affecting ganglions. The other plural form of ganglion is _____.
gli/o glial	**4.12** Neuroglia in the nervous system help hold together (glue together) the neurons, which are the primary nervous system cells. The combining term for glue is _____. A common adjective form is _____.
somat/o body	**4.13** Almost all functions in the body are regulated through the nervous system. The combining form meaning body is _____, as in the term psychosomatic, which refers to influences of the mind on the _____.
psych/o, thym/o mind mind faulty	**4.14** The three combining forms meaning mind are *phren/o*, _____, and _____, as in the terms schizophrenia, psychiatry, and dysthymia. Schizophrenia refers to a split _____. Psychiatry is the medical specialty centered on the diagnosis, treatment, and prevention of disorders of the _____. A dysthymia is a psychiatric disorder; the prefix *dys-* means painful, difficult, or _____.
schiz/o split	**4.15** The combining form meaning split is _____. The thoughts of a patient with schizophrenia are said to be _____ from reality.
gnos/o	**4.16** The combining form that means knowing and is the basis of the term gnosia (meaning the ability to perceive and recognize) is _____.
esthesi/o excessive	**4.17** All physical sensations throughout the body are perceived by the brain. The combining form meaning sensation is _____, as in the term hyperesthesia, an abnormally heightened sensitivity to sensations. The prefix *hyper-* means above or _____.
kinesi/o movement	**4.18** The nervous system also controls body movement. The combining form meaning movement is _____, as in the term kinesiology, which is the study of body _____.

ANSWERS	REVIEW
phas/o	**4.19** The combining form meaning speech is _____. Aphasia is a condition of language loss in which one is often unable to speak. (Recall that the prefix *a-* means _____.) Aphasic is the _____ form of the term.
without	
adjective	
phrase	**4.20** *Lex/o* is a combining form meaning word or _____. A person with a condition of difficulty understanding written or spoken words or phrases is said to have _____.
dyslexia	
phob/o	**4.21** Someone with a phobia has an exaggerated fear of or sensitivity to something. The combining form for phobia is _____.
somn/i	**4.22** Three specific combining forms mean sleep: *somn/o*, _____, and *hypn/o*. Polysomnography, for example, makes a _____ of various physiologic changes that occur during _____. Recall that the prefix *poly-* means _____. Hypnosis is the condition of being in a _____-like state by suggestion. Recall that the suffix *-osis* means increase or _____.
record	
sleep	
many	
sleep	
condition	
narc/o	**4.23** Different from the sleep state, a state of stupor can result in various conditions. The combining form meaning stupor is _____, as in the term narcotic, referring to a class of drugs that induce _____.
stupor	
carry	**4.24** The combining form *phor/o* means to bear or _____. Recall that the prefix *eu-* means normal or _____ (well). Thus, the term euphoria, meaning an exaggerated sense of well-being, originates from term parts meaning to carry well.
good	
stere/o	**4.25** The combining form meaning three-dimensional or solid is _____, as in the term stereotaxic, referring to an apparatus allowing precise localization in space.
ton/o	**4.26** The combining form meaning tone or tension is _____, as in the term monotone, which refers to speaking in an unchanging single _____. Recall that the prefix *mono-* means _____.
tone	
one	

ANSWERS	REVIEW
coordination without, condition of ataxia	**4.27** *Tax/o* is a combining form meaning order or _____. Combined with the prefix *a-*, meaning _____, and the suffix *-ia*, meaning _____, the term describing a condition of inability to coordinate muscle movements is _____.
top/o place	**4.28** The combining form for place is _____. For example, the term topesthesia refers to the ability to localize the _____ on which the skin is touched.
down	**4.29** The prefix *cata-* means _____. The term catatonia, for example, which means a state of being unresponsive and unmoving, comes from word roots meaning that all muscle activity is down.
-asthenia weakness	**4.30** The suffix meaning weakness is _____, as in the term myasthenia, which is a condition involving _____ of the muscles (*my/o* = muscle).
sleep -lepsy	**4.31** The term narcolepsy is made from the secondary meaning of the combining form *narc/o*, which is _____, and the suffix _____, meaning seizure. In narcolepsy, sleep comes on unexpectedly and suddenly, as in a seizure.
impulse or attraction death fear	**4.32** The term mania means a state of abnormal elation and increased activity. The suffix *-mania*, however, refers to an abnormal _____ toward something. For example, necromania is an abnormal attraction to _____. Compare this with necrophobia, which is an abnormal _____ of death.
-paresis half hemi-	**4.33** The suffix meaning a slight paralysis is _____, as in the term hemiparesis, meaning a slight paralysis in _____ of the body (right or left). Recall that the prefix meaning half is _____.
paralysis	**4.34** The suffix *-plegia* means _____, as in the term paraplegia, referring to paralysis of the legs and lower trunk.

Self-Instruction: Anatomic Terms

Study this table to prepare for the programmed review that follows.

TERM	MEANING
CENTRAL NERVOUS SYSTEM	
central nervous system (CNS) *sen'trăl něr'vŭs sis'tĕm*	brain and spinal cord
brain (see Figure 4-3)	portion of the central nervous system contained within the cranium
cerebrum *sĕ-rē'brŭm*	largest portion of the brain; divided into right and left halves, known as *cerebral hemispheres*, which are connected by a bridge of nerve fibers called the *corpus callosum*; lobes of the cerebrum are named after the skull bones they underlie
frontal lobe	anterior section of each cerebral hemisphere; responsible for voluntary muscle movement and personality
parietal lobe *pă-rī'ĕ-tăl lōb*	portion posterior to the frontal lobe; responsible for sensations such as pain, temperature, and touch
temporal lobe *tem'pŏ-răl lōb*	portion that lies below the frontal lobe; responsible for hearing, taste, and smell
occipital lobe *ok-sip'i-tăl lōb*	portion posterior to the parietal and temporal lobes; responsible for vision
cerebral cortex *se-rē'brăl kōr'teks*	outer layer of the cerebrum consisting of gray matter; responsible for higher mental functions (*cortex* = bark)
thalamus *thal'ă-mŭs*	each of two masses of gray matter deep within the brain between the cerebral hemispheres on either side of the third ventricle; responsible for relaying sensory information to the cortex

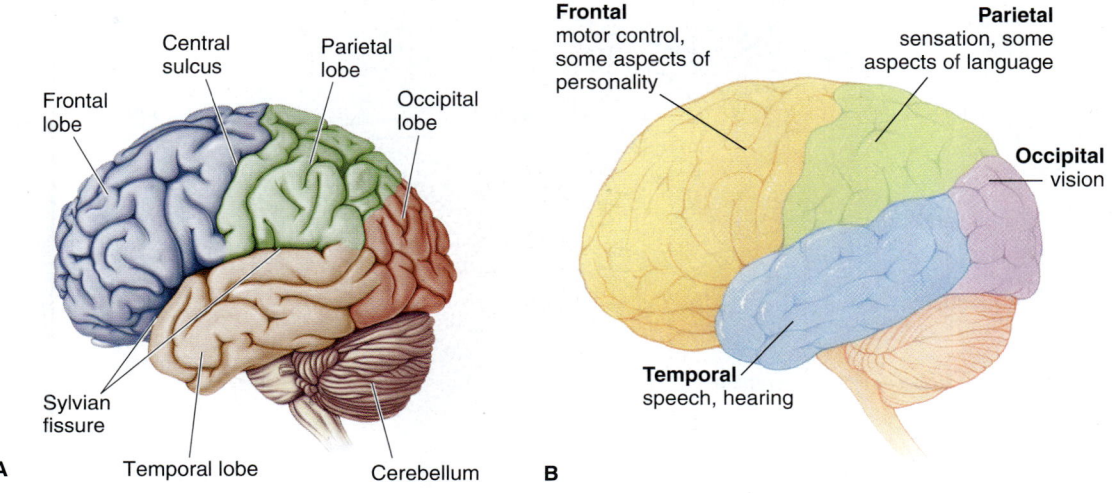

FIGURE 4-3 ■ The lobes and localized functions of the cerebrum. A. Note the Sylvian fissure that divides the frontal lobe from the temporal lobe. Also note the central sulcus that divides the frontal lobe from the parietal lobe. B. Each lobe is associated with specific functions.

TERM	MEANING
diencephalon *dī-en-sef′ă-lon*	area deep within the brain that contains the thalamus and hypothalamus and is the link between the cerebral hemispheres and the brainstem; responsible for directing sensory information to the cortex
gyri *jī′rī*	convolutions (mounds) of the cerebral hemispheres
sulci *sŭl′sī*	shallow grooves that separate gyri
fissures *fish′ŭrz*	deep grooves in the brain
cerebellum (see **Figure 4-3**) *ser-e-bel′ŭm*	portion of the brain located below the occipital lobes of the cerebrum; responsible for control and coordination of skeletal muscles
brainstem *brān′stem*	region of the brain that serves as a relay between the cerebrum, cerebellum, and spinal cord; responsible for breathing, heart rate, and body temperature; the three levels are the mesencephalon (midbrain), pons, and medulla oblongata
ventricles (see **Figure 4-4**) *ven′tri-kĕlz*	series of interconnected cavities within the cerebral hemispheres and brainstem filled with cerebrospinal fluid (CSF)
cerebrospinal fluid (CSF) *ser′ĕ-brō-spī′năl flū′id*	plasma-like clear fluid circulating in and around the brain and spinal cord

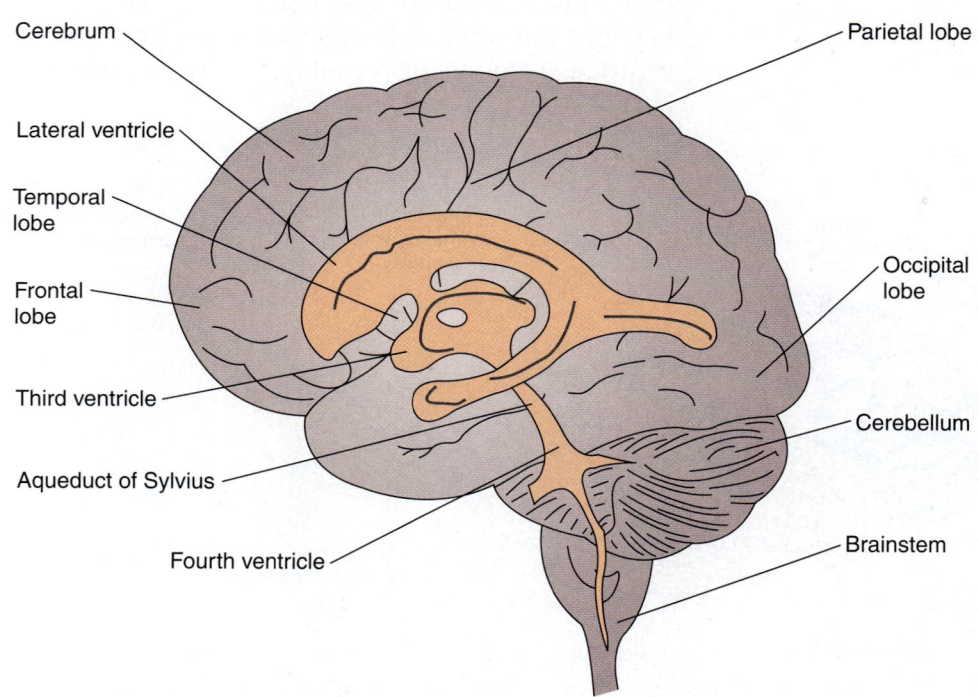

FIGURE 4-4 ■ Ventricles of the brain. Cerebrospinal fluid flows from the lateral ventricles into the third ventricle, then through the narrow aqueduct of Sylvius to the fourth ventricle.

CHAPTER 4 • NERVOUS SYSTEM AND PSYCHIATRY 137

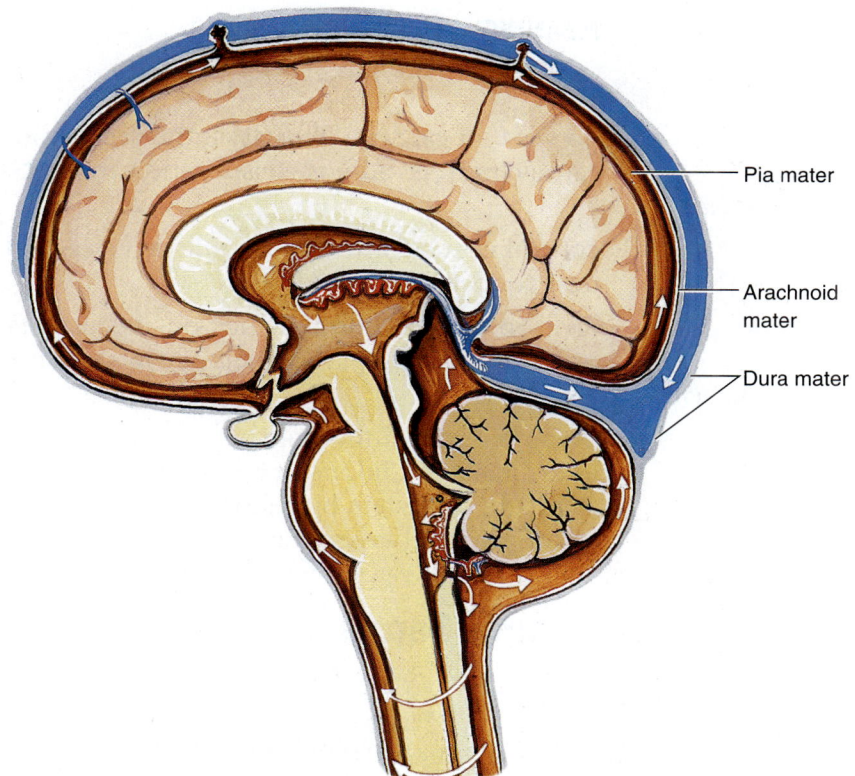

FIGURE 4-5 ■ The meninges protect the brain and spinal cord. *Arrows* indicate the flow of cerebrospinal fluid.

TERM	MEANING
spinal cord *spī′năl kōrd*	column of nervous tissue from the brainstem through the vertebrae; responsible for nerve conduction to and from the brain and the body
meninges (see Figure 4-5) *mĕ-nin′jēz*	three membranes that cover the brain and spinal cord, consisting of the dura mater, pia mater, and arachnoid mater
PERIPHERAL NERVOUS SYSTEM	
peripheral nervous system (PNS) *pĕ-rif′ĕ-răl nĕr′vŭs sis′tĕm*	nerves that branch from the central nervous system including nerves of the brain (cranial nerves) and spinal cord (spinal nerves)
cranial nerves *krā′nē-ăl nĕrvz*	12 pairs of nerves arising from the brain
spinal nerves *spī′năl nĕrvz*	31 pairs of nerves arising from the spinal cord
sensory nerves *sen′sŏ-rē nĕrvz*	nerves that conduct impulses from body parts and carry sensory information to the brain; also called *afferent nerves* (*ad* = toward; *ferre* = carry)
motor nerves *mō′ter nĕrvz*	nerves that conduct motor impulses from the brain to muscles and glands; also called *efferent nerves* (*e* = out; *ferre* = carry)

TERM	MEANING
AUTONOMIC NERVOUS SYSTEM	
autonomic nervous system (ANS) *aw-tō-nom′ik ner′vŭs sis′tĕm*	nerves that carry involuntary impulses to smooth muscle, cardiac muscle, adipose tissue, and various glands
hypothalamus *hī′pō-thal′ă-mŭs*	control center for the autonomic nervous system located near the pituitary gland
sympathetic nervous system *sim-pă-thet′ik ner′vŭs sis′tĕm*	division of the autonomic nervous system that is concerned primarily with preparing the body in stressful or emergency situations
parasympathetic nervous system *par-ă-sim-pă-thet′ik ner′vŭs sis′tĕm*	division of the autonomic nervous system that is most active in ordinary conditions; it counterbalances the effects of the sympathetic system by restoring the body to a restful state after a stressful experience

Programmed Review: Anatomic Terms

ANSWERS	REVIEW
central brain	**4.35** The brain and spinal cord comprise the _____ nervous system. The _____ is the part of the central nervous system within the cranium.
cerebrum frontal lobe	**4.36** The largest portion of the brain, the _____, is divided into the two cerebral hemispheres. The lobe at the front of each cerebral hemisphere, called the _____ _____, controls muscle movement and personality. Posterior to the frontal lobe is the parietal lobe.
parietal	**4.37** The lobe posterior to the frontal lobe, called the _____ lobe, is responsible for sensations such as pain, temperature, and touch. Inferior to the frontal lobe is the temporal lobe.
temporal	**4.38** The lobe below the frontal lobe, called the _____ lobe, is responsible for hearing, taste, and smell. Posterior to the parietal and temporal lobes is the occipital lobe.
occipital	**4.39** The lobe posterior to the parietal and temporal lobes, the _____ lobe, is responsible for vision.
cortex	**4.40** The Latin word cortex means bark, referring to an outer layer. The outer layer of the cerebrum is the cerebral _____, which is the gray matter responsible for higher mental functions. Sensory information is relayed to the cortex by the thalamus (diencephalon).

ANSWERS	REVIEW
thalamus, diencephalon thalami	**4.41** The two gray masses deep within the brain that relay sensory information to the cortex are called the _____ or _____. The plural of thalamus is _____.
gyri, gyrus sulci sulcus fissures	**4.42** Gyri, sulci, and fissures are physical characteristics of the cerebral hemispheres. Convolutions (mounds) of the hemispheres are called _____. The singular of gyri is _____. The shallow grooves that separate gyri are called _____. The singular of sulci is _____. The deep grooves in the brain are called _____.
cerebellum	**4.43** Below the occipital lobes is the cerebellum. The _____ is responsible for controlling skeletal muscles. The cerebellum and cerebrum both communicate with the spinal cord through the brainstem.
brainstem	**4.44** The spinal cord communicates with the cerebrum and cerebellum through the _____, which is also responsible for breathing, heart rate, and body temperature. Interconnected cavities within the brainstem and cerebral hemispheres are called ventricles.
ventricles cerebrospinal	**4.45** Cerebrospinal fluid fills the _____, which are the cavities in the cerebral hemispheres and brainstem. The plasma-like fluid circulating in and around the brain and spinal cord is called the _____ fluid.
spinal cord	**4.46** The column of nervous tissue that descends from the brainstem though the vertebrae of the spine is the _____ _____. The spinal cord and brain are covered by membranes called meninges.
meninges	**4.47** The three membranes covering the brain are called the _____.
peripheral cranial spinal	**4.48** Nerves branch from the central nervous system to the peripheral nervous system to reach all areas of the body. Cranial nerves, spinal nerves, sensory nerves, and motor nerves are all part of the _____ nervous system. The 12 pairs of nerves arising from the brain are the _____ nerves. The 31 pairs of nerves arising from the spinal cord are the _____ nerves.

ANSWERS	REVIEW
sensory motor	**4.49** The nerves in the peripheral nervous system that carry sensory information to the brain are the _____ nerves. The nerves that carry motor impulses from the brain to the muscles and glands are the _____ nerves.
autonomic	**4.50** The autonomic nervous system controls involuntary functions of smooth muscle, cardiac muscle, and various glands. The hypothalamus is the control center for the _____ nervous system.
hypothalamus below	**4.51** The autonomic nervous system is controlled by the _____, which is located below the thalamus. Recall that the prefix *hypo-* means _____ or deficient.
sympathetic parasympathetic	**4.52** The sympathetic nervous system and the parasympathetic nervous system are divisions of the autonomic nervous system. In stressful or emergency situations, the _____ nervous system prepares the body. In most ordinary conditions, the _____ nervous system is more active, counterbalancing the effects of the sympathetic nervous system.

Self-Instruction: Nervous System Symptomatic Terms

Study this table to prepare for the programmed review that follows.

TERM	MEANING
aphasia ă-fā′zē-ă	impairment because of localized brain injury that affects the understanding, retrieving, and formulating of meaningful and sequential elements of language, as demonstrated by an inability to use or comprehend words; occurs because of a stroke, head trauma, or disease
dysphasia dis-fā′zē-ă	impairment in speech production and inability to arrange words in an understandable way
coma kō′mă	a general term referring to levels of decreased consciousness with varying responsiveness; a common method of assessment is the Glasgow coma scale
Glasgow coma scale (GCS) (see **Figure 4-6**) glas′gō kō′mă skāl	a neurologic scale used to assess level of consciousness
delirium dē-lir′ē-ŭm	a state of mental confusion caused by disturbances in cerebral function; the many causes include fever, shock, and drug overdose (*deliro* = to draw the furrow awry when plowing, to go off the rails)

CHAPTER 4 • NERVOUS SYSTEM AND PSYCHIATRY

Glasgow Coma Scale	Best possible total score 15	Worst possible total score 3
Monitored performance	**Reaction**	**Score**
Eye opening	Spontaneous	4
	Open when spoken to	3
	Open at pain stimulus	2
	No reaction	1
Verbal performance	Coherent	5
	Confused, disoriented	4
	Disconnected words	3
	Unintelligible sounds	2
	No verbal reaction	1
Motor responsiveness	Follows instructions	6
	Intentional pain-avoidance	5
	Large motor movement	4
	Flexor synergism	3
	Extensor synergism	2
	No reaction	1

FIGURE 4-6 ■ The Glasgow coma scale (GCS). The GCS is scored between 3 and 15, with 3 being the worst score and 15 being the best score.

TERM	MEANING
dementia dē-men′shē-ă	an impairment of intellectual function characterized by memory loss, disorientation, and confusion (*dementio* = to be mad)
motor deficit mō′ter def′i-sit	loss or impairment of muscle function
sensory deficit sen′sŏ-rē def′i-sit	loss or impairment of sensation
neuralgia nū-ral′jē-ă	pain along the course of a nerve
paralysis pă-ral′i-sis	temporary or permanent loss of motor control
flaccid paralysis flak′sid pă-ral′i-sis	defective (flabby) or absent muscle control caused by a nerve lesion
spastic paralysis spas′tik pă-ral′i-sis	stiff and awkward muscle control caused by a central nervous system disorder
hemiparesis hem′ē-pă-rē′sis	partial paralysis of the right or left half of the body
sciatica sī-at′i-kă	pain that follows the pathway of the sciatic nerve, caused by compression or trauma of the nerve or its roots
seizure sē′zhŭr	sudden, transient disturbances in brain function resulting from an abnormal firing of nerve impulses; may or may not be associated with convulsion
convulsion kon-vŭl′shŭn	to pull together; type of seizure that causes a series of sudden, involuntary contractions of muscles
syncope sin′kŏ-pē	fainting
tactile stimulation tak′til stim-yū-lā′shŭn	evoking a response by touching

TERM	MEANING
hyperesthesia hī′pĕr-es-thē′zē-ă	increased sensitivity to stimulation such as touch or pain
paresthesia par-es-thē′zē-ă	abnormal sensation of numbness and tingling without objective cause

Programmed Review: Nervous System Symptomatic Terms

ANSWERS	REVIEW
speech without condition of aphasia	4.53 Linking *phas/o* (the combining form meaning _____) with *a-* (the prefix meaning _____) and *-ia* (the suffix meaning _____) forms the term describing one's inability to use or comprehend words due to localized brain injury (such as occurs as the result of a stroke): _____.
faulty dysphasia	4.54 The prefix *dys-* means painful, difficult, or _____. Impairment in speech production and inability to arrange words in an understandable way is termed _____.
coma	4.55 A decreased level of consciousness, measured with the Glasgow coma scale, is called a _____.
delirium dementia	4.56 Mental and intellectual function can be disturbed by medical or psychiatric conditions or drugs. A state of mental confusion resulting from disturbed cerebral function is called _____. The impairment of intellectual function characterized by memory loss and disorientation is _____.
motor, sensory	4.57 A deficit is a loss or impairment related to a nervous system problem. The loss of muscle function is called a _____ deficit. The loss of sensation is called a _____ deficit.
neur/o pain neuralgia	4.58 The combining form meaning nerve is _____. Recall that the suffix *-algia* means _____. Therefore, the term for pain along the course of a nerve is _____.
paralysis flaccid spastic	4.59 A temporary or permanent loss of motor control is called _____. A nerve lesion that causes a lack of muscle control, resulting in flabby muscles that do not move, is called _____ paralysis. Stiff, awkward muscle control caused by a central nervous system disorder is called _____ paralysis.

ANSWERS	REVIEW
-paresis hemi- hemiparesis	**4.60** The suffix meaning partial paralysis is _____. Recall that the prefix meaning half is _____. The term for partial paralysis of the right or left half of the body is _____.
sciatica	**4.61** The sciatic nerve runs down the leg. Pain along its pathway caused by compression or trauma to this nerve is called _____.
seizure convulsion	**4.62** A sudden, transient disturbance of brain function that results from abnormal firing of nerve impulses is called a _____. A type of seizure that involves sudden, involuntary muscle contractions is termed _____.
syncope	**4.63** The Greek word synkope means cutting short or swoon. From this word, the medical term for fainting is _____.
tactile	**4.64** The process of evoking a response by touching a person's skin is called _____ stimulation.
condition of esthesi/o excessive hyperesthesia	**4.65** Again, the suffix -ia means _____. The combining form meaning sensation is _____. The prefix hyper- means above or _____. From these three word parts comes the term meaning a condition of increased sensitivity to the sensations of touch and pain: _____.
abnormal paresthesia	**4.66** Recall that the prefix para- means alongside of or _____. The term for a condition of an abnormal sensation of numbness and tingling is _____.

Self-Instruction: Nervous System Diagnostic Terms

Study this table to prepare for the programmed review that follows.

TERM	MEANING
agnosia ag-nō′zē-ă	any of many types of loss of neurologic function involving interpretation of sensory information
astereognosis ă-stĕr′ē-og-nō′sis	inability to judge the form of an object by touch (e.g., a coin from a key)
atopognosis ă-top-og-nō′sis	inability to locate a sensation properly, such as an inability to locate a point touched on the body
Alzheimer disease awlz′hī-mĕr di-zēz′	disease of structural changes in the brain resulting in an irreversible deterioration that progresses from forgetfulness and disorientation to loss of all intellectual functions, total disability, and death

TERM	MEANING
amyotrophic lateral sclerosis (ALS) ă-mī-ō-trō′fik lat′ĕr-ăl sklĕ-rō′sis	condition of progressive deterioration of motor nerve cells resulting in total loss of voluntary muscle control; symptoms advance from muscle weakness in the arms and legs, to the muscles of speech, swallowing, and breathing, to total paralysis and death; also known as *Lou Gehrig disease*
cerebral palsy (CP) se-rē′brăl pawl′zē	condition of motor dysfunction caused by damage to the cerebrum during development or injury at birth; characterized by partial paralysis and lack of muscle coordination (*palsy* = paralysis)
cerebrovascular disease ser′ĕ-brō-vas′kyū-lăr di-zēz′	disorder resulting from a change within one or more blood vessels of the brain
cerebral arteriosclerosis se-rē′brăl ar-tēr′ē-ō-skler-ō′sis	hardening of the arteries of the brain
cerebral atherosclerosis se-rē′brăl ath′er-ō-skler-ō′sis	condition of lipid (fat) buildup within the blood vessels of the brain (*ather/o* = fatty [lipid] paste)
cerebral aneurysm se-rē′brăl an′yū-rizm	dilation of a blood vessel in the brain (*aneurysm* = dilation or widening)
cerebral embolism (see Figure 4-7) se-rē′brăl em′bo-lizm	obstruction of a blood vessel in the brain by an embolus (blood clot, air bubble, or fat deposit in a blood vessel) transported through the circulation
cerebral thrombosis (see Figure 4-7) se-rē′brăl throm-bō′sis	presence of a stationary clot in a blood vessel of the brain
cerebrovascular accident (CVA) (see Figure 4-8) ser′ĕ-brō-vas′kyū-lăr ak′si-dent	damage to the brain caused by cerebrovascular disease, such as occlusion of a blood vessel by a thrombus or embolus (ischemic stroke) or intracranial hemorrhage after rupture of an aneurysm (hemorrhagic stroke); also called *stroke*

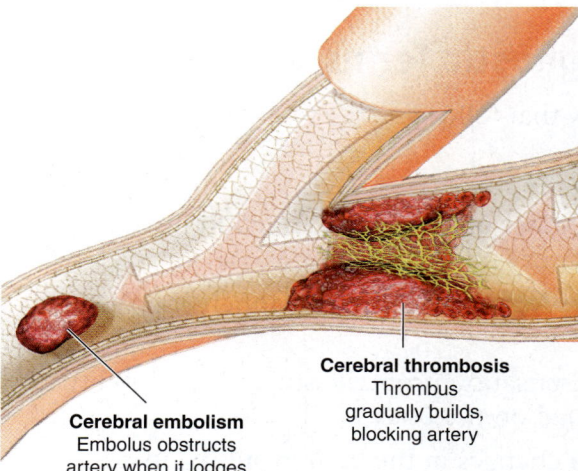

FIGURE 4-7 ■ Cerebral embolism and cerebral thrombosis.

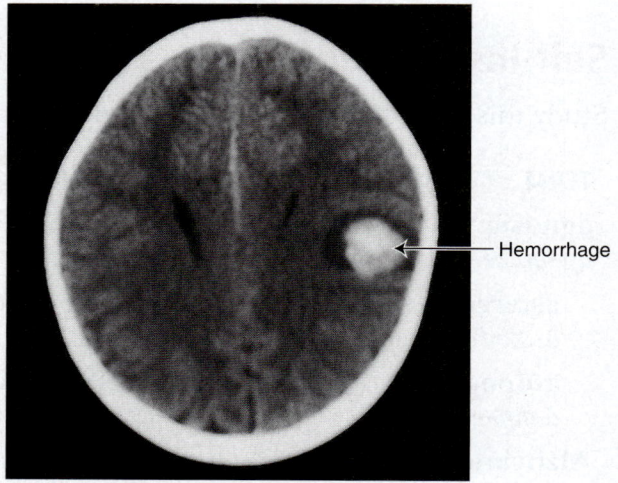

FIGURE 4-8 ■ Cerebrovascular accident (stroke). Computed tomography (CT) scan of the brain of a 4-year-old boy showing a large hemorrhage.

TERM	MEANING
stroke (see Figure 4-8) *strōk*	damage to the brain caused by cerebrovascular disease, such as occlusion of a blood vessel by a thrombus or embolus (ischemic stroke) or intracranial hemorrhage after rupture of an aneurysm (hemorrhagic stroke); also called *cerebrovascular accident* (CVA)
transient ischemic attack (TIA) *tranz′ē-ent is-kē′mik ă-tak′*	brief episode of loss of blood flow to the brain, usually caused by a partial occlusion that results in temporary neurologic deficit (impairment); often precedes a CVA
encephalitis *en-sef-ă-lī′tis*	inflammation of the brain
epilepsy *ep′i-lep′sē*	disorder affecting the central nervous system; characterized by recurrent seizures
tonic–clonic seizure *ton′ik-klon′ik sē′zhŭr*	stiffening-jerking; a major motor seizure involving all muscle groups; previously termed *grand mal (big bad) seizure*
absence seizure *ab′sens sē′zhŭr*	seizure involving a brief loss of consciousness without motor involvement; previously termed *petit mal (little bad) seizure*
partial seizure *par′shăl sē′zhŭr*	seizure involving only limited areas of the brain with localized symptoms
glioma *glī-ō′mă*	tumor of neuroglia (ependymal cells, oligodendrocytes, astrocytes, and microglia) graded according to degree of malignancy (see Figure 4-9)
herniated disc (disk) (see Figure 4-10) *hĕr′nē-ā-tĕd disk*	protrusion of a degenerated or fragmented intervertebral disk so that the nucleus pulposus protrudes, causing compression on the spinal nerve root
herpes zoster (see Figure 4-11) *hĕr′pēz zos′tĕr*	viral disease affecting the peripheral nerves, characterized by painful blisters that spread over the skin following the affected nerves, usually unilateral; also known as *shingles*

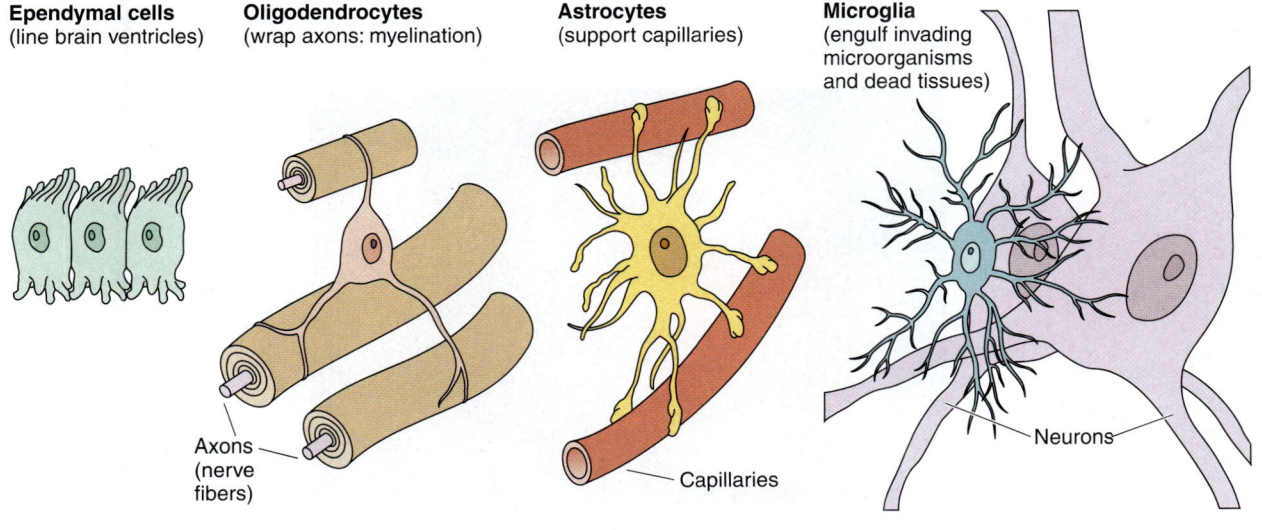

FIGURE 4-9 ■ Types of neuroglia.

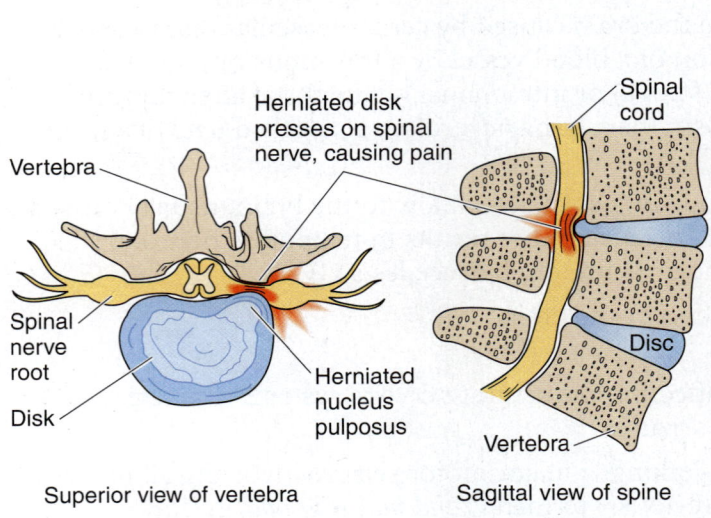

FIGURE 4-10 ■ View of a herniated disk.

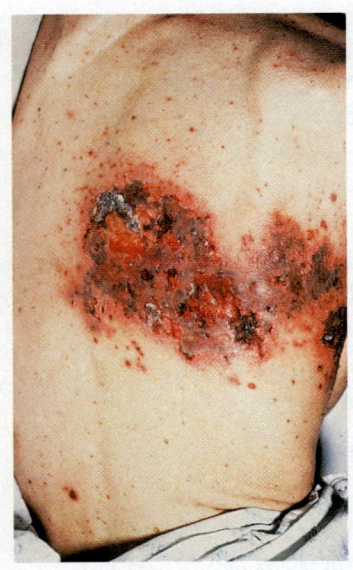

FIGURE 4-11 ■ Shingles. An outbreak of shingles with the primary skin lesions following the path of the affected nerves.

TERM	MEANING
Huntington disease (HD) hŭn′ting-tŏn di-zēz	hereditary disease of the central nervous system characterized by bizarre, involuntary body movements and progressive dementia (*choros* = dance); also called *Huntington chorea*
Huntington chorea hŭn′ting-tŏn kōr-ē′ă	hereditary disease of the central nervous system characterized by bizarre, involuntary body movements and progressive dementia (*choros* = dance); also called *Huntington disease*
hydrocephalus (see Figure 4-12) hī-drō-sef′ă-lŭs	abnormal accumulation of cerebrospinal fluid in the ventricles of the brain because developmental problems, infection, injury, or tumor
meningioma mĕ-nin′jē-ō′mă	benign tumor of the coverings of the brain (the meninges)

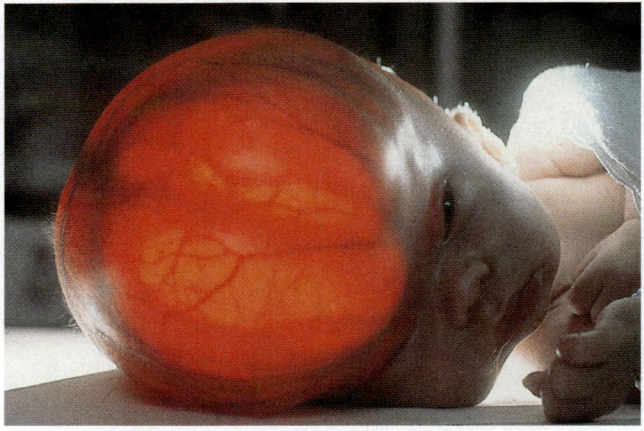

FIGURE 4-12 ■ An infant with hydrocephalus. An enlargement of the cerebral ventricles leads to hydrocephalus.

TERM	MEANING
meningitis men-in-jī′tis	inflammation of the meninges
migraine headache mī′grān hed′āk	paroxysmal (sudden, periodic) attacks of mostly unilateral headache, often accompanied by disordered vision, nausea, or vomiting, lasting hours or days and caused by dilation of arteries
multiple sclerosis (MS) mŭl′ti-pul sklĕ-rō′sis	disease of the central nervous system characterized by the demyelination (deterioration of the myelin sheath) of nerve fibers, with episodes of neurologic dysfunction (exacerbation) followed by recovery (remission)
myasthenia gravis mī-as-thē′nē-ă gra′vis	autoimmune disorder that affects the neuromuscular junction, causing a progressive decrease in muscle strength; activity resumes and strength returns after a period of rest
myelitis mī′ĕ-lī′tis	inflammation of the spinal cord
narcolepsy nar′kō-lep-sē	sleep disorder characterized by a sudden, uncontrollable need to sleep, attacks of paralysis (cataplexy), and dreams intruding while awake (hypnagogic hallucinations)
neural tube defects nūr′ăl tūb dē′fektz	congenital deformities of the brain and spinal cord caused by incomplete development of the neural tube, the embryonic structure that forms the nervous system
anencephaly an′en-sef′ă-lē	defect in closure of the cephalic portion of the neural tube that results in incomplete development of the brain and bones of the skull; the most drastic neural tube defect usually results in a stillbirth

spina bifida
    (see Figure 4-13)
    spī′nă bĭ fi-dă
	defect in development of the spinal column characterized by the absence of vertebral arches, often resulting in pouching of the meninges (meningocele) or of the meninges and spinal cord (meningomyelocele); considered to be the most common neural tube defect (*spina* = spine; *bifida* = split into two parts)

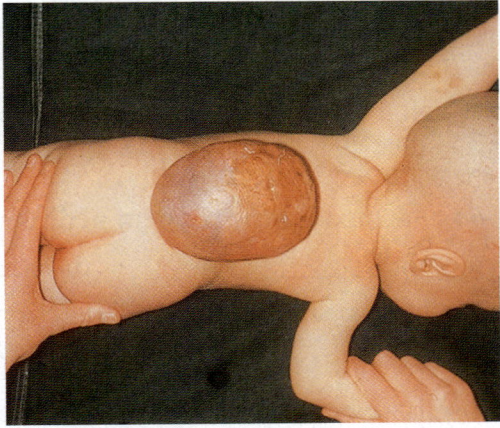

FIGURE 4-13 ■ Spina bifida with myelomeningocele. The infant also has hydrocephaly.

TERM	MEANING
Parkinson disease *pahr′kin-sĕn di-zēz′*	condition of slowly progressive degeneration in an area of the brainstem (substantia nigra) resulting in a decrease of dopamine (a chemical neurotransmitter necessary for proper movement); characterized by tremor, rigidity of muscles, and slow movements (bradykinesia); usually occurs later in life
plegia *plē′jē-ă*	paralysis
hemiplegia *hem-ē-plē′jē-ă*	paralysis on one side of the body
paraplegia *par-ă-plē′jē-ă*	paralysis from the waist down
quadriplegia *kwah′dri-plē′jē-ă*	paralysis of all four limbs
poliomyelitis *po′lē-ō-mī′ĕ-lī′tis*	inflammation of the gray matter of the spinal cord caused by a virus, often resulting in spinal and muscle deformity and paralysis (*polio* = gray)
polyneuritis *pol′ē-nū-rī-tis*	inflammation involving two or more nerves, often caused by a nutritional deficiency, such as lack of thiamine
sleep apnea *slēp ap′nē-ă*	periods of breathing cessation (10 seconds or more) that occur during sleep, often causing snoring

Programmed Review: Nervous System Diagnostic Terms

ANSWERS	REVIEW
gnos/o, without agnosia stere/o astereognosis top/o atopognosis	**4.67** Recall that the combining form that means knowing is _____. The prefix *a-* means _____. The general term for many types of loss of neurologic function (meaning "not knowing") is therefore _____. The combining form meaning three-dimensional is _____. The type of agnosia in which a person cannot judge the shape of an object by touch is termed _____. Recall that the combining form meaning place or location is _____. The type of agnosia in which a person cannot locate a sensation on the body is called _____.
Alzheimer	**4.68** Named for the German neurologist who researched dementia, _____ disease causes structural changes in the brain resulting in mental deterioration.
cerebral palsy	**4.69** Palsy means a partial paralysis. The condition of partial paralysis and lack of muscle coordination caused by damage to the cerebrum is called _____ _____ (CP).

ANSWERS	REVIEW
cerebrovascular condition arteriosclerosis cerebral atherosclerosis	**4.70** The combining form *vascul/o* refers to blood vessels. A disease affecting blood vessels in the cerebrum is called _____ disease. The combining form *scler/o* means hard. Recall that the suffix *-osis* means increase or _____. The term for a condition of hardening of the arteries in the brain is cerebral _____. The combining form *ather/o* means fatty paste. The condition of a hardening of a pasty lipid buildup in the blood vessels of the brain is called _____ _____.
aneurysm cerebral thrombosis embolism	**4.71** The dilation of a blood vessel in the brain is called a cerebral _____. The Greek word thrombos means a clot. A stationary blood clot in a blood vessel in the brain is called a _____ _____. A blood clot carried in the circulation that obstructs a blood vessel in the brain is called a cerebral _____.
cerebrovascular accident ischemic hemorrhagic	**4.72** Occlusion of a blood vessel in the brain by a thrombus, embolus, or bleeding after rupture of an aneurysm may cause brain damage known as a stroke or _____ _____ (CVA). Thrombotic and embolic strokes are classified as _____ strokes, because they result in a loss of blood flow to brain tissues. Damage caused by the hemorrhage of blood into brain tissue is called a _____ stroke.
transient ischemic attack	**4.73** Ischemia is a condition in which blood flow to an area is reduced. A brief episode of loss of blood flow to the brain caused by a partial occlusion of a blood vessel is called a _____ _____ _____ (TIA).
mening/o, -itis meningitis	**4.74** Recall that the combining form meaning meninges is _____. The suffix meaning inflammation is _____. Therefore, the term for inflammation of the meninges is _____.
head brain encephalitis	**4.75** Formed using the prefix *en-*, meaning in, and *cephal/o*, meaning _____, *encephal/o* is a combining form meaning the entire _____. The term for inflammation of the brain is _____.

ANSWERS	REVIEW
myel/o myelitis poliomyelitis	**4.76** The combining form for the spinal cord is _____. Inflammation of the spinal cord is termed _____. The combining form *poli/o* means gray. An inflammation of the gray matter of the spinal cord, caused by a virus, is called _____.
neur/o many polyneuritis	**4.77** The combining form meaning nerve is _____. The prefix *poly-* means _____. The term for inflammation of two or more nerves is _____.
epilepsy tension tonic–clonic absence partial	**4.78** The disorder of the central nervous system characterized by recurrent seizures is _____. Recall that the combining form *ton/o* refers to muscle tone or _____. The type of epileptic seizure in which muscles stiffen and jerk is called _____-_____ seizure. A type of epileptic seizure in which a brief loss of consciousness occurs (the person seems to be absent for a moment) is called an _____ seizure. A _____ seizure affects only limited areas of the brain with localized symptoms.
gli/o -oma glioma meningioma	**4.79** The combining form meaning glue is _____, the origin of the name for neuroglia, which are thought to "glue" together neurons. The suffix meaning tumor is _____. A malignant (cancerous) tumor of neuroglia is called a _____. A benign (noncancerous) tumor of the meninges is called _____. (Note: Word structuring alone does not indicate whether a tumor is cancerous. Rely on a good medical dictionary or oncology reference for clarification.)
herniated	**4.80** A hernia is a protrusion of a structure from its normal location. A degenerated or fragmented intervertebral disk that protrudes and compresses a nerve is called a _____ disk.
herpes zoster	**4.81** A herpes virus causes skin blisters following an affected nerve, often in a belt-like pattern on the skin. The Greek word *zoster* means girdle or belt. This condition is called _____ _____.

ANSWERS	REVIEW
	4.82 The term chorea comes from a Greek word meaning dance. A chorea is a spasmodic involuntary movement of muscles. A hereditary type of chorea that is characterized by bizarre body movements and progressive dementia
Huntington chorea	is called _____ _____ or
Huntington disease	_____ _____ (HD).
	4.83 The combining form *hydr/o* means water or fluid. The combining form *cephal/o* means head. These two combining forms are the origin of the term for an abnormal accumulation of cerebrospinal fluid in the brain:
hydrocephalus	_____.
	4.84 The kind of severe headache accompanied
migraine	by disordered vision, nausea, and vomiting is a _____ headache.
	4.85 Recall that *scler/o* is the combining form meaning
hard	_____. A disease of the central nervous system involving deterioration of the myelin sheath of nerve fibers and multiple patches of hard plaques in the brain and
multiple	spinal cord is called _____
sclerosis	_____ (MS).
	4.86 Formed by the combination of *a-*, meaning
without, muscle	_____, *my/o*, meaning _____, *troph/o*, meaning
nourishment	development or _____, and *-ic*, meaning
pertaining to	_____, the word amyotrophic is used in naming the neurologic condition characterized by the progressive deterioration of motor nerve cells that results in total loss of
amyotrophic lateral	voluntary muscle control: _____ _____
sclerosis	_____ (ALS). This condition is also called
Lou Gehrig	_____ _____ disease (named after the American baseball player who had the condition).
	4.87 The combining form *my/o* means muscle, and the suffix
weakness	*-asthenia* means _____. Thus, a term for muscle
myasthenia	weakness is _____. An autoimmune disorder that causes a progressive decrease in muscle strength is myasthenia
gravis	_____.

ANSWERS	REVIEW
sleep, seizure narcolepsy	**4.88** Recall that the combining form *narc/o* means stupor or _____. The suffix *-lepsy* means _____. A sleep disorder in which the person falls asleep as quickly as if in a seizure is called _____.
movement Parkinson	**4.89** Bradykinesia, a condition of slow _____, along with tremor and rigidity of muscles are symptoms first documented by the British physician for whom this slowly progressive, degenerative neurologic condition was named: _____ disease.
paralysis half hemiplegia paraplegia quadri- quadriplegia	**4.90** Recall that the suffix *-plegia* means _____. The prefix *hemi-* means _____, and paralysis of half (one side) of the body is called _____. Paralysis from the waist down is called _____. Recall that the prefix meaning four is _____. Therefore, the term for paralysis of all four limbs is _____.
sleep apnea	**4.91** The Greek word apnoia means want of breath. The term for a condition in which breathing stops for short periods during sleep is _____ _____.
nerve neural tube without entire brain process of anencephaly bifida pouching meningocele meningomyelocele	**4.92** Neural, the adjective pertaining to _____, is used to name the embryonic tube that forms the nervous system, called the _____ _____. Congenital deformities caused by its incomplete development are known as neural tube defects. The term formed by the combination of *an-*, meaning _____, *encephal/o* meaning _____ _____, and *-y*, meaning condition or _____ ____, describes the most drastic type of defect caused by the incomplete development of the brain and bones of the skull: _____. The word describing that which is split into two parts is used in the name for the most common neural tube defect, which is characterized by the absence of spinal vertebral arches: spina _____. The suffix *-cele*, meaning _____ or hernia, is used to describe conditions that often accompany spina bifida: pouching of the meninges (_____) or pouching of the meninges and spinal cord (_____).

Self-Instruction: Nervous System Diagnostic Tests and Procedures

Study this table to prepare for the programmed review that follows.

TEST OR PROCEDURE	EXPLANATION
electrodiagnostic procedures ē-lek′trō-dī-ag-nos′tik prō-sē′jŭrz	diagnostic procedures used to evaluate the function of the nervous system by recording the electrical signals produced in the brain, spinal cord, and peripheral nerves
electroencephalogram (EEG) (see Figure 4-14) ē-lek′trō-en-sef′ă-lō-gram	record of the minute electrical impulses of the brain measured as alpha, beta, delta, and theta waves; used to identify neurologic conditions that affect brain function and level of consciousness
evoked potentials ē-vokt′ pō-ten′shălz	record of minute electrical potentials (waves) that are extracted from ongoing EEG activity to diagnose auditory, visual, and sensory pathway disorders; also used to monitor the neurologic function of patients during surgery
polysomnography (PSG) (see Figure 4-15) pol′ē-som-nog′ră-fē	recording of various aspects of sleep (e.g., eye and muscle movements, respiration, and EEG patterns) to diagnose sleep disorders
lumbar puncture (LP) lŭm′bar pŭnk′chūr	introduction of a specialized needle into the spine in the lumbar region for diagnostic or therapeutic purposes, such as to obtain CSF for testing; also called *spinal tap*
magnetic resonance imaging (MRI) mag-net′ik rez′ō-nănts im′ăj-ing	nonionizing imaging technique using magnetic fields and radiofrequency waves to visualize anatomic structures (especially soft tissue), such as the tissues of the brain and spinal cord

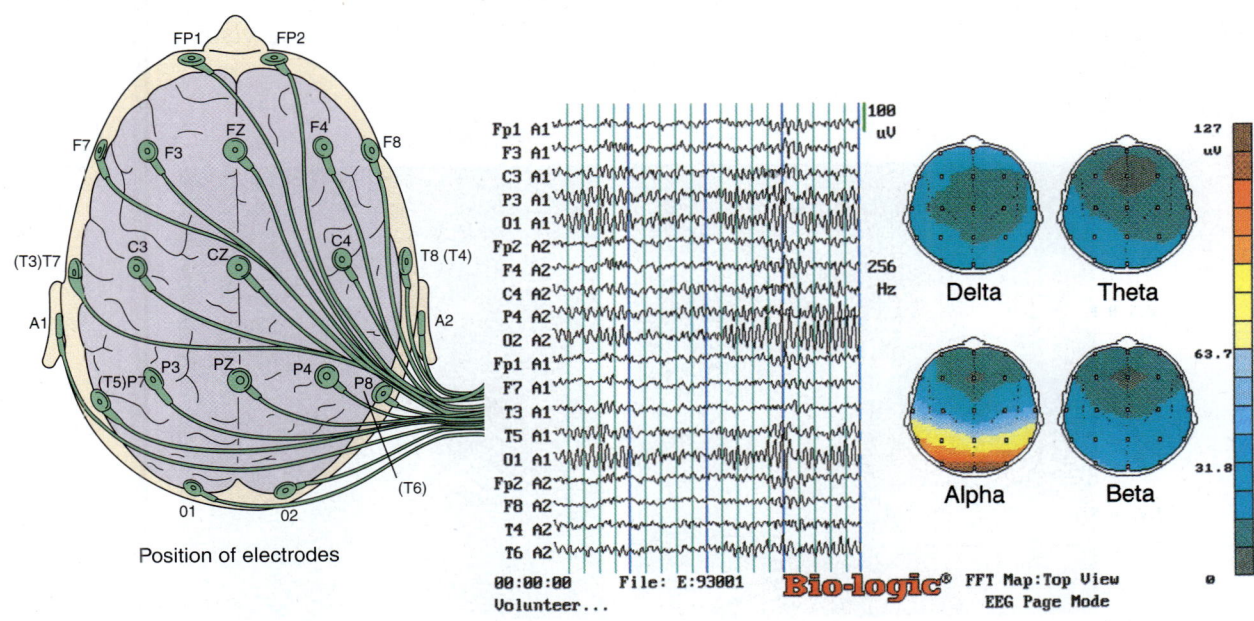

Normal EEG wave forms shown on left and computer compilation of frequency bands (delta, theta, alpha, and beta) mapped on right

FIGURE 4-14 ■ Electroencephalography (EEG).

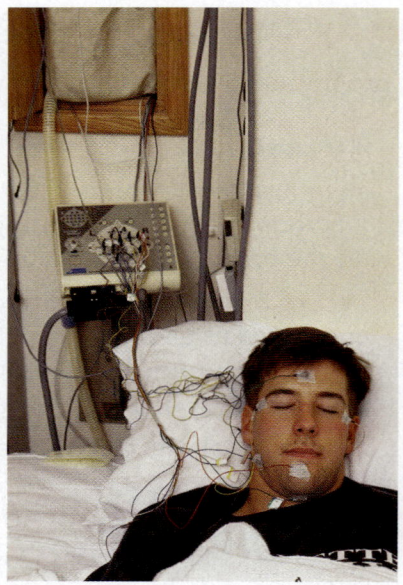

FIGURE 4-15 ■ Polysomnography (PSG). A patient undergoing polysomnography has electrodes affixed to the scalp, face, chest, and legs.

TEST OR PROCEDURE	EXPLANATION
magnetic resonance angiography (MRA) (see Figure 4-16) *mag-net′ik rez′ō-nănts an-jē-og′ră-fē*	magnetic resonance imaging of blood vessels to detect pathologic conditions, such as thrombosis and atherosclerosis
intracranial MRA (see Figure 4-16A) *in′tră-krā′nē-ăl em-ar-ā*	magnetic resonance image of the head to visualize the vessels of the cerebral arterial circle (circle of Willis), which is a common site of cerebral aneurysm, stenosis, or occlusion
extracranial MRA (see Figure 4-16B) *eks′tră-krā′nē-ăl em-ar-ā*	magnetic resonance image of the neck to visualize the carotid artery circulation

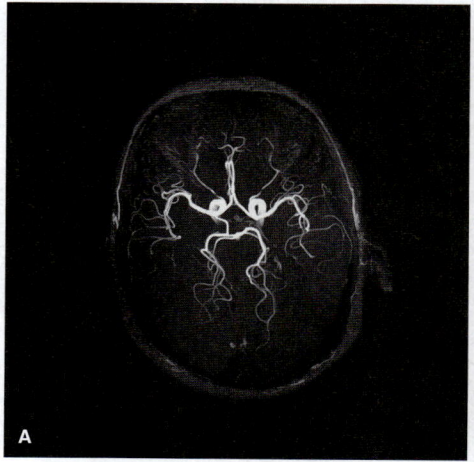
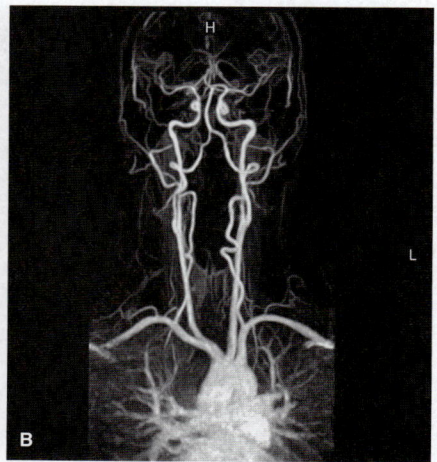

FIGURE 4-16 ■ Magnetic resonance angiography (MRA). **A.** Contrast-enhanced intracranial MRA showing circulation of the cerebral arterial circle (circle of Willis). **B.** Contrast-enhanced extracranial MRA showing carotid arterial circulation.

TEST OR PROCEDURE	EXPLANATION
nuclear medicine imaging nū′klē-ăr med′i-sen im′ăj-ing	radionuclide organ imaging
single-photon emission computed tomography (SPECT) brain scan sing′gel-fō′ton ē-mish′ŭn kom-pyūt′ĕd tō-mog′ră-fē brān skan	scan combining nuclear medicine and computed tomography to produce images of the brain after the administration of radioactive isotopes

positron-emission tomography (PET)
   (see Figure 4-17)
   poz′i-tron-ē-mish′ŭn tō-mog′ră-fē
	technique combining nuclear medicine and computed tomography to produce images of brain anatomy and corresponding physiology; used to study stroke, Alzheimer disease, epilepsy, metabolic brain disorders, chemistry of nerve transmissions in the brain, and so on; provides greater accuracy than SPECT, but is used less often because of cost and the limited availability of the radioisotopes

radiography rā′dē-og′ră-fē	x-ray imaging
cerebral angiogram se-rē′brăl an′jē-ō-gram	x-ray of blood vessels in the brain after intracarotid injection of contrast medium
computed tomography (CT) of the head kom-pyū′tĕd tō-mog′ră-fē	computed tomographic (x-ray) images of the head used to visualize abnormalities, such as brain tumors and malformations
myelogram mī′ĕ-lō-gram	x-ray of the spinal cord obtained after intraspinal injection of contrast medium

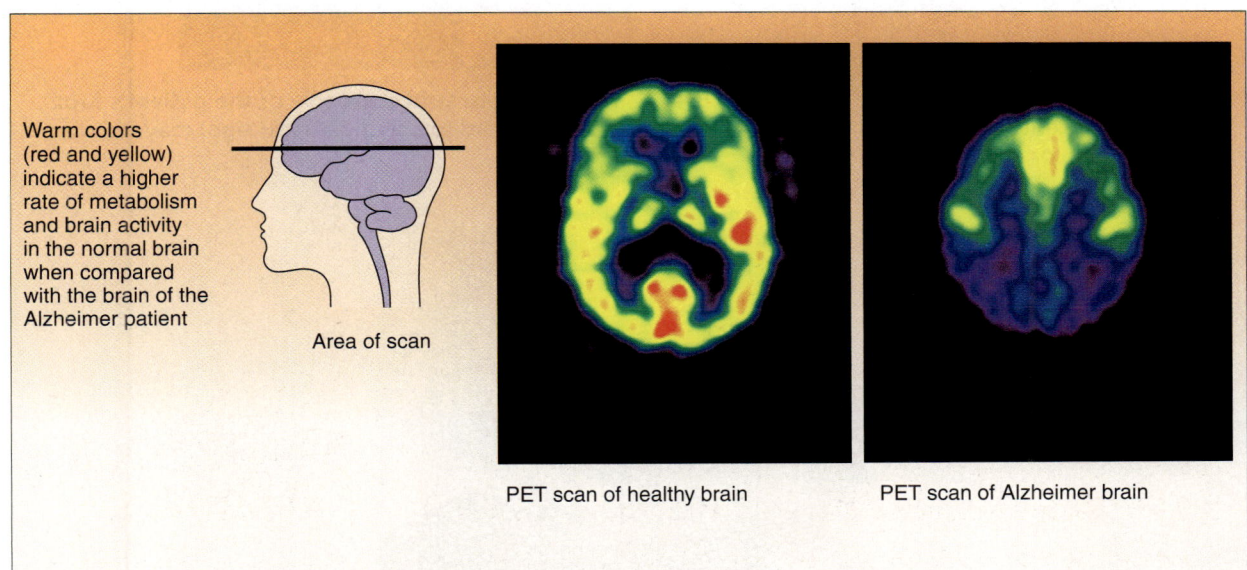

FIGURE 4-17 ■ Positron-emission tomography (PET) scans of the brain.

TEST OR PROCEDURE	EXPLANATION
reflex testing rē′fleks test′ing	test performed to observe the body's response to a stimulus
deep tendon reflexes (DTR) dēp ten′dŏn rē′fleks-ĕz	involuntary muscle contraction after percussion at a tendon (e.g., patella or Achilles) indicating function; positive findings are either no reflex response or an exaggerated response to stimulus; numbers are often used to record responses Ø = no response (absent reflex) 1+ = diminished response 2+ = normal response 3+ = more brisk than average response 4+ = hyperactive response

Babinski sign
   (see Figure 4-18)
   bă-bin′skē sīn
	pathologic response to stimulation of the plantar surface of the foot; a positive sign is indicated when the toes dorsiflex (curl upward); also called *Babinski reflex*

Babinski reflex bă-bin′skē rē′fleks	pathologic response to stimulation of the plantar surface of the foot; a positive sign is indicated when the toes dorsiflex (curl upward); also called *Babinski sign*
transcranial Doppler sonogram (see Figure 4-19) trans-krā′nē-ăl dop′lĕr son′ō-gram	image made by sending ultrasound beams through the skull to assess blood flow in intracranial vessels; used in the diagnosis and management of stroke and head trauma

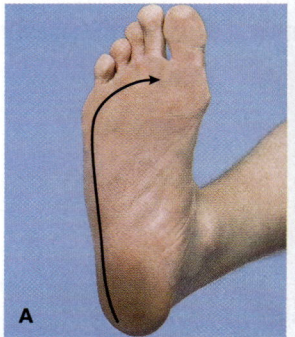 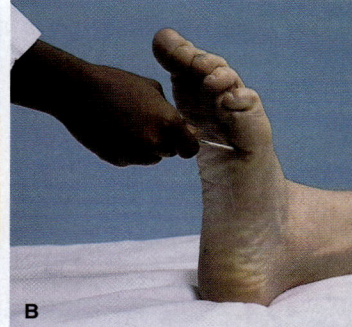 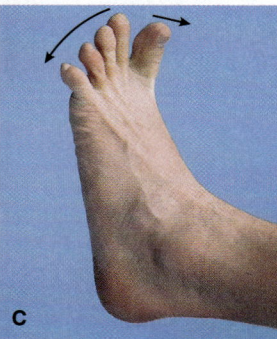

FIGURE 4-18 ■ Babinski sign. **A.** The clinician uses an instrument to stroke the sole of the patient's foot. **B.** Toe flexion (absent Babinski sign) is normal. **C.** Toes that fan outward (present Babinski sign) may indicate injury to the brain or spinal nerves.

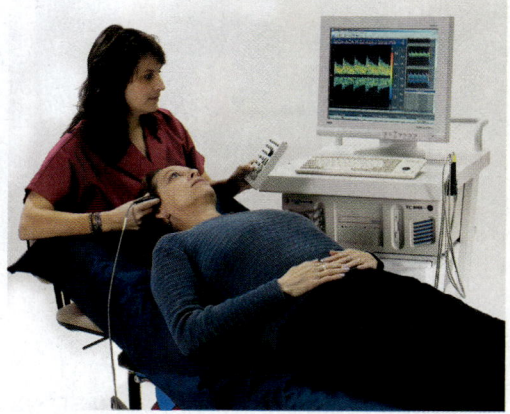

FIGURE 4-19 ■ Transcranial Doppler sonography.

Programmed Review: Nervous System Diagnostic Tests and Procedures

ANSWERS	REVIEW
encephal/o record electroencephalogram evoked	**4.93** A wide variety of tests and procedures are used to diagnose conditions of the nervous system, including several electrodiagnostic procedures. The combining form referring to electricity is *electr/o*. The combining form referring to the entire brain is _____. Recall that the suffix *-gram* means _____. An EEG is a record of electrical impulses in the brain; EEG is an abbreviation for _____. Minute electrical waves sorted out of the EEG activity to diagnose specific nerve pathway disorders are called _____ potentials. (Potential is a term referring to electrical charges.)
somn/o poly- recording polysomnography	**4.94** In addition to *hypn/o* and *somn/i*, a combining form meaning sleep is _____. The prefix meaning many is _____. The suffix *-graphy* means process of _____. From these three parts comes the term for another electrodiagnostic procedure that measures various physiologic aspects of sleep: _____ (PSG).
lumbar puncture	**4.95** The procedure in which a specialized needle is introduced into the lumbar spine, such as to obtain a sample of cerebrospinal fluid for examination, is called a _____ _____ (LP).
magnetic resonance	**4.96** A nonionizing imaging technique using magnetic fields to visualize structures such as tissues of the brain and spinal cord is called _____ _____ imaging (MRI).
magnetic resonance angiography crani/o, within intracranial outside extracranial	**4.97** An MRI technique for imaging blood vessels (including the combining form *angi/o*, meaning vessel) is termed _____ _____ _____ (MRA). The combining form for skull is _____. The prefix *intra-* means _____. Magnetic resonance imaging of the head to visualize the vessels of the circle of Willis is called _____ MRA. The prefix *extra-* means _____. The term for magnetic resonance imaging of the neck to depict the carotid arteries is called _____ MRA.

ANSWERS	REVIEW
medicine photon emission tomography	**4.98** Imaging a structure after administration of a radionuclide is called nuclear _____ imaging. A specialized brain scan that combines nuclear medicine with computed tomography (CT) is called single _____ _____ computed _____ (SPECT).
tomography	**4.99** Another technique that combines nuclear medicine and CT to study brain anatomy and physiology is positron emission _____ (PET).
process recording radiography cerebral angi/o cerebral angiogram	**4.100** Recall that the suffix *-graphy* means the _____ of _____. The process of recording x-ray images is called _____. The adjective form of cerebrum, pertaining to the largest part of the brain, is _____. Again, the combining form for blood vessel is _____. An x-ray of the blood vessels of the cerebrum is called a _____ _____.
computed tomography	**4.101** Cross-sectional x-ray images of the brain produced by _____ _____ are also used to visualize abnormalities, such as brain tumors.
myel/o, record myelogram	**4.102** The combining form meaning spinal cord is _____. Again, the suffix *-gram* means _____. An x-ray record of the spinal cord using an intraspinal contrast medium is called a _____.
Reflex deep tendon	**4.103** A reflex is the body's automatic response to a stimulus. _____ testing is performed to observe such responses. Reflexes that involve involuntary muscle contraction after percussion at a tendon are called _____ _____ reflexes (DTR).
Babinski	**4.104** A response to stimulation of the plantar surface of the foot is a pathologic reflex called the _____ sign, which is named for Babinski, the French neurologist who discovered it.
across transcranial sonogram	**4.105** Ultrasound is also called sonography. The prefix *trans-* means _____ or through. The record of an ultrasound image made by sending ultrasound waves through the skull is called a _____ _____.

Self-Instruction: Nervous System Operative Terms

Study this table to prepare for the programmed review that follows.

TERM	MEANING
carotid endarterectomy *ka-rot'id end'ar-těr-ek'tŏ-mē*	incision and coring of the lining of the carotid artery to clear a blockage caused by the buildup of atherosclerotic plaque or a clot; an open procedure used to treat patients who are at risk for stroke
craniectomy *krā'nē-ek'tō-mē*	excision of part of the skull to approach the brain
craniotomy *krā-nē-ot'ō-mē*	incision into the skull to approach the brain
discectomy or diskectomy *disk-ek'tŏ-mē*	removal of a herniated disk; often done percutaneously (*per* = through; *cutaneous* = skin)
endovascular neurosurgery *en'dō-vas'kyū-lar nŭr'ō-sŭr'jĕr-ē*	minimally invasive techniques for diagnosis and treatment of disorders within blood vessels of the neck, brain, and spinal cord using specialized catheters inserted percutaneously (through the skin) into the femoral artery (in the groin) and guided by angiographic imaging to the treatment site; performed in a specialized angiographic laboratory by interventional neuroradiologists; common procedures are: • percutaneous transluminal angioplasty (PTA) with stent (e.g., carotid PTA) • embolization (plugging) of intracranial aneurysms and vascular malformations
interventional neuroradiology *in'tĕr-ven'shŭn-ăl nū'rō-rā'dē-ol'ŏ-jē*	clinical subspecialty that uses CT and ultrasound to guide percutaneous procedures such as biopsies, fluid drainage, catheter insertion, and dilating or stenting narrowed ducts or vessels
laminectomy *lam'i-nek'tŏ-mē*	excision of one or more laminae of the vertebrae to approach the spinal cord
vertebral lamina (see Figure 4-6) *ver'tĕ-brăl lam'i-nă*	flattened posterior portion of the vertebral arch
microsurgery *mī'krō-sŭr'jĕr-ē*	use of a microscope to dissect minute structures during surgery
neuroplasty *nū'rō-plas-tē*	surgical repair of a nerve
spondylosyndesis (see Figure 4-20) *spon'di-lō-sin-dē'sis*	an operative procedure to create ankylosis (joint fixation) between two or more vertebrae; also called *spinal fusion*

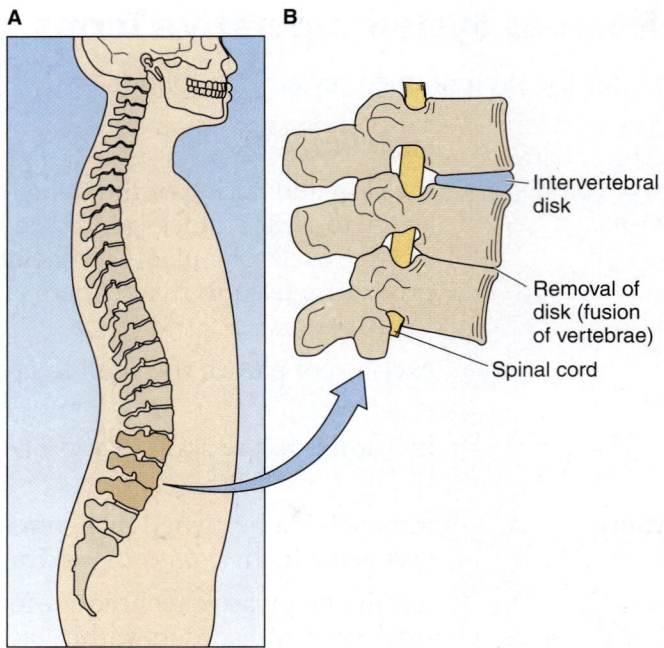

FIGURE 4-20 ■ Spondylosyndesis. **A.** Vertebral column. **B.** Spinal fusion.

Programmed Review: Nervous System Operative Terms

ANSWERS	REVIEW
within artery removal o endo-	**4.106** Endarterectomy, the open surgical technique that cuts out atherosclerotic blockage from the core lining of the carotid artery, was named by linking *endo-*, the prefix meaning _____, to *arteri/o*, the combining form meaning _____, and the suffix *-ectomy*, meaning excision or _____. Note that occasionally, when a prefix ends in a vowel and the root begins with a vowel, the final vowel is dropped from the prefix. Therefore, the letter ___ is dropped from the prefix _____ in this term.
-ectomy craniectomy	**4.107** The operative suffix meaning excision is _____. The excision of part of the skull, needed to reach the brain surgically, is termed _____.
diskectomy or discectomy	**4.108** The excision of a herniated spinal disk is termed a _____.
lamina laminectomy	**4.109** The flattened posterior portion of the vertebral arch is called a _____. The excision of one or more laminae is termed a _____.

CHAPTER 4 • NERVOUS SYSTEM AND PSYCHIATRY

ANSWERS	REVIEW
incision craniotomy	4.110 The operative suffix -*tomy* means _____. An incision into the skull to approach the brain is a _____.
microsurgery	4.111 Use of a microscope to dissect minute structures during surgery is called _____.
neur/o -plasty neuroplasty	4.112 The combining form meaning nerve is _____. Recall that the suffix for surgical repair or reconstruction is _____. The surgical repair of a nerve is called _____.
spondyl/o spondylosyndesis	4.113 The two combining forms meaning vertebra are *vertebr/o* and _____. Syndesis is a surgical technique of joining bones together. The medical term for spinal fusion, or surgically joining vertebrae together, is _____.
within vessel, pertaining to endovascular neuro radiology skin	4.114 Endovascular, a term formed by the combination of *endo-* (meaning _____) with *vascul/o* (meaning _____) and *-ar* (meaning _____ _____) is one of the words used to name the minimally invasive techniques for diagnosis and treatment of disorders within blood vessels of the neck, brain, and spinal cord, which are called _____ _____ surgery. The synonym for endovascular neurosurgery is interventional neuro_____, which is a term that identifies the technology used to guide the endovascular catheters to the treatment sites. The techniques are considered minimally invasive, because instruments are guided percutaneously (through the _____) into blood vessels, as opposed to "open" procedures that cut directly into tissues.

Self-Instruction: Nervous System Therapeutic Terms

Study this table to prepare for the programmed review that follows.

TERM	MEANING
chemotherapy kem-ō-thār′ă-pē	treatment of malignancies, infections, and other diseases with chemical agents to destroy selected cells or impair their ability to reproduce

TERM	MEANING
radiation therapy (see Figure 4-21) rā′dē-ā′shŭn thār′ă-pē	treatment of neoplastic disease using ionizing radiation to impede the proliferation of malignant cells
stereotactic radiosurgery ster′ē-ō-tak′tik rā′dē-ō-sŭr′jĕr-ē	radiation treatment to inactivate malignant lesions using multiple, precise external radiation beams focused on a target with the aid of a stereotactic frame and imaging such as CT, MRI, or angiography; used to treat inoperable brain tumors and other lesions; also called *stereotaxic radiosurgery*
stereotactic frame (see Figure 4-22) ster′ē-ō-tak′tik frām	mechanical device used to localize a point in space, targeting a precise site; also called *stereotaxic frame*
stereotaxic radiosurgery ster′ē-ō-tak′sik rā′dē-ō-sŭr′jĕr-ē	radiation treatment to inactivate malignant lesions using multiple, precise external radiation beams focused on a target with the aid of a stereotactic frame and imaging such as CT, MRI, or angiography; used to treat inoperable brain tumors and other lesions; also called *stereotactic radiosurgery*
stereotaxic frame (see Figure 4-22) ster′ē-ō-tak′sik frām	mechanical device used to localize a point in space, targeting a precise site; also called *stereotactic frame*

COMMON THERAPEUTIC DRUG CLASSIFICATIONS

analgesic an-ăl-jē′zik	drug that relieves pain
anticonvulsant an′tē-kon-vŭl′sant	drug that prevents or lessens convulsion
hypnotic hip-not′ik	drug that induces sleep

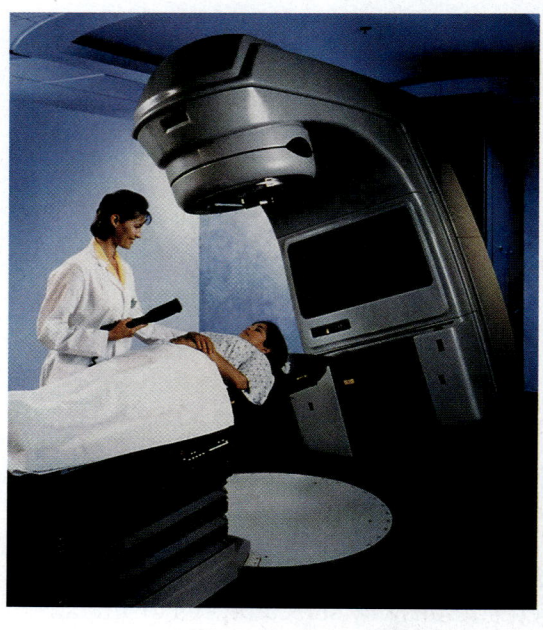

FIGURE 4-21 ■ Radiation therapy linear accelerator.

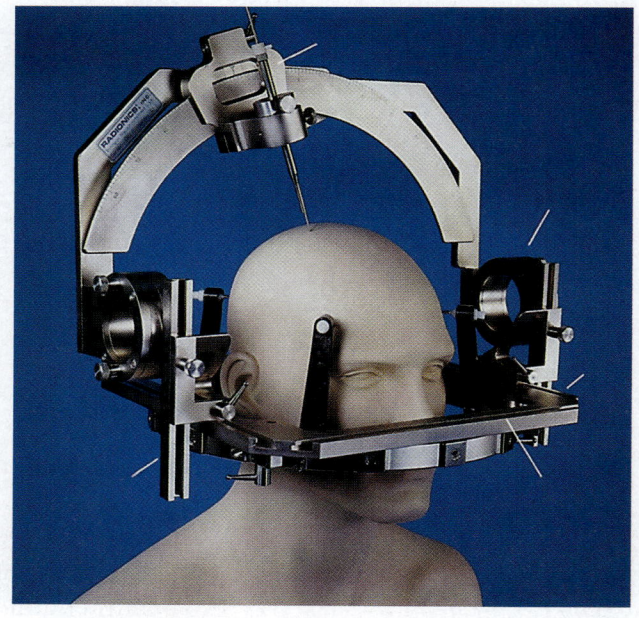

FIGURE 4-22 ■ Stereotactic frame.

Programmed Review: Nervous System Therapeutic Terms

ANSWERS	REVIEW
chemotherapy	**4.115** The combining form referring to chemical agents is *chem/o*. The treatment of malignancies, infections, and other diseases with chemical agents that destroy targeted cells is called _____.
radiation therapy	**4.116** Some kinds of cancer are treated with radiation, which deters the proliferation of malignant cells. This is called _____ _____.
stere/o stereotactic radiosurgery	**4.117** The combining form meaning three-dimensional or solid is _____, as in the term stereotactic (or stereotaxic) frame, which is an apparatus allowing precise localization in space. Radiation therapy given with precise localization of the radiation beam using a stereotactic frame is called _____ _____.
without analgesic	**4.118** The prefix *an-* means _____. The Greek word algesis means sensation of pain. A drug that relieves pain is called an _____.
against anticonvulsant	**4.119** Many drugs are named according to their action against a condition or symptom. The prefix *anti-* means _____. A drug that works to prevent or lessen convulsion is called an _____.
hypn/o hypnotic	**4.120** The combining forms meaning sleep are *somn/i, somn/o*, and _____. Formed from the last of these, the term for an agent that induces sleep is _____.

Self-Instruction: Psychiatric Symptomatic Terms

Study this table to prepare for the programmed review that follows.

TERM	MEANING
affect af′fekt	emotional feeling or mood
flat affect flat af′fekt	significantly dulled emotional tone or outward reaction
apathy ap′ă-thē	a lack of interest or display of emotion

TERM	MEANING
catatonia kat-ă-tō′nē-ă	a state of unresponsiveness to one's outside environment, usually including muscle rigidity, staring, and inability to communicate
delusion dē-lū′zhŭn	a persistent belief that has no basis in reality
grandiose delusion grăn-dē-ōs′ dē-lū′zhŭn	a person's false belief that he or she possesses great wealth, intelligence, or power

persecutory delusion
    pĕr-se-kyū-tōr′ē
    dē-lū′zhŭn
	a person's false belief that someone is plotting against him or her with the intent to harm

dysphoria dis-fōr′ē-ă	a restless, dissatisfied mood
euphoria yū-fōr′ē-ă	an exaggerated, unfounded feeling of well-being
hallucination ha-lū-si-nā′shŭn	a false perception of the senses for which there is no reality; most commonly hearing or seeing things (*alucinor* = to wander in mind)
ideation ī-dē-ā′shŭn	the formation of thoughts or ideas, such as suicidal ideation (thoughts of suicide)
mania mā′nē-ă	state of abnormal elation and increased activity
neurosis nū-rō′sis	a psychologic condition in which anxiety is prominent
psychosis sī-kō′sis	a mental condition characterized by distortion of reality resulting in the inability to communicate or function within one's environment
thought disorder thot dis-ōr′dĕr	thought that lacks clear processing or logical direction

Programmed Review: Psychiatric Symptomatic Terms

ANSWERS	REVIEW
affect emotional	**4.121** An emotional feeling or mood is called an _____. A flat affect is a significantly dulled _____ tone or outward reaction.
apathy	**4.122** A lack of interest or display of emotion is termed _____.
cata- ton/o catatonia	**4.123** Recall that the prefix meaning down is _____, and that the combining term for tone is _____. The original Greek term *katatonos* means stretching down. The medical term for a state of unresponsiveness that includes muscle rigidity is _____.

ANSWERS	REVIEW
false	**4.124** A delusion is a persistent _____ belief that has no basis in reality. A delusion that one has great wealth, intelligence, or power is called a _____ delusion. A delusion that one is being persecuted by others plotting against him or her is called a _____ _____.
grandiose	
persecutory delusion	
carry	**4.125** The combining form *phor/o* means to bear or _____. Recall that the prefix *dys-* means painful, difficult, or faulty. Thus, the term dysphoria originated from terms meaning to carry poorly. The medical term for a restless, dissatisfied mood is _____. Incorporating *eu-*, the prefix meaning good or _____, the term for an exaggerated, unfounded feeling of well-being is _____.
dysphoria	
normal	
euphoria	
hallucination	**4.126** From the Latin word *alucinor*, meaning to wander in mind, this medical term means a false perception of the senses: _____. Recall that the suffix *-ation* refers to _____.
process	
ideation	**4.127** The process of forming thoughts or ideas is called _____. For example, thoughts of suicide are called suicidal ideation.
condition of	**4.128** Again, the suffix *-ia* means _____ _____. A condition of abnormal elation and increased activity is called _____. The original Greek word mania means frenzy.
mania	
increase	**4.129** The suffix *-osis* means condition or _____. The combining form *neur/o* usually means _____, or, in this case, nervousness. The term for a psychologic condition in which anxiety is prominent is called _____, meaning the condition of nervousness.
nerve	
neurosis	
psych/o	**4.130** The combining forms meaning mind are *phren/o*, *thym/o*, and _____. The last of these is used with a suffix that means condition to make the term for a mental condition characterized by a distortion of reality resulting in an inability to function within one's environment: _____.
psychosis	
thought	**4.131** A disorder of thinking in which there is no clear processing or logical direction is called a _____ _____.
disorder	

Self-Instruction: Psychiatric Diagnostic Terms

Study this table to prepare for the programmed review that follows.

TERM	MEANING
MOOD DISORDERS	
major depression mā′jor dē-presh′ŭn **major depressive illness** mā′jor dē-pres′iv il′nes **clinical depression** klin′i-kăl dē-presh′ŭn **major affective disorder** mā′jor af-fek′tiv dis-ōr′děr	a disorder causing periodic disturbances in mood that affect concentration, sleep, activity, appetite, and social behavior; characterized by feelings of worthlessness, fatigue, and loss of interest.
dysthymia dis-thī′mē-ă	a milder affective disorder characterized by chronic depression
bipolar disorder (BD) bī-pō′lăr dis-ōr′děr	an affective disorder characterized by mood swings of mania and hypomania (extreme up and down states)
seasonal affective disorder (SAD) sē′zŏn-ăl af-fek′tiv dis-ōr′děr	an affective disorder marked by episodes of depression that most often occur during the fall and winter and that remit in the spring
ANXIETY DISORDERS	
generalized anxiety disorder (GAD) jen′ěr-ă-līzd ang-zī′ě-tē dis-ōr′děr	the most common anxiety disorder; characterized by chronic, excessive, uncontrollable worry about everyday problems; affects the ability to relax or concentrate, but does not usually interfere with social interactions or employment; physical symptoms include muscle tension, trembling, twitching, fatigue, headaches, nausea, and insomnia
panic disorder pan′ik dis-ōr′děr	a disorder of sudden, recurrent attacks of intense feelings, including physical symptoms that mimic a heart attack (rapid heart rate, chest pain, shortness of breath, chills, sweating, and dizziness) with a general sense of loss of control or feeling that death is imminent; often progresses to agoraphobia
phobia fō′bē-ă	exaggerated fear of a specific object or circumstance that causes anxiety and panic; named for the object or circumstance, such as agoraphobia (fear of the marketplace), claustrophobia (fear of confinement), and acrophobia (fear of high places)
posttraumatic stress disorder (PTSD) pōst-traw′măt-ik strĕs dis-ōr′děr	a condition resulting from an extremely traumatic experience, injury, or illness that leaves the sufferer with persistent thoughts and memories of the ordeal; may occur after a war, violent personal assault, physical or sexual abuse, serious accident, or natural disaster; symptoms include feelings of fear, detachment, exaggerated startle response, restlessness, nightmares, and avoidance of anything or anyone who triggers the painful recollections

TERM	MEANING
obsessive-compulsive disorder (OCD) ob-ses'iv-kom-pŭl'siv dis-ōr'dĕr	an anxiety disorder featuring unwanted, senseless obsessions accompanied by repeated compulsions; can interfere with all aspects of a person's daily life; for example, the thought that a door is not locked causing repetitive checking to make sure it is locked, or thoughts that one's body has been contaminated causing repetitive washing
hypochondriasis hī'pō-kon-drī'ă-sis	a preoccupation with thoughts of disease and concern that one is suffering from a serious condition that persists despite medical reassurance to the contrary

DISORDERS USUALLY DIAGNOSED IN CHILDHOOD

autism aw'tizm	a developmental disability, commonly appearing during the first 3 years of life, resulting from a neurologic disorder affecting brain function, as evidenced by difficulties with verbal and nonverbal communication and an inability to relate to anything beyond oneself (*auto* = self) in social interactions; persons with autism often exhibit body movements such as rocking and repetitive hand movements; persons commonly become preoccupied with observing parts of small objects or moving parts or with performing meaningless rituals
dyslexia dis-lek'sē-ă	a developmental disability characterized by difficulty in understanding written or spoken words, sentences, or paragraphs that affects reading, spelling, and self-expression
attention-deficit/ hyperactivity disorder (ADHD) ă-ten'shŭn-def'i-sit hī-pĕr-ak-tiv'i-tē dis-ōr'dĕr	a dysfunction characterized by consistent hyperactivity, distractibility, and lack of control over impulses, which interferes with ability to function normally at school, home, or work
intellectual disability in'te-lek'chū-ăl dis'ă-bil'i-tē	a condition of below average intelligence or mental ability and lack of skills necessary for day-to-day activities; there are varying degrees ranging from mild to profound

EATING DISORDERS

anorexia nervosa an-ō-rek'sē-ă nĕr-vō'să	a severe disturbance in eating behavior caused by abnormal perceptions about one's body weight, as evidenced by an overwhelming fear of becoming fat that results in a refusal to eat and body weight well below normal
bulimia nervosa bū-lē'mē-ă nĕr-vō'să	an eating disorder characterized by binge eating followed by efforts to limit digestion though induced vomiting, use of laxatives, or excessive exercise

SUBSTANCE ABUSE DISORDERS

substance abuse disorders sŭb'stans ă-byūs'dis-ōr'dĕrz	mental disorders resulting from abuse of substances such as drugs, alcohol, or other toxins, causing personal and social dysfunction; identified by the abused substance, such as alcohol abuse, amphetamine abuse, opioid (narcotic) abuse, and polysubstance abuse

TERM	MEANING
PSYCHOTIC DISORDERS	
schizophrenia *skiz-ō-frē′nē-ă*	a disease of brain chemistry causing a distorted cognitive and emotional perception of one's environment; symptoms include distortions of normal function (such as disorganized thought, delusions, hallucinations, and catatonic behavior), flat affect, apathy, and withdrawal from reality

Programmed Review: Psychiatric Diagnostic Terms

ANSWERS	REVIEW
clinical affective	**4.132** Psychiatrists use several terms when referring to major depression, which is a disorder causing mood disturbances that affects concentration, sleep, and activity and is characterized by feelings of worthlessness and apathy. Other terms include major depressive illness, _____ depression, and major _____ disorder.
manic bipolar	**4.133** The disorder in which a person experiences mood swings between depression and mania is called _____ depression or _____ disorder (BD).
thym/o faulty dysthymia	**4.134** Recall that the three combining forms meaning mind are *phren/o*, *psych/o*, and _____. The prefix *dys-* means painful, difficult, or _____. Another mood disorder, _____, uses the third combining form and is a milder affective disorder that is characterized by chronic depression.
seasonal affective disorder	**4.135** An affective disorder in which episodes of depression occur in seasonal cycles is called _____ _____ _____ (SAD).
generalized anxiety	**4.136** There are several anxiety disorders. The most common anxiety disorder occurs generally, not from a specific anxiety-producing situation. It causes excessive and uncontrollable worrying, and it may produce physical symptoms. This disorder is called _____ _____ disorder (GAD).
panic disorder	**4.137** Another anxiety disorder produces sudden attacks of intense feelings of anxiety and panic, with often dramatic physical symptoms. This disorder is called _____ _____.

ANSWERS	REVIEW
phob/o condition of phobia	**4.138** Recall that the combining form that means an exaggerated fear or sensitivity is _____. The suffix *-ia* means _____. The psychiatric condition in which one experiences an exaggerated fear of something is called a _____.
post- posttraumatic stress disorder	**4.139** After a traumatic experience, a person may develop a stressful condition involving persistent thoughts of the ordeal, fear, and other symptoms. Recall that a common prefix meaning after or behind is _____. This condition is termed _____ _____ _____ (PTSD).
obsessive-compulsive disorder	**4.140** An obsession is a persistent, uncontrollable thought. A compulsion is a persistent, uncontrollable behavior. An anxiety disorder characterized by obsession and compulsions that often interfere with all aspects of an individual's life is called _____-_____ _____ (OCD).
below presence hypochondriasis	**4.141** The combining form *chondr/o* refers to cartilage of the ribs. The prefix *hypo-* means deficient or _____. Thus, the term hypochondrium refers to the abdomen (beneath the ribs)—once thought to be the place where sensations of a distressing nature were experienced, such as the concern that one is suffering from a serious condition despite medical reassurance to the contrary. Recall that the suffix *-iasis* means formation of or the _____ of. The term for the condition when this concern is present is _____.
condition of autism	**4.142** The prefix *auto-* means self. Recall that the suffix *-ism* means _____. A developmental condition in which the person is unable to relate to anyone other than himself or herself is called _____.
lex/o difficult	**4.143** The combining form meaning word or phrase is _____. The prefix *dys-* means painful, faulty, or _____. The term for the developmental disability

ANSWERS	REVIEW
dyslexia condition of	of difficulty understanding written words or phrases is _____. The suffix -*ia* means _____ ___.
attention-deficit hyperactivity disorder excessive	4.144 Typically, ADHD is diagnosed in childhood, when the child has difficulty paying attention to things, is easily distracted, and is generally hyperactive. ADHD is the abbreviation for _____-_____/ _____ _____. Recall that the prefix *hyper-* means above or _____.
intellectual disability	4.145 A condition of below average intelligence or mental ability is called _____ _____.
without condition of anorexia nervosa	4.146 The Greek word *orexis* means appetite. Recall that the prefix *an-* means _____, and that the suffix -*ia* means _____ ___. Thus, the term for the condition of being without an appetite is _____. When this condition is caused by a psychologic disturbance ("nervous" condition) and fear of being fat, it is called anorexia _____.
bulimia	4.147 An eating disorder characterized by binge eating followed by efforts to limit the digestion of food is called _____ nervosa. Bulimia comes from two Greek words meaning hungry as an ox.
abuse	4.148 Substance abuse disorders are mental disorders resulting from an _____ of substances, such as drugs or alcohol, that leads to dysfunction.
split mind schizophrenia split	4.149 The combining form *schiz/o* means _____, and the combining form *phren/o* means _____. Thus, the term for a disease of brain chemistry that causes disorganized thinking, delusions, hallucinations, and other symptoms is _____. Some people mistakenly believe that schizophrenia means a mind that is split in two personalities (multiple personality disorder), but the term actually refers to a mind that is _____ from reality.

Self-Instruction: Psychiatric Therapeutic Terms

Study this table to prepare for the programmed review that follows.

TERM	MEANING
electroconvulsive therapy (ECT) ē-lek′trō-kon-vŭl′siv thār′ă-pē	electrical shock applied to the brain to induce convulsions; used to treat patients with severe depression
light therapy līt thār′ă-pē	use of specialized illuminating light boxes and visors to treat seasonal affective disorder
psychotherapy sī-kō-thār′ă-pē	treatment of psychiatric disorders using verbal and nonverbal interaction with patients, individually or in a group, employing specific actions and techniques
behavioral therapy bē-hāv′yōr-ăl thār′ă-pē	treatment to decrease or stop unwanted behavior
cognitive therapy kog′ni-tiv thār′ă-pē	treatment to change unwanted patterns of thinking
COMMON THERAPEUTIC DRUG CLASSIFICATIONS	
psychotropic drugs sī′kō-trop′ik drŭgz	medications used to treat mental illnesses (*trop/o* = a turning)
antianxiety agents an-tī-ang-zī′ĕ-tē ā′jentz	drugs used to reduce anxiety; also called *anxiolytic agents*
anxiolytic agents ang′zē-ō-lit′ik ā′jentz	drugs used to reduce anxiety; also called *antianxiety agents*
antidepressant an′tē-dē-pres′ănt	drug that counteracts depression
neuroleptic agents nū-rō-lep′tik ā′jentz	drugs used to treat psychosis, especially schizophrenia
sedative sed′ă-tiv	drug that has a calming effect and quiets nervousness

Programmed Review: Psychiatric Therapeutic Terms

ANSWERS	REVIEW
electroconvulsive	**4.150** The combining form *electr/o* refers to electricity. Therapy for patients with severe depression that uses a shock to the brain that induces convulsions is called _____ therapy (ECT).
light	**4.151** One theory for the depression of seasonal affective disorder is that the person suffers from reduced amounts of sunlight in the fall and winter. A treatment for this is therefore _____ therapy.

ANSWERS	REVIEW
psych/o psychotherapy	**4.152** The treatment modality for psychiatric patients using verbal and nonverbal interactions was originally named to mean therapy of the mind. Three combining forms meaning mind are *phren/o*, *thym/o*, and _____. Made with the third form, this therapy is termed _____.
behavioral	**4.153** Treatment emphasizing behavioral changes is called _____ therapy.
cognitive	**4.154** Treatment directed to change unwanted patterns of thinking is called _____ therapy. The term cognitive refers to thought processes.
psychotropic	**4.155** The suffix *-tropic* pertains to turning. The term for the class of drugs used in treating mental illnesses literally means turning of the mind: _____ drugs.
anti- antianxiety anxiolytic	**4.156** Drug classes are frequently named for their actions to cause something or their actions to prevent something. A common prefix meaning against or opposed to is _____. Drugs that work against anxiety, therefore, are termed _____ agents. Another term for these drugs uses the suffix *-lytic*, pertaining to breaking down something. Thus, the term for these drugs literally means breaking down anxiety: _____ agents.
antidepressant	**4.157** A drug that counteracts (works against) depression is called an _____.
neur/o neuroleptic	**4.158** The combining form meaning nerve is _____. Drugs used to treat psychosis, especially schizophrenia, are called _____ agents.
sedative	**4.159** A patient can be sedated to calm his or her anxious state. A drug that quiets nervousness is called a _____.

Chapter 4 Abbreviations

ABBREVIATION	EXPANSION
ADHD	attention-deficit/hyperactivity disorder
ALS	amyotrophic lateral sclerosis
ANS	autonomic nervous system
BD	bipolar disorder
CNS	central nervous system
CP	cerebral palsy
CSF	cerebrospinal fluid
CT	computed tomography
CVA	cerebrovascular accident
DTR	deep tendon reflexes
ECT	electroconvulsive therapy
EEG	electroencephalogram
GAD	generalized anxiety disorder
GCS	Glasgow coma scale
HD	Huntington disease
LP	lumbar puncture
MRA	magnetic resonance angiography
MRI	magnetic resonance imaging
MS	multiple sclerosis
NCV	nerve conduction velocity
OCD	obsessive-compulsive disorder
PET	positron-emission tomography
PNS	peripheral nervous system
PSG	polysomnography
PTSD	posttraumatic stress disorder
SAD	seasonal affective disorder
SPECT	single-photon emission computed tomography
TIA	transient ischemic attack

PRACTICE EXERCISES

For each of the following words, write out the term parts (prefixes [P], combining forms [CF], roots [R], and suffixes [S]) on the lines below the word. Then define the term according to the meaning of its parts.

EXAMPLE

anencephaly

an / encephala / y
P   R   S

DEFINITION: without/brain/condition or process of

1. catatonic

   _____ / _____ / _____
      P   R   S

   DEFINITION: _____

2. meningocele

   _____ / _____
      CF   S

   DEFINITION: _____

3. dyslexia

   _____ / _____ / _____
      P   R   S

   DEFINITION: _____

4. euphoria

   _____ / _____ / _____
      P   R   S

   DEFINITION: _____

5. myelopathy

   _____ / _____ / _____
      CF   R   S

   DEFINITION: _____

Write the correct medical term for each of the following definitions.

6. _____ excision of a herniated disk

7. _____ a slowly progressive degeneration of nerves in the brain characterized by tremor, rigidity of muscles, and slow movements

8. _____ a type of seizure that causes a series of sudden, involuntary contractions of muscles

9. _____ congenital neural tube defect of the spinal column characterized by the absence of vertebral arches

Complete each medical term by writing the missing word part.

10. electro_____gram = record of electrical brain impulses

11. crani_____ = excision of part of the skull

12. _____algesia = loss of sense of pain

Write the letter of the matching term in the space provided.

13. grand mal _____   a. tonic–clonic
14. flabby _____   b. CVA clot
15. stroke _____   c. Alzheimer disease
16. dementia _____   d. PSG
17. sleep study _____   e. flaccid

Write out the expanded term for each abbreviation.

18. CT _____
19. MRI _____
20. PET _____

Circle the combining form that corresponds to the meaning given.

21. brain
    a. encephal/o   b. crani/o   c. neur/o
22. movement
    a. esthesi/o   b. kinesi/o   c. somat/o
23. speech
    a. phas/o   b. plas/o   c. phag/o

Identify the meninges of the brain by writing the missing words in the spaces provided.

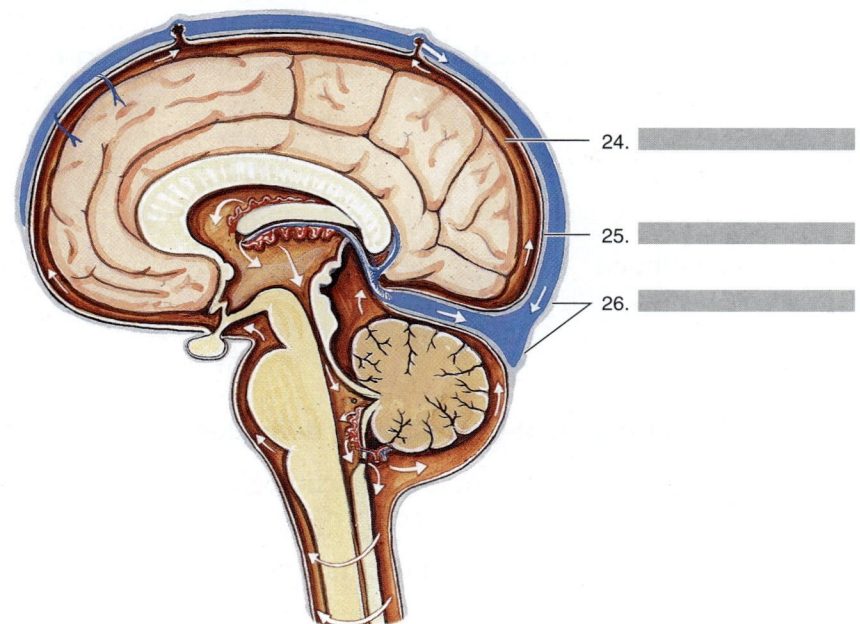

24. _____
25. _____
26. _____

Circle the correct spelling.

27. a. Alsheimer b. Alzheimer c. Alshiemer
28. a. skitzoprenia b. skizophrenia c. schizophrenia
29. a. quadraplegia b. quadriplega c. quadriplegia

Give the noun used to form each adjective.

30. epileptic
31. euphoric
32. cerebellar

Write the letter of the matching definition in the space provided after the name of the psychiatric symptom.

33. persecutory delusion _____
34. euphoria _____
35. flat affect _____
36. grandiose delusion _____

a. an exaggerated, unfounded feeling of well-being
b. dull emotional tone or outward reaction
c. false belief that one is very wealthy, intelligent, or powerful
d. false belief that one is being plotted against

Write out the expanded term for each abbreviation.

37. ECT _____
38. BD _____
39. PTSD _____

Write the letter of the matching psychiatric diagnosis in the space provided after the description.

40. anxiety disorder _____
41. bipolar disorder _____
42. psychosis _____
43. disorder identified in childhood _____
44. eating disorder _____
45. mild depression _____

a. hypochondriasis
b. bulimia nervosa
c. dysthymia
d. schizophrenia
e. manic depression
f. autism

Write the correct medical term for each of the following definitions.

46. _____ general term for a psychologic condition in which anxiety is a featured characteristic
47. _____ depression that occurs most during fall and winter

Match the illness with its treatment by writing the letter of the corresponding treatment in the space after the name of the psychiatric diagnosis.

48. anxiety   _____   a. behavioral therapy

49. seasonal affective disorder   _____   b. light therapy

50. bulimia   _____   c. anxiolytic agent

MEDICAL RECORD ANALYSIS

Medical Record 4-1

OUTPATIENT HISTORY AND PHYSICAL, NEUROLOGIC SERVICES

CC: numbness and tingling in feet and hands

HPI: This 44 y.o. right-handed female c/o numbness in her feet for the past 2 weeks with "pockets" of numbness in the abdomen. Her legs feel heavy and numb. Her hands started tingling a week ago, and she is feeling very nervous. She has had similar episodes over the past 3 years, lasting about a week at a time, often after stressful events or during hot weather.

PMH: Operations: none. No serious illness/accidents

FH: Father, age 71, L&W; Mother, age 66, is bipolar; her only sibling, a sister, age 28, has cerebral palsy.

SH: Denies smoking or use of street drugs, but drinks socially

OH: certified public accountant. Marital Status: single

ROS: noncontributory

VS: T 94.2°F., P 82, R 16, BP 110/68, Ht 5'2", Wt 138#

PE: HEENT: WNL. Neck: negative. Heart/Lungs: normal.

Cranial nerves intact. Reflexes: DTRs are increased, greater on the left than the right, without spasticity.

Toes upgoing bilaterally.

There is numbness to tactile pin stimulation over both extremities. She has no finger-to-nose ataxia. Her gait is steady.

A: R/O MS

P: Schedule MRI of the brain with and without gadolinium (contrast)

RTO for report and further evaluation ×1 week

Questions About Medical Record 4-1

1. Which medical term best describes the patient's symptom?
   a. hyperesthesia
   b. paresthesia
   c. ataxia
   d. hemiparesis
   e. neuralgia

2. What is noted in the history about the patient's mother?
   a. she is alive and well
   b. she suffers from depression
   c. she has mood swings of mania and depression
   d. she suffers from generalized anxiety
   e. she is a hypochondriac

3. Describe the sister's condition:
   a. disorder affecting the central nervous system characterized by seizures
   b. hereditary disease of the central nervous system characterized by bizarre involuntary body movements and progressive dementia
   c. abnormal accumulation of cerebrospinal fluid in the ventricles of the brain as a result of developmental abnormality
   d. condition of motor dysfunction caused by damage to the cerebrum during development or injury at birth
   e. slowly progressive degeneration of nerves in the brain characterized by tremor, rigidity, and slow movements

4. Which medical term describes the positive finding of the "toes upgoing" bilaterally?
   a. Babinski sign
   b. neuralgia
   c. hemiparesis
   d. spastic paralysis
   e. flaccid paralysis

5. What is the doctor's impression?
   a. the patient has multiple sclerosis
   b. the patient does not have multiple sclerosis
   c. the patient may have multiple sclerosis
   d. the patient may have hardening of the arteries in the brain
   e. the patient does not have hardening of the arteries in the brain

6. Describe the test noted in the Plan.
   a. x-ray
   b. nuclear image
   c. ultrasound scan
   d. tomographic radiograph
   e. scan produced by magnetic fields and radiofrequency waves

ANSWERS TO PRACTICE EXERCISES

1. P: cata
   R: ton
   S: ic
   DEFINITION: down/tone or tension/pertaining to

2. CF: meningo
   S: cele
   DEFINITION: meninges (membrane)/pouching or hernia

3. P: dys
   R: lex
   S: ia
   DEFINITION: painful, difficult, or faulty/speech/condition of

4. P: eu
   R: phor
   S: ia
   DEFINITION: good or normal/carry or bear/condition of

5. CF: myelo
   R: path
   S: y
   DEFINITION: spinal cord/disease/condition or process of

6. diskectomy or discectomy
7. Parkinson disease
8. convulsion
9. spina bifida
10. electroencephalogram

11. craniectomy
12. analgesia
13. a
14. e
15. b
16. c
17. d
18. computed tomography
19. magnetic resonance imaging
20. positron-emission tomography
21. encephal/o
22. kinesi/o
23. phas/o
24. pia mater
25. arachnoid mater
26. dura mater
27. Alzheimer
28. schizophrenia
29. quadriplegia
30. epilepsy
31. euphoria
32. cerebellum
33. d
34. a
35. b
36. c
37. electroconvulsive therapy
38. bipolar disorder
39. posttraumatic stress disorder
40. a
41. e
42. d
43. f
44. b
45. c
46. neurosis
47. seasonal affective disorder
48. c
49. b
50. a

ANSWERS TO MEDICAL RECORD 4-1

1. b
2. c
3. d
4. a
5. c
6. e

THE EYE

Learning Outcomes

After completing this chapter, you should be able to:

- Define terms parts related to the eye.
- Identify key eye anatomic structures and their functions.
- Define symptomatic and diagnostic terms related to the eye.
- Explain diagnostic tests, procedures, operative terms, and therapeutic terms related to the eye.
- Cite common abbreviations related to the eye and give the expansion of each.
- Explain terms used in medical records involving the eye.

OVERVIEW OF THE EYE

The eyes are the organs of sight that provide three-dimensional vision (see **Figure 5-1**):

- The eye has two chambers: the anterior chamber that contains a water fluid called aqueous humor and a posterior chamber that contains a gelatinous fluid called vitreous humor.
- The cornea is the transparent, outer covering of the anterior portion of the eye.
- Light enters the eye through an opening called the pupil. Muscles of the iris (the colored part of the eye) regulate the pupil's size.
- The sclera is the white, tough, fibrous outer eye layer that extends from the cornea to the optic nerve. The choroid is the pigmented vascular layer between the sclera and the retina.
- The conjunctiva is the mucous membrane that lines the eyelids and outer eye surface.
- The lens is a transparent structure posterior to the pupil that bends light rays on the retina to aid in focusing. The retina is the nerve tissue in the inner posterior part of the eye.

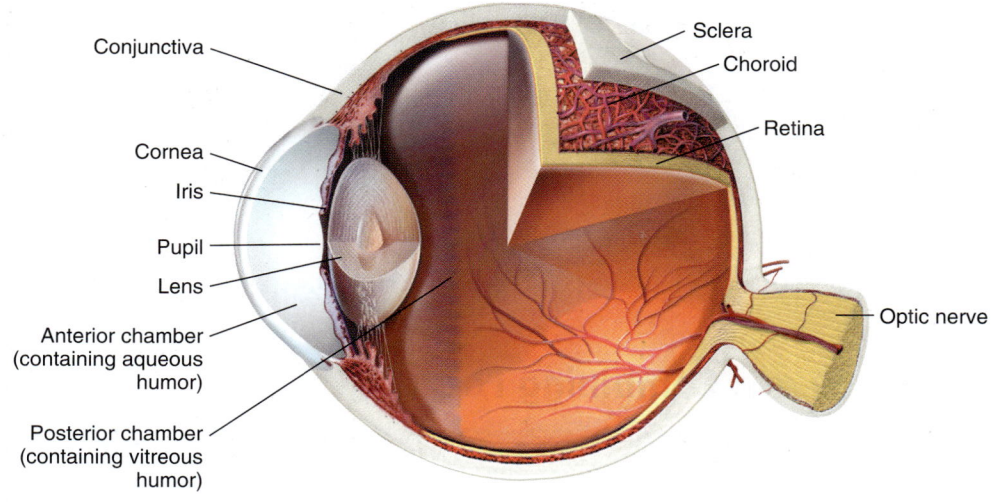

FIGURE 5-1 ■ Anatomy of the eye.

- Rods (for dim vision) and cones (for color vision) are the visual receptors (neurons) in the retina that respond to the light waves.
- Nerve fibers from the rods and cones join in the optic disc (blind spot; not shown in figure), from which the optic nerve carries transmissions to the brain.
- Other functions of the eye are performed by protective and lubricating structures.

Self-Instruction: Combining Forms

Study this table to prepare for the programmed review that follows.

COMBINING FORM	MEANING
aque/o	water
blephar/o	eyelid
conjunctiv/o	conjunctiva (to bind together)
corne/o	cornea
cycl/o	circle, ciliary body
dacry/o	tear
ir/o	colored circle, iris
irid/o	colored circle, iris
kerat/o	cornea
lacrim/o	tear
ocul/o	eye
ophthalm/o	eye
opt/o	eye
phac/o	lens (lentil)
phak/o	lens (lentil)
phot/o	light

COMBINING FORM	MEANING
presby/o	old age
retin/o	retina
scler/o	hard or sclera
vitre/o	glassy
-opia (suffix)	condition of vision

Programmed Review: Combining Forms

ANSWERS	REVIEW
ophthalm/o study, logist eye	5.1 The three combining forms meaning eye are *ocul/o*, *opt/o*, and _____. Ophthalmology defines the specialty related to the _____ of the eye. An ophthalmo_____ is a physician who specializes in the study and treatment (including surgery) of the _____.
opt/o measuring eye	5.2 Optometry is the profession that examines the eyes for vision problems and other disorders. The combining form referring to the eye in this term is _____. The suffix *-metry* generally refers to a process of _____. Optometrist is the title of the professional who specializes in measuring the _____.
pertaining to, ocul/o	5.3 The combining form used in ocular, an adjective meaning _____ ____ the eye, is _____.
eyelid, blephar/o inflammation blepharitis	5.4 A blepharospasm is an involuntary muscular contraction of the _____. The combining form for eyelid is _____. For example, the suffix *-itis* means _____, and the term for an inflamed eyelid is _____.
water	5.5 The combining form *aque/o* means _____ in reference to the eye.
cornea kerat/o keratoplasty	5.6 *Corne/o* is the Latin combining form used to name the part of the eye called the _____. The second combining form meaning cornea, from the Greek word kera (meaning horn or hard tissue), is _____. It is used in the term describing the surgical repair or reconstruction of the cornea: _____.

ANSWERS	REVIEW
lacrim/o dacryocystitis dacry/o	**5.7** As often happens, there are two combining forms for tears: one based on a Latin word and one based on a Greek word. The lacrimal gland (tear gland) comes from this combining form: _____. The term dacryocyst refers to the lacrimal sac (*cyst* = sac), where tears are collected before they flow to the nose. Inflammation of the lacrimal sac is therefore called _____. This second combining form for tears is _____.
lentil phac/o, phak/o dissolution breaking down lens	**5.8** The Greek word *phakos* means lentil or anything shaped like a lentil and, thus, is used for the lens of the eye, because it looks like a _____. As sometimes happens, two spellings evolved for this combining form: _____ and _____. Recall that the suffix *-lysis* means breaking down or _____. Phacolysis is therefore the _____ _____ of the lens. A phakoma is a tumor-like condition of the _____.
phot/o photophobia	**5.9** The combining form meaning light is _____. An abnormal fear or sensitivity to light is _____.
vision old condition	**5.10** The suffix *-opia* refers to a condition of _____. Because the combining form *presby/o* means _____ age, the term presbyopia refers to a vision _____ that is common in old age.
scler/o retin/o vitre/o	**5.11** Many combining forms are like the terms that express their meaning. For example, the combining form meaning the conjunctiva is *conjunctiv/o*. The combining form for the sclera is _____. The combining form meaning retina is _____, and the combining form referring to the vitreous (glassy substance) of the eye is _____.
circle incision cyclotomy	**5.12** *Cycl/o* is a combining form referring to a _____ or the ciliary body, a ring of tissue in the eye. Recall that *-tomy* is a suffix meaning _____. Therefore, an incision in the ciliary body is called a _____.
irid/o colored, iris inflammation excision or removal iridectomy	**5.13** *Ir/o* and _____ are the two combining forms referring to the _____ circle of the eye, which is known as the _____. Iritis refers to an _____ of the iris. The combination of the second combining form for iris with *-ectomy*, a suffix meaning _____, forms the term for an excision of a portion of the iris: _____.

Self-Instruction: Anatomic Terms

Study this table to prepare for the programmed review that follows.

TERM	MEANING
anterior chamber (see Figure 5-1) *an-tēr′ē-ōr chām′bĕr*	fluid-filled space between the cornea and iris
aqueous humor (see Figure 5-1) *ak′wē-ŭs hyū′mer*	watery liquid secreted by the ciliary processes that fills the anterior and posterior chambers of the eye and provides nourishment for the cornea, iris, and lens (*humor* = fluid)
scleral venous sinus *sklē′răl vē′nŭs sī′nŭs*	duct in the anterior chamber that carries filtered aqueous humor to the veins and bloodstream; also called *canal of Schlemm*
canal of Schlemm *kă-nal′ of shlem*	duct in the anterior chamber that carries filtered aqueous humor to the veins and bloodstream; also called *scleral venous sinus*
choroid *kō′royd*	vascular layer beneath the sclera that provides nourishment to the outer portion of the retina
ciliary body *sil′ē-ar-ē bod′ē*	ring of tissue behind the peripheral iris that is composed of ciliary muscle and ciliary processes
ciliary muscle *sil′ē-ar-ē mŭs′ĕl*	smooth muscle portion of the ciliary body, which contracts to assist in near vision
ciliary processes *sil′ē-ar-ē pros′es-ēz*	epithelial tissue folds on the inner surface of the ciliary body that secrete aqueous humor
conjunctiva (see Figure 5-1) *kon-jŭnk-tī′vă*	mucous membrane that lines the eyelids and outer surface of the eyeball
cornea (see Figure 5-1) *kōr′nē-ă*	transparent, anterior part of the eyeball covering the iris, pupil, and anterior chamber that functions to refract (bend) light to focus a visual image
eyelid *ī′lid*	movable, protective fold that opens and closes, covering the eye; also called *palpebra*
palpebra *pal′pĕ-bră*	movable, protective fold that opens and closes, covering the eye; also called *eyelid*
fovea centralis *fō′vē-ă sen-trā′lis*	pinpoint depression in the center of the macula lutea that is the site of sharpest vision (*fovea* = pit)
fundus *fŭn′dŭs*	interior surface of the eyeball, including the retina, optic disc, macula lutea, and posterior pole (curvature at the back of the eye) (*fundus* = base)
Zeis glands *zīs glanz*	oil glands opening into the follicles of the eyelashes
tarsal glands (see Figure 5-2) *tar′săl glanz*	oil glands located along the rim of the eyelids; also called *meibomian glands*
meibomian glands *mī-bō′mē-ăn glanz*	oil glands located along the rim of the eyelids; also called *tarsal glands*
iris *ī′ris*	colored circle; colored part of the eye located behind the cornea that contracts and dilates to regulate light passing through the pupil

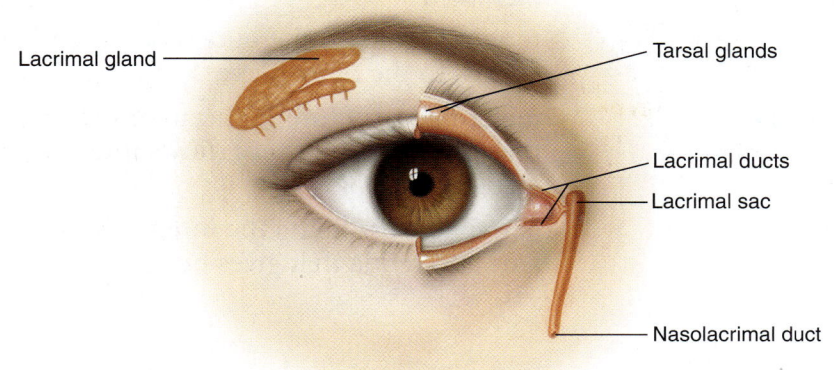

FIGURE 5-2 ■ The right lacrimal gland, lacrimal sac, and associated ducts.

TERM	MEANING
lacrimal gland (see **Figure 5-2**) *lak′ri-măl gland*	gland located in the upper outer region above the eyeball that secretes tears
lacrimal ducts (see **Figure 5-2**) *lak′ri-măl dŭkts*	tubes that carry tears to the lacrimal sac
lacrimal sac (see **Figure 5-2**) *lak′ri-măl sak*	structure that collects tears before emptying into the nasolacrimal duct
lens *lenz*	transparent structure behind the pupil that bends and focuses light rays on the retina
lens capsule *lenz kap′sūl*	capsule that encloses the lens
macula lutea (see **Figure 5-13B**) *mak′yū-lă lū′tĕ-ā*	central region of the retina; responsible for central vision; yellow pigment provides its color (*lutea* = yellow)
nasolacrimal duct (see **Figure 5-2**) *nā-zō-lak′ri-măl dŭkt*	passageway for tears from the lacrimal sac into the nose
optic disc (see **Figure 5-13B**) *op′tik disk*	exit site of retinal nerve fibers as well as entrance point for retinal arteries and exit point for retinal veins
optic nerve *op′tik nĕrv*	nerve responsible for carrying impulses for the sense of sight from the retina to the brain
posterior chamber (see **Figure 5-1**) *pos-tēr′ē-ōr chām′bĕr*	space between the back of the iris and the front of the vitreous chamber; filled with aqueous humor
pupil *pyū′pil*	black, circular opening in the center of the iris through which light passes as it enters the eye
retina (see **Figure 5-13B**) *ret′i-nă*	innermost layer that perceives and transmits light to the optic nerve
cones *kōnz*	cone-shaped cells within the retina that are color sensitive and respond to bright light
rods *rodz*	rod-shaped cells within the retina that respond to dim light

TERM	MEANING
sclera *sklēr'ă*	tough, fibrous, white outer coat extending from the cornea to the optic nerve
trabecular meshwork *tră-bek'yū-lăr mesh'wĕrk*	mesh-like structure in the anterior chamber that filters the aqueous humor as it flows into the scleral venous sinus
vitreous *vit'rē-ŭs*	jelly-like mass filling the inner chamber between the lens and retina that gives bulk to the eye

Programmed Review: Anatomic Terms

ANSWERS	REVIEW
cornea	**5.14** Let us look at the anatomy of the eye in the approximate order of structures involved as light waves enter the eye and result in nerve transmissions to the brain. Light first passes through a transparent outer covering over the iris, pupil, and anterior chamber called the _____.
anterior front aqueous water canal trabecular	**5.15** The _____ chamber is a fluid-filled space between the cornea and iris. It is called anterior because it is the _____ fluid chamber in the eye. The fluid within the anterior chamber is called _____ humor. Recall that the combining form *aque/o* means _____. This watery fluid is carried to the veins through the _____ of Schlemm. As the aqueous humor flows into this canal, it is filtered by a mesh-like structure called the _____ meshwork.
pupil iris light	**5.16** The light waves then pass through the black, circular opening in the center of the iris called the _____. The _____ surrounding the pupil is the colored part of the eye that contracts and dilates to regulate the amount of _____ that passes through the pupil.
posterior humor chamber behind or in back of	**5.17** Between the back of the iris and the upper and lower sections of the lens and vitreous chamber is the _____ chamber, which is also filled with aqueous _____. It is called the posterior _____ because it is _____ the anterior chamber.
lens	**5.18** Light waves passing through the pupil and anterior chamber reach the _____, a transparent structure that focuses

ANSWERS	REVIEW
capsule	the light rays on the retina. The lens is enclosed in a structure called the lens _____.
ciliary ciliary muscle	5.19 Tiny muscles control the shape of the lens, allowing it to change its focus for near and far vision. The ring of muscle around the lens, behind the iris, is called the _____ body, and its smooth muscle portion is called the _____ _____.
processes posterior Schlemm	5.20 Tissue folds on the inner surface of the ciliary body, called ciliary _____, secrete aqueous humor, which fills the anterior and _____ chambers and drains through the canal of _____.
vitreous glassy	5.21 Light waves focused by the lens now pass through the _____ chamber on the way to the retina. The vitreous is a jelly-like mass that fills this inner chamber and gives bulk to the eye. Recall that the combining form *vitre/o* means _____, referring to the vitreous of the eye.
retina rods bright, rods	5.22 The light waves passing through the vitreous chamber then strike the _____, the innermost layer at the back of the eye that contains visual receptor neurons that respond to light. These special cells are the _____ and cones. The cones respond to _____ light, and the _____ respond to dim light. These neuron reactions are transmitted to the optic nerve and then to the brain.
macula lutea fovea centralis	5.23 The central region of the retina, which has a yellow color (*lutea* = yellow), is called the _____ _____. At the center of the macula lutea is a pinpoint depression, which is the site of sharpest vision, called the _____ _____ (*fovea* = pit).
fundus choroid	5.24 The entire interior surface of the eyeball, including the retina, optic disc, and macula lutea, is termed the _____. The layer behind the retina that provides nourishment to the retina is called the _____.
disc optic	5.25 Nerve fibers from the retina come together at the optic _____, the site where the nerves exit the eye. The _____ nerve then carries the nerve impulses to the brain to create the sense of sight.

ANSWERS	REVIEW
sclera	**5.26** The tough outer layer of the eye extending from the cornea around the retina to the optic nerve is called the _____.
palpebra palpebrae	**5.27** Additional eye structures help to protect the eye from the environment. The medical term for eyelid is _____. The plural of this term is _____. The palpebrae can close over the eye.
meibomian Zeis	**5.28** The oil glands located along the rim of the eyelids are called the _____ glands. Other oil glands surrounding the eyelashes are called the glands of _____.
conjunctiva conjunctivitis	**5.29** The mucous membrane that lines the eyelids and outer surface of the eyeball is called the _____, from the combining form *conjunctiv/o*. Because this is the outermost structure of the eye, it is easily irritated by foreign substances, causing an inflammation called _____.
lacrim/o lacrimal glands	**5.30** There are two combining forms meaning tear or tears: *dacry/o*, which is Greek, and _____, which is Latin. Note that the Latin form is used to name the anatomy related to tears. For example, the glands that secrete tears, located in the upper outer region above the eyeball, are called the _____ _____.
ducts sac	**5.31** The tiny tubes that carry tears away from the eye are the lacrimal _____. These ducts carry tears to the lacrimal _____, which collects tears before emptying into the nasolacrimal duct.
nasolacrimal nose	**5.32** Tears from the lacrimal sac reach the nose through the _____ duct. The combining form *nas/o* means _____.

Self-Instruction: Symptomatic Terms

Study this table to prepare for the programmed review that follows.

TERM	MEANING
asthenopia as-thĕ-nō′pē-ă	eyestrain (*asthenia* = weak condition)
blepharospasm blef′ă-rō-spazm	involuntary contraction of the muscles surrounding the eye causing uncontrolled blinking and lid squeezing

TERM	MEANING
diplopia di-plō′pē-ă	double vision
exophthalmus ek-sof-thal′mos	abnormal protrusion of one or both eyeballs; also spelled *exophthalmus*
exophthalmos ek-sof-thal′mus	abnormal protrusion of one or both eyeballs; also spelled *exophthalmos*
lacrimation lak-ri-mā′shŭn	secretion of tears
nystagmus nis-tag′mŭs	involuntary, rapid, oscillating movement of the eyeball (*nystagmos* = a nodding)
photophobia fō-tō-fō′bē-ă	extreme sensitivity to, and discomfort from, light
scotoma skō-tō′mă	blind spot in vision (*skotos* = darkness)

Programmed Review: Symptomatic Terms

ANSWERS	REVIEW
vision diplopia	**5.33** Recall that the suffix *-opia* means a condition of _____. The combining form *dipl/o* means double. The condition of having double vision is termed _____.
asthenopia	**5.34** Based on the Greek word asthenia, which means weakness, the condition of eyestrain (weak vision) is called _____.
phot/o photophobia	**5.35** Recall that the combining form meaning light is _____. Extreme sensitivity to, and discomfort from, light is termed _____.
blephar/o blepharospasm	**5.36** Again, the combining form for eyelid is _____. The term for a sudden involuntary contraction of the muscles around the eyelid is _____.
ophthalm/o, out exophthalmos exophthalmus	**5.37** The three combining forms for eye are *ocul/o*, *opt/o*, and _____. The prefix *ex-* means _____ or away. Using the last combining form and this prefix, the term for the condition in which the eyeballs protrude out is termed _____ or _____ (alternate spelling).
tear process lacrimation	**5.38** *Lacrim/o* is a combining form meaning _____. The suffix *-ation* refers to a _____. The term for the process of secreting tears is _____.

ANSWERS	REVIEW
nystagmus	**5.39** The Greek word *nystagmos* means a nodding, such as the movement of the head up and down or sideways. The condition of rapid oscillation of the eyeballs is called _____.
scotoma	**5.40** The medical term for a visual blind (dark) spot comes from the Greek word that means darkness. The blind spot is called a _____.

Self-Instruction: Diagnostic Terms

Study this table to prepare for the programmed review that follows.

TERM	MEANING
refractive errors rē-frak′tiv er′ōrz	defects in the bending of light as it enters the eye, causing an improper focus on the retina
astigmatism ă-stig′mă-tizm	distorted vision caused by an oblong or cylindrical curvature of the lens or cornea that prevents light rays from coming to a single focus on the retina (*stigma* = point)
hyperopia (see **Figure 5-3B**) hī-pĕr-ō′pē-ă	farsightedness; difficulty seeing close objects when light rays are focused on a point behind the retina
myopia (see **Figure 5-3C**) mī-ō′pē-ă	nearsightedness; difficulty seeing distant objects when light rays are focused on a point in front of the retina
presbyopia prez-bē-ō′pē-ă	impaired vision caused by old age or loss of accommodation
accommodation ă-kom′ŏ-dā′shŭn	ability of the eye to adjust focus on near objects
amblyopia am-blē-ō′pē-ă	decreased vision in early life because of a functional defect that can occur as a result of strabismus, refractive errors (when one eye is more nearsighted, farsighted, or astigmatic than the other), or trauma; usually occurs in one eye; also known as *lazy eye* (*ambly/o* = dim)
aphakia ă-fā′kē-ă	absence of the lens, usually after cataract extraction

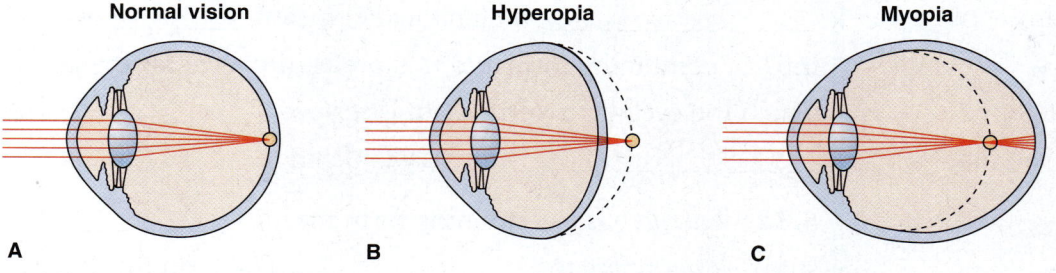

FIGURE 5-3 ■ Refraction. **A.** Proper focus of light rays on the retina. **B.** Light rays are focused on a point behind the retina in hyperopia. **C.** Light rays are focused at a point in front of the retina in myopia.

CHAPTER 5 • THE EYE

TERM	MEANING
blepharitis *blef′ă-rī′tis*	inflammation of the eyelid
blepharochalasis *blef′ă-rō-kal′ă-sis*	baggy eyelid; overabundance and loss of skin elasticity on the upper eyelid causing a fold of skin to hang down over the edge of the eyelid when the eyes are open (*chalasis* = a slackening)
blepharoptosis *blef′ă-rop′tō-sis*	drooping of the superior eyelid; usually caused by paralysis; also called *ptosis*
ptosis *tō′sis*	drooping of the superior eyelid; usually caused by paralysis; also called *blepharoptosis*
chalazion (see **Figure 5-4**) *ka-lā′zē-on*	chronic nodular inflammation of a tarsal gland, usually the result of a blocked duct; commonly presents as a swelling on the upper or lower eyelid (*chalaza* = hailstone)
cataract (see **Figures 5-5** and **5-6B**) *kat′ă-rakt*	opaque clouding of the lens causing decreased vision

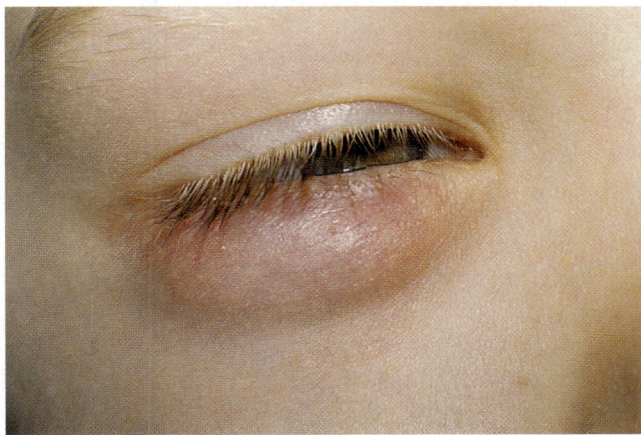

FIGURE 5-4 ■ Chalazion.

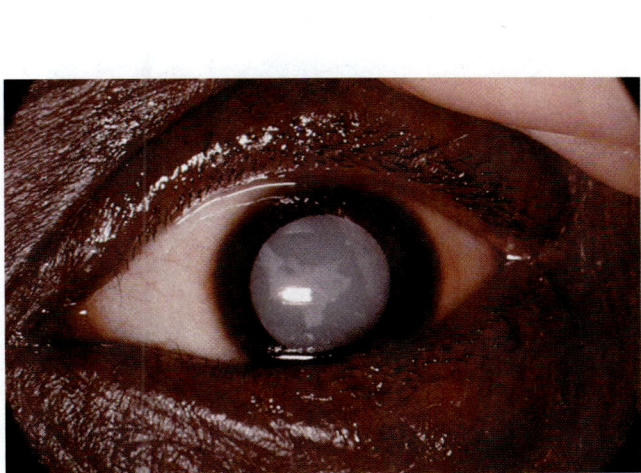

FIGURE 5-5 ■ Cataract.

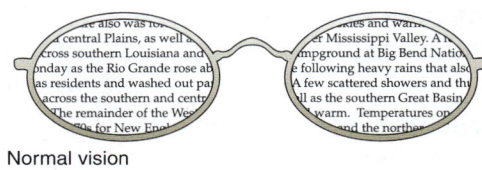

A Normal vision

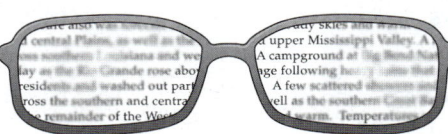

B Cataract (hazy vision)

C Diabetic retinopathy (retinal damage leads to blind spots)

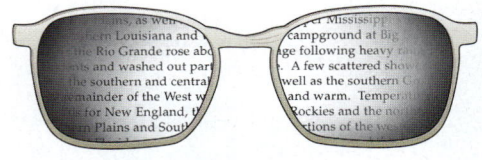

D Glaucoma (loss of peripheral vision)

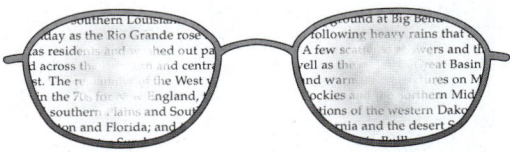

E Macular degeneration (loss of central vision)

FIGURE 5-6 ■ Simulations of vision loss (A–E).

TERM	MEANING
conjunctivitis kon-jŭnk-ti-vī′tis	inflammation of the conjunctiva; also called *pinkeye*
dacryoadenitis dak′rē-ō-ad-ĕ-nī′tis	inflammation of the lacrimal gland
dacryocystitis dak′rē-ō-sis-tī′tis	inflammation of the lacrimal sac
diabetic retinopathy (see **Figures 5-6C** and **5-13C**) dī-ă-bet′ik ret-i-nop′ă-thē	disease of the retina in people with diabetes characterized by capillary leakage, bleeding, and new vessel formation (neovascularization) leading to scarring and loss of vision
ectropion (see **Figure 5-7A**) ek-trō′pē-on	outward turning of the rim of the eyelid (*tropo* = turning)
entropion (see **Figure 5-7B**) en-trō′pē-on	inward turning of the rim of the eyelid
epiphora ē-pif′ō-ră	abnormal overflow of tears caused by blockage of the lacrimal duct (*epi* = upon; *phero* = to bear)
glaucoma (see **Figure 5-6D**) glaw-kō′mă	group of diseases of the eye characterized by increased intraocular pressure that results in damage to the optic nerve, producing defects in vision
hordeolum (see **Figure 5-8**) hōr-dē′ō-lŭm	an acute infection of a sebaceous gland of the eyelid; also called a *sty* (*hordeum* = barley)
iritis ī-rī′tis	inflammation of the iris
keratitis ker-ă-tī′tis	inflammation of the cornea
macular degeneration mak′yū-lăr dē-jen-ĕr-ā′shŭn	breakdown or thinning of the tissues in the macula lutea, resulting in partial or complete loss of central vision (see **Figure 5-6E**)
pseudophakia sū-dō-fak′ē-ă	an eye in which the natural lens is replaced with an artificial lens implant (*pseudo* = false)

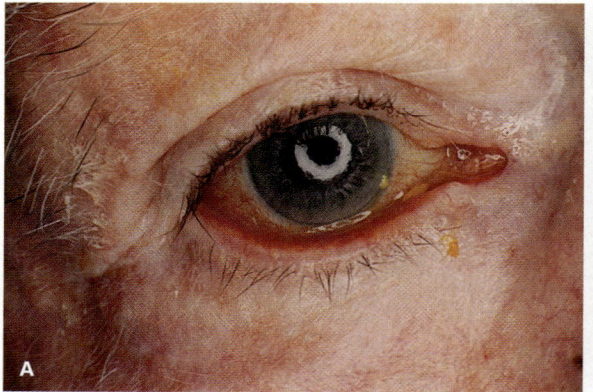 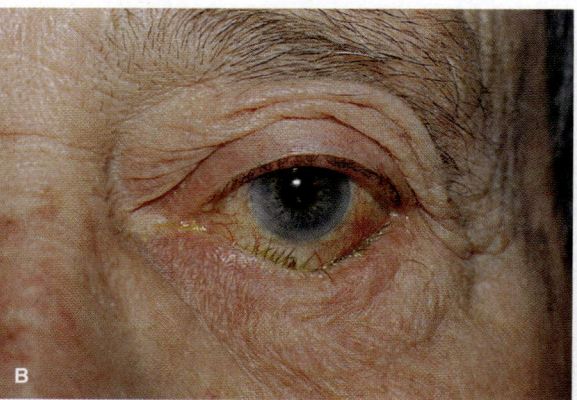

FIGURE 5-7 ■ **Eyelid abnormalities. A.** Severe bilateral lower-lid ectropion. **B.** Lower-lid entropion causing the lashes to rub on the cornea.

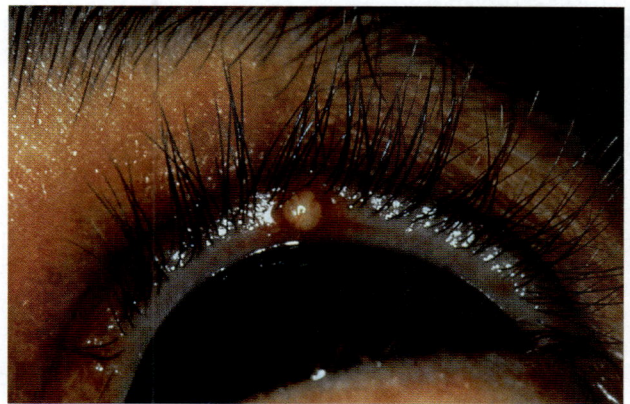

FIGURE 5-8 ■ Hordeolum on the upper eyelid.

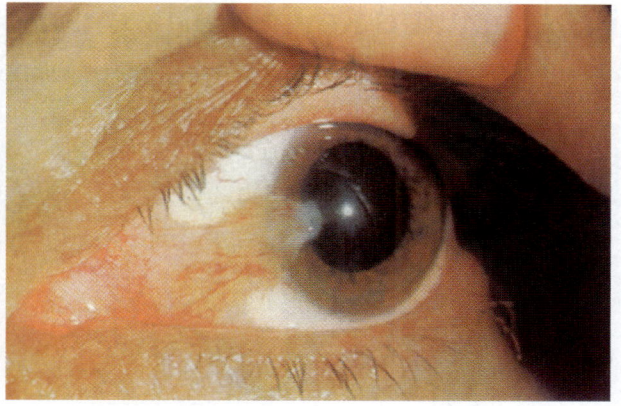

FIGURE 5-9 ■ Pterygium caused by ultraviolet light exposure and drying.

TERM	MEANING
pterygium (see Figure 5-9) tĕ-rij′ē-ŭm	fibrous, wing-shaped growth of conjunctival tissue that extends onto the cornea, developing most commonly from prolonged exposure to ultraviolet light
retinal detachment ret′i-năl dē-tach′ment	separation of the retina from the underlying epithelium, disrupting vision and resulting in blindness if not repaired surgically
retinitis ret-i-nī′tis	inflammation of the retina
strabismus stra-biz′mŭs	a condition of eye misalignment caused by intraocular muscle imbalance (*strabismus* = a squinting; *hetero* = other); also called *heterotropia* or *crossed eyes*
heterotropia het′ĕr-ō-trō′pē-ă	a condition of eye misalignment caused by intraocular muscle imbalance (*strabismus* = a squinting; *hetero* = other); also called *strabismus* or *crossed eyes*
esotropia (see Figure 5-10A) es-ō-trō′pē-ă	right or left eye deviates inward, toward nose (*eso* = inward; *tropo* = turning)
exotropia (see Figure 5-10B) ek-sō-trō′pē-ă	right or left eye deviates outward, away from nose (*exo* = out; *tropo* = turning)
scleritis sklĕ-rī′tis	inflammation of the sclera
trichiasis tri-kī′ă-sis	misdirected eyelashes that rub on the conjunctiva or cornea

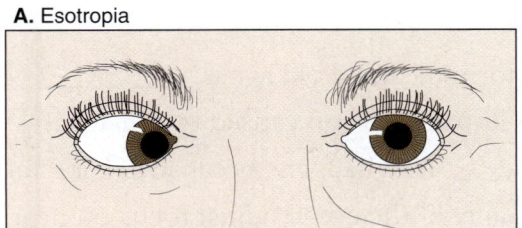

A. Esotropia

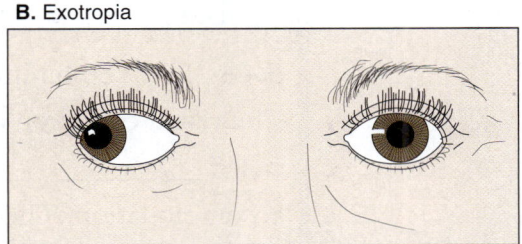

B. Exotropia

FIGURE 5-10 ■ Eye misalignment disorders. Esotropia is medial turning of the eye. Exotropia is lateral turning of the eye.

Programmed Review: Diagnostic Terms

ANSWERS	REVIEW
inflammation blepharitis conjunctivitis	**5.41** Recall that the suffix *-itis* means _____. Inflammation of the eyelid is therefore termed _____. Inflammation of the conjunctiva is called _____ (or pinkeye).
kerat/o keratitis	**5.42** In addition to *corne/o*, a combining form that means cornea is _____. The term for inflammation of the cornea uses this second form: _____.
ir/o iritis	**5.43** The two combining forms for the iris of the eye are *irid/o* and _____. The latter is used to make the term for inflammation of the iris: _____.
retinitis scleritis	**5.44** Inflammation of the retina is termed _____. Inflammation of the sclera is _____.
dacry/o dacryocyst dacryocystitis	**5.45** The two combining forms for tears are *lacrim/o* and _____. The combining form *cyst/o* means a sac. Using the latter form for tears, the tear sac is termed the _____. Inflammation of the tear sac is called _____.
inflammation lacrimal or tear	**5.46** The combining form *aden/o* means gland. Thus, the term dacryoadenitis means _____ of the _____ gland.
refractive vision beyond hyperopia myopia	**5.47** Conditions in which the eye incorrectly focuses light on the retina are called _____ errors. Recall that the suffix *-opia* means a condition of _____. The prefix *hyper-* means excessive or _____. The condition of farsightedness occurs when the light rays from near objects focus beyond the retina. This is called _____. The opposite condition of nearsightedness is called _____.
presby/o presbyopia accommodation	**5.48** The combining form meaning old age is _____. The visual condition of impaired vision caused by old age is called _____. This happens because of a loss of accommodation. The ability of the eye to adjust focus on near objects is called _____.

ANSWERS	REVIEW
blepharochalasis	**5.49** The Greek word chalasis means a slackening, such as with baggy skin. The term for a baggy eyelid (using the combining form for eyelid) is _____. The combining form *dermat/o* means skin.
downward blepharoptosis	**5.50** Recall that the suffix *-ptosis* means a falling or _____ displacement. The term for a drooping of the eyelid is _____. This is usually caused by paralysis.
chalazion chalazia	**5.51** From the Greek word for a small hailstone (chalazion), which it may resemble in appearance, comes the term for a chronic nodular inflammation of a meibomian gland: _____. The plural of chalazion is _____.
cataract	**5.52** The clouding of the lens that causes decreased vision is called a _____.
condition of disease retinopathy	**5.53** The combining form *path/o* means disease, and the suffix *-y* means process of or _____ _____. Thus, *-pathy* refers to a condition of _____. A retinal disease condition in diabetics caused by problems with the capillaries is called diabetic _____.
out ectropion within entropion	**5.54** The Greek word tropo means turning. The prefix *ec-* means away or _____. The condition of the eyelid rim turning outward is called _____. The prefix *en-*, however, means _____ or inward. The condition of the rim of the eyelid turning in is called _____.
upon epiphora	**5.55** If the lacrimal duct becomes blocked, tears that might otherwise flow to the lacrimal sac overflow. The term for this condition begins with the prefix *epi-*, which means _____. The tears flow upon and out of the outer surface of the eye. This condition is called _____.
glaucoma	**5.56** The group of diseases characterized by increased intraocular pressure, resulting in damage to the ocular nerve and causing visual defects, is called _____.

ANSWERS	REVIEW
phak/o condition of pseudophakia	**5.57** Recall that the combining forms for lens are *phac/o* and _____. The latter spelling along with the prefix *pseudo-* (false) and the suffix *-ia*, meaning _____, forms the term for an implanted artificial lens: _____.
strabismus condition of heterotropia esotropia exotropia	**5.58** From the Greek word *strabismos*, meaning a squinting, comes this term for a condition of eye misalignment: _____. Recall that the word root *tropo* means a turning, and that the suffix *-ia* means a _____. The combining form *heter/o* means the other. Another term for strabismus is named for the appearance of one eye turning toward the other: _____. If the eye turns inward (*eso* = inward) toward the nose, this is called _____. If the eye turns outward (*exo* = outward), this is called _____.
macular degeneration	**5.59** A breakdown of tissues in the macula lutea that causes a loss of central vision is called _____ _____.
detachment	**5.60** Separation of the retina from the underlying tissue, usually requiring surgical repair, is called retinal _____.
hordeolum	**5.61** The Latin word *hordeolus* means a little barley grain, which is similar in appearance to a sty, an acute infection of a sebaceous gland of the eyelid. The medical term for a sty is _____.
pterygium ultraviolet	**5.62** The combining form *pteryg/o* means wing-shaped. A triangular, or wing-shaped, fibrous growth of conjunctival tissue extending onto the cornea is called _____. Pterygia are most commonly caused by prolonged exposure to _____ light.
presence trichiasis	**5.63** Recall that the suffix *-iasis* means formation or _____ of. The combining form *trich/o* means hair. The presence of misdirected eyelashes that rub on the conjunctiva or cornea is called _____.
amblyopia	**5.64** *Ambly/o*, a combining form meaning dim, is the foundation of the term _____, commonly called lazy eye, that describes the condition of decreased vision in early life because of a functional defect (e.g., strabismus and refractive error).

Self-Instruction: Diagnostic Tests and Procedures

Study this table to prepare for the programmed review that follows.

TEST OR PROCEDURE	EXPLANATION
distance visual acuity (see Figure 5-11) dis′tănts vizh′yū-ăl ă-kyū′i-tē	measure of the ability to see the details and shape of identifiable objects from a specified distance, usually from 20 ft (6 m) using a Snellen eye chart; normal distance visual acuity is 20/20 (6/6)
fluorescein angiography (see Figure 5-12) flōr-es′ē-in an-jē-og′ră-fē	visualization and photography of retinal and intraocular vessels made as fluorescein dye, which is injected into a vein, circulates through the eye
ophthalmoscopy (see Figure 5-13) of-thăl-mos′kŏ-pē	use of an ophthalmoscope to view the interior of the eye
slit lamp biomicroscopy (see Figure 5-14) slit lamp bī′ō-mī-kros′kŏ-pē	combination of a microscope and a narrow beam of light used to examine the eye, especially the cornea, lens, fluids, and membranes
sonography sŏ-nog′ră-fē	use of high-frequency sound waves to detect pathology within the eye (e.g., foreign bodies and detached retina)
tonometry (see Figure 5-15) tō-nom′ĕ-trē	use of a tonometer to measure intraocular pressure, which is elevated in glaucoma

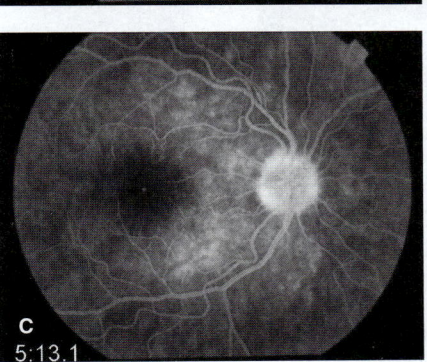

FIGURE 5-11 ■ Snellen eye chart for testing distance visual acuity.

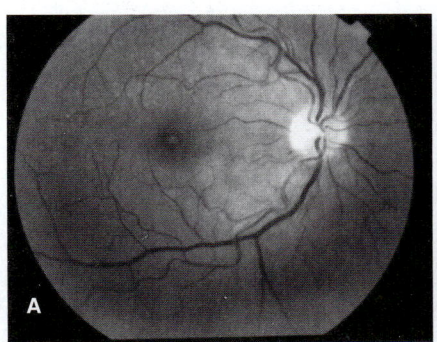

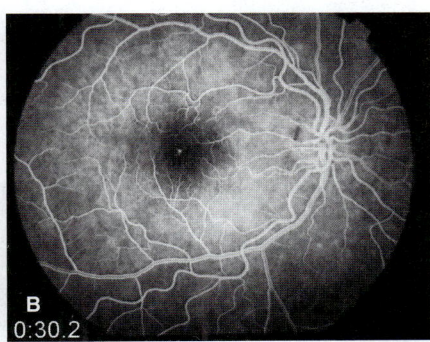

FIGURE 5-12 ■ Fluorescein angiography photographs. **A.** Right eye before injection of fluorescein. **B.** Maximal levels of fluorescein circulating through the retinal blood vessels 30 seconds after injection. **C.** Elimination of fluorescein after 5 minutes.

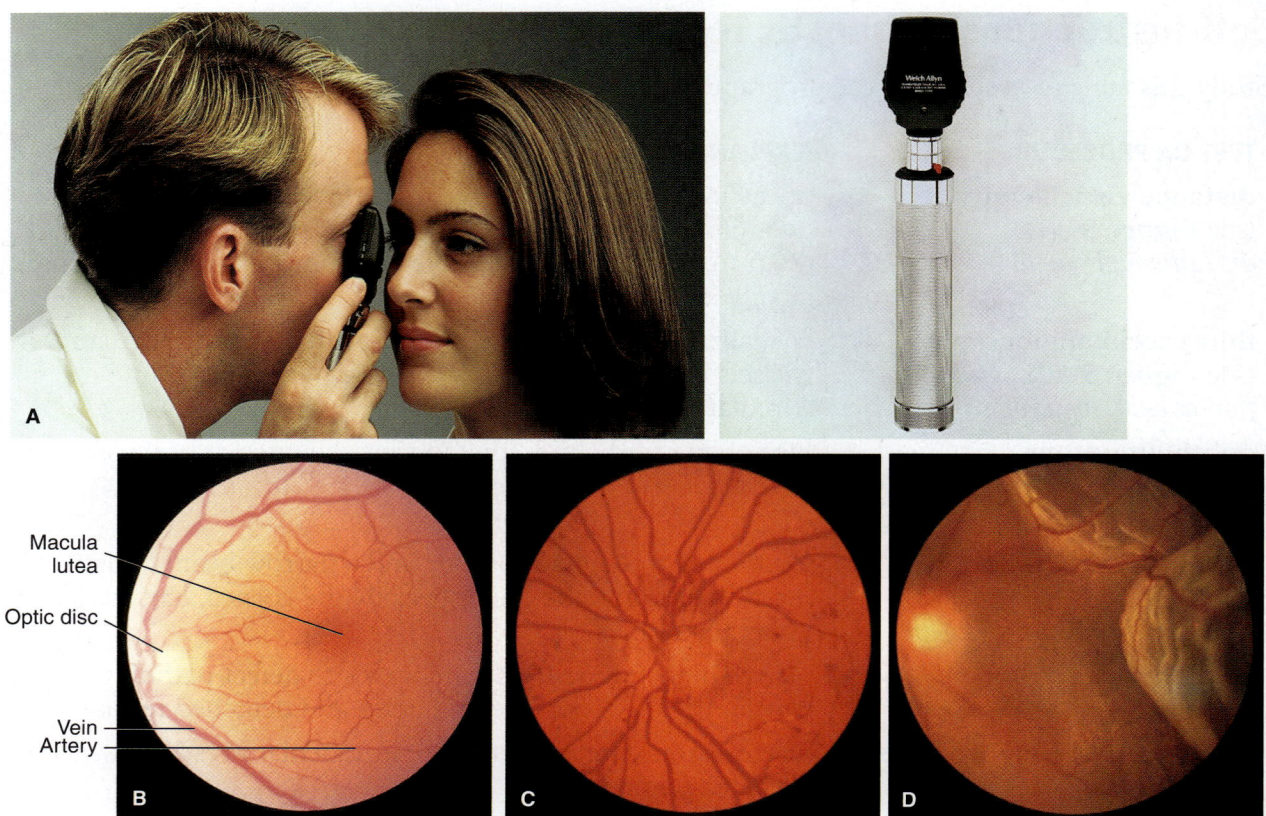

FIGURE 5-13 ■ **A.** Doctor performing ophthalmoscopy using an ophthalmoscope. **B.** Normal retina. **C.** Aneurysms seen in diabetic retinopathy. **D.** Retinal detachment.

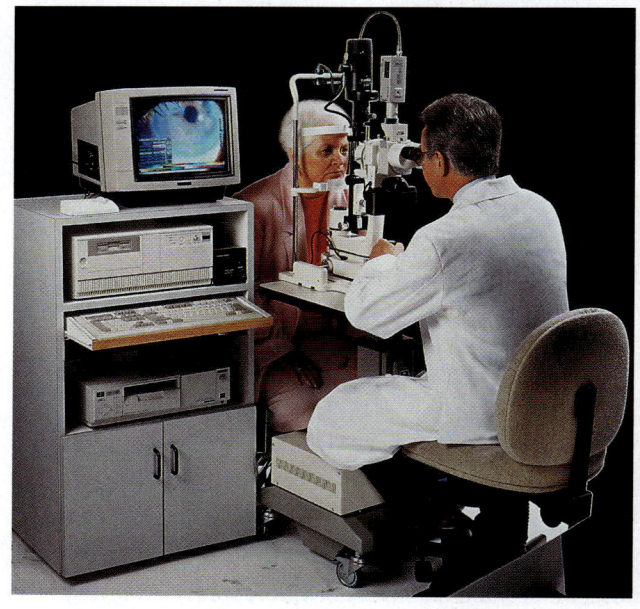

FIGURE 5-14 ■ Slit lamp biomicroscopy.

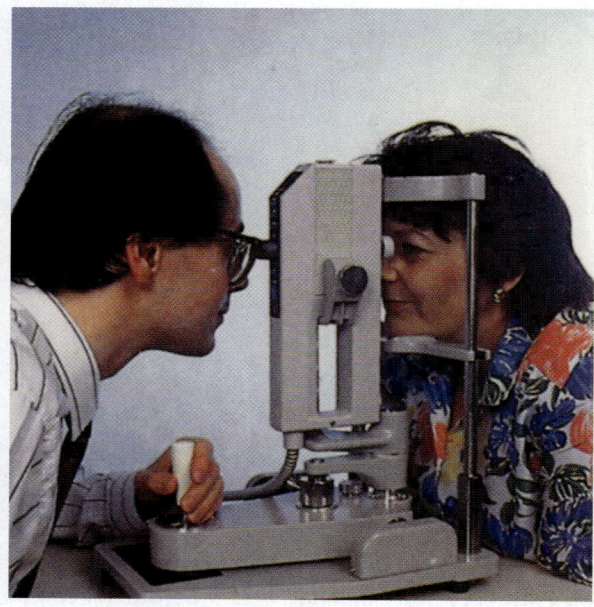

FIGURE 5-15 ■ Tonometry.

Programmed Review: Diagnostic Tests and Procedures

ANSWERS	REVIEW
ophthalm/o ophthalmoscopy	**5.65** Again, the three combining forms meaning eye are *ocul/o*, *opt/o*, and _____. The last one is used with the suffix that means the process of examination to make the term for use of an ophthalmoscope to view the interior of the eye: _____.
visual acuity normal	**5.66** The diagnostic test that measures the ability to see objects at a specified distance, usually from 20 ft (6 m), is called distance _____ _____. A result of 20/20 (6/6) represents _____ distance visual acuity.
fluorescein	**5.67** Angiography, which is radiography of blood vessels after injection of a contrast medium, is used in many body areas. The procedure used with the eye is called _____ angiography, which is named for the fluorescein dye that is injected into a vein to circulate through the eye.
sonography recording	**5.68** The use of high-frequency sound waves to make an image for detecting pathology in the eye is called _____, or ultrasound. The suffix *-graphy* means a process of _____.
tonometry process	**5.69** A tonometer measures intraocular pressure as a test for glaucoma. This procedure is called _____. The suffix *-metry* means a _____ of measuring.
biomicroscopy	**5.70** A special microscope is used to examine eye structures. This procedure is called slit lamp _____.

Self-Instruction: Operative Terms

Study this table to prepare for the programmed review that follows.

TERM	MEANING
blepharoplasty blef´ă-rō-plast-tē	surgical repair of an eyelid
cataract extraction kat´ă-rakt ek-strak´shŭn	excision of a cloudy lens from the eye
cryoretinopexy krī-ō-ret´i-nō-pek-sē	use of intense cold to seal a hole or tear in the retina; used to treat retinal detachment; also called *cryopexy*
cryopexy krī´ō-pek-sē	use of intense cold to seal a hole or tear in the retina; used to treat retinal detachment; also called *cryoretinopexy*

TERM	MEANING
dacryocystectomy *dak′rē-ō-sis-tek′tŏ-mē*	excision of a lacrimal sac
enucleation *ē-nū-klē-ā′shŭn*	excision of an eyeball
iridectomy *ir-i-dek′tŏ-mē*	excision of a portion of iris tissue
iridotomy *ir′i-dot′ŏ-mē*	incision into the iris (usually with a laser) to allow drainage of aqueous humor from the posterior to anterior chamber; used to treat a type of glaucoma
keratoplasty *ker′ă-tō-plas-tē*	corneal transplantation; replacement of a diseased or scarred cornea with a healthy one from a matched donor
laser surgery (see Figure 5-16) *lā′zĕr sŭr′jĕr-ē*	use of a laser to make incisions or destroy tissues; used to create fluid passages or to obliterate tumors or aneurysms
laser-assisted in situ keratomileusis (LASIK) *lā′zĕr-ă-sis′tĕd in sī′tū ker′ă-tō-mī-lū′sis (lā′sik)*	a technique using the excimer laser to reshape the surface of the cornea to correct refractive error (e.g., myopia, hyperopia, and astigmatism) (*smileusis* = carving)
intraocular lens (IOL) implant (see Figure 5-17) *in′tră-ok′yū-lăr lenz im′plant*	implantation of an artificial lens to replace a defective natural lens (e.g., after cataract extraction)

FIGURE 5-16 ■ Simulation of laser application.

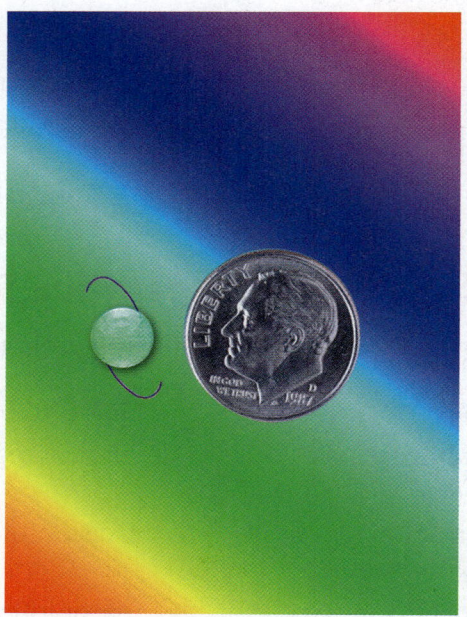

FIGURE 5-17 ■ Size comparison of an intraocular lens to a dime.

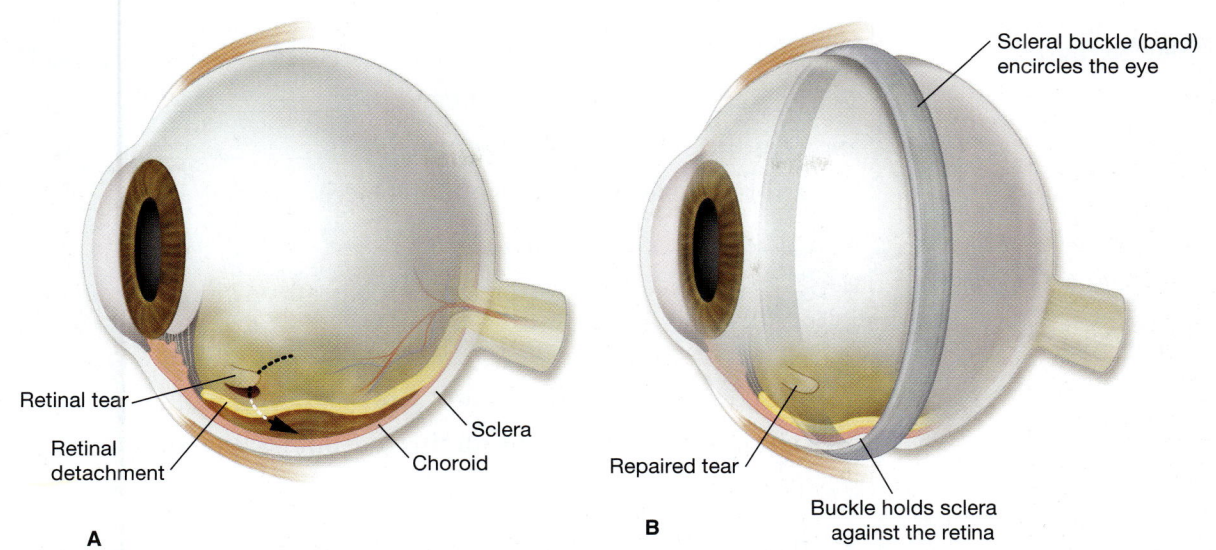

FIGURE 5-18 ■ Scleral buckle. **A.** Detached retina with an *arrow* showing the movement of fluid. **B.** Scleral buckling repairing a retinal tear by attaching a buckle (*band*) around the sclera to keep the retina from pulling away.

TERM	MEANING
phacoemulsification fak′ō-ē-mŭl-si-fi-kā′shŭn	use of ultrasound to shatter and break up a cataract, with aspiration and removal
scleral buckling (see Figure 5-18) sklēr′ăl bŭk′ling	surgery to treat retinal detachment by placing a band of silicone around the sclera to cinch it toward the middle of the eye and relieve pull on the retina; often combined with other techniques to seal retinal tears (e.g., cryoretinopexy)

Programmed Review: Operative Terms

ANSWERS	REVIEW
-plasty blepharoplasty	5.71 Recall that the suffix for surgical repair or reconstruction is _____. The surgical repair of an eyelid is termed _____.
-pexy cryoretinopexy	5.72 The combining form *cry/o* means cold. Recall that the operative suffix meaning suspension or fixation is _____. The operative procedure using intense cold to seal a hole in the retina is called _____, or simply cryopexy.
cataract intraocular lens, implant within	5.73 The excision of a cloudy lens from the eye is called a _____ extraction. After the lens has been excised, an artificial lens may be implanted in a procedure called an _____ _____ (IOL) _____. The prefix *intra-* means _____.

ANSWERS	REVIEW
lacrimal -ectomy dacryocystectomy	**5.74** Recall that *dacryocyst* means _____ sac, and that the surgical suffix for excision is _____. Therefore, the term for excision of a lacrimal sac is _____.
iridectomy	**5.75** The excision of a portion of iris tissue is _____.
-tomy iridotomy	**5.76** The surgical suffix meaning incision is _____. An incision into the iris to allow drainage from the posterior chamber is called an _____.
enucleation	**5.77** The Latin word *enucleo* means to remove the kernel, such as the kernel of a nut. The medical term for removing an entire structure, such as the eyeball (or a tumor), without rupturing it is _____.
kerat/o keratoplasty	**5.78** The two combining forms referring to the cornea are *corne/o* and _____, which also can mean hard. Combining the latter with the suffix for surgical repair or reconstruction yields this term for a corneal transplant: _____.
laser surgery in situ keratomileusis	**5.79** Lasers are used in many operative techniques to make incisions or destroy tissues. This is generally called _____ _____. A special technique using a laser to reshape the surface of the cornea is termed laser-assisted _____ _____ _____ (LASIK).
phacoemulsification	**5.80** The term emulsification refers to breaking up a substance and distributing it through another substance, generally a liquid. A surgical procedure uses ultrasound to shatter and break up a cataract such that after emulsification, it can be removed by aspiration. This procedure is called _____.
buckling	**5.81** A surgical procedure to treat retinal detachment by placing a "buckle-like" band of silicone around the sclera to cinch it toward the middle of the eye and relieve pull on the retina is simply called scleral _____.

Self-Instruction: Therapeutic Terms

Study this table to prepare for the programmed review that follows.

TERM	MEANING
contact lens kon′takt lenz	small, plastic, curved disc with optical correction that fits over the cornea; used to correct refractive errors
eye instillation ī in-sti-lā′shŭn	introduction of a medicated solution in the eye, usually administered by a drop (gt) or drops (gtt) in the affected eye or eyes
eye irrigation ī ir′i-gā′shŭn	washing of the eye with water or other fluid (e.g., saline)
COMMON THERAPEUTIC DRUG CLASSIFICATIONS	
antibiotic ophthalmic solution an′tē-bī-oť′ik of-thal′mik sŏ-lū′shŭn	antimicrobial agent in solution; used to treat bacterial infections (e.g., conjunctivitis) and corneal ulcers
cycloplegic sī-klō-plē′jik	agent that paralyzes the ciliary muscle and the powers of accommodation; commonly used in pediatric eye examinations
mydriatic mid′rē-at′ik	agent that causes dilation of the pupil; used for certain eye examinations
miotic mī-ot′ik	agent that causes the pupil to contract (*mio* = less)

Programmed Review: Therapeutic Terms

ANSWERS	REVIEW
contact lens	5.82 The plastic lens that the user fits over the cornea to correct refractive errors is called a _____ _____.
instillation, drop gtt irrigation	5.83 Introduction of a medicated solution in the eye is called an eye _____, usually administered by a _____ (gt) or drops (____) in the affected eye or eyes. Washing the eye with water or other fluid is called eye _____.
antibiotic ophthalmic	5.84 A solution composed of an antimicrobial agent in a fluid for treatment of bacterial eye infections is called an _____ _____ solution.
mydriatic	5.85 The term mydriasis means dilation of the pupil. A therapeutic drug that causes dilation of the pupil for an eye examination is called a _____ agent.

ANSWERS	REVIEW
miotic	**5.86** In contrast, miosis means contraction of the pupil. A therapeutic drug that causes the pupil to contract is called a _____ agent.
circle ciliary paralysis cycloplegic	**5.87** *Cycl/o* is a combining form referring either to a _____ or the _____ body, a ring-like structure in the eye that contains ciliary muscles. Recall from Chapter 4 that *-plegia* is a suffix meaning _____. The term pertaining to an agent that paralyzes the ciliary muscle and powers of accommodation during some eye examinations, using the adjective form of *-plegia*, is _____.

Chapter 5 Abbreviations

ABBREVIATION	EXPANSION
gt	drop
gtt	drops
IOL	intraocular lens
LASIK	laser-assisted in situ keratomileusis

PRACTICE EXERCISES

For each of the following words, write out the term parts (prefixes [P], combining forms [CF], roots [R], and suffixes [S]) on the lines below the word. Then define the term according to the meaning of its parts.

EXAMPLE
epikeratophakia
epi / kerato / phak / ia
P　　CF　　R　　S

DEFINITION: upon/cornea/lens/condition of

1. ophthalmology
   _____ / _____
   　　CF　　　　　　S
   DEFINITION: _____

2. lacrimal
   _____ / _____
   　　R　　　　　　S
   DEFINITION: _____

3. keratoplasty
   _____ / _____
   　　CF　　　　　　S
   DEFINITION: _____

4. iritis
   _____ / _____
   　　R　　　　　　S
   DEFINITION: _____

5. phacolysis
   _____ / _____
   　　CF　　　　　　S
   DEFINITION: _____

6. retinopathy
   _____ / _____ / _____
   　　CF　　　　　　R　　　　　　S
   DEFINITION: _____

7. conjunctivitis
   _____ / _____
   　　R　　　　　　S
   DEFINITION: _____

8. presbyopia
   _____ / _____
   　　R　　　　　　S
   DEFINITION: _____

9. aphakia

    _____ / _____ / _____
       P   R   S

    DEFINITION: _____

10. scleromalacia

    _____ / _____
       CF   S

    DEFINITION: _____

Write the letter of the definition that matches each of the following refractive disorders.

11. myopia   _____   a. loss of accommodation due to old age
12. strabismus _____   b. lazy eye
13. presbyopia _____   c. farsightedness
14. astigmatism _____   d. crossed eyes
15. hyperopia   _____   e. distorted vision
16. amblyopia   _____   f. nearsightedness

Complete each medical term by writing the missing part.

17. _____itis = inflammation of the cornea
18. dacryo_____ectomy = excision of a tear sac
19. _____ophthalmos = protrusion of the eyeball
20. _____chalasis = baggy eyelids

Briefly define the following medical terms.

21. diplopia _____
22. tonometer _____
23. ectropion _____
24. scotoma _____

Write the correct medical term for each of the following definitions.

25. _____ pinkeye
26. _____ inflammation of the eyelid
27. _____ agent that causes dilation of the pupil
28. _____ clouding of the lens causing decreased vision
29. _____ breakdown or thinning of the tissues in the macula lutea, resulting in partial or complete loss of central vision
30. _____ involuntary, rapid oscillating movement of the eyeball

Circle the combining form that corresponds to the meaning given.

31. eye
    a. or/o   b. opt/o   c. ot/o

32. light
    a. phon/o   b. phot/o   c. opt/o

33. lens (lentil)
    a. phac/o   b. scler/o   c. conjunctiv/o

34. tear
    a. dacry/o   b. hydr/o   c. aque/o

35. eyelid
    a. ocul/o   b. ophthalm/o   c. blephar/o

Identify the parts of the eye by writing the missing words in the spaces provided.

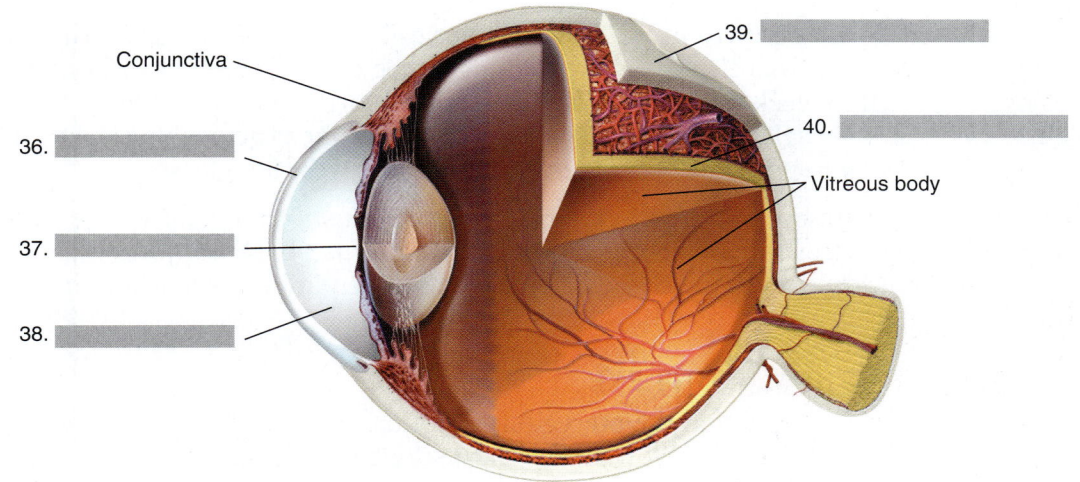

36. _____
37. _____
38. _____
39. _____
40. _____

For each of the following, circle the correct spelling of the term.

41. a. asthenopia   b. assthinopia   c. asthinopia
42. a. terigium   b. pterygium   c. pteregium
43. a. mydriatic   b. midriatic   c. myadriatic
44. a. epiphora   b. epifora   c. epifhora
45. a. opthalmoscope   b. ofthalmoscope   c. ophthalmoscope

Give the noun that is used to form each adjective.

46. conjunctival _____

47. myopic   _____

48. scleral   _____

49. macular   _____

50. exophthalmic _____

MEDICAL RECORD ANALYSIS

Medical Record 5-1

PROGRESS NOTE

S: This 51 y/o female c/o a growth in the corner of her right eye that is dry and irritated. She has had the feeling that there was "something in the eye" for about 4 months before noticing the growth 3 weeks ago. She wears contacts to correct farsightedness but has recently switched to eyeglasses because of the discomfort. She is active physically and loves tennis and water sports, but she does not frequently wear sunglasses.

O: Inspection of the right eye reveals an inflamed, raised, whitish, triangular wedge of fibrovascular tissue, the base of which lies within the interpalpebral conjunctiva and the apex of which encroaches on the cornea. A photo documentation is made and included in the chart.

A: INFLAMED PTERYGIUM, RIGHT EYE

1. P: The patient is advised that the pterygium is not dangerous, but that further growth could interfere with vision and warrant surgical excision. She was counseled on the importance of wearing UV blocking sunglasses and advised to avoid smoky or dusty areas as much as possible.
2. RX: fluorometholone, 0.1% suspension, 1 gt q4h OD during the day for inflammation; OTC artificial tears solution, prn dryness/irritation
3. RTO in 3 months for slit lamp evaluation, or sooner if symptoms persist.

Questions About Medical Record 5-1

1. Describe the refractive error noted in the subjective information:
   a. eyestrain
   b. inflammation of the cornea
   c. difficulty seeing distant objects
   d. difficulty seeing close objects
   e. blind spot in vision

2. Which action on the part of the patient likely contributed to the condition?
   a. wearing contact lenses
   b. removing contact lenses
   c. playing tennis
   d. not routinely wearing sunglasses
   e. strenuous physical activity

3. Which ophthalmologic procedure is included in the plan?
   a. use of laser to reshape the surface of the cornea
   b. use of an ophthalmoscope to view the interior of the eye
   c. use of a tabletop microscope to examine the eye, especially the cornea
   d. implantation of an artificial lens
   e. use of a tonometer to measure the intraocular pressure

4. How should the fluorometholone be administered?
   a. one drop every 4 hours
   b. four drops in the eye every morning
   c. one drop every day for 4 days
   d. as needed during the day
   e. one drop every other day for 4 days

5. When should the patient instill the artificial tears?
   a. every day
   b. every night
   c. during the day
   d. only as needed
   e. when feeling the need to cry

6. What caused the pterygium?
   a. misdirected eyelashes that rub on the conjunctiva or cornea
   b. intraocular muscle imbalance
   c. separation of the retina from the underlying epithelium
   d. abnormal overflow of tears
   e. ultraviolet exposure and drying

7. What was the patient told about the pterygium?
   a. it is cancerous
   b. it is not dangerous
   c. it must be removed
   d. both a and c
   e. none of the above

ANSWERS TO PRACTICE EXERCISES

1. ophthalmology
   CF: opthalmo
   S: logy
   DEFINITION: eye/study of
2. lacrimal
   R: lacrim
   S: al
   DEFINITION: tear/pertaining to
3. keratoplasty
   CF: kerato
   S: plasty
   DEFINITION: cornea/surgical repair or reconstruction
4. iritis
   R: ir
   S: itis
   DEFINITION: iris/inflammation
5. phacolysis
   CF: phaco
   S: lysis
   DEFINITION: lens (lentil)/breaking down or dissolution
6. retinopathy
   CF: retino
   R: path
   S: y
   DEFINITION: retina/disease/condition or process of
7. conjunctivitis
   R: conjunctiv
   S: itis
   DEFINITION: conjunctiva (to join together)/inflammation
8. presbyopia
   R: presby
   S: opia
   DEFINITION: old age/condition of vision
9. aphakia
   P: a
   R: phak
   S: ia
   DEFINITION: without/lens (lentil)/condition or process of
10. scleromalacia
    CF: sclero
    S: malacia
    DEFINITION: sclera/softening
11. f
12. d
13. a
14. e
15. c
16. b
17. keratitis
18. dacryocystectomy
19. exophthalmos
20. blepharochalasis
21. double vision

22. instrument to measure intraocular pressure
23. outward turning of the rim of the eyelid
24. blind spot in vision
25. conjunctivitis
26. blepharitis
27. mydriatic
28. cataract
29. macular degeneration
30. nystagmus
31. opt/o
32. phot/o
33. phac/o
34. dacry/o
35. blephar/o
36. cornea
37. pupil
38. anterior chamber (containing aqueous humor)
39. sclera
40. retina
41. asthenopia
42. pterygium
43. mydriatic
44. epiphora
45. ophthalmoscope
46. conjunctiva
47. myopia
48. sclera
49. macula lutea
50. exophthalmos or exophthalmos

ANSWERS TO MEDICAL RECORD 5-1

1. d
2. d
3. c
4. a
5. d
6. e
7. b

6

THE EAR

Learning Outcomes

After completing this chapter, you should be able to:
- Define terms parts related to the ear.
- Identify key ear anatomic structures and their functions.
- Define symptomatic and diagnostic terms related to the ear.
- Explain diagnostic tests, procedures, operative terms, and therapeutic terms related to the ear.
- Cite common abbreviations related to the ear and give the expansion of each.
- Explain terms used in medical records involving the ear.

OVERVIEW OF THE EAR

The ear is divided into three regions. These regions are the external ear, middle ear, and internal ear (see **Figure 6-1**).

- The **external ear** is made up of the auricle (*pinna*) and the external acoustic meatus. The auricle directs sound waves, and the external acoustic meatus is the passageway inward toward the tympanic membrane, which is the boundary between the external ear and the middle ear.
- The **middle ear** is the region between the external acoustic meatus and the internal ear. Sound waves reach the tympanic membrane, or eardrum, in the middle ear. The tympanic membrane transmits sound vibrations to the auditory ossicles, which are three little bones called the malleus, incus, and stapes. From here, vibrations are transmitted to the oval window, which stimulates the auditory fluids in the internal ear. Also in the middle ear, the auditory tube, also known as the *eustachian tube*, connects with the pharynx (throat) to maintain equal air pressure.

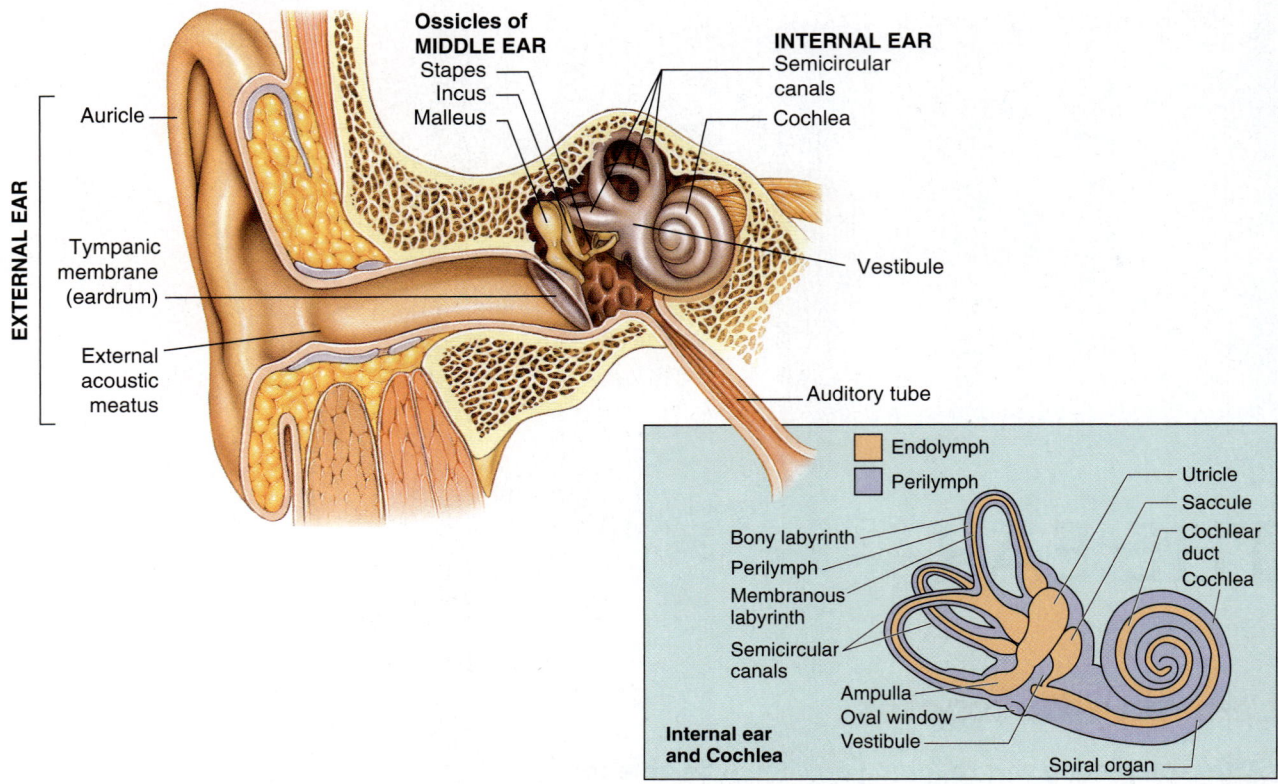

FIGURE 6-1 ■ Anatomy of the ear.

- The **internal ear**, also known as the *inner ear* or *labyrinth*, receives sound vibrations and passes them through intricate, intercommunicating tubes (semicircular canals) and chambers (vestibule) to the spiral organ (*organ of Corti*) within the cochlea. At the spiral organ, nerve impulses are generated and transmitted to the brain for processing. The internal ear also helps maintain the body's equilibrium by stimulating nerve impulses resulting from movement or changes in position.

Self-Instruction: Combining Forms

Study this table to prepare for the programmed review that follows.

COMBINING FORM	MEANING
acous/o	hearing
aer/o	air or gas
audi/o	hearing
aur/i	ear
cerumin/o	wax
myring/o	eardrum
ot/o	ear
salping/o	tube
tympan/o	eardrum
-acusis	hearing condition

Programmed Review: Combining Forms

ANSWERS	REVIEW
acous/o, audi/o -acusis -metry audiometry	**6.1** The two combining forms for hearing are used in many everyday words in addition to medical terms. People speak of the acoustics of a room, for example, and of audible noises. These two combining forms are _____ and _____. Related to the combining form *acous/o* is the suffix for a hearing condition: _____. The term *presbyacusis*, for example, means hearing loss because of old age. Recall that the suffix meaning process of measuring is _____. The medical process of measuring a person's hearing, using the other combining form, is _____.
aer/o anaerobe	**6.2** The combining form for air or gas is _____. This combining form is used in many medical terms. An aerobe, for example, is a microbe that lives in the presence of air, whereas a microbe that lives without air (formed with the prefix meaning without) is an _____.
ot/o otologist ear	**6.3** The two combining forms for ear are *aur/i* and _____. The medical study of the ear is called otology. The physician who specializes in the study and treatment of the ear is an _____. Otology is a subspecialty of otorhinolaryngology (otolaryngology), involving the study and treatment of the _____, nose, and throat (more commonly known as ENT).
aur/i	**6.4** The other combining form meaning ear is _____. The auricle, for example, is the outer, visible part of the ear.
cerumin/o -osis ceruminosis	**6.5** The combining form referring to ear wax comes from the Latin word cera, meaning wax. That combining form is _____. Recall that the suffix meaning condition or increase is _____; therefore, the term for a condition of excessive ear wax is _____.
salping/o salpingitis	**6.6** The combining form for the auditory tube comes from the Greek word salpinx, meaning trumpet. That combining form is _____. Using the common suffix for inflammation, the medical term for inflammation of the auditory tube in the ear is _____.

ANSWERS	REVIEW
tympan/o -tomy tympanotomy	**6.7** Kettledrums used in symphony orchestras are called tympani, from the Greek word for drum. The combining form for the eardrum is _____. Recall that the suffix for surgical incision is _____. An incision into the eardrum is therefore called a _____.
myring/o -ectomy myringectomy	**6.8** A second combining form for eardrum comes from the Latin word for drum membrane: myringa. That combining form is _____. Recall that the suffix for surgical excision is _____. Combine these term components to create the medical term for the excision of the eardrum: _____.

Self-Instruction: Anatomic Terms

Study this table to prepare for the programmed review that follows (see **Figure 6-1**).

TERM	MEANING
external ear eks-těr′ năl ēr	outer structures of the ear that collect sound
auricle aw′ri-kl	projected part of the external ear; also called *pinna* (*pinna* = feather)
pinna pin′ă	projected part of the external ear; also called *auricle* (little ear) (*pinna* = feather)
external acoustic meatus eks-těr′ năl ă-kūs′ tik mē-ā′ tŭs	external passage for sounds collected from the auricle to the tympanic membrane; also called *external auditory meatus*
external auditory meatus eks-těr′ năl aw′ di-tōr-ē mē-ā′ tŭs	external passage for sounds collected from the auricle to the tympanic membrane; also called *external acoustic meatus*
cerumen sě-rū′ men	a waxy substance secreted by glands located throughout the external canal
middle ear mid′ ěl ēr	structures in the middle of the ear that vibrate sound from the tympanic membrane to the internal ear
tympanic membrane tim-pan′ik mem′brān	eardrum; drum-like structure that receives sound collected in the external acoustic meatus and amplifies it through the middle ear; also called the *tympanum*
tympanum tim′pă-nŭm	eardrum; drum-like structure that receives sound collected in the external acoustic meatus and amplifies it through the middle ear; also called the *tympanic membrane*
malleus mal′ē-ŭs	first of the three auditory ossicles of the middle ear; also called the *hammer*
incus ing′kŭs	middle of the three auditory ossicles of the middle ear; also called the *anvil*
stapes stā′pēz	last of the three auditory ossicles of the middle ear; also called the *stirrup*

TERM	MEANING
eustachian tube yū-stā′shăn tūb	tube connecting the middle ear to the pharynx (throat); also called the *auditory tube*
auditory tube aw′di-tōr-ē tūb	tube connecting the middle ear to the pharynx (throat); also called the *eustachian tube*
oval window ō′val win′dō	membrane that covers the opening between the middle ear and internal ear
internal ear in-ter′năl ēr	intricate, fluid-filled, intercommunicating bony and membranous passages that function in hearing by relaying sound waves to auditory nerve fibers on a path to the brain for interpretation; also sense body movement and position to maintain balance and equilibrium (*labyrinth* = maze); also called the *labyrinth*
labyrinth lab′i-rinth	intricate, fluid-filled, intercommunicating bony and membranous passages that function in hearing by relaying sound waves to auditory nerve fibers on a path to the brain for interpretation; also sense body movement and position to maintain balance and equilibrium (*labyrinth* = maze); also called the *internal ear*
cochlea kok′lē-ă	coiled tubular structure of the internal ear that contains the spiral organ (organ of Corti) (*cochlea* = snail); cochlear duct is the membranous tube within the cochlea
perilymph per′i-limf	fluid that fills the bony labyrinth of the internal ear
endolymph en′dō-limf	fluid within the membranous labyrinth of the internal ear
spiral organ spī′răl ōr′gan	structure located in the cochlea; contains receptors (hair cells) that receive vibrations and generate nerve impulses for hearing; also called *organ of Corti*
organ of Corti ōr′gan of kōr′tē	structure located in the cochlea; contains receptors (hair cells) that receive vibrations and generate nerve impulses for hearing; also called *spiral organ*
vestibule ves′ti-byūl	middle part of the internal ear, in front of the semicircular canals and behind the cochlea, that contains the utricle and the saccule; functions to provide body balance and equilibrium
utricle ū′tri-kěl	the larger of two sacs within the membranous labyrinth of the vestibule in the internal ear (*uter* = leather bag)
saccule sak′yūl	the smaller of two sacs within the membranous labyrinth of the vestibule in the internal ear (*sacculus* = small bag)
semicircular canals sem′ē-sěr′kyū-lar kă-nalz′	three canals within the internal ear that contain specialized receptor cells that generate nerve impulses with body movement

Programmed Review: Anatomic Terms

ANSWERS	REVIEW
pinna pinnae	**6.9** The outer, projecting part of the external ear is called the auricle or _____. The plural form of this term is _____. The adjective form is pinnal.
external auditory or acoustic cerumen	**6.10** Sound waves travel from the pinna through the _____ _____ meatus toward the eardrum. Glands along this structure secrete a waxy substance called _____.
tympanum	**6.11** The tympanic membrane, or _____, is the beginning of the middle ear. Also called the eardrum, this structure amplifies sounds into the middle ear.
bones malleus incus stapes	**6.12** The middle ear has three ossicles, which are small _____, that are named because of their shapes. The first, named for its hammer shape, is the _____. The malleus receives sound vibrations from the tympanic membrane and transmits them to the anvil-shaped bone, called the _____, which transmits them to the stirrup-shaped bone, called the _____. The stapes transfers the vibrations to the internal ear.
eustachian auditory	**6.13** It is necessary to equalize air pressure outside of the body with that of the middle ear. The tube connecting the middle ear to the throat (pharynx) is the _____ tube (named for the Italian anatomist Eustachio). This is also called the _____ tube.
oval window internal	**6.14** The opening between the middle ear and the internal ear is covered with a membrane called the _____ _____, which is named for its rounded shape and window-like covering. The stapes transmits sound vibrations to the oval window and, thus, into the _____ ear.
labyrinth	**6.15** The internal ear is a network of interconnecting tubes and chambers that looks like a maze and is also called the _____.

ANSWERS	REVIEW
within perilymph endolymph cochlea	**6.16** The combining form *lymph/o* refers to clear liquid. The prefix *peri-* means around, and the prefix *endo-* means _____. The fluid that fills the bony labyrinth in the internal ear is called _____, and the fluid within the membranous labyrinth is called _____. The coiled, snail-shaped structure containing the spiral organ (organ of Corti) is the _____.
spiral organ	**6.17** Nerve receptors are located inside the _____ _____. This organ generates nervous impulses for hearing.
vestibule small utricle saccule	**6.18** The middle part of the internal ear that contains the utricle and saccule is the _____. Recall that the suffix *-ule* means _____. The larger of the two sacs in the vestibule is the _____, and the smaller of the two sacs is the _____.
semicircular canals	**6.19** The labyrinth structures with partially circular shapes that generate nerve impulses with body movement are called _____ _____. These nerve receptors help to maintain the body's balance and equilibrium.

Self-Instruction: Symptomatic Terms

Study this table to prepare for the programmed review that follows.

TERM	MEANING
otalgia ō-tal′jē-ă	earache; also called *otodynia*
otodynia ō-tō-din′ē-ă	earache; also called *otalgia*
otorrhagia ō-tō-rā′jē-ă	bleeding from the ear
otorrhea ō-tō-rē′ă	purulent drainage from the ear
tinnitus tin′i-tŭs	a ringing or buzzing in the ear; a jingling
vertigo věr′ti-gō	a turning round; dizziness

Programmed Review: Symptomatic Terms

ANSWERS	REVIEW
ear pain otalgia	**6.20** The combining form *ot/o* means _____. Recall that the suffix *-algia* means _____. Thus, the term for ear pain, or an earache, is _____.
bleeding or to burst forth otorrhagia	**6.21** The suffix *-rrhagia* means _____. The term for bleeding from the ear is _____.
-rrhea otorrhea	**6.22** Recall that the symptomatic suffix meaning discharge is _____. The term for a purulent drainage (discharge) from the ear is _____.
tinnitus	**6.23** The Latin word *tinnitus* means to jingle. The symptom of hearing a jingling, ringing, or buzzing sound in the ear is _____.
vertigo	**6.24** The Latin word *vertigo* means dizziness or turning around. The symptom of feeling that one is turning around, or feeling dizzy, is called _____.

Self-Instruction: Diagnostic Terms

Study this table to prepare for the programmed review that follows.

TERM	MEANING
EXTERNAL EAR	
otitis externa (see Figure 6-2) ō-tī′tis eks-tĕr′nă	inflammation of the external acoustic meatus
cerumen impaction sĕ-rū′men im-pak′shŭn	excessive buildup of wax in the ear that often reduces hearing acuity, especially in elderly persons

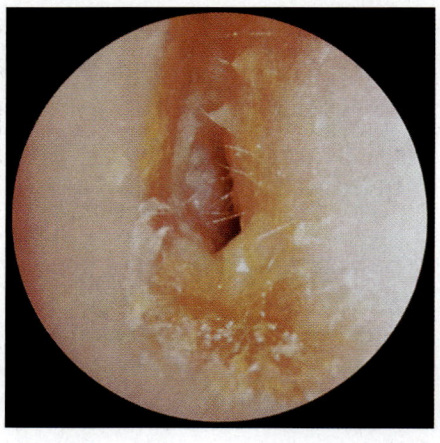

FIGURE 6-2 ■ Otitis externa.

TERM	MEANING
MIDDLE EAR	
myringitis mir-in-jī′tis	inflammation of the eardrum; also called *tympanitis*
tympanitis tim-pă-nī′tis	inflammation of the eardrum; also called *myringitis*
otitis media (see **Figure 6-3**) ō-tī′tis mē′dē-ă	inflammation of the middle ear
aerotitis media ār-o-tī′tis mē′dē-ă	inflammation of the middle ear from changes in atmospheric pressure; often occurs with frequent air travel
eustachian obstruction yū-stā′shăn ob-strŭk′shŭn	blockage of the auditory (eustachian) tube, usually resulting from infection, as in otitis media
otosclerosis ō′tō-sklĕ-rō′sis	hardening of the bony tissue in the ear
INTERNAL EAR	
acoustic neuroma ă-kūs′tik nū-rō′mă	benign, but life-threatening tumor of the vestibular division of the vestibulocochlear nerve (cranial nerve VIII) that causes vertigo, tinnitus, and hearing loss; also called *vestibular schwannoma*
labyrinthitis lab′i-rin-thī′tis	inflammation of the internal ear (labyrinth), usually accompanied by vertigo and deafness
Ménière disease měn-yār′ di-zēz′	disorder of the internal ear resulting from an excessive buildup of endolymph, causing episodes of vertigo, tinnitus, nausea, vomiting, and hearing loss; one or both ears can be affected, and attacks vary in both frequency and intensity (named after Prosper Ménière, the French physician who first described the condition)
GENERAL	
deafness def′nes	general term for partial or complete loss of hearing

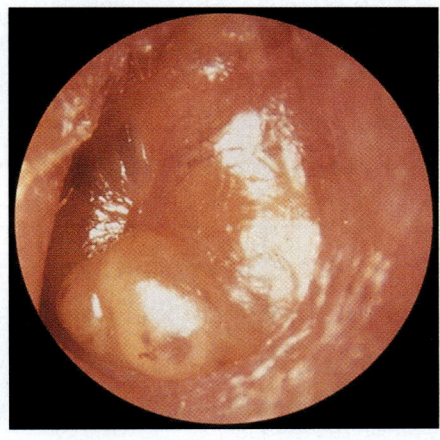

FIGURE 6-3 ■ Otitis media.

TERM	MEANING
conductive hearing loss kon-dŭk′tiv hēr′ing los	hearing impairment caused by interference with sound or vibratory energy in the external canal, middle ear, or ossicles
sensorineural hearing loss sen′sōr-i-nūr′ăl hēr′ing los	hearing impairment caused by lesions or dysfunction of the cochlea or cochlear (auditory) nerve
mixed hearing loss mikst hēr′ing los	combination of sensorineural and conductive hearing loss
presbyacusis prez′bē-ă-kū′sis	hearing impairment in old age; also called *presbycusis*
presbycusis prez-bē-kū′sis	hearing impairment in old age; also called *presbyacusis*

Programmed Review: Diagnostic Terms

ANSWERS	REVIEW
-itis myringitis, tympanitis	**6.25** Recall that the suffix for inflammation is _____. Using the two different combining forms meaning eardrum, two terms for an inflamed tympanic membrane are _____ and _____.
otitis externa otitis media inflammation labyrinthitis	**6.26** There are three different types of otitis, depending on whether the inflammation is in the external ear, middle ear, or internal ear. Inflammation of the external acoustic meatus is termed _____ _____, and inflammation of the middle ear is termed _____ _____. Otitis interna, or _____ of the internal ear, is more commonly known as inflammation of the labyrinth, or _____.
aerotitis media	**6.27** Using the combining forms for both air and ear, the term for inflammation of the middle ear caused by changes in atmospheric pressure is _____ _____.
cerumen impaction	**6.28** Ear wax can build up in the external acoustic meatus and become impacted. This condition of excessive ear wax is called _____ _____.
eustachian obstruction	**6.29** A middle ear infection, such as otitis media, may cause a blockage of the eustachian tube, which is called a _____ _____. This condition is common in young children when the tube is small and easily obstructed.

ANSWERS	REVIEW
increase otosclerosis	**6.30** The combining form for *scler/o* means hard. Recall that the suffix *-osis* means condition or _____. The medical term for the hardening (increased hardness) of bony tissue in the ear is therefore called _____.
hearing, pertaining to acoustic neuroma	**6.31** The two-word term describing a benign tumor on the vestibular division of the vestibulocochlear nerve (cranial nerve VIII) that causes vertigo, tinnitus, and hearing loss is formed by combining *acous/o*, the combining form meaning _____, and *-ic*, the suffix meaning _____, along with *neur/o*, the combining form meaning nerve and the suffix for tumor: _____ _____.
tinnitus vertigo Ménière	**6.32** Ringing in the ear, or _____, and dizziness, or _____, along with vomiting, nausea, and hearing loss are symptoms of an internal ear disorder resulting from an excessive buildup of endolymph called _____ disease (named for the French physician who first described the condition).
deafness conductive sensorineural mixed	**6.33** The general term for partial or complete hearing loss is _____, which is often called hearing impairment or hearing disabled. Hearing loss can be caused by mechanical factors that interfere with the transmission of sound vibrations through the external and middle ears. This is called _____ hearing loss. The term for hearing loss caused by dysfunction of the cochlea or cochlear (auditory) nerve is formed using combining forms referring to the senses and nerves: _____ hearing loss. A combination of sensorineural and conductive hearing loss is known as _____ hearing loss.
hearing condition presbyacusis presbycusis	**6.34** The suffix *-acusis* means _____ _____. Because the combining form *presby/o* means old age, the term for hearing impairment in old age is _____. The shortened form of this term is _____.

Self-Instruction: Diagnostic Tests and Procedures

Study this table to prepare for the programmed review that follows.

TEST OR PROCEDURE	EXPLANATION
audiometry (see **Figure 6-4**) *aw-dē-om′ě-trē*	process of measuring hearing
audiometer *aw′dē-om′ě-ter*	instrument to measure hearing
audiogram *aw′dē-ō-gram*	record of hearing measurement
audiologist *aw-dē-ol′ō-jist*	health professional who specializes in the study of hearing impairments
auditory acuity testing *aw′di-tōr-ē ă-kyū′i-tē test′ing*	physical assessment of hearing; useful in differentiating between conductive and sensorineural hearing loss
tuning fork (see **Figure 6-5**) *tū′ning fork*	a two-pronged, fork-like instrument that vibrates when struck; used to test hearing, especially bone conduction; two types are Webber test and Rinne test

FIGURE 6-4 ■ Audiometry: hearing screening.

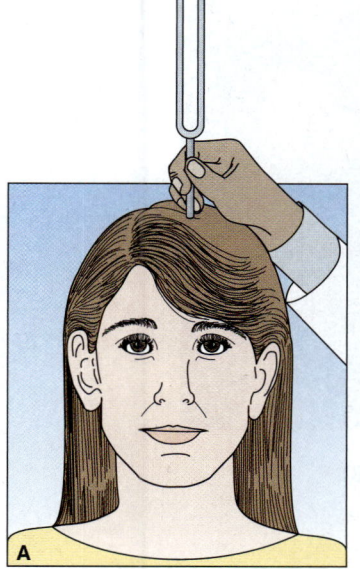
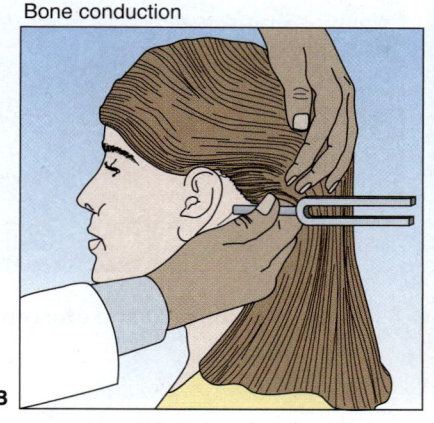
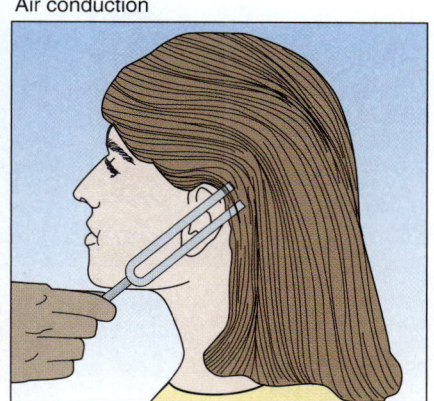

FIGURE 6-5 ■ Tuning fork testing. **A.** Webber test. **B.** Rinne test.

TEST OR PROCEDURE	EXPLANATION
brainstem auditory evoked potential (BAEP) (see Figure 6-6) *brān′stem aw′di-tōr-ē ē-vōkt′ pō-tent′shăl*	electrodiagnostic testing that uses computerized equipment to measure involuntary responses to sound within the auditory nervous system; commonly used to assess hearing in newborns; also called *brainstem auditory evoked response* (BAER)
brainstem auditory evoked response (BAER) *brān′stem aw′di-tōr-ē ē-vōkt′ rē-spons′*	electrodiagnostic testing that uses computerized equipment to measure involuntary responses to sound within the auditory nervous system; commonly used to assess hearing in newborns; also called *brainstem auditory evoked potential* (BAEP)

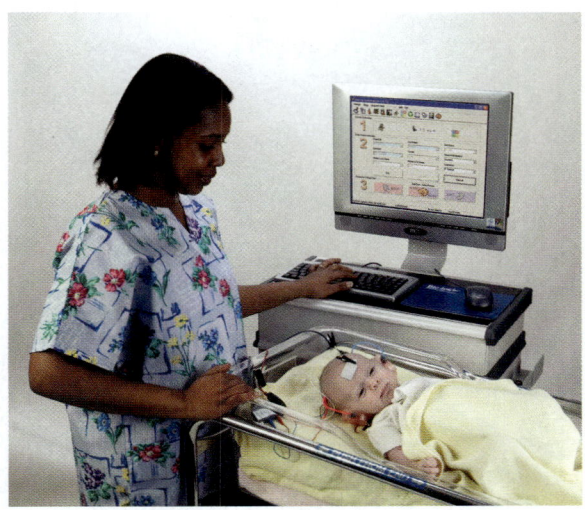

FIGURE 6-6 ■ Brainstem auditory evoked potential (BAEP) testing of a newborn.

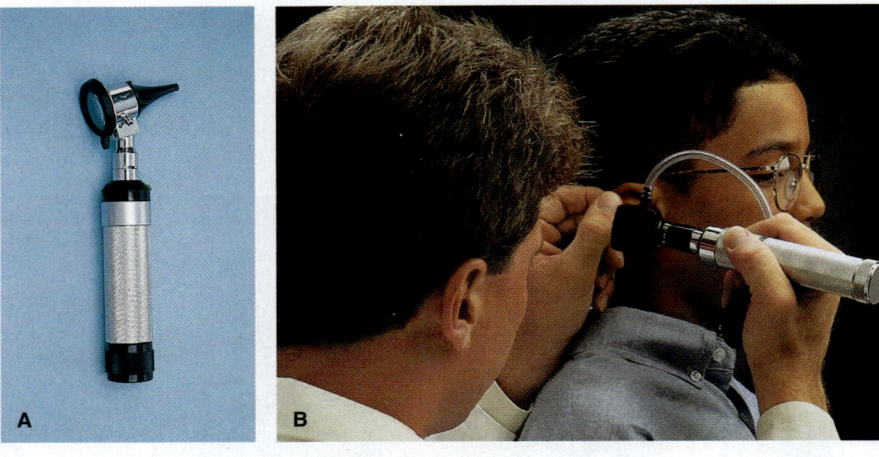

FIGURE 6-7 ■ An otoscope (A) and otoscopy (B).

TEST OR PROCEDURE	EXPLANATION
otoscope (see Figure 6-7A) ō′tō-skōp	instrument for examining the ear
otoscopy (see Figure 6-7B) ō-tos′kŏ-pē	use of an otoscope to examine the external acoustic meatus and tympanic membrane

pneumatic otoscopy
   (see Figure 6-8)
   nū-mat′ik ō-tos′kŏ-pē
	otoscopic observation of the tympanic membrane as air is released into the external acoustic meatus; immobility indicates the presence of middle ear effusion (fluid buildup), which occurs as a result of otitis media

tympanometry tim′pă-nom′ĕ-trē	measurement of the compliance and mobility (conductibility) of the tympanic membrane and ossicles of the middle ear by monitoring the response to external airflow pressures

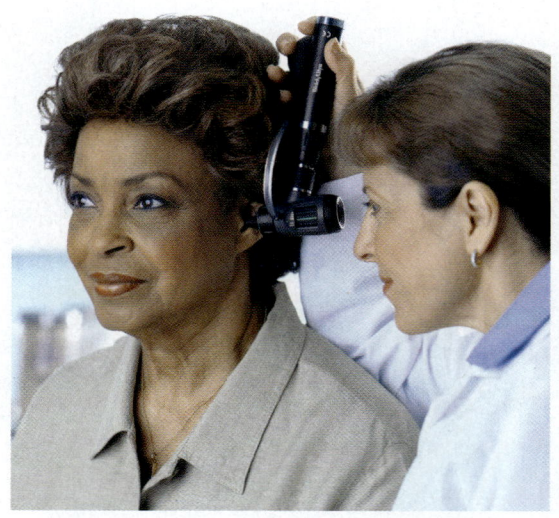

FIGURE 6-8 ■ Doctor performing pneumatic otoscopy.

Programmed Review: Diagnostic Tests and Procedures

ANSWERS	REVIEW
-metry audiometry	**6.35** Recall that the suffix referring to the process of measuring is _____. Thus, the term for the process of measuring hearing is _____.
-meter audiometer	**6.36** The suffix for an instrument for measuring is _____. Thus, the term for an instrument that measures hearing is _____.
-gram audiogram	**6.37** The suffix meaning a record is _____. Thus, the term for a record of hearing measurement is _____.
-logist audiologist	**6.38** The suffix for someone who specializes in the study or treatment of a certain subject area is _____. Thus, the term for a health professional who specializes in the study of hearing impairments is an _____.
-metry eardrum tympanometry	**6.39** Again, the suffix for the process of measuring is _____. *Tympan/o* is the combining form for _____ (also called the tympanic membrane or tympanum). The process of measuring the compliance and mobility (conductibility) of the tympanic membrane is called _____. This test may be used to help diagnose hearing loss.
auditory acuity middle, sensorineural	**6.40** A physical assessment of hearing that differentiates between conductive and sensorineural hearing loss is called _____ _____ testing. A conductive hearing loss is usually caused in the external or _____ ear, whereas a _____ hearing loss involves a problem in the cochlea or cochlear (auditory) nerve.
tuning fork bone	**6.41** The vibrating device that is used in acuity testing is a _____ _____. One test uses it to assess the conduction of vibration through _____.

ANSWERS	REVIEW
brainstem auditory evoked potential	**6.42** The electrodiagnostic test using computerized equipment to measure involuntary responses to sound within the auditory nervous system, such as commonly used to assess hearing in newborns, is called _____ _____ _____ _____ (BAEP).
ot/o otoscopy pneumatic	**6.43** The combining forms meaning ear are *aur/i* and _____. The latter is combined with the suffix referring to a process of examination to form this medical term for using an otoscope to examine the external acoustic meatus and tympanic membrane: _____. The term describing otoscopic observation of the tympanic membrane as air is released into the external acoustic meatus is called _____ otoscopy (including a combining form meaning lung or air).

Self-Instruction: Operative Terms

Study this table to prepare for the programmed review that follows.

TERM	MEANING
microsurgery mī-krō-sŭr′jĕr-ē	surgery with the use of a microscope used on delicate tissue, such as the ear
myringotomy mir-in-got′-mē	incision into the eardrum, most often for insertion of a small polyethylene (PE) tube to keep the canal open and prevent fluid buildup, such as occurs in otitis media; also called *tympanotomy*
tympanotomy (see **Figure 6-9**) tim′pă-not′ŏ-mē	incision into the eardrum, most often for insertion of a small polyethylene (PE) tympanostomy tube to keep the canal open and prevent fluid buildup, such as occurs in otitis media; also called *myringotomy*
otoplasty ō′tō-plas-tē	surgical repair of the external ear
stapedectomy stā-pĕ-dek′tō-mē	excision of the stapes to correct otosclerosis
tympanoplasty tim′pă-nō-plas-tē	surgical procedure to reconstruct the tympanic membrane and/or the auditory ossicles

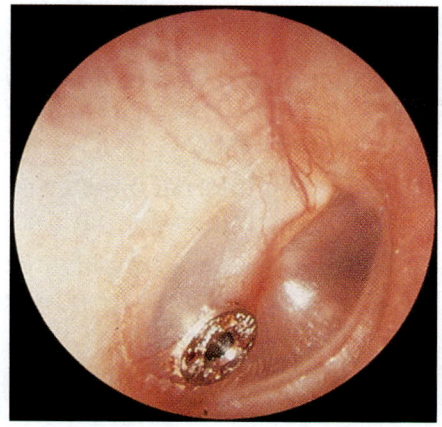

FIGURE 6-9 ■ View through otoscope shows placement of tympanostomy tube.

Programmed Review: Operative Terms

ANSWERS	REVIEW
-plasty otoplasty	**6.44** Recall that the suffix for surgical repair or reconstruction is _____. A surgeon might repair the external ear after trauma, for example. This is called an _____.
tympanoplasty	**6.45** A surgical repair of the tympanic membrane is a _____. This may include a graft to a scarred membrane to improve sound conduction.
microsurgery	**6.46** Many of the ear's internal structures are small and delicate, and surgery must be performed using a microscope. This type of surgery is called _____.
otitis media tomy otomy	**6.47** Small children often have middle ear infections with inflammation, which are called _____ _____. To drain fluids from the middle ear, small tubes are often inserted into the eardrum after a surgical incision through the eardrum. There are two terms that describe this procedure. One, using the suffix for incision, is myringo_____. The other, using the suffix describing the creation of an opening, is tympan_____.
-ectomy otosclerosis stapedectomy ossicles or bones middle	**6.48** The suffix meaning excision is _____. For the condition of hardening of the bony tissue of the ear, _____, the stapes may be excised to correct the hearing problem. This procedure is called a _____. The stapes is the last of the three auditory _____ in the _____ ear.

Self-Instruction: Therapeutic Terms

Study this table to prepare for the programmed review that follows.

TERM	MEANING
auditory prosthesis aw′di-tōr-ē pros′thē-sis	any internal or external device that improves or substitutes for natural hearing
hearing aid hēr′ing ād	an external amplifying device designed to improve hearing by more effective collection of sound into the ear
cochlear implant (see Figure 6-10) kok′lē-ăr im′plant	an electronic device implanted in the cochlea that provides sound perception to patients with severe or profound sensorineural (nerve) hearing loss in both ears
ear lavage ēr lă-vahzh′	irrigation of the external ear canal, often to remove excessive buildup of cerumen
ear instillation ēr in-sti-lā′shŭn	introduction of a medicated solution into the external canal, usually administered by drop (gt) or drops (gtt) in the affected ears

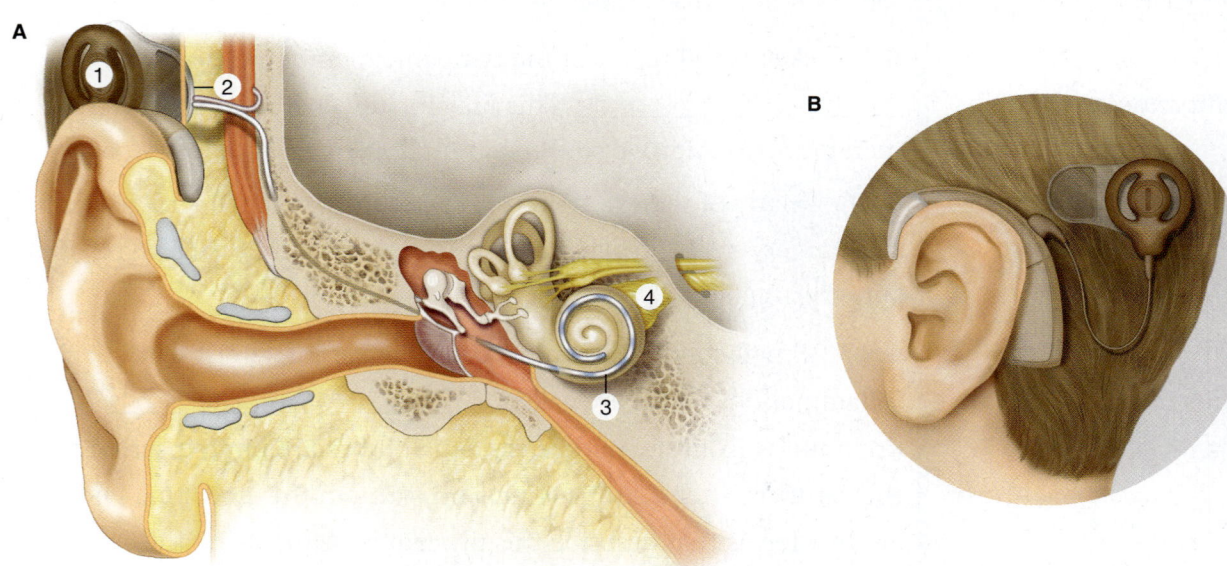

1. External speech processor captures sound and converts it into digital signals
2. Processor sends digital signal to internal implant
3. Internal implant converts signals into electrical energy, sending it to an electrode array inside the cochlea
4. Electrodes stimulate hearing nerve, bypassing damaged hair cells, and the brain perceives signals to hear sound

FIGURE 6-10 ■ Cochlear implant. **A.** Function of a cochlear implant. **B.** Side view showing placement of external speech processor.

TERM	MEANING
COMMON THERAPEUTIC DRUG CLASSIFICATIONS	
antibiotic an′tē-bī-ot′ik	a drug that inhibits the growth of or destroys microorganisms; used to treat diseases caused by bacteria (e.g., otitis media)
antihistamine an-tē-his′tă-mēn	a drug that blocks the effects of histamine
histamine his′tă-mēn	a regulatory body substance released in allergic reactions, causing swelling and inflammation of tissues; seen in hay fever and urticaria (hives)
anti-inflammatory an′tē-in-flam′ă-tō-rē	a drug that reduces inflammation
decongestant dē-kon-jes′tant	a drug that reduces congestion and swelling of membranes, such as those of the nose and auditory tube in an infection

Programmed Review: Therapeutic Terms

ANSWERS	REVIEW
auditory prosthesis hearing aid cochlear	**6.49** A prosthesis is an artificial replacement for a diseased or missing body part. The term used to refer to any device that is used to improve or substitute for natural hearing is an _____ _____. The external amplifying device designed to improve hearing by more effective collection of sound into the ear is called a _____ _____. The electronic device implanted in the cochlea that provides sound perception to patients with severe or profound sensorineural (nerve) hearing loss in both ears is called a _____ implant.
lavage cerumen impaction	**6.50** The Latin term *lavo* means to wash. The process by which a cavity or organ is washed out by irrigating it with water or other fluid is called lavage. The external ear canal is often irrigated to remove buildup of cerumen in a process called ear _____. An excessive buildup of earwax is called _____ _____.
instillation drop, gtt	**6.51** The administration of a medicated solution into the ear's external canal is an ear _____, usually introduced by _____ (gt) or drops (___) in the affected ear or ears.

ANSWERS	REVIEW
histamine antihistamine against	**6.52** A substance in the body that is released during allergic reactions and that causes swelling and inflammation of tissues is called _____. A drug that acts to inhibit the effects of histamine is an _____. The prefix *anti-* means _____ or opposed to.
anti-inflammatory	**6.53** Similarly, a drug that reduces inflammation is an _____-_____.
antibiotic	**6.54** The same prefix joined with the combining form for life (*bio*) denotes a drug class that kills or inhibits microbial life. This type of drug is called an _____.
not decongestant	**6.55** The prefix *de-* means from, down, or _____. A drug that is given to reduce congestion, such as may occur in the auditory tube during an infection, is a _____.

Chapter 6 Abbreviations

ABBREVIATION	EXPANSION
BAEP	brainstem auditory evoked potential
BAER	brainstem auditory evoked response
ENT	ear, nose, and throat
PE	polyethylene
TM	tympanic membrane

PRACTICE EXERCISES

For each of the following words, write out the term parts (prefixes [P], combining forms [CF], roots [R], and suffixes [S]) on the lines below the word. Then define the term according to the meaning of its parts.

EXAMPLE
macrotia
macr / ot / ia
P   R   S

DEFINITION: large or long/ear/condition of

1. aerotitis
   _____ / _____ / _____
     P   R   S
   DEFINITION: _____

2. otorrhea
   _____ / _____
     CF   S
   DEFINITION: _____

3. myringoplasty
   _____ / _____
     CF   S
   DEFINITION: _____

4. acoustic
   _____ / _____
     R   S
   DEFINITION: _____

5. ceruminolysis
   _____ / _____
     CF   S
   DEFINITION: _____

6. salpingoscope
   _____ / _____
     CF   S
   DEFINITION: _____

7. audiometry
   _____ / _____
     CF   S
   DEFINITION: _____

8. tympanocentesis
   _____ / _____
     CF   S
   DEFINITION: _____

9. otodynia

   _____ / _____
       CF   S
   DEFINITION: _____

10. auricle

    _____ / _____
        R   S
    DEFINITION: _____

11. myringotomy

    _____ / _____
        CF   S
    DEFINITION: _____

12. ceruminosis

    _____ / _____
        R   S
    DEFINITION: _____

13. audiology

    _____ / _____
        CF   S
    DEFINITION: _____

Complete each medical term by writing the missing part.

14. oto_____osis = condition of hardening of the bony tissue of the ear

15. aero_____ media = inflammation of the middle ear caused by changes in atmospheric pressure

16. _____logist = person who specializes in the study of hearing impairments

17. _____tomy = incision into the eardrum for the insertion of tubes

18. _____scope = instrument used to view the ear canal and tympanum

19. _____ neuroma = benign tumor of the auditory nerve

20. _____ otoscopy = observation of the tympanic membrane as air is released into the external auditory meatus

Write the correct medical term for each of the following definitions.

21. _____ inflammation of the labyrinth
22. _____ dizziness
23. _____ bleeding from the ear
24. _____ electronic device implanted in the cochlea to provide sound perception
25. _____ hearing impairment of old age
26. _____ ringing in the ear
27. _____ excision of stapes to correct otosclerosis

28. _____ excessive buildup of ear wax

29. _____ earache

30. _____ the study of hearing

31. _____ irrigation of the external ear canal

32. _____ disorder of the internal ear characterized by vertigo, tinnitus, nausea, vomiting, and hearing loss, named after the French physician who first described it

Circle the combining form that corresponds to the meaning given.

33. eardrum
    a. salping/o   b. ot/o   c. myring/o

34. hearing
    a. ot/o   b. audi/o   c. angi/o

35. wax
    a. cerumin/o   b. crin/o   c. scler/o

36. auditory tube
    a. tympan/o   b. myring/o   c. salping/o

37. ear
    a. rhin/o   b. ot/o   c. or/o

38. air
    a. acr/o   b. aur/i   c. aer/o

Identify the parts of the ear by writing the missing words in the spaces provided.

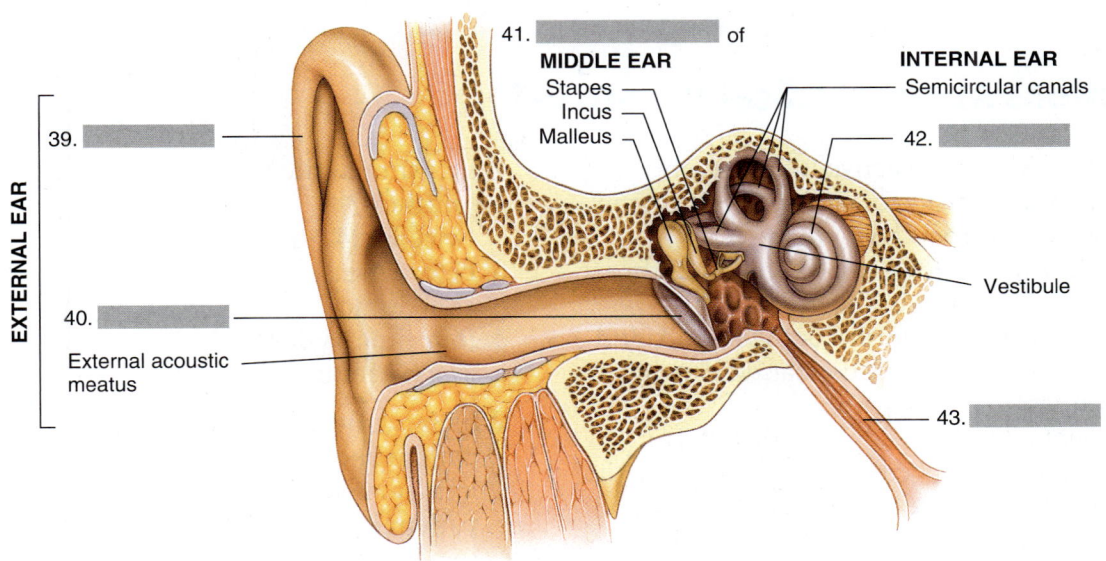

39. _____

40. _____

41. _____

42. _____

43. _____

Circle the correct spelling.

44. a. cerumen	b. ceramen	c. ceruman
45. a. myrimogotomy	b. mirongotomy	c. myringotomy
46. a. vertigo	b. vertago	c. verttigo
47. a. tinnitis	b. tinitus	c. tinnitus
48. a. stapedectomy	b. stapesectomy	c. stapedecktomy
49. a. defness	b. deafnass	c. deafness
50. a. eustation	b. eustachian	c. euhstation

MEDICAL RECORD ANALYSIS

Medical Record 6-1

PROGRESS NOTE

S: This 21 y.o. white male c/o a clogged ⓡ ear with increasing tinnitus. He has had a slight pharyngitis and nasal congestion × 7 d.

O: On PE, there was moist infectious debris in the ⓡ ear that was suctioned clear. The ⓡ tympanic membrane was dull and thickened. The external ear was clear and the tympanic membrane intact.

A: OTITIS MEDIA ⓡ ear

P: (1) Keep ears dry; (2) Rx Pen-VK 250 mg #24 1 p.o. q.i.d. p.c. and h.s.; (3) RTO in 10 d for follow-up (f/u)

Questions About Medical Record 6-1

1. Summarize the subjective information:
   a. patient complains of clogged and ringing ears, sore throat, and stuffy nose
   b. patient has a clogged right ear, sore throat, stuffy nose, and dizziness
   c. patient's right eardrum is thick, dull, and clogged with infectious matter, causing dizziness
   d. patient complains of a sore throat, stuffy nose, and a clogged right ear that is buzzing
   e. patient has a sore throat, stuffy nose, and purulent drainage from the right ear

2. What was the assessment?
   a. clogged right ear, sore throat, and stuffy nose
   b. inflammation of the right middle ear
   c. inflammation of the right external ear canal
   d. blockage of the auditory tube
   e. inflammation of the right eardrum

3. When should the patient take the prescribed medication?
   a. twice in 24 hours
   b. before meals
   c. at bedtime
   d. four times a day
   e. every 4 hours

4. Which is true of the plan?
   a. patient should return to the office immediately if a fever develops
   b. patient is given ear drops and advised not to get his ears wet for 10 days
   c. doctor wants to examine the patient again in 10 days
   d. patient is given an antibiotic and advised to increase fluid intake
   e. if not better in 10 days, patient will be referred to an otolaryngologist

ANSWERS TO PRACTICE EXERCISES

1. aerotitis
   P: aer
   R: ot
   S: itis
   DEFINITION: air or gas/ear/inflammation
2. otorrhea
   CF: oto
   S: rrhea
   DEFINITION: ear/discharge
3. myringoplasty
   CF: myringo
   S: plasty
   DEFINITION: eardrum/surgical repair or reconstruction
4. acoustic
   R: acous
   S: tic
   DEFINITION: hearing/pertaining to
5. ceruminolysis
   CF: cerumino
   S: lysis
   DEFINITION: wax/breaking down or dissolution
6. salpingoscope
   CF: salpingo
   S: scope
   DEFINITION: auditory tube/instrument for examination
7. audiometry
   CF: audio
   S: metry
   DEFINITION: hearing/process of measuring
8. tympanocentesis
   CF: tympano
   S: centesis
   DEFINITION: eardrum/puncture for aspiration
9. otodynia
   CF: oto
   S: dynia
   DEFINITION: ear/pain
10. auricle
    R: aur
    S: icle
    DEFINITION: ear/small
11. myringotomy
    CF: myringo
    S: tomy
    DEFINITION: eardrum/incision
12. ceruminosis
    R: cerumin
    S: osis
    DEFINITION: wax/condition or increase
13. audiology
    CF: audio
    S: logy
    DEFINITION: hearing/study of
14. otosclerosis
15. aerotitis media
16. audiologist
17. myringotomy
18. otoscope
19. acoustic neuroma
20. pneumatic otoscopy
21. labyrinthitis
22. vertigo
23. otorrhagia
24. cochlear implant
25. presbycusis
26. tinnitus
27. stapedectomy
28. cerumen impaction
29. otalgia
30. audiology
31. ear lavage
32. Ménière disease
33. myring/o
34. audi/o
35. cerumin/o
36. salping/o
37. ot/o
38. aer/o
39. auricle
40. tympanic membrane
41. ossicles
42. cochlea
43. auditory tube
44. cerumen
45. myringotomy
46. vertigo
47. tinnitus
48. stapedectomy
49. deafness
50. eustachian

ANSWERS TO MEDICAL RECORD 6-1

1. d
2. b
3. d
4. c

7

ENDOCRINE SYSTEM

Learning Outcomes

After completing this chapter, you should be able to:

- Define terms parts related to the endocrine system.
- Identify key endocrine system anatomic structures with their functions.
- Define symptomatic and diagnostic terms related to the endocrine system.
- Explain diagnostic tests; procedures; and operative and therapeutic terms related to the endocrine system.
- Cite common abbreviations related to the endocrine system and give the expansion of each.
- Explain terms used in medical records involving the endocrine system.

ENDOCRINE SYSTEM OVERVIEW

The endocrine system is made up of ductless glands that secrete hormones (chemical messengers) directly into the bloodstream. The endocrine system's collection of glands secretes numerous hormones that work at distant sites. That is, hormones secreted by one gland enter the bloodstream and target another organ elsewhere in the body. These hormones have a wide range of functions. Some regulate growth and metabolism, others are involved with tissue and sexual function, and some regulate reproduction, sleep, and mood. Overall, this system and its hormones influence nearly every cell, organ, and organ system in the body. Endocrine structures are shown in Figure 7-1. Figure 7-2 describes the functions of the endocrine glands.

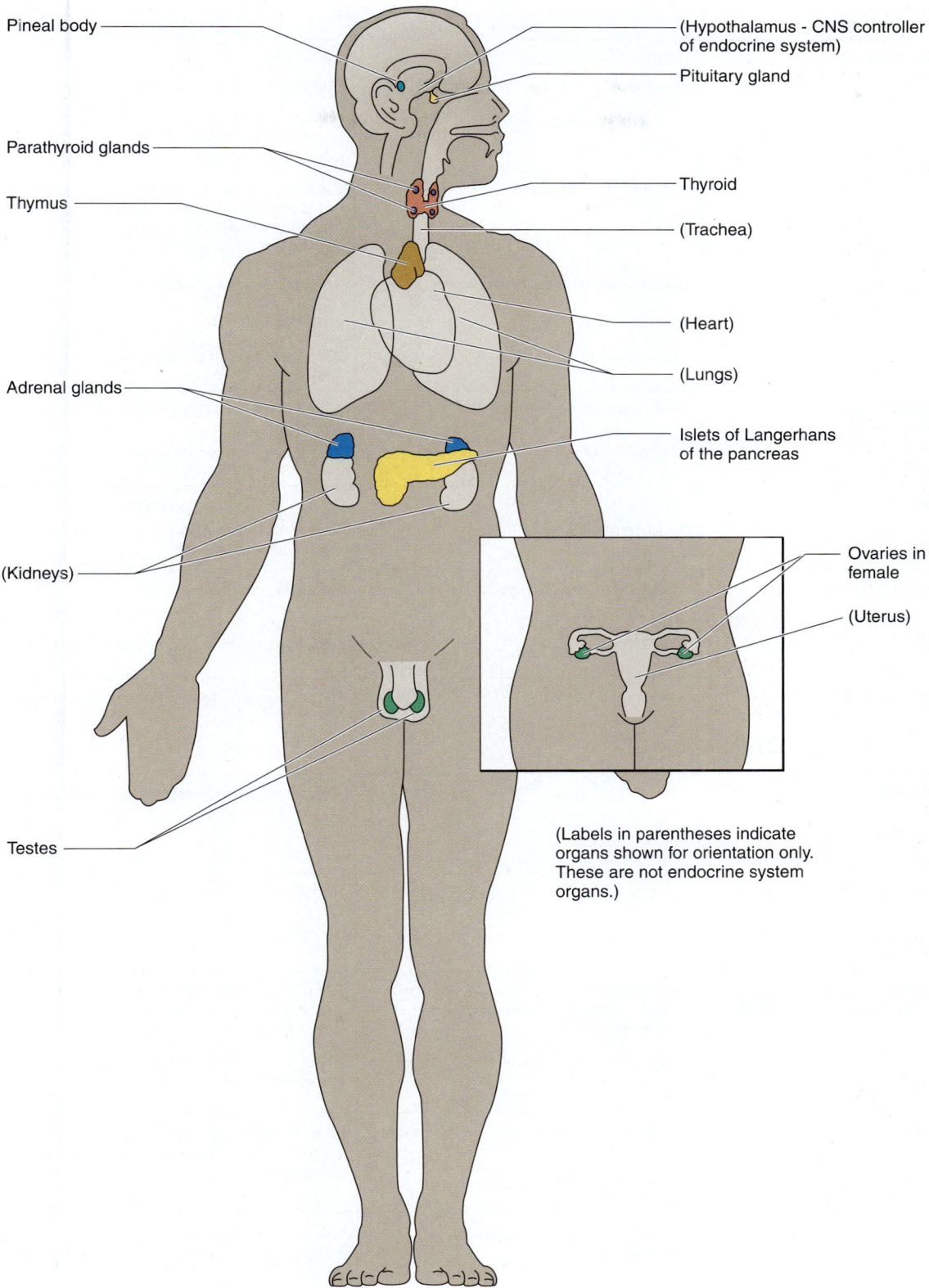

FIGURE 7-1 ■ The endocrine system.

Endocrine gland	Hormone	Function
*Anterior pituitary (adenohypophysis) 	Thyroid-stimulating hormone (TSH)	Stimulates secretion from thyroid gland
	Adrenocorticotrophic hormone (ACTH)	Stimulates secretion from adrenal cortex
	Follicle-stimulating hormone (FSH)	Initiates growth of ovarian follicle; stimulates secretion of estrogen in females and sperm production in males
	Luteinizing hormone (LH)	Causes ovulation; stimulates secretion of progesterone by corpus luteum (endocrine structure formed in ovary after ovulation); causes secretion of testosterone in testes
	Melanocyte-stimulating hormone (MSH)	Affects skin pigmentation
	Growth hormone (GH)	Influences growth
	Prolactin (PRL)	Stimulates breast development and milk secretion
*Posterior pituitary (neurohypophysis) 	Antidiuretic hormone (ADH)	Influences the absorption of water by kidney tubules
	Oxytocin (OXT)	Influences uterine contraction
Pineal body	Melatonin	Involved with circadian rhythm
	Serotonin	Constricts blood vessels and acts as a neurotransmitter
Thyroid gland 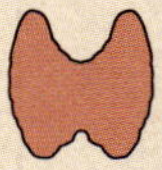	Triiodothyronine (T_3), thyroxine (T_4)	Regulate metabolism
	Calcitonin	Regulates calcium and phosphorus metabolism
Parathyroid glands 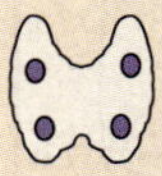	Parathyroid hormone (PTH)	Regulates calcium and phosphorus metabolism
Pancreas (islets of Langerhans) 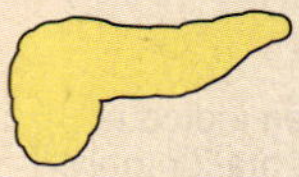	Insulin, glucagon	Regulates carbohydrate/sugar metabolism
Thymus gland 	Thymosin	Regulates immune response
Adrenal glands (suprarenal glands) 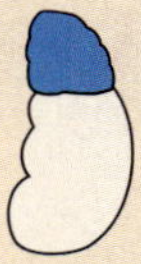	Steroid hormones: glucocorticoids, mineralocorticoids, androgens	Regulate carbohydrate metabolism and salt and water balance; androgrens affect male sex characteristics
	Epinephrine, norepinephrine	Affect sympathetic nervous system in stress response
Ovaries 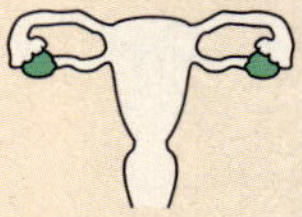	Estrogen, progesterone	Responsible for the development of female secondary sex characteristics and the regulation of reproduction
Testes 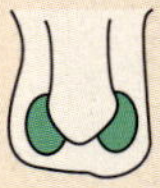	Testosterone	Affects masculinization and reproduction

* Release of hormones in pituitary is controlled by hypothalamus

FIGURE 7-2 ■ **Functions of the endocrine glands.**

Self-Instruction: Combining Forms

Study this table to prepare for the programmed review that follows.

COMBINING FORM	MEANING
aden/o	gland
adren/o	adrenal gland
adrenal/o	adrenal gland
andr/o	male
crin/o	to secrete
dips/o	thirst
gluc/o	glucose (sugar)
glucos/o	glucose (sugar)
glyc/o	glucose (sugar)
hormon/o	hormone (an urging on)
ket/o	ketone bodies
keton/o	ketone bodies
pancreat/o	pancreas
thym/o	thymus gland
thyr/o	thyroid gland (shield)
thyroid/o	thyroid gland (shield)

Programmed Review: Combining Forms

ANSWERS	REVIEW
aden/o -oma adenoma	7.1 The combining form meaning gland is _____. Put this together with the suffix referring to a tumor, _____, to create the term for a tumor of glandular tissue: _____.
adrenal near enlargement adrenomegaly inflammation adrenalitis	7.2 The combining forms *adren/o* and *adrenal/o* mean _____ gland. The prefix *ad-* used in these combining forms gives a clue that the gland is to, toward, or _____ the kidney. Using *adren/o* and the suffix *-megaly*, meaning _____, the term describing an enlargement of the adrenal gland is _____. Using the combining form *adrenal/o* and the suffix *-itis*, meaning _____, the term describing an inflammation of the adrenal gland is _____.
andr/o form pertaining to andromorphous	7.3 The combining form meaning male is _____. Linked to *morph/o*, the combining form meaning _____, and *-ous*, the suffix meaning _____, the term pertaining to male form or appearance is _____.

ANSWERS	REVIEW
secrete within endocrine	**7.4** The combining form *crin/o* means to _____. Recall that the prefix *endo-* means _____. Thus, the medical term for the _____ system refers to secreting within. The endocrine system secretes hormones and other substances from ductless glands.
dips/o many condition of polydipsia	**7.5** The combining form meaning thirst is _____. Recall that the prefix *poly-* means _____ or excessive, and that the suffix *-ia* means a _____. Thus, the term for a condition of excessive thirst is _____.
glucos/o production glucogenic hyper- blood glucose or sugar	**7.6** The three combining terms for sugar are *glyc/o*, *gluc/o*, and _____. Glucose is a form of sugar that is found in the blood and used for energy. The suffix *-genic* pertains to origin or _____. Combined with *gluc/o*, the term for something giving rise to or producing glucose is therefore _____. From the combining form *glyc/o* and the prefix _____, meaning too much or excessive, and the suffix *-emia*, referring to a _____ condition, comes the term hyperglycemia, a condition of too much _____ in the blood.
hormon/o adjective	**7.7** The combining form for hormone is _____, from a Greek word meaning "an urging on." (A hormone is a substance that urges an action to occur.) Hormonal is the _____ form.
keton/o ur/o condition of ketonuria	**7.8** The two combining forms meaning ketone bodies are *ket/o* and _____. Ketone bodies are chemical substances resulting from metabolism. Recall that the combining form for urine is _____, and that the suffix *-ia* means a _____. Therefore, the term for a condition of ketone bodies in the urine is _____.
pancreat/o -itis pancreatitis pancreatectomy	**7.9** The combining form meaning the pancreas is _____. Recall that the suffix for inflammation is _____. The term for inflammation of the pancreas is therefore _____. Removal of the pancreas is termed _____.
thymus thymoma	**7.10** The combining form *thym/o* means the _____ gland. A tumor of thymic tissue is called a _____.

ANSWERS	REVIEW
thyr/o thyroid/o shield, pertaining to, poison thyroid gland thyrotoxic inflammation thyroid	**7.11** The two combining forms meaning thyroid gland are _____ and _____. The Greek term at the origin of these combining forms means *shield*, and the thyroid gland is so named because it is resembles a _____. The suffix *-ic* means _____ _____. Combined with *tox/o*, a combining form meaning _____, and *thyr/o*, meaning _____ _____, the term pertaining to poison of the thyroid gland is _____. Thyroiditis describes an _____ of the _____ gland.

Self-Instruction: Anatomic Terms

Study this table to prepare for the programmed review that follows.

GLAND OR HORMONE	LOCATION OR FUNCTION
adrenal glands ă-drē′năl glanz	located on the superior surface of each kidney; the outer adrenal cortex secretes steroid hormones, and the inner adrenal medulla secretes epinephrine and norepinephrine; also called *suprarenal glands*
suprarenal glands sū′pră-rē′năl glanz	located on the superior surface of each kidney; the outer adrenal cortex secretes steroid hormones, and the inner adrenal medulla secretes epinephrine and norepinephrine; also called *adrenal glands*
steroid hormones stēr′oyd hōr′mōnz	hormones secreted by the adrenal cortex
glucocorticoids glū-kō-kōr′ti-koydz	hormones that regulate carbohydrate metabolism and have anti-inflammatory effects; cortisol is the most significant glucocorticoid
mineralocorticoid min′ěr-al-ō-kōr′ti-koyd	hormones that maintain salt and water balance
androgens an′drō-jenz	hormones that influence development and maintenance of male sex characteristics, for example, facial hair, deep voice
catecholamines kat-ě-kol′ă-mēnz	hormones secreted by the adrenal medulla that affect the sympathetic nervous system in stress response
epinephrine ep-i-nef′rin	hormone that is secreted in response to fear or physical injury; also called *adrenaline*
adrenaline ă-dren′ă-lin	hormone that is secreted in response to fear or physical injury; also called *epinephrine*
norepinephrine nōr′ep-i-nef′rin	hormone that is secreted in response to hypotension (low blood pressure) and physical stress

GLAND OR HORMONE	LOCATION OR FUNCTION
ovaries ō′vă-rēz	located on both sides of the uterus in the female pelvis; secrete estrogen and progesterone
estrogen es′trō-jen	hormone that is responsible for the development of female secondary sex characteristics
progesterone prō-jes′tĕr-ōn	hormone that regulates uterine conditions during pregnancy
islets of Langerhans of the pancreas ī′lets of lahng′ĕr-hahnz of the pan′krē-as	endocrine tissue within the pancreas (the organ located behind the stomach, in front of the 1st and 2nd lumbar vertebrae); secretes insulin and glucagon; also called *pancreatic islets*
insulin in′sŭ-lin	a hormone secreted by the beta cells of the islets of Langerhans that is responsible for regulating the metabolism of glucose (*insulin* = island)
glucagon glū′kă-gon	a hormone secreted by the alpha cells of the islets of Langerhans that regulates carbohydrate metabolism by raising blood sugar
parathyroid glands par-ă-thī′royd glanz	two paired glands located on the posterior aspect of the thyroid gland in the neck; secrete parathyroid hormone (PTH)
parathyroid hormone (PTH) par-ă-thī′royd hōr′mōn	hormone that regulates calcium and phosphorus metabolism
pineal gland pin′ē-ăl gland	located in the center of the brain; secretes melatonin and serotonin
melatonin mel-ă-tōn′in	hormone that is involved with circadian rhythm (24-hour cycle); affects the onset of puberty
serotonin sēr-ō-tō′nin	hormone that constricts blood vessels and acts as a neurotransmitter
pituitary gland pi-tū′i-tār-ē gland **hypophysis** hī-pof′i-sis	located at the base of the brain; considered the master gland as it secretes hormones that regulate the function of other glands, such as the thyroid, adrenal glands, ovaries, and testicles; the anterior pituitary secretes thyroid-stimulating hormone, adrenocorticotropic hormone, follicle-stimulating hormone, luteinizing hormone, melanocyte-stimulating hormone, growth hormone, and prolactin; the posterior pituitary releases antidiuretic hormone and oxytocin
anterior pituitary an-tēr′ē-ōr pi-tū′i-tār-ē	anterior lobe of the pituitary gland; also called *adenohypophysis*
adenohypophysis ad′ĕ-nō-hī-pof′i-sis	anterior lobe of the pituitary gland; also called *anterior pituitary*
thyroid-stimulating hormone (TSH) thī′royd-stim-yū′lā-ting hōr′mōn	hormone that stimulates secretion from thyroid gland
adrenocorticotropic hormone (ACTH) ă-drē′nō-kōr′ti-kō-trō′pik hōr′mōn	hormone that stimulates secretion from adrenal cortex

GLAND OR HORMONE	LOCATION OR FUNCTION
follicle-stimulating hormone (FSH) fol′i-kĕl-stim-yū′lā-ting hōr′mōn	hormone that initiates the growth of ovarian follicle; stimulates the secretion of estrogen in females and the production of sperm in males
luteinizing hormone (LH) lū-tē-nī′zing hōr′mōn	hormone that causes ovulation; stimulates the secretion of progesterone by the corpus luteum; causes the secretion of testosterone in the testes
melanocyte-stimulating hormone (MSH) mel′ă-nō-sīt-stim-yū′lā-ting hōr′mōn	hormone that affects skin pigmentation
growth hormone (GH) grōth hōr′mōn	hormone that influences growth
prolactin (PRL) prō-lak′tin	hormone that stimulates breast development and milk production during pregnancy; also called *lactogenic hormone*
lactogenic hormone lak-tō-jen′ik hōr′mōn	hormone that stimulates breast development and milk production during pregnancy; also called *prolactin*
posterior pituitary pos-tēr′ē-ŏr pi-tū′i-tār-ē	posterior lobe of the pituitary gland; also called *neurohypophysis*
neurohypophysis nūr′ō-hī-pof′i-sis	posterior lobe of the pituitary gland; also called *posterior pituitary*
antidiuretic hormone (ADH) an′tē-dī-yū-ret′ik hōr′mōn	hormone released by the posterior pituitary that influences the absorption of water by kidney tubules; also called *vasopressin*
vasopressin (VP) vā′sō-pres′in	hormone released by the posterior pituitary that influences the absorption of water by kidney tubules; also called *antidiuretic hormone* (ADH)
oxytocin (OXT) ok-sē-tō′sin	hormone released by the posterior pituitary that influences uterine contraction
testes tes′tēz	located on both sides within the scrotum in the male; secrete testosterone
testosterone tes-tos′tĕ-rōn	affects masculinization and reproduction
thymus thī′mŭs	located in the mediastinum (partition between the lungs) anterior to and above the heart; secretes thymosin
thymosin thī′mō-sin	hormone that regulates immune response
thyroid thī′royd	located in front of the neck; secretes triiodothyronine (T_3), thyroxine (T_4), and calcitonin
triiodothyronine (T_3) trī-ī′ō-dō-thī′rō-nēn	thyroid hormone similar to thyroxine but having greater potency; regulates metabolism
thyroxine (T_4) thī-rok′sēn	thyroid hormone that regulates metabolism
calcitonin kal-si-tō′nin	hormone that regulates calcium and phosphorus metabolism

Programmed Review: Anatomic Terms

ANSWERS	REVIEW
adrenal above	**7.12** The suprarenal, or _____, glands are located in the kidneys. The term *renal* refers to the kidneys, and the prefix *supra-* means _____. These glands secrete steroid hormones and other hormones.
corticoids steroids male	**7.13** Steroid hormones have several functions, including an effect on sex characteristics. They include gluco_____ and mineral cortico_____. Androgens are steroids that stimulate the development of _____ sex characteristics.
suprarenal norepinephrine nervous	**7.14** Also secreted by the adrenal, or _____, glands are epinephrine and _____, which are hormones that affect the _____ system in a stress response of the body. For example, epinephrine, also called adrenaline, stimulates the heart and breathing rates.
endocrine secrete progesterone female	**7.15** The ovaries in women are both reproductive and _____ organs, because they produce oocytes for reproduction and also _____ hormones. The hormones secreted by the two ovaries are estrogen and _____, which stimulate the development of _____ sex characteristics and help to regulate reproduction.
pancreas glucagon gluc/o	**7.16** The islets of Langerhans are groups of cells in the _____, an organ that is located behind (posterior to) the stomach. The pancreas secretes insulin and _____, which help to regulate carbohydrate and sugar metabolism. The condition diabetes mellitus involves abnormal utilization of insulin. The term glucagon is made from the combining form for sugar: _____.
alongside of parathyroid parathyroid	**7.17** Recall that the prefix *para-* means _____ _____. Located alongside of the thyroid in the neck are the _____ glands. They secrete _____ hormone (PTH), which regulates calcium and phosphorus metabolism.
pineal serotonin melatonin	**7.18** Located in the center of the brain is the _____ gland, which secretes the neurotransmitter _____. Also secreted by the pineal is the substance _____. This hormone affects the onset of puberty.

ANSWERS	REVIEW
hypophysis below anterior posterior	**7.19** The pituitary gland, located at the base of the brain, secretes a long list of hormones. It is also called the _____, a term using the prefix *hypo-*, meaning _____ (or deficient), because it hangs below the hypothalamus part of the brain. The front subdivision of the pituitary gland is called the _____ pituitary, or the adenohypophysis. The rear subdivision is called the _____ pituitary, or the neurohypophysis.
thyroid corticotropic follicle, hormone	**7.20** The anterior pituitary secretes seven hormones that are often identified by their abbreviations. TSH is _____-stimulating hormone. ACTH is adreno_____ hormone. FSH is _____-stimulating hormone. LH is luteinizing _____.
growth stimulating before, prolactin	**7.21** Also secreted by the anterior pituitary are _____ hormone (GH) and melanocyte-_____ hormone (MSH). The hormone that stimulates breast development and milk during pregnancy (from the combining form *lact/o* meaning milk and the prefix *pro-* meaning _____) is called _____.
neurohypophysis antidiuretic promotes	**7.22** The posterior pituitary, also called the _____, secretes two hormones. ADH, or _____ hormone, influences the absorption of water in the kidney. (Note that diuretic drugs stimulate the body to excrete water; thus, the term antidiuretic would involve an action that _____ the retention of water.)
oxytocin	**7.23** The other hormone released by the posterior pituitary is _____, which stimulates uterine contractions during labor (childbirth).
testes testosterone testis	**7.24** In males, located within the scrotum are the _____, which are two glands that secrete a hormone affecting masculinization and reproduction: _____. The singular of testes is _____. The testes are also called the testicles.
thymus	**7.25** Located in the mediastinum above (superior) and anterior to the heart is the _____. This gland secretes thymosin, which regulates the immune response.
thyroid thyroxine calcitonin	**7.26** From the combining form *thyr/o*, the _____ gland is located in front of the neck and secretes three hormones. Triiodothyronine (T_3) and _____ (T_4) regulate metabolism. The third hormone, called _____, regulates calcium metabolism and is from the same combining form as calcium.

Self-Instruction: Symptomatic Terms

Study this table to prepare for the programmed review that follows.

TERM	MEANING
exophthalmos (see Figure 7-3) *ek-sof-thal′mos*	protrusion of one or both eyeballs, often because of thyroid dysfunction or a tumor behind the eyeball; also called *exophthalmus*
exophthalmus (see Figure 7-3) *ek-sof-thal′mŭs*	protrusion of one or both eyeballs, often because of thyroid dysfunction or a tumor behind the eyeball; also called *exophthalmos*
glucosuria *glū-kō-syū′rē-ă*	glucose (sugar) in the urine; also called *glycosuria*
glycosuria *glī′kō-syū′rē-ă*	glucose (sugar) in the urine; also called *glucosuria*
hirsutism *hĭr′sū-tizm*	shaggy; an excessive growth of hair, especially in unusual places (e.g., a woman with a beard)
hypercalcemia *hī′pĕr-kal-sē′mē-ă*	an abnormally high level of calcium in the blood
hypocalcemia *hī′pō-kal-sē′mē-ă*	an abnormally low level of calcium in the blood
hyperglycemia *hī′pĕr-glī-sē′mē-ă*	an abnormally high level of glucose in the blood
hypoglycemia *hī′pō-glī-sē′mē-ă*	an abnormally low level of glucose in the blood
hyperkalemia *hī′pĕr-kă-lē′mē-ă*	an abnormally high level of potassium in the blood (*kalium* = potassium)
hypokalemia *hī′pō-kă-lē′mē-ă*	deficient level of potassium in the blood
hypersecretion *hī′pĕr-se-krē′shŭn*	abnormally increased secretion
hyposecretion *hī′pō-se-krē′shŭn*	abnormally decreased secretion

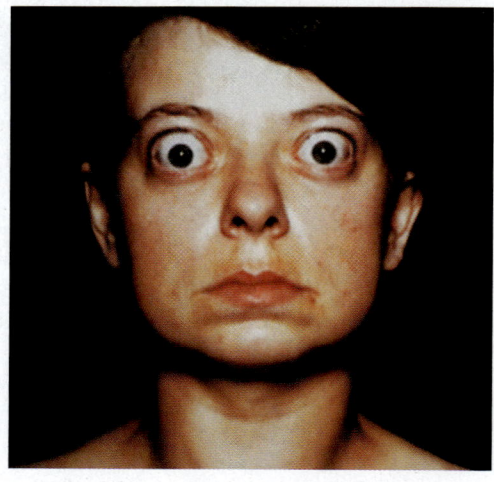

FIGURE 7-3 ■ Patient with exophthalmos.

TERM	MEANING
ketosis kē-tō′sis	presence of an abnormal amount of ketone bodies (acetone, beta-hydroxybutyric acid, and acetoacetic acid) in the blood and urine indicating an abnormal metabolism of carbohydrates, such as in uncontrolled diabetes and starvation (*keto* = alter); also called *ketoacidosis* and *diabetic ketoacidosis* (DKA)
ketoacidosis kē′tō-as-i-dō′sis	presence of an abnormal amount of ketone bodies (acetone, beta-hydroxybutyric acid, and acetoacetic acid) in the blood and urine indicating an abnormal metabolism of carbohydrates, such as in uncontrolled diabetes and starvation (*keto* = alter); also called *ketosis* and *diabetic ketoacidosis* (DKA)
diabetic ketoacidosis (DKA) dī′ă-bet′ik kē′tō-as-i-dō′sis	presence of an abnormal amount of ketone bodies (acetone, beta-hydroxybutyric acid, and acetoacetic acid) in the blood and urine indicating an abnormal metabolism of carbohydrates, such as in uncontrolled diabetes and starvation (*keto* = alter); also called *ketosis* and *ketoacidosis*
metabolism mě-tab′ō-lizm	all chemical processes in the body that result in growth, generation of energy, elimination of waste, and other body functions
polydipsia pol-ē-dip′sē-ă	excessive thirst
polyuria pol-ē-yū′rē-ă	excessive urination

Programmed Review: Symptomatic Terms

ANSWERS	REVIEW
away exophthalmos or exophthalmus	**7.27** One of the combining forms for eye is *ophthalm/o*. Recall that the prefix *ex-* means _____ or out. The term for the condition in which one or both eyeballs protrude, usually because of a thyroid dysfunction, is _____.
hirsutism condition of	**7.28** From the Latin word meaning shaggy (hirsutus), the term for an excessive growth of hair in an unusual place is _____. The suffix *-ism* means _____ ____.
metabolism after	**7.29** Using the same suffix (*-ism*), though not in reference to a medical condition in this case, the term for all chemical processes in the body involving growth and energy is _____. The prefix *meta-* means beyond, _____, or change. In this instance, metabolism refers to changes occurring in those chemical processes.

ANSWERS	REVIEW
	7.30 Recall that the combining form *ur/o* means
urine	_____, and that the suffix *-ia* means
condition of	_____ _____. The condition of glucose (sugar) in
glucosuria	the urine is called _____ or glycosuria.
many	**7.31** The prefix *poly-* means _____. The condition in which one urinates excessively many times
polyuria	is called _____.
	7.32 Using the same prefix (*-poly*) and suffix (*-ia*) as seen earlier, the term for the condition of excessive thirst
polydipsia	is _____.
	7.33 The most common prefix meaning above or
hyper-	excessive is _____. The opposite prefix, meaning
hypo-	below or deficient, is _____. These prefixes are used in many symptomatic terms related to levels of secretions and substances in the blood that are influenced by endocrine functions. Abnormally increased secretion
hypersecretion	is called _____, whereas abnormally
hyposecretion	decreased secretion is called _____.
	7.34 Recall that the suffix for a blood condition is
-emia	_____. An abnormally high blood level of calcium
hypercalcemia	is called _____, and an abnormally low
hypocalcemia	blood level of calcium is called _____.
	7.35 An abnormally low level of blood glucose is called
hypoglycemia	_____, whereas an abnormally high blood
hyperglycemia	glucose level is called _____.
	7.36 From the Latin root *kalium* for potassium, the term for an abnormally low level of potassium in the blood is
hypokalemia	_____, whereas an abnormally high level of
hyperkalemia	potassium in the blood is _____.
	7.37 The suffix *-osis* means condition or
increase	_____. The condition of an increased
ketosis	presence of ketone bodies is called _____, or
keto	_____ acidosis. The abbreviation DKA refers to diabetic
ketoacidosis	_____.

Self-Instruction: Diagnostic Terms

Study this table to prepare for the programmed review that follows.

TERM	MEANING
ADRENAL GLANDS	
Cushing syndrome (see Figure 7-4) *kush'ing sin'drōm*	a collection of signs and symptoms caused by an excessive level of cortisol hormone; may be due to excessive production by the adrenal gland (often because of a tumor), or, more commonly, occurs as a side effect of treatment with glucocorticoids (steroid hormones), such as prednisone for asthma, rheumatoid arthritis, lupus, or other inflammatory diseases; symptoms include upper body obesity, facial puffiness (moon-shaped appearance), hyperglycemia, weakness, thin and easily bruised skin with striae (stretch marks), hypertension, and osteoporosis
adrenal virilism *ă-drē'năl vir'i-lizm*	excessive output of the adrenal secretion of androgens (male sex hormones) in adult women caused by a tumor or hyperplasia (tissue enlargement); evidenced by amenorrhea (absence of menstruation), acne, hirsutism, and deepening of the voice (*virilis* = masculine)
PANCREAS	
diabetes mellitus (DM) *dī-ă-bē'tēz mel'i-tŭs*	metabolic disorder caused by the absence of or insufficient production of insulin secreted by the pancreas, resulting in hyperglycemia and glucosuria (*diabetes* = passing through; *mellitus* = sugar)
type 1 diabetes mellitus *tīp 1 dī-ă-bē'tēz mel'i-tŭs*	diabetes in which no beta-cell production of insulin occurs and the patient is dependent on insulin for survival; once known as *juvenile diabetes*
type 2 diabetes mellitus *tīp 2 dī-ă-bē'tēz mel'i-tŭs*	diabetes caused by either a lack of insulin or the body's inability to use insulin efficiently; patients may not require insulin replacement therapy to control the disorder if blood glucose level is controlled by diet and exercise

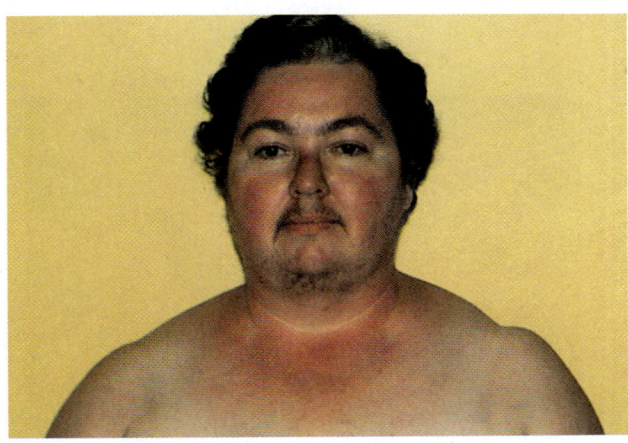

FIGURE 7-4 ■ Cushing syndrome. A patient with the characteristic upper body obesity and facial puffiness with a moon-shaped appearance is shown.

TERM	MEANING
hyperinsulinism hī′pĕr-in′sū-lin-izm	a condition resulting from an excessive amount of insulin in the blood that draws glucose out of the bloodstream, resulting in hypoglycemia, fainting, and convulsions; often caused by an overdose of insulin or by a tumor of the pancreas
pancreatitis pan′krē-ă-tī′tis	inflammation of the pancreas

PARATHYROID GLANDS

hyperparathyroidism hī′pĕr-par-ă-thī′royd-izm	hypersecretion of the parathyroid glands, usually caused by a tumor
hypoparathyroidism hī′pō-par-ă-thī′royd-izm	hyposecretion of the parathyroid glands

PITUITARY GLAND (HYPOPHYSIS)

acromegaly (see Figure 7-5) ak-rō-meg′ă-lē	disease characterized by enlarged features, especially of the face and hands, caused by hypersecretion of the pituitary growth hormone after puberty, when normal bone growth has stopped; most often caused by a pituitary tumor
gigantism (see Figure 7-6) jī′gan-tizm	a condition of hypersecretion of growth hormone during childhood bone development that leads to an abnormal overgrowth of bone, especially of the long bones; most often caused by a pituitary tumor; also called *giantism*

THYROID

goiter (see Figure 7-7) goy′tĕr	enlargement of the thyroid caused by thyroid dysfunction, tumor, lack of iodine in the diet, or inflammation (*goiter* = throat)
hyperthyroidism (hī-pĕr-thī′royd-izm	a condition of hypersecretion of thyroid hormone characterized by nervousness, weight loss, rapid pulse, protrusion of the eyeball (exophthalmos), and goiter. See Table 7-1.
Graves disease grāvz diz′ēz	the most common form of hyperthyroidism; caused by an autoimmune defect that creates antibodies that stimulate the overproduction of thyroid hormones; exophthalmos is a featured characteristic

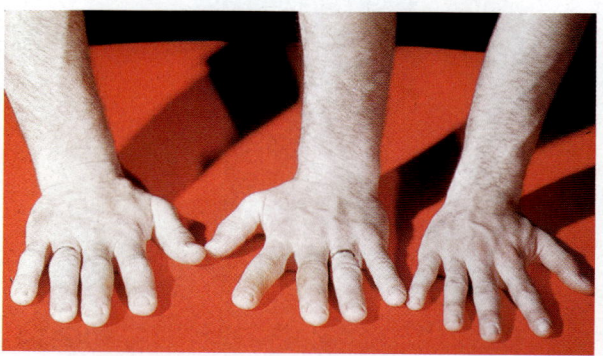

FIGURE 7-5 ■ Acromegaly. Enlarged hands of a person with acromegaly compared to the hand of a person without acromegaly (far right).

FIGURE 7-6 ■ Gigantism. A 22-year-old man with gigantism is shown next to his identical twin brother.

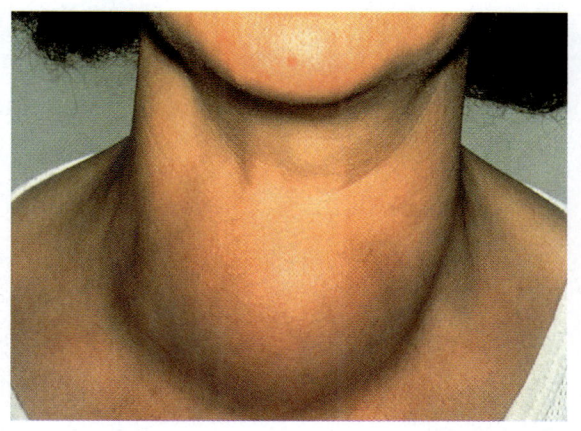

FIGURE 7-7 ■ Patient with goiter.

TERM	MEANING
hypothyroidism *hī′pō-thī′royd-izm*	a condition of hyposecretion of thyroid hormone resulting in sluggishness, slow pulse, and, often, obesity. See **Table 7-1**.
myxedema *mik-sĕ-dē′mă*	advanced hypothyroidism in adults characterized by sluggishness, slow pulse, puffiness in the hands and face, and dry skin (*myx* = mucus)
infantile hypothyroidism *in′făn-tīl hī′pō-thī′royd-izm*	condition of congenital hypothyroidism in children that results in a developmental disability and short physical stature; the thyroid is either congenitally absent or imperfectly developed

TABLE 7-1 Hyperthyroidism Versus Hypothyroidism

Hyperthyroidism	Hypothyroidism
Restless, nervous, irritable, fine tremor, insomnia	Lethargic, poor memory, slow, expressionless
Fine, silky hair with hair loss	Dry, brittle hair with hair loss
Warm, moist skin	Pale, cold, dry, and scaling skin
Increased perspiration	Decreased perspiration
Fast heart rate (tachycardia)	Slow heart rate (bradycardia)
Weight loss	Weight gain
Protrusion of the eyeball (exophthalmos)	Edema of the face and eyelids
Absence of menstruation (amenorrhea)	Heavy menstruation (menorrhagia)
Diffuse (whole gland) goiter	Thick tongue, slow speech

Programmed Review: Diagnostic Terms

ANSWERS	REVIEW
inflammation pancreatitis	**7.38** Recall that the suffix *-itis* means _____. Inflammation of the pancreas is called _____.
high glucose (sugar) diabetes mellitus 1, no insulin 2 resistance	**7.39** Most endocrine problems involve excessive or deficient secretion of hormones or the body's use of those hormones. The condition caused by the absence or insufficient production of insulin secreted by the pancreas resulting in hyperglycemia (_____ blood glucose) and glycosuria (_____ in the urine) is called _____ _____ (DM). Patients with type ____ diabetes mellitus produce ____ insulin and thereby are dependent on _____ for survival. Patients with type ____ diabetes mellitus produce insulin, but not enough, or have insulin _____ (a defective use of the insulin that is produced).
hyper- condition of hyperinsulinism hypoglycemia	**7.40** Recall that the prefix for excessive is _____, and that the suffix *-ism* refers to a _____ ____. The condition of having excessive insulin is called _____. This condition results in low blood glucose, which is called _____.
hypoparathyroidism hyperparathyroidism	**7.41** The terms for diagnostic conditions are formed from the combining form for the gland's name with the prefixes for deficient or excessive, referring to the gland's secretion. The condition of hyposecretion of the parathyroid glands is called _____, and hypersecretion of these glands is called _____.
hypothyroidism hyperthyroidism Graves exophthalmos or exophthalmus	**7.42** Similarly, hyposecretion of the thyroid gland is called _____, and hypersecretion of the thyroid gland is called _____. The most common form of hyperthyroidism is called _____ disease. A featured characteristic of Graves disease is the protrusion of the eyeballs, known as _____.

ANSWERS	REVIEW
infantile hypothyroidism	**7.43** Congenital hypothyroidism in children, characterized by reduced stature and poor mental development, is called _____ _____.
myxedema	**7.44** The term edema refers to a swollen body area caused by fluid retention. This root is used in the term for a form of advanced hypothyroidism in adults that involves swollen hands and face along with other symptoms: _____.
goiter	**7.45** The Latin word *guttur* means throat. The condition of an enlarged thyroid gland caused by thyroid dysfunction, tumor, or other causes, and characterized by the appearance of a swollen throat is _____.
Cushing	**7.46** Cortisol is a glucocorticoid hormone that is secreted by the adrenal gland. Excessive levels of cortisol, either caused by tumor or as a side effect of treatment with steroid hormones, result in a collection of signs and symptoms known as _____ syndrome.
andr/o, androgen adrenal virilism	**7.47** The adrenal glands also secrete a male sex hormone that is named using the combining form for male: _____. This hormone is called _____. Hypersecretion of androgen in adult women causes a condition that is named, in part, from the Latin word for masculine (virilis). This condition is called _____ _____.
enlargement acromegaly pituitary gigantism childhood hyper tumor	**7.48** The combining form *acr/o* refers to the extremities. Recall that the suffix *-megaly* means _____. The condition characterized by enlarged hands and face resulting from pituitary hypersecretion of growth hormone after puberty, when normal bone growth has stopped, is termed _____. The condition of hypersecretion of pituitary growth hormone during childhood bone development that leads to an abnormal overgrowth of bone, especially of the long bones, is called _____ _____. Acromegaly occurs in adulthood, and gigantism occurs in _____. Each is a result of _____ secretion of pituitary growth hormone, most often caused by a _____.

Self-Instruction: Diagnostic Tests and Procedures

Study this table to prepare for the programmed review that follows.

TEST OR PROCEDURE	EXPLANATION
LABORATORY TESTING	
blood sugar (BS) blŭd shu-găr	measurement of the level of sugar (glucose) in the blood; also called *blood glucose*
blood glucose blŭd glū′kōs	measurement of the level of sugar (glucose) in the blood; also called *blood sugar*
fasting blood sugar (FBS) fast-ing blŭd shu′găr	measurement of blood sugar (glucose) level after fasting (not eating) for 12 hours
postprandial blood sugar (PPBS) pōst-pran′dē-ăl blŭd shu-găr	measurement of blood sugar (glucose) level after a meal (commonly 2 hours later)
glucose tolerance test (GTT) glū′kōs tol′ĕr-ănts test	measurement of the body's ability to metabolize carbohydrates by administering a prescribed amount of glucose after a fasting period, then measuring blood and urine for glucose levels every hour thereafter for 4 to 6 hours
glycohemoglobin (HbAlc) glī′kō-hē-mō-glō′bin	a molecule (fraction) in hemoglobin, the level of which rises in the blood as a result of an increased level of blood sugar (glucose); a common blood test used in diagnosing and treating diabetes; also called *glycosylated hemoglobin* (HbA1c)
glycosylated hemoglobin (HbAlc) glī′kō-si-lāt-ĕd hē-mō-glō′bin	a molecule (fraction) in hemoglobin, the level of which rises in the blood as a result of an increased level of blood sugar (glucose); a common blood test used in diagnosing and treating diabetes; also called *glycohemoglobin* (HbA1c)
electrolyte panel ē-lek′trō-līt păn′el	measurement of the level of specific ions (sodium, potassium, and chloride) along with carbon dioxide (CO_2) (for indirect measure of bicarbonate ion) in the blood; electrolytes are essential for maintaining water balance (hydration) as well as nerve, muscle, and heart activity
thyroid function study thī′royd fŭnk′shŭn stŭd′el	measurement of thyroid hormone levels in blood plasma to determine the efficiency of glandular secretions, including T_3, T_4, and TSH
urine sugar and ketone studies yūr′in shu′găr and kē′tōn stŭd′ēz	chemical tests to determine the presence of sugar (glucose) or ketone bodies in urine; used as a screen for diabetes
IMAGING PROCEDURES	
computed tomography (CT) kom-pyū′tĕd tō-mog′ră-fē	CT of the head is used to obtain a transverse (horizontal) view of the pituitary gland

CHAPTER 7 • ENDOCRINE SYSTEM

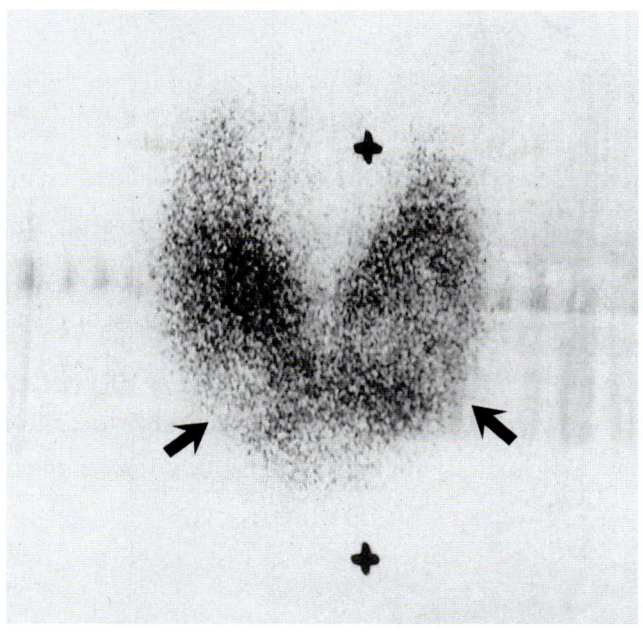

FIGURE 7-8 ■ Thyroid uptake and image detecting the presence of multiple nodules (*arrows*).

TEST OR PROCEDURE	EXPLANATION
magnetic resonance imaging (MRI) măg-nĕt′ik rĕz′ō-nănts im′ă-jing	nonionizing images of magnetic resonance are useful in identifying abnormalities of the pituitary gland, pancreas, adrenal glands, and thyroid
sonography sŏ-nŏg′ră-fē	sonographic images are used to identify endocrine pathology, such as with thyroid ultrasound
thyroid uptake and image (see Figure 7-8) thī′royd ŭp′tāk and im′ăj	radionuclide (nuclear medicine) scan of the thyroid to visualize the radioactive accumulation of previously injected isotopes to detect thyroid nodules or tumors

Programmed Review: Diagnostic Tests and Procedures

ANSWERS	REVIEW
glucose	**7.49** Several laboratory tests are used to diagnose problems in the endocrine system. Because diabetes is a serious and common disorder, blood sugar levels are particularly important for diagnostic purposes. Measurement of the level of sugar (glucose) in the blood is simply called a blood sugar (BS), or blood _____.
fasting blood sugar	**7.50** A measurement of the blood sugar level after a 12-hour fast is called a _____ _____ _____ (FBS).

ANSWERS	REVIEW
post-	**7.51** The prefix meaning "after" or "behind" is _____. The Latin word *prandium* means a meal. The medical adjective formed from these two parts is used when referring to a blood sugar test performed approximately 2 hours after a meal: _____ _____ _____ (PPBS).
postprandial blood sugar	
glucose tolerance test	**7.52** A more complex blood sugar test measures the body's ability to metabolize carbohydrates. Glucose is administered after a fasting period, and blood and urine glucose levels are measured hourly thereafter to determine how well the body tolerates this glucose. This is called a _____ _____ _____ (GTT).
glycohemoglobin HbA1c	**7.53** Another type of blood sugar test that examines the effect of blood sugar on hemoglobin is called a _____ test. This test is also known as a glycosylated hemoglobin (_____) test.
electrolyte	**7.54** The Greek word *lytos* means soluble (as in any substance that dissolves in water or blood). Some ions conduct electricity when they are dissolved. These substances are called electrolytes. Proper electrolyte levels are essential for balanced body function. Measurement of the level of specific ions, such as sodium and potassium, are part of an _____ panel.
thyroid function	**7.55** The laboratory study that measures thyroid hormone levels in the blood to determine how well the thyroid is functioning is called a _____ _____ study.
urine sugar ketone void	**7.56** Chemical measurements of sugar and ketones in the urine, which are used as a screen for diabetes, are called _____ _____ and _____ studies. Production of a urine specimen for these tests requires one to urinate or _____ (empty the bladder).
computed tomography	**7.57** In addition to these laboratory tests, several imaging procedures are used to diagnose endocrine disorders. The type of x-ray imaging using a computer to create a transverse view, such as of the pituitary gland, is called _____ _____ (CT).
magnetic resonance imaging	**7.58** Nonionizing images using _____ _____ _____ (MRI) may be used to identify abnormalities in several glands.

ANSWERS	REVIEW
son/o recording sonography	7.59 Recall that the combining form meaning sound is _____. The suffix *-graphy* refers to the process of _____. The imaging modality using very high sound frequencies to record images of the endocrine glands is called _____.
thyroid uptake image	7.60 A test of the thyroid involves injection of radioactive isotopes that are taken up in the thyroid, leading to production of a nuclear image. This is called a _____ _____ and _____.

Self-Instruction: Operative Terms

Study this table to prepare for the programmed review that follows.

TERM	MEANING
adrenalectomy ă-drē-năl-ek′tŏ-mē	removal of one or both adrenal glands
hypophysectomy hī′pof-i-sek′tŏ-mē	removal of the pituitary gland
pancreatectomy pan′krē-ă-tek′tŏ-mē	removal of the pancreas
parathyroidectomy pa′ră-thī-roy-dek′tŏ-mē	removal of the parathyroid glands
thymectomy thī-mek′tŏ-mē	removal of the thymus
thyroidectomy thī-roy-dek′tŏ-mē	removal of the thyroid

Programmed Review: Operative Terms

ANSWERS	REVIEW
removal adrenalectomy	7.61 Recall that the suffix *-ectomy* means _____. The removal of the adrenal gland is called an _____.
pancreatectomy	7.62 The surgical removal of the pancreas is called a _____.
thyroidectomy	7.63 The removal of the thyroid is called a _____.
parathyroid	7.64 A parathyroidectomy is the removal of the _____ glands.

ANSWERS	REVIEW
thymectomy	7.65 The removal of the thymus is called a _____.
hypophysis hypophysectomy	7.66 Recall that the pituitary gland is also called the _____. That combining form is used in the term for removal of the pituitary gland: _____.

Self-Instruction: Therapeutic Terms

Study this table to prepare for the programmed review that follows.

TERM	MEANING
continuous subcutaneous insulin infusion (CSII) (see Figure 7-9) kon-tin′yū-ŭs sŭb-kyū-tā′nē-ŭs in′sŭ-lin in-fyū′zhŭn	use of an insulin delivery device that is worn on the body (usually the abdomen) and subcutaneously infuses doses of insulin programmed according to the individual needs of the diabetic patient; also called *insulin pump therapy*
insulin pump therapy (see Figure 7-9) in′sŭ-lin pŭmp thār′ă-pē	use of an insulin delivery device that is worn on the body (usually the abdomen) and subcutaneously infuses doses of insulin programmed according to the individual needs of the diabetic patient; also called *continuous subcutaneous insulin infusion* (CSII)
radioiodine therapy rā′dē-ō-ī′ō-dīn thār′ă-pē	use of radioactive iodine to treat disease, such as to eradicate thyroid tumor cells; treatment is administered in a nuclear medicine facility

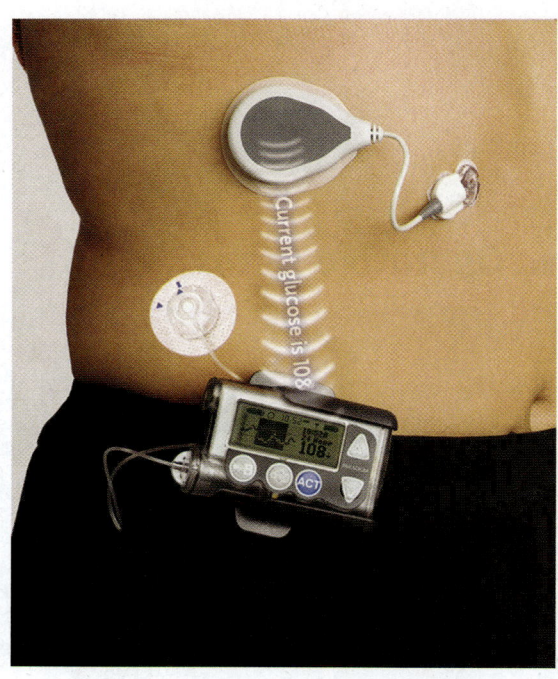

FIGURE 7-9 ■ Abdominal placement of an insulin pump (continuous subcutaneous insulin infusion).

TERM	MEANING
COMMON THERAPEUTIC DRUG CLASSIFICATIONS	
antidiabetic drug an-tē-dī-ă-bet′ ik drŭg	any of several agents used to control blood glucose levels in treatment of diabetes mellitus
antithyroid drug an-tē-thī′ royd drŭg	an agent that blocks the production of thyroid hormones; used to treat hyperthyroidism
hormone replacement therapy (HRT) hōr′ mōn rē-plās′ ment thār′ ă-pē	treatment with a hormone to correct a hormonal deficiency (e.g., estrogen, testosterone, and thyroid)
hypoglycemic hī′ pō-glī-sē′ mik	a drug that lowers the blood glucose level (e.g., insulin); also called *antihyperglycemic*
antihyperglycemic an′ tē-hī′ per-glī-sē′ mik	a drug that lowers the blood glucose level (e.g., insulin); also called *hypoglycemic*

Programmed Review: Therapeutic Terms

ANSWERS	REVIEW
continuous subcutaneous insulin infusion 1 diabetes mellitus	**7.67** An insulin pump is a device that subcutaneously infuses programmed doses of insulin through the skin. This therapy, which is called _____ _____ _____ _____ (CSII), is used in the treatment of type ___ _____ _____ (DM).
radioiodine nuclear	**7.68** Because the thyroid absorbs iodine, radioactive iodine that is administered into the body becomes localized in the thyroid, where it can kill thyroid tumor cells. This is called _____ therapy, and it is administered in a _____ medicine facility.
anti- antidiabetic -emia hyperglycemia antihyperglycemic hypoglycemic	**7.69** Drug classifications are often named by their action against some process or condition in the body. The prefix meaning *against* is _____. Any agent that works against the ill effects of diabetes mellitus by controlling blood glucose levels in called an _____ drug. The suffix for a blood condition is _____. Recall that the condition of high blood glucose is called _____. A drug that works against this condition by lowering the blood glucose level is an _____ drug. Another term for this is a _____ drug.

ANSWERS	REVIEW
antithyroid	**7.70** An agent that blocks the production of thyroid hormones is called an _____ drug.
hormone replacement therapy	**7.71** A patient with a deficiency of a particular hormone may be treated by administration of that hormone to replace what is missing. This treatment is referred to as _____ _____ _____ (HRT).

Chapter 7 Abbreviations

ABBREVIATION	EXPANSION
ACTH	adrenocorticotropic hormone
ADH	antidiuretic hormone
BS	blood sugar
CO_2	carbon dioxide
CSII	continuous subcutaneous insulin infusion
CT	computed tomography
DKA	diabetic ketoacidosis
DM	diabetes mellitus
FBS	fasting blood sugar
FSH	follicle-stimulating hormone
GH	growth hormone
GTT	glucose tolerance test
HbA1c	glycosylated hemoglobin
HRT	hormone replacement therapy
LH	luteinizing hormone
MRI	magnetic resonance imaging
MSH	melanocyte-stimulating hormone
OXT	oxytocin
PPBS	postprandial blood sugar
PRL	prolactin
PTH	parathyroid hormone
T_3	triiodothyronine
T_4	thyroxine
TSH	thyroid-stimulating hormone
VP	vasopressin

PRACTICE EXERCISES

For each of the following words, write out the term parts (prefixes [P], combining forms [CF], roots [R], and suffixes [S]) on the lines below the word. Then define the term according to the meaning of its parts.

EXAMPLE

parathyroid

para / thyr / oid

P   R   S

DEFINITION: alongside of/thyroid gland/resembling

1. adenitis

    _____ / _____
        R   S

    DEFINITION: _____

2. hyperglycemia

    _____ / _____ / _____
        P   R   S

    DEFINITION: _____

3. thyrotoxicosis

    _____ / _____ / _____
       CF   R   S

    DEFINITION: _____

4. polydipsia

    _____ / _____ / _____
        P   R   S

    DEFINITION: _____

5. hormonal

    _____ / _____
        R   S

    DEFINITION: _____

6. ketosis

    _____ / _____
        R   S

    DEFINITION: _____

7. polyuria

    _____ / _____ / _____
        P   R   S

    DEFINITION: _____

8. endocrine

    _____ / _____ / _____
        P   R   S

    DEFINITION: _____

9. thyroptosis

   _____ / _____
   CF   S

   DEFINITION: _____

10. thymoma

    _____ / _____
    R   S

    DEFINITION: _____

Write the correct medical term for each of the following definitions.

11. _____ advanced hypothyroidism in adults

12. _____ congenital hypothyroidism

13. _____ most common form of hyperthyroidism

14. _____ condition resulting from an excessive level of cortisol hormone characterized by obesity, hyperglycemia, and weakness

15. _____ disease characterized by enlarged features, caused by hypersecretion of the pituitary growth hormone after puberty

Write the letter of the matching term in the space after the meaning.

16. congenital hypothyroidism _____   a. gigantism
17. polydipsia _____   b. hirsutism
18. hyperthyroidism _____   c. enlarged thyroid
19. hypophysis _____   d. depends on insulin
20. goiter _____   e. infantile hypothyroidism
21. adult hypothyroidism _____   f. pituitary
22. adrenal virilism _____   g. does not usually depend on insulin
23. type 2 diabetes _____   h. excessive thirst
24. pituitary hypersecretion _____   i. myxedema
25. type 1 diabetes _____   j. Graves disease

Complete each medical term by writing the missing part.

26. poly_____ia = excessive thirst

27. _____secretion = abnormally increased secretion

28. _____glycemia = low blood glucose

29. glucos_____ = glucose in the urine

30. _____secretion = decreased secretion

Write out the expanded term for each abbreviation.

31. CSII _____
32. HRT _____
33. FBS _____
34. DM _____
35. PPBS _____

Write the correct terms for the anatomic structures indicated.

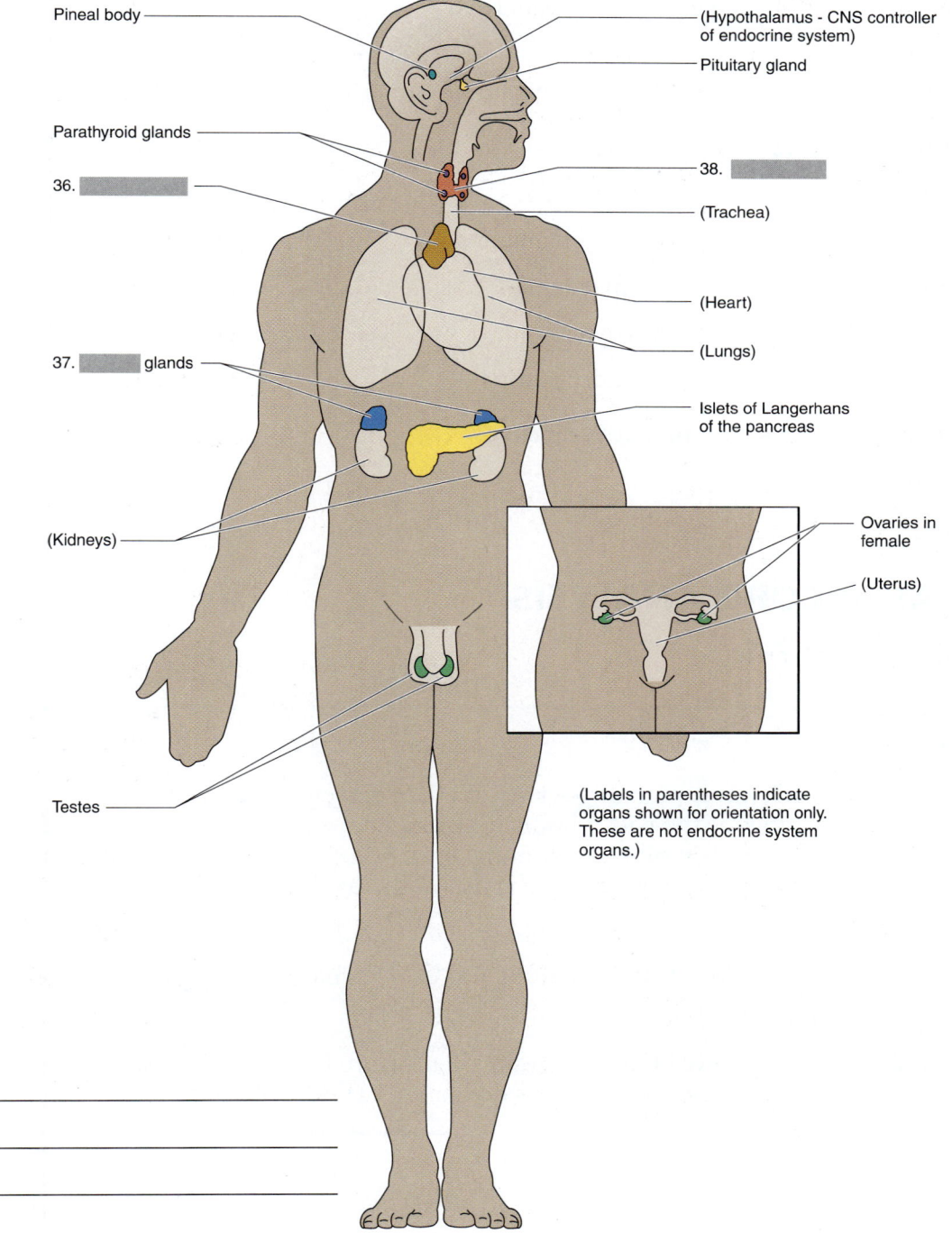

36. _____
37. _____
38. _____

Circle the meaning that corresponds to the combining form given.

39. adren/o
    a. male
    b. extremity
    c. adrenal gland

40. thyr/o
    a. nourishment
    b. shield
    c. chest

41. crin/o
    a. blue
    b. cell
    c. secrete

42. gluc/o
    a. stomach
    b. sugar
    c. pancreas

43. dips/o
    a. thirst
    b. ketones
    c. secrete

Circle the correct spelling.

44. a. hirsutism   b. hirsuitism   c. hirsitism
45. a. exopthalmos   b. exopthamamos   c. exophthalmos
46. a. myexedema   b. mixedema   c. myxedema
47. a. goiter   b. goyter   c. goitir
48. a. androgenius   b. androgenous   c. andreogenous

Give the noun that is used to form each adjective.

49. metabolic _____
50. diabetic _____

MEDICAL RECORD ANALYSIS
Medical Record 7-1

PROGRESS NOTE

S: This is a 27 y.o. female with a known Hx of diabetes seen in the ER with nausea and vomiting for the past 3 hours. She has skipped two doses of her insulin because BS levels monitored at home have been low. She is now experiencing a cephalalgia similar to what she has had in the past before coma.

O: T 35.5°C, P 90, R 2 0, BP 126/68

Lab blood sodium 130, potassium 4.1, CO_2 9, chloride 102, glucose 296 studies:

A: Diabetic ketoacidosis

P: Admit to ICU: give 10 units insulin IV; measure BS 1° p̄ insulin given, then q4h; check urine for sugar and ketosis q void; repeat electrolytes in AM.

Questions About Medical Record 7-1

1. What is the CC?
   a. nausea, vomiting, and headache
   b. nausea, vomiting, and dizziness
   c. nausea, vomiting, and high blood pressure
   d. nausea, vomiting, and ringing in the ears
   e. nausea, vomiting, and unconsciousness

2. What is the diagnosis?
   a. hyperglycemia
   b. hypoglycemia
   c. type 1 DM with ketone bodies in the blood
   d. type 2 DM without ketone bodies in the blood
   e. combination of hyperglycemia and glucosuria

3. Where will the patient be admitted?
   a. neuropsychiatric facility
   b. coronary care facility
   c. emergency room
   d. recovery room
   e. intensive care unit

4. Which of the following are electrolytes?
   1. sodium 2. potassium 3. chloride 4. glucose
   a. only 1, 2, and 3 are electrolytes
   b. only 1 and 3 are electrolytes
   c. only 2 and 4 are electrolytes
   d. only 4 is an electrolyte
   e. all are electrolytes

5. Why were the blood electrolyte studies performed?
   a. to examine the electrical impulses of the brain
   b. to measure the level of ions in the blood in evaluation of metabolism
   c. to measure hormone levels and determine glandular efficiency
   d. to visualize the accumulation of radioactive isotopes to eliminate the presence of tumor
   e. to measure the level of glucose in the blood

6. How should the insulin be administered?
   a. within the skin
   b. absorption through unbroken skin
   c. within the muscle
   d. within the vein
   e. under the skin

7. How often should the blood glucose be measured?
   a. 1 hour after insulin administration, then every 4 hours thereafter
   b. once each morning
   c. each time the patient urinates
   d. 1 hour before insulin administration, then four times a day thereafter
   e. 1 hour before insulin administration, then every 4 hours thereafter

ANSWERS TO PRACTICE EXERCISES

1. adenitis
   R: aden
   S: itis
   DEFINITION: gland/inflammation

2. hyperglycemia
   P: hyper
   R: glyc
   S: emia
   DEFINITION: above or excessive/sugar/blood condition

3. thyrotoxicosis
   CF: thyro
   R: toxic
   S: osis
   DEFINITION: thyroid gland (shield)/poison/condition or increase

4. polydipsia
   P: poly
   R: dips
   S: ia
   DEFINITION: many/thirst/condition of

5. hormonal
   R: hormon
   S: al
   DEFINITION: hormone (an urging on)/pertaining to

6. ketosis
   R: ket
   S: osis
   DEFINITION: ketone bodies/condition or increase

7. polyuria
   P: poly
   R: ur
   S: ia
   DEFINITION: many/urine/condition of
8. endocrine
   P: endo
   R: crin
   S: e
   DEFINITION: within/to secrete/noun marker
9. thyroptosis
   CF: thyro
   S: ptosis
   DEFINITION: thyroid gland (shield)/falling or downward displacement
10. thymoma
    R: thym
    S: oma
    DEFINITION: thymus gland/tumor
11. myxedema
12. infantile hypothyroidism
13. Graves disease
14. Cushing syndrome
15. acromegaly
16. e
17. h
18. j
19. f
20. c
21. i
22. b
23. g
24. a
25. d
26. polydipsia
27. hypersecretion
28. hypoglycemia
29. glucosuria
30. hyposecretion
31. continuous subcutaneous insulin infusion
32. hormone replacement therapy
33. fasting blood sugar
34. diabetes mellitus
35. postprandial blood sugar
36. thymus
37. adrenal
38. thyroid
39. adrenal gland
40. shield
41. secrete
42. sugar
43. thirst
44. hirsutism
45. exophthalmos
46. myxedema
47. goiter
48. androgenous
49. metabolism
50. diabetes

ANSWERS TO MEDICAL RECORD 7-1

1. a
2. c
3. e
4. a
5. b
6. d
7. a

BLOOD AND LYMPHATIC SYSTEM

Learning Outcomes

After completing this chapter, you should be able to:

- Define term parts related to blood and the lymphatic system.
- Identify key blood and lymphatic system anatomic structures with their functions.
- Define symptomatic and diagnostic terms related to blood and the lymphatic system.
- Explain diagnostic tests; procedures; and operative and therapeutic terms related to blood and the lymphatic system.
- Cite common abbreviations related to blood and the lymphatic system and give the expansion of each.
- Explain terms used in medical records involving blood and the lymphatic system.

BLOOD AND LYMPHATIC SYSTEM OVERVIEW

The blood:

- Transports oxygen, nutrients, and hormones to body cells
- Carries wastes and carbon dioxide away from the cells

The lymphatic system:

- Protects the body by filtering microorganisms and foreign particles from the lymph, a clear fluid collected from body tissues
- Supports the activities of the lymphocytes in the immune response

- Maintains the body's internal fluid environment as an intermediary between the blood in the capillaries and tissue cells
- Carries fats away from digestive organs

Self-Instruction: Combining Forms

Study this table to prepare for the programmed review that follows.

COMBINING FORM	MEANING
blast/o (also a suffix, -blast)	germ or bud
chrom/o	color
chromat/o	color
chyl/o	juice
cyt/o	cell
hem/o	blood
hemat/o	blood
immun/o	immune, resistant
lymph/o	clear fluid
morph/o	form
myel/o	bone marrow or spinal cord
phag/o	eat or swallow
plas/o	formation
reticul/o	a net
splen/o	spleen
thromb/o	clot
thym/o	thymus

Programmed Review: Combining Forms

ANSWERS	REVIEW
blast/o	8.1 The combining form meaning *germ* or *bud* is _____, as in the term blastogenesis, which refers to the origin or production of cells by budding. The suffix from this combining
-blast	form is _____. Hemocytoblasts (a term formed from the
blood	combination of *-blast* with *hem/o* meaning _____ and *cyt/o*,
cell	meaning _____) are the primitive stem cells in the bone marrow that develop into blood cells. An erythroblast develops
red	into an erythrocyte, or a _____ blood cell.

CHAPTER 8 • BLOOD AND LYMPHATIC SYSTEM

ANSWERS	REVIEW
chromat/o color condition of	**8.2** The combining form *chrom/o* or _____ means _____. For example, chromone refers to plant pigments. Recall that the suffix *-ism* means _____ __; therefore, chromatism is a condition of abnormal pigmentation.
juice blood chyle	**8.3** The combining form *chyl/o* means _____ or fluid. Chyle is a pale yellow fluid from the intestine that is carried by the lymphatic system. The suffix *-emia* refers to a _____ condition; thus, chylemia means the presence of _____ in the blood.
hemat/o hem/o formation blood	**8.4** Hematology, a term made from the combining form _____, meaning blood, is the medical study of the blood. Another combining form for blood is _____, as in hemostat, which is an agent or device that stops the flow of blood from a vessel. Recall that the suffix *-poiesis* means _____. Therefore, hemopoiesis refers to the process of formation and development of various types of _____ cells.
immun/o immunocompromised	**8.5** The combining form meaning immune or resistant is _____. The immune system helps the body resist infectious disease. Both the blood and lymphatic systems are involved in the immune system. Someone whose immune system has been compromised by disease is said to be _____.
clear lymphoma	**8.6** The combining form *lymph/o* means _____ fluid. Lymph is a clear fluid, collected from body tissues, that flows through lymphatic vessels and, eventually, into the venous blood circulation. Using the suffix that means *tumor*, a neoplasm of the lymphatic system is called a _____.
eat cell eats condition of	**8.7** The combining form *phag/o* means _____ or swallow. The suffix *-cyte* refers to a _____. A phagocyte therefore is a cell that _____ bacteria, foreign particles, and other cells. Using the suffix *-osis*, which generally means increase or _____ __, phagocytosis is the process or condition of phagocytes ingesting other solid substances.

ANSWERS	REVIEW
formation without condition of	**8.8** *Plas/o* is a combining form meaning _____. Using the prefix *a-*, meaning _____, and the suffix *-ia*, meaning _____ _____, aplasia is a condition in which a formation (tissue or organ) is absent or defective.
form study of	**8.9** *Morph/o* is a combining form meaning _____. Combined with *-logy*, the suffix meaning _____ _____, morphology is the study of form, including the size and shape of a specimen, such as blood cells.
myel/o cell bone marrow	**8.10** The combining form referring to either bone marrow or the spinal cord is _____. Bone marrow is the tissue within the cavities of bones, where many types of blood cells are produced. Combined with *cyt/o*, which is the combining form meaning _____, a myelocyte is an immature blood cell in the _____ _____.
net erythro reticulo red	**8.11** *Reticul/o* is a combining form meaning a _____. A network of substances influences the development of red blood cells from a primitive _____blast (red bud or germ) to a _____cyte (from the combining form meaning a net). Reticulocytes are immature _____ blood cells, or erythrocytes.
splen/o enlargement spleen splenectomy	**8.12** The spleen is a key organ of the lymphatic system. It filters the blood and performs other functions. The combining form for spleen is _____. Recalling that the suffix *-megaly* means _____, splenomegaly is an enlarged _____. Use the common suffix for excision or removal to construct the word that means the removal of the spleen: _____.
cell thromb/o, clot	**8.13** Thrombocytes, or platelets, are blood _____ fragments that function to clot the blood. The combining form meaning clot is _____. A thrombus is a blood _____ inside a blood vessel.
thym/o thymoma	**8.14** The thymus is a gland in the lymphatic system; the term comes from the combining form _____. A tumor of thymus tissue is called a _____.

Self-Instruction: Anatomic Terms in Whole Blood

Study this table to prepare for the programmed review that follows.

TERM	MEANING
TERMS RELATED TO BLOOD FLUID (see Figure 8-1)	
blood *blŭd*	circulating tissue of the body consisting of fluid with formed elements (red blood cells, white blood cells, and platelets) suspended in the fluid
plasma *plaz'mă*	liquid portion of the blood and lymph; contains water, proteins, and cellular components (i.e., white blood cells, red blood cells, and platelets)
serum *sēr'ŭm*	liquid portion of the blood that remains after clotting
CELLULAR COMPONENTS OF THE BLOOD (see Figure 8-2)	
red blood cell (RBC) *red blŭd sel*	transports oxygen and carbon dioxide; also called *erythrocyte*
erythrocyte *ĕ-rith'rō-sīt*	transports oxygen and carbon dioxide; also called *red blood cell*
hemoglobin *hē-mō-glō'bin*	the protein–iron compound in erythrocytes that transports oxygen and carbon dioxide

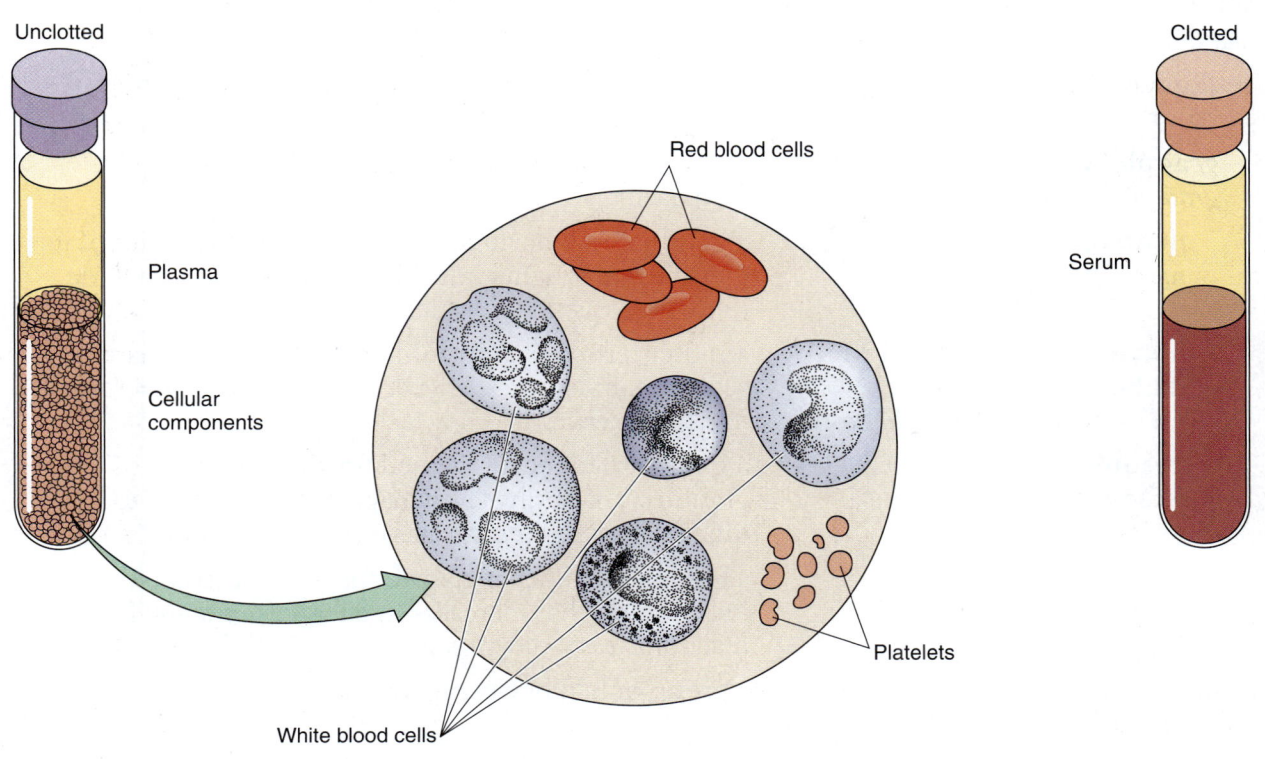

FIGURE 8-1 ■ Components of whole blood.

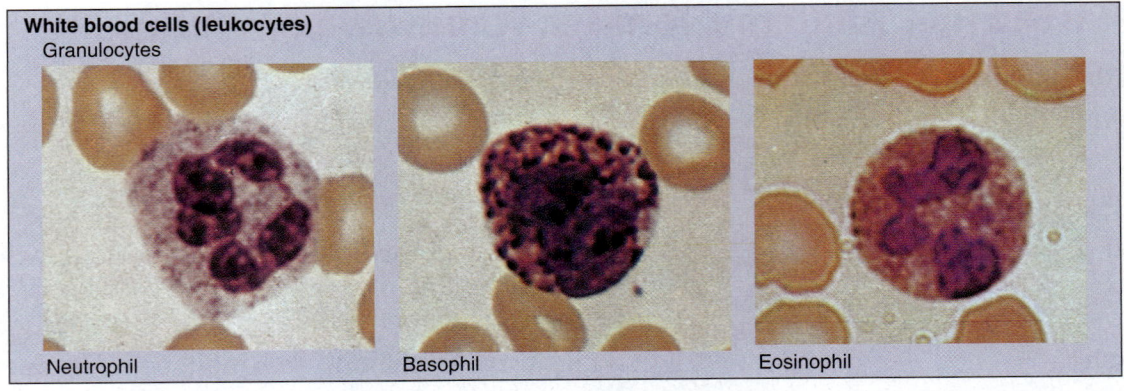
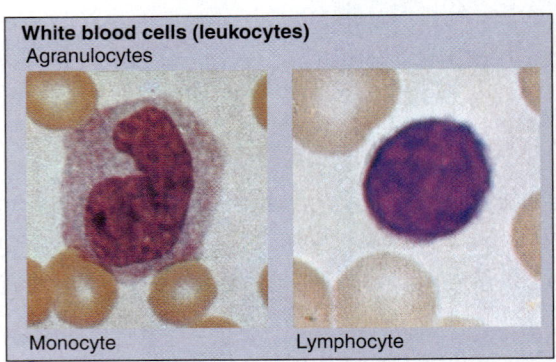
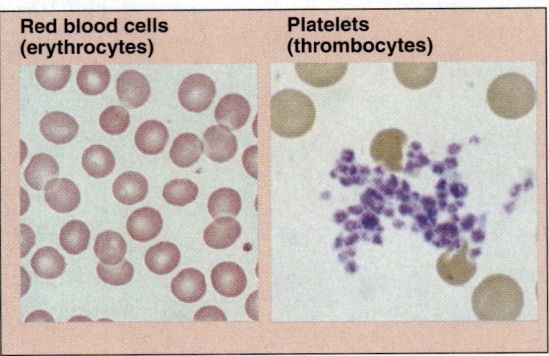

FIGURE 8-2 ■ Cellular components of the blood.

TERM	MEANING
white blood cell wīt blŭd sel	protects the body from harmful invading substances; also called *leukocyte*
leukocyte lū′kō-sīt	protects the body from harmful invading substances; also called *white blood cell*
granulocytes gran′yū-lō-sītz	a group of leukocytes containing granules in their cytoplasm
neutrophil nū′trō-fil	a granular leukocyte, named for the neutral stain of its granules, that fights infection by swallowing bacteria (phagocytosis) (*neutr* = neither; *phil* = attraction for)
polymorphonuclear (PMN) leukocyte pol′ē-mōr′fō-nū′klē-ăr lū′kō-sīt	another term for neutrophil, referring to the many segments in its nucleus (*poly* = many; *morpho* = form; *nucleus* = kernel)
basophil bā′sō-fil	a granular leukocyte, named for the dark stain of its granules, that brings anticoagulant substances to inflamed tissues (*baso* = base; *phil* = attraction for)
eosinophil ē-ō-sin′ō-fil	a granular leukocyte, named for the rose-colored stain of its granules, that increases in allergic and some infectious reactions (*eos* = dawn-colored [rosy]; *phil* = attraction for)
agranulocytes ā-grăn′ū-lō-sītz	a group of leukocytes without granules in their nuclei
monocyte mon′ō-sīt	an agranulocytic leukocyte that performs phagocytosis to fight infection (*mono* = one)

TERM	MEANING
lymphocyte *lim′ fō-sīt*	an agranulocytic leukocyte that is active in the process of immunity; the three categories of lymphocytes are T cells (thymus-dependent), B cells (bone marrow–derived), and natural killer (NK) cells
platelets *plāt′ lets*	cell fragments in the blood that are essential for blood clotting (coagulation); also called *thrombocytes*

Programmed Review: Anatomic Terms in Whole Blood

ANSWERS	REVIEW
plasma serum	**8.15** The liquid portion of the blood and lymph is called _____. The plasma contains proteins, cells, and other substances. After blood clots, the liquid portion that remains is called _____.
cell red red, cell hemoglobin blood	**8.16** Recall that *-cyt/o* is a combining form meaning _____, and that *erythr/o* is a combining form meaning _____. Therefore, an erythrocyte is a _____ blood _____. Erythrocytes transport oxygen and carbon dioxide. Oxygen and carbon dioxide bond to the protein–iron compound contained in the erythrocytes, which is called _____ (from the combining form *hem/o*, meaning _____).
white leukocyte granulocytes, without agranulocytes	**8.17** The combining form *leuk/o* means _____; thus, a white blood cell is a _____. There are many types of leukocytes in the blood, but they can be divided into two general categories: those with granules in their cytoplasm and those without granules in their cytoplasm. Leukocytes with granules are called _____. Because the prefix *a-* means _____, the term for leukocytes without granules is _____.
eosinophil basophil	**8.18** Several types of leukocytes are named according to how they appear when stained, or by which stain they attract (*phil* = attraction for). A neutrophil is a leukocyte in which the granules stain neutrally or without color; a neutrophil has an attraction for neither (*neutr*) color stain. An _____ is a leukocyte in which the granules stain (attract) a rose color (*eos* = rosy color). Finally, another type of leukocyte has granules that stain (attract) a dark base color (*baso* = base); this type is called a _____.

ANSWERS	REVIEW
polymorphonuclear	**8.19** Another term for a neutrophil is _____ (PMN) leukocyte. This term comes from the many segments in the nucleus.
lymphocyte infection	**8.20** An agranulocytic leukocyte in the lymphatic system that is active in the process of immunity is called a _____. A monocyte, which is another agranulocytic leukocyte, performs phagocytosis to fight _____.
platelet clot clotting	**8.21** Another term for a thrombocyte is _____. The combining form *thromb/o* means _____; therefore, platelets function in blood _____.

Self-Instruction: Anatomic Terms in the Lymphatic System

Study this table to prepare for the programmed review that follows (see **Figure 8-3**).

TERM	MEANING
ORGANS OF THE LYMPHATIC SYSTEM	
lymphatic system lim-fat′ik sis′tĕm	consists of lymph vessels, nodes, and tissues through which lymph drains into the blood
thymus thī′mŭs	primary gland of the lymphatic system, located within the mediastinum, that helps to maintain the body's immune response by producing T lymphocytes
spleen splēn	organ between the stomach and the diaphragm that filters out aging blood cells, removes cellular debris by phagocytosis, and provides an environment for lymphocytes to initiate immune responses
STRUCTURES OF THE LYMPHATIC SYSTEM	
lymph limf	fluid that is circulated through the lymph vessels
lymph capillaries limf kap′i-lār-ēz	microscopic vessels that draw lymph from tissues to the lymph vessels
lymph vessels limf ves′ĕlz	vessels that receive lymph from the lymph capillaries and circulate it to the lymph nodes; also called *lymphatic vessels*
lacteals lak′tē-ălz	specialized lymph vessels in the small intestine that absorb fat into the bloodstream (*lacteus* = milky)
chyle kīl	white or pale yellow substance in lymph that contains fatty substances absorbed by the lacteals
lymph nodes limf nōdz	many small, oval structures that filter lymph from the lymph vessels; major locations include the cervical, axillary, and inguinal regions

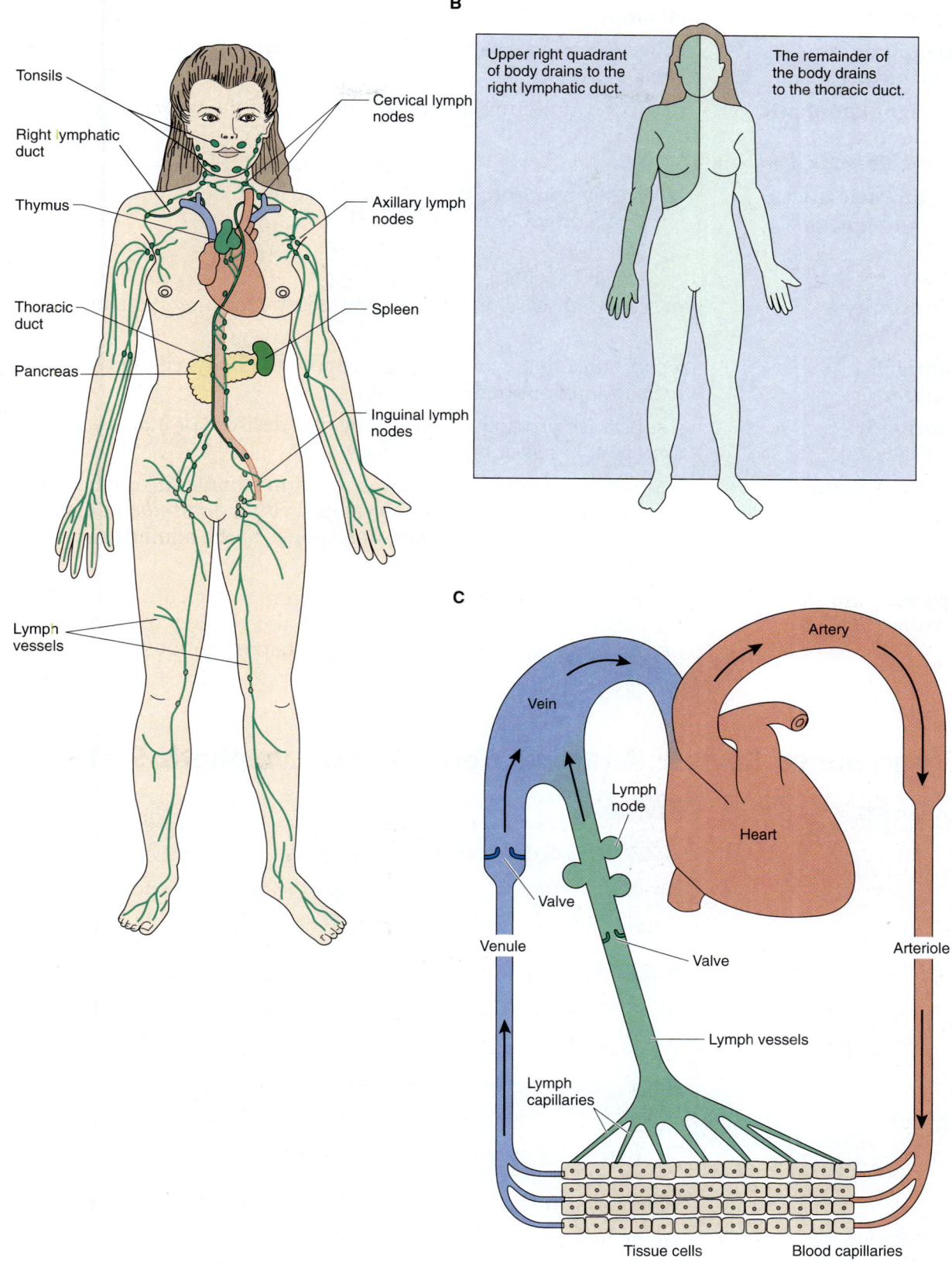

FIGURE 8-3 ■ **Lymphatic system. A. Lymphatic structures. B. Lymph drainage. C. Blood and lymph circulation.**

TERM	MEANING
lymph ducts limf dŭktz	collecting channels that carry lymph from the lymph nodes to the veins
right lymphatic duct rīt lim-fat′ik dŭkt	receives lymph from the right upper part of the body
thoracic duct thō-ras′ik dŭkt	receives lymph from the left side of the head, neck, chest, abdomen, left arm, and lower extremities
IMMUNITY	
immunity i-myū′ni-tē	process of disease protection induced by exposure to an antigen
antigen an′ti-jen	a substance that, when introduced into the body, causes the formation of antibodies against it
antibody an′tē-bod-ē	a substance produced by the body that destroys or inactivates an antigen that has entered the body
active immunity ak′tiv i-myū′ni-tē	a long-lasting immunity that results from stimulating the body to produce its own antibodies; developed either *naturally*, in response to an infection, or *artificially*, in response to the administration of a vaccine
passive immunity pas′iv i-myū′ni-tē	a short-lasting immunity that results from foreign antibodies that are conveyed either *naturally*, through the placenta to a fetus, or *artificially*, by injection of a serum containing antibodies

Programmed Review: Anatomic Terms in the Lymphatic System

ANSWERS	REVIEW
thymus thym/o	8.22 Located in the mediastinum, the _____ is a gland that produces T lymphocytes for the body's immune response. This term comes from the combining form _____.
spleen splenectomy	8.23 Aging blood cells are filtered out in the _____, which also removes cellular debris by phagocytosis. The removal of this organ is called a _____.
lymph clear	8.24 The fluid circulating through the lymph vessels is called _____. The meaning of the combining form *lymph/o* reminds us that this fluid is _____.
capillaries	8.25 The microscopic vessels that draw lymph from body tissues to the lymph vessels are called lymph _____. The same term is used in the cardiovascular system for the tiny vessels connecting arteries and veins.

CHAPTER 8 • BLOOD AND LYMPHATIC SYSTEM

ANSWERS	REVIEW
lacteals chyle	**8.26** In addition to lymph capillaries, which collect lymph from body tissues, special lymph vessels in the intestine, called _____, absorb fat. This liquid in lymph absorbed by the lacteals is called _____.
nodes ducts, lymphatic thoracic extremities	**8.27** Lymph vessels carry lymph to the lymph _____, which filter the lymph. Lymph is then carried from the lymph nodes to the veins via lymph _____. The right _____ duct receives lymph from the right upper part of the body, and the _____ duct receives lymph from the left side of the head, neck, chest, left arm, and lower _____.
antibody immunity antigen, antibody	**8.28** The body protects itself from infectious disease in several ways. An antigen is a substance that, when introduced into the body, causes formation of an _____ against it. This process of disease protection is called _____. Exposure to an _____ starts the process, and the _____ destroys or inactivates the antigen.
active passive	**8.29** Antibodies that develop naturally, after contracting an infection, or artificially, after administering a vaccine, result in _____ immunity. Antibodies that are conveyed naturally through the placenta to a fetus result in _____ immunity. The difference between active and passive in this case is whether the body itself actively makes the antibodies or passively receives them from outside.

Self-Instruction: Symptomatic Terms

Study this table to prepare for the programmed review that follows.

TERM	MEANING
RELATED TO BLOOD	
microcytosis (see **Figure 8-4**) mī′krō-sī-tō′sis	presence of small red blood cells
hypochromic (see **Figure 8-4**) hī′pō-krō′mik	pale in color; lighter in color than normal
macrocytosis (see **Figure 8-5**) mak′rō-sī-tō′sis	presence of large red blood cells

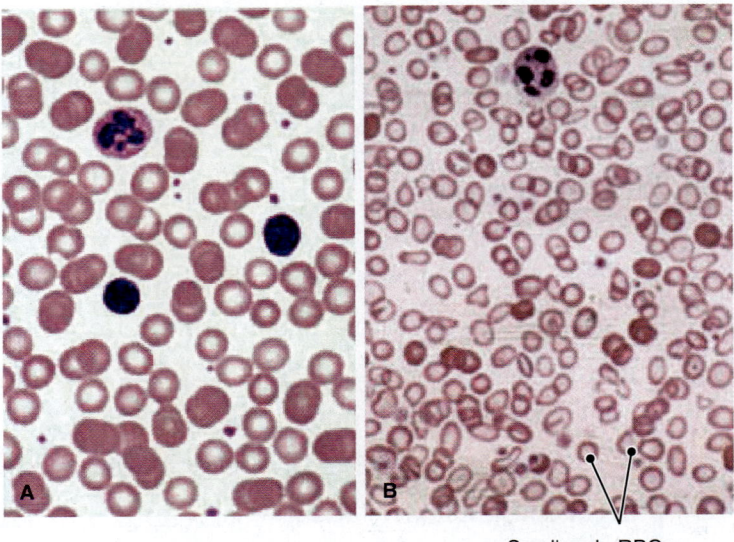

FIGURE 8-4 ■ The blood in iron deficiency anemia. **A.** Normal blood smear. **B.** Microcytic (small) and hypochromic (pale) red blood cells (RBCs).

TERM	MEANING
anisocytosis *an-ī′sō-sī-tō′sis*	presence of red blood cells of unequal size (*an* = not, without; *iso* = equal)
poikilocytosis *poy′ki-lō-sī-tō′sis*	presence of large, irregularly shaped red blood cells (*poikilo* = irregular)
reticulocytosis *re-tik′ū-lō-sī-tō′sis*	an increased number of immature erythrocytes in the blood

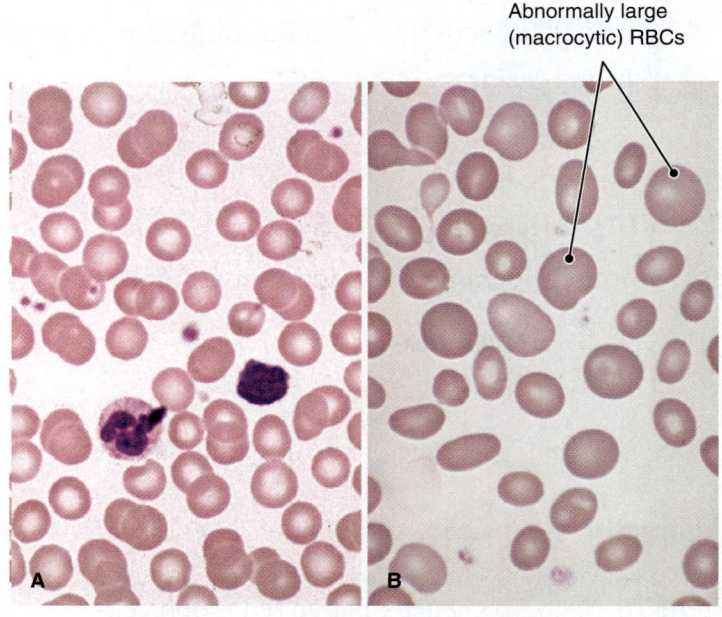

FIGURE 8-5 ■ The blood in pernicious anemia. **A.** Normal blood smear. **B.** Macrocytic (abnormally large) red blood cells (RBCs).

TERM	MEANING
erythropenia ĕ-rith-rō-pē′nē-ă	an abnormally reduced number of red blood cells
lymphocytopenia lim′fō-sī-tō-pē′nē-ă	an abnormally reduced number of lymphocytes
neutropenia nū′trō-pē′nē-ă	a decreased number of neutrophils
pancytopenia pan′sī-tō-pē′nē-ă	an abnormally reduced number of all cellular components in the blood
thrombocytopenia throm′bō-sī-tō-pē′nē-ă	an abnormally decreased number of platelets in the blood, impairing the clotting process
hemolysis hē-mol′i-sis	breakdown of the red blood cell membrane

RELATED TO THE LYMPHATIC SYSTEM

immunocompromised im′yū-nō-kom′prō-mīzd	impaired immunologic defenses caused by an immunodeficiency disorder or by therapy with immunosuppressive agents
immunosuppression im′yū-nō-sŭ-presh′ŭn	impaired ability to provide an immune response
lymphadenopathy lim-fad′ĕ-nop′ă-thē	enlarged (diseased) lymph nodes
splenomegaly splē-nō-meg′ă-lē	enlargement of the spleen

Programmed Review: Symptomatic Terms

ANSWERS	REVIEW
increase cytosis macrocytosis	8.30 The suffix -*osis* can mean either a *condition of* or an _____. In either case, the suffix is used with symptomatic terms to indicate an abnormal or unusual condition. The presence of small red blood cells is called micro_____, and the presence of large red blood cells is called _____.
anisocytosis poikilocytosis	8.31 Red blood cells also may be present in unequal sizes. The presence of red blood cells of unequal size (*aniso* = unequal) is termed _____. The presence of large, irregularly shaped (*poikilo* = irregular) red blood cells is called _____.

ANSWERS	REVIEW
net	**8.32** The combining form *reticul/o* means _____. As mentioned previously, a reticulocyte is a young red blood cell (so named because of the network of substances in the cell). The condition of an increased number of immature erythrocytes in the blood is called _____.
reticulocytosis	
reduction	**8.33** Recall that the suffix *-penia* means an abnormal _____. Several symptomatic terms involving blood cells are formed with this suffix. An abnormally reduced number of lymphocytes is called _____. An abnormal reduction in the number of platelets (thrombocytes) is termed _____. An abnormally reduced number of erythrocytes can be termed erythrocytopenia, but the shorter term, _____, is generally used.
lymphocytopenia	
thrombocytopenia	
erythropenia	
all	**8.34** The prefix *pan-* means _____. An abnormally reduced number of all types of blood cells is therefore called _____. Like the shorter term erythropenia, the term for a reduced number of neutrophils uses just one combining form with the suffix *-penia*: _____.
pancytopenia	
neutropenia	
-lysis	**8.35** The suffix meaning breakdown or dissolution is _____. The term for the breakdown of the red blood cell membrane uses the combining form for blood (in effect, the blood itself breaks down): _____.
hemolysis	
immunosuppression	**8.36** Some drugs or disease states suppress the body's ability to provide an immune response; this is called _____. A patient with impaired immunologic defenses caused by a disorder or by immunosuppressive agents is said to be _____.
immunocompromised	
lymphadenopathy	**8.37** The combining form *path/o* simply means *disease*, as in the term pathology. The combining form *aden/o* means gland or node. A disease state in which lymph nodes are enlarged is called _____.
enlargement	**8.38** The symptomatic suffix *-megaly* refers to an _____. An enlarged spleen, which may result from several different diseases, is called _____.
splenomegaly	

Self-Instruction: Diagnostic Terms

Study this table to prepare for the programmed review that follows.

TERM	MEANING
acquired immunodeficiency syndrome (AIDS) ă-kwīrd' im'yŭ-nō-dē-fish'en-sē sin'drōm	a syndrome caused by the human immunodeficiency virus (HIV) that renders immune cells ineffective, permitting opportunistic infections, malignancies, and neurologic diseases to develop; transmitted sexually or through contaminated blood
anemia ă-nē'mē-ă	a condition of reduced numbers of red blood cells, hemoglobin, or packed red cells in the blood, resulting in a diminished ability of red blood cells to transport oxygen to the tissues
aplastic anemia ā-plas'tik ă-nē'mē-ă	a normocytic-normochromic type of anemia characterized by the failure of bone marrow to produce red blood cells

iron deficiency anemia
     (see Figure 8-4)
     ī'ĕrn de-fish'en-sē ă-nē'mē-ă
	a microcytic-hypochromic type of anemia characterized by a lack of iron that affects the production of hemoglobin and is characterized by small red blood cells containing low amounts of hemoglobin

pernicious anemia
     (see Figure 8-5)
     pĕr-nish'ŭs ă-nē'mē-ă
	a macrocytic-normochromic type of anemia characterized by an inadequate supply of vitamin B_{12}, causing red blood cells to become large, varied in shape, and reduced in number

autoimmune disease aw-tō-i-myūn' di-zēz'	any disorder characterized by abnormal function of the immune system that causes the body to produce antibodies against itself, resulting in tissue destruction or loss of function; rheumatoid arthritis and lupus are examples of autoimmune diseases (*auto* = self)
erythroblastosis fetalis ĕ-rith'rō-blas-tō'sis fē-tă'lis	a disorder that results from the incompatibility of a fetus with Rh-positive blood and a mother with Rh-negative blood, causing red blood cell destruction in the fetus; a blood transfusion is necessary to save the fetus
Rh factor r-h fak'tōr	the antigen on the surface of red blood cells of the Rh blood group system; its presence can cause a reaction between Rh-positive blood and Rh-negative blood; Rh is derived from Rhesus monkey, in which the antigen was first observed
Rh positive (Rh$^+$) r-h poz'i-tiv	presence of antigens
Rh negative (Rh$^-$) r-h neg'ă-tiv	absence of antigens
hemochromatosis hē'mō-krō-mă-tō'sis	hereditary disorder with an excessive buildup of iron deposits in the body
hemophilia hē-mō-fil'ē-ă	a group of hereditary bleeding disorders caused by a defect in clotting factors necessary for the coagulation of blood

TERM	MEANING
leukemia lū-kē′mē-ă	chronic or acute malignant (cancerous) disease of the blood-forming organs, characterized by abnormal leukocytes in the blood and bone marrow
myelodysplasia mī′ĕ-lō-dis-plā′zē-ă	disorder within the bone marrow characterized by a proliferation of abnormal stem cells (cells that give rise to different types of blood cells); usually develops into a specific type of leukemia
lymphoma lim-fō′mă	any neoplastic disorder of lymph tissue, usually malignant, as in Hodgkin disease
metastasis mĕ-tas′tă-sis	process by which cancer cells are spread by blood or lymph circulation to a distant organ; the plural form, metastases, indicates spreading to two or more distant sites
mononucleosis mon′ō-nū-klē-ō′sis	condition caused by the Epstein–Barr virus (EBV) and characterized by an increase in mononuclear cells (monocytes and lymphocytes) in the blood along with enlarged lymph nodes (lymphadenopathy), fatigue, and sore throat (pharyngitis)
polycythemia pol′ē-sī-thē′mē-ă	increased number of erythrocytes and hemoglobin in the blood
septicemia sep-ti-sē′mē-ă	systemic disease caused by infection with microorganisms and their toxins in circulating blood

Programmed Review: Diagnostic Terms

ANSWERS	REVIEW
acquired immunodeficiency syndrome	**8.39** AIDS is the acronym for _____ _____ _____, which is caused by the human immunodeficiency virus (HIV).
without anemia iron deficiency pernicious aplastic	**8.40** The prefix *an-* means _____ or reduction. The general term for a blood condition in which there is a reduction in the number of red blood cells, hemoglobin, or the volume of packed red blood cells is _____. Several types of anemia are common. Anemia characterized by a lack of iron, affecting the production of hemoglobin, is called _____ _____ anemia. Anemia characterized by an inadequate supply of vitamin B_{12} is called _____ anemia. Another type is described by the term formed in part by *a-* (without) and *plas/o* (formation): _____ anemia.

ANSWERS	REVIEW
immune resistant autoimmune	**8.41** *Auto-*, a prefix meaning self, is used in combination with *immun/o*, the combining form meaning _____ or _____, to name the disorder characterized by abnormal function of the immune system that causes the body to produce antibodies against itself: _____ disease.
erythroblastosis fetalis factor Rh negative	**8.42** A disorder resulting from incompatibility of a fetus with Rh-positive blood and a mother with Rh-negative blood, named in part because of the large number of erythroblasts that are found in the fetal blood, is called _____ _____. The Rh _____ is said to be positive when Rh antigens are present on the surface of red blood cells. The absence of such antigens is called _____ _____.
hemochromatosis	**8.43** One hereditary blood disorder results in an excessive buildup of iron deposits in the body. Because this condition can cause skin pigmentation changes, the term used to describe it uses the combining form meaning color and the combining form meaning blood. This condition is called _____.
clotting	**8.44** Hemophilia is a group of hereditary bleeding disorders with a defect in _____ factors necessary for coagulation.
blood leukemia formation myelodysplasia	**8.45** The diagnostic suffix *-emia* refers to a _____ condition. A malignant blood disease marked by abnormal white blood cells (leukocytes) is called _____. A disorder in the bone marrow that usually develops into leukemia is built from the combining form *myel/o*, meaning bone marrow; the prefix *dys-*, meaning faulty; and the suffix *-plasia*, meaning a condition of _____. This disorder is called _____.
many, polycythemia	**8.46** Also built with the suffix *-emia,* the term for an increase in hemoglobin and the number of erythrocytes in the blood begins with the prefix *poly-*, which means _____. This disorder is called _____.

ANSWERS	REVIEW
-oma lymphoma	**8.47** Recall that the suffix meaning *tumor* is _____. A tumor of lymph tissue is called a _____.
beyond metastasis	**8.48** The prefix *meta-* means _____, after, or change. The term for the spread of cancer cells beyond the original site of the tumor through blood or lymph is _____.
mononucleosis increase	**8.49** Monocytes and lymphocytes are mononuclear cells. The viral condition characterized by an increase in both types is called _____. The suffix *-osis* means condition of or _____.
septicemia	**8.50** Sepsis is from the Greek word for putrefaction, indicating infection. A systemic condition caused by infection in the blood is therefore termed _____.

Self-Instruction: Diagnostic Tests and Procedures

Study this table to prepare for the programmed review that follows.

TEST OR PROCEDURE	EXPLANATION
BLOOD STUDIES	
phlebotomy fle-bot′ŏ-mē	incision into or puncture of a vein to withdraw blood for testing; also called *venotomy*
venotomy vē-not′ŏ-mē	incision into or puncture of a vein to withdraw blood for testing; also called *phlebotomy*
blood chemistry blŭd kem′is-trē	test of the fluid portion of blood to measure the amounts of its chemical constituents (e.g., glucose and cholesterol)
blood chemistry panels blŭd kem′is-trē păn′elz	specialized batteries of automated blood chemistry tests performed on a single sample of blood; used as a general screen for disease or to target specific organs or conditions (e.g., metabolic panel, lipid panel, and arthritis panel)
basic metabolic panel (BMP) bā′sik met-ă-bol′ik păn′el	battery of tests used as a general screen for disease; includes tests for calcium, carbon dioxide (CO_2), chloride, creatinine, glucose, potassium, sodium, and blood urea nitrogen (BUN)

comprehensive metabolic panel (CMP)
    (see **Figure 8-6**)
    kom-prē-hen′siv met-ă-bol′ik păn′el
	tests performed in addition to the basic panel for expanded screening: albumin, bilirubin, alkaline phosphatase, protein, alanine aminotransferase (ALT), and aspartate aminotransferase (AST)

```
CENTRAL MEDICAL CENTER
211 Medical Center Drive • Central City, US  90000-1234 • PHONE:  (012) 125-6784 • FAX:  (012) 125-9999

11/02/20xx
14:27


NAME    : TEST, PATIENT     LOC: TEST         DOB: 02/03/xx        AGE: 38Y
MR#     : TEST-221                                                 SEX: M
ACCT#   : H111111111


M63561 COLL: 11/02/20xx  13:24      REC: 11/02/20xx  13:25

  COMPREHENSIVE METABOLIC PANEL

  Blood Urea Nitrogen               *30          [5 - 25]          mg/dl
  (BUN)
    Sodium                          139          [135 - 153]       mEq/L
    Potassium                       4.2          [3.5 - 5.3]       mEq/L
    Chloride                        105          [101 - 111]       mEq/L
    Carbon Dioxide (CO₂)            27           [24 - 31]         mmol/L
    Glucose, Random                 *148         [70 - 110]        mg/dl
    Creatinine                      *1.5         [< 1.5]           mg/dl
    SGOT (AST)                      18           [10 - 42]         U/L
    SGPT (ALT)                      *8           [10 - 60]         U/L
    Alkaline Phosphatase            58           [42 - 121]        U/L
    Total Protein                   6.5          [6.0 - 8.0]       G/dl
    Albumin                         3.7          [3.5 - 5.0]       G/dl
    Amylase                         33           [< 129]           U/L
    Bilirubin, Total                0.7          [< 1.5]           mg/dl
    Calcium, Total                  9.7          [8.6 - 10.6]      mg/dl


  TEST, PATIENT    TEST-221                 END OF REPORT                     PAGE 1
  11/02/20xx  14:27

  INTERIM REPORT COMPLETED
```

FIGURE 8-6 ■ Comprehensive metabolic panel report. Normal ranges are in brackets [ ].

TEST OR PROCEDURE	EXPLANATION
blood culture *blŭd kŭl′chĕr*	test to determine if infection is present in the bloodstream by isolating a specimen of blood in an environment that encourages the growth of microorganisms; the specimen is observed, and the organisms that grow in the culture are identified
CD4 cell count *c-d-fōr sel kownt*	a measure of the number of cluster of differentiation (CD4) cells (a subset of T lymphocytes) in the blood; used in monitoring the course of HIV and in timing the treatment of AIDS; the normal adult range is 600–1,500 cells in a given volume of blood
erythrocyte sedimentation rate (ESR) *ĕ-rith′rō-sīt sed′i-men-tā′shŭn rāt*	timed test that measures the rate at which red blood cells settle through a volume of plasma
partial thromboplastin time (PTT) *par′shăl throm-bō-plas′tin tīm*	test to determine coagulation defects, such as platelet disorders
thromboplastin *throm-bō-plas′tin*	substance present in tissues, platelets, and leukocytes that is necessary for coagulation

TEST OR PROCEDURE	EXPLANATION
prothrombin time (PT) *prō-throm'bin tīm*	test to measure activity of prothrombin in the blood
prothrombin *prō-throm'bin*	protein substance in the blood that is essential to the clotting process
complete blood count (CBC) (see **Figure 8-7**) *kom-plēt' blŭd kownt*	a common laboratory blood test performed as a screen of general health or for diagnostic purposes and typically includes the component tests that follow; test results are usually reported along with normal values so that the clinician can interpret the results based on the instrumentation used by the laboratory; normal ranges also may vary depending on the region and climate
white blood count (WBC) *wīt blŭd kownt*	a count of the number of white blood cells in a given volume of blood obtained via manual or automated laboratory methods

---

CENTRAL MEDICAL CENTER
211 Medical Center Drive • Central City, US 90000-1234 • PHONE: (012) 125-6784 • FAX: (012) 125-9999

11/02/20xx
14:27

NAME   : TEST, PATIENT   LOC: TEST   DOB: 2/2/xx   AGE: 27Y
MR#   : TEST-221   SEX: M
ACCT#   : H111111111

M63558 COLL: 11/2/20xx 13:23   REC: 11/2/20xx 13:24

HEMOGRAM
CBC
```
  WBC        *11.5      [4.5 - 10.5]       K/UL
  RBC         5.84      [4.6 - 6.2]        M/UL
  HGB        17.2       [14.0 - 18.0]      G/DL
  HCT        50.8       [42.0 - 52.0]      %
  MCV        87         [82 - 92]          FL
  MCH        29.5       [27 - 31]          PG
  MCHC       33.9       [32 - 36]          G/DL
  PLT       202         [150 - 450]        K/UL


  Auto Lymph %    15       [20 - 40]       %
  Auto Mono %      2       [1 - 11]        %
  Auto Neutro %   82       [50 - 75]       %
  Auto Eos %       1       [0 - 6]         %
  Auto Baso %      0       [0 - 2]         %
  Auto Lymph #     1.7     [1.5 - 4.0]     K/UL
  Auto Mono #      0.2     [0.2 - 0.9]     K/UL
  Auto Neutro #    9.4     [1.0 - 7.0]     K/UL
  Auto Eos #       0.1     [0 - 0.7]       K/UL
  Auto Baso #      0.0     [0 - 0.2]       K/UL
```

TEST, PATIENT   TEST-221   END OF REPORT   PAGE 1
11/02/20xx   14:27   INTERIM REPORT

INTERIM REPORT COMPLETE

FIGURE 8-7 ■ Complete blood count (CBC) report. Normal ranges are in brackets [ ].

TEST OR PROCEDURE	EXPLANATION
red blood count (RBC) rĕd blŭd kownt	a count of the number of red blood cells in a given volume of blood obtained via manual or automated laboratory methods
hemoglobin (HGB or Hgb) hē-mō-glō′bin	a test to determine the blood level of hemoglobin (expressed in grams)
hematocrit (HCT or Hct) hē-mat′ō-krit	a measurement of the percentage of packed red blood cells in a given volume of blood
blood indices blŭd in′di-sēz	calculations of RBC, HGB, and HCT results to determine the average size, hemoglobin concentration, and content of red blood cells to classify an anemia (Note: in the entries below, the term corpuscular pertains to a blood cell)
mean corpuscular (cell) volume (MCV) mēn kōr-pŭs′kū-lăr (sel) vol′yŭm	calculation of the volume (size) of individual red blood cells using HCT and RBC results: MCV = HCT/RBC
mean corpuscular (cell) hemoglobin (MCH) mēn kōr-pŭs′kū-lăr (sel) hē-mō-glō′bin	calculation of the content (weight) of hemoglobin in the average red blood cell using HGB and RBC results: MCH = HGB/RBC
mean corpuscular (cell) hemoglobin concentration (MCHC) mēn kōr-pŭs′kū-lăr (sel) hē-mō-glō′bin kon-sen-trā′shŭn	calculation of the average hemoglobin concentration in each red blood cell using HGB and HCT results: MCHC = HGB/HCT
differential count dif-ĕr-en′shăl kownt	determination of the number of each type of white blood cell (leukocyte) in a stained blood smear; each type is counted and reported as a percentage of the total examined Type of Leukocyte Normal Range lymphocytes: 25–33% monocytes: 3–7% neutrophils: 54–75% eosinophils: 1–3% basophils: 0–1%
red cell morphology rĕd sel mōr-fol′-jē	as part of identifying and counting the white blood cells, the condition, size, and shape of red blood cells in the background of the smeared slide are noted (e.g., anisocytosis, poikilocytosis)
platelet count (PLT) plāt′let kownt	calculation of the number of thrombocytes in the blood; the normal adult range is 150,000–450,000 platelets in a given volume of blood

TEST OR PROCEDURE	EXPLANATION
BONE AND LYMPH STUDIES	
bone marrow aspiration (see **Figure 8-8**) bōn mar′ō as-pi-rā′shŭn	needle aspiration of bone marrow tissue for pathologic examination
bone marrow biopsy bōn mar′ō bī′op-sē	pathologic examination of bone marrow tissue
lymphangiogram lim-fan′jē-ō-gram	an x-ray image of a lymph node or lymph vessel obtained after injection of a contrast dye
DIAGNOSTIC IMAGING	
computed tomography (CT) kom-pyū′tĕd tō-mog′ra-fē	full body x-ray CT images are used to detect tumors and cancers such as lymphoma
positron-emission tomography (PET) poz′i-tron ē-mish′ŭn tō-mog′ră-fē	scanning technique combining nuclear medicine and computed tomography technology to produce images of anatomy and metabolic function within the body; useful in determining the recurrence of cancers or to measure response to therapy; commonly used in evaluating lymphoma

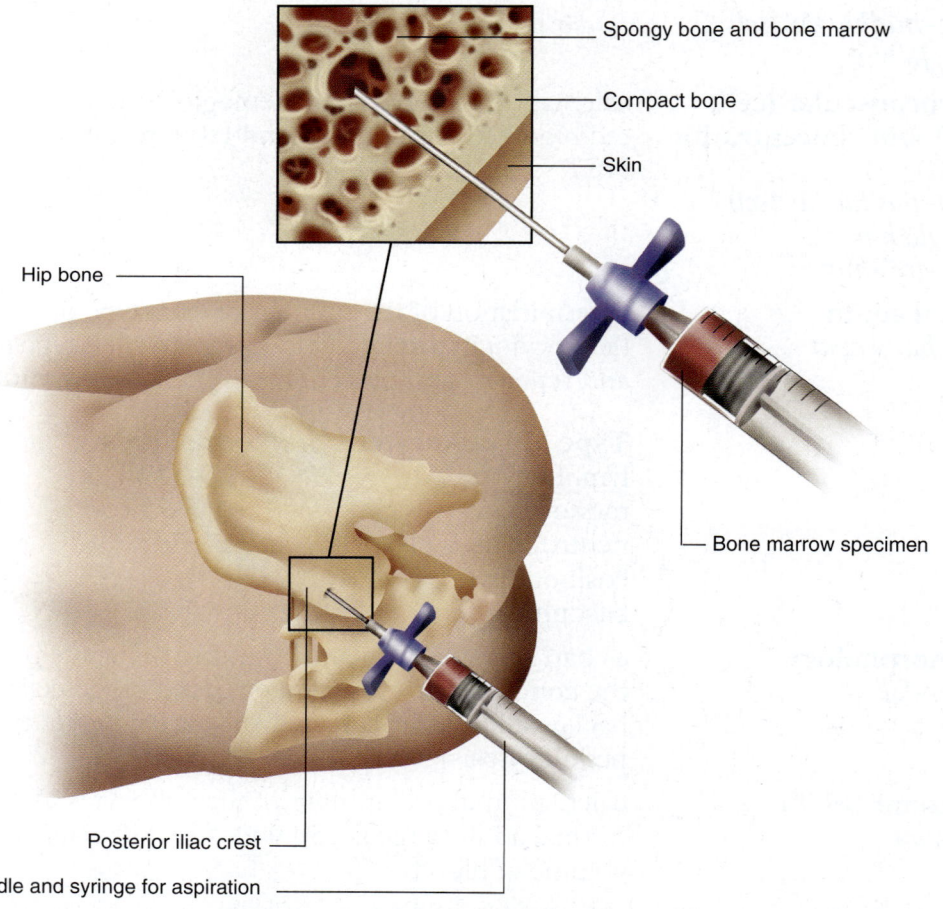

FIGURE 8-8 ■ Bone marrow aspiration. Posterior view of the pelvic region showing a common site for bone marrow aspiration.

Programmed Review: Diagnostic Tests and Procedures

ANSWERS	REVIEW
venotomy, phlebotomy incision	**8.51** Blood studies are tests performed with samples of blood. The blood sample, often drawn by a phlebotomist, is obtained through a needle puncture (or incision) of a vein, which is called a _____ or a _____. Recall that the suffix *-tomy* refers to an _____.
chemistry panel metabolic comprehensive metabolic panel	**8.52** Blood studies generally examine the chemical constituents of the blood or the physical properties of different kinds of blood cells. A test of the fluid portion of blood for the presence of chemical constituents is called a blood _____. A blood chemistry _____ includes a battery of chemistry tests using a single sample of blood. Some panels target specific organs or conditions, such as a lipid or arthritis panel. Two panels of chemistry tests are used as a general or expanded screen for disease: a basic _____ panel (BMP), and a _____ _____ _____ (CMP).
culture	**8.53** To determine the presence and type of an infection in the blood, a blood sample may be put in an environment that encourages the growth of microorganisms. This test is called a blood _____.
CD4 AIDS	**8.54** Cluster of differentiation (CD4) cells are a subset of T lymphocytes in the blood that are increased in patients who are positive for HIV. The measure of these cells, which is known as a _____ cell count, is used in monitoring the course of HIV infection and in timing the treatment of acquired immunodeficiency syndrome (_____).
erythrocytes erythrocyte sedimentation	**8.55** Red blood cells are also called _____. A diagnostic test that measures how fast red blood cells settle through plasma is called the _____ _____ rate.
thromb/o thromboplastin partial thromboplastin prothrombin prothrombin time	**8.56** The combining form for clot is _____. That root is part of the term for the substance in tissues, platelets, and leukocytes that is necessary for coagulation: _____. The test for coagulation defects is called a _____ _____ time (PTT). The term for a protein substance in blood that is essential for clotting comes from a prefix meaning before and the combining form for clot: _____. The diagnostic test that measures the activity of this protein is called a _____ _____ (PT).

ANSWERS	REVIEW
blood count	**8.57** A complete _____ _____ (CBC) is a diagnostic test that is often performed as a general screen. It includes several component tests. The RBC is a count of the number of _____
red	
blood	_____ cells in a given volume of blood. A WBC is a count of
white, cells	the number of _____ blood _____ in a given volume of blood. The test of the blood level of hemoglobin is often simply
HGB, Hgb	called a hemoglobin, and it is abbreviated as _____ or _____. The measurement of the percentage of packed red blood cells in a
hematocrit	given volume of blood is called the _____ (HCT or Hct).
	8.58 Different values in the CBC are used to calculate the size, makeup, and content of red blood cells to classify an anemia. These
indices	calculations are called blood _____. The calculation
mean	of the volume (size) of individual cells is called the _____
corpuscular (cell)	_____ volume (MCV). The term mean refers to average. The calculation of the weight of hemoglobin in an average red blood
mean, hemoglobin	cell is called the _____ corpuscular (cell) _____ (MCH). The calculation of the mean hemoglobin concentration
hemoglobin	in each cell is called the mean corpuscular (cell) _____
concentration	_____ (MCHC).
	8.59 Thrombocytes are counted as part of a CBC. Another term for
platelet	thrombocyte is _____. Thus, this measure is simply called a
platelet count	_____ _____ (PLT).
white	**8.60** Recall that there are several kinds of leukocytes (_____
cytes	blood cells), such as lymphocytes, mono_____, neutrophils,
phils	eosino_____, and basophils. The study that determines the percentage of each type present in a smear of blood is called a
differential count	_____ _____.
	8.61 When the differential count is done, the size and shape of red blood cells in the sample are also noted. This is called the red cell
morphology	_____.
	8.62 The removal of bone marrow tissue by a needle for
aspiration	pathologic examination is called a bone marrow _____.
bone	Pathologic examination of bone marrow tissue is called a _____
marrow biopsy	_____ _____.

ANSWERS	REVIEW
-gram lymphangiogram	8.63 The combining form *angi/o* refers to either blood or lymph vessels. The suffix meaning a record is _____. Using these two components along with the combining form for lymph, the term _____ is an x-ray of a lymph node or vessel.
computed tomography cancers positron emission tomography	8.64 Full body CT (_____ _____), a specialized ionizing x-ray image of the whole body, is commonly used to detect tumors and _____, such as lymphoma. Another ionizing imaging modality is the use of whole body PET (_____-_____ _____) to determine the recurrence of cancers or to measure the response to therapy.

Self-Instruction: Operative Terms

Study this table to prepare for the programmed review that follows.

TERM	MEANING
bone marrow transplant bōn mar′ō tranz′plant	transplantation of healthy bone marrow from a compatible donor to a diseased recipient to stimulate blood cell production
lymphadenectomy lim-fad′ĕ-nĕk′tŏ-mē	removal of a lymph node
lymphadenotomy lim-fad′ĕ-not′ŏ-mē	incision into a lymph node
lymph node dissection limf nōd di-sek′shŭn	removal of possible cancer-carrying lymph nodes for pathologic examination
splenectomy splē-nek′tŏ-mē	removal of the spleen
thymectomy thī-mek′tŏ-mē	removal of the thymus

Programmed Review: Operative Terms

ANSWERS	REVIEW
removal splenectomy thymectomy lymphadenectomy	8.65 The suffix *-ectomy* means _____ or excision. The removal of the spleen is called a _____. The removal of the thymus is called a _____. The removal of a lymph node is called a _____.
incision lymphadenotomy	8.66 The suffix *-tomy*, on the other hand, means _____. An incision into a lymph node is called a _____.

ANSWERS	REVIEW
dissection	**8.67** Removal of possible cancer-carrying lymph nodes for pathologic examination is called a lymph node _____.
bone marrow	**8.68** To stimulate blood cell production inside bones, a _____ _____ transplant is made from a compatible donor to a diseased recipient.

Self-Instruction: Therapeutic Terms

Study this table to prepare for the programmed review that follows.

TERM	MEANING
blood transfusion blŭd trans-fyū′zhŭn	introduction of blood products into the circulation of a recipient whose blood volume is reduced or deficient in some manner
autologous blood aw-tol′ŏ-gŭs blŭd	blood donated by and stored for a patient for future personal use (e.g., upcoming surgery) (*auto* = self)
homologous blood hō-mol′ō-gŭs blŭd	blood voluntarily donated by any person for transfusion to a compatible recipient (*homo* = same)
blood component therapy blŭd kom-pō′nent thār′ă-pē	transfusion of a specific blood component, such as packed red blood cells, platelets, or plasma
cross-matching kros-match′ing	method of matching a donor's blood to the recipient by mixing a sample in a test tube to determine compatibility
chemotherapy kem′ō-thār-ă-pē	treatment of malignancies, infections, and other diseases with chemical agents to destroy selected cells or to impair their ability to reproduce
immunotherapy im′ū-nō-thār′ă-pē	use of biologic agents to prevent or treat disease by stimulating the body's own defense mechanisms, as seen in the treatment of AIDS, cancer, or allergy
plasmapheresis plaz′mă-fĕ-rē′sis	removal of plasma from the body with separation and extraction of specific elements (e.g., platelets) followed by reinfusion (*apheresis* = a withdrawal)
COMMON THERAPEUTIC DRUG CLASSIFICATIONS	
anticoagulant an′tē-kō-ag′yū-lant	a drug that prevents clotting of the blood
hemostatic hē-mō-stat′ik	a drug that stops the flow of blood within the vessels
vasoconstrictor vā′sō-kon-strik′tŏr	a drug that causes a narrowing of blood vessels, thereby decreasing blood flow
vasodilator vā′sō-dī-lā′tŏr	a drug that causes dilation of blood vessels, thereby increasing blood flow

Programmed Review: Therapeutic Terms

ANSWERS	REVIEW
transfusion autologous homologous	**8.69** The general term for giving blood or blood products to a recipient whose blood is in some way deficient is blood _____. There are several types of blood transfusions. A patient's own blood removed for his or her own personal use in a later transfusion is called _____ blood (*auto* = self). Blood from a compatible donor (i.e., a donor with the same blood type) is called _____ blood (*homo* = same).
component	**8.70** The transfusion of specific blood components, such as platelets or plasma, is called blood _____ therapy.
cross-matching	**8.71** The process of determining compatibility between donated blood and the recipient's blood is called _____-_____. This must be done to ensure the recipient does not suffer a potentially fatal transfusion reaction.
chemotherapy	**8.72** The treatment of neoplasms and other diseases with chemical agents that destroy the targeted cells is called _____. Chemotherapy is used for many forms of cancer in virtually all body systems.
immune, immunotherapy	**8.73** The term describing the use of biologic agents to prevent or treat disease by stimulating the body's own defense mechanisms was coined by combining *-therapy* with *immun/o*, the combining form meaning _____. Therefore, the term is _____.
plasmapheresis	**8.74** The root *apheresis* means withdrawal. The withdrawal of blood plasma from the body to separate out specific components before reinfusing the plasma is called _____.
against anticoagulant	**8.75** Recall that the prefix *anti-* means _____. Drug classes are frequently named by their actions against something. A drug that prevents blood clotting or coagulation is an _____.
vasoconstrictor vasodilator	**8.76** Drug classes are also named for their specific actions. The combining form for blood vessel is *vas/o*. A drug that narrows or constricts blood vessels is a _____. A drug that widens or dilates blood vessels is a _____.

ANSWERS	REVIEW
-stasis hem/o hemostatic	**8.77** Recall that the suffix that means stop or stand is _____. The combining form for blood is *hemat/o* or _____. A type of drug that stops blood from flowing within a vessel is called a _____ drug.

Chapter 8 Abbreviations

ABBREVIATION	EXPANSION
AIDS	acquired immunodeficiency syndrome
ALT	alanine aminotransferase (enzyme)
AST	aspartate aminotransferase (enzyme)
BMP	basic metabolic panel
BUN	blood urea nitrogen
CBC	complete blood count
CD	cluster of differentiation
CMP	comprehensive metabolic panel
CO_2	carbon dioxide
CT	computed tomography
ESR	erythrocyte sedimentation rate
HCT or Hct	hematocrit
HGB or Hgb	hemoglobin
HIV	human immunodeficiency virus
MCH	mean corpuscular (cell) hemoglobin
MCHC	mean corpuscular (cell) hemoglobin concentration
MCV	mean corpuscular (cell) volume
NK	natural killer (cell)
PET	positron-emission tomography
PLT	platelet count
PMN	polymorphonuclear (leukocyte)
PT	prothrombin time
PTT	partial thromboplastin time
RBC	red blood cell; red blood count
Rh^+	Rh positive
Rh^-	Rh negative
RRR	relative risk reduction, regular rate and rhythm
RTO	return to office
WBC	white blood cell; white blood count

PRACTICE EXERCISES

For each of the following words, write out the term parts (prefixes [P], combining forms [CF], roots [R], and suffixes [S]) on the lines below the word. Then define the term according to the meaning of its parts.

EXAMPLE
dyshematopoiesis
dys / hemato / poiesis
P   CF   S

DEFINITION: painful, difficult, or faulty/blood/formation

1. erythroblastosis
   _____ / _____ / _____
     CF   R   S
   DEFINITION: _____

2. chylopoiesis
   _____ / _____
     CF   S
   DEFINITION: _____

3. hemocytometer
   _____ / _____ / _____
     CF   CF   S
   DEFINITION: _____

4. splenorrhagia
   _____ / _____
     CF   S
   DEFINITION: _____

5. lymphadenitis
   _____ / _____ / _____
     R   R   S
   DEFINITION: _____

6. immunotoxic
   _____ / _____ / _____
     CF   R   S
   DEFINITION: _____

7. reticulocytosis
   _____ / _____ / _____
     CF   R   S
   DEFINITION: _____

8. thymopathy
   _____ / _____ / _____
     CF   R   S
   DEFINITION: _____

9. leukocytic

    _____ / _____ / _____
       CF   R   S
    DEFINITION: _____

10. lymphangiogram

    _____ / _____ / _____
       R   CF   S
    DEFINITION: _____

Name the three calculations that are part of the blood indices.

11. _____

12. _____

13. _____

Fill in the blanks with the correct medical terms and abbreviations.

14. The procedure of counting the number of leukocytes in the blood is called a _____ _____ _____ and is abbreviated as _____.

15. The blood study that determines the amount of pigment in red blood cells is called a _____ and is abbreviated as _____ or _____.

Write out the expanded term for each abbreviation.

16. PT _____

17. ESR _____

Write the letter of the matching definition in the space after the term.

18. microcytosis _____   a. large RBCs
19. poikilocytosis _____   b. thrombocyte
20. neutrophil _____   c. WBC with rose-stained granules
21. monocyte _____   d. RBC
22. eosinophi _____   e. an agranulocyte active in immunity
23. lymphocyte _____   f. WBC with dark-stained granules
24. basophil _____   g. WBC termed "one cell"
25. platelet _____   h. RBCs of unequal size
26. erythrocyte _____   i. WBC with granules
27. granulocyte _____   j. large, irregular RBCs
28. anisocytosis _____   k. a polymorphonuclear WBC
29. macrocytosis _____   l. small RBCs

Write the correct medical term for each of the following definitions.

30. _____ a decrease in the number of neutrophils
31. _____ blood donated by a person and stored for his or her future use
32. _____ impaired ability to provide an immune response

Circle the combining form that corresponds to the meaning given.

33. eat or swallow
    a. phas/o b. phag/o c. plas/o
34. clot
    a. thromb/o b. thym/o c. lymph/o
35. juice
    a. lymph/o b. hemat/o c. chyl/o
36. formation
    a. plas/o b. troph/o c. thromb/o

Circle the correct spelling.

37. a. hematopoesis b. hematopoiesis c. hematoepoisis
38. a. platelets b. plattelets c. plateletts
39. a. anissocytosis b. aniscocytosis c. anisocytosis
40. a. polkulocytosis b. poikilocytosis c. poiekilocytosis
41. a. hemalysis b. hemoliesis c. hemolysis
42. a. lymphadenpathy b. lymphadenopathy c. lymphoadenopathy

Give the noun used to form each adjective.

43. leukemic _____
44. immunosuppressive _____
45. plasmapheretic _____

Write the correct terms for the components of blood shown in the illustration.

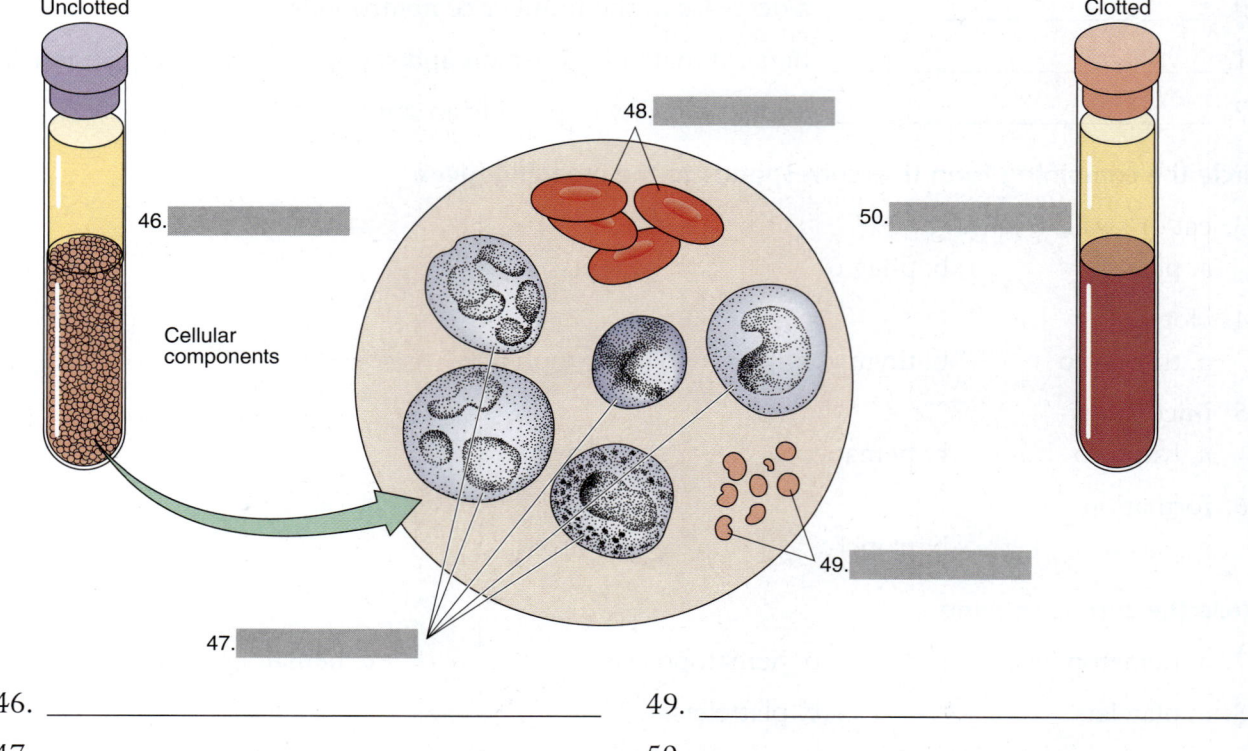

46. _____
47. _____
48. _____
49. _____
50. _____

MEDICAL RECORD ANALYSIS

Medical Record 8-1

PROGRESS NOTE

CC: Fatigue

S: This 43 y/o female c/o feeling run down with lack of energy × 1 mo. Pt denies fever, chills, nausea, vomiting, diarrhea, constipation and reports no weight loss. She has had very heavy menstrual periods lasting 5 days since DC of birth control pills 1 year ago.

    PMH: mononucleosis at age 14, NKDA. FH: father, age 68, died of MI; mother, age 74, has myelodysplasia; sister, age 45, L&W

    SH: married × 8 yr, no children; ETOH–wine with dinner, denies smoking.

O: VS: T 98.8°F, P 81, R 15, BP 136/62. WDWN female in NAD. HEENT—WNL

    Neck: supple s̄ lymphadenopathy. Lungs: clear. Heart: RRR s̄ murmur

    Abdomen: soft and tender s̄ organomegaly. Extremities: no edema.

A: Etiology of fatigue and decreased energy unclear. Possible iron deficiency anemia in light of heavy menstrual periods.

P: Blood studies to include comprehensive metabolic panel, CBC c̄ differential. RTO in 1 wk for lab results.

Questions About Medical Record 8-1

1. Which of the following is not mentioned in the history?
   a. type of treatment the patient received for mononucleosis
   b. patient's consumption of alcohol
   c. how long the patient has been married
   d. health status of the patient's sister

2. Describe the condition of the patient's mother.
   a. She has leukemia.
   b. She has a bleeding disorder characterized by an abnormally decreased number of platelets in the blood.
   c. She has a hereditary disorder characterized by an excessive buildup of iron deposits in the body.
   d. She has a disorder within the bone marrow characterized by a proliferation of abnormal stem cells, which usually develops into leukemia.

3. Which of the following describes the findings of the physical examination?
   a. swollen lymph glands
   b. normal examination
   c. fast heart rate
   d. heart murmur

4. What is the possible cause of the patient's fatigue?
   a. viral condition characterized by an increase in mononuclear cells (monocytes and lymphocytes) in the blood
   b. macrocytic-normochromic type of anemia characterized by an inadequate supply of vitamin B_{12}, causing red blood cells to become large, varied in shape, and reduced in number
   c. microcytic-hypochromic type of anemia characterized by small red blood cells containing low amounts of hemoglobin because of a lack of iron in the body
   d. normocytic-normochromic type of anemia characterized by the failure of bone marrow to produce red blood cells

5. Identify the subjective information most significantly linked to the assessment.
   a. enlarged lymph glands
   b. heavy menstrual periods
   c. fatigue
   d. the patient quit taking birth control pills

6. Which of the following tests is part of the plan?
   a. test to determine coagulation defects, such as platelet disorders
   b. test to diagnose an infection in the bloodstream by culturing a specimen of blood
   c. needle aspiration of bone marrow tissue for pathologic examination
   d. expanded battery of automated blood chemistry tests used as a general screen for disease

ANSWERS TO PRACTICE EXERCISES

1. erythroblastosis
   CF: erythro
   R: blast
   S: osis
   DEFINITION: red/germ or bud/condition or increase
2. chylopoiesis
   CF: chylo
   S: poiesis
   DEFINITION: juice/formation
3. hemocytometer
   CF: hemo
   CF: cyto
   S: meter
   DEFINITION: blood/cell/instrument for measuring
4. splenorrhagia
   CF: spleno
   S: rrhagia
   DEFINITION: spleen/to burst forth
5. lymphadenitis
   R: lymph
   R: aden
   S: itis
   DEFINITION: clear fluid/gland/inflammation
6. immunotoxic
   CF: immuno
   R: tox
   S: ic
   DEFINITION: immune, resistant/poison/pertaining to
7. reticulocytosis
   CF: reticulo
   R: cyt
   S: osis
   DEFINITION: a net/cell/condition or increase
8. thymopathy
   CF: thymo
   R: path
   S: y
   DEFINITION: thymus/disease/condition or process of
9. leukocytic
   CF: leuko
   R: cyt
   S: ic
   DEFINITION: white/cell/pertaining to
10. lymphangiogram
    R: lymph
    CF: angio
    S: gram
    DEFINITION: clear fluid/vessel/record
11. mean corpuscular (cell) volume (MCV)
12. mean corpuscular (cell) hemoglobin (MCH)
13. mean corpuscular (cell) hemoglobin concentration (MCHC)
14. white blood count, WBC
15. hemoglobin, HGB, Hgb
16. prothrombin time
17. erythrocyte sedimentation rate
18. l
19. j
20. k
21. g
22. c
23. e
24. f
25. b
26. d
27. i
28. h
29. a
30. neutropenia
31. autologous blood
32. immunosuppression
33. phag/o
34. thromb/o
35. chyl/o
36. plas/o
37. hematopoiesis
38. platelets
39. anisocytosis
40. poikilocytosis
41. hemolysis
42. lymphadenopathy
43. leukemia
44. immunosuppression
45. plasmapheresis
46. plasma
47. leukocytes or white blood cells
48. erythrocytes or red blood cells
49. thrombocytes or platelets
50. serum

ANSWERS TO MEDICAL RECORD 8-1

1. a
2. d
3. b
4. c
5. b
6. d

CARDIOVASCULAR SYSTEM

Learning Outcomes

After completing this chapter, you should be able to:

- Define terms parts related to the cardiovascular system.
- Identify key cardiovascular system anatomic structures with their functions.
- Define symptomatic and diagnostic terms related to the cardiovascular system.
- Explain diagnostic tests; procedures; and operative and therapeutic terms related to the cardiovascular system.
- Cite common abbreviations related to the cardiovascular system and give the expansion of each.
- Explain terms used in medical records involving the cardiovascular system.

CARDIOVASCULAR SYSTEM OVERVIEW

The cardiovascular system consists of the heart and blood vessels, which work together to transport blood throughout the body (see **Figure 9-1**).

- The heart is a muscular organ that pumps blood throughout the body.
- The heart consists of four chambers: the **right atrium** and **left atrium** (upper chambers), and the **right ventricle** and **left ventricle** (lower chambers).
- The **interatrial septum** and **interventricular septum** divide the heart into right and left portions.
- Heart valves (mitral, tricuspid, aortic, and pulmonary) open and close to maintain the one-way flow of blood through the heart (see **Figure 9-2**).

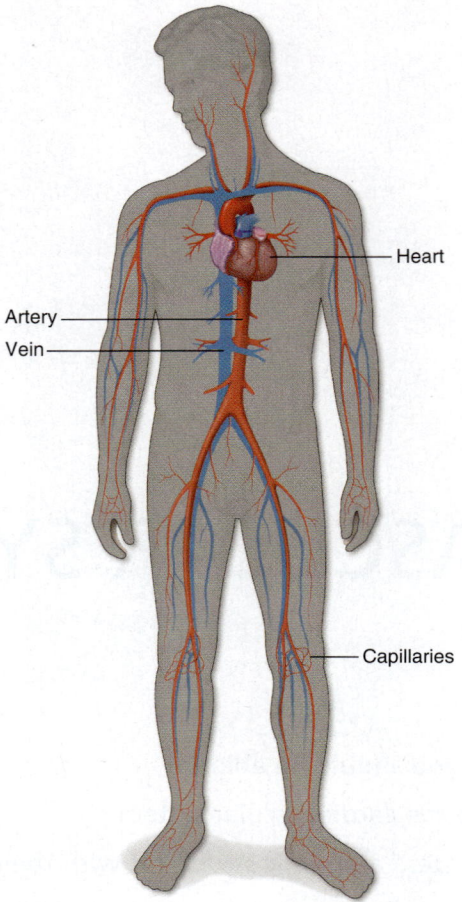

FIGURE 9-1 ■ **An overview of the cardiovascular system.**

- The heart has three layers: the **endocardium**, which lines the interior cavities of the heart; the **myocardium**, which is the thick, muscular layer; and the **epicardium**, which is the outer membrane (see **Figure 9-2**).
- Enclosing the heart is a loose, protective sac called the **pericardium.**

Blood, which transports essential elements within the body, flows through the heart as follows:

- Deoxygenated blood from the body enters the heart through the **superior vena cava** and **inferior vena cava** into the right atrium.
- During atrial contraction, the **tricuspid valve** opens to allow blood to flow into the **right ventricle**.
- Contraction of the ventricle pushes blood through the **pulmonary valve** into the pulmonary artery.
- The pulmonary circulation is the passage of blood from the right ventricle through the **pulmonary artery** to the **lungs** (where blood is oxygenated) and back through the **pulmonary veins** to the left atrium.
- With atrial contraction, the **mitral** (or bicuspid) **valve** opens to allow blood to flow into the **left ventricle**.
- Contraction of the left ventricle pushes blood through the **aortic valve** into the **aorta** and on to all parts of the body through the systemic circulation, the circulation of blood through the arteries, arterioles (small arteries), capillaries, venules (small veins), and veins throughout the body. Blood then returns to the right atrium (see **Figure 9-3**).
- The **coronary circulation** supplies blood to the heart, which is the first organ to receive oxygenated blood via the right and left coronary arteries. These arteries and their branches distribute blood throughout the entire heart (see **Figure 9-4**).

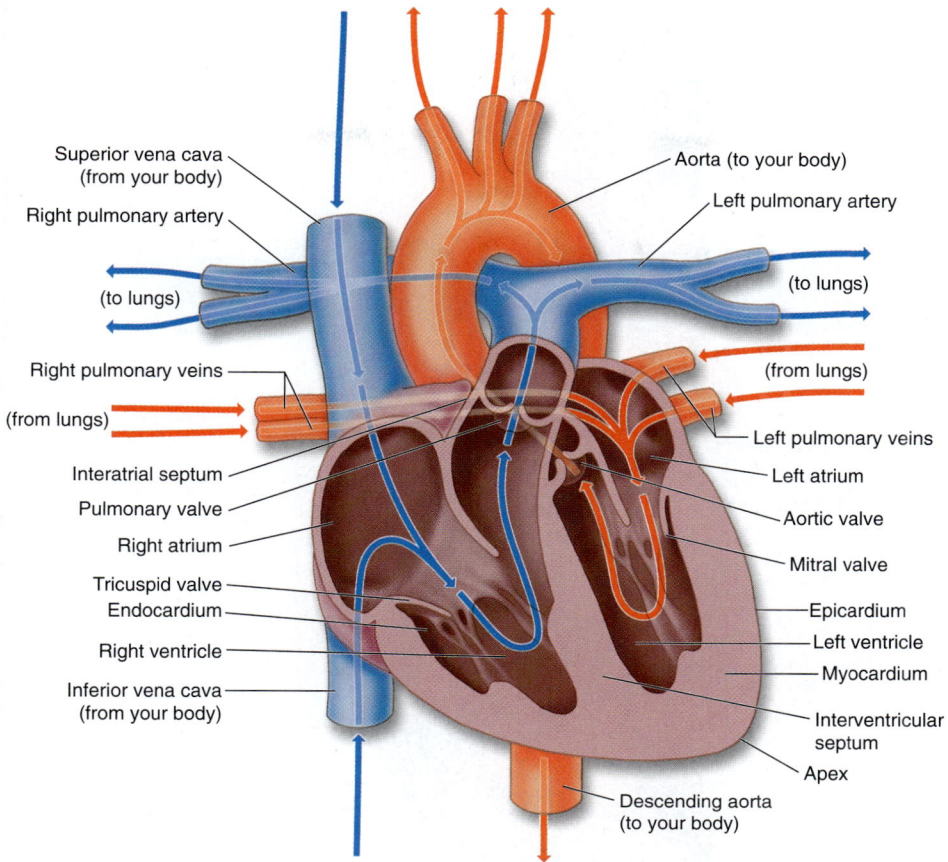

FIGURE 9-2 ■ Heart structures and major blood vessels. Red blood vessels and *arrows* indicate oxygenated blood, while blue blood vessels and *arrows* indicate deoxygenated blood.

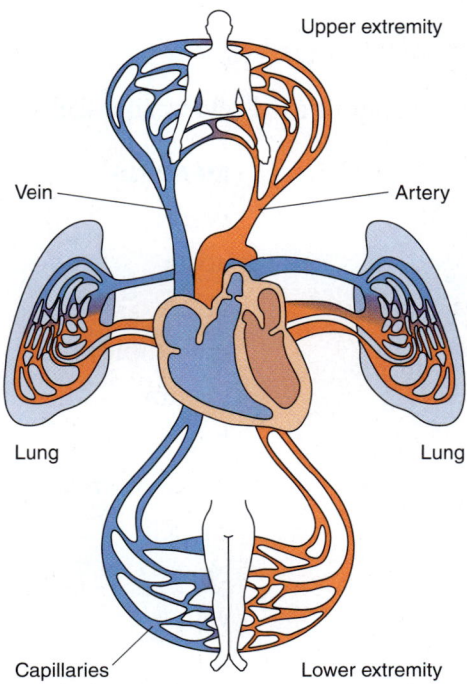

FIGURE 9-3 ■ An illustration showing the systemic circulation pattern.

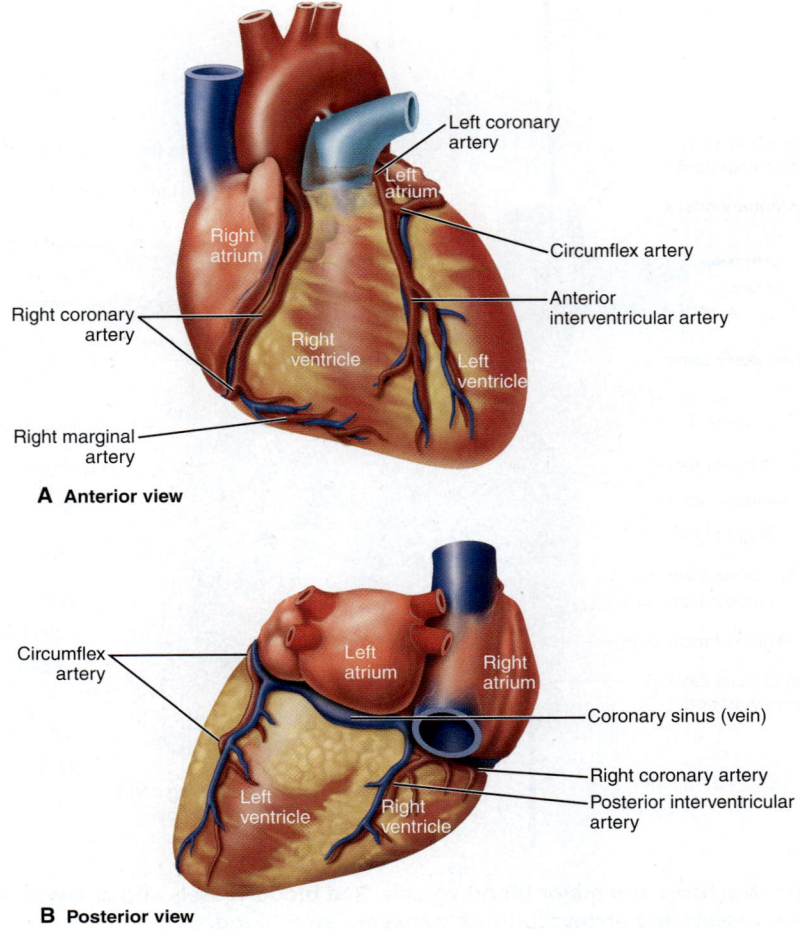

FIGURE 9-4 ■ Anterior (A) and posterior (B) views of the major vessels of the coronary circulatory loop.

Self-Instruction: Combining Forms

Study this table to prepare for the programmed review that follows.

COMBINING FORM	MEANING
angi/o	vessel
aort/o	aorta
arteri/o	artery
ather/o	fatty (lipid) paste
atri/o	atrium
cardi/o	heart
coron/o	circle or crown
my/o	muscle
pector/o	chest
phleb/o	vein
sphygm/o	pulse
steth/o	chest

COMBINING FORM	MEANING
thromb/o	clot
varic/o	swollen, twisted vein
vas/o	vessel
vascul/o	vessel
ven/o	vein
ventricul/o	ventricle (belly or pouch)

Programmed Review: Combining Forms

ANSWERS	REVIEW
heart	9.1 A cardiologist is a physician who specializes in the study of the _____.
angiogram	9.2 Formed from *angi/o*, an _____ is an x-ray record of a blood vessel.
vessel	9.3 A vasospasm is an involuntary contraction of a blood _____.
Cardiology	9.4 _____ is the medical specialty dealing with the study of the heart.
Thromb/o breaking down or dissolution	9.5 _____, the combining form meaning clot, is the subject of thrombolysis, a term referring to the _____ _____ of a clot or clots.
ventricle ventricul/o cardiologist	9.6 Someone with a congenital ventricular defect is born with an imperfection of a _____ in the heart. (The combining form in this term is _____.) That person would likely be under the care of a _____.
fatty or lipid	9.7 Atherosclerosis is a condition in which hardened _____ paste builds up inside blood vessels.
veins phleb/o, vein	9.8 A phlebotomist is someone trained to draw blood samples from the _____. This term comes from the combining form _____, meaning _____.
varic/o	9.9 Varicose veins, from the combining form _____, are so named because they are swollen and twisted.
ven/o arteries	9.10 Veins (named from the combining form _____) return blood to the heart from all around the body. Based on the root *arteri/o*, _____ carry blood in the other direction (from the heart to the body or lungs).

ANSWERS	REVIEW
pector/o steth/o	**9.11** The heart is in the chest, behind the area of the pectoral muscle. The pectoral muscles get their name from the combining form _____, which means chest. Another combining form that means chest is _____, which is the subject of the term stethoscope, an instrument used to listen to the heart or to breathing within the chest.
atria atri/o ventricul/o	**9.12** The heart has four chambers: two ventricles and two _____, which is the plural form of atrium. Atrium comes from the combining form _____, and ventricle comes from the combining form _____.
aorta myocardium circle or crown, coronary	**9.13** The _____, from the combining form *aort/o*, is the large blood vessel through which blood leaves the heart for delivery to all parts of the body. The coronary arteries branch from the aorta and supply the heart's muscular tissue, or the _____, with blood. The original meaning of *coron/o* refers to a _____. The _____ arteries are so named because they seem to encircle the heart like a crown.
sphygm/o veins vascul/o	**9.14** Each beat of the heart produces a pulse. The combining form that means pulse is _____. This is the key combining form in the term sphygmomanometer, an instrument that measures blood pressure (BP) based on its pressurized pulse through an artery. Arteries and _____ are the two types of larger blood vessels. Along with the capillaries, they are sometimes referred to collectively as the vasculature, from the combining form _____, meaning vessel.

Self-Instruction: Anatomic Terms

Study this table to prepare for the programmed review that follows.

TERM	MEANING
SEPTA AND LAYERS OF THE HEART (See Figure 9-2)	
atrium ā′trē-ŭm	upper right or left chamber of the heart

TERM	MEANING
endocardium en-dō-kar′dē-ŭm	membrane lining the cavities of the heart
epicardium ep-i-kar′dē-ŭm	membrane forming the outer layer of the heart
interatrial septum in-tĕr-ā′trē-ăl sep′tŭm	partition between the right and left atria
interventricular septum in-tĕr-ven-trik′yū-lăr sep′tŭm	partition between the right and left ventricles
myocardium mī′ō-kar′dē-ŭm	heart muscle
pericardium per-i-kar′dē-ŭm	protective sac enclosing the heart composed of two layers with fluid between; not shown on figure
visceral pericardium vis′ĕr-ăl per-i-kar′dē-ŭm	layer of the pericardial sac closest to the heart (*visceral* = pertaining to organ)
parietal pericardium pă-rī′ĕ-tăl per-i-kar′dē-ŭm	outer layer (*parietal* = pertaining to wall)
pericardial cavity per-i-kar′dē-ăl kav′i-tē	fluid-filled cavity between the pericardial layers
ventricle ven′tri-kĕl	lower right or left chamber of the heart

VALVES OF THE HEART AND VEINS (See Figure 9-2)

heart valves hart valvz	structures within the heart that open and close with the heartbeat to regulate the one-way flow of blood
aortic valve ā-ōr′tik valv	heart valve between the left ventricle and the aorta
mitral valve mī′trăl valv	heart valve between the left atrium and the left ventricle (*cuspis* = point); also called the *bicuspid valve*
bicuspid valve bī-kŭs′pid valv	heart valve between the left atrium and the left ventricle (*cuspis* = point); also called the *mitral valve*
pulmonary valve pul′mō-nār-ē valv	heart valve opening from the right ventricle to the pulmonary artery (*luna* = moon); also called the *pulmonary semilunar valve*
tricuspid valve trī-kŭs′pid valv	valve between the right atrium and the right ventricle
valves of the veins valvz of the vānz	valves located at intervals within the lining of veins, especially in the legs, which constrict with muscle action to move the blood returning to the heart

BLOOD VESSELS (See Figure 9-5)

arteries ar′tĕr-ēz	vessels that carry blood away from the heart to the arterioles
aorta ā-ōr′tă	large artery that is the main trunk of the arterial system branching from the left ventricle

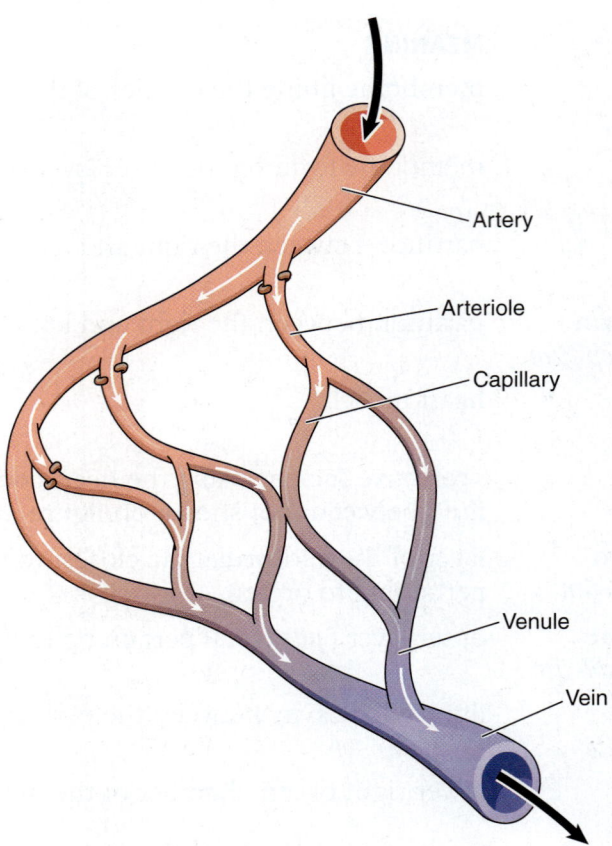

FIGURE 9-5 ■ The blood vessels.

TERM	MEANING
arterioles *ar-tēr′ē-ōlz*	small vessels that receive blood from the arteries
capillaries *kap′i-lār-ēz*	tiny vessels that join arterioles and venules
venules *ven′ūlz*	small vessels that gather blood from the capillaries into the veins
veins *vānz*	vessels that carry blood to the heart from the venules
CIRCULATION	
systemic circulation *sis-tem′ik sr-kyū-lā′shŭn*	circulation of blood throughout the body via arteries, arterioles, capillaries, venules, and veins to deliver oxygen and nutrients to body tissues (see Figure 9-3)
coronary circulation *kōr′o-nār-ē ser-kyū-lā′shŭn*	circulation of blood through the coronary blood vessels to deliver oxygen and nutrients to the heart muscle tissue (see Figure 9-4)
pulmonary circulation *pul′mō-nār-ē ser-kyū-lā′shŭn*	circulation of blood from the pulmonary artery through the vessels in the lungs and back to the heart via the pulmonary vein, providing for the exchange of gases (see Figure 9-3)

Programmed Review: Anatomic Terms

ANSWERS	REVIEW
atri/o atria upper	9.15 The term atrium is from the combining form _____. The plural form of atrium is _____. The right and left atria are the _____ chambers of the heart.
within heart tissue -ium	9.16 Recall that the prefix *endo-* means _____. Combined with *cardi/o*, it refers to something within the _____. The endocardium is the structure or _____ that lines the cavities of the heart. The suffix denoting structure or tissue is _____.
epi- suffix structure, tissue	9.17 A common prefix that means upon is _____. Combined with *cardi/o* and the _____ *-ium*, it forms the term epicardium, which is the _____ or _____ forming the outer layer of the heart.
muscle myocardium	9.18 *My/o* is a combining form meaning _____. The term for heart muscle tissue is _____.
around heart pericardium pericardial	9.19 *Peri-* is a prefix that means _____. The pericardium is a protective sac that encloses the _____. It has two layers with fluid between. Using the term that means pertaining to organ, the layer closest to the heart is called the visceral pericardium. The outer layer uses the term that means pertaining to wall and is called the parietal _____. Using the term that means pertaining to the pericardium, the fluid-filled space between these two layers is called the _____ cavity.
ventricul/o lower	9.20 The ventricles of the heart are so named from the combining form _____, meaning belly or pouch. The ventricles are the two _____ chambers of the heart.
between, atria interventricular chambers	9.21 The term septum refers to an anatomic partition. The interatrial septum is the partition _____ the left and right _____. Between the left and right ventricles is the _____ septum. The two atria and two ventricles are the four _____ of the heart.
valves aortic	9.22 The one-way blood flow from one heart chamber to another, or from a heart chamber to an artery, is regulated by heart _____, which open and close as the heart beats. The valve between the left ventricle and the aorta is called the _____ valve.

ANSWERS	REVIEW
bicuspid right right	**9.23** The mitral, or _____, valve is between the left atrium and the left ventricle. The tricuspid valve is between the _____ atrium and the _____ ventricle.
pulmonary	**9.24** The pulmonary valve is between the right ventricle and the _____ artery.
veins	**9.25** Other valves that open and close with muscle action to move blood back to the heart are known as the valves of the _____.
arteries ven/o	**9.26** The names of blood vessels are easy to remember because they are similar to the combining forms. The _____, which carry blood from the heart, get their name from the combining form *arteri/o*. The veins, which carry blood to the heart, are so named from the combining form _____.
arterioles capillaries venules small	**9.27** The _____, also from the combining form *arteri/o*, are the small vessels that receive blood from the arteries. The blood then flows to the _____, the tiniest vessels. Next, the blood is gathered from the capillaries into the _____, which are small vessels that connect to the veins. The suffixes *-ole* and *-ule* are used to indicate something _____.
aorta	**9.28** As blood leaves the heart to be distributed to the rest of the body, it first passes through the _____, a large artery that leads to the arteries that will carry the blood throughout the body.
systemic lungs coronary	**9.29** The term circulation refers to the flow of blood through the vessels. Blood flow through the body (except the lungs) is called _____ circulation. Pulmonary circulation is blood flow through the _____. Blood flow to the heart muscle, based on the combining form *coron/o*, is called _____ circulation.

Self-Instruction: Blood Pressure Terms

Study this table to prepare for the programmed review that follows.

TERM	MEANING
blood pressure (BP) *blŭd presh′ŭr*	measure of the blood within the systemic arteries maintained by the force and rate of the heartbeat and the diameter and elasticity of arterial walls; measured with a sphygmomanometer (blood pressure cuff) for diagnostic purposes (see **Figure 9-6**)

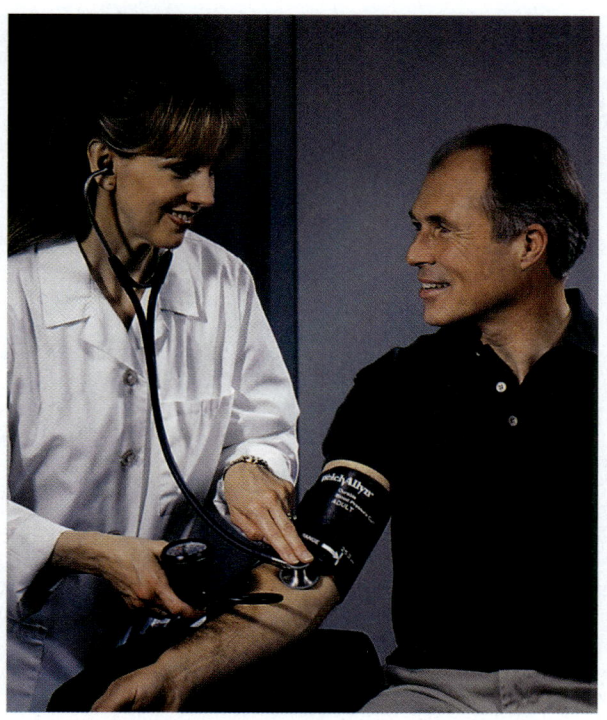

FIGURE 9-6 ■ Using a sphygmomanometer to measure blood pressure.

TERM	MEANING
diastole dī-as′tō-lē	to expand; period during the cardiac cycle (complete heart beat) when blood enters the relaxed ventricles from the atria
systole sis′tō-lē	to contract; period during the cardiac cycle (complete heart beat) when the heart is in contraction and blood is ejected through the aorta and the pulmonary artery
normotension nōr-mō-ten′shŭn	normal blood pressure
hypotension hī′pō-ten′shŭn	low blood pressure
hypertension (HTN) hī′pĕr-ten′shŭn	high blood pressure

Programmed Review: Blood Pressure Terms

ANSWERS	REVIEW
BP systole, diastole	9.30 Blood pressure, which is abbreviated as _____, is a measurement of the pressure on the walls of the arteries during contraction (_____) and relaxation (_____) of the heart.

ANSWERS	REVIEW
blood pressure systole diastole suffix pertaining to systolic diastolic	9.31 When BP, or _____ _____, is recorded, the contraction phase, or _____, is written first, followed by a slash, followed by the relaxation phase, or _____. The _____ -ic is used to modify the terms to mean _____ _____. The term that means pertaining to the contraction phase is _____, and the term that means pertaining to the relaxation phase is _____.
normo 120 80, hyper hypo	9.32 A blood pressure of 120/80 or below is considered a normal blood pressure and is termed _____tension. The numbers reflect a systolic reading of _____ and a diastolic reading of _____. High blood pressure is called _____ tension, and low blood pressure is called _____tension.

CARDIAC CONDUCTION

Cardiac conduction provides the electrical stimulus that is necessary to cause the heart muscle to pump blood by the continual contraction (systole) and relaxation (diastole) of myocardial (heart muscle) cells (see **Figure 9-7**).

Repeated electrical impulses are conducted:

from the sinoatrial (SA) node (the pacemaker of the heart)
↓
to the atrioventricular (AV) node
↓
to the atrioventricular (AV) bundle (bundle of His)
↓
to the right and left bundle branches
↓
to the Purkinje fibers

The impulses cause each myocardial cell to change:

from a resting state (polarization)
↓
to a contracting state (depolarization)
↓
back to a resting state by recharging (repolarization)

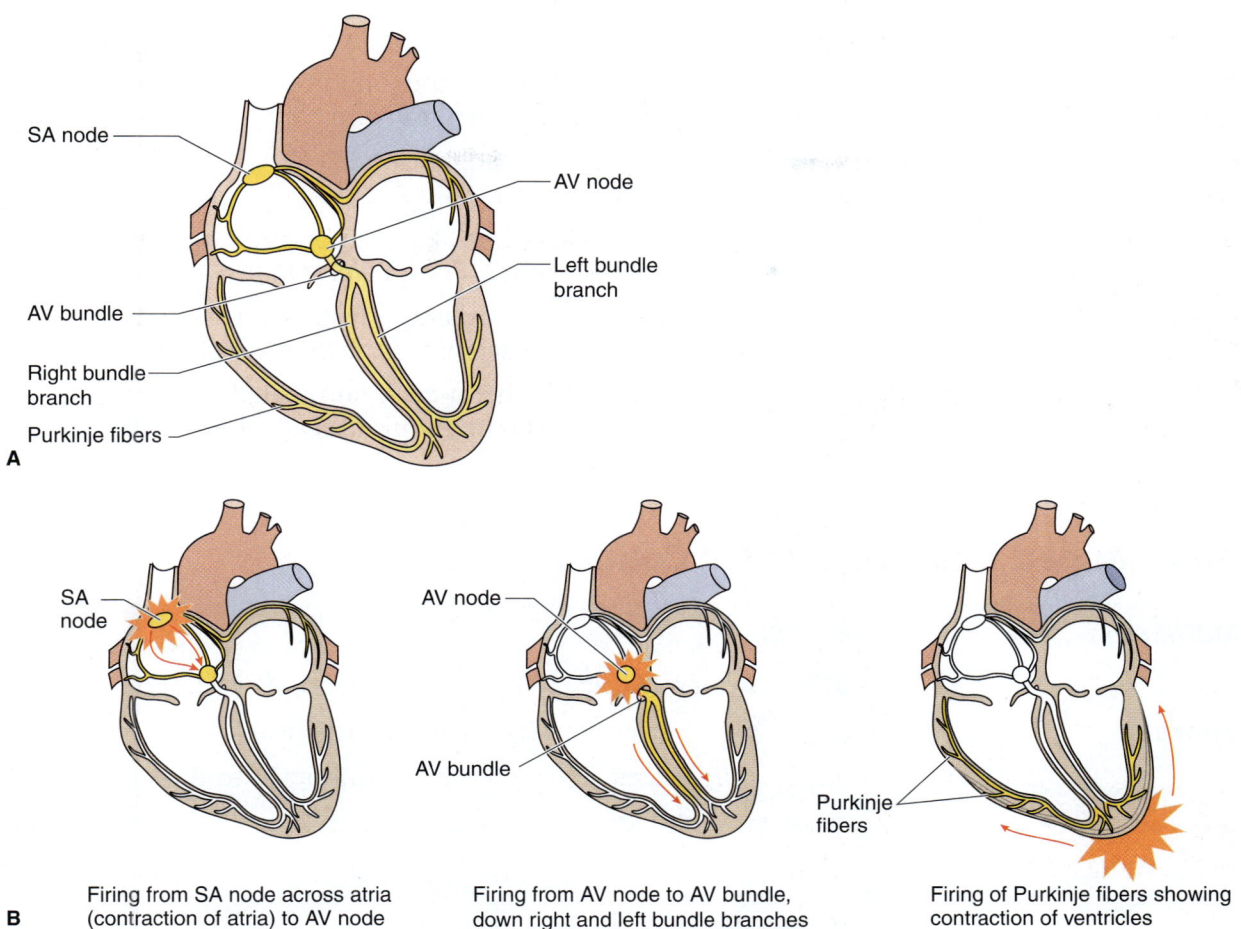

FIGURE 9-7 ■ Cardiac conduction. **A.** Anatomy. **B.** Conduction pathway.

Self-Instruction: Cardiac Conduction Terms

Study this table to prepare for the programmed review that follows.

TERM	MEANING
sinoatrial (SA) node *sī′nō-ā′trē-ăl nōd*	the pacemaker; highly specialized, neurologic tissue embedded in the wall of the right atrium; responsible for initiating electrical conduction of the heartbeat, causing the atria to contract and firing conduction of impulses to the atrioventricular (AV) node
atrioventricular (AV) node *ā′trē-ō-ven-trik′yū-lăr nōd*	neurologic tissue in the center of the heart that receives and amplifies the conduction of impulses from the SA node to the atrioventricular bundle (bundle of His)
atrioventricular (AV) bundle *ā′trē-ō-ven-trik′yū-lăr bŭn′dĕl*	neurologic fibers extending from the AV node to the right and left bundle branches that fire the impulse from the AV node to the Purkinje fibers; also called *bundle of His*
bundle of His *bŭn′dĕl of hiz*	neurologic fibers extending from the AV node to the right and left bundle branches that fire the impulse from the AV node to the Purkinje fibers; also called *atrioventricular (AV) bundle*

TERM	MEANING
Purkinje fibers pĕr-kin′jē fī′bĕrz	fibers in the ventricles that transmit impulses to the right and left ventricles, causing them to contract
polarization pō′lăr-i-zā′shŭn	resting; resting state of a myocardial cell
depolarization dē-pō′lăr-i-zā′shŭn	change of a myocardial cell from a polarized (resting) state to a state of contraction (*de* = not; *polarization* = resting)
repolarization rē′pō-lăr-i-zā′shŭn	recharging of the myocardial cell from a contracted state back to a resting state (*re* = again; *polarization* = resting)
normal sinus rhythm (NSR) nōr′măl sī′nŭs rith′ŭm	regular rhythm of the heart cycle stimulated by the SA node (average rate of 60–100 beats/minute) (see **Figure 9-11**)

Programmed Review: Cardiac Conduction Terms

ANSWERS	REVIEW
sinoatrial AV atri/o, ventricul/o	9.33 Review **Figure 9-7**. The term SA node refers to the _____ node, which is where the heart's electrical impulse originates. This impulse is conducted to the atrioventricular, or _____, node, a term made from the combining forms _____ and _____.
Purkinje contract	9.34 The impulse then moves from the atrioventricular bundle down the right and left bundle branches to the _____ fibers, which transmit impulses to the ventricles and cause them to _____. This rhythmic contraction is the heartbeat.
muscle heart heart muscle	9.35 The combining form *my/o* means _____, and the combining form *cardi/o* means _____. Myocardial cells comprise the _____ _____.
depolarization, repolarization	9.36 The resting state of the myocardial cells is called polarization. When each cell contracts, it changes to a state of _____. The stage of _____ is the change back to a resting state.
sinoatrial normal sinus	9.37 The normal regular heart rhythm produced by this continued simulation of heart muscle by electrical impulses originating in the _____, or SA, node is called _____ _____ rhythm, or NSR.

Self-Instruction: Symptomatic Terms

Study this table to prepare for the programmed review that follows.

TERM	MEANING
aneurysm (see Figure 9-8) an′yū-rizm	a widening; a bulging of the wall of an artery caused by a congenital defect or acquired weakness
saccular aneurysm (see Figure 9-8) sak-yū-lăr an′yū-rizm	a sac-like bulge on one side of an artery
fusiform aneurysm (see Figure 9-8) fyū′si-fōrm an′yū-rizm	a spindle-shaped bulge of an artery
dissecting aneurysm (see Figure 9-8) di-sek′ting an′yū-rizm	a split or tear of the arterial wall
constriction (see Figure 9-9A) kon-strik′shŭn	compression of a part that causes narrowing (stenosis)
angina pectoris an′ji-nă pek′tō-ris	chest pain caused by a temporary loss of oxygenated blood to heart muscle; often caused by narrowing of the coronary arteries (*angina* = to choke)
arteriosclerosis ar-tēr′ē-ō-skler-ō′sis	thickening, loss of elasticity, and calcification (hardening) of arterial walls
atherosclerosis ath′er-ō-skler-ō′sis	a form of arteriosclerosis characterized by the buildup of fatty substances that harden within the walls of arteries
atheromatous plaque (see Figure 9-9A) ath-ĕr-ō′mă-tŭs plak	a swollen area within the lining of an artery caused by the buildup of fat (lipids)
claudication klaw-di-kā′shŭn	limping; pain in a limb (especially the calf) while walking that subsides after rest; caused by inadequate blood supply
diaphoresis dī′ă-fō-rē′sis	profuse sweating (perspiration)

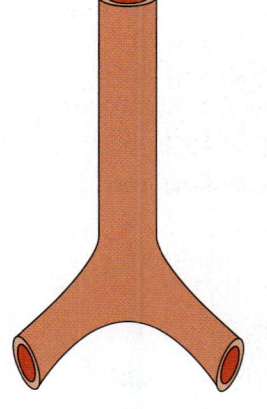
Normal artery

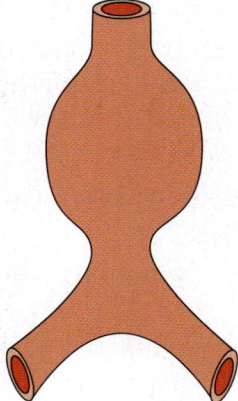
Artery with aneurysm

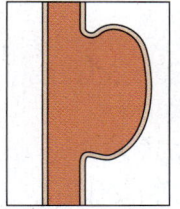
Saccular

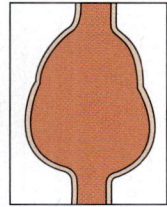
Fusiform

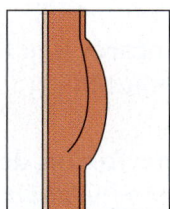
Dissecting

FIGURE 9-8 ■ Common types of aneurysms.

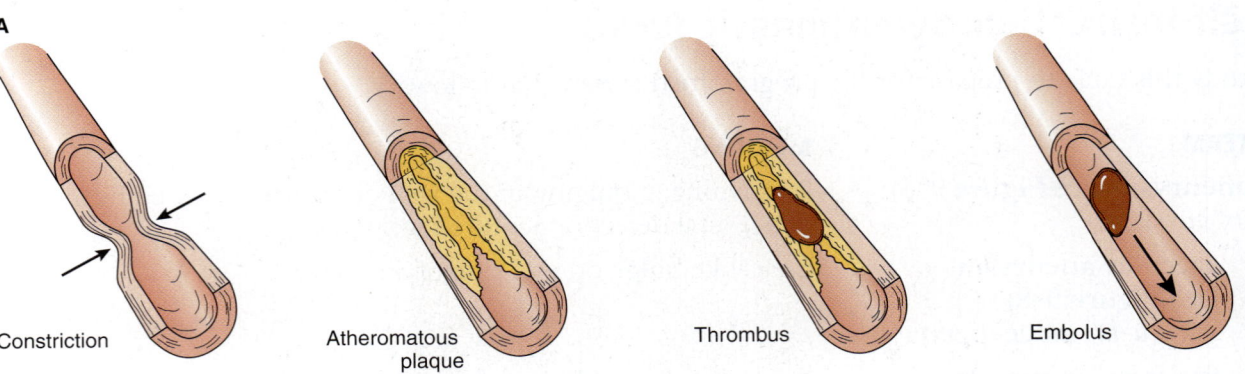
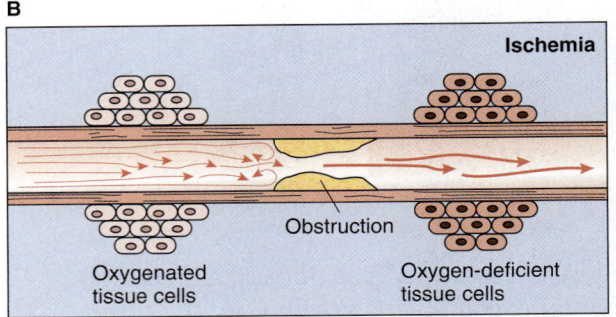
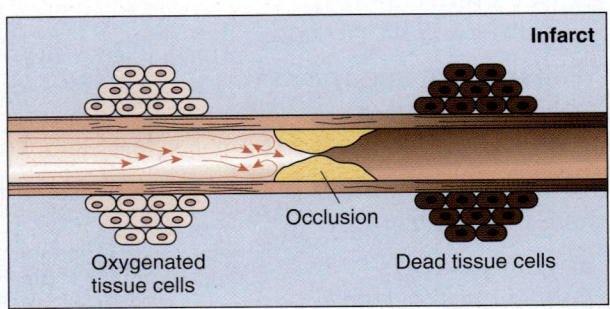

FIGURE 9-9 ■ Blood flow obstruction. **A.** Examples of conditions that cause reduced blood flow. **B.** Effects of reduced blood flow.

TERM	MEANING
thrombus (see Figure 9-9A) *throm'bŭs*	a stationary blood clot
embolus (see Figure 9-9A) *em'bō-lŭs*	a clot (e.g., air, fat, or a foreign object) carried in the bloodstream that obstructs the flow of blood when it lodges (*embolus* = a stopper)
heart murmur *hart mŭr'mŭr*	an abnormal sound from the heart produced by defects in the chambers or valves
ischemia (see Figure 9-9B) *is-kē'mē-ă*	decreased blood flow to tissue caused by obstruction or constriction of a blood vessel; to hold back blood
occlusion (see Figure 9-9B) *ŏ-klū'zhŭn*	plugging; an obstruction or a closing off
infarct (see Figure 9-9B) *in'farkt*	a localized area of necrosis (dead tissue cells) caused by ischemia resulting from occlusion of a blood vessel; to stuff into
perfusion deficit *pĕr-fyū'zhŭn def'i-sit*	lack of flow through a blood vessel caused by narrowing, occlusion, or obstruction
palpitation *pal-pi-tā'shŭn*	subjective experience of pounding, skipping, or racing heartbeats
stenosis *ste-nō'sis*	condition of narrowing of a part
vegetation (see Figure 9-10) *vej-ĕ-tā'shŭn*	an abnormal growth of tissue around a valve, generally resulting from infection; to grow

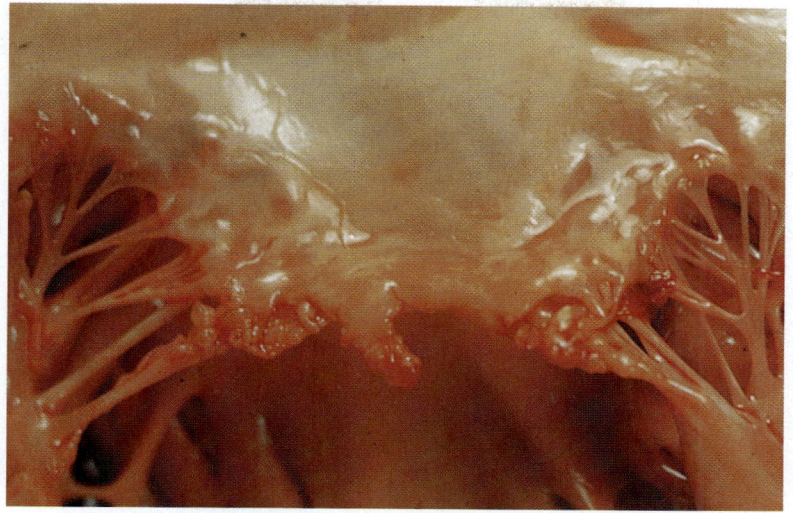

FIGURE 9-10 ■ The mitral valve shows destructive growths known as vegetations that have eroded through the margins of the valve in a patient with bacterial endocarditis.

Programmed Review: Symptomatic Terms

ANSWERS	REVIEW
hard artery or arterial fatty or lipid atherosclerosis	9.38 *Scler/o*, a combining form meaning _____, is a key component in the term arteriosclerosis, which refers to thickening, loss of elasticity, and hardening of _____ walls. *Ather/o*, a combining form meaning _____ paste, is used in the term that specifically describes a condition or increase of hardened fatty substances built up within the walls of arteries: _____.
embolus stationary	9.39 An _____ is a clot of any sort carried in the bloodstream that obstructs the flow of blood when it lodges. A thrombus, on the other hand, is a _____ blood clot.
  stenosis constriction narrowing plugging or obstruction	9.40 Blood flow through a vessel can be affected by various kinds of restrictions. A condition or narrowing is called _____. Stenotic conditions can be the result of a compression or _____ of a vessel. A buildup of atherosclerotic substances can also cause stenosis, a condition of _____. An occlusion, which is the _____ of a vessel, also might occur.

ANSWERS	REVIEW
ischemia deficit	**9.41** If blood flow is reduced to tissue, _____ occurs. When diagnostic tests detect the lack of blood flow from a vessel to tissue cells, it is called a perfusion _____. Perfusion refers to tissues with an adequate circulation of blood.
angina pector/o	**9.42** A heart condition of chest pain may occur when a temporary or transient restriction of blood flow to heart muscle occurs, which is called _____ pectoris. Recall that the combining form _____ refers to the chest. Therefore, this chest pain is called angina pectoris.
death infarct	**9.43** When prolonged or total ischemia occurs in an area, tissue necrosis or _____ results. The area of scarring from necrosis is called an _____.
bulge or widen saccular dissecting fusiform	**9.44** An aneurysm can occur in an artery because of a weakness in the wall. This causes the wall to _____. The type of aneurysm with a sac-like bulge is called a _____ aneurysm. If the bulge causes a split or tear of the vessel wall, it is called a _____ aneurysm. The bulge of a _____ aneurysm is spindle-shaped.
pain	**9.45** Various symptoms help cardiologists to determine what condition a patient is experiencing. Claudication is _____ in a limb, sometimes causing a limp, that results during movement because of an inadequate blood supply to the limb.
palpitation	**9.46** The subjective symptom of the heart pounding, skipping, or racing is called _____. Be careful not to confuse this term with palpation, the word meaning to touch or feel.
diaphoresis	**9.47** Sweating brought on by physical activity or a high-temperature environment is perfectly normal; however, profuse sweating, known as _____, accompanied by chest pain, shortness of breath, or heart palpitations, is a significant symptom of heart disease.
murmur	**9.48** The physician, when listening to the heart through a stethoscope, might hear an abnormal sound, called a heart _____, which is produced by a defect in the heart chambers or valves.

Self-Instruction: Diagnostic Terms

Study this table to prepare for the programmed review that follows.

TERM	MEANING
RELATED TO THE HEART AND ARTERIES	
acute coronary syndrome (ACS) ă-kyūt′ kōr′o-nār-ē sin′drōm	signs and symptoms indicating an active process of atherosclerotic plaque buildup or formation of a thrombus, or spasm within a coronary artery, causing a reduction or loss of blood flow to myocardial tissue; includes unstable angina and other pathologic events leading to myocardial infarction (MI); early diagnosis and rapid treatment are critical to avoid or minimize damage to heart muscle
arrhythmia (see Figure 9-11) ă-rith′mē-ă	any of several kinds of irregularity or loss of rhythm of the heartbeat; also called *dysrhythmia*
dysrhythmia dis-rith′mē-ă	any of several kinds of irregularity or loss of rhythm of the heartbeat; also called *arrhythmia*
bradycardia brad-ē-kar′dē-ă	slow heart rate (less than 60 beats/minute)
fibrillation fi-bri-lā′shŭn	chaotic, irregular contractions of the heart, as in atrial or ventricular fibrillation
atrial flutter ā′trē-ăl flŭt′ĕr	rapid regular atrial contractions occurring at rates between 250 and 330/minute
premature ventricular contraction (PVC) prē-mă-tūr′ ven-trik′ū-lăr kon-trak′shŭn	a ventricular contraction preceding the normal impulse initiated by the SA node (pacemaker)
tachycardia tak-i-kar′dē-ă	fast heart rate (greater than 100 beats/minute)
bacterial endocarditis bak-tēr′ē-ăl en′dō-kar-dī′tis	a bacterial inflammation that affects the endocardium or the heart valves (see Figure 9-10)
cardiac tamponade kar′dē-ak tam′pŏ-nād	compression of the heart produced by the accumulation of fluid in the pericardial sac, as results from pericarditis or trauma, causing rupture of a blood vessel within the heart (*tampon* = a plug)
cardiomyopathy kar′dē-ō-mī-op′ă-thē	a general term for disease of the heart muscle, such as alcoholic cardiomyopathy (damage to the heart muscle caused by excessive consumption of alcohol)
congenital anomaly of the heart kon-jen′i-tăl ah-nom′ah-lē of the hart	malformations of the heart that are present at birth (*congenital* = born with; *anomaly* = irregularity)
atrial septal defect (ASD) ā′trē-ăl sep′tăl dē′fekt	an opening in the septum separating the atria
coarctation of the aorta kō-ark-tā′shŭn of the ā-ōr′tă	narrowing of the descending portion of the aorta, resulting in a limited flow of blood to the lower part of the body

Normal sinus rhythm (NSR)

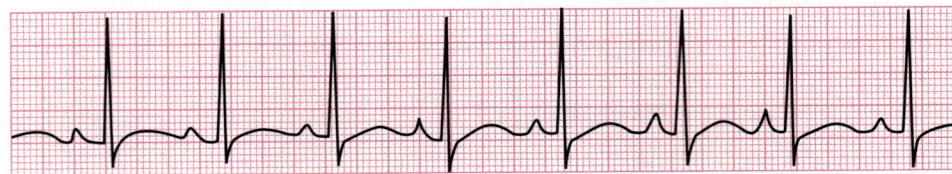

Bradycardia

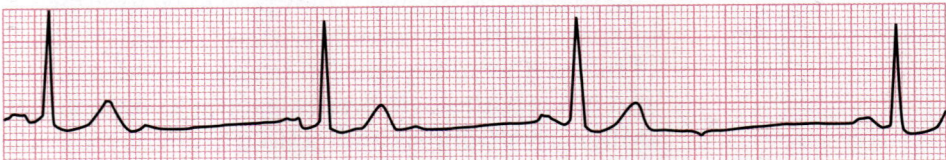

Ventricular fibrillation

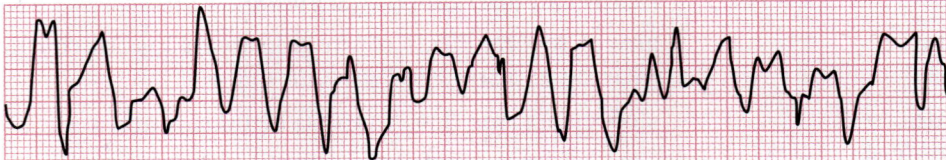

Atrial flutter

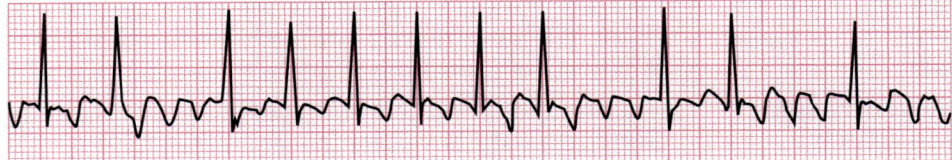

Premature ventricular contraction (PVC)

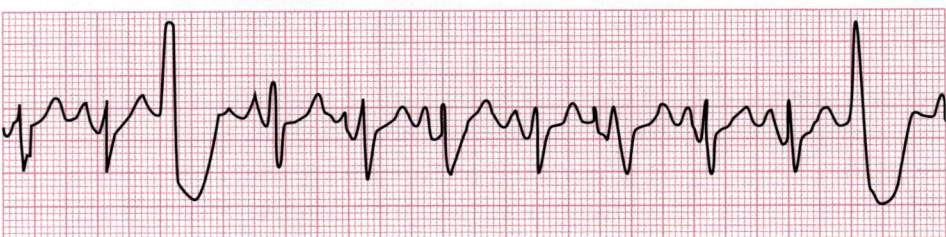

Tachycardia (sinus)

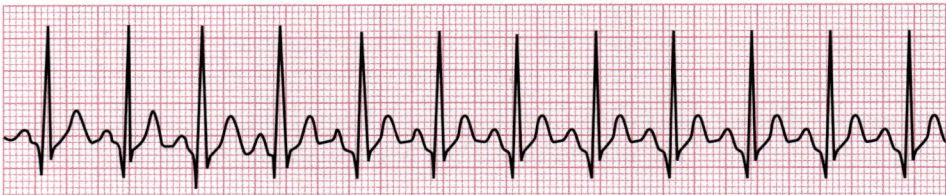

FIGURE 9-11 ■ Electrocardiogram (ECG or EKG) tracings showing common types of arrhythmia.

TERM	MEANING
patent ductus arteriosus (PDA) pā′tent dŭk′tŭs ar-tē′rē-ō′sŭs	an abnormal opening between the pulmonary artery and the aorta caused by failure of the fetal ductus arteriosus (a vessel that connects the left pulmonary artery with the descending aorta) to close after birth (*patent* = open)
ventricular septal defect (VSD) ven-trik′yū-lăr sep′tăl dē′fekt	an opening in the septum separating the ventricles
congestive heart failure (CHF) kon-jes′tiv hart fāl′yūr	failure of the heart to pump an adequate amount of blood to meet the demands of the body, resulting in congestion and edema in lower portions of the body; also called *cardiac failure* and *cardiac insufficiency*
left ventricular failure left ven-trik′yū-lăr fāl′yūr	failure of the left ventricle to pump an adequate amount of blood to meet the demands of the body, resulting in an increased pressure in the pulmonary (lung) circulation causing pulmonary congestion and pulmonary edema; also called *left-sided failure*
cor pulmonale kōr pul-mō-nā′lē right ventricular failure rīt ven-trik′yū-lăr fāl′yūr	enlargement of the right ventricle, resulting from chronic disease within the lungs, that causes congestion within the pulmonary circulation and resistance of blood flow to the lungs (*cor* = heart)
coronary artery disease (CAD) (see Figure 9-12) kōr′o-nār-ē ar′tĕr-ē di-zēz′	a condition affecting arteries of the heart that reduces the flow of blood and the delivery of oxygen and nutrients to the myocardium; most often caused by atherosclerosis (plaque buildup in arterial wall)
hypertension (HTN) hī′pĕr-ten′shŭn	persistently high blood pressure
essential hypertension ĕ-sen′shăl hī′pĕr-ten′shŭn	high blood pressure with no known cause; risks include smoking, obesity, increased salt intake, hypercholesterolemia, and hereditary factors; also called *primary hypertension* or *idiopathic hypertension*

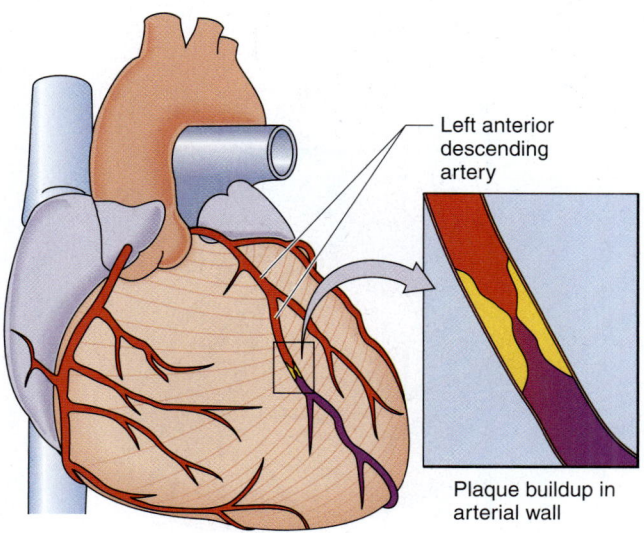

FIGURE 9-12 ■ Coronary artery disease (CAD).

TERM	MEANING
primary hypertension *prī′mār-ē hī′pĕr-ten′shŭn*	high blood pressure with no known cause; risks include smoking, obesity, increased salt intake, hypercholesterolemia, and hereditary factors; also called *essential hypertension* or *idiopathic hypertension*
secondary hypertension *sĕk′un-dār′ē hī′pĕr-ten′shŭn*	high blood pressure caused by the effects of another disease (e.g., kidney disease)
mitral valve prolapse (MVP) *mī′trăl valv prō′lapz*	protrusion of one or both cusps of the mitral valve back into the left atrium during ventricular contraction, resulting in incomplete closure and backflow of blood
myocardial infarction (MI) (see Figure 9-13) *mī-ō-kar′dē-ăl in-fark′shŭn*	death of myocardial tissue (infarction) caused by ischemia (loss of blood flow) that results from an occlusion (plugging) of a coronary artery; usually caused by atherosclerosis; symptoms include pain in the chest or upper body (shoulders, neck, and jaw), shortness of breath, diaphoresis, and nausea; also called *heart attack*
myocarditis *mī′ō-kar-dī′tis*	inflammation of myocardium; most often caused by viral or bacterial infection
pericarditis *per′i-kar-dī′tis*	inflammation of the pericardium
rheumatic heart disease *rū-mat′ik hart di-zēz′*	damage to heart muscle and heart valves by rheumatic fever (a streptococcal infection)
sudden cardiac arrest (SCA) *sŭd′dĕn kar′dē-ak ă-rest′*	the abrupt cessation of any cardiac output (CO), most commonly as the result of ventricular fibrillation; causes sudden death unless defibrillation is initiated immediately

RELATED TO THE VEINS

deep vein thrombosis (DVT) *dēp vān throm-bō′sis*	formation of a clot in a deep vein of the body, occurring most often in the femoral and iliac veins
phlebitis *fle-bī′tis*	inflammation of a vein

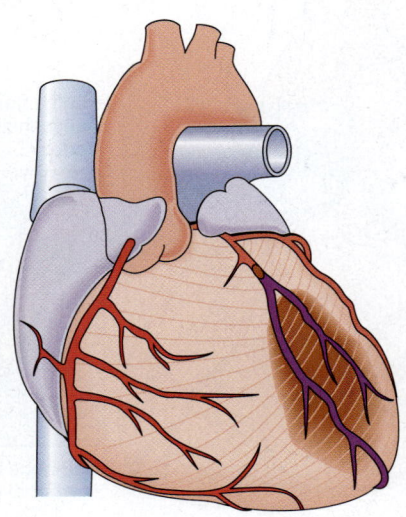

FIGURE 9-13 ■ Anterolateral myocardial infarction (MI) (*darkened area*) caused by occlusion of a branch of the left coronary artery.

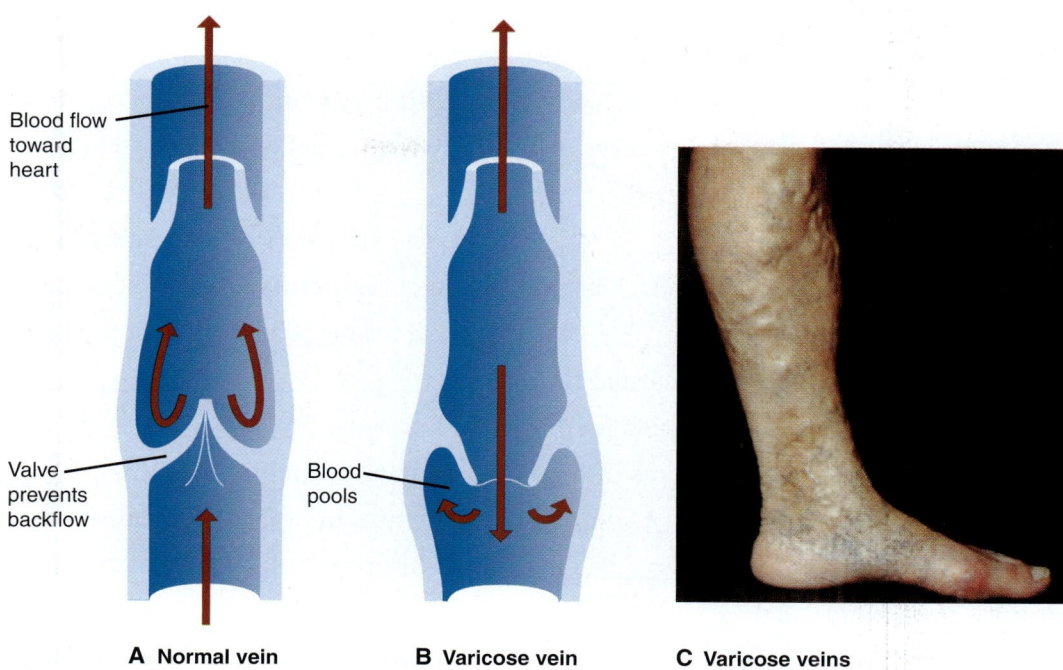

FIGURE 9-14 ■ Varicose veins. **A.** In a healthy vein, the valves help blood to flow back toward the heart and prevent it from pooling. **B.** In varicose veins, the valves no longer function properly, allowing the blood to pool. **C.** The pooling of blood in the veins causes them to become swollen and "knotty" in appearance.

TERM	MEANING
thrombophlebitis *throm′bō-fle-bī′tis*	inflammation of a vein associated with a clot formation
varicose veins (see Figure 9-14) *var′i-kōs vānz*	abnormally swollen, twisted veins with defective valves; most often seen in the legs

Programmed Review: Diagnostic Terms

ANSWERS	REVIEW
inflammation myocardium pericarditis endocardium	**9.49** The suffix *-itis* refers to an _____. Myocarditis therefore means an inflammation of the _____. Inflammation of the pericardium is called _____. Bacterial endocarditis is a bacterial inflammation affecting the _____ and heart valves.
coronary artery disease atherosclerosis	**9.50** The condition of reduced blood flow through the arteries that supply the heart muscle is called _____ _____ _____ (CAD). It most commonly results from a hardening of fatty substances within the lining of the arteries, a condition known as _____.

ANSWERS	REVIEW
	9.51 Atherosclerotic buildup within the wall of one or more coronary arteries can lead to a partial or total obstruction, which
occlusion	is called an _____. The resulting loss of blood flow, or
ischemia	_____, deprives the affected heart muscle of the oxygen it needs to survive. Prolonged ischemia leads to necrosis, the
death	_____ of myocardial tissue. The term describing the death
myocardial infarction	of myocardial tissue is _____ _____
heart attack	(MI), which is commonly known as a _____ _____.
chest	Symptoms of myocardial infarction include angina (_____
pain	_____), shortness of breath, nausea, and profuse sweating
diaphoresis	(_____). The abbreviation ACS, which stands for
acute coronary syndrome	_____ _____ _____, includes the signs and symptoms that indicate an active process of the pathologic events leading to myocardial infarction.
muscle	**9.52** Myopathy refers to a condition of diseased _____. The general term for a condition of diseased heart muscle is
cardiomyopathy	_____.
	9.53 The word root *tampon* means a plug (obstruction), and the term tamponade refers to an obstruction. A compression of the heart produced by accumulated fluid in the pericardial sac is
tamponade	called a cardiac _____.
	9.54 Another word root that means heart is *cor*. The condition
pulmonale	called cor _____ is caused by congestion in the pulmonary circulation that results in right ventricular failure. The
enlarged	right ventricle becomes _____ because of the increased effort to pump blood to the diseased lungs.
heart	**9.55** Congestive _____ failure (CHF) is a failure of the left ventricle to pump enough blood to the body. This condition is
failure	also called left ventricular _____.
	9.56 The term anomaly means irregularity (not normal). The term congenital pertains to something a person is born
with	_____. There are several congenital anomalies of the heart. An atrial septal defect (ASD) is an irregularity in the
partition, atria	septum, or _____, which separates the _____.
ventricular	A _____ septal defect (VSD) is an opening in the septum separating the ventricles.

ANSWERS	REVIEW
coarctation	**9.57** A narrowing of the descending portion of the aorta that restricts blood flow to the lower body is called a _____ of the aorta.
close	**9.58** Patent ductus arteriosus (PDA) is an abnormal opening between the pulmonary artery and the aorta. The term patent means open. PDA results if the fetal ductus arteriosus fails to _____ after birth.
without dysrhythmia brady-, slow fast tachycardia	**9.59** The prefix *a-* means without. An arrhythmia is a heartbeat _____ a normal rhythm. The synonym for arrhythmia, which is formed using the prefix describing painful, difficult, or faulty, is _____. There are several types of heart arrhythmias or dysrhythmias. The prefix meaning slow is _____. Therefore, bradycardia is a condition of _____ heart rate. *Tachy-* is the prefix meaning _____, so _____ is a condition of fast heart rate.
fibrillation	**9.60** Fast, chaotic, irregular contractions of the heart occur in a condition called _____.
contraction node	**9.61** Another common arrhythmia is a premature ventricular _____ (PVC). In this case, the contraction precedes the normal impulse initiated by the sinoatrial (SA) _____.
sudden cardiac arrest	**9.62** Ventricular fibrillation is a lethal arrhythmia that causes the ventricles to quiver rapidly (to fibrillate) instead of contracting and to be unable to pump blood. The term describing the abrupt cessation of any cardiac output (CO) as caused by ventricular fibrillation is _____ _____ _____ (SCA).
hypertension, HTN essential Secondary	**9.63** The condition of persistently high blood pressure is called _____ and is abbreviated as _____. Primary, or _____, hypertension cannot be attributed to a single cause. _____ hypertension, however, is caused by another condition, such as kidney disease.
rheumatic	**9.64** Rheumatic fever can cause damage to heart muscle and valves. This is called _____ heart disease.

ANSWERS	REVIEW
vein phlebitis thrombophlebitis	9.65 *Phleb/o* is a combining form for _____. Combined with the suffix for inflammation, this forms the term _____, which means inflammation of a vein. If that inflammation is associated with a clot formation, the condition is called _____.
deep vein thrombosis thrombus embolus	9.66 The condition of a formed clot in a deep vein of the body is called _____ _____ _____ (DVT). The danger of any clot (_____) formation in a vein is that it can break loose to become a traveling _____.

Self-Instruction: Diagnostic Tests and Procedures

Study this table to prepare for the programmed review that follows.

TEST OR PROCEDURE	EXPLANATION
stethoscope *steth′ō-skōp*	instrument used to listen for sounds in the body
auscultation (see **Figure 9-15**) *aws-kŭl-tā′shŭn*	physical examination method of listening to sounds within the body with a stethoscope (e.g., auscultation of the chest for heart and lung sounds)
gallop *gal′ŏp*	abnormal heart sound that mimics the gait of a horse; related to abnormal ventricular contraction
electrocardiogram (ECG or EKG) (see **Figures 9-11** and **9-16**) *ē-lek-trō-kar′dē-ō-gram*	an electrical picture of the heart represented by positive and negative deflections on a graph labeled with the letters P, Q, R, S, and T, which correspond to events of the cardiac cycle (a complete round of heart contraction, relaxation, and the intervals between)

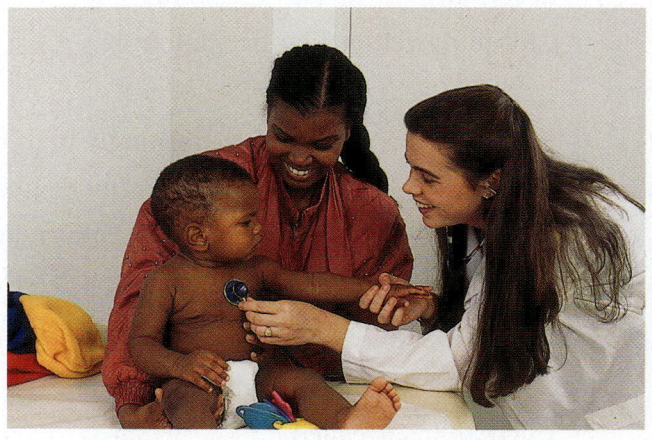

FIGURE 9-15 ■ **Auscultating heart sounds.**

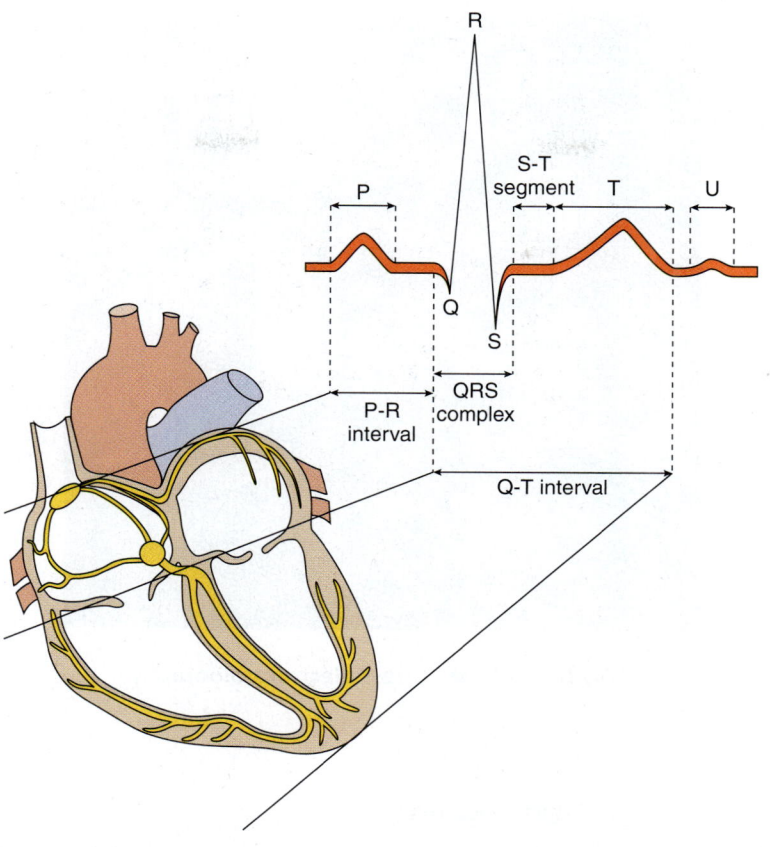

FIGURE 9-16 ■ Events of the cardiac cycle shown via electrocardiography. The P wave is the first complex of the electrocardiogram and represents atrial depolarization. The P-R interval is the time elapsing between the beginning of the P wave and the beginning of the QRS complex. The QRS complex represents ventricular depolarization. The S-T segment is the part of the ECG between the QRS complex and the T wave. The T wave is the next deflection after the QRS complex and represents ventricular repolarization. The Q-T interval is the time from the Q wave to the end of the T wave corresponding to electrical systole. The U wave is a positive wave following an upright T wave.

TEST OR PROCEDURE	EXPLANATION
stress electrocardiogram (stress ECG or EKG) (see Figure 9-17) *stres ē-lek-trō-kar′dē-ō-gram*	electrocardiogram (ECG or EKG) of the heart recorded during the induction of controlled physical exercise using a treadmill or bicycle; useful in detecting heart conditions (e.g., ischemia or infarction)
Holter monitor *hōl′ter mon′i-tŏr*	portable electrocardiograph worn by the patient that monitors electrical activity of the heart over 24 hours; useful in detecting periodic abnormalities
intracardiac electrophysiologic study (EPS) *in′tră-kar′dē-ak ē-lek′trō-fiz′ē-ō-loj′ik stŭd′ē*	invasive procedure involving placement of catheter-guided electrodes within the heart to evaluate and map the electrical conduction of cardiac arrhythmias; intracardiac catheter ablation may be performed at the same time to treat the arrhythmia
intracardiac catheter ablation *in′tră-kar′dē-ak kath′ĕ-tĕr ab-lā′shŭn*	use of radiofrequency waves sent through a catheter within the heart to treat arrhythmias by selectively destroying myocardial tissue at sites that generate abnormal electrical pathways

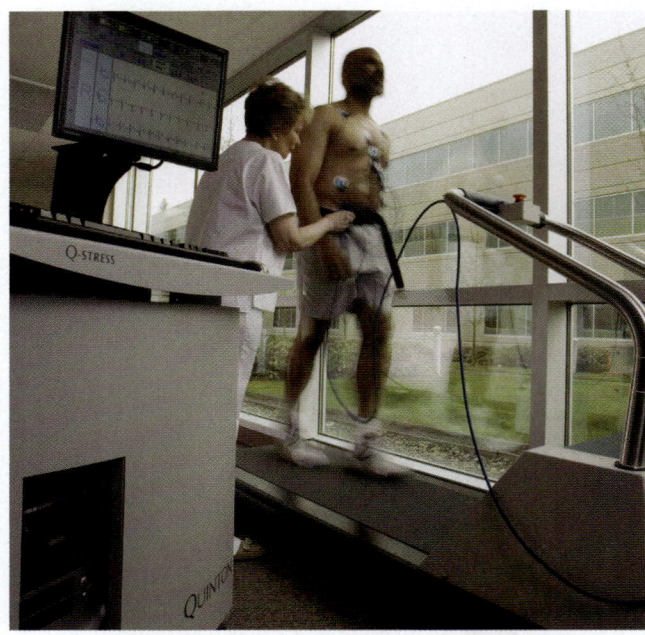

FIGURE 9-17 ■ Stress electrocardiography.

TEST OR PROCEDURE	EXPLANATION
magnetic resonance angiography (MRA) *mag-net′ik rez′ō-nănts an-jē-og′ră-fē*	magnetic resonance imaging of the heart and blood vessels for evaluation of pathology (see **Figure 4-16**)
nuclear medicine imaging *nū′klē-ĕr med′i-sin im′ă-jing*	radionuclide organ imaging of the heart after administration of radioactive isotopes to visualize structures and to analyze functions
myocardial radionuclide *mī-ō-kar′dē-ăl rā′dē-ō-nū′klīd pĕr-fyū′zhŭn skan*	scan of the heart made after an intravenous (IV) injection of an isotope (e.g., thallium) as it is absorbed by myocardial cells in proportion to blood flow throughout the heart; useful in evaluating coronary artery disease (CAD)
myocardial radionuclide perfusion stress scan *mī-ō-kar′dē-ăl rā′dē-ō-nū′klīd pĕr-fyū′zhŭn stres skan*	nuclear perfusion scan of the heart that is made before and after the induction of controlled physical exercise (treadmill or bicycle) or a pharmaceutical agent that produces the effect of exercise stress in patients who are unable to ambulate
multiple-gated acquisition (MUGA) scan *mŭl′ti-pul-gāt′ĕd ak′wi-zi′shŭn skan*	nuclear image of the beating heart in motion made as radioactive isotopes are injected in the bloodstream and traced through the heart's chambers; useful in evaluating the pumping function of the ventricles
positron-emission tomography (PET) scan of the heart *poz′i-tron-ē-mish′ŭn tō-mog′ră-fē skan of the hart*	use of specialized nuclear isotopes and computed tomographic techniques to produce perfusion (blood flow) images and to study the cellular metabolism of the heart; can be performed at rest or with stress

TEST OR PROCEDURE	EXPLANATION
radiology rā′dē-ol′ŏ-jē	x-ray imaging
angiography an-jē-og′ră-fē	process of x-ray imaging a blood vessel after injection of contrast dye, most commonly after catheter placement
angiogram an′jē-ō-gram	record obtained by angiography

coronary angiogram
        (see Figure 9-18)
        kōr′o-nār-ē an′jē-ō-gram
	x-ray image of the blood vessels of the heart using a catheter to inject contrast; see percutaneous transluminal coronary angioplasty (PTCA) listed under Self-Instruction: Operative Terms

arteriogram ar-tēr′ē-ō-gram	x-ray image of a particular artery (e.g., coronary arteriogram or renal arteriogram)
aortogram ā-ōr′tō-gram	x-ray image of the aorta
venogram vē′nō-gram	x-ray image of a vein
cardiac catheterization (see Figure 9-19) kar′dē-ak kath′ĕ-ter-ī-zā′shŭn	introduction of a flexible, narrow tube (or catheter) through a vein or artery into the heart to withdraw samples of blood, to measure pressures within the heart chambers or vessels, and to inject contrast dye for fluoroscopic radiography and cine film (motion picture) imaging of the chambers of the heart and coronary arteries; often includes interventional procedures, such as angioplasty and atherectomy; see percutaneous coronary intervention (PCI) procedures listed under Self-Instruction: Operative Terms
left heart catheterization left hart kath′ĕ-ter-ī-zā′shŭn	x-ray imaging of the left ventricular cavity and coronary arteries

PERCUTANEOUS TRANSLUMINAL CORONARY ANGIOPLASTY (PTCA)

Predilation angiogram revealing 99% stenosis of the right coronary artery (RCA).

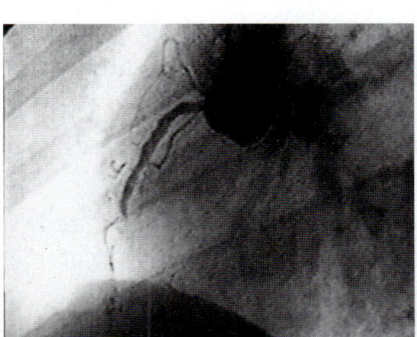

PTCA procedure showing catheter placement and straddling of the balloon at the occluded site.

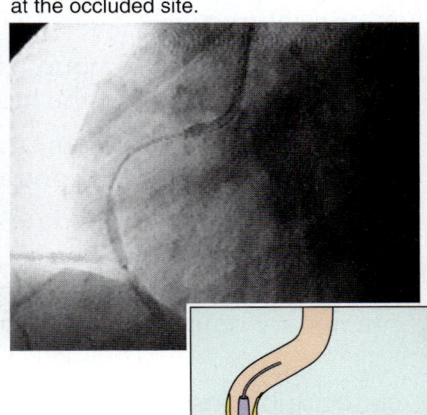

Catheter and wire placement with balloon inflation.

Post-PTCA angiogram showing successful dilation.

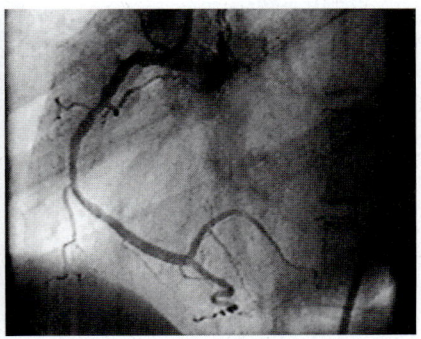

FIGURE 9-18 ■ Angiograms illustrating angioplasty.

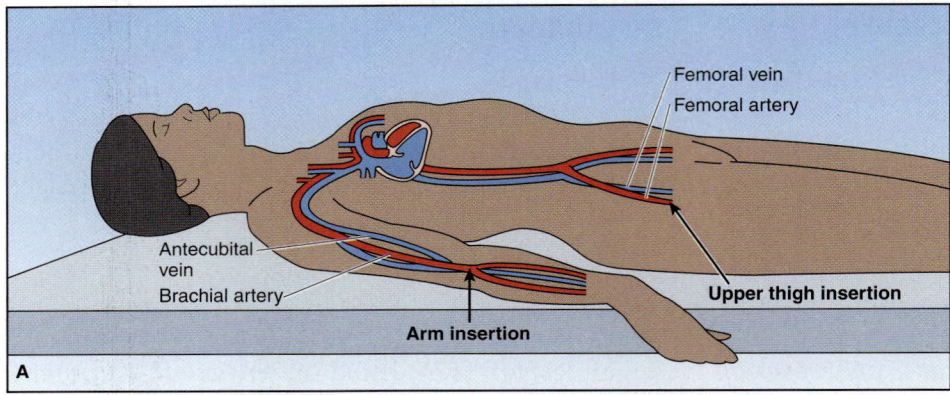

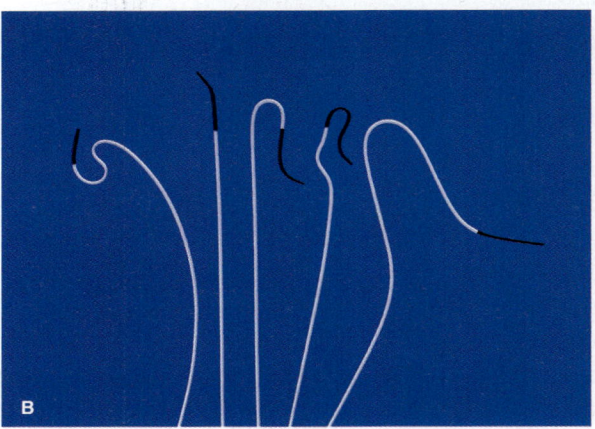

FIGURE 9-19 ■ Cardiac catheterization. **A.** Possible insertion sites for cardiac catheterization. **B.** Angiographic catheters.

TEST OR PROCEDURE	EXPLANATION
right heart catheterization rīt hart kath′ĕ-ter-ī-zā′shŭn	measurement of oxygen saturation and pressure readings of the right side of the heart
ventriculogram ven-trik′ū-lō-gram	x-ray image of the ventricles
stroke volume (SV) strōk vol′yŭm	measurement of the amount of blood ejected from a ventricle in one contraction
cardiac output (CO) kr′dē-ak owt′put	measurement of the amount of blood ejected per minute from either ventricle of the heart
ejection fraction ē-jek′shŭn frak′shŭn	measurement of the volume percentage of left ventricular blood ejected with each contraction
computed tomographic angiography (CTA) (see **Figure 9-20**) kom-pyū′tĕd tō-mo-grăf′ik an-jē-og′ră-fē	specialized, noninvasive, three-dimensional (3-D) computed tomographic scan of the heart and circulation of the "greater" blood vessels, such as the coronary arteries, aorta, and pulmonary veins; performed with or without contrast
sonography sŏ-nog′ră-fē	sonographic imaging; using high-frequency sound waves to visualize internal structures

echocardiography (echo)
    (see **Figure 9-21**)
    ek′ō-kar-dē-og′ră-fē
	recording of sound waves through the heart to evaluate structure and motion

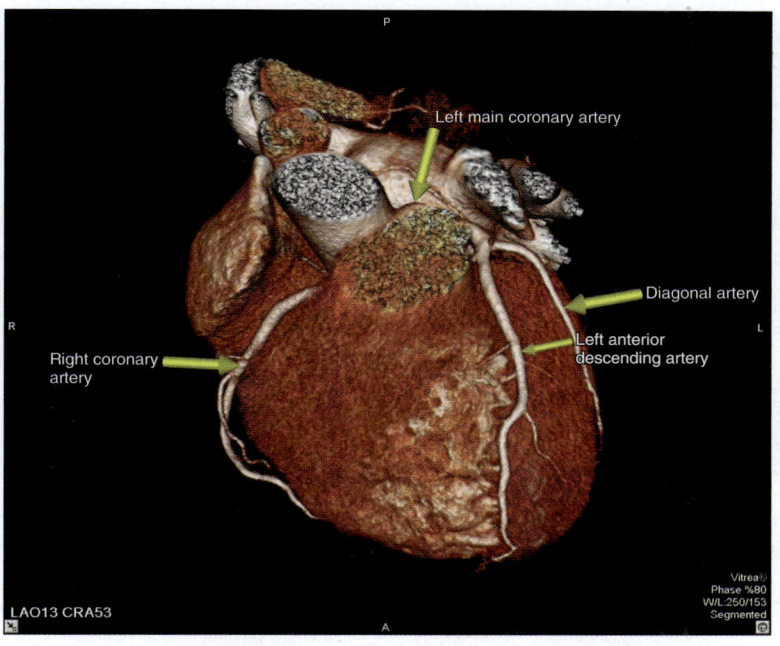

FIGURE 9-20 ■ Computed tomographic angiography (CTA) of normal heart. *Arrows* point to right coronary artery (RCA), left main coronary artery, diagonal artery, and left anterior descending artery.

TEST OR PROCEDURE	EXPLANATION
stress echocardiogram (stress echo) *stres ek-ō-kar′dē-ō-gram*	echocardiogram of the heart recorded during the induction of controlled physical exercise (treadmill or bicycle) or a pharmaceutical agent that produces the effect of exercise stress in patients who are unable to ambulate; useful in detecting conditions such as ischemia or infarction
transesophageal echocardiogram (TEE) *trans-e-sof′ăj-ē-ăl ek-ō-kar′dē-ō-gram*	echocardiogram of the heart after placement of an ultrasonic transducer at the end of an endoscope inside the esophagus
Doppler sonography (see Figure 9-22) *dop′lĕr sŏ-nog′ră-fē*	ultrasound technique used to evaluate blood flow to determine the patency (openness) and luminal (central cavity within a vessel) diameter; used to check for a deep vein thrombosis (DVT), carotid insufficiency, or to determine blood flow through structures

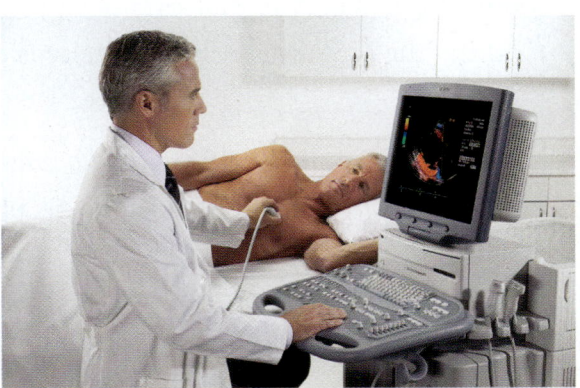

FIGURE 9-21 ■ Echocardiography.

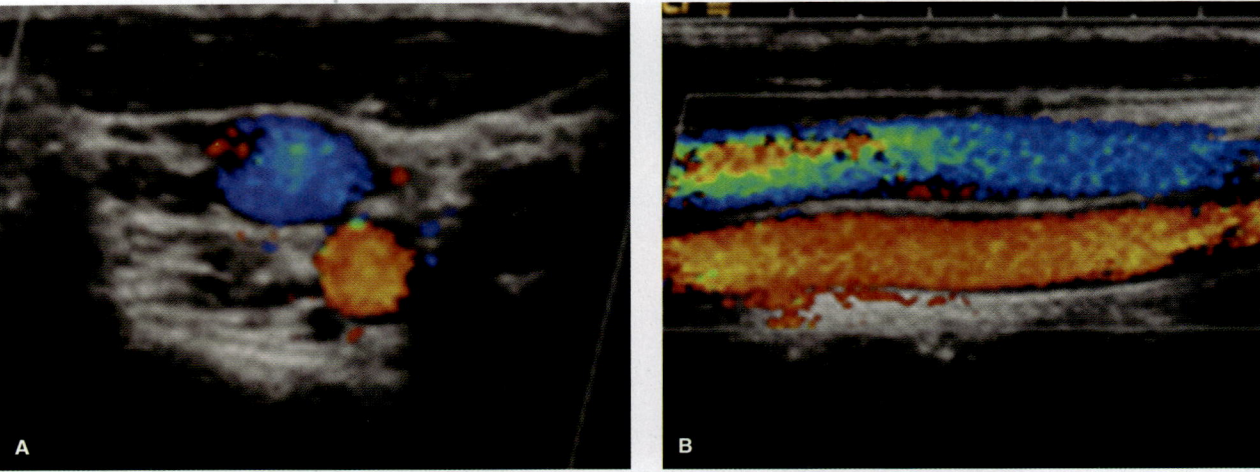

FIGURE 9-22 ■ Color flow Doppler image of the common carotid artery and jugular vein. Longitudinal (A) and transverse (B) images. Flow in the jugular vein is assigned a blue color, because blood is moving away from the transducer. Flow in the carotid artery is toward the transducer and is red. Color Doppler sonography helps to assess patency and luminal diameter.

Programmed Review: Diagnostic Tests and Procedure

ANSWERS	REVIEW
chest, stethoscope auscultation	9.67 Recall that the combining form *steth/o* means _____, and that a _____ is an instrument for listening to sounds within the chest or elsewhere in the body. This procedure, from the Greek word meaning to listen, is called _____.
gallop	9.68 Auscultation can be used to detect a heart murmur or other abnormal heart sound, such as that which mimics the gait of a horse, called a _____.
record heart electrocardiogram stress electrocardiogram	9.69 The suffix *-gram* refers to a _____. The combining form *cardi/o* refers to the _____. A record of the electrical conductivity of the heart is called an _____ (ECG or EKG). A special kind of electrocardiogram obtained during the physical stress of exercise is called a _____ _____.
vessel angiography angiogram heart	9.70 The combining form *angi/o* refers to a _____. The suffix *-graphy* refers to the diagnostic process of making a record, such as by x-ray imaging. The process of x-ray imaging a blood vessel is called _____, and the record itself is called an _____. A coronary angiogram is an x-ray image of the blood vessels encircling the _____.

ANSWERS	REVIEW
aortogram venogram	**9.71** An x-ray of a particular artery is called an arteriogram. An x-ray image of the aorta is called an _____. An x-ray image of a vein is called a _____.
cardiac catheterization right oxygen	**9.72** A catheter can be introduced into the heart for diagnostic purposes. This process is called _____ _____. Left heart catheterization is usually done to obtain a radiograph of the left ventricular cavity and coronary arteries, and _____ heart catheterization is usually done to measure _____ saturation and pressure.
ventriculogram -gram	**9.73** An x-ray image of the ventricles is called a _____, from the combining form *ventricul/o* and the suffix _____.
contraction, output left, ejected	**9.74** Cardiac catheterization also allows for measurement of stroke volume (SV), or how much blood is ejected from a ventricle in one _____. Cardiac _____ (CO) measures the amount of blood ejected per minute from either ventricle; ejection fraction measures the volume percentage of the _____ ventricular contents _____ with each contraction.
magnetic resonance imaging angiography computed tomography three-dimensional heart	**9.75** The abbreviation MRI stands for _____ _____ _____. The abbreviation MRA stands for magnetic resonance _____, which is specialized imaging of the heart and blood vessels. The abbreviation CT stands for _____ _____. The process abbreviated as CTA provides a specialized _____-_____ x-ray image of the _____ and greater vessels.
radionuclide organ imaging function radionuclide heart, intravenous myo, blood	**9.76** Nuclear medicine imaging, or _____ _____ _____, uses radioactive isotopes to visualize body structures and to analyze _____. A myocardial _____ perfusion scan is made of the _____ after _____ (IV) injection of an isotope is absorbed by _____cardial cells in proportion to _____ flow.

ANSWERS	REVIEW
motion, pumping positron emission tomography isotopes stress	A MUGA scan provides a nuclear image of the beating heart in _____ and is useful in evaluating the _____ function of the ventricles. The abbreviation PET stands for _____ _____ _____, which is a nuclear scan that uses radioactive _____ and computed tomographic (CT) technology. PET is used in cardiology to study the cellular metabolism of the heart. These scans can be made with the patient at rest or after exercise or _____.
ultrasound sound echo	9.77 Sonography, or diagnostic _____, is the imaging modality using high-frequency _____ waves to visualize body tissues. The recording of sound waves through the heart to evaluate structure and motion is called _____ cardiography.
echocardiogram stress transesophageal	9.78 A record of the heart made with echocardiography (echo) is called an _____. If made during controlled exercise, it is called a _____ echocardiogram. If made after passing the transducer through the esophagus, it is called a _____ echocardiogram (TEE).
Doppler	9.79 The type of sonography that uses ultrasound to evaluate blood flow is called _____ sonography.
within heart arrhythmias electrophysiologic study intracardiac ablation	9.80 Intracardiac means pertaining to _____ the _____. Physiologic means pertaining to function. The invasive procedure involving the placement of a catheter within the heart to map the electrical conduction of cardiac dysrhythmias, or _____, is abbreviated as EPS, which stands for intracardiac _____ _____. The myocardial tissue generating abnormal electrical pathways can be treated at the time of an intracardiac electrophysiologic study by using high-frequency waves sent through a catheter to ablate or destroy myocardial tissue responsible for generating the abnormal conduction. This treatment is called _____ catheter _____.

Self-Instruction: Operative Terms

Study the following:

TERM	MEANING
PROCEDURES PERFORMED IN THE TRADITIONAL OPERATING ROOM	
coronary artery bypass graft (CABG) (see Figure 9-23) kōr′o-nār-ē ar′tĕr-ē bī′pas graft	grafting a portion of a blood vessel retrieved from another part of the body (e.g., a length of saphenous vein from the leg or mammary artery from the chest wall) to bypass an occluded coronary artery, restoring circulation to myocardial tissue; the traditional method includes temporary arrest of the heart with circulation (bypass) of the patient's blood through a heart–lung machine during the procedure; an alternative, off-pump approach uses a stabilizer to perform the procedure on the beating heart; the abbreviation CABG is pronounced "cabbage"
anastomosis ă-nas′tō-mō′sis	the joining of two blood vessels to allow flow from one to the other; opening
endarterectomy end′ar-tĕr-ek′tŏ-mē	surgical removal of the lining of an artery to clear a blockage caused by a clot or atherosclerotic plaque buildup
valve replacement valv rē-plās′ment	surgery to replace a diseased heart valve with an artificial valve; there are two types of artificial valves: tissue valves, most commonly made from animal tissue (e.g., porcine [pig] or bovine [cow]), and mechanical valves, made from synthetic material
valvuloplasty val′vyū-lō-plas-tē	surgical repair of a defective heart valve
PROCEDURES PERFORMED IN A CATHETERIZATION LABORATORY	
percutaneous coronary intervention (PCI) (see Figure 9-24) per′kyū-tā′nē-ŭs kōr′o-nār-ē in′tĕr-ven′shn	interventional procedures used to treat coronary artery disease (CAD) performed at the time of cardiac catheterization in a specialized laboratory setting (or "cath lab") instead of the traditional operating room
angioscopy an-jē-os′kō-pē	use of a flexible fiberoptic angioscope (accompanied by an irrigation system, camera, video recorder, and monitor) that is guided through a specific blood vessel to visually assess a lesion and to select the mode of therapy; also called *vascular endoscopy*
vascular endoscopy vas′kyū-lăr en-dos′kŏ-pē	use of a flexible fiberoptic angioscope (accompanied by an irrigation system, camera, video recorder, and monitor) that is guided through a specific blood vessel to visually assess a lesion and to select the mode of therapy; also called *angioscopy*
atherectomy (see Figure 9-24A) ath-e-rek′tō-mē	excision of atheromatous plaque from within an artery utilizing a device housed in a flexible catheter that selectively cuts away or pulverizes tissue buildup

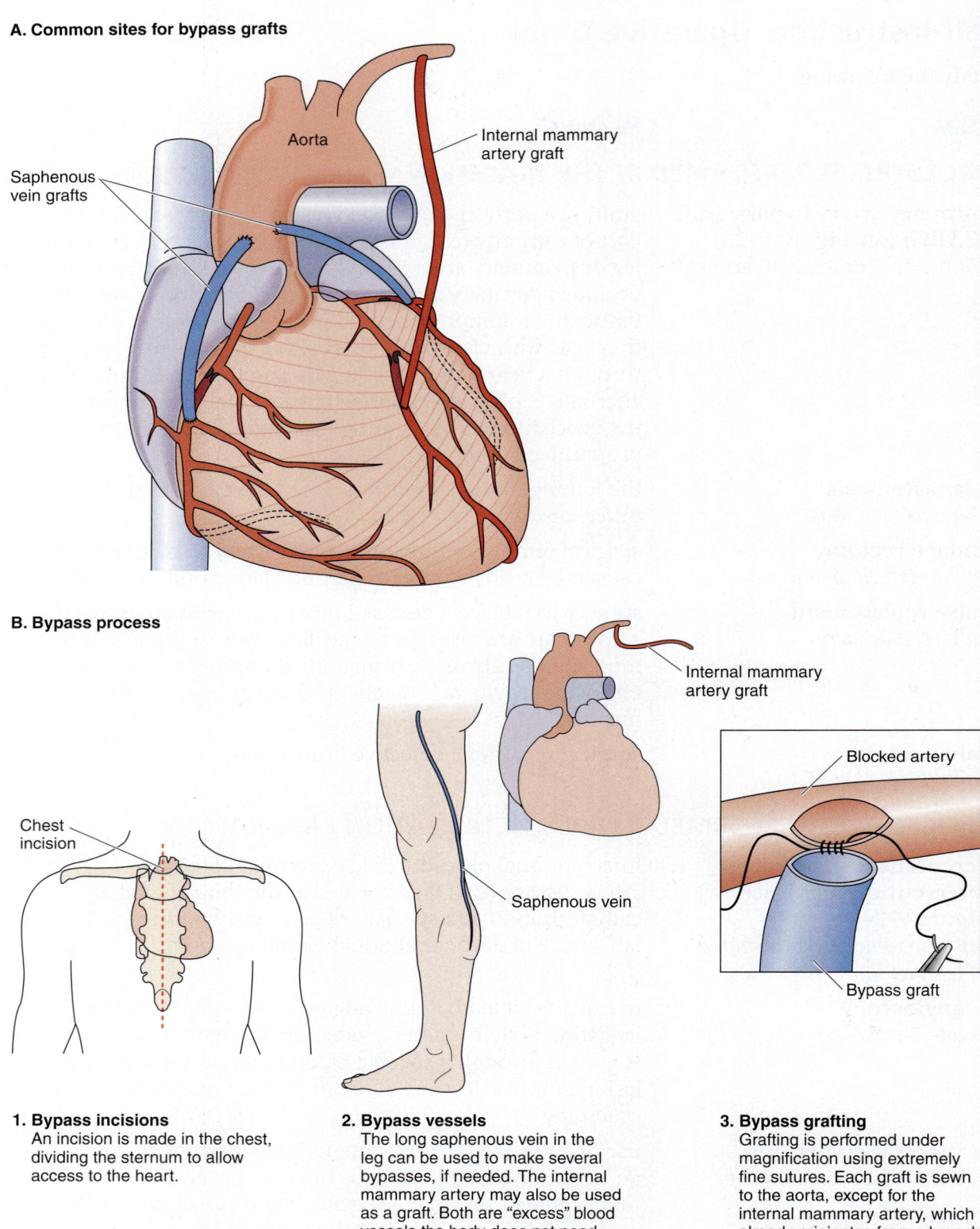

FIGURE 9-23 ■ Traditional methods of coronary artery bypass graft (CABG). **A.** Common sites for grafts on the heart. **B.** Bypass incisions (*1*), vessels (*2*), and grafting (*3*).

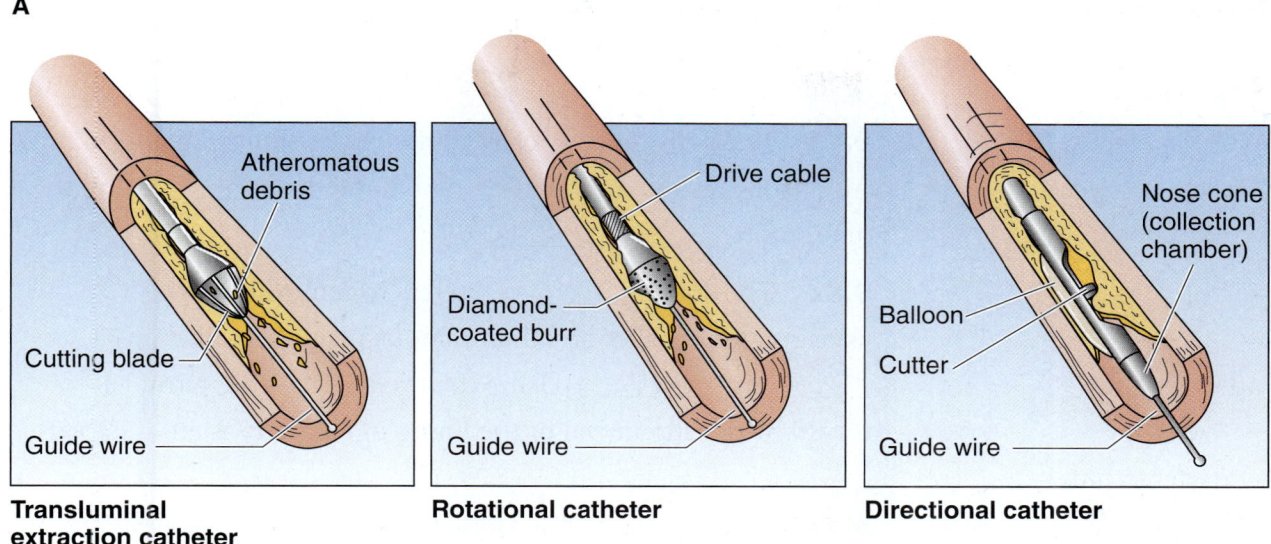

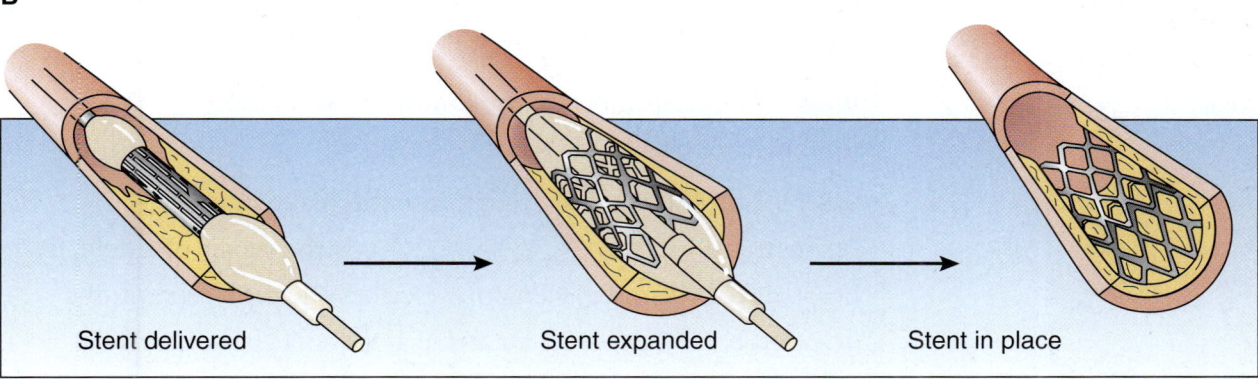

FIGURE 9-24 ■ Examples of devices used in percutaneous coronary interventional procedures. **A.** Atherectomy devices. **B.** Intravascular stent.

TERM	MEANING
percutaneous transluminal coronary angioplasty (PTCA) (see Figures 9-18 and 9-24) pĕr-kyū-tā′nē-ŭs tranz′lū-men′ăl kōr′o-nār-ē an′jē-ō-plas-tē	a method for treating the narrowing of a coronary artery by inserting a specialized catheter with a balloon attachment, then inflating the balloon to dilate and open the narrowed portion of the vessel and restore blood flow to the myocardium; most often includes the placement of a stent
intravascular stent placement (see Figure 9-24B) in′tră-vas′kyū-lăr stent plās′ment	implantation of a device used to reinforce the wall of a vessel and assure its patency (openness); most often used to treat a stenosis or a dissection (a split or tear in the wall of a vessel) or to reinforce patency of a vessel after angioplasty

Programmed Review: Operative Terms

ANSWERS	REVIEW
vessel angioscope	9.81 The suffix -scopy refers to the process of examination. Angioscopy is the examination of a blood _____ using a fiberoptic _____.
-ectomy atherectomy endarterectomy	9.82 The suffix _____ refers to removal or excision. Removal of an atheromatous plaque is called an _____. Using the prefix endo-, the term for the surgical removal of the lining of an artery is an _____.
bypass graft	9.83 CABG is the abbreviation for a coronary artery _____ _____, in which a portion of a blood vessel is grafted in place to bypass an occluded coronary artery.
vessels	9.84 An anastomosis is the joining of two blood _____ to flow from one to the other.
valvuloplasty tissue pig, cow	9.85 The suffix -plasty refers to a surgical repair or reconstruction. A _____ is the repair of a defective heart valve. Valve replacement describes the replacement of a diseased heart valve with an artificial valve. Types of artificial valves include mechanical ones, tissue made from synthetic material, and _____ valves made from animal tissue, such as porcine (_____) or bovine (_____).
vessel coronary angioplasty	9.86 An angioplasty is the surgical repair of a blood _____. A specialized procedure called a percutaneous transluminal _____ _____ (PTCA) is a treatment for a narrowed coronary artery.
stent	9.87 An intravascular _____ is implanted to keep a blood vessel open and to reinforce the vessel's wall.

Self-Instruction: Therapeutic Terms

Study this table to prepare for the programmed review that follows.

TERM	MEANING
defibrillation (see Figure 9-25) dē-fib-ri-lā′shŭn	termination of ventricular fibrillation by delivering an electrical stimulus to the heart; most commonly, this is done by applying the electrodes of the defibrillator externally to the chest wall, but it can also be performed internally, such as during open heart surgery or via an implanted device
defibrillator dē-fib′ri-lā-tŏr	device that delivers the electrical stimulus in defibrillation
cardioversion kar′dē-ō-ver′zhŭn	restoration of a fast or irregular heart rate to a normal rhythm, either by pharmaceutical means or by delivery of electrical energy
implantable cardioverter defibrillator (ICD) im-plan′t-bĕl kar′dē-ō-ver′ter dē-fib′ri-lā′tŏr	an implanted, battery-operated device with rate-sensing leads; the device monitors cardiac impulses and initiates an electrical stimulus as needed to stop ventricular fibrillation or tachycardia
pacemaker (see Figure 9-26) pās′mā-kĕr	a device used to treat slow heart rates (bradycardia) by electrically stimulating the heart to contract; most often, it is implanted with lead wires and battery circuitry under the skin, but it can also be placed on a temporary basis externally with lead wires inserted into the heart via a vein

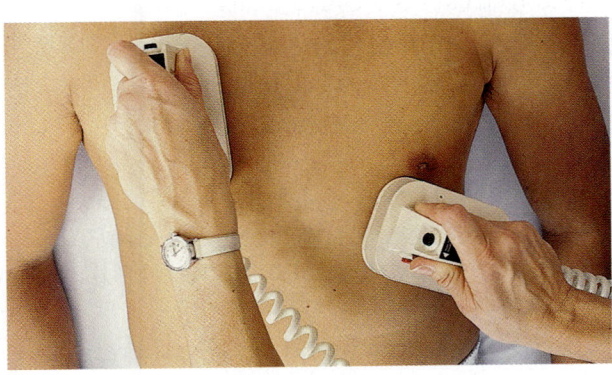

FIGURE 9-25 ■ Defibrillation. Standard paddle placement for defibrillation.

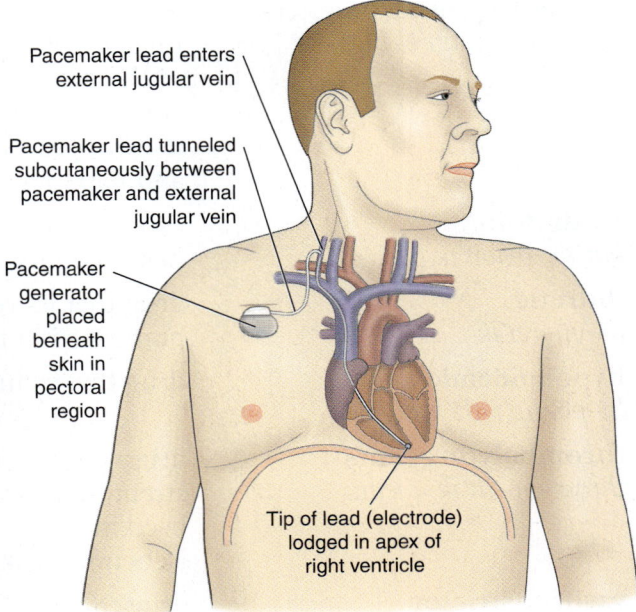

FIGURE 9-26 ■ Insertion of a pacemaker.

TERM	MEANING
COMMON THERAPEUTIC DRUG CLASSIFICATIONS	
angiotensin-converting enzyme (ACE) inhibitor an′jē-ō-ten′sin-kon-vert′ing en′zīm in-hib′i-tŏr	drug that suppresses the conversion of angiotensin in the blood by the angiotensin-converting enzyme (ACE); used in the treatment of hypertension
antianginal an′tē-an′ji-năl	drug that dilates coronary arteries, restoring oxygen to the tissues to relieve the pain of angina pectoris
antiarrhythmic an′tē-ă-rith′mik	drug that counteracts cardiac arrhythmia
anticoagulant an′tē-kō-ag′yū-lant	drug that prevents clotting of the blood; commonly used in the treatment of thrombophlebitis and myocardial infarction
antihypertensive an′tē-hī-per-ten′siv	drug that lowers blood pressure
beta-adrenergic blocking agents bā′tă-ad-rĕ-nĕr′jik blok′ing ā′jentz	agents that inhibit responses to sympathetic adrenergic nerve activity, causing a slowing of electrical conduction and heart rate and a lowering of the pressure within the walls of the vessels; used to treat angina pectoris and hypertension; the Greek small letter *beta* is commonly used in the names of these agents (i.e., β-blockers); also called *beta-blockers*
beta-blockers bā′tă-blok′ĕrz	agents that inhibit responses to sympathetic adrenergic nerve activity, causing a slowing of electrical conduction and heart rate and a lowering of the pressure within the walls of the vessels; used to treat angina pectoris and hypertension; the Greek small letter *beta* is commonly used in the names of these agents (i.e., β-blockers); also called *beta-adrenergic blocking agents*
calcium-channel blockers kal′sē-ŭm-chan′ĕl blok′ĕrz	agents that inhibit the entry of calcium ions into heart muscle cells, causing a slowing of the heart rate, a lessening of the demand for oxygen and nutrients, and a relaxing of the smooth muscle cells of the blood vessels to cause dilation; used to prevent or treat angina pectoris, some arrhythmias, and hypertension
cardiotonic kar′dē-ō-ton′ik	drug that increases the force of myocardial contractions in the heart; commonly used to treat congestive heart failure (CHF)
diuretic dī-yū-ret′ik	drug that increases the secretion of urine; commonly prescribed in treating hypertension
hypolipidemic hī-pō-lip′i-dē′mik	drug that reduces serum fat and cholesterol
thrombolytic agents throm-bō-lit′ik ā′jentz	drugs used to dissolve thrombi (blood clots) (e.g., streptokinase or tissue plasminogen activator [TPA or tPA]); used in acute management of myocardial infarction (MI) and ischemic stroke; commonly called "clot busters"
vasoconstrictor vā′sō-kon-strik′tŏr	drug that causes a narrowing of the blood vessels, thereby decreasing blood flow
vasodilator vā′sō-dī-lā′tŏr	drug that causes dilation of the blood vessels, thereby increasing blood flow

Programmed Review: Therapeutic Terms

ANSWERS	REVIEW
bradycardia pacemaker	**9.88** The term for a condition of slow heart is _____. A device that is surgically implanted to make a slow heart maintain an adequate pace is called a _____.
fast cardioversion	**9.89** Tachycardia is a condition of _____ heart rate. Version is a process of turning. The method of turning an abnormally fast or irregular heart rate back to normal by use of a drug or delivery of electrical energy is called _____.
fibrillation, not defibrillator	**9.90** Chaotic, irregular contractions of the heart are called _____. The prefix *de-* means from, down, or _____. A device used on a patient to stop ventricular fibrillation is called a _____. The process of doing so is called defibrillation.
implantable cardioverter defibrillator	**9.91** An implantable device that initiates an electrical stimulus to stop ventricular fibrillation or tachycardia is called an _____ _____ _____ (ICD).
against or opposed to coagulation or clotting hypertensive	**9.92** The prefix *anti-* means _____. Drugs in the class known as anticoagulants work to prevent _____. A drug that lowers high blood pressure is called an anti_____.
chest pain antianginal dilator myocardium	**9.93** Recall that angina pectoris is _____ _____. Drugs that treat this pain are classified as _____ drugs. Nitroglycerin is a common antianginal medication. It acts as a vaso_____, causing the coronary arteries to expand and, thereby, increasing the flow of blood to the heart muscle tissue, also known as the _____.
arrhythmic	**9.94** A drug that counteracts a cardiac arrhythmia is called an anti_____.
beta-blockers	**9.95** Several different drug classifications are used to treat hypertension. Beta-adrenergic blocking agents, also called, more simply, _____-_____, work by inhibiting responses to a nerve activity and slowing electrical conduction and heart rate.

ANSWERS	REVIEW
calcium-channel	**9.96** Another type of antihypertensive drug works by inhibiting the entry of calcium ions into heart muscle cells, thereby slowing the heart and causing other changes. These are called _____-_____ blockers.
urine	**9.97** Another antihypertensive drug, called a diuretic, works by increasing the secretion of _____ from the body.
tonic	**9.98** Congestive heart failure (CHF) is often treated with drugs that increase the force of ventricular contractions. These drugs are called cardio_____ agents.
hypolipid	**9.99** Recall that lipids are fats. Using the prefix *hypo-*, the term for a drug that lowers the amount of fat in the blood is a _____emic agent.
breaking down clots thrombo clot busters myocardial infarction	**9.100** The suffix *-lysis* means _____ _____. Drugs that work to dissolve thrombi or _____ in the blood are called _____lytic agents. Thrombolytics, commonly known as _____ _____, are used in acute management of ischemic stroke and _____ _____ (MI).

Chapter 9 Abbreviations

ABBREVIATION	EXPANSION
ACE	angiotensin-converting enzyme
ACS	acute coronary syndrome
ASD	atrial septal defect
AV	atrioventricular
BP	blood pressure
CABG	coronary artery bypass graft
CAD	coronary artery disease
CCU	coronary care unit; critical care unit
CHF	congestive heart failure
CO	cardiac output
CTA	computed tomographic angiography

ABBREVIATION	EXPANSION
CXR	chest x-ray
DVT	deep vein thrombosis
ECG	electrocardiogram
ECHO	echocardiography
EKG	electrocardiogram
EPS	electrophysiologic study
HTN	hypertension
ICD	implantable cardioverter defibrillator
IV	intravenous
MI	myocardial infarction
MRA	magnetic resonance angiography
MUGA	multiple-gated acquisition (scan)
MVP	mitral valve prolapse
NSR	normal sinus rhythm
PCI	percutaneous coronary intervention
PDA	patent ductus arteriosus
PET	positron-emission tomography
PTCA	percutaneous transluminal coronary angioplasty
PVC	premature ventricular contraction
RCA	right coronary artery
SA	sinoatrial
SCA	sudden cardiac arrest
STAT	immediately
SV	stroke volume
TEE	transesophageal echocardiogram
tPA or TPA	tissue plasminogen activator
VSD	ventricular septal defect

PRACTICE EXERCISES

For each of the following words, write out the term parts (prefixes [P], combining forms [CF], roots [R], and suffixes [S]) on the lines below the word. Then define the term according to the meaning of its parts.

EXAMPLE

pericardial

peri / cardi / al
P   R   S

DEFINITION: around/heart/pertaining to

1. angiography

    _____ / _____
         CF   S

    DEFINITION: _____

2. varicosis

    _____ / _____
         R   S

    DEFINITION: _____

3. pectoral

    _____ / _____
         R   S

    DEFINITION: _____

4. vasospasm

    _____ / _____
         CF   S

    DEFINITION: _____

5. venous

    _____ / _____
         R   S

    DEFINITION: _____

Write the letter of the matching meaning in the space after the term.

6. atherosclerosis _____   a. traveling clot that obstructs when it lodges

7. infarct _____   b. buildup of fat

8. hypotension _____   c. growth of tissue

9. vegetation _____   d. low blood pressure

10. embolus _____   e. scar left by necrosis

Write the correct medical term for each of the following definitions.

11. _____ malformations of the heart present at birth

12. _____ thickening, loss of elasticity, and calcification (hardening) of arterial walls

13. _____ irregularity or loss of rhythm of the heartbeat
14. _____ a general term for disease of the heart muscle
15. _____ joining of two blood vessels to allow flow from one vessel to the other

Write the correct terms for the anatomic structures indicated.

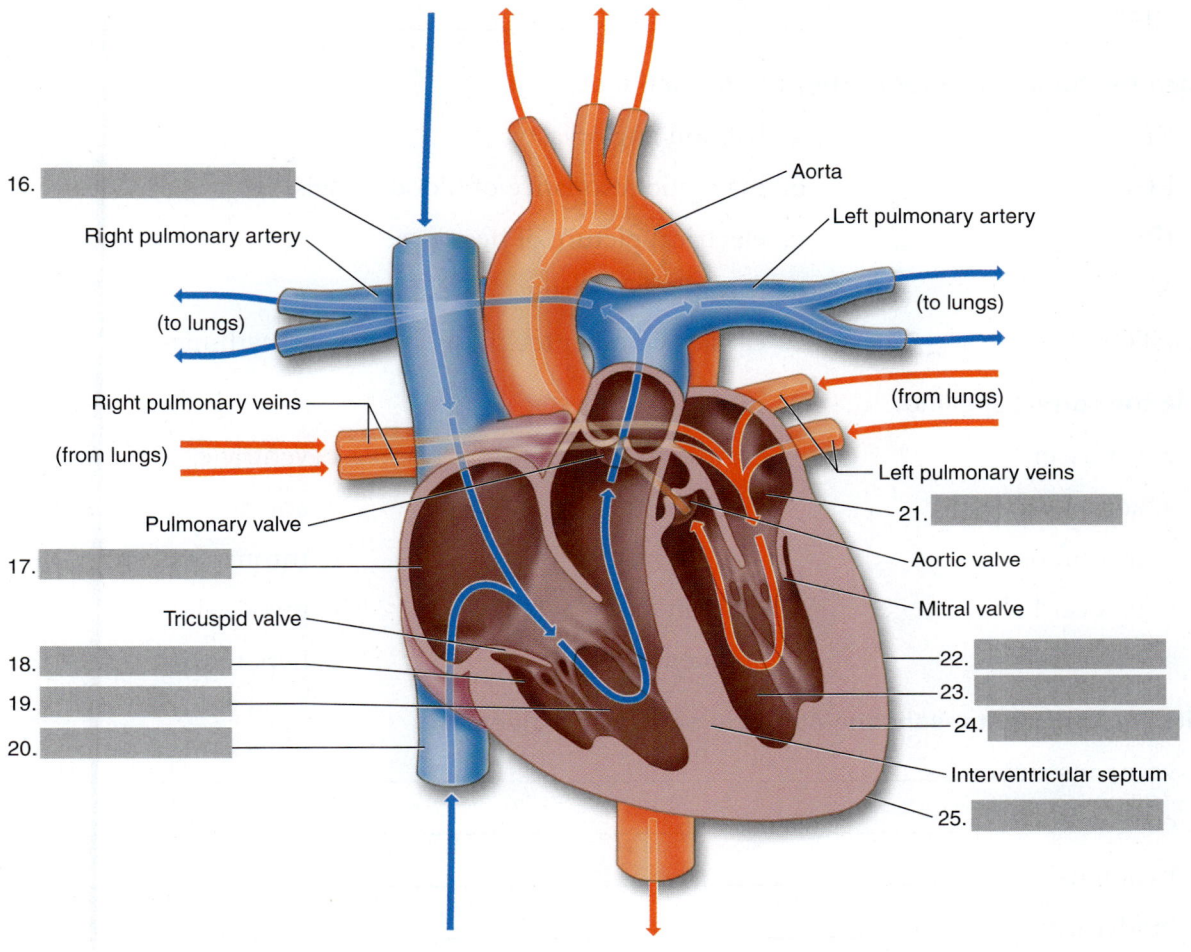

16. _____
17. _____
18. _____
19. _____
20. _____
21. _____
22. _____
23. _____
24. _____
25. _____

Write out the expanded term for each abbreviation.

26. PVC _____
27. PDA _____
28. ACS _____
29. ICD _____
30. CHF _____

Match the following abbreviations with their meanings.

31. EPS _____   a. balloon angioplasty
32. ECG _____   b. magnetic resonance of blood vessels
33. tPA _____   c. electrical picture of heart
34. MRA _____   d. thrombolytic drug
35. PTCA _____   e. cardiac catheter technique to map arrhythmias

Circle the correct spelling.

36. a. ventricel   b. ventrical   c. ventricle
37. a. aorta   b. aorto   c. aorrta
38. a. thrombos   b. thrombus   c. thrommbus
39. a. myocardial   b. mycardial   c. myocardiol
40. a. hypatension   b. hyptension   c. hypotension

Write the term that means the opposite of the term given.

41. vasoconstriction _____
42. coagulant _____
43. hypotension _____
44. bradycardia _____
45. diastole _____

Circle the combining form that corresponds to the meaning given.

46. chest
    a. phleb/o   b. sphygm/o   c. pector/o
47. vein
    a. aort/o   b. phleb/o   c. varic/o
48. vessel
    a. angi/o   b. arteri/o   c. coron/o
49. heart
    a. ven/o   b. coron/o   c. cardi/o
50. fatty paste
    a. aort/o   b. ather/o   c. atri/o

MEDICAL RECORD ANALYSIS
Medical Record 9-1

PROGRESS NOTE

S: This 54 y/o male was admitted to CCU with onset of acute anterior chest pain radiating to the left shoulder and SOB; pt underwent a CABG × 4, 6 months ago.

O: BP 190/110, P 100, R 72, T 38°C
On PE, pt was in moderate to severe distress. An ECG showed sinus tachycardia, and a CXR revealed left ventricular hypertrophy.

A: R/O MI

P: Order blood enzyme measurement STATE chocardiogram
CT scan of chest

Questions About Medical Record 9-1

1. What is the patient's CC?
   a. severe angina
   b. angina developing slowly over time
   c. enlargement of the heart
   d. fast heart rate
   e. slow heart rate

2. Describe the procedure that the patient underwent 6 months ago.
   a. surgery to dilate and open narrowed portions of coronary arteries
   b. diversion of blood flow around occluded coronary arteries
   c. replacement of a diseased heart valve
   d. coring of the lining of an artery to remove a clot
   e. heart transplant

3. Where was the patient treated?
   a. outpatient medical office
   b. outpatient emergency room
   c. inpatient intensive care
   d. inpatient coronary care
   e. outpatient cardiology department

4. What type of physician is most appropriate to provide initial care and assessment of this patient?
   a. ER physician
   b. internist
   c. gerontologist
   d. cardiovascular surgeon
   e. cardiologist

5. What did the electrical picture of the heart reveal?
   a. extremely rapid but regular contractions of the heart
   b. slow heart rate
   c. chaotic, irregular contractions of the heart
   d. fast heart rate
   e. interference with normal electrical conduction of the heart known as a block

6. What was the assessment?
   a. patient may have had a heart attack
   b. patient may be suffering from right heart failure
   c. patient has congestive heart failure
   d. patient may have high blood pressure
   e. patient may have an enlarged heart

7. What were the objective findings of the chest radiograph?
   a. unknown
   b. increase in size of left ventricle
   c. vessel disease
   d. dead heart muscle
   e. fast heart rate

8. Identify the x-ray imaging procedure ordered in the plan.
   a. sonogram of heart
   b. chest radiography
   c. blood pressure
   d. computed tomography
   e. biochemistry panel

ANSWERS TO PRACTICE EXERCISES

1. angiography
   CF: angio
   S: graphy
   DEFINITION: vessel/process of recording
2. varisocis
   R: varic
   S: osis
   DEFINITION: swollen, twisted vein/condition or increase
3. pectoral
   R: pector
   S: al
   DEFINITION: chest/pertaining to
4. vasospasm
   CF: vaso
   S: spasm
   DEFINITION: vessel/involuntary contraction
5. venous
   R: ven
   S: ous
   DEFINITION: vein/pertaining to
6. b
7. e
8. d
9. c
10. a
11. congenital anomalies
12. arteriosclerosis
13. arrhythmia or dysrhythmia
14. cardiomyopathy
15. anastomosis
16. superior vena cava
17. right atrium
18. endocardium
19. right ventricle
20. inferior vena cava
21. left atrium
22. epicardium
23. left ventricle
24. myocardium
25. apex
26. premature ventricular contraction
27. patent ductus arteriosus
28. acute coronary syndrome
29. implantable cardioverter defibrillator
30. congestive heart failure
31. e
32. c
33. d
34. b
35. a
36. ventricle
37. aorta
38. thrombus
39. myocardial
40. hypotension
41. vasodilation
42. anticoagulant
43. hypertension
44. tachycardia
45. systole
46. pector/o
47. phleb/o
48. angi/o
49. cardi/o
50. ather/o

ANSWERS TO MEDICAL RECORD 9-1

1. a
2. b
3. d
4. e
5. d
6. a
7. b
8. d

10

RESPIRATORY SYSTEM

After completing this chapter, you should be able to:
- Define terms parts related to the respiratory system.
- Identify key respiratory system anatomic structures with their functions.
- Define symptomatic and diagnostic terms related to the respiratory system.
- Explain diagnostic tests; procedures; and operative and therapeutic terms related to the respiratory system.
- Cite common abbreviations related to the respiratory system and give the expansion of each.
- Explain terms used in medical records involving the respiratory system.

RESPIRATORY SYSTEM OVERVIEW

Our body's cells require oxygen, and the job of the respiratory system is to make sure the oxygen requirements are met. Carbon dioxide is a byproduct of cellular metabolism, and the respiratory system plays a role in the exchange of oxygen for carbon dioxide. In physiology, we refer to the exchange of air between the lungs and the atmosphere as *respiration*. Respiration in this sense can also be called *breathing* or *ventilation*. Here is an overview of the respiratory system (see **Figure 10-1**).

- It is divided into an upper respiratory tract and a lower respiratory tract.
- The respiratory system supplies oxygen to body cells and tissues by via the bloodstream.
- Oxygen is brought into the body as air is inhaled (inspiration) into the lungs and is passed into the bloodstream.

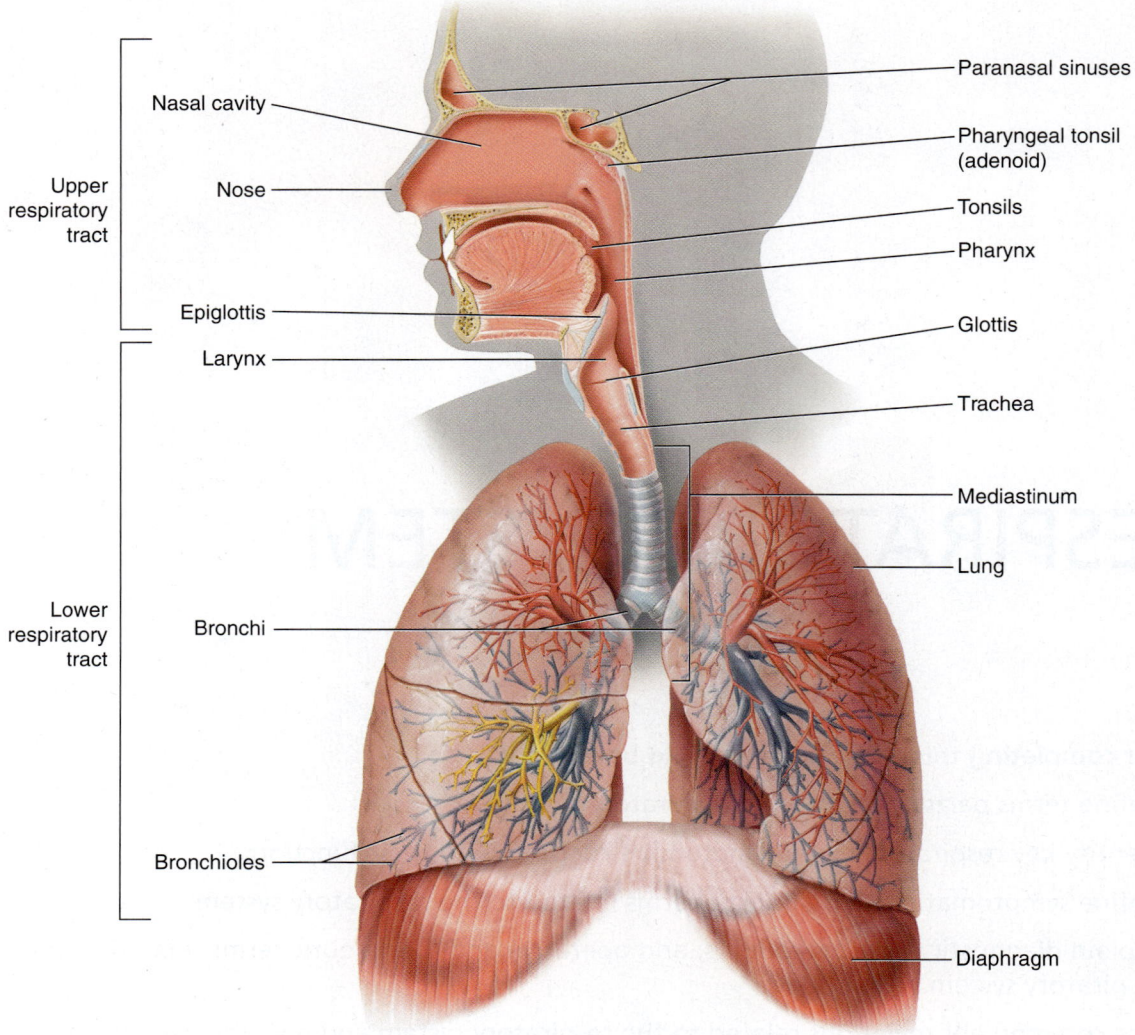

FIGURE 10-1 ■ Structures of the respiratory system.

- Carbon dioxide is eliminated through exhalation (expiration) as the lungs received carbon dioxide that has diffused out of the blood.
- The larynx and vocal cords make sounds possible as air passes across them.

Self-Instruction: Combining Forms

Study this table to prepare for the programmed review that follows.

COMBINING FORM	MEANING
alveol/o	alveolus (air sac)
bronch/o	bronchus (airway)
bronchi/o	bronchus (airway)
bronchiol/o	bronchiole (little airway)
capn/o	carbon dioxide
carb/o	carbon dioxide

COMBINING FORM	MEANING
laryng/o	larynx (voice box)
lob/o	lobe (a portion)
nas/o	nose
or/o	mouth
ox/o	oxygen
palat/o	palate
pector/o	chest
pharyng/o	pharynx (throat)
phren/o	diaphragm (also mind)
pleur/o	pleura (lining of lungs)
-pnea	breathing
pneum/o	air or lung
pneumon/o	air or lung
pulmon/o	lung
rhin/o	nose
sinus/o	sinus (cavity)
spir/o	breathing
steth/o	chest
thorac/o	chest
tonsill/o	tonsil
trache/o	trachea (windpipe)
uvul/o	uvula

Programmed Review: Combining Forms

ANSWERS	REVIEW
pulmon/o pneum/o, pneumon/o inflammation	10.1 The lungs are the primary organs of the respiratory system. A pulmonologist is a medical specialist who is concerned with the lungs. The combining form for lung is _____. The two combining forms that can refer to either air or lung are _____ and _____. For example, pneumothorax describes air in the chest (pleural cavity). Pneumonitis is an _____ of the lung.
lob/o excision lobectomy	10.2 The combining form for lobe (as in a lung lobe) is _____. Because the suffix -ectomy means an _____ or removal, the removal of a lung lobe is called a _____.

ANSWERS	REVIEW
	10.3 Several different combining forms refer to the chest and are the basis of terms related to the respiratory system. A
incision	thoracotomy is an _____ into the chest; the term
thorac/o	uses the combining form _____. A stethoscope, from the
steth/o	combining form _____, is an instrument used to listen to lung sounds through the chest wall. Because the suffix -*algia*
pain	refers to _____, pectoralgia, from the combining form
pector/o	_____, means chest pain.
ox/o	**10.4** The combining form meaning oxygen is _____.
deficient or below	Using the prefix *hypo-*, which means _____, and
condition of	the suffix -*ia*, which means _____ ____, the term for
hypoxia	a condition of deficient oxygen levels is _____. (Note that occasionally, when a prefix ends in a vowel and the root begins with a vowel, the final vowel is dropped from the prefix.)
blood	Because the suffix -*emia* refers to a _____ condition, the term for a condition of deficient oxygen in the blood is
hypoxemia	_____.
	10.5 The lungs move oxygen into the blood and carbon dioxide out of the blood. The combining forms for carbon
capn/o, carb/o	dioxide are _____ and _____. Hypercapnia,
much	for example, is a condition of too _____ carbon dioxide in the blood; hypercarbia is a synonym. The term for a condition of
hypocapnia	too little carbon dioxide in the blood is _____ or
hypocarbia	_____.
breathing	**10.6** The combining form *spir/o* means _____.
measuring	Because -*metry* refers to the process of _____ something, the term for the measuring of breathing is
spirometry, -pnea	_____. A suffix related to breathing is _____, as
difficult, painful, or faulty	in the term dyspnea, meaning _____ breathing.
	10.7 Many combining forms are the basis of anatomic terms related to the respiratory system. The combining form meaning
or/o	mouth or oral cavity is _____. The combining form meaning
nas/o	nose or nasal cavity is _____. From the Greek word *rhis*
rhin/o	comes a second combining term for nose: _____. Rhinitis,
inflammation	for example, is an _____ of the nose.

ANSWERS	REVIEW
sinus/o -itis sinusitis	**10.8** The combining form for sinus is _____. Because the suffix meaning an inflammation is _____, the term for an inflammation of a sinus is _____. (Remember that a combining vowel is *not* used before a suffix that begins with a vowel.)
palat/o palatoplasty	**10.9** The palate is the roof of the mouth, from the combining form _____. Recall that the suffix *-plasty* refers to a surgical repair or reconstruction; the term for reconstruction of the palate is _____.
pharyng/o pharyngitis laryng/o laryngitis	**10.10** The combining form for the pharynx (throat) is _____. An inflamed pharynx is called _____. Beneath the pharynx is the larynx (voice box), from the combining form _____. An inflamed larynx is _____.
tonsill/o uvul/o trache/o	**10.11** Many anatomic terms are virtually identical to their combining forms. The combining term for tonsil is _____. The combining term for uvula is _____. The combining term for trachea (windpipe) is _____. These are all structures of the airway.
bronch/o bronchi bronchiol/o	**10.12** The combining form for bronchus (airway) is _____ or *bronchi/o*. The plural of bronchus is _____. A related term, bronchiole (little airway), is derived from the combining form _____.
alveol/o	**10.13** An alveolus is a small air sac in the lungs, from the combining form _____. The common adjective form is alveolar.
pleur/o pleurae	**10.14** Pleura is a membrane enclosing the lungs, from the combining form _____. The plural of pleura is _____.
phren/o phrenalgia or phrenodynia	**10.15** The Greek word *phren* can mean either the mind or the diaphragm, a muscular partition below the lungs. The combining form for diaphragm is _____. Using the common suffix for pain, the term for pain in the diaphragm is _____.

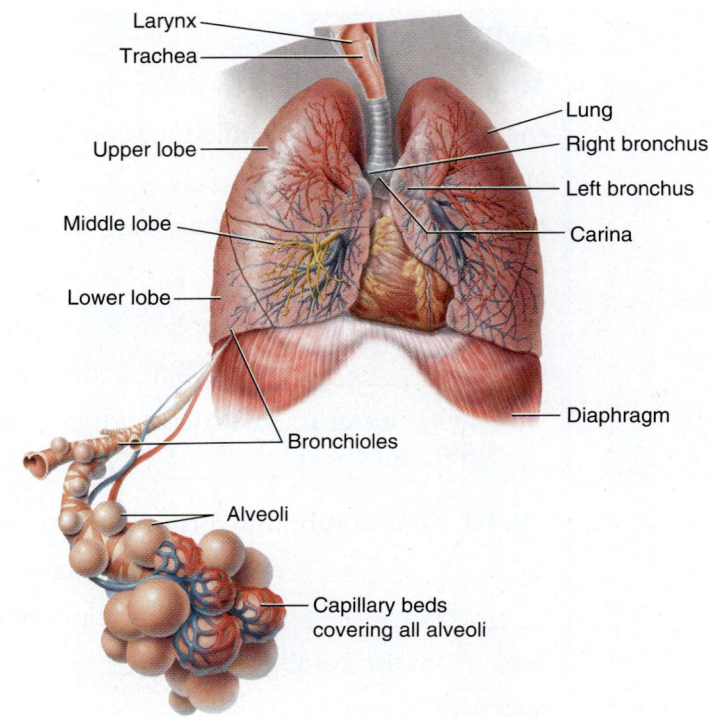

FIGURE 10-2 ■ Structures of the lower respiratory tract.

Self-Instruction: Anatomic Terms

Study this table to prepare for the programmed review that follows (see Figures 10-1 and 10-2).

TERM	MEANING
nose *nōz*	structure that warms, moistens, and filters air as it enters the respiratory tract; also houses the olfactory receptors for the sense of smell
paranasal sinuses *par′ ă-nā′ săl sī′ nŭs-ĕz*	air-filled spaces in the skull that open into the nasal cavity
palate *pal′ ăt*	roof of the mouth; partition between the oral and nasal cavities; divided into the hard and soft palate
hard palate *hard pal′ ăt*	bony anterior (front) portion of the palate
soft palate *soft pal′ ăt*	muscular posterior (back) portion of the palate
pharynx *far′ ingks*	throat; passageway for food to the esophagus and for air to the larynx
nasopharynx *nā-zō-far′ ingks*	part of the pharynx directly behind the nasal passages
oropharynx *ōr′ ō-far′ ingks*	central portion of the pharynx between the roof of the mouth and the upper edge of the epiglottis
laryngopharynx *lă-ring′ gō-far′ ingks*	lower part of the pharynx, just below the oropharyngeal opening into the larynx and esophagus

TERM	MEANING
tonsils *ton′silz*	oval lymphatic tissues on each side of the pharynx that filter air to protect the body from bacterial invasion; also called *palatine tonsils*
adenoid *ad′ĕ-noyd*	lymphatic tissue on the back of the pharynx behind the nose; also called *pharyngeal tonsil*
uvula *yū′vyū-lă*	small projection hanging from the posterior middle edge of the soft palate; named for its grape-like shape
larynx *lar′ingks*	voice box; passageway for air moving from the pharynx to the trachea; contains the vocal cords
glottis *glot′is*	opening between the vocal cords in the larynx
epiglottis *ep-i-glot′is*	a lid-like structure that covers the larynx during swallowing to prevent food from entering the airway
carina *kă-rī′nă*	cartilaginous ridge at the point where the trachea divides into the two (right and left) bronchi
trachea *trā′kē-ă*	windpipe; passageway for air from the larynx to the area of the carina, where it splits into the right and left bronchi in the lungs
bronchial tree *brong′kē-ăl trē*	branched airways that lead from the trachea to the microscopic air sacs called alveoli
right bronchus and left bronchus *rīt brong′kŭs and left brong′kŭs*	two primary airways branching from the area of the carina into the lungs
bronchioles *brong′kē-ōlz*	progressively smaller tubular branches of the airways
alveoli *al-vē′ō-lī*	thin-walled, microscopic air sacs that exchange gases
lungs *lŭngz*	two spongy organs in the thoracic cavity enclosed by the diaphragm and rib cage; responsible for breathing
lobes *lōbz*	subdivisions of the lung, with two on the left and three on the right
pleura (see **Figure 10-3**) *plūr′ă*	membranes enclosing the lung (visceral pleura) and lining the thoracic cavity (parietal pleura)
pleural cavity *plūr′ăl kav′i-tē*	potential space between the visceral and parietal layers of the pleura
diaphragm *dī′ă-fram*	muscular partition that separates the thoracic cavity from the abdominal cavity and that moves upward and downward to aid in breathing
mediastinum *mē′dē-as-tī′nŭm*	partition that separates the thorax into two compartments (containing the right and left lungs) and that encloses the heart, esophagus, trachea, and thymus gland
mucous membranes *myū′kus mem′brānz*	thin sheets of tissue that line respiratory passages and secrete mucus, a viscid (sticky) fluid

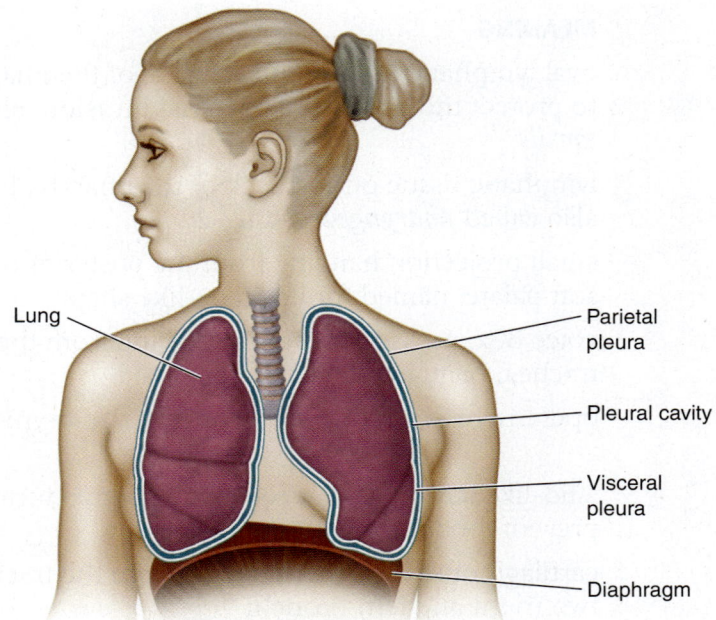

FIGURE 10-3 ■ The pleural membranes associated with the lungs.

TERM	MEANING
cilia sil′ē-ă	hair-like processes from the surface of epithelial cells, such as those of the bronchi, to move mucus upward
parenchyma pă-reng′ki-mă	functional tissues of any organ, such as the tissues of the bronchioles, alveoli, ducts, and sacs, that perform respiration

Programmed Review: Anatomic Terms

ANSWERS	REVIEW
paranasal sinuses palate soft	10.16 Air enters the respiratory system at the mouth and nose, which filters and warms the air. The air-filled cavities in the skull that open into the nasal cavity are called _____ _____. The roof of the mouth is called the _____, which is divided into two parts: the hard palate and the _____ palate.
pharynx nasopharynx oropharynx	10.17 Air then passes through the throat, or _____. The part of this structure located behind the nasal passages includes the combining form for nose in its name; it is called the _____. The part of the pharynx between the roof of the mouth and the upper edge of the epiglottis includes the combining form for mouth in its name; it is called the _____.

ANSWERS	REVIEW
larynx laryngopharynx tonsils adenoid uvula	**10.18** The air moves from the pharynx to the structure called the voice box, the medical term for which is _____. Appropriately, the lower part of the pharynx, where it meets the larynx, is called the _____. The oval lymphatic tissues on each side of the pharynx that help to filter bacteria from the air are the _____. Another area of lymphatic tissue on the back of the pharynx behind the nose is the _____. Hanging from the posterior middle edge of the soft palate is a small tissue projection called the _____.
vocal cords epiglottis upon	**10.19** The glottis is the opening between the _____ _____ in the larynx. A related term for the lid-like structure that covers the larynx during swallowing to prevent food from entering the trachea is the _____. The prefix *epi-* means _____. The epiglottis lies upon the trachea to close it like a lid during swallowing.
trachea bronchi bronchial bronchioles -ole	**10.20** The air then enters the windpipe, or _____, which splits into the right and left _____, which are the two primary airways to the lungs. Note in **Figure 10-1** how the bronchi soon split into more and more branches. The branching structure is called the _____ tree. The smallest tubular branches are the _____. The suffix _____ means small.
alveoli alveolus lungs lobes three	**10.21** At the ends of the bronchioles are thin-walled, microscopic air sacs called _____, where oxygen and carbon dioxide are exchanged. The singular form of this term is _____. The alveoli comprise much of the right and left _____. The left lung is divided into two sections, called _____; the right lung has _____ lobes.
pleura pleural	**10.22** The membranes enclosing the lung and lining the thoracic cavity are called _____. Between these two layers of pleura is a potential space called the _____ cavity.
diaphragm	**10.23** The lungs are in the thoracic cavity. Between the thoracic cavity and the abdominal cavity below is a muscular partition that moves up and down to help with breathing. This partition is called the _____.

ANSWERS	REVIEW
mediastinum	**10.24** The term medial means relating to the middle. Using the same combining form, the term for the partition in the middle of the thorax that separates the thorax into two compartments is the _____.
mucous membranes mucous cilia	**10.25** Lining the inside of respiratory passages are membranes that secrete mucus, called _____ _____. Note the difference between the noun mucus and the adjective form _____. Mucus traps microorganisms and other materials, and tiny hair-like processes, called _____, move this mucus up and out of the respiratory tract to be expelled from the body.
tissue alveoli	**10.26** The term parenchyma refers to functional _____ of any organ. In the lungs, the parenchyma includes the bronchioles and, most importantly, the _____, where gas exchange takes place.

Self-Instruction: Symptomatic Terms

Study this table to prepare for the programmed review that follows.

TERM	MEANING
BREATHING	
eupnea *yūp-nē′ă*	normal breathing
bradypnea *brad-ip-nē′ă*	slow breathing
tachypnea *tak-ip-nē′ă*	fast breathing
hypopnea *hī-pop′nē-ă*	shallow breathing
hyperpnea *hī-pĕr-nē′ă*	deep breathing
dyspnea *disp-nē′ă*	difficulty breathing
apnea *ap′nē-ă*	inability to breathe
orthopnea *ōr-thop-nē′ă*	ability to breathe only in an upright position; (orth/o = straight)
Cheyne–Stokes respiration *chān-stōks res-pi-rā′shŭn*	pattern of breathing characterized by a gradual increase of depth and, sometimes, in rate to a maximum level, followed by a decrease, resulting in apnea

TERM	MEANING
Lung Sounds	
crackles *krak'ĕlz*	popping sounds heard on auscultation of the lung when air enters diseased airways and alveoli; occurs in disorders such as bronchiectasis or atelectasis; also called *rales*
rales *rahlz*	popping sounds heard on auscultation of the lung when air enters diseased airways and alveoli; occurs in disorders such as bronchiectasis or atelectasis; also called *crackles*
wheezes *wēz'ez*	high-pitched, musical sounds heard on auscultation of the lung as air flows through a narrowed airway; occurs in disorders such as asthma or emphysema
rhonchi *rong'kī*	added sound with a musical pitch during inhaling or exhaling heard on auscultation of the chest caused by air passing through narrowed bronchi or due to mucus buildup; if low-pitched it is called *sonorous rhonchus* and if high-pitched with a whistle or squeaky quality it is called *sibilant rhonchus*
stridor *strī'dōr*	high-pitched, crowing sound that occurs with an obstruction in the upper airway (trachea or larynx)
GENERAL SYMPTOMATIC TERMS	
caseous necrosis *kā'sē-ŭs nĕ-krō'sis*	degeneration and death of tissue with a cheese-like appearance
cyanosis *sī-ă-nō'sis*	bluish coloration of the skin caused by a deficient amount of oxygen in the blood
dysphonia *dis-fō'nē-ă*	hoarseness (*phon/o* = voice or sound)
epistaxis *ep-i-stak'sis*	nosebleed (*epi* = upon; *stazo* = to drip)
expectoration *ek-spek-tō-rā'shŭn*	coughing up and spitting out of material from the lungs
sputum *spyū'tŭm*	material expelled from the lungs by coughing
hemoptysis *hē-mop'ti-sis*	coughing up and spitting out blood that originates in the lungs (*ptysis* = to spit)
hypercapnia *hī-pĕr-kap'nē-ă*	excessive level of carbon dioxide in the blood (*capno* = smoke; *carbo* = coal); also called *hypercarbia*
hypercarbia *hī-pĕr-kar'bē-ă*	excessive level of carbon dioxide in the blood (*capno* = smoke; *carbo* = coal); also called *hypercapnia*
hyperventilation *hī'pĕr-ven-ti-lā'shŭn*	excessive movement of air into and out of the lungs, causing hypocapnia
hypocapnia *hī-pō-kap'nē-ă*	deficient level of carbon dioxide in the blood; also called *hypocarbia*
hypocarbia *hī-pō-kar'bē-ă*	deficient level of carbon dioxide in the blood; also called *hypocapnia*
hypoventilation *hī'pō-ven-ti-lā'shŭn*	deficient movement of air into and out of the lungs, causing hypercapnia

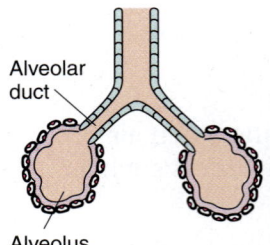
A Normal
Bronchioles and alveolar ducts are open, allowing air to reach alveoli and alveolar capillaries; alveoli and ducts are elastic, pushing air out of the lungs during exhalation

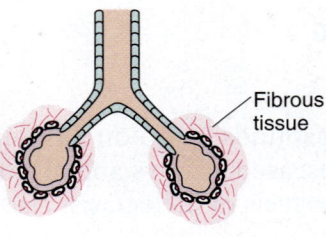
B Pneumoconiosis
Chronic inhalation of dust particles results in the formation of fibrous tissue surrounding the alveoli, limiting their ability to stretch and restricting the intake of air

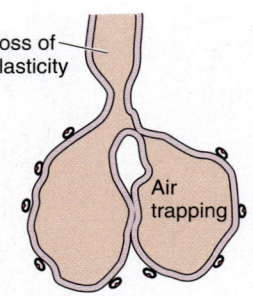
C Emphysema
Alveoli lose their elasticity, making it difficult to push air out of the lungs and obstructing exhalation of air

FIGURE 10-4 ■ Comparison of normal alveoli (A) with alveoli in restrictive (B) and obstructive (C) lung disorders.

TERM	MEANING
hypoxemia hī-pok-sē′mē-ă	deficient amount of oxygen in the blood
hypoxia hī-pok′sē-ă	deficient amount of oxygen in tissue cells
obstructive lung disorder (see Figure 10-4 A–C) ob-strŭk′tiv lŭng dis-ōr′děr	condition blocking the flow of air moving out of the lungs
restrictive lung disorder (see Figure 10-4 A–C) rē-strik′tiv lŭng dis-ōr′děr	condition limiting the intake of air into the lungs
pulmonary edema pŭl′mō-nār-ē e-dē′mă	fluid filling the spaces around the alveoli and, eventually, flooding into the alveoli
pulmonary infiltrate (see Figure 10-8) pŭl′mō-nār-ē in-fil′trāt	density on an x-ray image representing the consolidation of matter within the air spaces of the lungs, usually resulting from an inflammatory process
rhinorrhea rī-nō-rē′ă	thin, watery discharge from the nose (runny nose)

Programmed Review: Symptomatic Terms

ANSWERS	REVIEW
breathing fast brady- tachypnea, bradypnea	**10.27** To review, the suffix *-pnea* refers to _____. Many symptomatic terms use this suffix to identify different breathing problems. Recall that the prefix *tachy-* means _____, and that the prefix for slow is _____. Therefore, fast breathing is called _____, and slow breathing is called _____.

ANSWERS	REVIEW
deficient hyper- hypopnea hyperpnea	**10.28** The prefix *hypo-* means below or _____, and the opposite prefix, meaning above or excessive, is _____. The term for shallow (or deficient) breathing therefore is _____, and the term for deep (or excessive) breathing is _____.
normal difficult eupnea dyspnea	**10.29** The prefix *eu-* means good or _____, and the prefix *dys-* means painful, faulty, or _____. Therefore, the term for normal breathing is _____, and the term for difficulty breathing is _____.
without apnea stopped upright	**10.30** The prefix *a-* means _____. The term for an inability to breathe is _____, and in an apneic patient, breathing has _____ entirely. Orthopnea refers to an inability to breathe in any position but an _____ one.
Cheyne Stokes	**10.31** A pattern of breathing in which depth and, sometimes, rate gradually increase and then decrease is called _____-_____ respiration.
chest crackles rhonchi stridor	**10.32** Recall that with a stethoscope, one can listen to sounds in the _____. Lung sounds are often symptomatic of respiratory problems. The popping sounds caused by air entering diseased airways and alveoli are called _____ or rales. High-pitched musical sounds resulting from air flowing through a narrowed airway, such as in asthma or emphysema, are called wheezes or _____. The high-pitched crowing sound that occurs with an obstructed upper airway is called _____.
capn/o condition of hypercapnia hypercarbia	**10.33** The two combining forms for carbon dioxide are *carb/o* and _____. Using the prefix meaning above or excessive and the suffix *-ia*, meaning _____, a condition of having too much carbon dioxide in the blood is called _____ or _____.
deficient condition of ox/o hypoxia blood deficient, oxygen	**10.34** *Hypo-* is a prefix meaning below or _____. The suffix *-ia* means _____. Join these with the combining form for oxygen, or _____, to build the term describing a condition of deficient oxygen in the tissues, or _____. Hypoxemia is the term that describes the initial effect or condition of the _____ when there is a _____ amount of _____. A related term

ANSWERS	REVIEW
blue increase cyanosis cyanotic	links *cyan/o*, the combining form meaning _____, with *-osis*, the suffix meaning condition or _____, to form the term describing a bluish coloration of the skin caused by a deficient amount of oxygen in the blood: _____. The adjective form is _____.
hyperventilation hypoventilation	**10.35** Ventilation is the movement of air into and out of the lungs. Excessive movement of air is called _____, whereas deficient movement of air is called _____.
dys- dysphonia	**10.36** The prefix meaning difficult, painful, or faulty is _____. Combined with the combining form *phon/o*, meaning voice or sound, and the suffix for condition, the term for a condition of hoarseness (difficult or painful voice) is _____.
epi- epistaxis	**10.37** The term for nosebleed does *not* use the combining form for nose. It literally means "drip upon," combining the prefix for upon, _____, with *stazo*, a root meaning to drip. The medical term for nosebleed is _____.
expectoration sputum hemoptysis	**10.38** The cilia lining the structures of the airway move mucus and other material up and out of the airway and lungs, where it can be coughed up and spit out of the body. The process of coughing up and spitting out such material is termed _____. The material expelled from the lungs by coughing is called _____. Using the combining form for blood (*hem/o*), the term for coughing up blood from the lungs is _____.
obstructive restrictive lung	**10.39** A condition in which the flow of air is blocked from moving out of the lungs is called an _____ lung disorder. A condition limiting the intake of air into the lungs is a _____ _____ disorder.
pulmonary	**10.40** Edema is the presence of excessive watery fluid. Edema in the lungs is called _____ edema.
infiltrate inflammation	**10.41** Density on an x-ray image representing the consolidation of matter within the air spaces of the lungs is called a pulmonary _____. Pulmonary infiltrates usually indicate a process of _____ in the lung.

ANSWERS	REVIEW
necr/o caseous necrosis condition or increase	**10.42** The word *caseous* means cheese-like in appearance. Recall that the combining form meaning death is _____. The term for dead and degenerating tissue with a cheese-like appearance is _____ _____. The suffix *-osis* means _____ or _____.
discharge rhinorrhea	**10.43** Recall that the suffix *-rrhea* means _____. This suffix joins with the Greek combining form for nose to create the term for watery discharge from the nose: _____.

Self-Instruction: Diagnostic Terms

Study this table to prepare for the programmed review that follows.

TERM	MEANING
asthma (see **Figure 10-5**) *az′mă*	panting; obstructive pulmonary disease caused by a spasm of the bronchial tubes or by swelling of the mucous membrane; characterized by paroxysmal (sudden, periodic) attacks of wheezing, dyspnea, and cough
atelectasis *at-ĕ-lek′tă-sis*	collapse of lung tissue (alveoli) (*atele* = imperfect; *-ectasis* = expansion or dilation)
bronchiectasis (see **Figure 10-6**) *brong-kē-ek′tă-sis*	abnormal dilation of the bronchi with accumulation of mucus

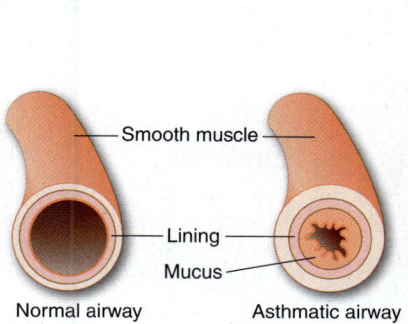

FIGURE 10-5 ■ Bronchial asthma. A normal bronchus and the bronchus of a patient with asthma. Bronchial inflammation associated with edema, mucus production, and obstruction are seen in the asthmatic airway.

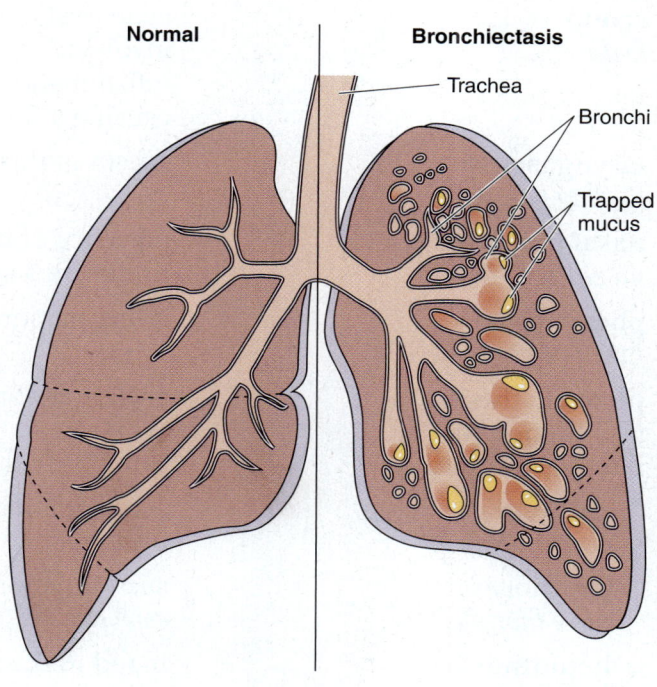

FIGURE 10-6 ■ Bronchiectasis.

TERM	MEANING
bronchitis *brong-kī′tis*	inflammation of the bronchi
bronchogenic carcinoma *brong-kō-jen′ik kar-si-nō′mă*	lung cancer; cancer originating in the bronchi
bronchospasm *brong′kō-spazm*	constriction of bronchi caused by spasm (involuntary contraction) of the peribronchial smooth muscle
emphysema (see Figure 10-4C) *em-fi-sē′mă*	obstructive pulmonary disease characterized by overexpansion of the alveoli with air and destructive changes in their walls, resulting in loss of lung elasticity and decreased gas exchange (*emphysan* = to inflate)
chronic obstructive pulmonary disease (COPD) *kron′ik ob-strŭk′tiv pūl′mō-nār-ē di-zēz′*	permanent, destructive pulmonary disorder that is a combination of chronic bronchitis and emphysema
cystic fibrosis *sis′tik fī-brō′sis*	inherited condition of exocrine gland malfunction causing secretion of abnormally thick, viscous (sticky) mucus that obstructs passageways within the body, commonly affecting the lungs and digestive tract; mucus that obstructs the airways leads to infection, inflammation, and damage of lung tissue
laryngitis *lar-in-jī′tis*	inflammation of the larynx
laryngotracheobronchitis (LTB) *lă-ring′gō-trā′kē-o-brong-kī′tis*	acute respiratory infection involving the larynx, trachea, and bronchi causing inflammation; creates a funnel-shaped elongation of tissue causing a distinct "seal bark" cough; referred to as *croup* in infants and young children
croup *krūp*	acute respiratory infection in infants and young children involving the larynx, trachea, and bronchi causing inflammation; creates a funnel-shaped elongation of tissue causing a distinct "seal bark" cough
laryngospasm *lă-ring′gō-spazm*	spasm of the laryngeal muscles, causing a constriction
nasal polyposis *nā′zăl pol′i-pō′sis*	presence of numerous polyps in the nose (a polyp is a tumor on a stalk)
pharyngitis *far′in-jī′tis*	inflammation of the pharynx
pleural effusion (see Figure 10-7) *plūr′ăl e-fū′zhŭn*	accumulation of fluid in the pleural cavity
empyema *em-pī-ē′mă*	accumulation of pus in the pleural cavity; also called *pyothorax*
pyothorax *pī-ō-thōr′aks*	accumulation of pus in the pleural cavity; also called *empyema*
hemothorax *hē-mō-thōr′aks*	blood in the pleural cavity

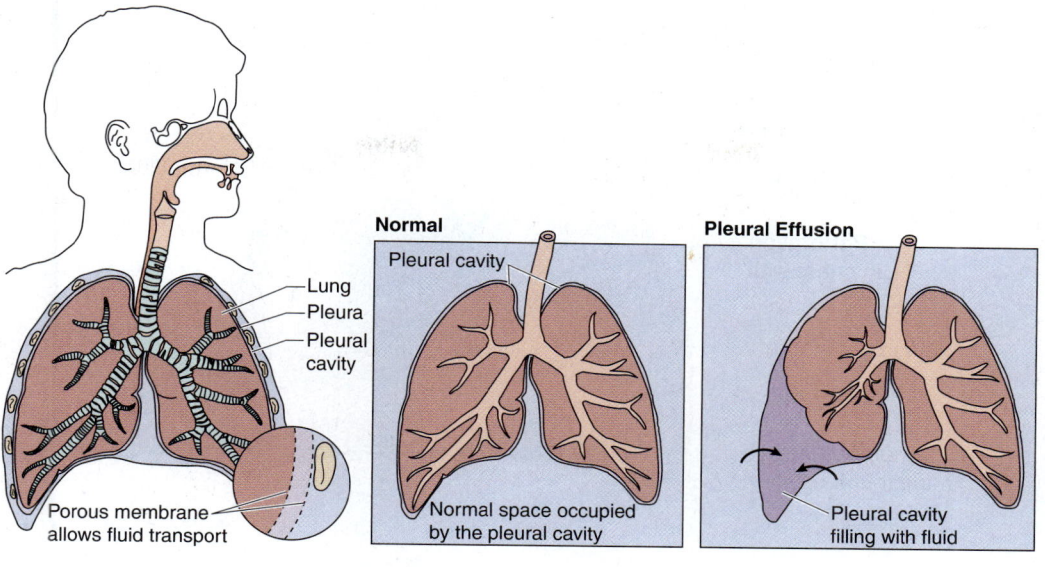

FIGURE 10-7 ■ Pleural effusion.

TERM	MEANING
pleuritis plū-rī′tis	inflammation of the pleura; also called *pleurisy*
pleurisy plūr′i-sē	inflammation of the pleura; also called *pleuritis*
pneumoconiosis (see Figure 10-4B) nū′mō-kō-nē-ō′sis	chronic restrictive pulmonary disease resulting from prolonged inhalation of fine dusts, such as coal, asbestos (asbestosis), or silicone (silicosis) (*conio* = dust)
pneumonia (see Figure 10-8) nū-mō′nē-ă	inflammation in the lung resulting from infection by bacteria, viruses, fungi, or parasites or from aspiration of chemicals
Pneumocystis jiroveci **pneumonia** (PCP) nū-mō-sis′tis jir-ō-vess′ī nū-mō′nē-ă	pneumonia caused by the *Pneumocystis jiroveci* organism, a common opportunistic infection in those who are positive for the human immunodeficiency virus (HIV)

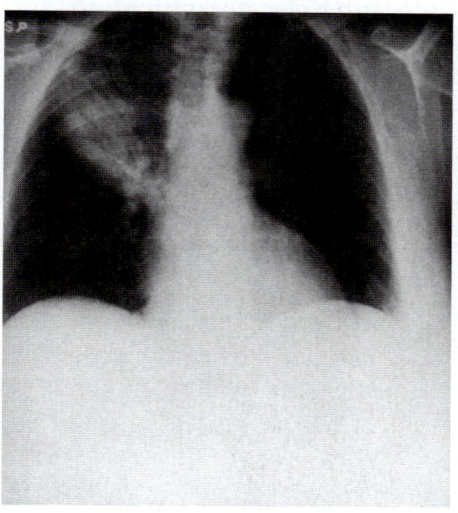

FIGURE 10-8 ■ Chest x-ray image showing pulmonary infiltrates in right upper lobe consistent with lobar pneumonia. Dense material (inflammatory exudate) absorbs radiation, whereas normal alveoli do not.

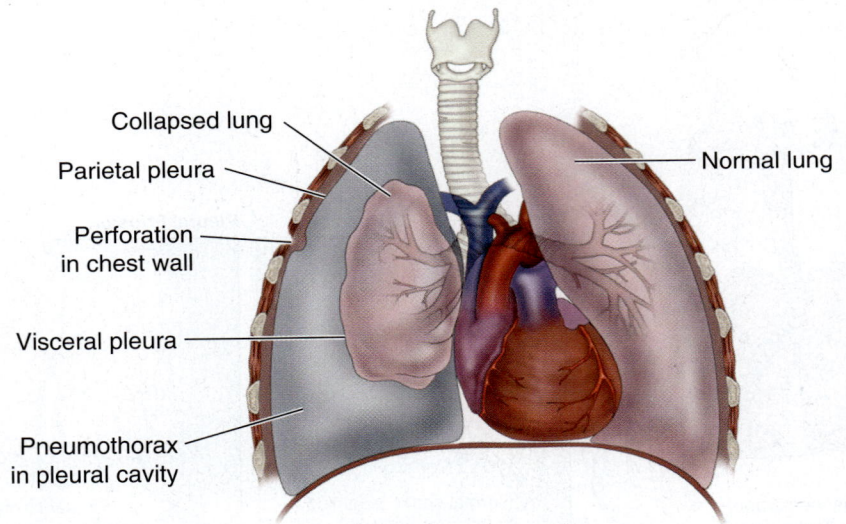

FIGURE 10-9 ■ Pneumothorax. A pneumothorax can be caused by many factors, including lung disease or a perforation in the chest wall.

TERM	MEANING
pneumothorax (see Figure 10-9) nū-mō-thōr′aks	air in the pleural cavity caused by a puncture of the lung or chest wall
pneumohemothorax nū′mō-hē-mō-thōr′aks	air and blood in the pleural cavity
pneumonitis nū-mō-nī′tis	inflammation of the lung, often caused by hypersensitivity (allergy) to chemicals or dusts
pulmonary embolism (PE) pul′mō-nār-ē em′bō-lizm	occlusion in the pulmonary circulation, most often caused by a blood clot
pulmonary tuberculosis (TB) pul′mō-nār-ē tū-bĕr-kyū-lō′sis	disease caused by the presence of *Mycobacterium tuberculosis* in the lungs; characterized by the formation of tubercles, inflammation, and necrotizing caseous lesions (caseous necrosis)
sinusitis sī′nŭs-ī′tis	inflammation of the sinuses
sleep apnea slēp ap′nē-ă	periods of breathing cessation (10 seconds or more) that occur during sleep, often resulting in snoring
tonsillitis ton-si-lī′tis	acute or chronic inflammation of the tonsils
upper respiratory infection (URI) up′er rĕs-par′uh-tōr-ē in-fek′shŭn	infectious disease of the upper respiratory tract involving the nasal passages and pharynx, marked by sneezing, watery eyes, and profuse secretion of watery mucus; usually associated with the common cold

Programmed Review: Diagnostic Terms

ANSWERS	REVIEW
upper respiratory infection	**10.44** URI is the abbreviation for _____ _____ _____, an infection of the upper respiratory tract involving the nasal passages, pharynx, and bronchi.
-itis sinusitis tonsillitis pharyngitis laryngitis bronchitis	**10.45** Recall that the suffix for inflammation is _____. Many individual structures of the respiratory system can become inflamed, often by an infection. Inflammation of the sinuses is called _____. Inflammation of the tonsils is called _____. Inflammation of the pharynx is called _____. Inflammation of the larynx is called _____. Inflammation of the bronchi is called _____.
pleuritis pleurisy	**10.46** Inflammation of the pleura is called _____. Another term for this condition is _____.
pneumonitis laryngotracheobronchitis croup	**10.47** The term for inflammation of the lung is built from the combining form meaning either air or lung. This term is _____. Another "itis" inflammation involving the larynx, trachea, and bronchi causes a distinctive, seal-like bark. The longer term for this condition, _____, uses all three combining forms; the shorter term for this condition is _____.
pneumonia pneumocystis pneumoconiosis	**10.48** Several other diagnostic terms are built from the combining form meaning air or lung. Using a suffix indicating a condition of, the term for an inflammation of the lung caused by infection with bacteria or viruses, or by exposure to chemicals, is _____. One kind of pneumonia caused by the *Pneumocystis jiroveci* organism is called _____ pneumonia. A chronic restrictive disease resulting from inhaling dust (*conio* = dust) is called _____.
pneumothorax pneumohemothorax hemothorax	**10.49** This same combining form for air is used to build the terms referring to air in a body cavity. Air in the thorax caused by a puncture of the lung or chest wall is called _____. The term for both air and blood (*hem/o* = blood) in the thorax is _____. The presence of blood alone in the pleural cavity of the chest is called _____.

ANSWERS	REVIEW
bronchitis -spasm bronchospasm -ectasis bronchiectasis, carcinoma bronchogenic carcinoma	**10.50** In addition to inflammation of the bronchi, called _____, several other diagnostic conditions can occur in the bronchi. Recall that the suffix for an involuntary contraction is _____. A constriction of the bronchi caused by contraction of the smooth muscle around the bronchi is called _____. Recall that the diagnostic suffix for expansion or dilation is _____; thus, the condition of abnormal dilation of the bronchi with an accumulation of mucus is called _____. Recall that _____ means cancer tumor. Lung cancer originating in the bronchi is called _____ _____.
-spasm laryngospasm	**10.51** Again, the suffix for an involuntary contraction is _____. A contraction of laryngeal muscles, causing a constriction, is termed _____.
-ectasis atelectasis	**10.52** Recall that the suffix for expansion or dilation is _____. Therefore, the term for a collapse of lung tissue uses this suffix combined with the root *atele* (meaning imperfect): _____.
asthma emphysema chronic obstructive pulmonary disease	**10.53** There are several types of obstructive pulmonary disease. Caused by a spasm of the bronchial tubes or by swelling of their mucous membrane, _____ is characterized by sudden attacks of wheezing, dyspnea, and cough. Another condition, characterized by overexpansion of the alveoli with air and destructive changes in their walls, is called _____. The permanent destructive pulmonary disorder that is a combination of emphysema and chronic bronchitis is called _____ _____ _____ _____ (COPD).
condition nasal polyposis	**10.54** The diagnostic suffix *-osis* means _____ or increase. The condition of numerous polyps in the nose is called _____ _____.
cystic fibrosis	**10.55** Another use for *-osis* is in the term describing the hereditary condition of exocrine gland malfunction that causes secretion of abnormally thick mucus in the lungs, obstructing the airways and leading to infection and damage to lung tissue: _____ _____.

ANSWERS	REVIEW
	10.56 Fluid, pus, blood, or air can accumulate in the pleural cavity. The term for blood in this cavity in the thorax is
hemothorax	_____. The combining form meaning pus is *py/o*; thus, the accumulation of pus in the pleural cavity is
pyothorax	called _____, or empyema. An accumulation of
pleural effusion	fluid in the pleural cavity is called a _____ _____.
apnea sleep apnea	**10.57** Recall that the term for an inability to breathe is _____. The condition in which this happens for short periods during sleep is called _____ _____.
pulmonary tuberculosis	**10.58** The bacteria *Mycobacterium tuberculosis* causes the lung disease _____ _____.
pulmonary embolism	**10.59** A blood clot that lodges in the pulmonary circulation, causing an occlusion, is called a _____ _____ (PE).

Self-Instruction: Diagnostic Tests and Procedures

Study this table to prepare for the programmed review that follows.

TEST OR PROCEDURE	EXPLANATION
arterial blood gas (ABG) ar-tē′rē-ăl blŭd gas	analysis of arterial blood to determine the adequacy of lung function in the exchange of gases
pH	abbreviation for the potential of hydrogen; measurement of blood acidity or alkalinity
PaO_2	abbreviation for partial pressure of oxygen; measurement of the amount of oxygen in the blood
$PaCO_2$	abbreviation for partial pressure of carbon dioxide; measurement of the amount of carbon dioxide in the blood
endoscopy en-dos′kŏ-pē	examination inside a body cavity with a flexible endoscope for diagnostic or treatment purposes
bronchoscopy (see **Figure 10-10**) brong-kos′kŏ-pē	use of a flexible endoscope, called a bronchoscope, to examine the airways
nasopharyngoscopy nā′zō-far′ing-gos′kŏ-pē	use of a flexible endoscope to examine the nasal passages and the pharynx (throat) to diagnose structural abnormalities, such as obstructions, growths, and cancers

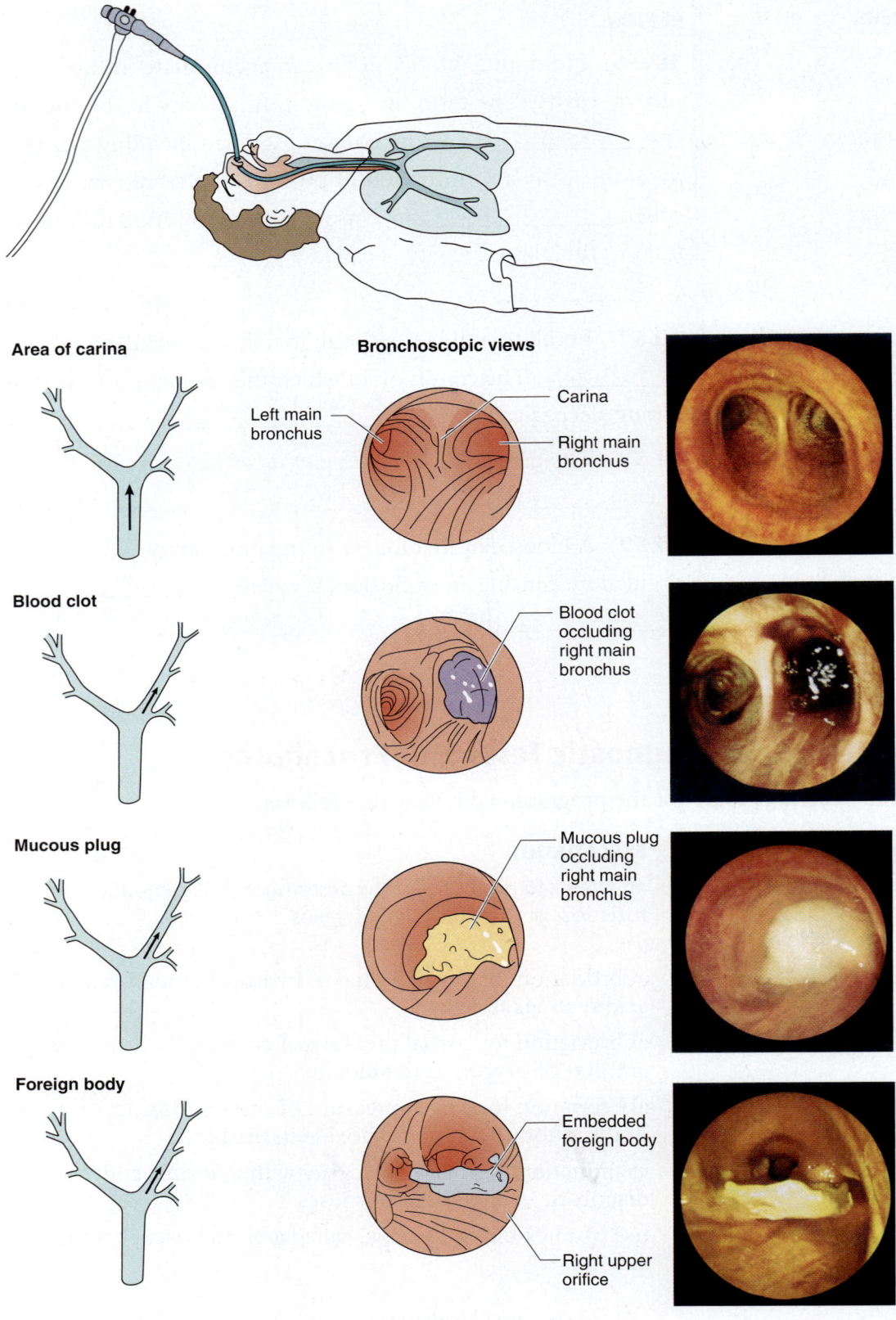

FIGURE 10-10 ■ Bronchoscopy.

TEST OR PROCEDURE	EXPLANATION
examination methods ek-zam-i-nā'shŭn meth'ŏdz	techniques used during physical examination to objectively evaluate the respiratory system
auscultation aws-kŭl-tā'shŭn	to listen; a physical examination method of listening to the sounds within the body with the aid of a stethoscope, such as auscultation of the chest for heart and lung sounds
percussion pĕr-kŭsh'ŭn	a physical examination method of tapping the body to elicit vibrations and sounds to estimate the size, border, or fluid content of a cavity, such as the chest
lung biopsy (Bx) lŭng bī'op-sē	removal of a small piece of lung tissue for pathologic examination
lung scan (see Figure 10-11 A,B) lŭng skan	a two-part nuclear (radionuclide) scan of the lungs to detect abnormalities of ventilation (breathing) or perfusion (blood flow) made after radioactive material is injected in the patient's blood, and as the patient breathes radioactive material into the airways; comparison of the two scans indicates whether an abnormality exists in the airways or the pulmonary circulation; also called *ventilation–perfusion scan*
ventilation–perfusion (V/Q) scan (see Figure 10-11 A,B) ven-ti-lā'shŭn-per-fyū'zhŭn skan	a two-part nuclear (radionuclide) scan of the lungs to detect abnormalities of ventilation (breathing) or perfusion (blood flow) made after radioactive material is injected in the patient's blood, and as the patient breathes radioactive material into the airways; comparison of the two scans indicates whether an abnormality exists in the airways or the pulmonary circulation; also called *lung scan*
magnetic resonance imaging (MRI) mag-net'ic rez'ō-nănts im'ăj-ing	nonionizing image of the lung to visualize lung lesions
polysomnography (PSG) pol'ē-som-nog'ră-fē	recording of various aspects of sleep (i.e., eye and muscle movements, respiration, and brain-wave patterns) for diagnosis of sleep disorders (*somn/o* = sleep) (see Chapter 4, Figure 4-15)

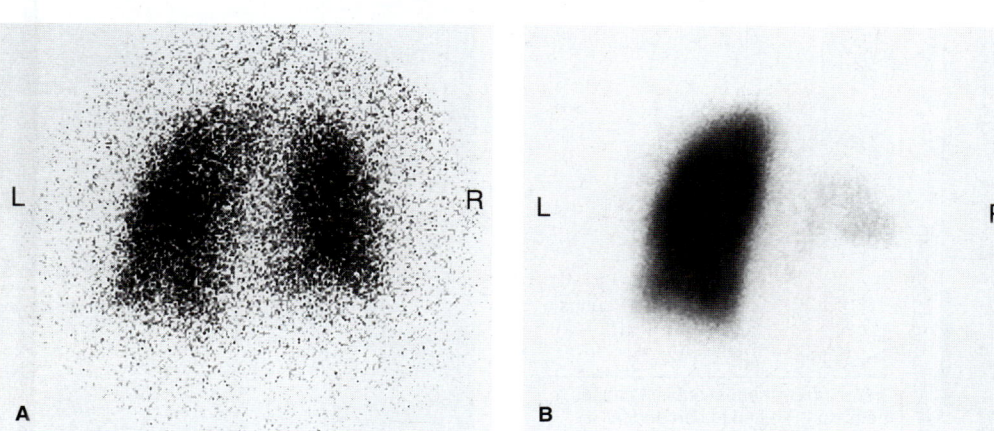

FIGURE 10-11 ■ Posterior lung scan in a patient with an embolus in the right lung. **A.** Ventilation image shows a normal pattern. **B.** Absence of blood flow to the right lung is apparent on perfusion scan. *L*, left; *R*, right.

TEST OR PROCEDURE	EXPLANATION
pulmonary function testing (PFT) pŭl'mō-nār-ē fŭnk'shŭn test'ing	direct and indirect measurements of lung volumes and capacities

spirometry
    (see Figure 10-12 A,B)
    spī-rom'ĕ-trē
	direct measurement of lung volume and capacity

tidal volume
    (TV or V_T)
    tī'dăl vol'yŭm
	amount of air exhaled after a normal inspiration

vital capacity (VC) vīt-ăl kă-pas'i-tē	amount of air exhaled after a maximal inspiration
peak flow (PF) pēk flō	measure of the fastest flow of exhaled air after a maximal inspiration; also called *peak expiratory flow rate*
peak expiratory flow rate (PEFR) pēk ek-spī'ră-tō-rē flō rāt	measure of the fastest flow of exhaled air after a maximal inspiration; also called *peak flow*
pulse oximetry (see Figure 10-13 A,B) pŭls ok-sim'ĕ-trē	noninvasive method of estimating the percentage of oxygen saturation in the blood using an oximeter with a specialized probe attached to the skin at a site of arterial pulsation, commonly the finger; used to monitor hypoxemia
radiology rā'dē-ol'ŏ-jē	x-ray imaging

chest x-ray (CXR)
    chest x-rā
	x-ray imaging of the chest to visualize the lungs; directional terms identify the path of the x-ray beam to produce the radiograph:
	    PA (posterior–anterior) = from back to front
	    AP (anterior–posterior) = from front to back
	    lateral = toward the side (e.g., left lateral)

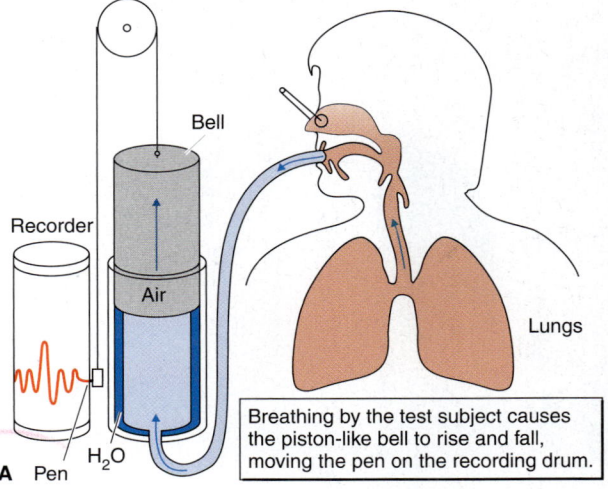
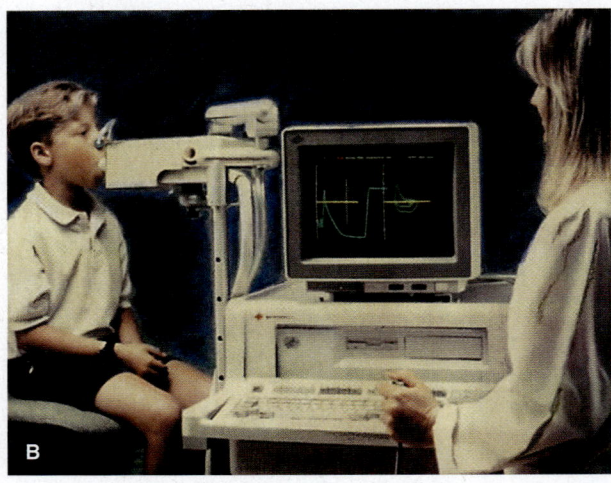

FIGURE 10-12 ■ Spirometry. **A.** Principles of spirometry. **B.** Modern spirometry.

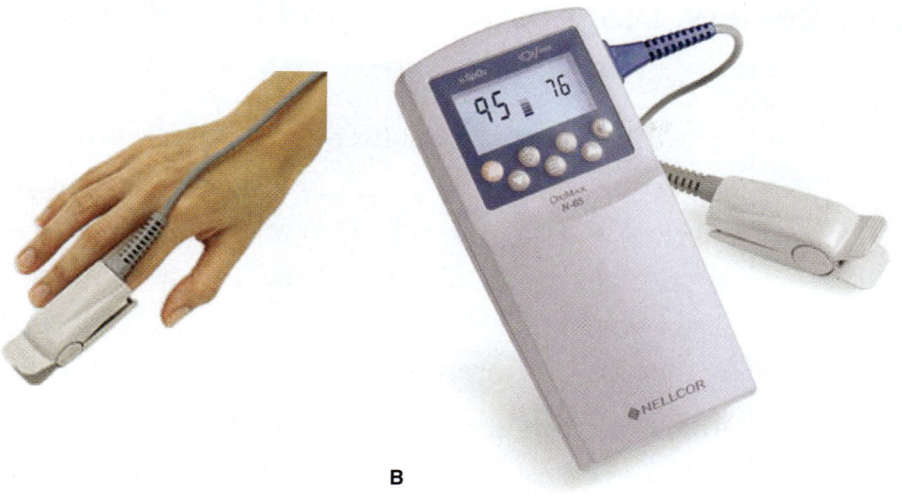

FIGURE 10-13 ■ Pulse oximetry. **A.** Placement of a sensor on the patient's finger. **B.** Oxygen saturation reading on a portable monitor.

TEST OR PROCEDURE	EXPLANATION
computed tomography (CT) *kom-pyū′tĕd tō-mog′ră-fē*	CT of the thorax is used to detect lesions in the lung; CT of the head is used to visualize the structures of the nose and sinuses
pulmonary angiography (see Figure 10-14) *pul′mō-nār-ē an-jē-og′ră-fē*	x-ray imaging of the blood vessels of the lungs after the injection of contrast dye

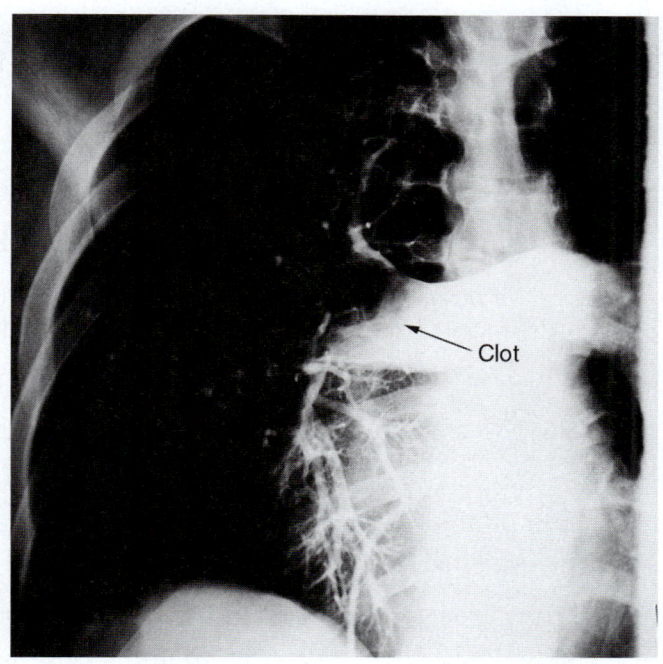

FIGURE 10-14 ■ Pulmonary angiogram showing an embolus obstructing pulmonary circulation (*arrow*).

Programmed Review: Diagnostic Tests and Procedures

ANSWERS	REVIEW
-scopy endoscopy bronchoscopy nasopharyngoscopy	**10.60** Recall that the suffix meaning a process of examination (with an instrument) is _____. Because *endo-* is the prefix for within, the general term for examination within a body cavity using a scope is _____. Use of a special endoscope to examine the airways and bronchi is called _____. Examination of the nasal and throat passages is _____.
chest auscultation	**10.61** A stethoscope is used to listen to _____ sounds. The physical examination procedure for doing this is called _____.
percussion	**10.62** Another physical examination method uses tapping of the body to listen to the resulting sounds and vibrations to make observations about underlying organs and masses. This is called _____.
gases pH PaO_2 $PaCO_2$	**10.63** Laboratory tests analyze arterial blood _____ (ABGs) to determine the adequacy of their function in the lung. The _____ is a measure of blood acidity or alkalinity. The amount of oxygen in the blood is measured as the partial pressure of oxygen and is referred to as _____. The partial pressure of carbon dioxide is referred to as _____.
biopsy	**10.64** Removal of a small sample of lung tissue for pathologic examination is called a lung _____. Many different organs and tissues in the body can be biopsied.
many -graphy polysomnography	**10.65** The combining form *somn/o* means sleep, and the prefix *poly-* means _____. The suffix referring to the process of recording is _____. Using these three word parts, the procedure that records many aspects of sleep (breathing, muscle movements, and so on) is called _____.
pulmonary function spirometry tidal	**10.66** Measurement of lung volumes and capacities is called _____ _____ testing (PFT). Formed from the combining term for breathing and the suffix for the process of measuring, the term for the direct measurement of lung volume and capacity is _____. The amount of air exhaled after a normal inspiration is called _____ volume. The amount of air exhaled

CHAPTER 10 • RESPIRATORY SYSTEM 375

ANSWERS	REVIEW
vital capacity	after a maximal inspiration is called _____ _____. The measure of the fastest flow of exhaled air after a maximal
peak expiratory flow	inspiration is called peak flow or _____ _____ _____ rate (PEFR).
pulse oximetry	**10.67** A noninvasive method of estimating the percentage of oxygen saturation in the blood uses an oximeter attached to the skin at a site of arterial pulsation. This procedure is called _____ _____.
lung scan ventilation, perfusion	**10.68** Several different imaging modalities are used to visualize the lungs and other respiratory structures. A two-part nuclear scan of the lungs to detect perfusion or ventilation abnormalities is simply called a _____ _____, or a V/Q scan, in which V stands for _____ (breathing) and Q stands for _____ (blood flow). A nonionizing image of the lungs using magnetic fields and radiofrequency waves is produced using a
magnetic resonance imaging	modality called _____ _____ _____ (MRI).
radiology, record	**10.69** Using *radi/o*, a combining form meaning x-ray, and the suffix meaning study of, the term for x-ray imaging is _____. A radiogram is an x-ray _____; however, recall that the suffix meaning instrument for recording,
-graph	_____, is used in the preferred term for an x-ray image:
radiograph	_____. An x-ray of the full thorax to visualize the
chest x-ray	lungs is a _____ _____ (CXR). The abbreviations
posterior-anterior	PA, for _____-_____, and AP, for
anterior-posterior	_____-_____, indicate the path of the x-ray beam in producing the radiograph. Anterior refers to the
front, back	_____, and posterior refers to the _____. AP, then, indicates that the x-ray passed from the front of the chest to the
side	back of the chest. A left lateral CXR is taken from the left _____ of the chest. X-ray imaging of the blood vessels of the lungs taken after injection of a contrast medium is called pulmonary
angiography	_____. The form of x-ray imaging in which a computer creates cross-sectional images of structures such as the lungs is
computed tomography	called _____ _____ (CT).

Self-Instruction: Operative Terms

Study this table to prepare for the programmed review that follows.

TERM	MEANING
adenoidectomy *ad′ĕ-noy-dek tŏ-mē*	an operation to remove adenoid tissue from the nasopharynx
lobectomy *lō-bek′tŏ-mē*	removal of a lobe of a lung
nasal polypectomy *nā′zăl pol′i-pek′tŏ-mē*	removal of a nasal polyp
pneumonectomy *nū′mō-nek′tō-mē*	removal of an entire lung
thoracentesis (see **Figure 10-15**) *thōr′ă-sen-tē′sis*	puncture for aspiration of the chest (pleural cavity)
thoracoplasty *thōr′ă-kō-plas-tē*	repair of the chest involving fixation of the ribs
thoracoscopy *thōr-ă-kos′kŏ-pē*	endoscopic examination of the pleural cavity using a thoracoscope (endoscope for viewing intrathoracic structures)
thoracostomy (see **Figure 10-15**) *thōr-ă-kos′tŏ-mē*	surgical opening in the chest, usually to insert a tube
thoracotomy *thōr-ă-kot′ŏ-mē*	incision into the chest
tonsillectomy *ton-si-lek′tŏ-mē*	removal of the tonsils

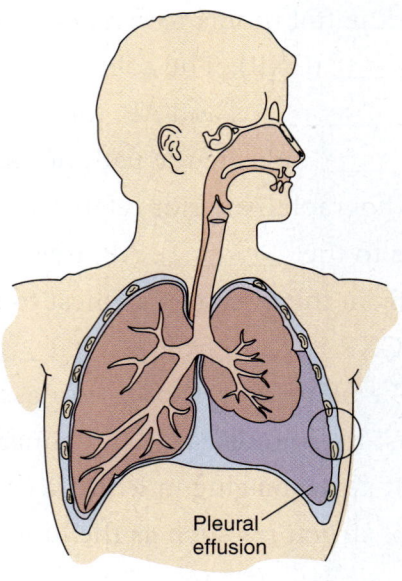
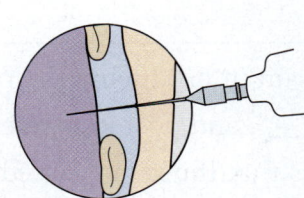
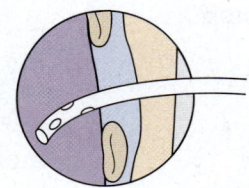

FIGURE 10-15 ■ Common treatments of pleural effusion.

Tracheotomy
Incision of the trachea for exploration, removal of a foreign body, or obtaining a biopsy specimen

Tracheostomy
Incision of the trachea and insertion of a tube to facilitate passage of air or removal of secretions

Sagittal view, with tracheostomy tube in place

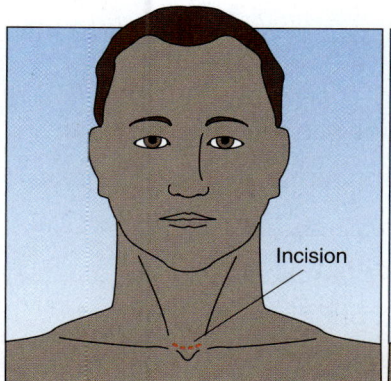
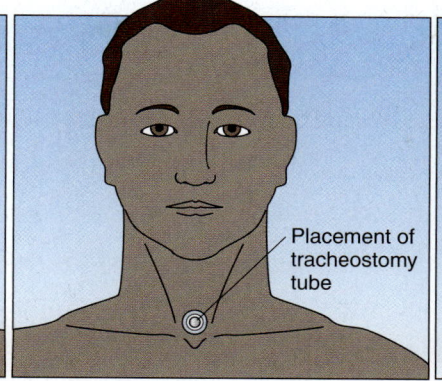
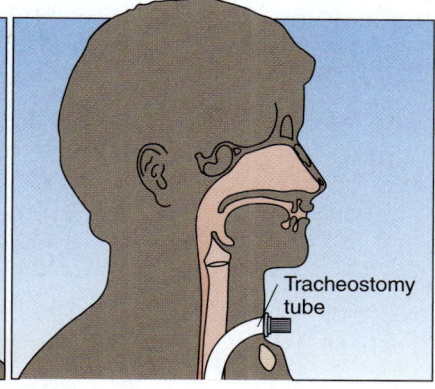

FIGURE 10-16 ■ Operative procedures related to the trachea.

TERM	MEANING
tonsillectomy and adenoidectomy (T and A) *ton-si-lek′tŏ-mē and ad′ĕ-noy-dek′tŏ-mē*	removal of the tonsils and adenoid tissue
tracheotomy (see Figure 10-16) *trā′kē-ot′ŏ-mē*	incision into the trachea
tracheostomy (see Figure 10-16) *trā′kē-os′tŏ-mē*	an operation to make an opening into the trachea, usually to insert a tube

Programmed Review: Operative Terms

ANSWERS	REVIEW
excision	**10.70** Recall that the suffix *-ectomy* means _____ or removal. The term for the surgical removal of the adenoids is
adenoidectomy	_____. The term for removal of a nasal polyp is
nasal polypectomy	_____ _____. Formed using the combining form that means either air or lung, the term for removal of an entire
pneumonectomy	lung is _____. The removal of the tonsils is called a
tonsillectomy	_____. Sometimes, the tonsils and adenoid tissue are
tonsillectomy and adenoidectomy	removed at the same time in a procedure called a _____ _____ _____ (T and A). The removal of a lung lobe is
lobectomy	called a _____.

ANSWERS	REVIEW
incision thoracotomy tracheotomy	**10.71** The suffix *-tomy* refers to an _____. An incision into the chest is called a _____. An incision into the trachea is a _____.
opening tracheostomy thoracostomy	**10.72** The operative suffix *-stomy* means surgical creation of an _____. The creation of an opening into the trachea, most often to insert a tube, is called a _____. The surgical creation of an opening into the chest is called _____. (Note that *-tomy* and *-stomy* have related but distinctly different meanings.)
-plasty thoracoplasty	**10.73** The suffix denoting surgical repair or reconstruction is _____. Thus, the surgical repair of the chest that involves fixing the ribs is called a _____.
puncture thoracentesis	**10.74** The suffix *-centesis* means a _____ for aspiration. A puncture that is made surgically for aspiration of fluid or air from the chest (pleural cavity) is called a _____. (Note that thoracocentesis is an acceptable term but is used less often than the shortened form: thoracentesis.)
examination thoracoscopy	**10.75** Recall that the suffix *-scopy* means process of _____. The endoscopic examination of the pleural cavity is called _____. Thoracoscopy is a surgical procedure because an incision must be made for insertion of the endoscope. In contrast, bronchoscopy and nasopharyngoscopy are diagnostic procedures because the scope is inserted through natural body openings.

Self-Instruction: Therapeutic Terms

Study this table to prepare for the programmed review that follows.

TERM	MEANING
cardiopulmonary resuscitation (CPR) kar′dē-ō-pul′mo-nār-ē rē-sŭs-i-tā′shŭn	method of artificial respiration and chest compressions to move oxygenated blood to vital body organs when breathing and the heart have stopped
continuous positive airway pressure (CPAP) therapy (see Figure 10-17) kon-tin′yū-ŭs poz′i-tiv ār′wā presh′ŭr thār′ă-pē	use of a device with a mask that pumps a constant pressurized flow of air through the nasal passages; commonly used during sleep to prevent airway closure in sleep apnea

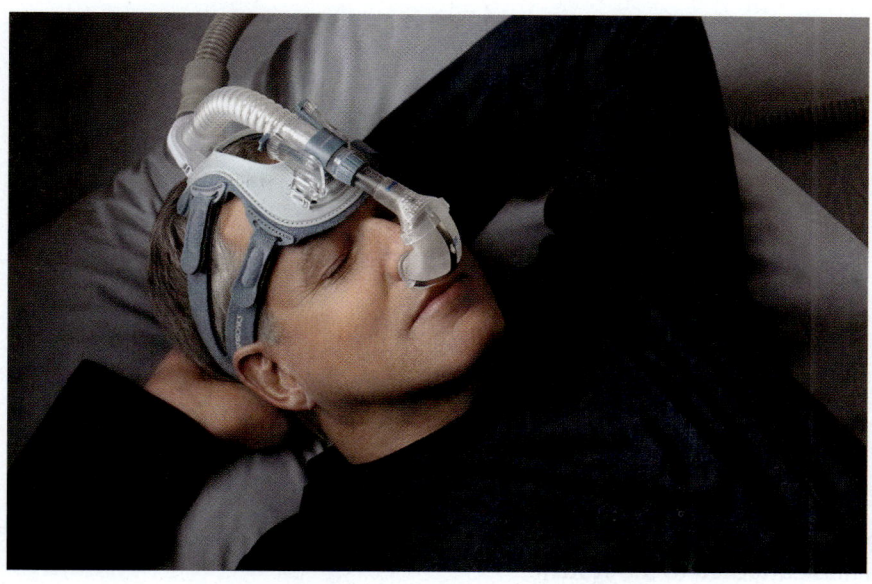

FIGURE 10-17 ■ Patient wearing a continuous positive airway pressure (CPAP) mask.

TERM	MEANING
endotracheal intubation *en′dō-trā′kē-ăl* *in-tū-bā′shŭn*	passage of a tube into the trachea via the nose or mouth to open the airway for delivering gas mixtures to the lungs (e.g., oxygen, anesthetics, or air)
incentive spirometry (see **Figure 10-18**) *in-sen′tiv spī-rom′ĕ-trē*	a common postoperative breathing therapy using a specially designed spirometer to encourage the patient to inhale and hold an inspiratory volume to exercise the lungs and prevent pulmonary complications

FIGURE 10-18 ■ Incentive spirometry.

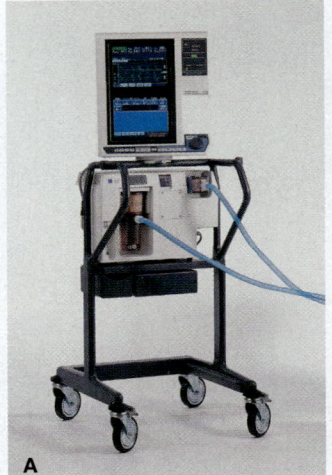
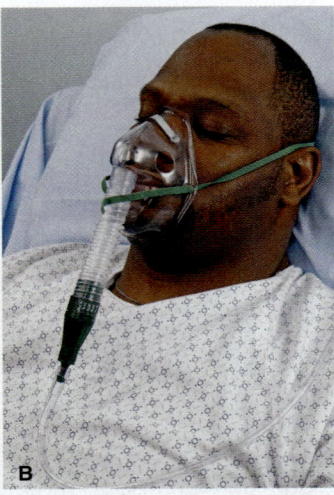

FIGURE 10-19 ■ Mechanical ventilation. **A.** Mechanical ventilation system. **B.** Patient on mechanical ventilation via mask attached to the system.

TERM	MEANING
mechanical ventilation (see **Figure 10-19 A,B**) mĕ-kan′i-kăl ven-ti-lā′shŭn	mechanical breathing using a ventilator
COMMON THERAPEUTIC DRUG CLASSIFICATIONS	
antibiotic an′tē-bī-ot′ik	a drug that kills or inhibits the growth of microorganisms
anticoagulant an′tē-kō-ag′yū-lant	a drug that dissolves, or prevents the formation of, thrombi or emboli in the blood vessels (e.g., heparin)
antihistamine an-tē-his′tă-mēn	a drug that neutralizes or inhibits the effects of histamine
histamine his′tă-mēn	a chemical in the body that is released by injured cells during allergic reactions and injury causing constriction of bronchial smooth muscle and dilation of blood vessels
bronchodilator brong-kō-dī-lā′ter	a drug that dilates the muscular walls of the bronchi
expectorant ek-spek′tō-rănt	a drug that increases bronchial secretions and promotes coughing them out

Programmed Review: Therapeutic Terms

ANSWERS	REVIEW
cardiopulmonary resuscitation	10.76 CPR stands for _____ _____, a method of artificial respiration and chest compressions to move oxygenated blood to vital body organs when breathing and the heart have stopped.

ANSWERS	REVIEW
continuous positive airway stopped	**10.77** A patient with sleep apnea may use a device that pumps pressurized air through the nasal passages to prevent airway closure during sleep. This treatment is called _____ _____ _____ pressure (CPAP) therapy. Recall that apnea means _____ breathing.
within endotracheal intubation	**10.78** The prefix *endo-* means _____. The passage of a tube within the trachea via the nose or mouth to deliver oxygen to the lungs is called _____ _____.
measurement incentive spirometry	**10.79** Recall that spirometry is the direct _____ of lung volume and capacity. A similar spirometer is used in postoperative breathing therapy to motivate the patient to inhale and hold a larger inspiratory volume. This therapy is called _____ _____.
mechanical ventilation	**10.80** Mechanical breathing using a ventilator machine is called _____ _____.
against anticoagulant antibiotic	**10.81** Recall that the prefix *anti-* means _____ or opposed to. Drug classes are commonly named for their actions, such as acting against some thing or process. A drug that acts to prevent the process of coagulation (forming of blood clots) is called an _____. The same prefix joined with the combining form for life (*bio*) denotes a drug class that acts to kill or inhibit bacterial life. This drug is called an _____.
histamine antihistamine	**10.82** A substance in the body that is released in allergic reactions, and that causes constriction of bronchial muscles, is called a _____. A drug that acts to inhibit the effects of histamine is called an _____.
bronchodilator	**10.83** A person who has asthma may experience constriction of the bronchi during an attack. A therapeutic drug that counteracts this constriction by dilating the muscular walls of the bronchi is called a _____.
coughing expectorant	**10.84** Recall that expectoration means _____ up and spitting out material from the lungs. A type of drug that increases mucus production to promote coughing and expelling is called an _____.

Chapter 10 Abbreviations

ABBREVIATION	EXPANSION
ABG	arterial blood gas
AP	Anterior–posterior
Bx	biopsy
COPD	chronic obstructive pulmonary disease
CPAP	continuous positive airway pressure
CPR	cardiopulmonary resuscitation
CT	computed tomography
CXR	chest x-ray
HIV	human immunodeficiency virus
LTB	laryngotracheobronchitis
MRI	magnetic resonance imaging
PA	Posterior–anterior
$PaCO_2$	partial pressure of carbon dioxide
PaO_2	partial pressure of oxygen
PCP	*Pneumocystis jiroveci* pneumonia
PE	pulmonary embolism
PEFR	peak expiratory flow rate
PF	peak flow
PFT	pulmonary function testing
pH	potential of hydrogen
PSG	polysomnography
T and A	tonsillectomy and adenoidectomy
TB	tuberculosis
TV or V_T	tidal volume
URI	upper respiratory infection
VC	vital capacity
V/Q	ventilation–perfusion (scan)

PRACTICE EXERCISES

For each of the following words, write out the term parts (prefixes [P], combining forms [CF], roots [R], and suffixes [S]) on the lines below the word. Then define the term according to the meaning of its parts.

EXAMPLE
Intranasal

intra / nas / al
P   R   S

DEFINITION: within/nose/pertaining to

1. pulmonology

    _____ / _____
       CF   S
    DEFINITION: _____

2. thoracocentesis

    _____ / _____
       CF   S
    DEFINITION: _____

3. pleuritis

    _____ / _____
       R   S
    DEFINITION: _____

4. hypercarbia

    _____ / _____ / _____
       P   R   S
    DEFINITION: _____

5. tracheotomy

    _____ / _____
       CF   S
    DEFINITION: _____

6. thoracostomy

    _____ / _____
       CF   S
    DEFINITION: _____

7. bronchospasm

    _____ / _____
       CF   S
    DEFINITION: _____

8. pneumonic

    _____ / _____
       R   S
    DEFINITION: _____

9. nasopharyngoscopy

_____ / _____ / _____
   CF   CF   S

DEFINITION: _____

10. uvulopalatopharyngoplasty

_____ / _____ / _____ / _____
   CF   CF   CF   S

DEFINITION: _____

Write the correct medical term for each of the following definitions.

11. _____ air in pleural space
12. _____ pus in pleural space
13. _____ blood in pleural space
14. _____ listening to sounds within the body
15. _____ endoscope used to examine the airways

Complete each medical term by writing the missing word part or parts.

16. _____ coni _____ = lung condition caused by prolonged inhalation of dust
17. bronchi _____ = dilation of bronchus
18. _____ plasty = surgical repair of the chest
19. _____ itis = inflammation of the lung
20. _____ metry = process of measuring breathing

Write out the expanded term for each abbreviation.

21. PEFR _____
22. VC _____
23. TB _____

Write the standard abbreviations for the following descriptions.

24. _____ chest x-ray
25. _____ analysis of the blood to determine the adequacy of lung function in the exchange of gases
26. _____ surgical removal of the tonsils and adenoids

Write the letter of the matching term or term part in the space provided.

27. crackles   _____   a. naso
28. stetho   _____   b. hyperventilation
29. hypercapnia   _____   c. hypercarbia
30. hyperpnea   _____   d. thoraco
31. rhino   _____   e. rales

Circle the correct spelling in each set of words.

32. a. auskucation   b. auscultation   c. ascultation
33. a. tackypnea   b. tachypenia   c. tachypnea
34. a. eupnea   b. eupenia   c. eupneia
35. a. plurisy   b. plurisey   c. pleurisy

Give the noun that is used to form each adjective.

36. orthopneic _____
37. asthmatic _____
38. hypoxic _____

Write the correct terms for the anatomic structures indicated.

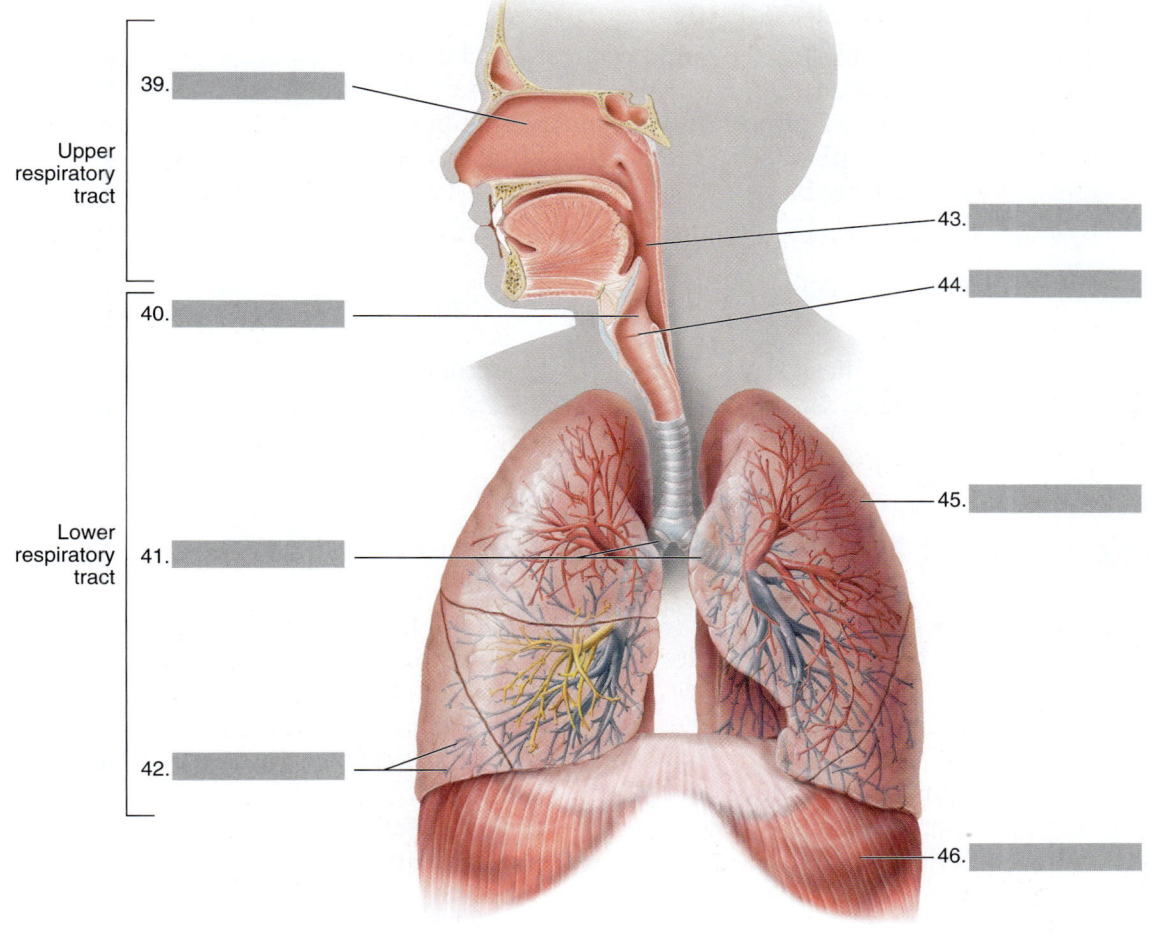

39. _____   43. _____
40. _____   44. _____
41. _____   45. _____
42. _____   46. _____

Circle the combining form that corresponds to the meaning given.

47. nose	a. ren/o	b. rhin/o	c. nos/o
48. air or lung	a. aden/o	b. pneum/o	c. thorac/o
49. throat	a. thorac/o	b. laryng/o	c. pharyng/o
50. chest	a. thorac/o	b. pneum/o	c. lapar/o

MEDICAL RECORD ANALYSIS

Medical Record 10-1

PROGRESS NOTE

S: This is a 26 y/o male c/o a nonproductive cough, dyspnea, and fever × 2 d; pt does not smoke and has otherwise been in good health.

O: T 101°F, BP 100/64, R 25, P 104

Tachypnea is accompanied by mild cyanosis, and inspiratory crackles are noted upon auscultation. WBC 31,000; Hct 37%; platelet count 109,000. CXR shows diffuse infiltrates at the bases of both lungs. An ABG taken while the patient was breathing room air showed a pH of 10.54, $PaCO_2$ of 20, PaO_2 of 74. Sputum specimen contains 3+ WBC but no bacteria.

A: Pneumonia of unknown etiology

P: IV erythromycin STAT

admit to ICU

deliver O_2 by face mask and monitor for hypoxemia

Questions About Medical Record 10-1

1. What is the patient's chief complaint?
   a. afebrile with a dry cough and difficulty breathing
   b. febrile with a dry cough and difficulty breathing
   c. cannot breathe, has a fever, and is coughing up material from the lungs
   d. hoarse throat, dry cough, and fever
   e. febrile, coughing up sputum, and breathing fast

2. What are the findings upon PE?
   a. slow breathing, blue skin, and rhonchi heard in the lungs as the patient exhales
   b. fast breathing, blue skin, and musical sounds heard in the lungs as the patient inhales
   c. slow breathing, blue skin, and rales heard in the lungs as the patient holds her breath
   d. fast heart, blue skin, and rales heard in the lungs as the patient inhales
   e. fast breathing, blue skin, and popping sounds heard in the lungs as the patient inhales

3. What did the chest x-ray show?
   a. tuberculosis
   b. asthma
   c. density representing solid material usually indicating inflammation
   d. fluid filling spaces around the lungs
   e. lung cancer

4. What is the impression?
   a. dilation of the bronchi with an accumulation of mucus
   b. inflammation of the bronchi
   c. inflammation of the pleura
   d. inflammation of the lungs because of sensitivity to dust or chemicals
   e. inflammation of the lungs of unknown cause

5. What is an ABG?
   a. analysis of blood to determine the adequacy of lung function in the exchange of gases
   b. measurement of lung volume and capacity
   c. measurement of the flow of air during inspiration
   d. scan to detect breathing abnormalities
   e. image of the lungs used to visualize lung lesions

6. Describe the condition for which the patient was monitored while undergoing oxygen therapy.
   a. blockage of airflow out of the lungs
   b. excessive movement of air into and out of the lungs
   c. deficient amount of oxygen in the blood
   d. deficient amount of oxygen in the tissue cells
   e. excessive level of carbon dioxide in the blood

7. What is the Sig: on the erythromycin?
   a. not mentioned
   b. inject into a vein immediately
   c. take four immediately
   d. insert into the vagina immediately
   e. inject into a muscle immediately

ANSWERS TO PRACTICE EXERCISES

1. pulmonology
   CF: pulmono
   S: logy
   DEFINITION: lung/study of

2. thoracocentesis
   CF: thoraco
   S: centesis
   DEFINITION: chest/puncture for aspiration

3. pleuritis
   R: pleur
   S: itis
   DEFINITION: pleura/inflammation

4. hypercarbia
   P: hyper
   R: carb
   S: ia
   DEFINITION: above or excessive/carbon dioxide/condition of

5. tracheotomy
   CF: tracheo
   S: tomy
   DEFINITION: trachea/incision

6. thoracostomy
   CF: thoraco
   S: stomy
   DEFINITION: chest/creation of an opening

7. bronchospasm
   CF: broncho
   S: spasm
   DEFINITION: bronchus (airway)/involuntary contraction

8. pneumonic
   R: pneumon
   S: ic
   DEFINITION: air or lung/pertaining to

9. nasopharyngoscopy
   CF: naso
   CF: pharyngo
   S: scopy
   DEFINITION: nose/pharynx (throat)/process of examination

10. uvulopalatopharyngoplasty
    CF: uvulo
    CF: palato
    CF: pharyngo
    S: plasty
    DEFINITION: uvula (grape)/palate/throat/surgical repair or reconstruction
11. pneumothorax
12. empyema or pyothorax
13. hemothorax
14. auscultation
15. bronchoscope
16. pneumoconiosis
17. bronchiectasis
18. thoracoplasty
19. pneumonitis
20. spirometry
21. peak expiratory flow rate
22. vital capacity
23. tuberculosis
24. CXR
25. ABG
26. T and A
27. e
28. d
29. c
30. b
31. a
32. auscultation
33. tachypnea
34. eupnea
35. pleurisy
36. orthopnea
37. asthma
38. hypoxia
39. nasal cavity
40. larynx
41. bronchi
42. bronchioles
43. pharynx
44. trachea
45. lung
46. diaphragm
47. rhin/o
48. pneum/o
49. pharyng/o
50. thorac/o

ANSWERS TO MEDICAL RECORD 10-1

1. b
2. e
3. c
4. e
5. a
6. c
7. b

DIGESTIVE SYSTEM

Learning Outcomes

After completing this chapter, you should be able to:

- Define term parts related to the digestive system.
- Identify key digestive system anatomic structures with their functions.
- Define symptomatic and diagnostic terms related to the digestive system.
- Explain diagnostic tests; procedures; and operative and therapeutic terms related to the digestive system.
- Cite common abbreviations related to the digestive system and give the expansion of each.
- Explain terms used in medical records involving the digestive system.

DIGESTIVE SYSTEM OVERVIEW

The digestive system, also called the *gastrointestinal system*, is made up of the digestive tract, also known as the gastrointestinal (GI) tract, and its associated structures. Its functions include:

- **Digestion**, which is the process of breaking down food by chewing, swallowing, and mixing in digestive juices to convert some of the food into absorbable molecules.
- **Absorption**, which is the passage of digested food molecules through the walls of the intestines and into the bloodstream to be carried to cells of the body.
- **Excretion**, which is the elimination of nonabsorbable nutrients and wastes from the body.

Self-Instruction: Combining Forms

Study this table to prepare for the programmed review that follows.

COMBINING FORM	MEANING
abdomin/o	abdomen
an/o	anus
appendic/o	appendix
bil/i	bile
bucc/o	cheek
celi/o	abdomen
cheil/o	lip
chol/e	bile
col/o	colon
colon/o	colon
cyst/o	bladder or sac
dent/i	teeth
doch/o	duct
duoden/o	duodenum
enter/o	small intestine
esophag/o	esophagus
gastr/o	stomach
gingiv/o	gum
gloss/o	tongue
hepat/o	liver
hepatic/o	liver
herni/o	hernia
ile/o	ileum
inguin/o	groin
jejun/o	jejunum (empty)
lapar/o	abdomen
lingu/o	tongue
lith/o	stone
or/o	mouth
pancreat/o	pancreas
peritone/o	peritoneum
phag/o	eat or swallow
proct/o	anus and rectum
pylor/o	pylorus (gatekeeper)
rect/o	rectum
sial/o	saliva

COMBINING FORM	MEANING
sigmoid/o	sigmoid colon (resembles)
steat/o	fat
stomat/o	mouth
-emesis (suffix)	vomiting

Programmed Review: Combining Forms

ANSWERS	REVIEW
gastr/o enter/o GI	11.1 A gastroenterologist specializes in the gastrointestinal tract. The term is built from the combining forms for stomach and intestine. The combining form meaning stomach is _____. The combining form meaning small intestine is _____. The abbreviation for gastrointestinal is _____.
pertaining to adjective duodenal	11.2 Many combining forms related to the digestive system are similar to the English words for their meaning. For example, the combining form for duodenum is *duoden/o*. Recall that the suffix *-al*, meaning _____ _____, makes an _____ ending. The adjective form of duodenum is _____.
herni/o hernia	11.3 There are many other combining forms that are also similar to their meaning. The combining form meaning hernia is _____. For example, a herniorrhaphy is the suturing of a repaired _____.
ile/o ileostomy	11.4 The combining form for ileum is _____. For example, the surgical creation of an opening for the ileum is _____.
jejun/o inflammation jejunitis	11.5 The combining form for the jejunum is _____. Recall that the suffix *-itis* means _____. Inflammation of the jejunum is called _____.
pancreat/o pancreatitis	11.6 The combining form for pancreas is _____. Inflammation of the pancreas is called _____.
an/o anal, rectum rectal proct/o anus, rectum	11.7 The combining form for anus is _____. The common adjective form is _____. *Rect/o*, the combining form for _____, is derived from the Latin word rectus, meaning straight. The rectum is so named for its straight passage from the lower bowel to the anus. The common adjective form is _____. The combining form referring to the anus and rectum is _____. A proctologic examination involves the study of the _____ and the _____.

ANSWERS	REVIEW
appendic/o appendicitis	**11.8** The combining form for appendix is _____. Inflammation of the appendix is called _____.
peritone/o examination peritoneoscopy	**11.9** The combining form for peritoneum is _____. Link this combining form with *-scopy*, the suffix meaning process of _____, to build the term describing the endoscopic examination of the peritoneum: _____.
pylor/o adjective pertaining to pyloric	**11.10** The combining form for pylorus is _____. Recall that the suffix *-ic* is an _____ ending that means _____ ____. The adjective form of pylorus is _____.
sigmoid/o sigmoidoscopy	**11.11** The combining form for sigmoid colon is _____. The process of examining the sigmoid colon with a sigmoidoscope is called a _____.
esophag/o pertaining to adjective esophageal	**11.12** The combining form for esophagus is _____. Recall that the suffix *-eal*, meaning _____ ____, makes an _____ ending. The adjective form of esophagus is _____.
puncture abdominocentesis celi/o, lapar/o	**11.13** In many cases, two or more combining forms have the same meaning. One combining form meaning abdomen is *abdomin/o*. Recall that the suffix *-centesis* means a _____ for aspiration. A puncture of the abdomen for aspiration of an abdominal fluid is called _____. Two other combining forms for abdomen are _____ and _____, as in the terms celiocentesis and laparoscopy.
col/o colon colon/o	**11.14** There are two combining forms for colon. An inflammation of the colon is termed colitis, which is made with the combining form _____. The second combining form is used in the term colonoscopy, which means examination of the _____. That combining form is _____.
bil/i presence, stone	**11.15** There are two combining forms for bile. The term referring to the production of bile is biligenic, which is made from the combining form _____. The second combining form is used to make the term cholelithiasis. Recall that the suffix *-iasis* means formation of or _____ of, and the combining form *lith/o* means _____. Therefore, the term cholelithiasis refers to the presence of a stone in the

ANSWERS	REVIEW
bile chol/e	gallbladder or _____ ducts. The combining form for bile used in this term is _____.
gloss/o under lingu/o	**11.16** There are two combining forms for tongue. An inflammation of the tongue is called glossitis. The combining form used to create this term is _____. The other combining form is used in the term sublingual, which means _____ the tongue. This second combining form is _____.
or/o pain, mouth stomat/o	**11.17** There are two combining forms for mouth. One is used in the common adjective form oral. That combining form is _____. The other is used, for example, in the term stomalgia, which refers to a condition of _____ in the _____. The combining form meaning mouth in this term is _____.
enlargement hepat/o incision hepatic/o	**11.18** There are two similar combining forms meaning liver. The term hepatomegaly, which means an _____ of the liver, is made from the combining form _____. The other is used to make the term hepaticotomy, which refers to an _____ into the liver. That combining form is _____.
bucc/o	**11.19** The adjective buccal pertains to the cheek. The combining form for cheek is _____.
repair cheil/o	**11.20** Recall that the suffix *-plasty* refers to surgical _____ or reconstruction. The term cheiloplasty means repair of the lip. The combining form for lip is _____.
chol/e doch/o	**11.21** A choledochotomy is an incision into a bile duct. The combining form for bile used here is _____. The combining form meaning duct is _____.
dent/i	**11.22** The adjective dental refers to the teeth. The combining form used to make this term is _____.
bile, bladder	**11.23** A cholecystectomy is the excision of the gallbladder. Chol/e means _____, and *cyst/o* means _____ or sac. Put together, these two combining forms refer to the gallbladder, which holds bile.
gums gingiv/o	**11.24** Gingivitis is inflammation of the _____. The combining form meaning gum is _____.
sial/o	**11.25** A sialolith is a stone of the salivary gland or duct. The combining form for saliva is _____.

ANSWERS	REVIEW
inguin/o	**11.26** The adjective inguinal pertains to the groin. The combining form meaning groin is _____.
condition of without phag/o	**11.27** The term aphagia means the condition of being unable to eat. Recall that the suffix *-ia* means _____, and the prefix *a-* means _____. The combining form meaning to eat or to swallow is _____.
dissolution steat/o	**11.28** Recall that the suffix *-lysis* means breaking down or _____. The term steatolysis refers to the breaking down of fat in digestion. The combining form for fat is _____.
blood -emesis	**11.29** The term hematemesis refers to the vomiting of blood. (*Hemat/o* is the combining form for _____.) The suffix meaning vomiting is _____.

Self-Instruction: Anatomic Terms

Study this table to prepare for the programmed review that follows (see **Figures 11-1** to **11-3**).

TERM	MEANING
oral cavity ōr′ ăl kav′i-tē	cavity that receives food for digestion; also called *mouth*

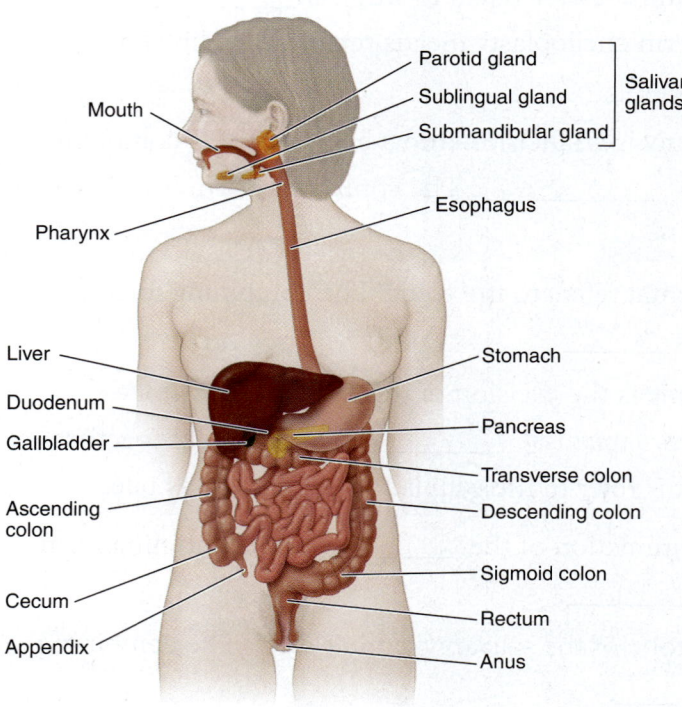

FIGURE 11-1 ■ The digestive system.

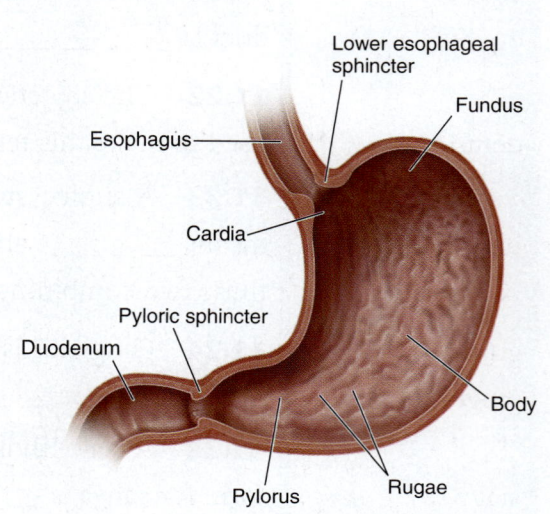

FIGURE 11-2 ■ The stomach.

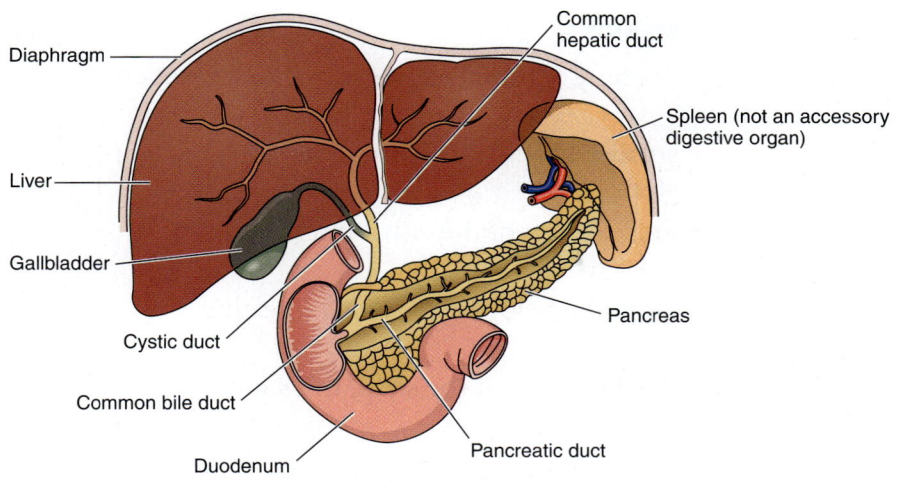

FIGURE 11-3 ■ Accessory organs of digestion and biliary ducts.

TERM	MEANING
mouth *mowth*	cavity that receives food for digestion; also called *oral cavity*
salivary glands *sal'i-vār-ē glanz*	three pairs of exocrine glands in the mouth that secrete saliva: the parotid, the submandibular, and the sublingual glands
cheeks *chēks*	lateral walls of the mouth
lips *lips*	fleshy structures surrounding the mouth
palate *pal'ăt*	structure that forms the roof of the mouth; divided into the hard palate and the soft palate
uvula *ū'vyū-lă*	small projection hanging from the posterior middle edge of the soft palate
tongue *tŭng*	muscular structure of the floor of the mouth covered by mucous membrane and secured by a band-like membrane known as the frenulum
gums *gŭmz*	tissue surrounding the necks of the teeth in the upper and lower jaws; also called *gingivae*
teeth *tēth*	hard bony projections in the jaws for masticating (chewing) food
pharynx *far'ingks*	throat; passageway for food traveling to the esophagus and for air traveling to the larynx
esophagus *ē-sof'ă-gŭs*	muscular tube that moves food from the pharynx to the stomach
stomach (see **Figure 11-2**) *stŭm'ăk*	sac-like organ that mechanically mixes and chemically prepares food received from the esophagus; the stomach has four regions: fundus, cardia, body, and pylorus
lower esophageal sphincter (LES) *lō'wĕr ĕ-sof'ă-jē'ăl sfingk'tĕr*	opening from the esophagus to the stomach (*sphincter* = band); also called the *cardiac sphincter*

TERM	MEANING
pyloric sphincter *pī-lōr′ik sfingk′tĕr*	opening from the stomach into the duodenum
small intestine *smawl in-tes′tin*	smaller tubular structure that digests food received from the stomach
duodenum *dū-ō-dē′nŭm*	first portion of the small intestine
jejunum *jĕ-jū′nŭm*	second portion of the small intestine
ileum *il′ē-ŭm*	third portion of the small intestine
large intestine *larj in-tes′tin*	larger tubular structure that receives the liquid waste products of digestion, reabsorbs water and minerals, and forms and stores feces for defecation
cecum *sē′kŭm*	first part of the large intestine
appendix *ă-pen′diks*	worm-like projection of lymphatic tissue hanging off the cecum; may help to resist infection (*vermi* = worm); also called *vermiform appendix*
colon *kō′lon*	portions of the large intestine extending from the cecum to the rectum; identified by direction or shape
ascending colon *a-sen′ding kō′lon*	portion of the colon that extends upward from the cecum
transverse colon *trans-vĕrs′ kō′lon*	portion of the colon that extends across from the ascending cecum
descending colon *dē-send′ing kō′lon*	portion of the colon that extends downward from the transverse colon
sigmoid colon *sig′moyd kō′lon*	portion of the colon (resembling an "S" in shape) that terminates at the rectum
rectum *rek′tŭm*	distal (end) portion of the large intestine
anus *ā′nŭs*	opening of the rectum to the outside of the body
feces *fē′sēz*	waste formed by the absorption of water in the large intestine; usually solid
defecation *def-ĕ-kā′shŭn*	evacuation of feces from the rectum
peritoneum *per′i-tō-nē′ŭm*	membrane surrounding the entire abdominal cavity and consisting of the parietal layer (lining the abdominal wall) and the visceral layer (covering each organ in the abdomen)
peritoneal cavity *per′i-tō-nē′ăl kav′i-tē*	space between the parietal and visceral peritoneum
omentum *ō-men′tŭm*	an extension of the peritoneum attached to the stomach and connecting it with other abdominal organs

TERM	MEANING
liver liv'ĕr	organ in the upper right quadrant that produces bile, which is secreted into the duodenum during digestion
gallbladder gawl'blad-ĕr	receptacle that stores and concentrates the bile produced in the liver
pancreas pan'krē-as	gland that secretes pancreatic juice into the duodenum via the pancreatic duct, where it mixes with bile to digest food
biliary ducts (see Figure 11-3) bil'ē-ār-ē dŭkts	ducts that convey bile; include the common hepatic, cystic, and common bile ducts

Programmed Review: Anatomic Terms

ANSWERS	REVIEW
oral salivary palate uvula	**11.30** Let us trace the anatomy of the digestive system from beginning to end. Food is taken in at the _____ cavity, or mouth, where the digestive process begins as food is chewed and saliva from the _____ glands is mixed with the food. Structures of the mouth include the cheeks, lips, tongue, teeth, and gums. The roof of the mouth, or the _____, is divided into the hard palate and the soft palate. The small tissue projection hanging from the back edge of the soft palate is called the _____.
pharynx esophagus lower esophageal stomach	**11.31** Chewed food then passes through the throat to the esophagus and then to the stomach. The medical term for the throat is the _____. From the pharynx, the food reaches the _____, which is a muscular tube descending to the stomach. At the inferior portion of the esophagus is the _____ _____ sphincter, the opening from the esophagus to the _____.
stomach pyloric	**11.32** The sac-like organ that mixes and prepares food received from the esophagus is called the _____. From the stomach, food moves next to the small intestine through the _____ sphincter.
sphincter, duodenum jejunum ileum	**11.33** The small intestine does most of the digestive work and has three segments. The first, connected to the stomach at the pyloric _____, is called the _____. After the duodenum comes the second portion, the _____. After the jejunum comes the third portion, the _____. From the ileum, the food passes into the large intestine.

ANSWERS	REVIEW
liver biliary gallbladder duodenum	**11.34** Other organs produce substances to help the small intestine digest food. Bile is produced in the _____ and is conveyed through the _____ ducts to the gallbladder. The _____ stores and concentrates the bile that is produced in the liver, which is then conveyed to the first portion of the small intestine, the _____.
pancreas	**11.35** Pancreatic juice, which is produced in the _____, is also secreted into the duodenum. This assists in digestion as well.
large cecum appendix	**11.36** After leaving the small intestine, the digested food enters the _____ intestine, where water and minerals are reabsorbed and wastes are formed into feces for defecation. The first part of the large intestine is called the _____. Hanging from the cecum is a projection of tissue, which is called the vermiform _____.
colon ascending transverse descending sigmoid rectum	**11.37** The next part of the large intestine, the _____, is identified in four sections that are named for their direction or shape. The portion of the colon extending upward from the cecum is called the _____ colon. The portion that extends from the ascending portion across the body is the _____ colon. The portion extending downward from the transverse colon is the _____ colon. The S-shaped portion at the end of the descending colon is the _____ colon. The sigmoid colon terminates at the _____, which is the end of the large intestine.
anus feces defecation	**11.38** Waste leaves the body through the opening of the rectum, called the _____. The waste formed in the large intestine is called _____. The evacuation of feces from the rectum is called _____.
peritoneum abdominal peritoneal peritoneum	**11.39** Surrounding the entire abdominal cavity is a membrane called the _____. The peritoneum lines not only the _____ cavity (the parietal layer) but also each organ in the abdomen (the visceral layer). The space between the parietal and visceral peritoneum is called the _____ cavity. The omentum is an extension of the _____ that is attached to the stomach, connecting it with other abdominal organs.

ANATOMIC AND CLINICAL DIVISIONS OF THE ABDOMEN

Anatomic and clinical divisions of the abdomen provide reference points to describe abdominal locations. There are nine specific anatomic divisions and four general clinical divisions (see Figures 11-4 to 11-6). All references are based on the patient's right or left.

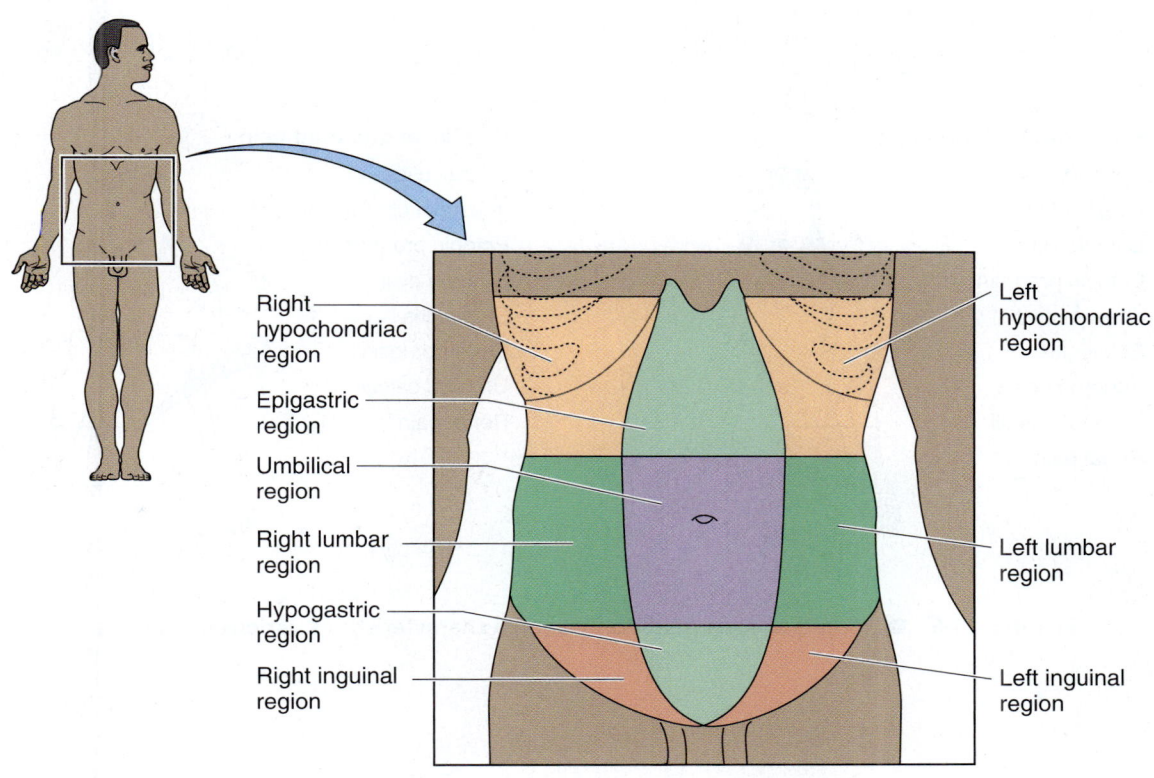

FIGURE 11-4 ■ Anatomic divisions of the abdomen.

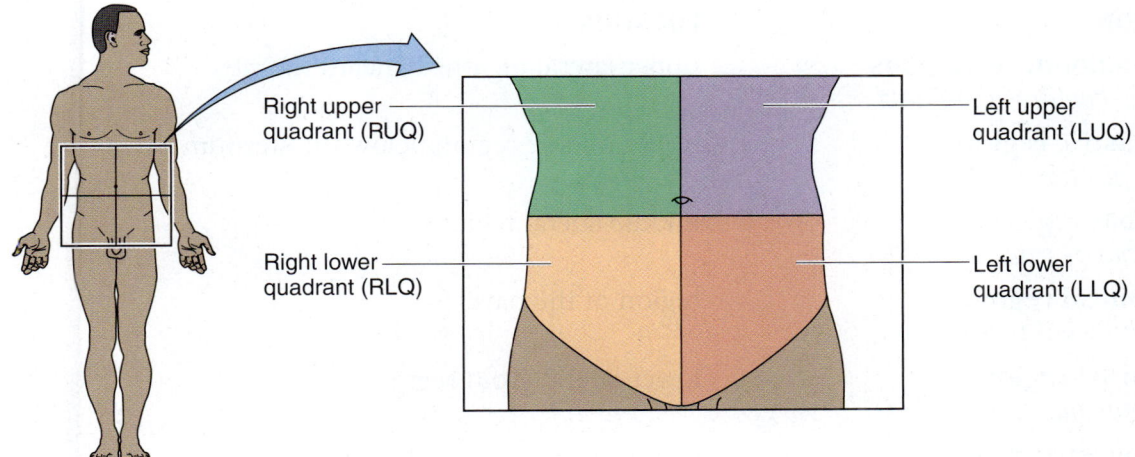

FIGURE 11-5 ■ Clinical divisions of the abdomen.

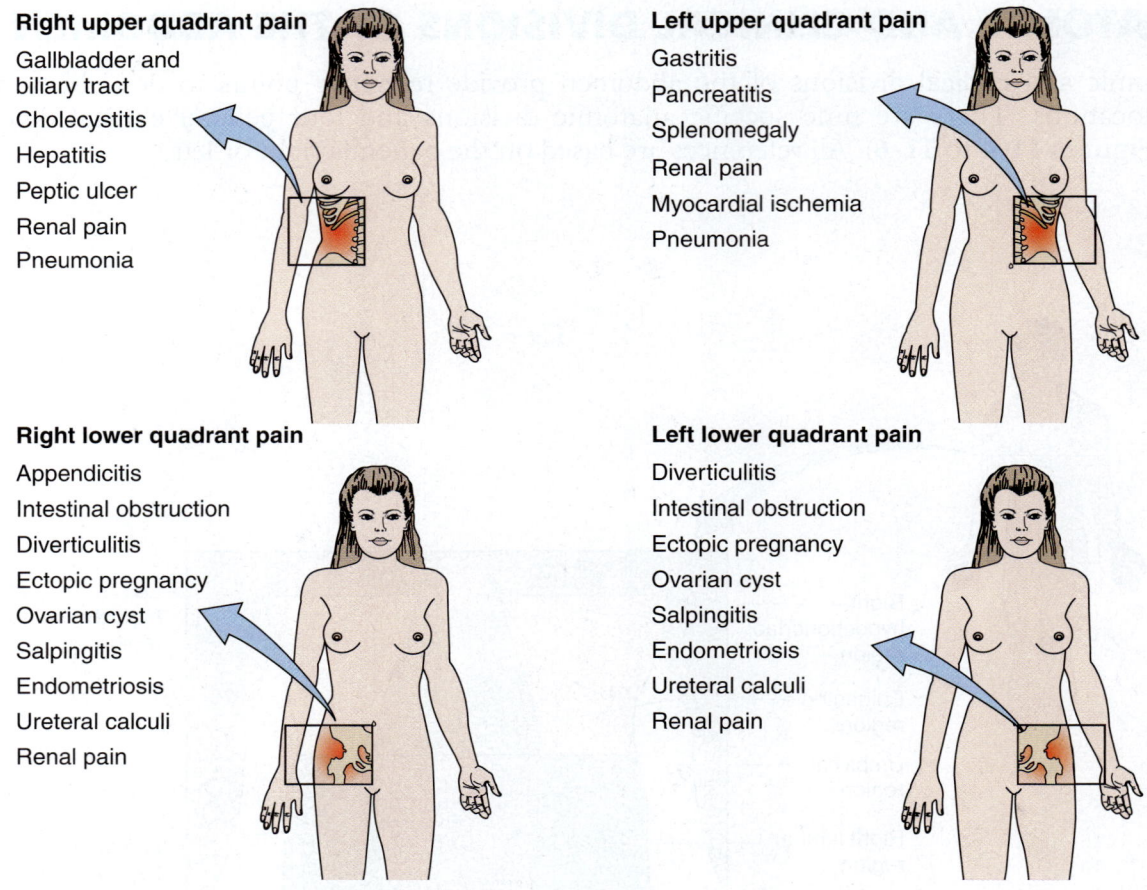

FIGURE 11-6 ■ Common sites of abdominal pain characteristic of various conditions.

Self-Instruction: Anatomic Divisions

Study this table to prepare for the programmed review that follows (see **Figure 11-4**).

REGION	LOCATION
hypochondriac regions hī-pō-kon′drē-ak rē′jŭnz	upper lateral regions beneath the ribs
epigastric region ep-i-gas′trik rē′jŭn	upper middle region below the sternum
lumbar regions lŭm′bar rē′jŭnz	middle lateral regions
umbilical region ŭm-bil′i-kăl rē′jŭn	region of the navel
inguinal regions ing′gwi-năl rē′jŭnz	lower lateral groin regions
hypogastric region hī-pō-gas′trik rē′jŭn	region below the navel

Programmed Review: Anatomic Divisions

ANSWERS	REVIEW
below hypochondriac	11.40 The abdomen is divided into several anatomic regions for reference purposes. Recall that the prefix *hypo-* means _____ or deficient. The upper lateral regions beneath the ribs (*chondro* = cartilaginous) are called the _____ regions.
upon gastr/o epigastric	11.41 The prefix *epi-* means _____. The combining form meaning stomach is _____. Thus, the name for the upper middle region below the sternum and lying approximately upon the stomach is the _____ region.
lumbar	11.42 The middle lateral areas of the abdomen, to each side of the lumbar spine, are the _____ regions.
umbilical	11.43 The medical term for the navel is the umbilicus. The anatomic area in the region of the navel is called the _____ region.
inguin/o inguinal	11.44 The combining form for groin is _____. The lower lateral groin regions are the _____ regions.
hypo- gastr/o hypogastric	11.45 The prefix for below is _____, and the combining form for stomach is _____. Thus, the area below the navel, approximately below the stomach, is called the _____ region.

Self-Instruction: Symptomatic Terms

Study this table to prepare for the programmed review that follows.

TERM	MEANING
anorexia an-ō-rek′sē-ă	loss of appetite (*orexia* = appetite)
aphagia ă-fā′jē-ă	inability to swallow
ascites (see Figure 11-7) ă-sī′tēz	accumulation of fluid in the peritoneal cavity (*ascos* = bag)
buccal bŭk′ăl	in the cheek
diarrhea dī-ă-rē′ă	frequent loose or liquid stools
constipation kon-sti-pā′shŭn	infrequent or incomplete bowel movements characterized by hardened, dry stool that is difficult to pass (*constipo* = to press together)

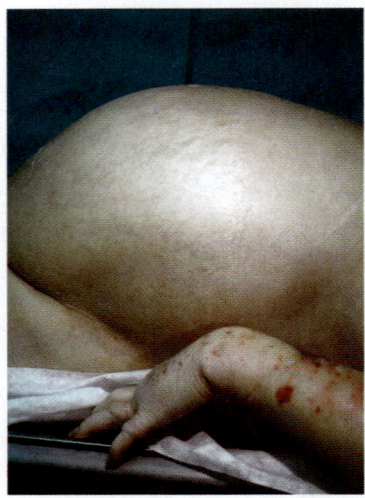

FIGURE 11-7 ■ Patient showing massive ascites and distention of abdomen.

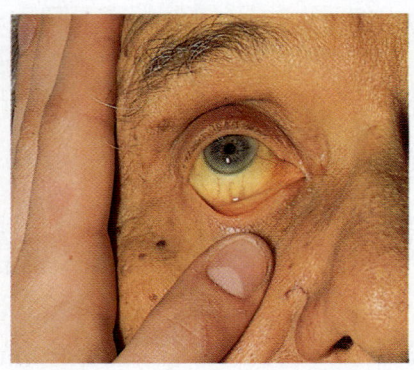

FIGURE 11-8 ■ The yellow color of jaundice (icterus) is easily seen in the sclera of this patient and in the patient's skin as contrasted with the examiner's hand.

TERM	MEANING
dyspepsia *dis-pep′sē-ă*	indigestion (*pepsis* = digestion)
dysphagia *dis-fā′jē-ă*	difficulty in swallowing
eructation *ē-rŭk-tā′shŭn*	belch
flatulence *flat′yū-lents*	gas in the stomach or intestines (*flatus* = a blowing)
halitosis *hal-i-tō′sis*	bad breath (*halitus* = breath)
hematemesis *hē′mă-tem′ĕ-sis*	vomiting blood
hematochezia *hē′mă-tō-kē′zē-ă*	red blood in stool (*chezo* = defecate)
hepatomegaly *hep′ă-tō-meg′ă-lē*	enlargement of the liver
hyperbilirubinemia *hī′pĕr-bil′i-rū-bi-nē′mē-ă*	excessive level of bilirubin (bile pigment) in the blood
icterus (see **Figure 11-8**) *ik′tĕr-ŭs*	yellow discoloration of the skin, sclera (white of the eye), and other tissues caused by excessive bilirubin in the blood (*jaundice* = yellow); also called *jaundice*
jaundice *jawn′dis*	yellow discoloration of the skin, sclera (white of the eye), and other tissues caused by excessive bilirubin in the blood (*jaundice* = yellow); also called *icterus*
melena *me-lē′nă*	dark-colored, tarry stool caused by old blood

TERM	MEANING
nausea *naw′zē-ă*	feeling sick in the stomach
steatorrhea *stē′ă-tō-rē′ă*	feces containing fat
sublingual *sŭb-ling′gwăl*	under the tongue; also called *hypoglossal*
hypoglossal *hī-pō-glos′ăl*	under the tongue; also called *sublingual*

Programmed Review: Symptomatic Terms

ANSWERS	REVIEW
condition of without phag/o aphagia	**11.46** Recall that the suffix *-ia* means _____ _____. The prefix *a-* means _____. Again, the combining form meaning to eat or swallow is _____. Therefore, the term for the condition of being unable to swallow (without swallowing) is _____.
faulty dysphagia	**11.47** The prefix *dys-* means painful, difficult, or _____. The term for the condition of having difficulty swallowing, then, is _____.
anorexia	**11.48** The condition of loss of (or without) appetite (*orexia* = appetite) is called _____.
dyspepsia	**11.49** The condition of indigestion, or of painful digestion (*pepsis* = digestion), is called _____.
adjective pertaining to bucc/o buccal	**11.50** The suffix *-al* is an _____ ending meaning _____ _____. The combining form meaning cheek is _____. The adjective form meaning pertaining to the cheek is _____.
ascites	**11.51** Formed from the root *ascos* (meaning bag), the term for an accumulation of fluid in the peritoneal cavity is _____.
eructation	**11.52** From the Latin word *eructo* comes the term for belch: _____.
flatulence	**11.53** From the Latin word *flatus* (meaning a blowing) comes the term for gas in the stomach or intestines: _____.
condition halitosis	**11.54** The suffix *-osis* means increase or _____. The condition of having bad breath is called _____.

ANSWERS	REVIEW
-emesis hematemesis	**11.55** A combining form for blood is *hemat/o*. Again, the suffix meaning vomiting is _____. The term for vomiting blood is _____.
hematochezia	**11.56** Formed from the root word *chezo* (meaning defecate) comes this term for the condition of having red blood in the stool: _____.
hepat/o, -megaly hepatomegaly	**11.57** The two combining forms for liver are *hepatic/o* and _____. Recall that the suffix for enlargement is _____. Using the latter combining form for liver, the term for enlargement of the liver is _____.
-emia excessive hyperbilirubinemia	**11.58** Recall that the suffix meaning blood condition is _____. The prefix *hyper-* means above or _____. The condition of having excessive bilirubin in the blood is _____.
icterus	**11.59** When there is excessive bilirubin in the blood, the skin is discolored yellow. This is called jaundice, or _____.
melena	**11.60** From the Greek word *melaina* (meaning black) comes this term for dark-colored, tarry stool caused by old blood: _____.
nausea	**11.61** From a Greek word originally referring to seasickness comes the term for feeling sick in the stomach: _____.
steat/o discharge steatorrhea	**11.62** Again, the combining form for fat is _____. Recall that the suffix *-rrhea* means _____. The term for fat in the feces (a discharge of fat) is _____.
lingu/o below or under sublingual	**11.63** The two combining forms for tongue are *gloss/o* and _____. The prefix *sub-* means _____. Made with the latter combining form, the term for under the tongue is _____.
through discharge diarrhea constipation	**11.64** Formed from the prefix *dia-*, meaning across or _____, and the suffix *rrhea-*, meaning _____, the term describing frequent loose or liquid stool is _____. In contrast, the term describing hardened, dry stool that is difficult to pass is _____.

Self-Instruction: Diagnostic Terms

Study this table to prepare for the programmed review that follows.

TERM	MEANING
RELATED TO THE UPPER DIGESTIVE TRACT	
ankyloglossia *ang′ki-lō-glos′ē-ă*	tongue-tie; a defect of the tongue characterized by a short, thick frenulum (*ankyl/o* = crooked or stiff)
cheilitis *kī-lī′tis*	inflammation of the lip
esophageal varices (see Figure 11-17) *ē-sof′ă-jē′ăl var′i-sēz*	swollen, twisted veins in the esophagus that are especially susceptible to ulceration and hemorrhage
esophagitis *ē-sof-ă-jī′tis*	inflammation of the esophagus
gastritis (see Figure 11-17) *gas-trī′tis*	inflammation of the stomach
gastroesophageal reflux disease (GERD) *gas′trō-ē-sof-ă-jē′ăl rē′fluks di-zēz′*	backflow of contents of the stomach into the esophagus, often resulting from abnormal function of the lower esophageal sphincter, causing burning pain in the esophagus
gingivitis *jin-ji-vī′tis*	inflammation of the gums
glossitis *glo-sī′tis*	inflammation of the tongue
parotiditis *pă-rot-i-dī′tis*	inflammation of the parotid gland; also called *mumps* and *parotitis*
parotitis *par-ō-tī′tis*	inflammation of the parotid gland; also called *mumps* and *parotiditis*
peptic ulcer disease (PUD) *pep′tik ŭl′sĕr di-zēz′*	sore on the mucous membrane of the stomach, duodenum, or any other part of the gastrointestinal system exposed to gastric juices; commonly caused by infection with *Helicobacter pylori* bacteria (*pept/o* = to digest)

gastric ulcer
     (see Figure 11-9)
     gas′trik ŭl′sĕr
	ulcer located in the stomach

duodenal ulcer *dū′ō-dē′năl ŭl′sĕr*	ulcer located in the duodenum
pyloric stenosis *pī-lōr′ik ste-nō′sis*	narrowed condition of the pylorus
sialoadenitis *sī′ă-lō-ad-ĕ-nī′tis*	inflammation of a salivary gland
stomatitis *stō-mă-tī′tis*	inflammation of the mouth

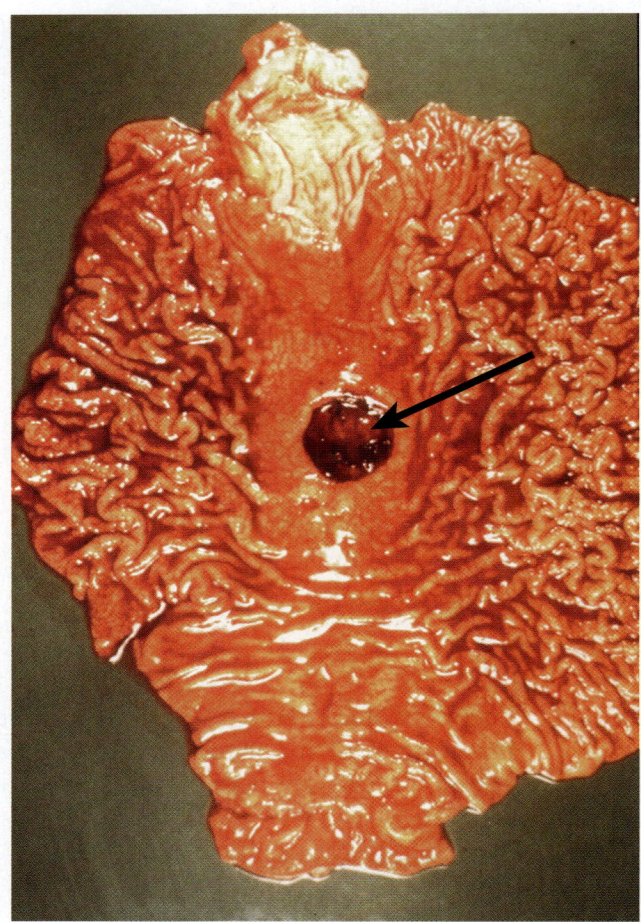

FIGURE 11-9 ■ Gastric ulcer. The stomach has been opened to reveal a deep gastric ulcer. The *arrow* is pointing at the area of ulceration.

TERM	MEANING
RELATED TO THE LOWER DIGESTIVE TRACT	
anal fistula ā′năl fis′tyū-lă	an abnormal, tube-like passageway from the anus that may connect with the rectum (*fistula* = pipe)
appendicitis ă-pen-di-sī′tis	inflammation of the appendix
colitis kō-lī′tis	inflammation of the colon (large intestine)
ulcerative colitis ŭl′sĕr-ă-tiv kō-lī′tis	chronic inflammation of the colon with ulcerations
colorectal polyps (see Figure 11-17) kol′ō-rek′tăl pol′ips	benign tissue growths on the mucous membrane lining the large intestine and rectum; adenomatous types are precancerous and likely to develop into malignancy
pediculated polyp pĕ-dik′yū-lā′tĕd pol′ip	polyp that is projected on a stalk (*ped/o* = foot)
sessile polyp ses′il pol′ip	polyp lying flat on the surface (*sessilis* = low growing)

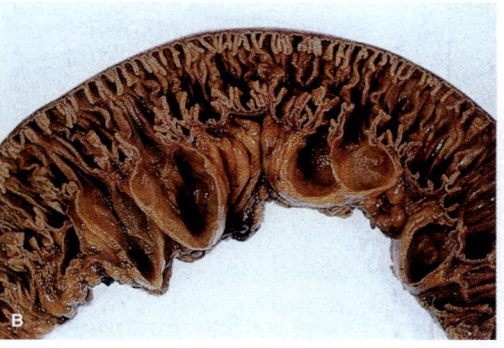

FIGURE 11-10 ■ Diverticulosis. **A.** Multiple outpouchings along the border of the jejunum. **B.** Cut section showing thin-walled diverticular outpouchings.

TERM	MEANING
diverticulum dī-vĕr-tik′yū-lŭm	an abnormal side pocket in the gastrointestinal tract; usually related to a low dietary fiber intake
diverticulosis (see **Figures 11-10 A,B** and **11-17**) dī′vĕr-tik-ū-lō′sis	presence of diverticula in the gastrointestinal tract, especially the colon
diverticulitis dī′vĕr-tik-yū-lī′tis	inflammation of diverticula
dysentery dis′en-ter-ē	inflammation of the intestine characterized by frequent, bloody stools; most often caused by bacteria or protozoa (e.g., amebic dysentery)
enteritis en-tĕr-ī′tis	inflammation of the small intestine
hemorrhoid (see **Figure 11-11**) hem′-royd	swollen, twisted vein (varicosity) in the anal region (*haimorrhois* = a vein likely to bleed)

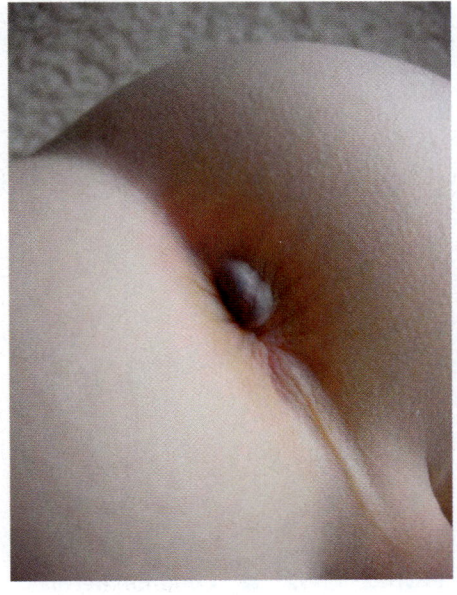

FIGURE 11-11 ■ External hemorrhoid in a 2-year-old boy with recurrent straining due to chronic constipation.

TERM	MEANING
hernia hĕr′nē-ă	protrusion of an organ part from its normal location
hiatal hernia (see **Figures 11-12** and **11-20**) hī-ā′tăl hĕr′nē-ă	protrusion of a part of the stomach upward through the opening in the diaphragm
inguinal hernia (see **Figure 11-12**) ing′gwi-năl hĕr′nē-ă	protrusion of a loop of the intestine through layers of the abdominal wall in the inguinal region
incarcerated hernia in-kar′sĕr-ā-tĕd hĕr′nē-ă	hernia that is swollen and fixed within a sac, causing an obstruction
strangulated hernia strang′gyū-lā-tĕd hĕr′nē-ă	hernia that is constricted, cut off from circulation, and likely to become gangrenous
umbilical hernia ŭm-bil′i-kăl hĕr′nē-ă	protrusion of the intestine through a weakness in the abdominal wall around the umbilicus (navel)

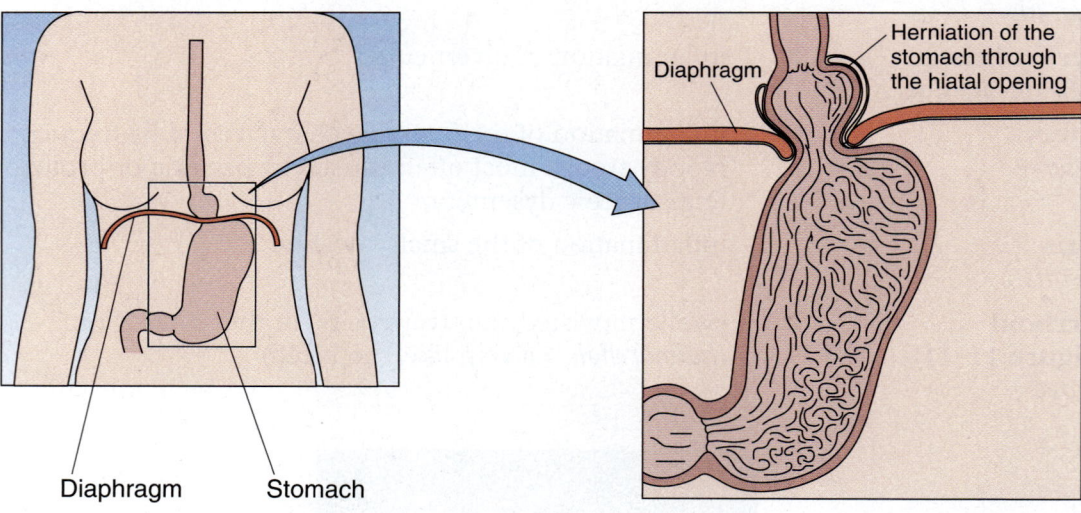

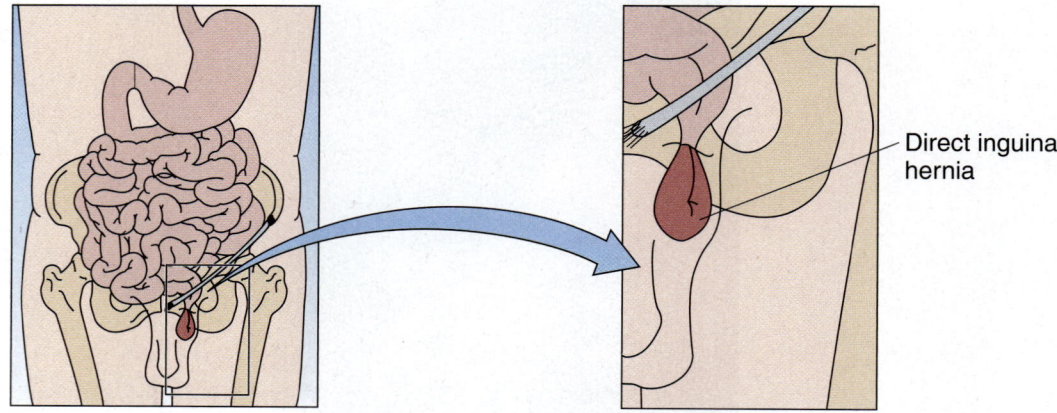

FIGURE 11-12 ■ Common hernias.

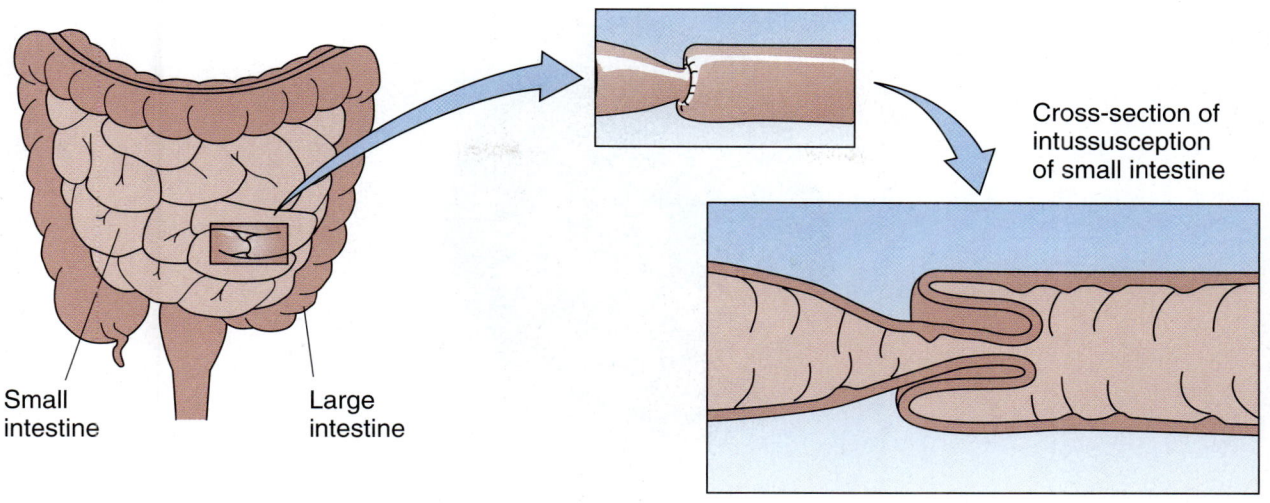

FIGURE 11-13 ■ Intussusception.

TERM	MEANING
ileitis *il-ē-ī′tis*	inflammation of the lower portion of the small intestine
intussusception (see Figure 11-13) *in′tŭs-sŭs-sep′shŭn*	prolapse of one part of the intestine into the lumen of the adjoining part (*intus* = within; *suscipiens* = to take up)
peritonitis *per′i-tō-nī′tis*	inflammation of the peritoneum
proctitis *prok-tī′tis*	inflammation of the rectum and the anus
volvulus (see Figure 11-14) *vol′vyū-lŭs*	twisting of the bowel on itself, causing obstruction (*volvo* = to roll)

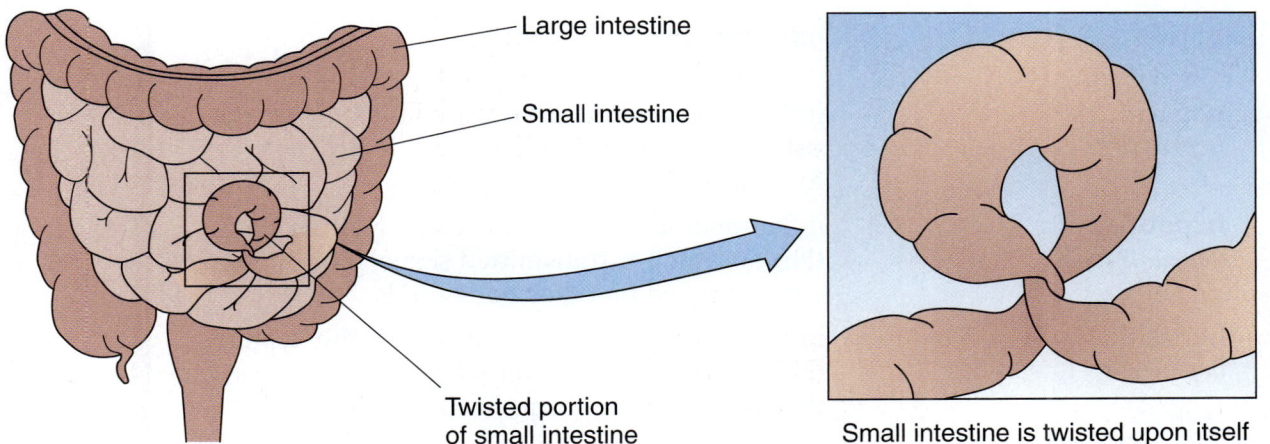

FIGURE 11-14 ■ Volvulus.

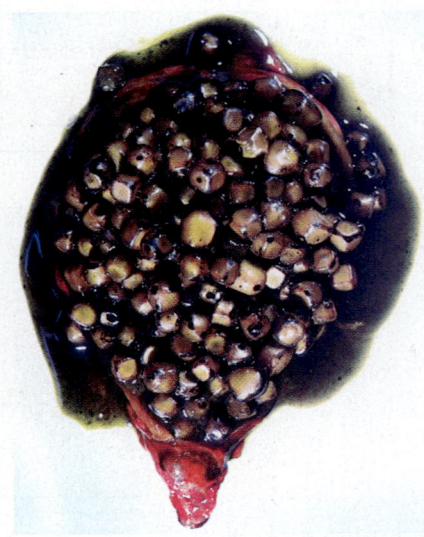

FIGURE 11-15 ■ Cholelithiasis. The gallbladder has been opened to reveal numerous gallstones made up of cholesterol.

TERM	MEANING
RELATED TO THE ACCESSORY ORGANS OF THE GASTROINTESTINAL SYSTEM	
cholangitis *kō-lan-jī′tis*	inflammation of the bile ducts
cholecystitis *kō′lē-sis-tī′tis*	inflammation of the gallbladder
choledocholithiasis (see Figure 11-17) *kō-led′ō-kō-lith-ī′ă-sis*	presence of stones in the common bile duct
cholelithiasis (see Figure 11-15) *kō′lē-li-thī′ă-sis*	presence of stones in the gallbladder or bile ducts
cirrhosis *sir-rō′sis*	chronic disease characterized by degeneration of liver tissue; most often caused by alcoholism or a nutritional deficiency (*cirrho* = yellow)
hepatitis *hep-ă-tī′tis*	inflammation of the liver
hepatitis A *hep-ă-tī′tis A*	inflammation of the liver caused by the hepatitis A virus (HAV), usually transmitted orally through fecal contamination of food or water
hepatitis B *hep-ă-tī′tis B*	inflammation of the liver caused by the hepatitis B virus (HBV), which is transmitted sexually or by exposure to contaminated blood or body fluids
hepatitis C *hep-ă-tī′tis C*	inflammation of the liver caused by the hepatitis C virus (HCV), which is transmitted by exposure to infected blood; this strain is rarely contracted sexually
pancreatitis *pan′krē-ă-tī′tis*	inflammation of the pancreas

Programmed Review: Diagnostic Terms

ANSWERS	REVIEW
-itis	**11.65** The suffix for inflammation is _____. Many parts of the gastrointestinal system can become inflamed; thus, there are many diagnostic terms for inflammation of different organs. The two combining forms for mouth are *or/o* and _____. Made with the latter, the term for inflammation of the mouth is _____.
stomat/o	
stomatitis	
sial/o	**11.66** The combining form for saliva is _____. Using that combining form along with *aden/o*, meaning gland, the term for inflammation of a salivary gland is _____. Inflammation of the parotid gland is called _____ (also known as mumps).
sialoadenitis	
parotiditis or parotitis	
cheil/o	**11.67** The combining form meaning lip is _____. Inflammation of the lip is called _____.
cheilitis	
gloss/o	**11.68** The two combining forms for tongue are *lingu/o* and _____. Using the latter, the term for inflammation of the tongue is _____. The combining form for gums is _____, and the term for inflammation of the gums is _____.
glossitis	
gingiv/o	
gingivitis	
esophag/o	**11.69** The combining form for esophagus is _____, and the term for inflammation of the esophagus is _____. The combining form for stomach is _____, and the term for inflammation of the stomach is _____.
esophagitis	
gastr/o	
gastritis	
enter/o	**11.70** The combining form for small intestine is _____, and the term for inflammation of the small intestine is _____.
enteritis	
ile/o	**11.71** The combining form for the ileum is _____, and inflammation of the ileum (the lower portion of the small intestine) is called _____. The two combining forms for the colon are *colon/o* and _____. Made from the latter form, the term for inflammation of the colon is _____. When this occurs chronically along with ulcerations, it is called _____ _____.
ileitis	
col/o	
colitis	
ulcerative colitis	

ANSWERS	REVIEW
condition of diverticulosis diverticulitis	**11.72** Recall that the suffix *-osis* means increase or _____ ____. The condition of having diverticula (abnormal little pockets in the gastrointestinal tract) is called _____. If the diverticula are inflamed, this is called _____.
appendic/o appendicitis peritone/o, inflammation peritoneum	**11.73** The combining form for the appendix is _____, and inflammation of the appendix is called _____. The combining form for the peritoneum is _____. Peritonitis describes _____ of the _____.
proct/o proctitis	**11.74** The combining form referring to the anus and rectum is _____. It is used in the term for inflammation of the rectum and the anus: _____.
gallbladder cholecystitis cholangitis	**11.75** *Cholecyst/o* refers to the _____. Inflammation of the gallbladder is termed _____. Formed from *chol/e* (bile) and *angi/o* (vessels), which, when combined, refer to the bile ducts, the term for inflammation of the bile ducts is _____.
pancreat/o pancreatitis	**11.76** The combining form for pancreas is _____. Inflammation of the pancreas is _____.
hepat/o hepatitis A, fecal B sexually blood, C blood	**11.77** The two combining forms for liver are *hepatic/o* and _____. Made from the latter, the term for inflammation of the liver is _____. The different types of hepatitis are named after the viruses that cause them. The hepatitis ____ virus (HAV) is transmitted orally through _____ contamination of food or water. Hepatitis ____ virus (HBV) is transmitted _____ or by exposure to contaminated _____ or body fluids. Hepatitis ____ virus (HCV) is transmitted primarily through exposure to infected _____.
condition of cirrhosis	**11.78** Again, the suffix *-osis* refers to an increase or _____ ____. The chronic liver condition that causes yellowing (*cirrho* = yellow) of tissues is called _____. It is usually caused by alcoholism or a nutritional deficiency.

ANSWERS	REVIEW
colon rectum pertaining to colorectal polyps pediculated sessile malignancy or cancer	**11.79** *Col/o* is a combining form referring to the _____. Combined with *rect/o*, meaning _____, and the suffix *-al*, meaning _____, the adjective referring to the colon and the rectum is _____. The mucous membranes lining the colon and the rectum are common sites for the development of benign tissue growths called _____. Those that project from a stalk are called _____ polyps, and those that lie flat on the surface are called _____ polyps. Adenomatous types are likely to develop into a _____.
pyloric stenosis	**11.80** Stenosis refers to a narrowed condition of an organ. A narrowing of the pylorus is termed _____ _____.
condition of gloss/o ankyloglossia	**11.81** The combining form *ankyl/o* means crooked or stiff. Recall that the suffix *-ia* means a _____. The two combining forms for tongue are *lingu/o* and _____. Made from the latter, the term for a condition of a tongue-tie defect with a stiff, short frenulum is _____.
esophageal varices	**11.82** Varices are swollen, twisted veins. When they occur in the esophagus, this condition is called _____ _____.
gastroesophageal reflux disease	**11.83** Reflux is a backflow. When stomach contents flow back into the esophagus, this is called _____ _____ _____ (GERD).
peptic ulcer disease gastric duodenal	**11.84** An ulcer is a sore on the skin or a mucous membrane. The disease characterized by ulcer formation on the mucous membrane of the stomach, duodenum, or any other part of the GI system exposed to gastric juices is called _____ _____ _____ (PUD). An ulcer located in the stomach is called a _____ ulcer, and an ulcer in the duodenum is called a _____ ulcer.
enter/o condition of or process of dysentery	**11.85** The prefix *dys-* means painful, difficult, or faulty. The combining form for small intestine is _____. The suffix *-y* means _____. The condition of a painful inflammation of the intestine (usually caused by bacteria or protozoa) is called _____.

ANSWERS	REVIEW
hernia	**11.86** The protrusion of an organ part from its normal location is termed a _____. Hernias are often named according to the location of the protrusion. The protrusion of a part of the stomach upward through the opening in the diaphragm (hiatus) is called a _____ hernia. Protrusion of a loop of intestine through the abdominal wall in the inguinal region is an _____ hernia. Protrusion of the intestine through a weakness in the abdominal wall around the umbilicus is called an _____ hernia.
hiatal	
inguinal	
umbilical	
incarcerated	**11.87** A hernia that is swollen and becomes fixed within a sac is called an _____ hernia. A hernia that becomes constricted and cut off from circulation is called a _____ hernia.
strangulated	
intussusception	**11.88** A section of intestine may prolapse into the lumen of an adjoining section, causing an _____. If a section of intestine twists upon itself, an obstruction may result; this condition is called _____ (*volvo* = to roll).
volvulus	
anal fistula	**11.89** A fistula (*fistula* = pipe) is an abnormal connection. A fistula from the anus to the rectum is called an ___ ___.
hemorrhoid	**11.90** *Hem/o* is a combining form referring to blood. A swollen, twisted vein in the anal region that is liable to bleed is called a _____.
bile	**11.91** The combining form *chol/e* means _____. The combining form for stone is _____. The suffix meaning formation of or presence of is _____. Therefore, the term for the presence of stones in the gallbladder or bile ducts is _____.
lith/o	
-iasis	
cholelithiasis	
choledocholithiasis	**11.92** The combining forms *chol/e* and *doch/o* together refer to the common bile duct. The term for the presence of stones in the common bile duct is _____.

Self-Instruction: Diagnostic Tests and Procedures

Study this table to prepare for the programmed review that follows.

TEST OR PROCEDURE	EXPLANATION
BIOPSY	
biopsy (Bx) bī′op-sē	removal and microscopic study of tissue for pathologic examination
incisional biopsy in-sizh′ŭn-ăl bī′op-sē	removal of a portion of a lesion
excisional biopsy ek-sizh′ŭn-ăl bī′op-sē	removal of an entire lesion
needle biopsy (see Figure 11-16) nē′děl bī′op-sē	percutaneous removal of tissue or fluid using a special, hollow needle (e.g., for liver biopsy)
ENDOSCOPY	
endoscopy (see Figure 11-17) en-dos′kŏ-pē	examination within a body cavity with a flexible endoscope for diagnosis or treatment; used in the gastrointestinal tract to detect abnormalities and to perform procedures such as biopsy, excision of lesions, and therapeutic interventions
Lower Gastrointestinal Endoscopy	
colonoscopy kō′lon-os′kŏ-pē	examination of the colon using a flexible colonoscope
proctoscopy prok-tos′kŏ-pē	examination of the rectum and anus with a proctoscope
sigmoidoscopy sig′moy-dos′kŏ-pē	examination of the sigmoid colon with a rigid or flexible sigmoidoscope

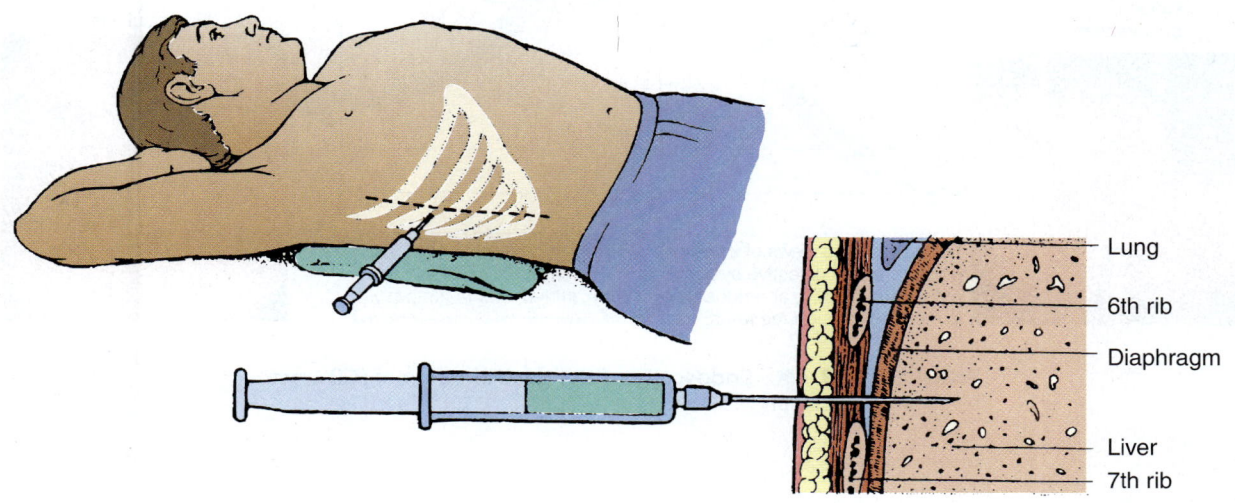

FIGURE 11-16 ■ Needle biopsy of the liver.

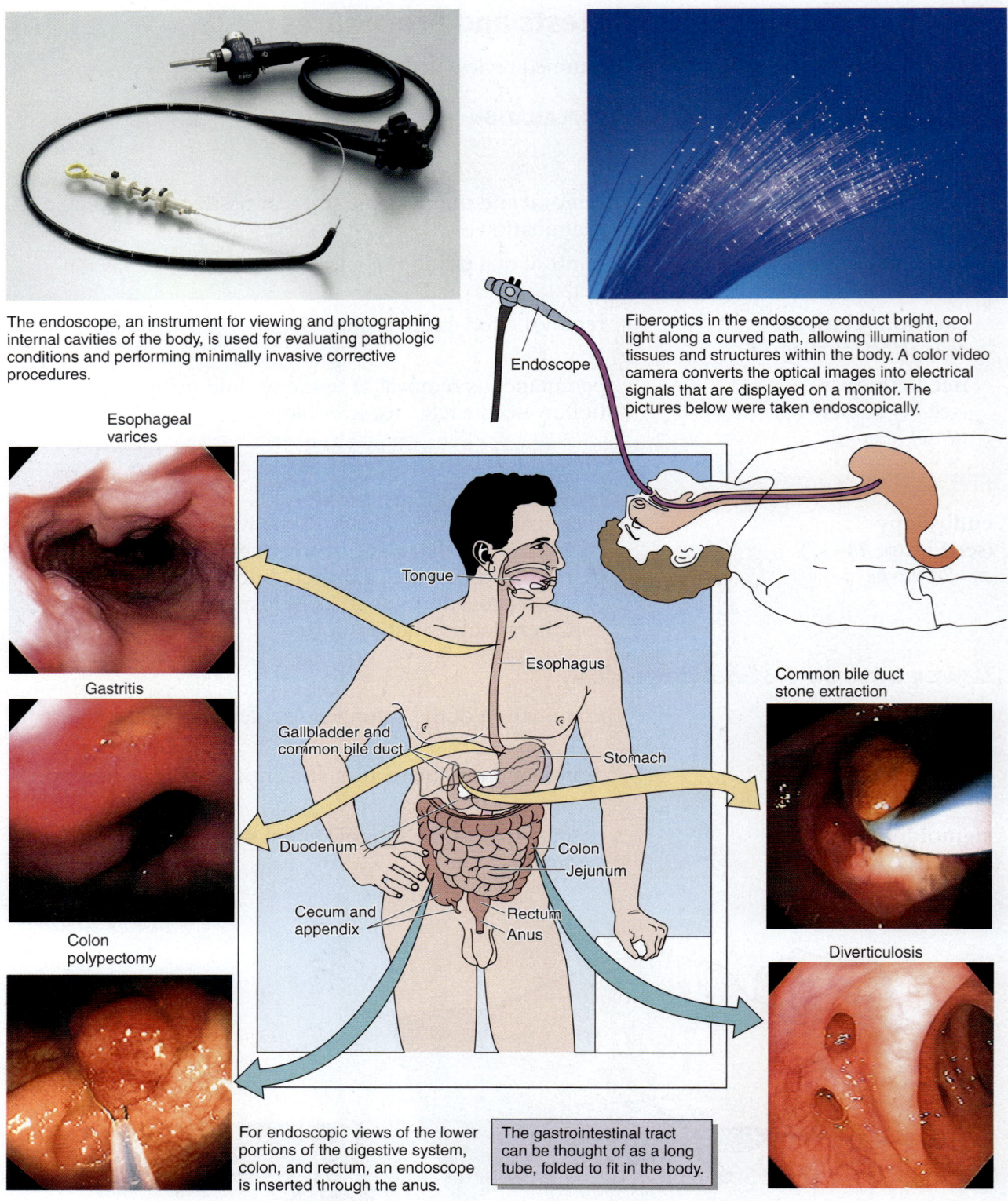

FIGURE 11-17 ■ Endoscopy of the gastrointestinal (GI) tract.

TEST OR PROCEDURE	EXPLANATION
Upper Gastrointestinal Endoscopy	
esophagogastroduodenoscopy (EGD) ē-sof′ă-gō-gas′trō-dū′ō-den-os-kŏ-pē	examination of the lining of the esophagus, stomach, and duodenum with a flexible endoscope for diagnostic and/or therapeutic purposes, such as biopsy, excision of lesions, removal of swallowed objects, dilation of obstructions, stent placement, measures to control hemorrhage, and so forth.
capsule endoscopy kap′sūl en-dos′kŏ-pē	examination of the small intestine made by a tiny video camera placed in a capsule and then swallowed; images are transmitted to a waist-belt recorder and then downloaded onto a computer for assessment of possible abnormalities; traditional endoscopy cannot completely access the small intestine because of its length and complexity
ENDOSCOPY OF THE ACCESSORY ORGANS AND ABDOMEN	
endoscopic retrograde cholangiopancreatography (ERCP) en-dō-skop′ik ret′rō-grād kō-lan′jē-ō-pan-krē-ă-tog′ră-fē	endoscopic procedure including x-ray fluoroscopy to examine the ducts of the liver, gallbladder, biliary ducts, and pancreas; includes use of instruments to obtain tissue samples, extract biliary stones, relieve obstructions, and so forth.
laparoscopy (see Figure 11-18) lap′ă-ros′kŏ-pē	examination of the abdominal cavity with a laparoscope for diagnostic purposes and/or to perform surgery
IMAGING STUDIES	
magnetic resonance imaging (MRI) mag-net′ik rez′ō-nănts im′ă-jing	nonionizing imaging technique for visualizing the abdominal cavity to identify disease or deformity in the gastrointestinal tract
radiography (see Figure 11-19) rā′dē-og′ră-fē	x-ray imaging used to detect a condition or anomaly within the gastrointestinal tract
upper gastrointestinal (GI) series (see Figure 11-20) ŭp′ĕr gas′trō-in-tes′ti-năl sēr′ēz	x-ray of the esophagus, stomach, and duodenum after the patient has swallowed a contrast medium; barium is the most commonly used medium

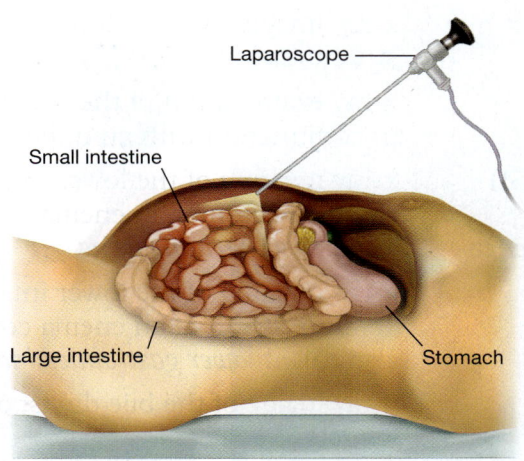

FIGURE 11-18 ■ Laparoscopy.

ANSWERS	REVIEW
upper gastrointestinal, series	obtained after the patient swallows barium is called an _____ _____ (GI) _____.
small bowel series	**11.105** Bowel is another term for intestine. Using the term bowel, the x-ray examination of the small intestine is called a _____ _____ _____.
lower gastrointestinal	**11.106** Barium contrast can also be introduced into the lower gastrointestinal tract through an enema. An x-ray image of the colon after a barium enema has been administered is called either a barium enema or a _____ _____ (GI) series.
record cholangiogram cholecystogram	**11.107** The suffix *-gram* means _____. Using the combining form referring to bile ducts, an x-ray record of bile ducts is called a _____. Using the combining form referring to the gallbladder, an x-ray image of the gallbladder is called a _____.
fluoroscopy	**11.108** The type of x-ray examination using a fluorescent screen to visualize structures in motion is called _____.
computed tomography	**11.109** The process of obtaining computer cross-sectional x-ray images of the abdomen is called _____ _____ (CT) of the abdomen.
recording sonography abdominal sonogram endoscopic ultrasonography	**11.110** The suffix *-graphy* means process of _____. Another term for ultrasound imaging is _____. An ultrasound image of the abdomen is called an _____ _____. When the sonographic transducer is placed inside an endoscope for examining a body cavity with ultrasound, this is called _____ _____ (EUS).
stool culture sensitivity	**11.111** Stool specimens can be diagnostically examined to detect pathology. Isolation of a specimen in a culture medium to grow and identify microorganisms and to determine the drugs to which they are sensitive is called a _____ _____ and _____ (C&S).
occult blood	**11.112** The term occult means hidden or not obvious. A chemical test of a stool specimen to detect unseen blood and, thereby, bleeding in the GI tract is called a stool _____ _____ study.

Self-Instruction: Operative Terms

Study this table to prepare for the programmed review that follows.

TERM	MEANING
abdominocentesis ab-dom′i-nō-sen-tē′sis	puncture of the abdomen for aspiration of fluid
abdominal paracentesis ab-dom′i-năl par′ă-sen-tē′sis	puncture of the abdomen for aspiration of fluid in the peritoneal cavity (e.g., fluid accumulated in ascites)
anal fistulectomy ā′năl fis-tyū-lek′tŏ-mē	excision of an anal fistula
anastomosis ă-nas′tō-mō′sis	union of two hollow vessels; a technique used in bowel surgery
appendectomy ap-pen-dek′tō-mē	excision of a diseased appendix
bariatric surgery bar-ē-at′rik sūr′jĕr-ē	treatment of morbid obesity by surgery to the stomach and/or intestines; procedures include restrictive techniques that limit the size of the stomach and malabsorptive techniques that limit the absorption of food (*baros* = weight; *iatric* = pertains to treatment)
cheiloplasty kī′lō-plas-tē	repair of the lip
cholecystectomy kō′lē-sis-tek′tō-mē	excision of the gallbladder; common treatment for symptomatic gallbladder disease (e.g., cholelithiasis, cholecystitis, and cholangitis)
laparoscopic cholecystectomy lap′ă-rō-skop′ik kō′lē-sis-tek′tō-mē	excision of the gallbladder through a laparoscope
colostomy (see **Figure 11-23**) kō-los′tō-mē	creation of an opening in the colon through the abdominal wall to create an abdominal anus, allowing stool to bypass a diseased portion of the colon; performed to treat ulcerative colitis, cancer, or obstructions
esophagoplasty ē-sof′ă-gō-plas-tē	repair of the esophagus
gastrectomy gas-trek′tŏ-mē	partial or complete removal of the stomach
gastric resection gas′trik rē-sek′shŭn	partial removal and repair of the stomach
gastroenterostomy gas′trō-en-tĕr-os′tō-mē	formation of an artificial opening between the stomach and small intestine; often performed at the time of gastrectomy to route food from the remainder of the stomach to the intestine; also performed to repair a perforated duodenal ulcer
glossectomy glo-sek′tō-mē	excision of all or part of the tongue
glossorrhaphy glo-sōr′ă-fē	suture of the tongue

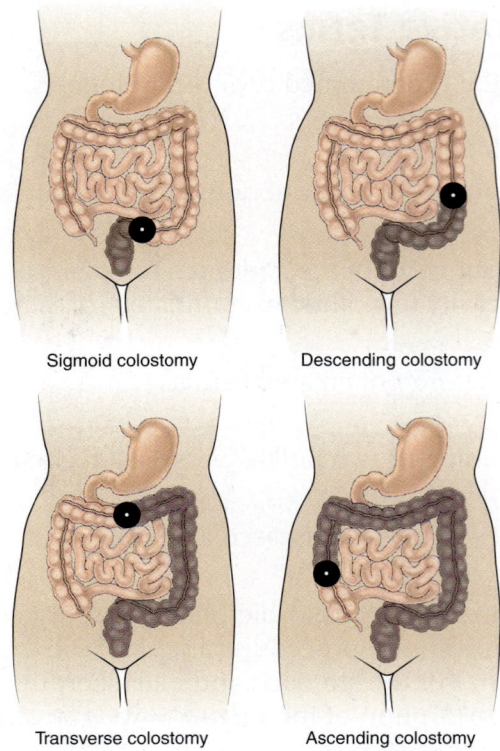

FIGURE 11-23 ■ Common colostomy sites.

TERM	MEANING
hemorrhoidectomy hem′ō-roy-dek′tŏ-mē	excision of hemorrhoids
hepatic lobectomy he-pat′ik lō-bek′tŏ-mē	excision of a lobe of the liver
herniorrhaphy hĕr′nē-ōr′ă-fē	repair of a hernia; also called *hernioplasty*
hernioplasty hĕr′nē-ō-plas-tē	repair of a hernia; also called *herniorrhaphy*
ileostomy il-ē-os′tŏ-mē	surgical creation of an opening on the abdomen to which the end of the ileum is attached, providing a passageway for ileal discharges; performed after removal of the colon, such as to treat chronic inflammatory bowel diseases (e.g., ulcerative colitis)
laparoscopic surgery lap′ă-rō-skop′ik sūr′jĕr-ē	abdominal surgery using a laparoscope
laparotomy lap-ă-rot′ō-mē	incision into the abdomen
pancreatectomy pan′krē-ă-tek′tō-mē	excision of the pancreas
polypectomy (see **Figure 11-17**) pol′i-pek′tŏ-mē	excision of polyps
proctoplasty prok′tō-plas-tē	repair of the anus and rectum

Programmed Review: Operative Terms

ANSWERS	REVIEW
gastr/o -ectomy gastrectomy	**11.113** Recall that the combining form for stomach is _____. The suffix for excision is _____. The surgical excision of part or all the stomach is called _____.
hemorrhoidectomy	**11.114** Excision of hemorrhoids is called _____.
pancreat/o pancreatectomy	**11.115** The combining form for pancreas is _____. Surgical excision of the pancreas is called _____.
gloss/o glossectomy	**11.116** The two combining forms for tongue are *lingu/o* and _____. Made from the latter, the term for surgical excision of all or part of the tongue is _____.
cholecystectomy laparoscopic	**11.117** Excision of the gallbladder is called _____. When performed through a laparoscope, it is called _____ cholecystectomy.
lobectomy	**11.118** Excision of a lobe of the liver is called a hepatic _____.
appendic/o appendectomy	**11.119** The combining form for appendix is _____. Surgical excision of the appendix is termed _____. (*Note:* The "*ic*" in the combining form is removed to prevent the unwieldy "*ic-ec*" sound.)
polypectomy	**11.120** The procedure of surgical excision of polyps is called _____.
anal fistulectomy	**11.121** Excision of an anal fistula is termed an _____ _____.
-plasty, cheiloplasty esophagoplasty hernioplasty proctoplasty	**11.122** Recall that the suffix for surgical repair or reconstruction is _____. Surgical repair of the lip is termed _____. Repair of the esophagus is called _____. Repair of a hernia is called _____. Repair of the anus and rectum is called _____.
-rrhaphy glossorrhaphy herniorrhaphy	**11.123** Recall that the suffix meaning suture is _____. Suture of the tongue is therefore called _____. Surgical repair and suture of a hernia is called _____.

ANSWERS	REVIEW
gastric resection	**11.124** Resection typically involves less tissue removal than a full excision. The procedure of partial removal and repair of the stomach is called _____ _____.
opening colostomy ileostomy	**11.125** Recall that the operative suffix *-stomy* means creation of an _____. The surgical creation of an opening in the colon through the abdominal wall, allowing stool to bypass a diseased portion of the colon, is called a _____. The creation of an opening from the end of the ileum to the abdomen, done when the colon has been removed, is called an _____.
gastroenterostomy	**11.126** The term for the creation of an artificial opening between the stomach and the small intestine is built from the combining forms for both the stomach and the intestine. This procedure is called a _____.
-tomy lapar/o laparotomy	**11.127** The operative suffix meaning incision is _____. Recall that the three combining forms meaning abdomen are *adomin/o*, *celi/o*, and _____. Formed from the last of these, the term for an incision into the abdomen is _____.
-centesis abdomin/o abdominocentesis paracentesis puncture of aspiration	**11.128** Recall that the suffix meaning puncture for aspiration is _____. The three combining forms meaning abdomen are *celi/o*, *lapar/o*, and _____. Made from the last of these, the term for puncture of the abdomen for the aspiration of a fluid is _____. Another general term for the aspiration of fluid from any cavity is _____. Abdominal paracentesis describes _____ ____ the abdomen for the _____ of fluid (e.g., the fluid that accumulates in ascites).
anastomosis	**11.129** The term for the operative procedure in which two hollow vessels are joined is _____. This technique is often used in bowel surgery.
laparoscopic	**11.130** A general term for abdominal surgery performed using a laparoscope is _____ surgery.
weight treatment, bariatric	**11.131** The term describing surgery to the stomach and/or intestines to treat morbid obesity is formed by joining *baros*, a combining form meaning _____, with *-iatric*, a suffix meaning _____, creating the term _____ surgery.

Self-Instruction: Therapeutic Terms

Study this table to prepare for the programmed review that follows.

TERM	MEANING
gastric lavage *gas′trik lă-vahzh′*	oral insertion of a tube into the stomach for examination and treatment, such as to remove blood clots from the stomach or to monitor bleeding (*lavage* = to wash)
nasogastric (NG) intubation *nă′sō-gas′trik in′tū-bā′shŭn*	insertion of a tube through the nose and into the stomach for various purposes, such as to obtain a gastric fluid specimen for analysis
COMMON THERAPEUTIC DRUG CLASSIFICATIONS	
antacid *ant-as′id*	drug that neutralizes stomach acid
antiemetic *an′tē-ĕ-met′ik*	drug that prevents or stops vomiting
antispasmodic *an′tē-spaz-mod′ik*	drug that decreases motility in the gastrointestinal tract to arrest spasm or diarrhea
cathartic *kă-thar′tik*	drug that causes movement of the bowels; also called a *laxative*

Programmed Review: Therapeutic Terms

ANSWERS	REVIEW
gastric lavage	**11.132** The word lavage means to wash. The therapeutic procedure in which a tube is inserted into the stomach from the mouth to remove fluids, such as blood clots, is termed _____ _____.
nasogastric intubation	**11.133** A tube can be inserted through the nose to the stomach for purposes such as obtaining a gastric fluid specimen for analysis. This is called _____ (NG) _____.
anti-	**11.134** Therapeutic drug classifications are often named for their actions against some process or condition. The common prefix meaning against is _____.
pertaining to antiemetic	**11.135** Recall that *-emesis* means vomiting and that the suffix *-ic*, which is often used in names of drug classes, means _____ _____. A drug that prevents or stops vomiting (against vomiting) is called an _____.

ANSWERS	REVIEW
antispasmodic	**11.136** Similarly, a drug used to stop spasms (of the gastrointestinal tract) is called an _____.
antacid	**11.137** A drug that works against excess stomach acid by neutralizing it is called an _____. (*Note:* In this case, the *-ic* ending is not used.)
cathartic	**11.138** The Greek word katharsis means purification by purging. A drug that purges the large intestine by stimulating a bowel movement is called a _____; such a drug is also called a laxative.

Chapter 11 Abbreviations

ABBREVIATION	EXPANSION
Bx	biopsy
C&S	culture and sensitivity
CT	computed tomography
EGD	esophagogastroduodenoscopy
ERCP	endoscopic retrograde cholangiopancreatography
EUS	endoscopic ultrasonography
GERD	gastroesophageal reflux disease
GI	gastrointestinal
HAV	hepatitis A virus
HBV	hepatitis B virus
HCV	hepatitis C virus
LES	lower esophageal sphincter
LLQ	left lower quadrant
LUQ	left upper quadrant
MRI	magnetic resonance imaging
NG	nasogastric
PUD	peptic ulcer disease
RLQ	right lower quadrant
RUQ	right upper quadrant
WDWN	well-developed and well-nourished

PRACTICE EXERCISES

For each of the following words, write out the term parts (prefixes [P], combining forms [CF], roots [R], and suffixes [S]) on the lines below the word. Then define the term according to the meaning of its parts.

EXAMPLE
sublingual
sub / lingu / al
P   R   S

DEFINITION: below or under/tongue/pertaining to

1. transabdominal
   _____ / _____ / _____
     P   R   S
   DEFINITION: _____

2. proctocolectomy
   _____ / _____ / _____
     CF   R   S
   DEFINITION: _____

3. sialolithotomy
   _____ / _____ / _____
     CF   CF   S
   DEFINITION: _____

4. glossorrhaphy
   _____ / _____
     CF   S
   DEFINITION: _____

5. hematemesis
   _____ / _____
     R   S
   DEFINITION: _____

Write the correct medical term for each of the following definitions.

6. _____ inflammation of the stomach
7. _____ loss of appetite
8. _____ inability to swallow
9. _____ in the cheek
10. _____ gas in the stomach or intestines

Complete each medical term by writing the missing word or word part.

11. hemi_____ectomy = removal of half of the stomach
12. _____itis = inflammation of the appendix
13. pyloric_____ = narrowed condition of the pylorus

429

Name the anatomic divisions of the abdomen.

14. lower lateral groin regions _____
15. upper lateral regions beneath the ribs _____
16. upper middle region below the sternum _____
17. region below the navel _____
18. middle lateral regions _____
19. region of the navel _____

Name the four clinical divisions of the abdomen.

20. Name the two upper clinical divisions of the abdomen _____
21. Name the two lower clinical divisions of the abdomen _____

Write the letter of the matching term in the space provided.

22. cathartic _____ a. appendectomy
23. herniorrhaphy _____ b. hernioplasty
24. appendicitis _____ c. barium enema
25. lower gastrointestinal series _____ d. jaundice
26. icterus _____ e. laxative

An endoscope is an instrument used to examine within the body. Name the specific type of endoscope used to examine the body parts listed here.

27. abdomen _____
28. anus _____

Write out the expanded term for each abbreviation.

29. NG _____
30. ERCP _____
31. GERD _____
32. LUQ _____
33. GI _____

Circle the combining form that corresponds to the meaning given.

34. abdomen
    a. gastr/o   b. lapar/o   c. stomat/o
35. tongue
    a. gloss/o   b. proct/o   c. gingiv/o
36. small intestine
    a. col/o   b. appendic/o   c. enter/o

37. teeth
    a. dent/i   b. chol/e   c. lingu/o
38. stomach
    a. lapar/o   b. stomat/o   c. gastr/o

Write the correct terms for the anatomic structures indicated.

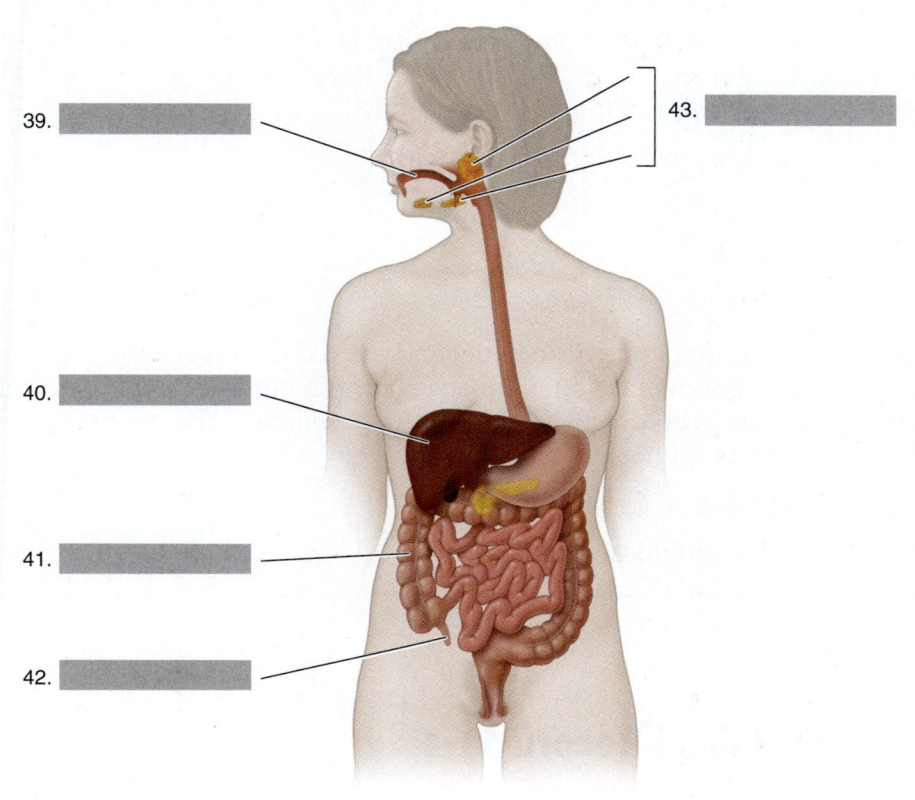

39. _____   42. _____
40. _____   43. _____
41. _____

Circle the correct spelling.

44. a. anorexia   b. annorexia   c. anorrexia
45. a. asites   b. ascitis   c. ascites
46. a. hematochesia   b. hemochezia   c. hematochezia
47. a. icterus   b. ickterus   c. icteris

Give the noun used to form each adjective.

48. fecal _____
49. icteric _____
50. endoscopic _____

MEDICAL RECORD ANALYSIS
Medical Record 11-1

EMERGENCY ROOM REPORT

S: This is a 36 y/o male with a complaint of abdominal pain. He describes having lifted a 75-lb beam yesterday at work. He noticed a sharp pain in his navel but continued to work. The pain intensified as the day went on and persisted through last night and today. He claims his navel now bulges forward. He denies fever, chills, dysphagia, anorexia, or vomiting.

PMH: No hospitalizations or surgeries

Meds: none

Allergies: NKDA

O: T 97.5°F, P 87, R 18, BP 128/86

WDWN male in moderate distress secondary to abdominal pain. Upon palpation, the abdomen is soft, with spasm of the muscles in the periumbilical region, and there is an obvious bulge in the umbilicus. The omentum is also palpable. There is no hepatosplenomegaly.

A: Incarcerated umbilical hernia

P: Admit for STAT umbilical hernia repair

Questions About Medical Record 11-1

1. Which of the following summarizes the subjective information?
   a. pain in stomach
   b. pain in abdomen
   c. pain in the groin area
   d. generalized abdominal pain with chills and fever
   e. stomach pain and has difficulty swallowing

2. What kind of an appetite does the patient have?
   a. normal
   b. increased
   c. decreased

3. What is the condition of the patient's liver?
   a. not stated
   b. enlarged
   c. not enlarged
   d. inflamed
   e. ruptured

4. What were the objective findings?
   a. involuntary contraction of the muscles around the navel
   b. pouching of the muscles under the navel
   c. contraction of abdominal muscles and enlargement of the spleen
   d. protrusion of the navel and enlargement of the liver
   e. pouching of the stomach and omentum

5. Which of the following best describes the diagnosis?
   a. a portion of the bowel has protruded through the abdominal wall and been cut off from circulation
   b. one part of the intestine has prolapsed into the lumen of the adjoining part
   c. a portion of the intestine has protruded through a weakness in the abdominal wall around the navel and is swollen and fixed in a sac
   d. a portion of the bowel has twisted on itself, causing obstruction
   e. the stomach and small intestine are inflamed

6. Which of the following medical terms describes the planned surgery?
   a. laparotomy
   b. gastroenterostomy
   c. hernioplasty
   d. ileostomy
   e. abdominal paracentesis

ANSWERS TO PRACTICE EXERCISES

1. transabdominal
   P: trans
   R: abdomin
   S: al
   DEFINITION: through/abdomen/pertaining to
2. proctocolectomy
   CF: procto
   R: col
   S: ectomy
   DEFINITION: rectum/col/ectomy
3. sialolithotomy
   CF: sialo
   CF: litho
   S: tomy
   DEFINITION: saliva/stone/incision
4. glossorrhaphy
   CF: glosso
   S: rrhaphy
   DEFINITION: tongue/suture
5. hematemesis
   R: hemat
   S: emesis
   DEFINITION: blood/vomiting
6. gastritis
7. anorexia
8. aphagia
9. buccal
10. flatulence
11. hemigastrectomy
12. appendicitis
13. pyloric stenosis
14. inguinal regions
15. hypochondriac regions
16. epigastric region
17. hypogastric region
18. lumbar regions
19. umbilical region
20. right upper quadrant (RUQ) and left upper quadrant (LUQ)
21. right lower quadrant (RLQ) and left lower quadrant (LLQ)
22. e
23. b
24. a
25. c
26. d
27. laparoscope
28. anoscope or proctoscope
29. nasogastric
30. endoscopic retrograde cholangiopancreatography
31. gastroesophageal reflux disease
32. left upper quadrant
33. gastrointestinal
34. lapar/o
35. gloss/o
36. enter/o
37. dent/i
38. gastr/o
39. mouth
40. liver
41. ascending colon
42. appendix
43. salivary glands
44. anorexia
45. ascites
46. hematochezia
47. icterus
48. feces
49. icterus
50. endoscopy

ANSWERS TO MEDICAL RECORD 11-1

1. b
2. a
3. c
4. a
5. c
6. c

URINARY SYSTEM

Learning Outcomes

After completing this chapter, you should be able to:

- Define term parts related to the urinary system.
- Identify key urinary system anatomic structures with their functions.
- Define symptomatic and diagnostic terms related to the urinary system.
- Explain diagnostic tests; procedures; and operative and therapeutic terms related to the urinary system.
- Cite common abbreviations related to the urinary system and give the expansion of each.
- Explain terms used in medical records involving the urinary system.

URINARY SYSTEM OVERVIEW

The urinary system includes the organs and structures involved in the formation and elimination of urine (see Figure 12-1). These structures with their functions include the following:

- The kidneys filter the blood and secrete water and nitrogenous wastes in urine.
- The kidneys regulate the levels of important substances, such as water, sodium, and potassium, in the blood.
- The ureters carry urine from the kidneys.
- The urinary bladder holds urine until it is expelled.
- The urethra carries urine from the urinary bladder to the body exterior.

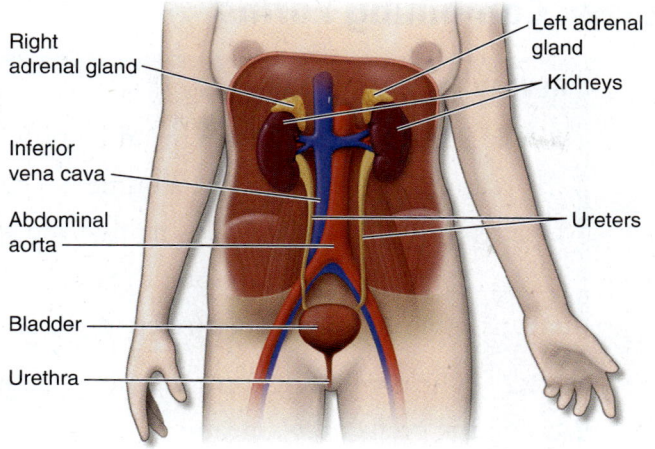

FIGURE 12-1 ■ Urinary system. The adrenal glands, inferior vena cava, and abdominal aorta are labeled for orientation purposes, but they are not part of the urinary system.

Self-Instruction: Combining Forms

Study this table to prepare for the programmed review that follows.

COMBINING FORM	MEANING
albumin/o	protein
bacteri/o	bacteria
cyst/o	bladder or sac
dips/o	thirst
glomerul/o	glomerulus (small ball)
gluc/o	glucose (sugar)
glucos/o	glucose (sugar)
glyc/o	glucose (sugar)
ket/o	ketone bodies
keton/o	ketone bodies
lith/o	stone
meat/o	meatus (opening)
nephr/o	kidney
py/o	pus
pyel/o	renal pelvis (basin)
ren/o	kidney
ur/o	urine
ureter/o	ureter
urethr/o	urethra
urin/o	urine
vesic/o	bladder or sac

Programmed Review: Combining Forms

ANSWERS	REVIEW
albumin/o resembling, albuminoid	**12.1** The combining form meaning protein comes from the Latin term for egg white: albumen. That combining form is _____. Recall that the suffix *-oid* means _____. Therefore, the term _____ means resembling albumin (referring to any protein).
bacteri/o against pertaining to antibacterial	**12.2** The combining form meaning bacteria is _____. Using the prefix *anti-*, meaning _____, and the suffix *-al*, meaning _____, an agent such as a soap that kills bacteria is called an _____.
bladder -scope cystoscope	**12.3** The combining form *cyst/o* means sac or _____. Using the suffix referring to an instrument for examination, _____, the term for the special kind of endoscope that is used to examine the bladder is _____.
vesic/o -tomy vesicotomy or cystotomy	**12.4** Another combining form meaning bladder or sac is _____ (from the Latin word *vesica*, meaning bladder). Using the operative suffix for incision, _____, the term for an incision into the bladder is _____.
dips/o many, condition of polydipsia	**12.5** The combining form meaning thirst (from the Greek word *dipsa*) is _____. Recall that the suffix *poly-* means _____. The suffix *-ia* refers to a _____. Thus, the term for excessive thirst (the need to drink many times) is _____.
urine -logist urologist urin/o	**12.6** *Ur/o* is a combining form meaning _____. Recall that the suffix for a specialist in the study of a special area is _____. The physician who specializes in conditions of the urinary system is therefore called a _____. Used to form the adjective urinary, a second combining form for urine is _____.
glucos/o urine condition of sugar	**12.7** The three combining terms for sugar are *glyc/o*, *gluc/o*, and _____. Glucose is a form of sugar that is found in the blood and used for energy. Because the combining form *ur/o* means _____ and the suffix *-ia* means a _____, the term glucosuria therefore refers to a condition of _____ in the urine.

ANSWERS	REVIEW
glomerul/o, glomeruli	**12.8** The combining form that means glomerulus (a small, ball-shaped cluster of capillaries in the kidney) is _____. The plural of glomerulus is _____. Because each nephron in the kidney has a glomerulus, each kidney has as many as 1,000,000 glomeruli.
keton/o urine condition of ketonuria	**12.9** The two combining forms meaning ketone bodies are *ket/o* and _____. Ketone bodies are chemical substances resulting from metabolism. Recall that *ur/o* is a combining form meaning _____. Combined with *-ia*, the suffix meaning _____ _____, the term for a condition of ketone bodies in the urine is _____.
increase ketosis	**12.10** Recall that the suffix *-osis* means condition or _____. Therefore, the term for the condition of increased ketone bodies in the body is _____.
lith/o lithiasis	**12.11** The combining form meaning stone is _____ (from the Greek word for stone, *lithos*). The suffix meaning formation of, or presence of, is *-iasis*. Therefore, the term for the formation of any stone is _____.
ureter/o ureterolithiasis	**12.12** Two similar words refer to different urinary system structures that carry urine. The ureters carry urine from the kidneys to the bladder. The urethra carries urine from the bladder to the outside of the body. The combining form for ureter is _____. The condition of having a stone form in the ureter is _____.
urethr/o -algia, -dynia urethralgia urethrodynia	**12.13** The combining form for urethra is _____. Recall that there are two suffixes meaning pain: _____ and _____. Each suffix is used to form synonyms meaning pain in the urethra: _____ or _____.
meat/o urine	**12.14** The combining form that means opening is _____ (from the Latin word *meatus*). The urethral meatus is the structure through which _____ leaves the body.

ANSWERS	REVIEW
ren/o	**12.15** Two different combining forms refer to the kidneys: *nephr/o* and _____. As often happens, these two forms come from Greek and Latin roots, both of which mean the kidneys. Recall that the suffix *-osis* refers to an increase or a
condition of	_____ _____; it is combined with the first combining
nephrosis	form to make this term for a kidney condition: _____. The second form combines with the common suffix *-al* to create
renal	this common adjective referring to the kidney: _____.
py/o	**12.16** The Greek word *pyon* is the origin of the combining form referring to pus: _____. This form is combined with *nephr/o* and the suffix for inflammation to create the term for suppurative
pyonephritis	(forming pus) inflammation of the kidney: _____.
pyel/o	**12.17** The combining form meaning basin is _____. This combining form also can refer to the pelvis, although it usually refers to the renal pelvis, a basin-like portion of the ureter within the kidney. Recall that the suffix for surgical repair or
-plasty	reconstruction is _____. Thus, a surgical repair of the renal
pyeloplasty	pelvis is called a _____.

Self-Instruction: Anatomic Terms

Study this table to prepare for the programmed review that follows (see **Figure 12-2 A,B**).

TERM	MEANING
kidneys kid′nēz	two structures located on each side of the lumbar region that excrete urine, remove wastes from the blood, and reclaim important electrolytes and water
renal cortex rē′năl kōr′teks	outer part of the kidney (*cortex* = bark)
hilum hī′lŭm	indented opening in the kidney where vessels enter and leave
renal artery rē′năl ar′ter-ē	one of two blood vessels that branch off the abdominal aorta that supplies the kidney with blood
renal vein rē′năl vān	one of two blood vessels that drain the kidney and connect to the inferior vena cava
renal medulla rē′năl me-dūl′ă	inner part of the kidney
calyces or calices kal′i-sēz	funnel-shaped ducts that carry urine from the nephrons to the renal pelvis (*kalyx* = cup of a flower)

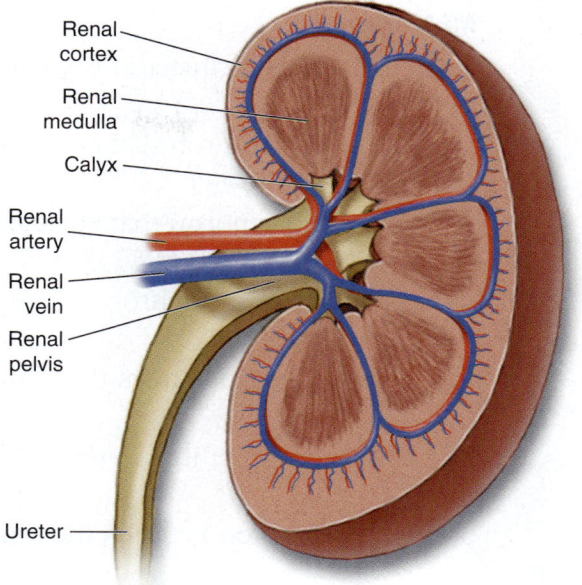
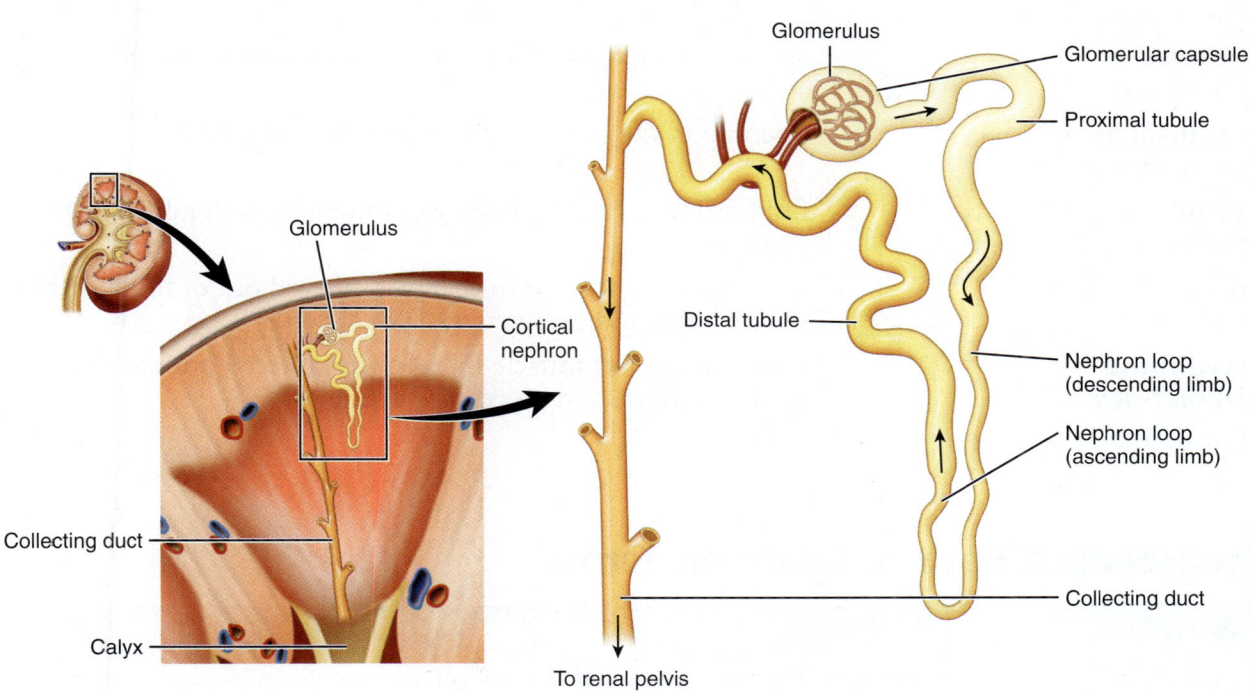

FIGURE 12-2 ■ Kidney and nephron. **A.** Kidney structures. **B.** Nephron structures.

TERM	MEANING
nephron *nef'ron*	microscopic functional unit of the kidney; long, convoluted tubular structure consisting of the renal corpuscle (glomerulus and glomerular capsule), proximal tubule, nephron loop, and distal tubule
collecting duct	tubule that connects the nephrons to the renal pelvis

TERM	MEANING
glomerulus glō-mer′yū-lŭs	small, ball-shaped cluster of capillaries located at the top of each nephron
glomerular capsule glō-mer′yū-lăr kap′sūl	top part of the nephron that encloses the glomerulus; also called *Bowman capsule*
Bowman capsule bō′măn kap′sūl	top part of the nephron that encloses the glomerulus; also called *glomerular capsule*
renal tubule rē′năl tū′byūl	stem portion of the nephron
ureter yū-rē′tĕr	tube that carries urine from the kidney to the bladder
renal pelvis rē′năl pel′vis	basin-like portion of the ureter within the kidney
ureteropelvic junction yū-rē′tĕr-ō-pel′vik jŭngk′shŭn	point of connection between the renal pelvis and the ureter
urinary bladder yūr′i-nār-ē blad′ĕr	sac that holds the urine
urethra yū-rē′thră	single canal that carries urine to the outside of the body
urethral meatus yū-rē′thrăl mē-ā′tŭs	opening in the urethra to the outside of the body
urine yūr′in	fluid produced by the kidneys, containing water and waste products
urea yū-rē′ă	waste product formed in the liver, filtered out of the blood by the kidneys, and excreted in urine
creatinine krē-at′i-nēn	waste product of muscle metabolism, filtered out of the blood by the kidneys, and excreted in urine

Programmed Review: Anatomic Terms

ANSWERS	REVIEW
kidneys cortex medulla medullae	**12.18** The two structures to the sides of the lumbar region that filter blood to remove wastes are the _____. The outer part of the kidney is called the renal _____ (from a word originally meaning bark, as tree bark is the outer part of a tree trunk). The inner part, where the urine is collected, is called the renal _____. (This same term, meaning middle, is used to refer to the middle part of a body structure.) The plural of medulla is _____.
hilum	**12.19** The indented opening in the kidney where vessels enter and leave is called the _____.

ANSWERS	REVIEW
nephrons glomerulus capsule renal tubule kidney	**12.20** Inside the cortex of the kidneys are the microscopic functional units that form urine; these units are called _____. At the top of each nephron is a ball-shaped cluster of capillaries, called a _____, that carries blood to and away from each nephron. Enclosing each glomerulus is a structure called the glomerular _____. From the glomerular capsule, the urine flows through the _____ _____. Recall that the adjective renal refers generally to the _____.
urine urea creatinine	**12.21** The fluid secreted by the nephrons that contains water and waste products is called _____. The waste product formed in the liver but filtered from the blood in the kidneys is called _____. A second waste product filtered from the blood in the kidneys is a product of muscle metabolism: _____.
calyces or calices calyx or calix	**12.22** Urine flows through the renal tubules from each nephron through a system of ducts called _____. The singular form of this term is _____. The calyces (also spelled calices) carry the urine to the renal pelvis, the basin-like portion of the ureter within the kidney.
renal pelvis ureteropelvic	**12.23** The basin-like portion of the ureter collecting urine from the calyces is called the _____ _____. The point of connection between the renal pelvis and the ureter is called the _____ junction.
ureter hilum	**12.24** From the renal pelvis, urine moves through the _____ to the bladder, a sac that holds the urine before its excretion. Each kidney has one ureter, which exits the kidney at the same point where the arteries and veins enter it, at the _____ of the kidney.
bladder urethra	**12.25** The sac that holds urine is called the urinary _____. From the bladder, the urine exits through a canal called the _____.
urethral meatus	**12.26** Made from the combining forms meaning urethra and opening, the opening from the urethra to the outside of the body, through which urine leaves the body, is called the _____ _____.

Self-Instruction: Symptomatic Terms

Study this table to prepare for the programmed review that follows.

TERM	MEANING
albuminuria al-bū-min-yū′rē-ă	presence of albumin in the urine, such as occurs in renal disease or in normal urine after heavy exercise; also called *proteinuria*
proteinuria prō-tēn-yu′rē-ă	presence of albumin in the urine, such as occurs in renal disease or in normal urine after heavy exercise; also called *albuminuria*
anuria an-yū′rē-ă	absence of urine formation
bacteriuria bak-tēr-ē-yū′rē-ă	presence of bacteria in the urine
dysuria dis-yū′rē-ă	painful urination
enuresis en-yū-rē′sis	involuntary discharge of urine, usually referring to a lack of urinary bladder control
nocturnal enuresis nok-tūr′năl en-yū-rē′sis	bed-wetting during sleep
glucosuria glū-kō-syū′rē-ă	glucose (sugar) in the urine; also called *glycosuria*
glycosuria glī′kō-syū′rē-ă	glucose (sugar) in the urine; also called *glucosuria*
hematuria (see Figure 12-3) hē′mă-tyū′rē-ă	presence of blood in the urine

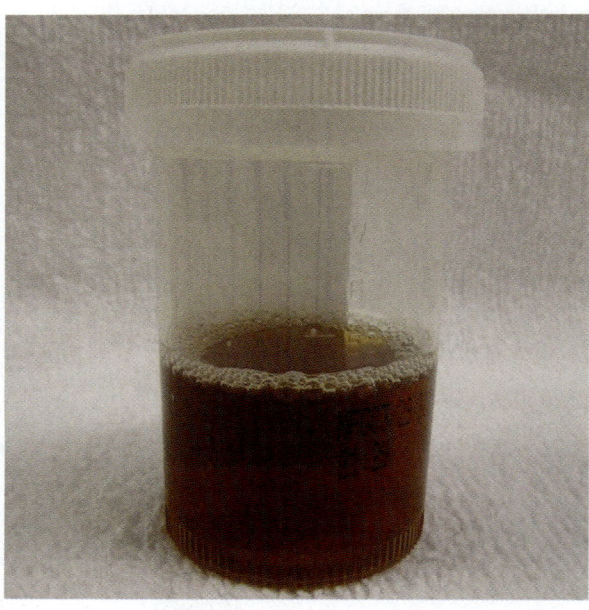

FIGURE 12-3 ■ Hematuria.

TERM	MEANING
incontinence in-kon′ti-nens	involuntary discharge of urine or feces
stress urinary incontinence (SUI) stres yūr′i-nār-ē in-kon′ti-nens	involuntary discharge of urine with coughing, sneezing, and/or strained exercise
ketonuria kē′tō-nyū′rē-ă	presence of ketone bodies in the urine
ketone bodies kē′tōn bod′ēz	acetone, beta-hydroxybutyric acid, and acetoacetic acid; products of metabolism that appear in the urine from the body's abnormal utilization of carbohydrates, such as occurs in uncontrolled diabetes or starvation; also called *ketone compounds*
ketone compounds kē′tōn kom′powndz	acetone, beta-hydroxybutyric acid, and acetoacetic acid; products of metabolism that appear in the urine from the body's abnormal utilization of carbohydrates, such as occurs in uncontrolled diabetes or starvation; also called *ketone bodies*
nocturia nokt-yū′rē-ă	urination at night after waking from sleep
oliguria ol′i-gyū′rē-ă	decreased urine production
polyuria pol-ē-yū′rē-ă	condition of excessive urination
pyuria pī-yū′rē-ă	presence of white cells in the urine, usually indicating infection
urinary retention yūr′i-nār-ē rē-ten′shŭn	retaining of urine resulting from an inability to void (urinate) naturally because of spasm or obstruction

Programmed Review: Symptomatic Terms

ANSWERS	REVIEW
urine condition of bacteriuria	**12.27** *Ur/o* is a combining form for _____. The suffix *-ia* refers to a _____ _____. Many symptomatic terms therefore end in *-uria*, referring to the presence of abnormal amounts of a substance in the urine. For example, the presence of bacteria in the urine is called _____.
hematuria	**12.28** A combining form meaning blood is *hemat/o*. The presence of blood in the urine is called _____.
py/o pyuria	**12.29** The combining form for pus is _____. Pus consists mostly of white blood cells that fight infection. The presence of white blood cells in the urine is therefore termed _____, which often indicates a urinary tract infection (UTI).

ANSWERS	REVIEW
albumin/o albuminuria	**12.30** The combining form meaning protein is _____. The presence of protein in the urine is therefore termed _____. Another term for protein in the blood is proteinuria.
without anuria nocturia	**12.31** The ending -*uria* is also used with other urinary conditions, not just with those indicating the presence of some substance in the urine. The prefix *an-* means _____; therefore, the term for absence of urine formation (being without urine) is _____. Another term modified by -*uria* describes excessive voluntary urination at night after waking from sleep: _____.
within enuresis nocturnal	**12.32** The term *uresis* is synonymous with urination. When combined with *en-*, the prefix meaning _____, the term referring to involuntary urinating because of lack of bladder control is _____. An involuntary discharge of urine during sleep is called _____ enuresis (bed-wetting).
glycosuria	**12.33** The presence of glucose (sugar) in urine is not a normal finding. The two synonyms used to indicate the presence of sugar in urine are glucosuria and _____.
painful dysuria	**12.34** Recall that the prefix *dys-* means difficult, faulty, or _____. The term for a condition of painful urination is _____.
deficient oliguria	**12.35** Recall that *oligo-* is a prefix meaning few or _____. Therefore, the term for a condition of decreased urine production is _____. (Recall that the final vowel is occasionally dropped from the prefix when joined with a root that begins with a vowel.)
urine polyuria	**12.36** Again, -*uria* is a common word ending that refers to a condition of _____. It is linked to the prefix meaning many to describe a condition of excessive urination: _____.
urine incontinence stress	**12.37** Enuresis is the involuntary discharge of _____; however, the general term for the involuntary discharge of urine or feces is _____. When an involuntary discharge of urine occurs during the stress of coughing, sneezing, or exercise, it is called _____ urinary incontinence (SUI).

ANSWERS	REVIEW
urine	**12.38** Urinary retention is the retention of _____ resulting from an inability to void (urinate) naturally because of spasm, an obstruction, or other factors.
ketone ketonuria	**12.39** The combining form *ket/o* means _____ bodies or ketone compounds. These are metabolic products that may appear in the urine because of abnormal use of carbohydrates. The condition in which ketone bodies appear in the urine is called _____.

Self-Instruction: Diagnostic Terms

Study this table to prepare for the programmed review that follows.

TERM	MEANING
adult polycystic kidney disease (APKD) ă-dŭlt′ pol-ē-sis′tik kid′nē di-zēz′	inherited condition of multiple cysts that gradually form in the kidney, causing destruction of normal tissue that leads to renal failure; diagnosed in adults presenting with hypertension, kidney enlargement, and recurrent urinary tract infections (UTIs)
glomerulonephritis glō-mer′yū-lō-nef-rī′tis	form of nephritis involving the glomerulus
hydronephrosis (see Figure 12-4) hī′drō-ne-frō′sis	pooling of urine in dilated areas of the renal pelvis and calices of one or both kidneys caused by an obstructed outflow of urine

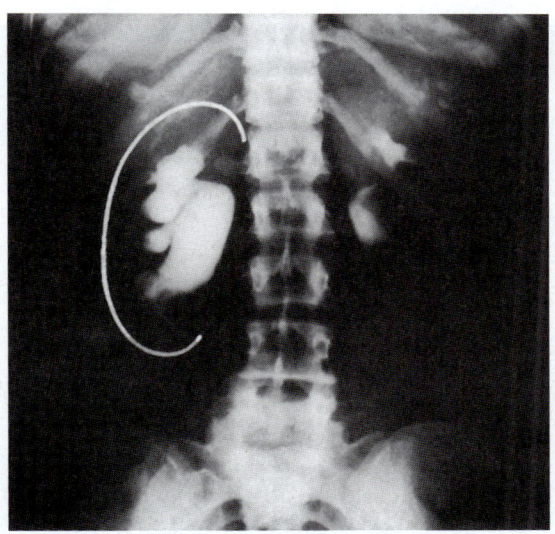

FIGURE 12-4 ■ Hydronephrosis. Collection of contrast media in the kidney displays an extraordinary amount of material, which indicates right-sided hydronephrosis caused by obstruction of the ureter.

TERM	MEANING
nephritis *ne-frī′tis*	inflammation of the kidney
pyelonephritis *pī′ĕ-lō-ne-frī′tis*	inflammation of the renal pelvis
nephrosis *ne-frō′sis*	degenerative disease of the renal tubules
nephrolithiasis (see **Figure 12-5**) *nef′rō-li-thī′ă-sis*	presence of kidney stones
cystitis *sis-tī′tis*	inflammation of the bladder
urethritis *yū-rē-thrī′tis*	inflammation of the urethra
urethrocystitis *yū-rē′thrō-sis-tī′tis*	inflammation of the urethra and bladder
urethral stenosis *yū-rē′thrăl ste-nō′sis*	narrowed condition of the urethra
urinary tract infection (UTI) *yūr′i-nār-ē trakt in-fek′shŭn*	invasion of pathogenic organisms (commonly bacteria) in the urinary tract, especially the urethra and bladder; symptoms include dysuria, urinary frequency, and malaise
uremia *yū-rē′mē-ă*	excess of urea and other nitrogenous waste in the blood caused by kidney failure; also called *azotemia*
azotemia *az-ō-tē′mē-ă*	excess of urea and other nitrogenous waste in the blood caused by kidney failure; also called *uremia*

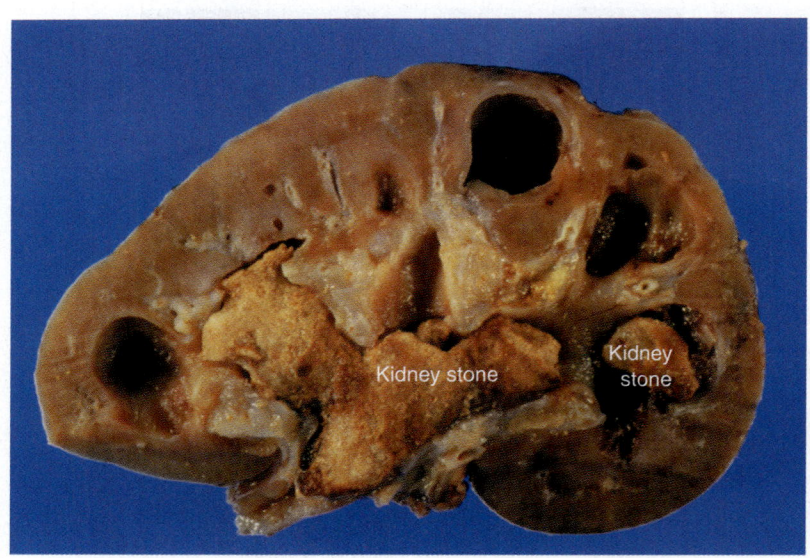

FIGURE 12-5 ■ Nephrolithiasis. This kidney has been cut open to reveal kidney stones.

Programmed Review: Diagnostic Terms

ANSWERS	REVIEW
sac many adult polycystic kidney disease	**12.40** *Cyst/o* is a combining form meaning either bladder or _____. *Cyst*, a root word, describes an abnormal sac. The term polycystic therefore pertains to _____ cysts. This term describes the inherited disease of multiple cysts that gradually form in the kidney, causing destruction of normal tissue and renal failure. Most commonly diagnosed in adulthood, this disease is called _____ _____ _____ _____ (APKD).
-itis nephr/o nephritis glomerulonephritis	**12.41** Recall that the suffix meaning inflammation is _____. Many diagnostic terms are formed by adding this suffix to the combining forms for anatomic structures. In addition to the combining form *ren/o*, another combining form meaning kidney is _____. Using that form, the term for inflammation of the kidney is _____. A form of nephritis involving the glomerulus is called _____.
cyst/o cystitis	**12.42** In addition to the combining form *vesic/o*, another combining form for the bladder is _____. Using that form, the term for inflammation of the bladder is _____.
urethritis	**12.43** Inflammation of the urethra is called _____.
urethrocystitis	**12.44** Inflammation of both the urethra and the bladder is called _____.
pyel/o renal pelvis pyelonephritis	**12.45** Recall that the combining form meaning basin is _____. The basin-like portion of the ureter is called the _____ _____. Therefore, the term for inflammation of the renal pelvis area of the kidney is _____.
condition nephrosis	**12.46** Recall that the suffix *-osis* means an increase or _____. That suffix is used to make the term for degenerative disease of the kidney (specifically, the renal tubules): _____.
condition of hydronephrosis	**12.47** A combining form meaning water (or watery fluid) is *hydr/o*. Recall that the suffix *-osis* means _____ _____ or increase. The term referring to a condition of urine pooling in the renal pelvis because of an outflow obstruction is _____.

ANSWERS	REVIEW
lith/o -iasis nephrolithiasis	**12.48** Recall that the combining form for stone is _____. The suffix for formation of or presence of is _____. These word parts, along with the combining form *nephr/o*, create the term for the presence of stones in the kidney: _____.
urethral stenosis	**12.49** A general medical term for the condition of a narrowed structure is stenosis. A narrowed condition of the urethra is called _____ _____.
urinary tract infection	**12.50** The invasion of pathogenic bacteria into urinary structures is called a _____ _____ _____ (UTI).
-emia uremia, azotemia	**12.51** Recall that the suffix for a blood condition is _____. Using the combining form for urine (in this case, referring to urea and waste products normally excreted in urine), the condition of nitrogenous wastes in the blood because of kidney failure is _____. A synonym for uremia is _____, a term that is made with the prefix *azo-*, which refers to a nitrogen molecule.

Self-Instruction: Diagnostic Tests and Procedures

Study this table to prepare for the programmed review that follows.

TEST OR PROCEDURE	EXPLANATION
cystoscopy (see Figure 12-6) *sis-tos′kŏ-pē*	examination of the bladder using a rigid or flexible cystoscope
kidney biopsy (Bx) *kid′nē bī′op-sē*	removal of kidney tissue for pathologic examination; also called *renal biopsy*

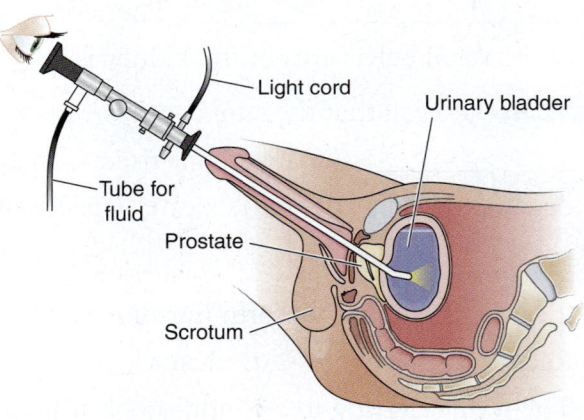

FIGURE 12-6 ■ Cystoscopy. A lighted cystoscope is inserted into the urinary bladder of a male. Sterile fluid is used to inflate the urinary bladder.

TEST OR PROCEDURE	EXPLANATION
renal biopsy (Bx) *rē′năl bī′op-sē*	removal of kidney tissue for pathologic examination; also called *kidney biopsy*
RADIOGRAPHY	
intravenous pyelogram (IVP) (see Figure 12-7) *in′tră-vē′nŭs pī′el-ō-gram*	x-ray image of the urinary tract obtained after an iodine contrast dye has been injected into the bloodstream; the contrast passes through the kidney and may reveal an obstruction, evidence of trauma, or some other pathology; also called *intravenous urogram (IVU)*
intravenous urogram (IVU) (see Figure 12-7) *in′tră-vē′nŭs yūr′ō-gram*	x-ray or computed tomography (CT) image of the urinary tract obtained after an iodine contrast dye has been injected into the bloodstream; the contrast passes through the kidney and may reveal an obstruction, evidence of trauma, or some other pathology; also called *intravenous pyelogram (IVP)*
kidneys, ureters, bladder (KUB) (see Figure 12-7) *kid′nēz, yū-rē′tĕrz, blad′ĕr*	abdominal x-ray or CT image of the kidneys, ureters, and bladder
scout film *skowt film*	plain-film x-ray image obtained to detect any obvious pathology before further imaging (e.g., a KUB before an IVP)
renal angiogram *rē′năl an′jē-ō-gram*	x-ray image of the renal vessels obtained after injection of a contrast dye
renal arteriogram *rē′năl ar-tēr′ē-ō-gram*	x-ray image of the renal artery obtained after injecting contrast dye into a catheter in the artery

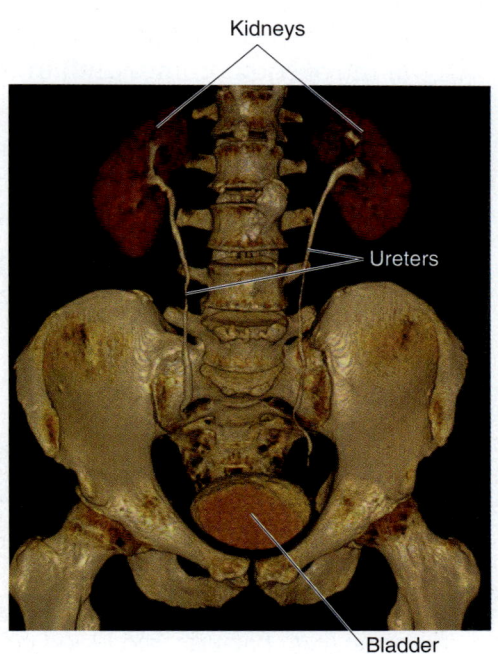

FIGURE 12-7 ■ Computed tomography intravenous pyelogram.

TEST OR PROCEDURE	EXPLANATION
retrograde pyelogram (RP) *ret′rō-grād pī′el-ō-gram*	x-ray image of the bladder, ureters, and renal pelvis obtained after contrast dye has been injected up to the kidney by way of a small catheter passed through a cystoscope; used to detect the presence of stones, obstruction, or some other pathology; also called *retrograde urogram*
retrograde urogram *ret′rō-grād yūr′ō-gram*	x-ray image of the bladder, ureters, and renal pelvis obtained after contrast dye has been injected up to the kidney by way of a small catheter passed through a cystoscope; used to detect the presence of stones, obstruction, or some other pathology; also called *retrograde pyelogram* (RP)
voiding cystourethrogram (VCU or VCUG) *voyd′ing sis-tō-yū-rēth′rō-gram*	x-ray image of the bladder and urethra obtained during urination (*voiding* = urinating)
abdominal sonogram *ab-dom′i-năl son′ō-gram*	abdominal ultrasound image of the urinary tract, including the kidney and bladder

LABORATORY TESTING

urinalysis (UA) (see Figure 12-8) *yūr′i-nal′i-sis*	physical, chemical, and microscopic examination of urine
specific gravity (SpGr) *spĕ-sif′ik grav′i-tē*	measure of the concentration or dilution of urine
pH	measure of the acidity or alkalinity of urine
glucose *glū′kōs*	chemical test used to detect sugar in the urine; most often used to screen for diabetes (*glucose* = sugar)
albumin (alb) *al-byū′min*	chemical test used to detect the presence of albumin (a type of protein) in the urine
protein *prō′tēn*	chemical test used to detect the presence of protein (a nitrogenous compound) in the urine
ketones *kē′tōnz*	chemical test used to detect the presence of ketone bodies in the urine; positive test indicates that fats are being used by the body instead of carbohydrates, which occurs during starvation or an uncontrolled diabetic state
urine occult blood *yūr′in ŏ-kŭlt′ blŭd*	chemical test for the presence of hidden blood in the urine resulting from red blood cell hemolysis; indicates bleeding in the kidneys (*occult* = hidden)
bilirubin *bil-i-rū′bin*	chemical test used to detect bilirubin in the urine; seen in gallbladder and liver disease
urobilinogen *yūr′ō-bī-lin′ō-jen*	chemical test used to detect bile pigment in the urine; increased amounts are seen in gallbladder and liver disease
nitrite *nī′trīt*	chemical test to determine the presence of bacteria in the urine
microscopic findings *mī′krō-skop′ik find′ings*	microscopic identification of abnormal constituents in the urine (e.g., bacteria, red blood cells, white blood cells, and casts); reported per high- or low-power field (hpf or lpf, respectively)

CENTRAL MEDICAL CENTER
211 Medical Center Drive • Central City, US 90000-1234 • PHONE: (012) 125-6784 • FAX: (012) 125-9999

11//02/20xx
13:49

NAME : TEST, PATIENT   LOC: TEST   DOB: 2/2/XX   AGE: 38Y
MR#   : TEST-221   SEX: M
ACCT # : H111111111

M63560 COLL: 11/2/20xx 13:24   REC: 11/2/20xx 13:25

URINE BASIC
- Color   STRAW
- Appearance   CLEAR
- Specific Gravity   1.010   [1.003 - 1.035]
- pH   5.5   [5.0 - 9.0]
- Protein   NEG   [0 - 10]   MG/DL
- Glucose   NEG   [NEG]
- Ketones   NEG   [NEG]
- Bilirubin   NEG   [NEG]
- Urine Occult Blood NEG   [NEG]
- Nitrites   NEG

URINE MICROSCOPIC
- Epithelial Cells   3 to 4   /HPF
- WBCs   0 to 1   /HPF
- RBCs   0   /HPF
- Bacteria   0
- Mucous Threads   0

TEST, PATIENT   TEST-221   END OF REPORT   PAGE 1
11/02/20xx   13:49   INTERIM REPORT
INTERIM REPORT COMPLETED

FIGURE 12-8 ■ Sample urinalysis (UA) report.

TEST OR PROCEDURE	EXPLANATION
urine culture and sensitivity (C&S) yūr′in kŭl′chŭr and sen-si-tiv′i-tē	isolation of a urine specimen in a culture medium to propagate the growth of microorganisms; organisms that grow in the culture are identified, as are drugs to which they are sensitive
blood urea nitrogen (BUN) blŭd yū-rē′ă nī′trō-jen	blood test to determine the level of urea in the blood; a high BUN indicates the inability of one or both kidneys to excrete urea
creatinine, serum krē-at′i-nēn, sēr′ŭm	test to determine the level of creatinine in the blood; useful in assessing kidney function
creatinine, urine krē-at′i-nēn, yūr′in	test to determine the level of creatinine in the urine
creatinine clearance testing krē-at′i-nēn klēr′ănts test′ing	measurements of the level of creatinine in the blood and in a 24-hour urine specimen to determine the rate at which creatinine is "cleared" from the blood by the kidneys

Programmed Review: Diagnostic Tests and Procedures

ANSWERS	REVIEW
vesic/o cystoscopy	**12.52** Recall that the two combining forms for bladder are *cyst/o* and _____. The first of these, combined with the suffix for process of examination with an instrument, forms the term for examination of the bladder with a special scope: _____.
biopsy renal	**12.53** The general term for removal of any body tissue for pathologic examination is _____ (Bx). The removal of kidney tissue is called a kidney biopsy or a _____ biopsy.
recording radiography	**12.54** Recall that the suffix *-graphy* means the process of _____ (e.g., an image). The process of making x-ray studies of internal body structures, such as the urinary tract, is termed _____.
scout KUB	**12.55** A plain-film x-ray image obtained to detect any obvious pathology before further imaging is called a _____ film. An abdominal x-ray image of the kidneys, ureters, and bladder (called a _____) is often obtained as a scout film before additional images are taken using a contrast medium.

ANSWERS	REVIEW
record renal pelvis intravenous pyelogram urogram within	**12.56** Recall that the suffix *-gram* means a _____. The combining form *pyel/o* means basin, referring to the basin-like portion of the ureter in the kidney known as the _____ _____. These components are used to name a type of x-ray image of the urinary tract that is obtained after contrast iodine has been injected into the bloodstream to reveal obstruction, trauma, or other problems in the kidney: _____ _____ (IVP). The other term for this x-ray, using the combining form for urine, is intravenous _____. Recall that the prefix *intra-* means _____, referring in this case to the contrast medium administered within a vein.
vessel renal angiogram arteriogram	**12.57** The term angiogram comes from the combining form *angi/o*, meaning _____; angiograms are x-ray images of blood vessels in many parts of the body. Therefore, the general term describing an x-ray image of the renal artery that is obtained after a contrast medium has been injected into it is _____ _____. The specific term uses the combining for artery: renal _____.
retrograde pyelogram	**12.58** The type of x-ray image of urinary structures that is obtained after a contrast medium is sent up (backward) through a catheter is called a _____ _____ (RP). The word retrograde refers to the insertion of the medium in a direction against the usual flow (of urine in this case).
urinate voiding cystourethrogram	**12.59** To void means to _____. An x-ray image of the bladder and urethra (using the combining forms for both) that is obtained during urination is called a _____ _____ (VCU or VCUG).
abdominal sonogram	**12.60** Ultrasound is also used with the urinary tract. An ultrasound image of the abdomen showing the kidneys and bladder is called an _____ _____.
urinalysis	**12.61** Many different laboratory tests are conducted on the urine to aid in diagnosing conditions of the urinary system. The term for a full set of physical, chemical, and microscopic examinations of urine is _____ (UA).

ANSWERS	REVIEW
specific gravity	**12.62** The measurement of the concentration of urine, showing the kidney's ability to concentrate or dilute urine, is called _____ _____ (SpGr).
pH	**12.63** The measurement of the acidity or alkalinity of any fluid is called its _____. Urinalysis (UA) includes the urine pH.
glucose	**12.64** Sugar in the blood or urine is called _____. When detected in the urine, glucose may be an indication of diabetes.
albumin/o albumin	**12.65** Recall that the combining form meaning protein is _____. The test in urinalysis (UA) that detects the presence of protein in the urine is called an _____ or protein test.
ketones	**12.66** The test to detect the presence of ketone bodies in the urine is simply called _____.
breaking down urine occult blood	**12.67** Recall that the suffix -*lysis* means dissolution or _____ _____. Hemolysis occurs when the intact membranes of red blood cells break down. The cells, once intact, are now hidden. The presence of free-flowing hemoglobin (the pigment normally contained within red blood cells) is a clue to their hidden state. The chemical test of urine to determine the presence of these once intact and now hidden blood cells is called _____ _____ _____.
bilirubin	**12.68** Bilirubin is a component of bile, which is secreted by the liver and is not normally present in urine. During urinalysis (UA), the chemical test for its presence in urine is simply called _____.
urobilinogen liver	**12.69** The chemical test for the presence of a bile pigment in the urine is called _____. Increased amounts of urobilinogen are seen in gallbladder and _____ disease.
bacteriuria nitrite	**12.70** The presence of bacteria in the urine is termed _____. Nitrite is a waste product that is produced by bacteria. The chemical test to determine the presence of this waste product in urine, thereby indicating bacteriuria, is simply called _____.

ANSWERS	REVIEW
microscopic findings	**12.71** Urine is examined under a microscope to identify abnormal constituents, such as blood cells. The results of this examination are called _____ _____.
urine culture sensitivity	**12.72** The isolation of a urine specimen in a culture medium to grow microorganisms and to identify drugs to which they are sensitive is called _____ _____ and _____ (C&S).
creatinine urine creatinine	**12.73** Recall that a waste product of muscle metabolism is _____. The test that determines the level of creatinine in the urine is called _____ _____.
serum creatinine creatinine clearance	**12.74** Blood tests (serum tests) also help to diagnose problems in the urinary system. The test to determine the level of creatinine in the blood is called _____ _____. Measurements taken in the blood and in a 24-hour urine specimen are used to determine the rate at which creatinine is cleared by the kidneys; this is called _____ _____ testing.
blood urea nitrogen	**12.75** BUN is the abbreviation for _____ _____ _____, a blood test to determine the level of urea in the blood. The results of this test may indicate a kidney disorder.

Self-Instruction: Operative Terms

Study this table to prepare for the programmed review that follows.

TERM	MEANING
urologic endoscopic surgery (see Figure 12-9) *yūr-ō-loj′ik en-dō-skop′ik sŭr′jĕr-ē*	use of specialized endoscopes (e.g., resectoscope) within the urinary tract to perform various surgical procedures, such as resection of a tumor, repair of an obstruction, stone retrieval, or stent
resectoscope *rē-sek′tŏ-skōp*	urologic endoscope inserted through the urethra to resect (cut and remove) lesions of the bladder, urethra, or prostate
intracorporeal lithotripsy (see Figure 12-10 A,B) *in′tră-kōr-pō′rē-ăl lith′ō-trip-sē*	method of destroying stones within the urinary tract using discharges of electrical energy that are transmitted to a probe within a flexible endoscope; most commonly used to pulverize bladder stones
nephrotomy *ne-frot′ŏ-mē*	incision into the kidney
nephrorrhaphy *nef-rōr′ă-fē*	suture of an injured kidney

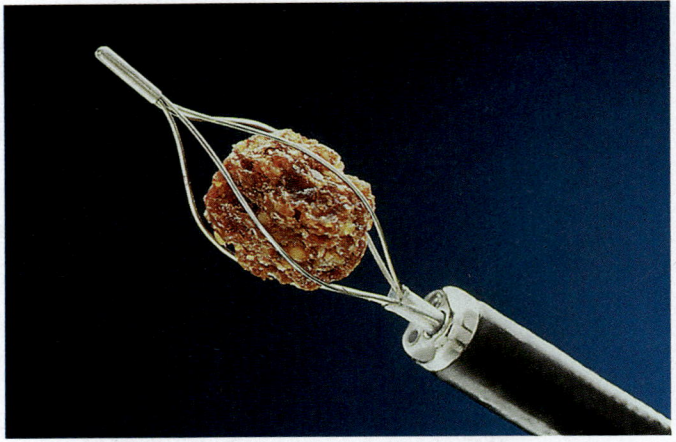

FIGURE 12-9 ■ Stone basket used in kidney stone retrieval.

TERM	MEANING
nephrolithotomy nef′rō-li-thot′ŏ-mē	incision into the kidney for the removal of stones
nephrectomy ne-frek′tō-mē	excision of a kidney
pyeloplasty pī′e-lō-plas-tē	surgical reconstruction of the renal pelvis
stent placement (see Figure 12-11) stent plās′ment	use of a device (stent) to hold open vessels or tubes (e.g., an obstructed ureter)
kidney transplantation kid′nē tranz-plan-tā′shŭn	transfer of a kidney from the body of one person (donor) to another (recipient); also called *renal transplantation*
renal transplantation rē′năl tranz-plan-tā′shŭn	transfer of a kidney from the body of one person (donor) to another (recipient); also called *kidney transplantation*

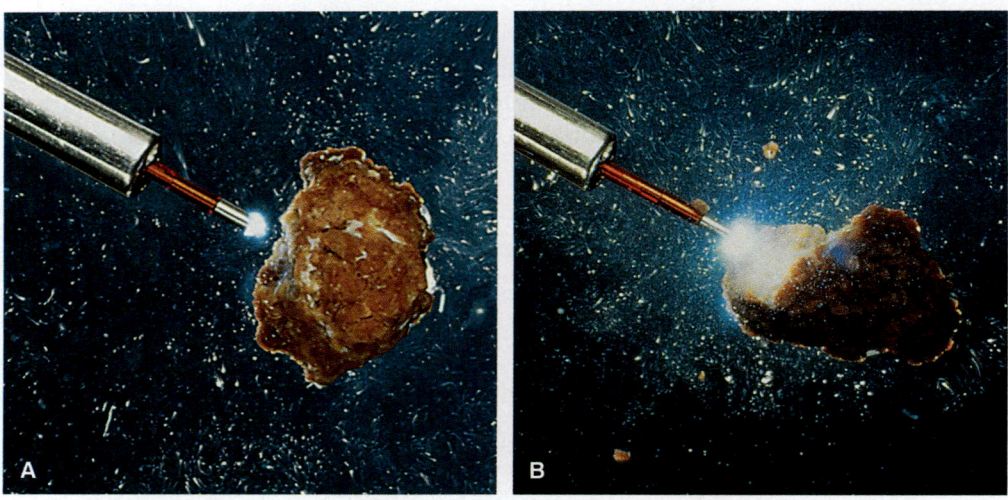

FIGURE 12-10 ■ Intracorporeal lithotripsy. **A.** Electrical energy is discharged. **B.** Simulation of the pulverizing of stones.

CHAPTER 12 • URINARY SYSTEM 457

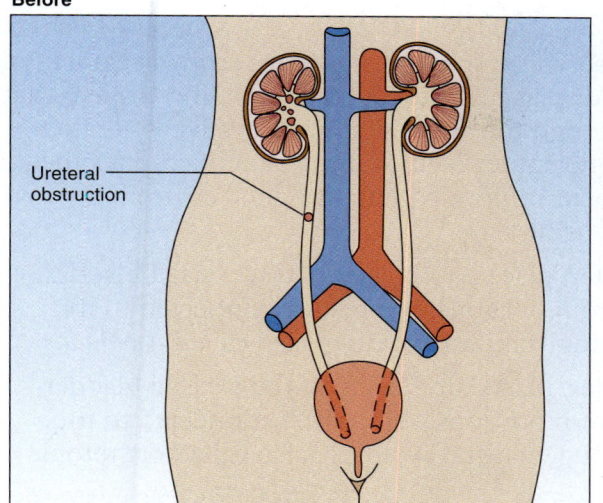
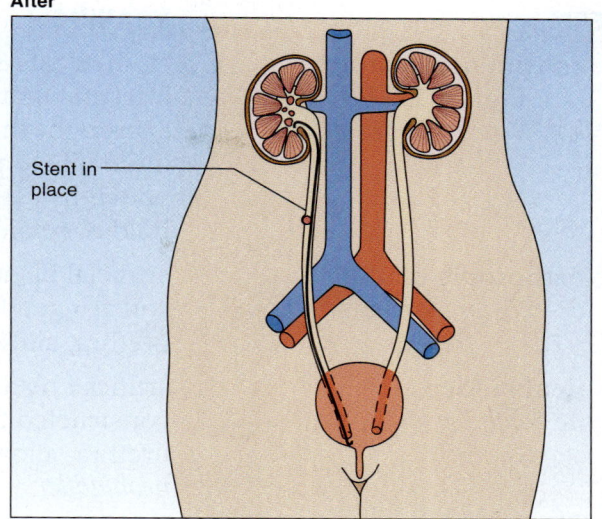

FIGURE 12-11 ■ Placement of a double-J stent to relieve ureteral obstruction (kidney stone).

TERM	MEANING
urinary diversion yūr′i-nār-ē di-věr′zhŭn	creation of a temporary or permanent diversion of the urinary tract to provide a new passage through which urine exits the body; used to treat defects or diseases (e.g., bladder cancer)
noncontinent ileal conduit (see Figure 12-12) non-kon′ti-nent il′e-ăl kon′dū-it	removal of a portion of the ileum to use as a conduit to which the ureters are attached at one end; the other end is brought through an opening (stoma) created in the abdomen; urine drains continually into an external appliance (bag); noncontinent indicates that urine cannot be held and drains continually

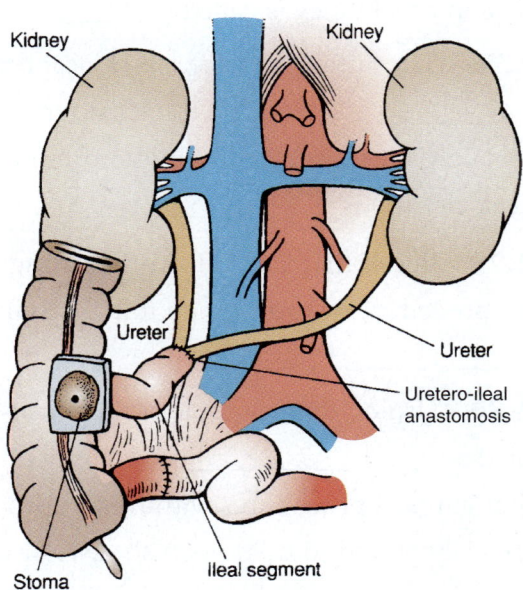

FIGURE 12-12 ■ Urostomy: Ileal conduit. A segment of ileum is isolated from terminal ileum, and continuity of the bowel is re-established with an end-to-end anastomosis. Ureters are joined to the proximal end of the ileal segment, and the distal end is brought out to the skin as a stoma.

TERM	MEANING
continent urostomy (see Figure 12-12) kon′ti-nent yū-ros-tō′mē	an internal reservoir (pouch) constructed from a segment of intestine that diverts urine through an opening (stoma) that is brought through the abdominal wall; a valve is created internally to prevent leakage, and the patient empties the pouch by catheterization; continent refers to the ability to hold or retain urine
orthotopic bladder ōr-thō-top′ik blad′ĕr	artificial bladder, placed at the site of the excised bladder, constructed from portions of intestine connected to the urethra, allowing "natural" voiding; also called *neobladder*
neobladder nē′ō-blad′ĕr	artificial bladder, placed at the site of the excised bladder, constructed from portions of intestine connected to the urethra, allowing "natural" voiding; also called *orthotopic neobladder*

Programmed Review: Operative Terms

ANSWERS	REVIEW
-tomy nephrotomy lith/o nephrolithotomy	12.76 Recall that the suffix meaning incision is _____. The term for an incision into the kidney is therefore _____. The combining form meaning stone is _____. An incision into the kidney to remove a stone (using the combining forms for both kidney and stone) is therefore _____.
excision or removal nephrectomy	12.77 The suffix *-ectomy* means _____. Therefore, the excision of a kidney is called _____.
-plasty pyeloplasty	12.78 The suffix referring to surgical repair or reconstruction is _____. Therefore, the term for surgical reconstruction of the renal pelvis (using the combining form meaning basin, for this basin-like structure) is _____.
-rrhaphy nephrorrhaphy	12.79 Recall that the suffix for suturing is _____. The procedure of suturing an injured kidney is therefore called _____.
resectoscope stent resecto	12.80 Urologic endoscopic surgery uses a specialized endoscope, called a _____, to resect tumors or to perform other surgical procedures within the urinary tract. A device that is surgically placed to hold open a vessel or tube is called a _____. Urologic stent placement also may be performed through the _____scope.

ANSWERS	REVIEW
within intracorporeal lithotripsy intracorporeal lithotripsy	**12.81** Stones within the urinary tract may be destroyed by the transmission of electrical energy through an endoscope. The prefix *intra-* means _____, and *corpor/o* combined with the suffix *-eal* pertains to the body. Thus, this process, performed within the body, is described as _____. The suffix *-tripsy* means crushing; thus, the crushing of a stone is termed _____. Together, these two terms form the name for the procedure of electrically destroying stones within the urinary tract, usually in the bladder: _____ _____.
kidney or renal transplantation	**12.82** In patients with two diseased kidneys, a kidney from a donor may be surgically implanted in the patient. This procedure is called _____ _____.
bladder ileal conduit continent	**12.83** Defects or diseases such as bladder cancer can require the temporary or permanent surgical diversion of the urinary tract. When cystectomy, or removal of the _____, is required, it is necessary to create a new permanent passage for urine to exit the body. One method that uses a portion of the ileum as a conduit, diverting urine from the ureters to the outside of the body is called an _____ _____. The term continent refers to the ability to hold or retain urine. This method is considered non_____, because urine cannot be held and drains continually into a bag.
urostomy continent	**12.84** The internal reservoir constructed of intestine that diverts urine to a stoma on the abdomen with a valve attachment to allow catheter draining is called _____. Because the reservoir retains urine, the procedure is called _____ urostomy.
neo urination, orthotopic correct pertaining to	**12.85** Construction of a new bladder, or a _____bladder, provides a straight connection to the urethra, allowing a more natural voiding or _____. A neobladder is also called an _____ bladder, a term formed from the combination of *orth/o*, meaning straight, normal, or _____; *top/o*, meaning place; and *-ic*, meaning _____ _____.

Self-Instruction: Therapeutic Terms

Study this table to prepare for the programmed review that follows.

TERM	MEANING
extracorporeal shock wave lithotripsy (ESWL) eks′ tră-kōr-pō′ rē-ăl shok wāv lith′ ō-trip′ sē	procedure using ultrasound outside the body to bombard and disintegrate a stone within; most commonly used to treat urinary stones above the bladder
kidney dialysis kid′ nē dī-al′ i-sis	methods of filtering impurities from the blood, replacing the function of one or both kidneys lost in renal failure
hemodialysis hē′ mō-dī-al′ i-sis	method of removing impurities by pumping the patient's blood through a dialyzer, the specialized filter of the artificial kidney machine (hemodialyzer)
peritoneal dialysis per′ i-tō-nē′ ăl dī-al′ i-sis	method of removing impurities using the peritoneum as the filter; a catheter inserted in the peritoneal cavity delivers cleansing fluid (dialysate) that is washed in and out in cycles
urinary catheterization yūr′ i-nār-ē kath′ ĕ-ter-ī-zā′ shun	methods of placing a tube into the bladder to drain or collect urine
straight catheter strāt kath′ ĕ-tĕr	a type of catheter that is inserted through the urethra into the bladder to relieve urinary retention or to collect a sterile specimen of urine for testing; the catheter is removed immediately after the procedure
Foley catheter fō′ lē kath′ ĕ-tĕr	indwelling catheter inserted through the urethra and into the bladder that includes a collection system allowing urine to be drained into a bag; the catheter can remain in place for an extended period
suprapubic catheter sū′ pră-pyū′ bik kath′ ĕ-tĕr	indwelling catheter inserted directly in the bladder through an abdominal incision above the pubic bone that includes a collection system that allows urine to be drained into a bag; used in patients requiring long-term catheterization
COMMON THERAPEUTIC DRUG CLASSIFICATIONS	
analgesic an-ăl-jē′ zik	drug that relieves pain
antibiotic an′ tē-bī-ot′ ik	drug that kills or inhibits the growth of microorganisms
antispasmodic an′ tē-spaz-mod′ ik	drug that relieves spasm
diuretic dī-yū-ret′ ik	drug that increases the secretion of urine

Programmed Review: Therapeutic Terms

ANSWERS	REVIEW
body, outside extracorporeal extracorporeal shock wave lithotripsy	**12.86** Recall that the term *intracorporeal* pertains to within the _____. In contrast, the prefix *extra-* means _____. Therefore, the term for outside the body is _____. The procedure using the shock waves of ultrasound from outside the body to break up urinary stones is termed _____ _____ _____ (ESWL).
kidney dialysis hemodialysis	**12.87** Dialysis is a general medical term that means filtration. This process of filtering impurities from the blood in patients with renal failure is called _____ _____. The combining form for blood is *hem/o*, which is used to create the term for the process of pumping a patient's blood through an artificial kidney machine: _____.
peritoneal dialysis	**12.88** Another method for removing impurities uses the patient's peritoneum (an abdominal cavity) for a filtering bath and is called _____ _____.
urinary, catheterization	**12.89** A catheter is a tube that is placed in a body cavity or vessel to allow passage of fluid through it. The process is called catheterization. Catheter placement in the bladder to drain or collect urine is therefore called _____ _____.
straight	**12.90** The type of catheter that is inserted straight through the urethra and into the bladder to relieve urinary retention or to collect a sterile specimen of urine for testing and that is removed immediately after the procedure is simply called a _____ catheter.
Foley catheter	**12.91** An indwelling catheter is one that is left in place. One type is named for its developer, Dr. Frederick Foley, and is inserted through the urethra and into the bladder and includes a collection system that allows urine to be drained into a bag. This type of catheter, called a _____ _____, can remain in place for an extended period.
above suprapubic	**12.92** Another type of indwelling catheter is used when the patient needs long-term catheterization. It is inserted directly in the bladder through an abdominal incision made above the pubic bone. *Supra-*, a prefix meaning excessive or _____, is used in the name of this catheter in reference to its placement above the pubic bone: _____ catheter.

ANSWERS	REVIEW
against	**12.93** Recall that the prefix *anti-* means _____ or opposed to. Drug classes are commonly named for their actions, such as acting against some thing or process. A drug that acts to prevent or relieve a spasm is called an _____.
antispasmodic	
antibiotic	The same prefix when joined with the combining form for life (*bio*) denotes a drug class that acts to kill or inhibit microbial life. This drug is called an _____.
without	**12.94** The Greek word algesis means sensation of pain. Recall that the prefix *an-* means _____. A type of drug that relieves pain is called an _____.
analgesic	
diuretic	**12.95** A drug that increases the secretion of urine is called a _____. Other common substances, such as coffee and alcohol, also have diuretic effects.

Chapter 12 Abbreviations

ABBREVIATION	EXPANSION
alb	albumin
APKD	adult polycystic kidney disease
BUN	blood urea nitrogen
Bx	biopsy
C&S	culture and sensitivity
ESWL	extracorporeal shock wave lithotripsy
hpf	high-power field
IVP	intravenous pyelogram
IVU	intravenous urogram
KUB	kidneys, ureters, bladder
lpf	low-power field
RP	retrograde pyelogram
SpGr	specific gravity
SUI	stress urinary incontinence
UA	urinalysis
UTI	urinary tract infection
VCU or VCUG	voiding cystourethrogram

PRACTICE EXERCISES

For each of the following words, write out the term parts (prefixes [P], combining forms [CF], roots [R], and suffixes [S]) on the lines below the word. Then define the term according to the meaning of its parts.

EXAMPLE

pericystitis

peri / cyst / itis

P   R   S

DEFINITION: around/bladder or sac/inflammation

1. pyuria

    _____ / _____ / _____
    R   R   S

    DEFINITION: _____

2. bacteriosis

    _____ / _____
    R   S

    DEFINITION: _____

3. transurethral

    _____ / _____ / _____
    P   R   S

    DEFINITION: _____

4. urogram

    _____ / _____
    CF   S

    DEFINITION: _____

5. urethrocystitis

    _____ / _____ / _____
    CF   R   S

    DEFINITION: _____

6. nephroptosis

    _____ / _____
    CF   S

    DEFINITION: _____

Write the correct medical term for each of the following definitions.

7. _____ inflammation of the bladder
8. _____ urinating at night
9. _____ involuntary discharge of urine
10. _____ suture of a torn kidney
11. _____ degenerative disease of the kidney without inflammation

Complete each medical term by writing the missing word part or word.

12. _____scopy = examination of the bladder
13. Urethral _____osis = a narrowed condition of the urethra
14. Extracorporeal shock wave _____ = procedure for disintegration of stones
15. _____scope = specialized endoscope used to cut and remove lesions from the bladder, urethra, or prostate
16. _____uria = scanty urination

Give the appropriate abbreviation for the following.

17. Kidney x-ray image obtained after contrast medium is sent "backward" through a cystoscope _____
18. Cytologic study of kidney tissue _____
19. Physical, chemical, and microscopic study of urine _____

Write the letter of the matching term in the space provided.

20. sugar _____   a. cyst/o
21. proteinuria _____   b. albuminuria
22. uremia _____   c. glyc/o
23. ren/o _____   d. nephr/o
24. vesic/o _____   e. azotemia

Write out the expanded term for each abbreviation.

25. C&S _____
26. VCU _____
27. BUN _____
28. IVU _____
29. ESWL _____

Circle the combining form that corresponds to the meaning given.

30. urine
    a. hydr/o   b. ur/o   c. ren/o
31. thirst
    a. dips/o   b. crin/o   c. hidr/o
32. pus
    a. pyel/o   b. py/o   c. albumin/o
33. bladder
    a. cyt/o   b. vesic/o   c. nephr/o
34. protein
    a. albumin/o   b. lip/o   c. bacteri/o

Write the correct terms for the anatomic structures indicated.

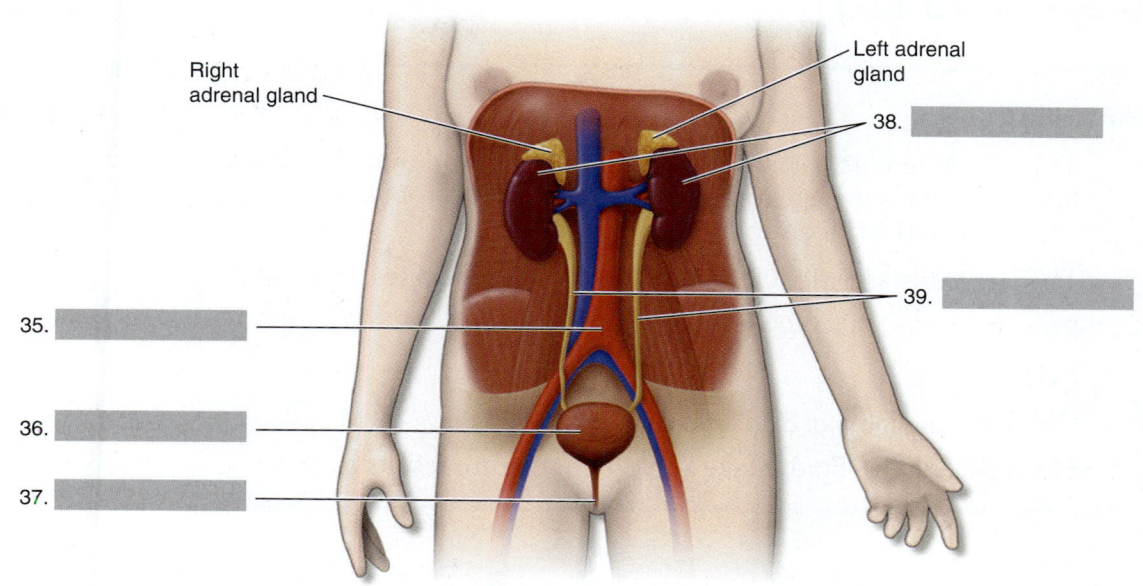

35. _____   38. _____
36. _____   39. _____
37. _____

Circle the correct spelling in each set of words.

40. a. cystascope   b. cystoskope   c. cystoscope
41. a. pyleogram   b. pyelogram   c. pielogram
42. a. oliguria   b. oleguria   c. oligouria
43. a. hydronefrosis   b. hidronephrosis   c. hydronephrosis
44. a. azootemia   b. azothemia   c. azotemia

Give the noun used to form each adjective.

45. urinary   _____
46. glomerular   _____
47. meatal   _____
48. uremic   _____
49. urethral   _____
50. nephrotic   _____

MEDICAL RECORD ANALYSIS

Medical Record 12-1

CHART NOTE

S: This 70 y/o female has had polyuria, nocturia, and dysuria × 2–3 d. She had a similar infection 6 months ago and was treated with Macrobid, 50 mg, q.i.d. × 3 d. She has occasional stress incontinence with hard sneezing.

O: The patient is afebrile. UA shows a trace of leukocytes and blood.

A: R/O recurrent UTI

P: C&S
Cipro 500 mg tab p.o. b.i.d. pending culture
Pt instructed to ↑ fluid intake and call for culture results in 48 h

1. What is the patient's CC?
   a. presence of red and white blood cells in her urine
   b. a urinary tract infection
   c. pain when she urinates, with the need to go often, even at night
   d. urinary retention

2. What were the objective findings?
   a. culture showed leukocytes and blood in the urine
   b. urinalysis indicated red and white blood cells present in urine
   c. infection of the bladder and urethra
   d. return of infection of the bladder and urethra

3. What was the doctor's impression?
   a. leukocytes and blood in the patient's urine
   b. patient has pain when she urinates, with the need to go often, even at night
   c. patient has a bladder infection
   d. patient may have another bladder infection

4. Which medical terms describe the UA findings?
   a. pyuria and hematuria
   b. dysuria and enuresis
   c. bacteriuria and hematuria
   d. bacteriuria and nocturia

5. To what does C&S refer?
   a. condition of urinary stress
   b. isolation of microorganisms in the urine
   c. inflammation of the bladder
   d. physical, chemical, and microscopic study of urine

6. How should the Cipro be administered?
   a. two, by mouth every day
   b. one, by mouth two times a day
   c. one, by mouth three times a day
   d. one, by mouth four times a day

7. Was the patient's temperature elevated?
   a. yes
   b. no
   c. nothing is stated about the patient's temperature

ANSWERS TO PRACTICE EXERCISES

1. pyuria
   R: py
   R: ur
   S: ia
   DEFINITION: pus/urine/condition of
2. bacteriosis
   R: bacteri
   S: osis
   DEFINITION: bacteria/condition or increase
3. transurethral
   P: trans
   R: urethr
   S: al
   DEFINITION: across or through/urethra/pertaining to
4. urogram
   CF: uro
   S: gram
   DEFINITION: urine/record
5. urethrocystitis
   CF: urethro
   R: cyst
   S: itis
   DEFINITION: urethra/bladder/inflammation
6. nephroptosis
   CF: nephro
   S: ptosis
   DEFINITION: kidney/falling or downward displacement
7. cystitis
8. nocturia
9. enuresis
10. nephrorrhaphy
11. nephrosis
12. cystoscopy
13. stenosis
14. lithotripsy
15. resectoscope
16. oliguria
17. RP
18. renal Bx or kidney Bx
19. UA
20. c
21. b
22. e
23. d
24. a
25. culture and sensitivity
26. voiding cystourethrogram
27. blood urea nitrogen
28. intravenous urogram
29. extracorporeal shock wave lithotripsy
30. ur/o
31. dips/o
32. py/o
33. vesic/o
34. albumin/o
35. abdominal aorta
36. urinary bladder
37. urethra
38. kidneys
39. ureters
40. cystoscope
41. pyelogram
42. oliguria
43. hydronephrosis
44. azotemia
45. urine
46. glomerulus
47. meatus
48. uremia
49. urethra
50. nephrosis

ANSWERS TO MEDICAL RECORD 12-1

1. c
2. b
3. d
4. a
5. b
6. b
7. b

13

MALE REPRODUCTIVE SYSTEM

Learning Outcomes

After completing this chapter, you should be able to:

- Define terms parts related to the male reproductive system.
- Identify key male reproductive system anatomic structures with their functions.
- Define symptomatic and diagnostic terms related to the male reproductive system.
- Explain diagnostic tests; procedures; and operative and therapeutic terms related to the male reproductive system.
- Cite common abbreviations related to the male reproductive system and give the expansion of each.
- Explain terms used in medical records involving the male reproductive system.

MALE REPRODUCTIVE SYSTEM OVERVIEW

The male reproductive organs have several functions. These functions include:
- Producing and storing **sperm**, the male reproductive cells.
- Introducing sperm into the female reproductive tract to fertilize the female **oocyte** (egg cell).
- Secreting hormones necessary for the development of secondary sexual characteristics.

Self-Instruction: Combining Forms

Study this table to prepare for the programmed review that follows.

COMBINING FORM	MEANING
balan/o	glans penis
epididym/o	epididymis
orch/o	testis or testicle
orchi/o	testis or testicle
orchid/o	testis or testicle
perine/o	perineum
prostat/o	prostate
sperm/o	sperm (seed)
spermat/o	sperm (seed)
test/o	testis or testicle
vas/o	vessel

Programmed Review: Combining Forms

ANSWERS	REVIEW
balan/o -plasty balanoplasty	**13.1** The combining form meaning glans penis comes from the Greek word *balanos*, which means acorn. This word was apparently used because the glans has a somewhat acorn shape. That combining form is _____. Recall that the suffix meaning a surgical repair or reconstruction is _____. Thus, the term for surgical reconstruction of the glans penis is _____.
epididym/o epididymides epididymitis	**13.2** The Greek word *epididymos* has an interesting origin: *epi-* means upon, and *didymos* means twins (referring to the two testicles). The epididymis is a structure on each testicle. The combining form meaning epididymis is _____. The plural of epididymis is _____. Using the common suffix meaning inflammation with this combining form, the term for inflammation of the epididymis is _____.
orch/o, orchi/o orchid/o	**13.3** Three different combining forms have evolved from the Greek word *orchis*, meaning testis (testicle): _____, _____, and _____. Having three slightly different forms makes it a little more difficult to know how to form medical terms from them. For example, the term orchitis is from the combining form

ANSWERS	REVIEW
orch/o, orchi/o orchid/o	_____, the term orchiopexy is from _____, and the term orchidectomy is from _____.
perine/o	**13.4** The adjective perineal comes from the combining form _____, referring to the perineum, an anatomic area between the scrotum and the anus in males.
prostat/o, pain prostatalgia	**13.5** The Latin term *prostata* has its origins in a Greek word that means one who stands before. Perhaps the prostate gland was so named because it stands before the opening for sperm leaving the body to exit through the penis. The combining form for prostate is _____. Recall that the suffix *-algia* means _____. Using this combining form, the term for a painful prostate is _____.
sperm/o, spermat/o sperm/o spermat/o	**13.6** The Greek word sperma means seed; thus, sperm are the reproductive "seed" of males. The two combining forms for sperm are _____ and _____. The combining form used to make the term oligospermia, meaning too few sperm in the semen, is _____. The combining form used to make the adjective form spermatic is _____.
vas/o -rrhaphy vasorrhaphy	**13.7** The Latin word vas refers to vessel, which includes ducts as well as blood vessels. The combining term for vessel is _____. Recall that the surgical suffix meaning suture is _____. Thus, the procedure of suturing a vessel is called a _____.

Self-Instruction: Anatomic Terms

Study this table to prepare for the programmed review that follows (see **Figure 13-1**).

TERM	MEANING
scrotum *skrō'tŭm*	skin-covered pouch in the groin divided into two sacs, each containing a testis and an epididymis
testis *tes'tis*	one of the two male reproductive glands, located in the scrotum, that produce sperm and the hormone testosterone; also called *testicle*
testicle *tes'tĭ-kĕl*	one of the two male reproductive glands, located in the scrotum, that produce sperm and the hormone testosterone; also called *testis*
sperm (see **Figure 13-2**) *sperm*	male gamete or sex cell produced in the testes that unites with the oocyte in the female to produce offspring; also called *spermatozoon*

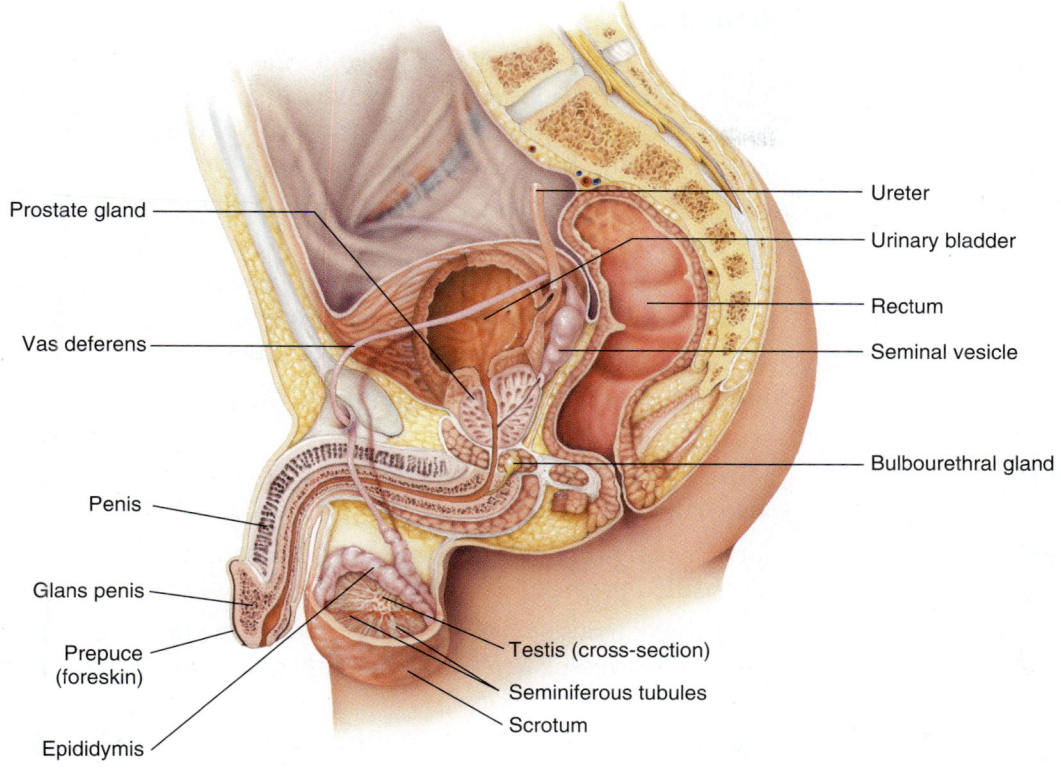

FIGURE 13-1 ■ Male reproductive system.

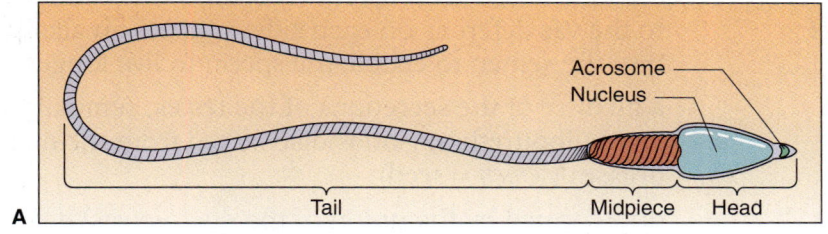

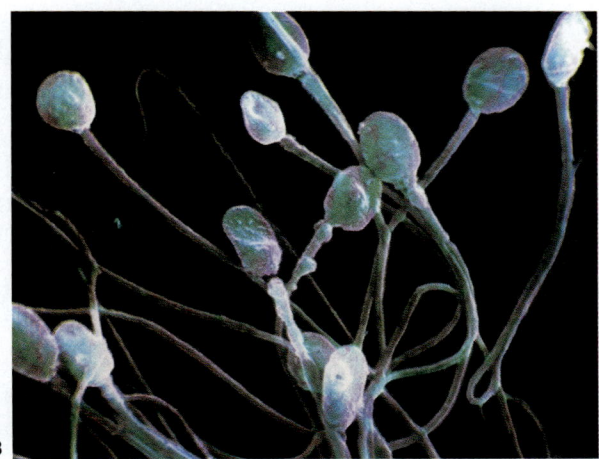

FIGURE 13-2 ■ Sperm. **A.** A typical sperm (magnified drawing). **B.** Prepared slide with sperm. Each sperm cell has a whip-like "tail," called a flagellum, that allows it to move. The ability to move is important for sperm because they need to travel through the woman's vagina, into the uterus, and then into the uterine tubes to meet the oocyte.

TERM	MEANING
spermatozoon (see **Figure 13-2**) *spĕr′mă-tō-zō′on*	male gamete or sex cell produced in the testes that unites with the oocyte in the female to produce offspring; composed of a head, midpiece, and tail (flagellum), with the head containing the acrosome (tip) and nucleus; also called *sperm*
epididymis *ep-i-did′i-mis*	coiled duct on the top and at the side of the testis that stores sperm before emission
penis *pē′nis*	erectile tissue (corpus spongiosum and corpora cavernosa) covered with skin that contains the urethra for urination and the ducts for secretion of seminal fluid (semen)
glans penis *glanz pē′nis*	bulging structure at the distal end of the penis (*glans* = acorn)
prepuce *prē′pūs*	loose casing that covers the glans penis; removed by circumcision; also called *foreskin*
foreskin *fōr′skin*	loose casing that covers the glans penis; removed by circumcision; also called *prepuce*
vas deferens *vas def′ĕr-ens*	duct that carries sperm from the epididymis to the ejaculatory duct (*vas* = vessel; *deferens* = carrying away); also called *ductus deferens*
ductus deferens *dŭk′tŭs def′ĕr-ens*	duct that carries sperm from the epididymis to the ejaculatory duct (*vas* = vessel; *deferens* = carrying away); also called *vas deferens*
seminal vesicle *sem′i-năl ves′i-kĕl*	one of two sac-like structures behind the bladder and connected to the vas deferens on each side; secretes an alkaline substance into the semen to enable the sperm to live longer
semen *sē′mĕn*	a mixture of the secretions of the testes, seminal vesicles, prostate, and bulbourethral glands discharged from the male urethra during orgasm (*semen* = seed)
ejaculatory duct *ē-jak′yū-lă-tōr-ē dŭkt*	duct formed by the union of the ductus (vas) deferens with the duct of the seminal vesicle; its fluid is carried into the urethra
prostate gland *pros′tāt gland*	trilobular gland that encircles the urethra just below the bladder and secretes an alkaline fluid into the semen (*pro* = before; *stat* = to stand); also called *prostate*
prostate *pros′tāt*	trilobular gland that encircles the urethra just below the bladder and secretes an alkaline fluid into the semen (*pro* = before; *stat* = to stand); also called *prostate gland*
bulbourethral glands *bŭl′bō-yū-rē′thrăl glanz*	pair of glands below the prostate, with ducts opening into the urethra, that adds a viscid (sticky) fluid to the semen; also called *Cowper glands*
Cowper glands *kow′per glanz*	pair of glands below the prostate, with ducts opening into the urethra, that adds a viscid (sticky) fluid to the semen; also called *bulbourethral glands*
perineum *per′i-nē′ŭm*	external region between the scrotum and anus in a male and between the vulva (external genitals) and anus in a female

CHAPTER 13 • MALE REPRODUCTIVE SYSTEM

> **TERM TIP:** **Prostrate Versus Prostate**
>
> **Prostate**, a Greek word that literally means "to stand before," describes the gland encircling the male urethra at the base of the urinary bladder. Its spelling is often confused with **prostrate** (with 2 r's) which describes lying stretched out on the ground face downward or a state of helplessness or exhaustion (*pro* = before; *stratus* = to strew).

Programmed Review: Anatomic Terms

ANSWERS	REVIEW
scrotum	**13.8** The testicles (or testes), which produce sperm and testosterone, are enclosed inside the skin-covered pouch called the _____.
testis testes	**13.9** Sperm are produced by each _____ (testicle). The plural of testis is _____.
sperm, spermatozoon	**13.10** Produced by the testes, the male gamete (sex cell) is called _____ or _____.
epididymis epididymides	**13.11** On each testis is a coiled duct that stores the sperm before emission and is called an _____. The plural of epididymis is _____.
vas deferens vessel	**13.12** The duct that carries the sperm from the epididymis to the ejaculatory duct is called the _____ _____. Recall that the combining form *vas/o* means _____ (or duct). Deferens means carrying away.
ejaculatory duct	**13.13** From the epididymis, the sperm is carried by the vas deferens to the _____ _____.
semen	**13.14** Various secretions are mixed with the sperm to make the fluid called _____, which is discharged through the male urethra during orgasm. The semen is sometimes called the male seed.
seminal	**13.15** Connected to the vas deferens on each side is another structure that secretes an alkaline substance into the semen. This is called the _____ vesicle. This alkaline substance enables the sperm to live longer.
prostate	**13.16** The trilobular gland encircling the urethra below the bladder, which also secretes an alkaline substance into the semen, is called the _____ gland. Malignancies of this gland, called prostate cancer, are common in men.

ANSWERS	REVIEW
bulbourethral Cowper	13.17 Finally, a pair of glands below the prostate, with ducts opening into the urethra, secrete a viscous fluid into the semen. These are called the _____ glands, or the _____ glands.
penis glans prepuce	13.18 The semen containing sperm and various secretions exits the body through the urethra, which passes through the skin-covered erectile tissue in the male called the _____. The acorn-shaped end of the penis where semen is ejaculated from the urethra is called the _____ penis. The medical term for foreskin, which covers the glans penis and is removed by circumcision in some men, is the _____.
perineum	13.19 Between the scrotum and the anus is the external area called the _____.

Self-Instruction: Symptomatic Terms

Study this table to prepare for the programmed review that follows.

TERM	MEANING
aspermia ā-spĕr′mē-ă	inability to secrete or ejaculate sperm
azoospermia ā-zō-ō-spĕr′mē-ă	semen without living spermatozoa; a sign of infertility in a male (*zoo* = life)
oligospermia ol′i-gō-spĕr′mē-ă	decreased production and expulsion of sperm
mucopurulent discharge myū-kō-pū′rū-lent dis′charj	drainage of mucus and pus

Programmed Review: Symptomatic Terms

ANSWERS	REVIEW
without condition of aspermia	13.20 Recall that the prefix *a-* means _____, and that the suffix *-ia* means _____. Use the shorter combining form for sperm to create the term for the condition in which one is unable to produce or ejaculate sperm (without sperm): _____.

ANSWERS	REVIEW
sperm or seed condition of azoospermia	**13.21** *Zoo* is a term component meaning animal life. Join this term component with *sperm/o* (a combining form meaning _____) and then modify it with the prefix meaning without and *-ia* (a suffix meaning _____) to create the term for a condition of semen without living sperm: _____.
few or deficient oligospermia	**13.22** Recall that the prefix *oligo-* means _____. The condition of deficient production and expulsion of sperm is called _____.
mucopurulent	**13.23** The term purulent refers to pus. The combining form for mucus is *muc/o*. The drainage of mucus and pus is called a _____ discharge.

Self-Instruction: Diagnostic Terms

Study this table to prepare for the programmed review that follows.

TERM	MEANING
anorchism *an-ōr′kizm*	absence of one or both testes
balanitis *bal-ă-nī′tis*	inflammation of the glans penis
cryptorchism (see **Figure 13-3**) *krip-tōr′kizm*	undescended testicle, or failure of a testis to descend into the scrotal sac during fetal development; the testis most often remains lodged in the abdomen or inguinal canal, requiring surgical repair (*crypt* = to hide); also called *cryptorchidism*

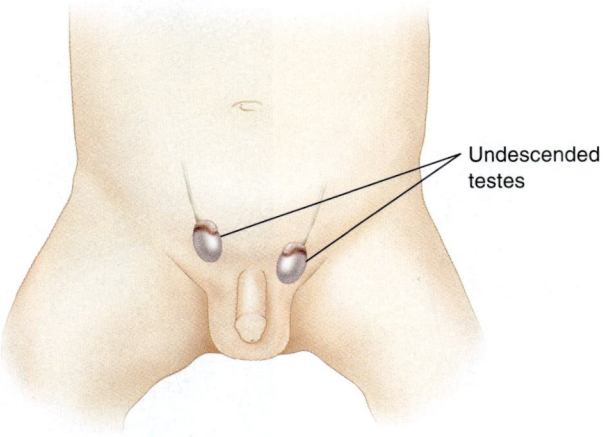

FIGURE 13-3 ■ Cryptorchism (cryptorchidism).

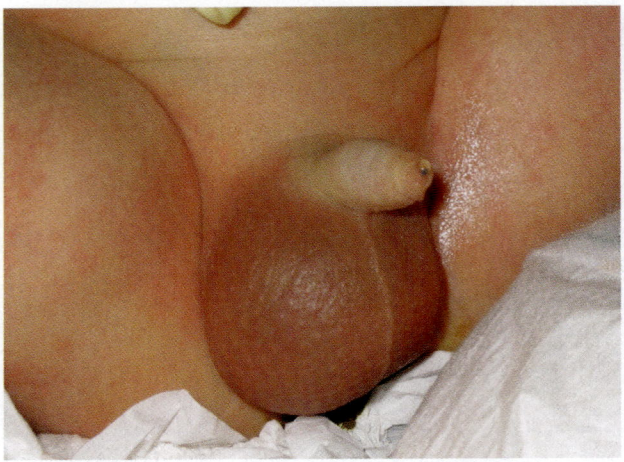

FIGURE 13-4 ■ Hydrocele.

TERM	MEANING
cryptorchidism (see Figure 13-3) *krip-tōr′ki-dizm*	undescended testicle, or failure of a testis to descend into the scrotal sac during fetal development; the testis most often remains lodged in the abdomen or inguinal canal, requiring surgical repair (*crypt* = to hide); also called *cryptorchism*
epididymitis *ep′i-did-i-mī′tis*	inflammation of the epididymis
erectile dysfunction (ED) *ē′rek-tīl dis-fŭnk′shŭn*	failure to initiate or maintain an erection until ejaculation because of physical or psychologic dysfunction; formerly termed impotence (*im* = not; *potis* = able)
hydrocele (see Figure 13-4) *hī′drō-sēl*	hernia of fluid in the testis or in the tubes leading from the testis
hypospadias (see Figure 13-5) *hī′pō-spā′dē-ăs*	congenital abnormal opening of the male urethra on the undersurface of the penis (*spadias* = to draw away)
Peyronie disease (see Figure 13-6) *pā-rō-nē′ di-zēz′*	disorder characterized by a buildup of hardened fibrous tissue in the corpus cavernosum, causing pain and a defective curvature of the penis, especially during erection

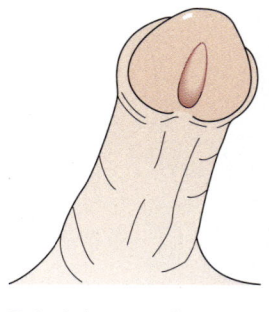
Balanic hypospadias

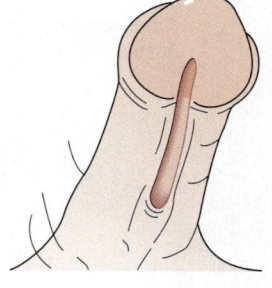
Penile hypospadias

FIGURE 13-5 ■ Hypospadias.

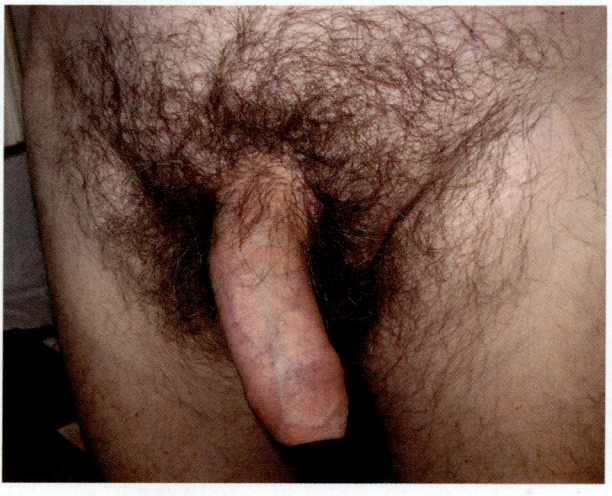

FIGURE 13-6 ■ Peyronie disease.

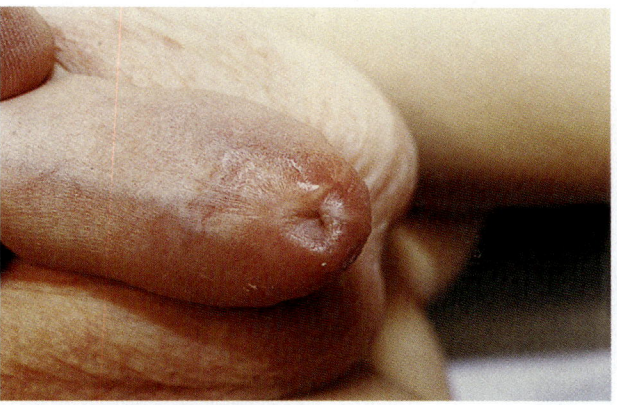

FIGURE 13-7 ■ Phimosis. With phimosis, the foreskin cannot be retracted over the penis tip.

TERM	MEANING
phimosis (see Figure 13-7) *fĭ-mō′sis*	a narrowed condition of the prepuce (foreskin) resulting in its inability to be drawn over the glans penis, often leading to infection; commonly requires circumcision (*phimo* = muzzle)
benign prostatic hyperplasia (BPH) (see Figure 13-8) *bē-nīn′ pros-tat′ik hī-pĕr-plā′zhē-ă*	enlargement of the prostate gland, common in older men, causing urinary obstruction; also called *benign prostatic hypertrophy* (BPH)
benign prostatic hypertrophy (BPH) (see Figure 13-8) *bē-nīn′ pros-tat′ik hī-pĕr′trō-fē*	enlargement of the prostate gland, common in older men, causing urinary obstruction; also called *benign prostatic hyperplasia* (BPH)
prostate cancer *pros′tāt kan′sĕr*	malignancy of the prostate gland

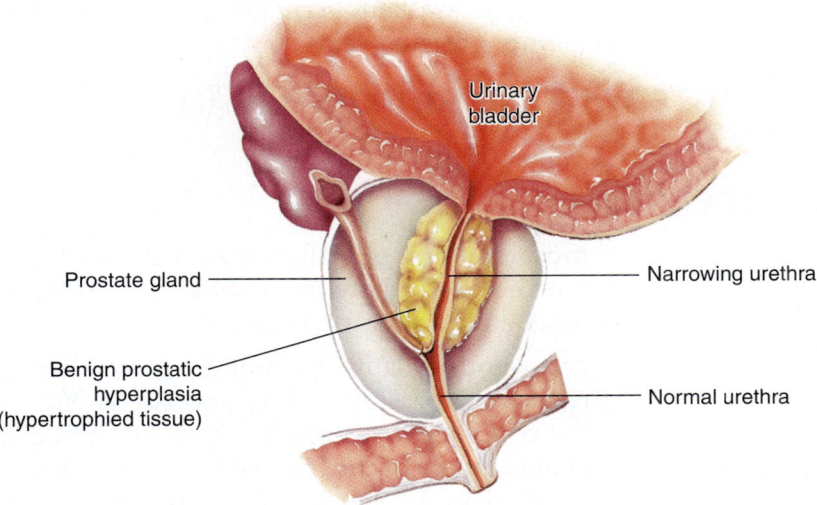

FIGURE 13-8 ■ Benign prostatic hyperplasia (BPH).

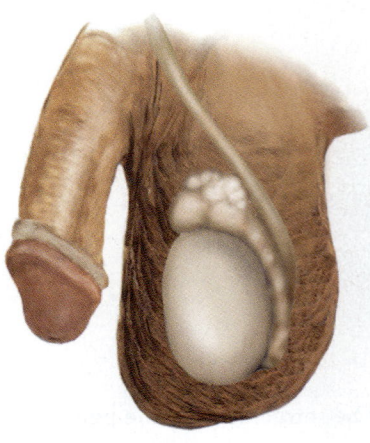

FIGURE 13-9 ■ Spermatocele. The mass located just above the testis indicates a spermatocele that contains sperm.

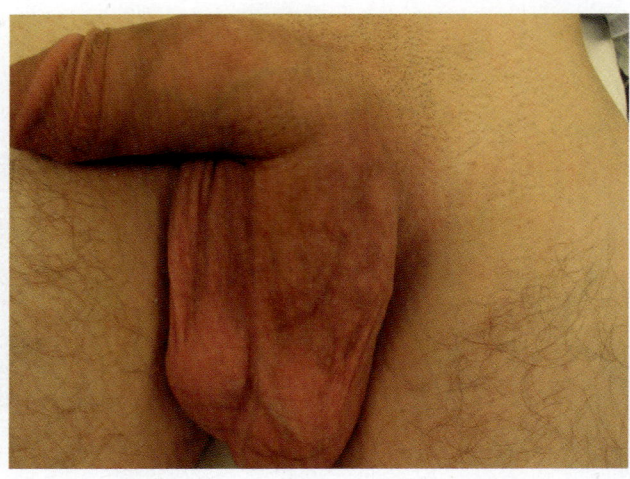

FIGURE 13-10 ■ Varicocele with characteristic "bag of worms" appearance within the testicle.

TERM	MEANING
prostatitis *pros-tă-tī′tis*	inflammation of the prostate
spermatocele (see Figure 13-9) *spĕr′mă-tō-sēl*	painless, benign cystic mass containing sperm lying above and posterior to, but separate from, the testicle
testicular cancer *tes-tik′yū-lăr kan′sĕr*	malignant tumor in one or both testicles commonly developing from the germ cells that produce sperm; classified in two groups according to growth potential
seminoma *sem-i-nō′mă*	most common type of testicular tumor, composed of immature germ cells; highly treatable with early detection
nonseminoma *non-sem-i-nō′mă*	testicular tumor arising from more mature germ cells; these tumors have a tendency to be more aggressive than seminomas and often develop earlier in life; includes choriocarcinoma, embryonal carcinoma, teratoma, and yolk sac tumors
varicocele (see Figure 13-10) *var′i-kō-sēl*	enlarged, swollen, herniated veins near the testis (*varico* = twisted vein)

SEXUALLY TRANSMITTED DISEASE (STD) OR SEXUALLY TRANSMITTED INFECTION (STI)

Major Bacterial STDs (STIs)

chlamydia *kla-mid′ē-ă*	most common sexually transmitted bacterial infection in North America; often occurs with no symptoms and is treated only after it has spread
gonorrhea *gon-ō-rē′ă*	contagious inflammation of the genital mucous membranes caused by invasion of the gonococcus *Neisseria gonorrhoeae*; the condition was named for the urethral discharge characteristic of the infection, which was first thought to be a leakage of semen (*gono* = seed; *rrhea* = discharge); the genus is named for the Polish dermatologist Albert Neisser

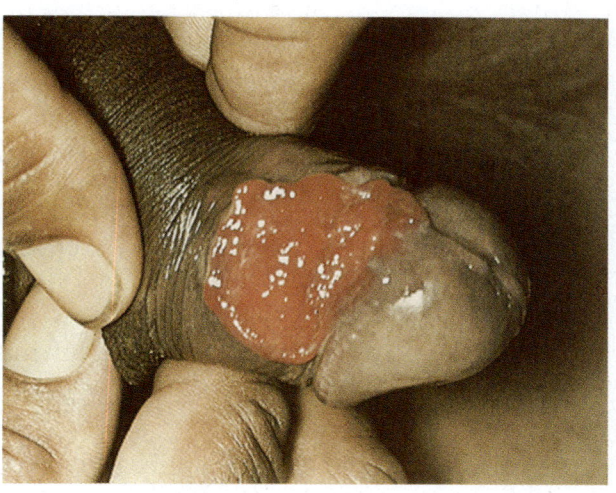

FIGURE 13-11 ■ Syphilitic chancre.

TERM	MEANING
syphilis (see Figure 13-11) sĭf′ĭ-lĭs	sexually transmitted infection caused by a spirochete and which may involve any organ or tissue over time; usually manifests first on the skin, with the appearance of small, painless, red papules that erode and form bloodless ulcers called chancres
Major Viral STDs (STIs)	
hepatitis B virus (HBV) hep-ă-tī′tis B vī′rŭs	virus that causes inflammation of the liver; transmitted through any body fluid, including vaginal secretions, semen, and blood
herpes simplex virus type 2 (HSV-2) (see Figure 14-9) her′pēz sim′pleks vī′rŭs tīp 2	virus that causes ulcer-like lesions of the genital and anorectal skin and mucosa; after initial infection, the virus lies dormant in the nerve cell root and may recur at times of stress
human immunodeficiency virus (HIV) hyū′măn im′yū-nō-dē-fish′en-sē vī′rŭs	virus that causes acquired immunodeficiency syndrome (AIDS), which permits various opportunistic infections, malignancies, and neurologic diseases; contracted through exposure to contaminated blood or body fluid (e.g., semen or vaginal secretions)
human papillomavirus (HPV) (see Figure 14-10) hyū′măn pap-i-lō′mă vī′rŭs	virus transmitted by direct sexual contact that causes an infection that can occur on the skin or mucous membranes of the genitals
condyloma acuminatum (pl. condylomata acuminata) kon-di-lō′mă ă-kū-mi-nā′tŭm (kon-di-lō-mah′tă ă-kū-mi-nā′tă)	lesion that appears as a result of human papillomavirus; on the skin, lesions appear as cauliflower-like warts, and on mucous membranes, they have a flat appearance; also known as *venereal warts* or *genital warts*

Programmed Review: Diagnostic Terms

ANSWERS	REVIEW
-itis balan/o balanitis	**13.24** Recall that the suffix meaning inflammation is _____. The combining form for glans penis is _____. Inflammation of the glans penis is therefore called _____.
epididymitis	**13.25** Inflammation of the epididymis is called _____.
prostatitis	**13.26** Inflammation of the prostate gland is called _____.
condition of, without testis anorchism	**13.27** Recall that the suffix -*ism* means _____. The prefix *an-* means _____. The combining form *orch/o* means _____. The medical term for the condition in which one or both testes are absent is _____.
condition of cryptorchism or cryptorchidism	**13.28** The combining form *crypt/o* means hidden. Again, the suffix -*ism* means _____. The condition in which a testicle does not descend during development but remains "hidden" in the abdomen is called _____.
hernia hydrocele varicocele sperm spermatocele	**13.29** Recall that the suffix -*cele* means pouching or _____. The combining form *hydr/o* refers to water or fluid. A hernia of fluid in the testis or tubes leading from the testis is called a _____. The combining form *varic/o* means swollen, twisted vein. A condition of swollen, herniated veins near the testis is therefore called _____. *Spermat/o*, a combining form meaning _____, is used in the term describing a painless, benign cystic mass containing sperm and lying near the testicle: _____.
hypospadias	**13.30** The congenital condition in which the urethra opens on the undersurface of the penis is called _____.
erectile dysfunction	**13.31** Impotence is a term formerly used to describe a failure to have or maintain an erection until ejaculation. This condition is now called _____ _____ (ED).

ANSWERS	REVIEW
disease	**13.32** The disorder characterized by a buildup of hardened fibrous tissue in the corpus cavernosum, causing pain and a defective curvature of the penis, is called Peyronie _____.
condition of phimosis	**13.33** Phimos, a word meaning muzzle, combined with *-osis*, the suffix meaning _____ ____, was used to name a narrowed condition of the prepuce that results in its inability to be drawn over the glans penis: _____.
benign above excessive benign prostatic hyperplasia or hypertrophy	**13.34** The opposite of malignant is _____. Recall that the prefix *hyper-* means _____ or _____. Hyperplasia refers to a condition of excessive formation of tissue. Hypertrophy refers to the excessive growth or enlargement of a structure. Using either of these terms, the nonmalignant enlargement of the prostate gland is called _____ _____ _____ (BPH).
prostate cancer	**13.35** Malignancy of the prostate is called _____ _____.
-oma seminoma	**13.36** Recall that the suffix for tumor is _____. The term for a malignant tumor of the testicle uses the root for semen instead of testicle: _____.
chlamydia	**13.37** Most sexually transmitted diseases (STDs) are caused by bacteria or viruses. The most common bacterial STD in North America, which often occurs without symptoms, is _____. Like many bacterial diseases, chlamydia gets its name from the Latin genus name for the bacteria: *Chlamydia*.
gonorrhoeae	**13.38** The name for another bacterial STD, the genus of which was named for the Polish dermatologist Albert Neisser, was coined in ancient times based on the thought that the urethral discharge characteristic of the infection was a leakage of semen: *Neisseria* _____.
syphilis	**13.39** The bacterial STD caused by a spirochete that can, over time, involve any body tissue or organ is _____.
hepatitis B	**13.40** Several viruses also cause STDs. The virus that causes inflammation of the liver, which can be spread through any body fluid, is _____ ____ virus (HBV).

ANSWERS	REVIEW
herpes simplex virus	**13.41** HSV-2 is the abbreviation for this sexually transmitted virus, which typically lies dormant after the initial infection but recurs at times of stress: _____ _____ _____ type 2.
human immunodeficiency virus	**13.42** The virus that causes acquired immunodeficiency syndrome (AIDS) is _____ _____ _____ (HIV).
papilloma	**13.43** HPV is the abbreviation for human _____ virus, which causes an STD characterized by lesions on the skin or mucous membranes. A condyloma is a warty growth; the
condylomata acuminata	plural of this term is _____. Condylomata _____ are warty growths in the genital area caused by HPV.

Self-Instruction: Diagnostic Tests and Procedures

Study this table to prepare for the programmed review that follows.

TEST OR PROCEDURE	EXPLANATION
biopsy (Bx) bī′op-sē	tissue sampling used to identify neoplasia
biopsy of the prostate (see Figure 13-12) bī′op-sē of the pros′tāt	needle biopsy of the prostate gland; often performed using ultrasound guidance
testicular biopsy tes-tik′yū-lăr bī′op-sē	biopsy of a testicle

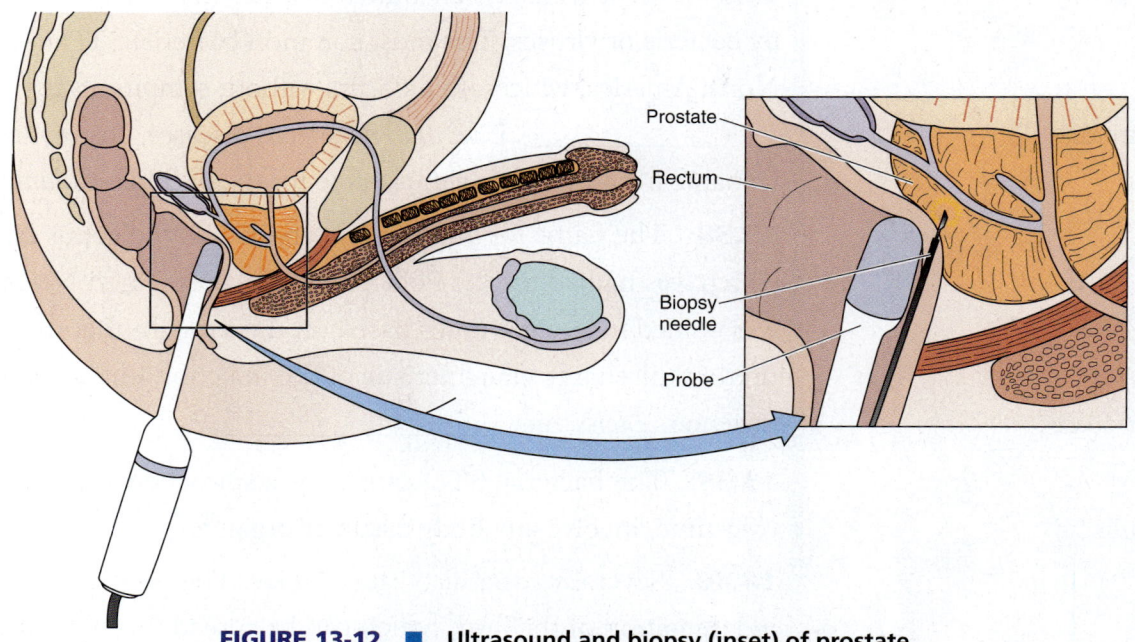

FIGURE 13-12 ■ Ultrasound and biopsy (inset) of prostate.

TEST OR PROCEDURE	EXPLANATION
digital rectal examination (DRE) *dij′i-tăl rek′tăl ek-zam′*	insertion of a finger into the male rectum to palpate the rectum and prostate
prostate-specific antigen (PSA) test *pros′tāt-spĕ-sif′ik an′ti-jen test*	blood test used to screen for prostate cancer; an elevated level of the antigen indicates the possible presence of tumor
urethrogram *yū-rē′thrō-gram*	x-ray of the urethra and prostate
semen analysis *sē′mĕn ă-nal′i-sis*	study of semen, including a sperm count with observation of morphology (form) and motility; usually performed to rule out male infertility
endorectal sonogram of the prostate (see Figure 13-12) *en′dō-rek′tăl son′ō-gram of the pros′tāt*	scan of the prostate made after introducing an ultrasonic transducer into the rectum; also used to guide needle biopsy; also called *transrectal sonogram of the prostate*
transrectal sonogram of the prostate (see Figure 13-12) *tranz-rek′tăl son′ō-gram of the pros′tāt*	scan of the prostate made after introducing an ultrasonic transducer into the rectum; also used to guide needle biopsy; also called *endorectal sonogram of the prostate*

Programmed Review: Diagnostic Tests and Procedures

ANSWERS	REVIEW
biopsy testicular	**13.44** The general term for removal of any body tissue for pathologic examination is _____, which is abbreviated Bx. The removal of testicular tissue is called a _____ biopsy.
prostate	**13.45** A needle biopsy of the prostate, often performed with ultrasound guidance, is called a _____ biopsy. This may be performed if prostate cancer is suspected.
prostate specific antigen	**13.46** Prostate cancer often causes the blood level of a specific antigen to become elevated. Thus, the _____-_____ _____ (PSA) test may indicate the possible presence of a prostate tumor.
digital rectal	**13.47** The physical examination procedure involving the physician inserting a finger (digit) into the rectum to palpate the rectum and prostate is called a _____ _____ examination (DRE). An enlarged or tender prostate can be detected with this examination.

ANSWERS	REVIEW
within endorectal sonogram	**13.48** Recall that the prefix *endo-* means _____. Another type of examination of the prostate involves introducing an ultrasonic transducer within the rectum to produce an _____ (or transrectal) _____ of the prostate, which can also be used to guide a needle biopsy.
record urethrogram	**13.49** Recall that the suffix *-gram* means a _____. An x-ray record of the urethra and prostate is called a _____.
semen analysis	**13.50** A study of semen that includes a sperm count and other characteristics of sperm is called a _____ _____. This analysis is often performed to help determine a man's fertility.

Self-Instruction: Operative Terms

Study this table to prepare for the programmed review that follows.

TERM	MEANING
circumcision (see Figure 13-13) ser-kŭm-sizh′ŭn	removal of the foreskin (prepuce), exposing the glans penis
epididymectomy ep′i-did-i-mek′tŏ-mē	removal of an epididymis
orchiectomy ōr-kē-ek′tŏ-mē	removal of a testicle; also called *orchidectomy*
orchidectomy ōr′ki-dek′tŏ-mē	removal of a testicle; also called *orchiectomy*
orchioplasty ōr′kē-ō-plas-tē	repair of a testicle
orchiopexy ōr′kē-ō-pek′sē	fixation of an undescended testis in the scrotum

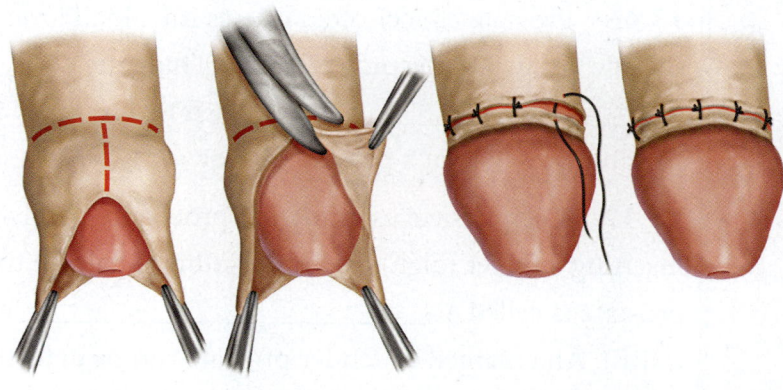

FIGURE 13-13 ■ Circumcision.

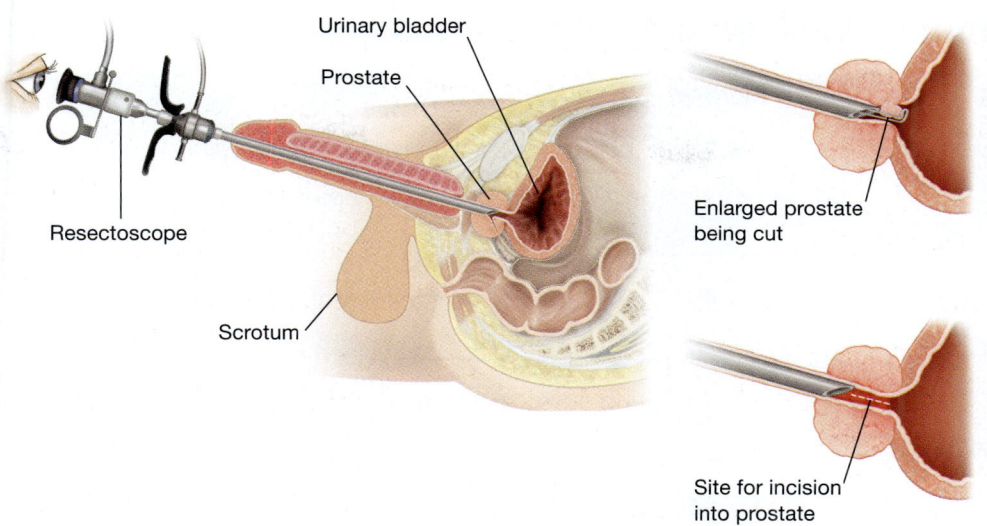

FIGURE 13-14 ■ Transurethral resection of prostate (TURP).

TERM	MEANING
prostatectomy pros′tă-tek′tŏ-mē	removal of the prostate gland
transurethral resection of the prostate (TURP) (see Figure 13-14) tranz-yū-rē′thral rē-sek′shŭn of the pros′tāt	removal of prostatic gland tissue through the urethra using a resectoscope, a specialized urologic endoscope; common treatment for benign prostatic hyperplasia/hypertrophy (BPH)
vasectomy (see Figure 13-15) va-sek′tŏ-mē	removal of a segment of the vas (ductus) deferens to produce sterility in the male
vasovasostomy vă′sō-vă-sos′tŏ-mē	restoration of the function of the vas deferens to regain fertility after a vasectomy

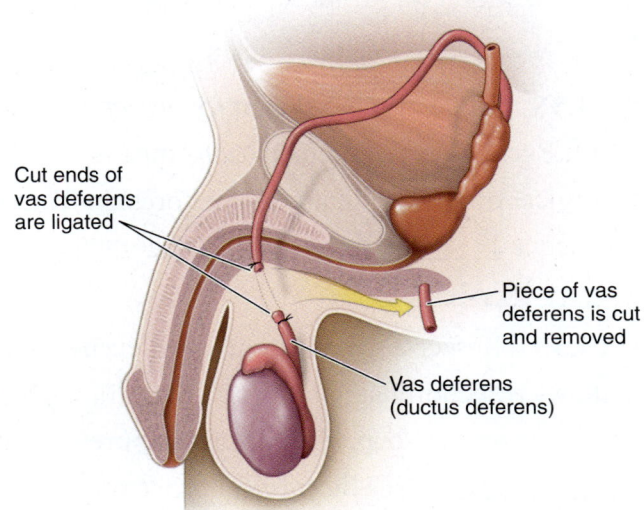

FIGURE 13-15 ■ Vasectomy. In a vasectomy, a piece of the vas deferens is cut and removed, and the loose ends are ligated (tied).

Programmed Review: Operative Terms

ANSWERS	REVIEW
removal epididymectomy	**13.51** Recall that the operative suffix *-ectomy* means _____ or excision. The removal of an epididymis is termed an _____.
orchiectomy orchidectomy	**13.52** The removal of a testicle is called an _____ or _____.
prostatectomy	**13.53** The surgical removal of the prostate gland is called a _____.
vasectomy	**13.54** Removal of part of the vas deferens is called a _____. This is done to produce male sterility.
opening vasovasostomy	**13.55** In contrast, the operative suffix *-stomy* means to create an _____. The operation performed to restore the function of the vas deferens after a vasectomy (to restore fertility) is called a _____. The combining form *vas/o* is used twice in the term to refer to both free ends of the vas deferens (which had been cut during the vasectomy), as both ends must be reopened so that they can be reattached.
repair orchioplasty	**13.56** Recall that the suffix *-plasty* means surgical reconstruction or _____. The surgical repair of a testicle is called _____.
-pexy orchiopexy	**13.57** The suffix for surgical fixation or suspension is _____. The fixation of an undescended testis in the scrotum is called an _____.
around circumcision prepuce	**13.58** The Latin word root for *-cision* (e.g., incision) means to cut. Recall that the prefix *circum-* means _____. The surgical procedure that cuts the foreskin from around the penis is called a _____. The medical term for the foreskin is _____.
through transurethral resection	**13.59** Resect is synonymous with excise. A specialized endoscope allows resection using an instrument through the scope; this is called a resectoscope. Recall that the prefix *trans-* means across or _____. The surgical procedure of removing prostatic gland tissue using a resectoscope through the urethra is called a _____ _____ of the prostate (TURP).

Self-Instruction: Therapeutic Terms

Study this table to prepare for the programmed review that follows.

TERM	MEANING
chemotherapy kem′ō-thār-ă-pē	treatment of malignancies, infections, and other diseases with chemical agents that destroy selected cells or impair their ability to reproduce
radiation therapy rā′dē-ā′shŭn thār′ă-pē	treatment of neoplastic disease using radiation, usually from a cobalt source, to stop the proliferation of malignant cells
brachytherapy brak-ē-thār′ă-pē	radiation therapy technique involving internal implantation of radioactive isotopes, such as radioactive seeds to treat prostate cancer; *brachy-*, meaning short distance, refers to localized application
hormone replacement therapy (HRT) hōr′mōn rē-plās′ment thār′ă-pē	use of a hormone to remedy a deficiency or regulate production (e.g., testosterone)
penile prosthesis pē′nīl pros′thē-sis	implantation of a device designed to provide an erection of the penis; used to treat physical impotence
penile self-injection pē′nīl self-in-jek′shŭn	intracavernosal (into the columns of penile erectile tissue) injection therapy causing an erection; used in treatment of erectile dysfunction

Programmed Review: Therapeutic Terms

ANSWERS	REVIEW
chemotherapy	**13.60** The combining form referring to chemical agents is *chem/o*. The treatment of malignancies, infections, and other diseases with chemical agents that destroy targeted cells is called _____.
radiation therapy brachytherapy	**13.61** Some kinds of cancer are also treated with radiation, which deters the proliferation of malignant cells. This is called _____ _____. *Brachy-*, a term component meaning short distance, is used to name the technique involving internal implantation of radioactive isotopes, such as radioactive seeds to treat prostate cancer. Signaling its localized application, this therapy is called _____.
hormone replacement	**13.62** If a patient is deficient in the production of a hormone, such as testosterone, treatment may involve administering a replacement hormone. This is called _____ _____ therapy (HRT).

ANSWERS	REVIEW
penile prosthesis	**13.63** A prosthesis is an artificial substitute for a nonfunctioning or missing body part or organ. A device that is implanted in the penis to provide an erection because the penis cannot become erect naturally is called a _____ _____.
penile	**13.64** Another therapy to treat erectile dysfunction involves self-injection of a medication into the corpus cavernosum to cause an erection. This therapy is called _____ self-injection.

Chapter 13 Abbreviations

ABBREVIATION	EXPANSION
BPH	benign prostatic hyperplasia; benign prostatic hypertrophy
Bx	biopsy
DRE	digital rectal examination
ED	erectile dysfunction
HBV	hepatitis B virus
HIV	human immunodeficiency virus
HPV	human papillomavirus
HRT	hormone replacement therapy
HSV-2	herpes simplex virus type 2
PSA	prostate-specific antigen
STD	sexually transmitted disease
TURP	transurethral resection of the prostate

PRACTICE EXERCISES

For each of the following words, write out the term parts (prefixes [P], combining forms [CF], roots [R], and suffixes [S]) on the lines below the word. Then define the term according to the meaning of its parts.

EXAMPLE
synorchism
syn / orch / ism
P   R   S

DEFINITION: together/testis or testicle/condition of

1. oligospermia
   _____ / _____ / _____
      P   R   S
   DEFINITION: _____

2. perineoplasty
   _____ / _____
      CF   S
   DEFINITION: _____

3. testalgia
   _____ / _____
      R   S
   DEFINITION: _____

4. balanic
   _____ / _____
      R   S
   DEFINITION: _____

5. prostatomegaly
   _____ / _____
      CF   S
   DEFINITION: _____

Write the correct medical term for each of the following definitions.

6. _____ absence of a testicle
7. _____ inflammation of the glans penis
8. _____ failure to maintain an erection
9. _____ enlarged, herniated veins near the testicle
10. _____ most common type of testicular cancer tumor

Complete each medical term by writing the missing word(s) or word part.

11. _____ orchism = undescended testicle

12. _____ _____ examination = insertion of a finger into the male rectum to palpate the rectum and prostate

13. _____ sonogram of the prostate = ultrasound scan of prostate made after introduction of the transducer into the rectum

14. _____ penis = bulging structure at the distal end of the penis

15. _____ spermia = inability to secrete or ejaculate semen

Match the medical term with its synonym or closely associated term.

16. semen analysis _____   a. orchiopexy
17. testis   _____   b. foreskin
18. testo   _____   c. sperm morphology
19. BPH   _____   d. testes
20. cryptorchism   _____   e. TURP
21. prepuce   _____   f. orchido

Write out the expanded term for each abbreviation.

22. PSA _____
23. BPH _____
24. TURP _____
25. DRE _____
26. Bx   _____

Circle the combining form that corresponds to the meaning given.

27. testis
    a. prostat/o   b. epididym/o   c. orchi/o

28. perineum
    a. peritone/o   b. perine/o   c. prostat/o

29. sperm
    a. test/o   b. orchi/o   c. spermat/o

30. vessel
    a. aden/o   b. angin/o   c. vas/o

31. glans penis
    a. prostat/o   b. orchid/o   c. balan/o

32. epididymis
    a. sperm/o   b. vas/o   c. epididym/o

Write the correct terms for the anatomic structures indicated.

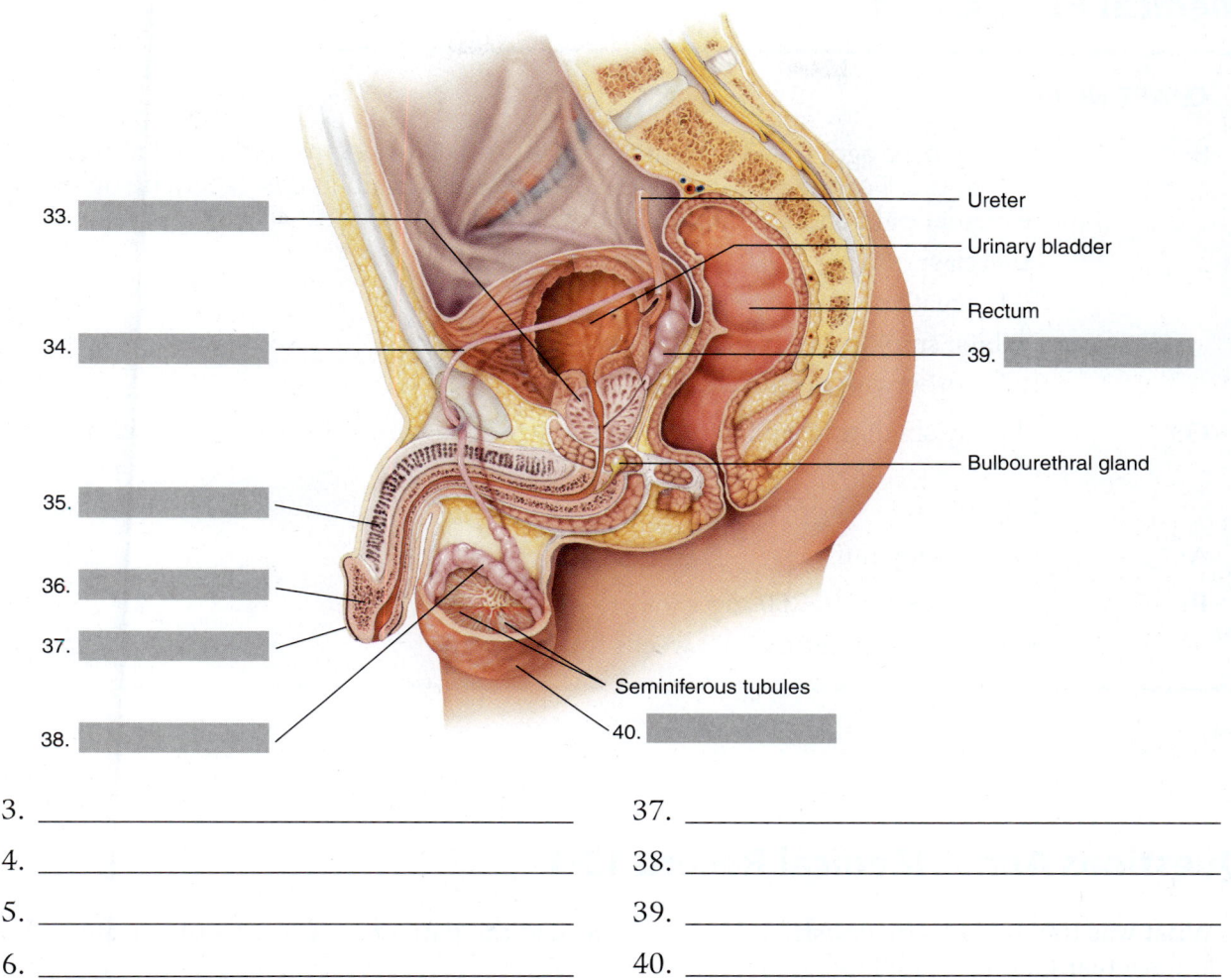

33. _____   37. _____
34. _____   38. _____
35. _____   39. _____
36. _____   40. _____

Circle the correct spelling in each set of words.

41. a. fimosis   b. phemosis   c. phimosis
42. a. oligspermia   b. oligospermia   c. oligispermia
43. a. azospermia   b. asospermia   c. azoospermia
44. a. anorchesm   b. anorchism   c. anorschizm
45. a. balanitis   b. balanitus   c. balantis

Give the noun used to form each adjective.

46. prostatic   _____
47. epididymal   _____
48. perineal   _____
49. penile   _____
50. gonorrheal   _____

MEDICAL RECORD ANALYSIS
Medical Record 13-1

CHART NOTE

S: Twelve days ago, this 34 y/o male had a flu-like syndrome that lasted about 2 to 3 hours. For the past 2 days, he has felt lousy again and is experiencing left testicular pain and swelling without voiding
Allergies: none
PH: negative
Habits: smoking—no alcohol—occasional beer
ROS: otherwise negative

O: Slightly small testes bilaterally; tender left epididymis; normal circumcised penis
UA: WNL

A: Left epididymitis

P: Rx: Ciprofloxacin 250 mg
Sig: bid × 14 d; return in 2 weeks for follow-up

Questions About Medical Record 13-1

1. What was the patient's diagnosis?
   a. testicular pain and swelling
   b. inflammation of the testicle
   c. swollen veins near the testis
   d. inflammation of the coiled duct that stores sperm
   e. fluid hernia in a testicle

2. What was the condition of the patient's penis?
   a. small but normal
   b. prepuce had been excised
   c. inflamed
   d. swollen and tender
   e. not stated

3. What was the Sig: on the prescription?
   a. one tablet twice a day for 14 days
   b. two immediately, then one a day for 14 days
   c. one immediately, then one a day for 14 days
   d. one as needed every day for 14 days

4. Did the patient have any trouble urinating?
   a. yes
   b. no

5. What was the condition of the right testicle?
   a. inflamed
   b. enlarged
   c. small
   d. normal
   e. had been excised

6. What was the result of the urinalysis?
   a. not stated
   b. normal
   c. not performed, because the patient could not void
   d. hematuria
   e. glucosuria

ANSWERS TO PRACTICE EXERCISES

1. oligospermia
   P: oligo
   R: sperm
   S: ia
   DEFINITION: few or deficient/sperm/condition of
2. perineoplasty
   CF: perineo
   S: plasty
   DEFINITION: perineum/surgical repair or reconstruction
3. testalgia
   R: test
   S: algia
   DEFINITION: testis or testicle/pain
4. balanic
   R: balan
   S: ic
   DEFINITION: glans penis/pertaining to
5. prostatomegaly
   CF: prostato
   S: megaly
   DEFINITION: prostate/enlargement
6. anorchism
7. balanitis
8. erectile dysfunction
9. varicocele
10. seminoma
11. cryptorchism or cryptorchidism
12. digital rectal examination
13. endorectal or transrectal sonogram of prostate
14. glans penis
15. aspermia
16. c
17. d
18. f
19. e
20. a
21. b
22. prostate-specific antigen
23. benign prostatic hyperplasia or hypertrophy
24. transurethral resection of the prostate
25. digital rectal examination
26. biopsy
27. orchi/o
28. perine/o
29. spermat/o
30. vas/o
31. balan/o
32. epididym/o
33. prostate gland
34. vas deferens
35. penis
36. glans penis
37. glans penis
38. epididymis
39. seminal vesicle
40. scrotum
41. phimosis
42. oligospermia
43. azoospermia
44. anorchism
45. balanitis
46. prostate
47. epididymis
48. perineum
49. penis
50. gonorrhea

ANSWERS TO MEDICAL RECORD 13-1

1. d
2. b
3. a
4. b
5. c
6. b

14

FEMALE REPRODUCTIVE SYSTEM AND OBSTETRICS

Learning Outcomes

After completing this chapter, you should be able to:

- Define term parts related to the female reproductive system and obstetrics.
- Identify key female reproductive system anatomic structures with their functions.
- Define symptomatic and diagnostic terms related to the female reproductive system and obstetrics.
- Explain diagnostic tests; procedures; and operative and therapeutic terms related to the female reproductive system and obstetrics.
- Cite common abbreviations related to the female reproductive system and obstetrics and give the expansion of each.
- Explain terms used in medical records involving the female reproductive system and obstetrics.

FEMALE REPRODUCTIVE SYSTEM AND OBSTETRICS OVERVIEW

This chapter focuses on the female reproductive system and obstetrics. Functions of the female reproductive system include:

- Producing female sex hormones.
- Propagating life by producing oocytes, the female sex cells.

- Providing a place for the implantation and nurturing of the fertilized oocyte, now called an ovum, through the embryonic and fetal stages to birth.
- Producing an infant's first source of nutrition.

Self-Instruction: Combining Forms

Study this table to prepare for the programmed review that follows.

COMBINING FORM	MEANING
-arche (suffix)	beginning
cervic/o	neck or cervix
colp/o	vagina (sheath)
episi/o	vulva (covering)
gynec/o	woman
hyster/o	uterus
lact/o	milk
mamm/o	breast
mast/o	breast
men/o	menstruation, menses
metr/o	uterus
obstetr/o	midwife
oo-	egg, ovary
oophor/o	ovary
ov/i	egg
ov/o	egg
ovari/o	ovary
pelv/i	pelvis (basin); hip bone
salping/o	uterine (fallopian) tube; also, Eustachian tube
toc/o	labor or birth
uter/o	uterus
vagin/o	vagina (sheath)
vulv/o	vulva (covering)

Programmed Review: Combining Forms

ANSWERS	REVIEW
cervic/o	**14.1** The Latin word cervix means neck; the cervix in the female is like a neck between the vagina and the uterus. The combining term for cervix is _____. The common adjective form, for example, is cervical.

ANSWERS	REVIEW
vagin/o colp/o -scope colposcope	**14.2** As often happens, there are two combining forms for vagina, one from a Latin word and one from a Greek word. The Latin word *vagina* means sheath (the vagina sheaths the penis during intercourse); the combining form is _____. The Greek word *kolpos* means a hollow; the combining form is _____. Using the latter combining form and the suffix for an instrument of examination, _____, forms the term for a special kind of scope designed to examine the vagina: _____.
episi/o, incision episiotomy	**14.3** The Greek term *epision*, meaning pubic region, is the origin for the combining form for the vulva (the external female genitalia): _____. The operative suffix *-tomy* means _____. Using this combining form, an incision made in the perineum to facilitate childbirth is an _____.
vulv/o	**14.4** A second combining form meaning vulva comes from the Latin word *vulva*: _____. It is used, for example, to create the common adjective form vulvar.
women gynec/o midwife	**14.5** A gynecologist is a physician who specializes in the reproductive system of _____. The combining form meaning "woman" is _____. Obstetrics is the specialty pertaining to the care and treatment of mother and fetus throughout pregnancy, childbirth, and the immediate postpartum period. *Obstetr/o* is a combining form meaning _____. OB-GYN is the abbreviation for the combined field of obstetrics (OB) and gynecology (GYN).
uter/o hyster/o excision or removal	**14.6** The uterus is the hollow organ (the womb) where the woman carries the fetus before childbirth. The Latin combining form used to name the uterus is _____. A hysterectomy is the surgical removal of the uterus; this term is made from the Greek combining form _____ plus the suffix *-ectomy*, which means _____.
metr/o uterus	**14.7** The Greek word for the uterus, *metra*, is the origin of a third combining form for uterus: _____. The term metrorrhagia, for example, refers to irregular bleeding from the _____ not occurring during menstruation.

ANSWERS	REVIEW
production milk lactogenic	**14.8** The suffix *-genic* (a combination of *gen/o* and *-ic*) pertains to origin or _____. It is used to modify the combining form *lact/o*, meaning _____, to form the adjective pertaining to the production of milk: _____.
mast/o, mamm/o pain -gram	**14.9** There are two combining forms meaning breast, again from Greek and Latin roots. The two combining forms for breast are _____ and _____. Because the suffix *-dynia* means _____, mastodynia means breast pain. The common suffix for a record resulting from an examination technique is _____. Thus, a mammogram is an x-ray of the breast.
menstruation men/o menopause	**14.10** From the Greek word *men*, meaning month, comes the combining form that means _____, which generally occurs about once a month in the adult female. The combining form is _____. The time later in life when menstruation permanently stops (pauses) is _____.
ovari/o oophor/o -itis ovary	**14.11** Once again, the two combining forms for the ovary come from Latin and Greek roots. The adjective ovarian is built from the combining form _____, which is from the Latin word for ovary. The Greek word *oophoros* means egg-bearing, giving rise to the combining form _____. Recall that the common suffix for inflammation is _____. Oophoritis is an inflammation of the _____.
sex cell ov/i, ov/o oocyte	**14.12** An oocyte is the woman's _____ _____, which is produced in the ovary. When fertilized by a sperm, an ovum is produced. The two combining forms for egg are very similar: _____ and _____. Ovigenesis, also called oogenesis, is the process of the formation and development of the _____.
salping/o inflammation	**14.13** The Greek word *salpinx* means trumpet or tube. It gives rise to the combining form _____, which refers to the uterine or fallopian tube, which carries the ovum from the ovary to the uterus. Salpingitis is an _____ of the uterine or fallopian tube.

ANSWERS	REVIEW
basin pertaining to pelvic	**14.14** *Pelv/i*, a Latin combining form referring to the shape of a _____, was used to name the pelvis, a basin-like ring of skeletal bones at the base of the spine that is bordered on each side by the hip bones. The reproductive organs are contained in the space formed by these bones. Using the combining form meaning pelvis combined with the suffix *-ic*, meaning _____, the term for this space is the _____ cavity.
toc/o difficult condition of dystocia	**14.15** The combining form for birth is _____. Tocophobia, for example, is a morbid fear of childbirth. Recall that the prefix *dys-* means faulty, painful, or _____, and the suffix *-ia* refers to a _____. Therefore, the term for a difficult childbirth is _____.
-arche menarche	**14.16** The suffix meaning beginning is _____. Using the combining form for menstruation, the term for the beginning of menstruation is _____.

Self-Instruction: Anatomic Terms

Study this table to prepare for the programmed review that follows (see **Figures 14-1 through 14-5**).

TERM	MEANING
uterus (see **Figure 14-1 A,B**) yū′tĕr-ŭs	womb; a pear-shaped organ in the pelvic cavity in which the embryo and fetus develops
fundus fŭn′dŭs	upper portion of the uterus above the entry to the uterine tubes
endometrium en-dō-mē′trē-ŭm	lining of the uterus, which is shed approximately every 28 to 30 days in a nonpregnant female during menstruation
myometrium mī-ō-mē′trē-ŭm	muscular wall of the uterus
uterine tubes yū′tĕr-in tūbz	tubes extending from each side of the uterus toward the ovary that provide a passage for ova to the uterus; also called *fallopian tubes*
fallopian tubes fă-lō′pē-ăn tūbz	tubes extending from each side of the uterus toward the ovary that provide a passage for ova to the uterus; also called *uterine tubes*
adnexa ad-nek′să	uterine tubes and ovaries (uterine appendages)
right uterine appendage rīt yū′tĕr-in ă-pen′dij	right uterine tube and ovary
left uterine appendage left yū′tĕr-in ă-pen′dij	left uterine tube and ovary

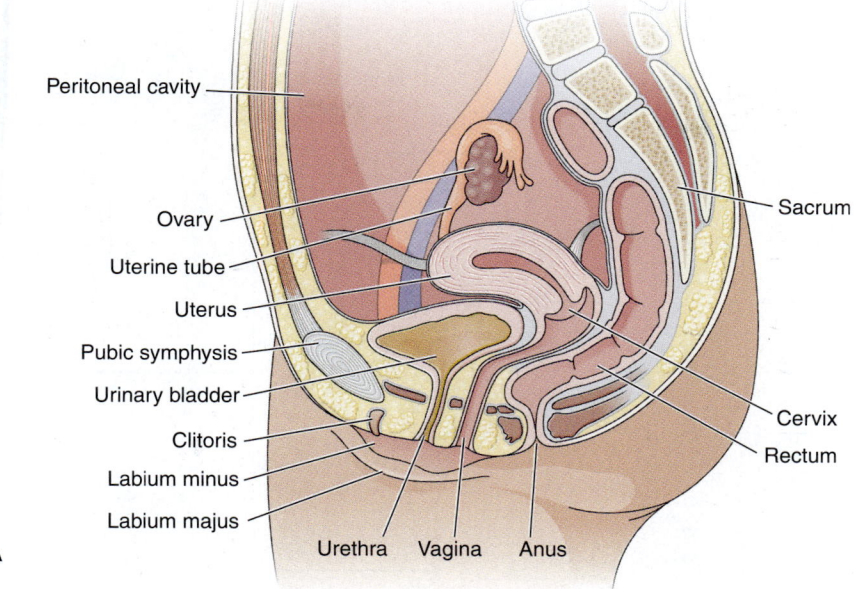
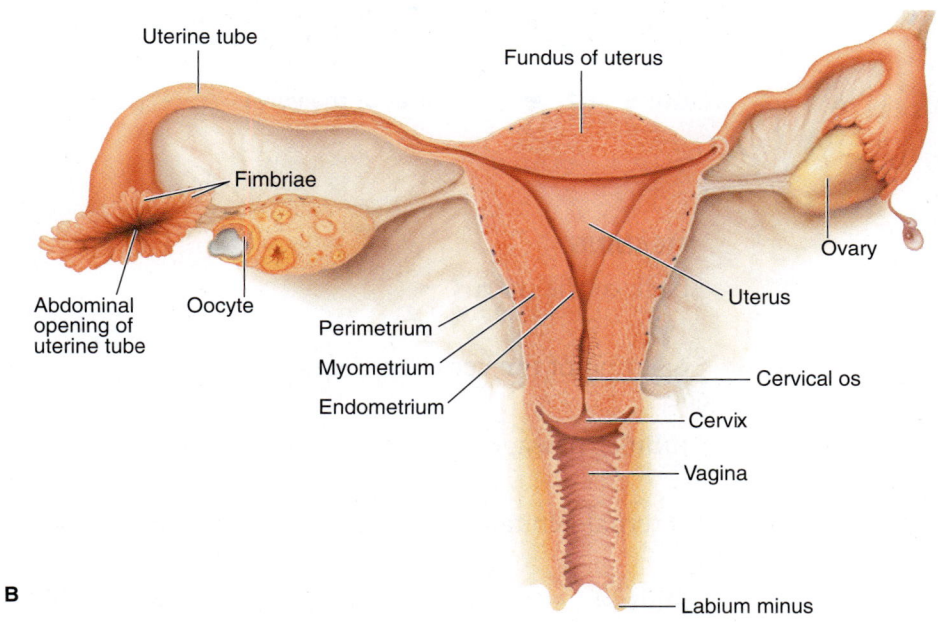

FIGURE 14-1 ■ Female reproductive system. **A.** Sagittal view of reproductive organs. **B.** The ovaries, uterine tubes, uterus, and vagina.

TERM	MEANING
ovary ō′vă-rē	one of two glands located on each side of the pelvic cavity that produce oocytes and female sex hormones
oocyte ō′ō-sīt	female gamete (sex cell); when fertilized by a sperm, it develops into an ovum and is capable of developing into a new individual
ovum ō′vŭm	imprecise term for a fertilized oocyte that is capable of implanting within the uterine wall

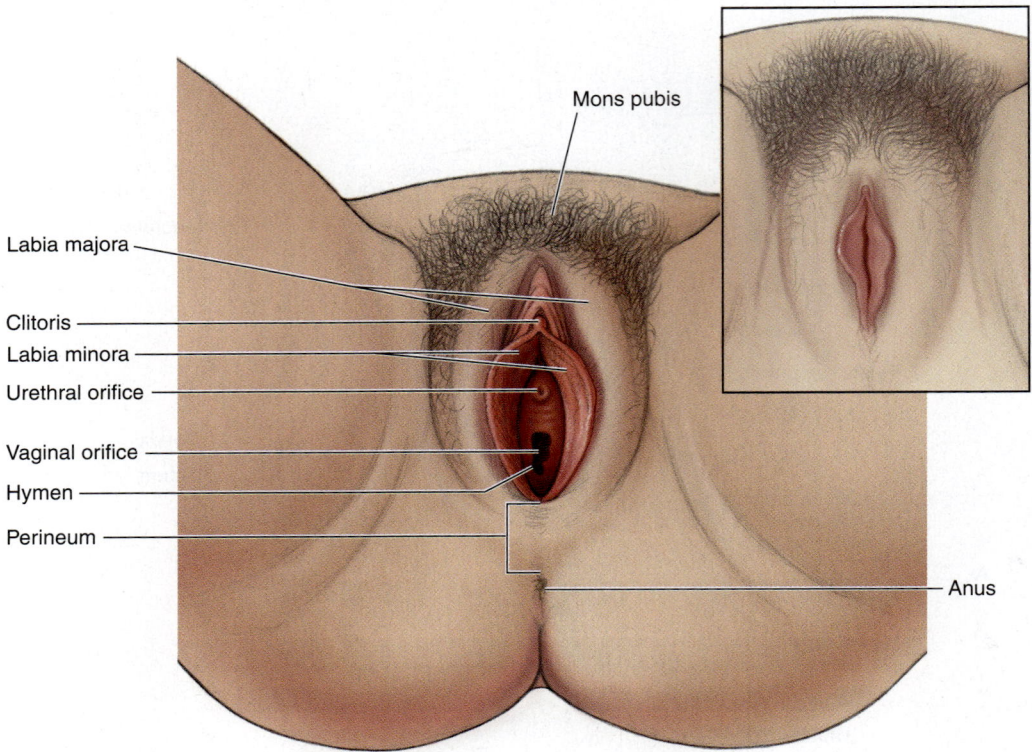

FIGURE 14-2 ■ Structures of the vulva.

TERM	MEANING
cervix sĕr′viks	neck of the uterus
cervical os sĕr′vi-kăl oz	opening of the cervix to the uterus
vagina vă-jī′nă	tubular passageway from the cervix to the outside of the body
vulva (see **Figure 14-2**) vŭl′vă	external genitalia of the female; term means "wrapper"
labia lā′bē-ă	folds of tissue on either side of the vaginal opening; known as the labia majora and labia minora
mons pubis monz pyū′bis	rounded mound of fatty tissue that covers the pubic bone
clitoris klit′ō-ris	female erectile tissue in the anterior portion of the vulva
hymen hī′men	fold of mucous membrane that encircles the entrance to the vagina
vaginal orifice vaj′i-năl or′i-fis	opening to the vagina; also called *introitus*
introitus in-trō′i-tŭs	opening to the vagina; also called *vaginal orifice*

TERM	MEANING
greater vestibular glands grāt-er ves-tib′yū-lăr glanz	two glands located on either side of the vaginal opening that secrete a lubricant during intercourse; also called *Bartholin glands*
Bartholin glands bahr′thō-lin glanz	two glands located on either side of the vaginal opening that secrete a lubricant during intercourse; also called *greater vestibular glands*
perineum per-i-nē′ŭm	region between the vulva and anus
breasts (see Figure 14-3) brests	protruding organs that contained the modified sweat glands called mammary glands that produce milk
mammary glands mam′ă-rē glanz	two glands in the female breasts (one in each breast) that are capable of producing milk
nipple nip′ĕl	projection (mammary papilla) on the breast surface through which milk can be secreted; lactiferous ducts carry breast milk to the nipple and lactiferous sinuses are expanded chambers that converge on the nipple surface
areola ă-rē′ō-lă	dark-pigmented area around the nipple

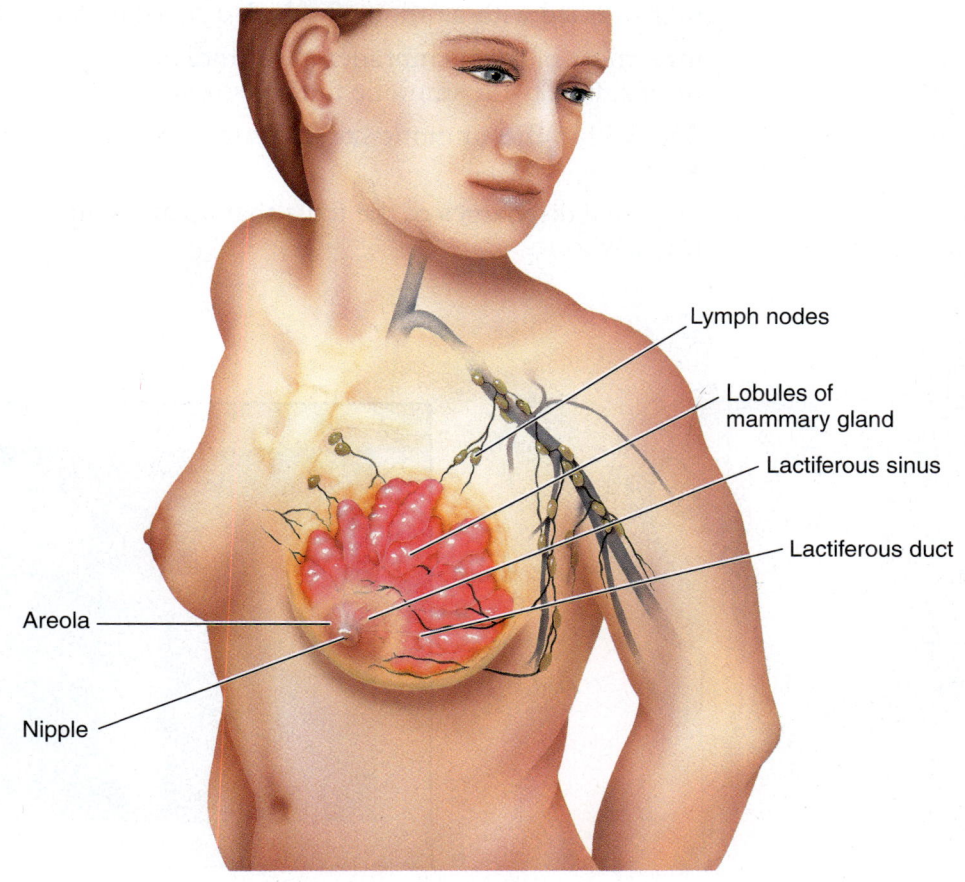

FIGURE 14-3 ■ Frontal view of the breasts.

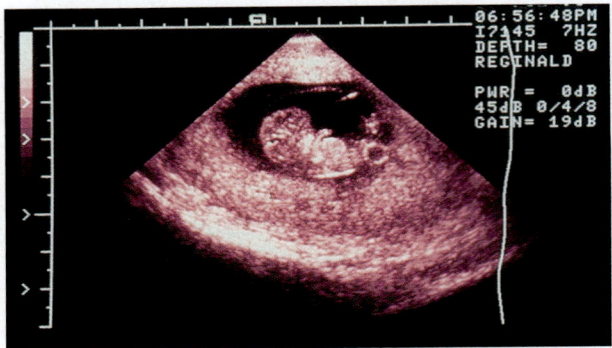

FIGURE 14-4 ■ Two-dimensional sonogram of an 8-week embryo.

TERM	MEANING
embryo (see Figure 14-4) em′brē-ō	the developing organism from fertilization to the end of the eighth week
fetus fē′tŭs	the developing organism from the ninth week to birth
placenta (see Figure 14-5 A,B) plă-sen′tă	vascular organ that develops in the uterine wall during pregnancy to provide nourishment for the fetus (*placenta* = cake)
amnion am′nē-on	innermost of the membranes surrounding the embryo in the uterus, filled with amniotic fluid; also called *amniotic sac*
amniotic sac am-nē-ot′ik sak	innermost of the membranes surrounding the embryo in the uterus, filled with amniotic fluid; also called *amnion*
amniotic fluid am-nē-ot′ik flū′id	fluid within the amniotic sac that surrounds and protects the fetus
meconium mē-kō′nē-ŭm	intestinal discharges of the fetus that form the first stools in the newborn

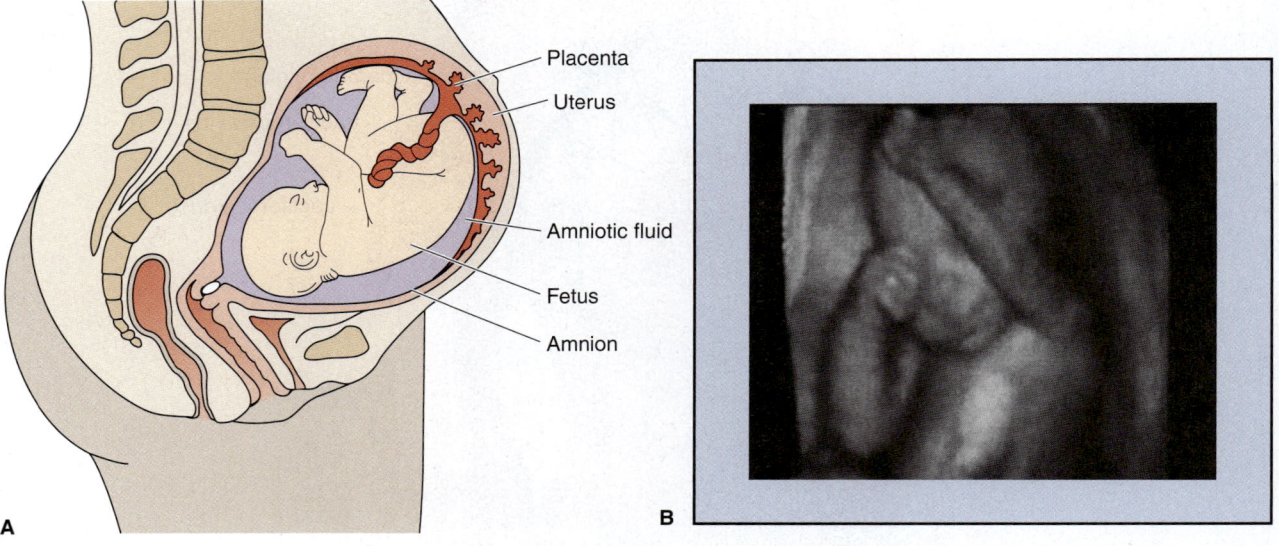

FIGURE 14-5 ■ **A.** Placenta and fetus in utero. **B.** Three-dimensional sonogram of fetus "waking up."

Programmed Review: Anatomic Terms

ANSWERS	REVIEW
vulva perineum	**14.17** The external genitalia of the female are collectively called the _____. The region between the vulva in the female (the scrotum in the male) and the anus is called the _____.
labia clitoris	**14.18** The vulva consists of the folds of tissue on either side of the vaginal opening, called the _____ majora and minor, and the female erectile tissue, called the _____. The labia majora are the larger tissue folds, and within them are the labia minora, the smaller tissue folds.
hymen	**14.19** Inward from the labia, the fold of mucous membrane encircling the entrance to the vagina is called the _____.
introitus Bartholin	**14.20** Another term for the entrance to the vagina, or vaginal orifice, is used in medical language for the entrance to other hollow organs as well. It comes from the Latin *intro-eo*, meaning to go into. This term is _____. Two glands located on either side of the vaginal opening, called _____ glands, secrete a lubricant during intercourse.
cervix neck cervical os	**14.21** The vagina is a tubular passageway between the _____ and the outside of the body, where the penis is inserted during intercourse. The cervix is the _____ of the uterus. The term for the opening of the cervix to the uterus, using the Latin word *os* (meaning mouth) is _____ _____. The term os is used in other anatomic areas to indicate an opening to a hollow organ or canal.
uterus fundus fundi	**14.22** The cervix is the neck of the _____ (the womb), where, after conception, the embryo and fetus develop. The upper part of the uterus, above the uterine tubes, is called the _____, from the Latin word *fundus*, referring to the largest part of a sac farthest from the opening. The plural of fundus is _____.
uterus myometrium within endometrium	**14.23** The combining form *metr/o* refers to the _____. The suffix *-ium* refers to a structure or tissue. The combining form *my/o* means muscle. Therefore, the term for the muscular wall of the uterus is the _____. Recall that the prefix *endo-* means _____. Within the uterus is a tissue that forms its lining, which is shed during menstruation and is called the _____.

ANSWERS	REVIEW
oocytes ovaries ovum	**14.24** Human eggs, called _____, are produced in each of the two _____. The ovaries also secrete female sex hormones. Fertilized oocytes are called *ova*. The singular of ova is _____.
fallopian appendage uterine adnexa	**14.25** The tubes through which the ova move from the ovaries to the uterus are called the _____ or uterine tubes. The right tube and ovary collectively are called the right uterine _____. The left tube and ovary are called the left _____ appendage. The collective term for both uterine appendages is the _____.
uterus oocyte	**14.26** Sperm deposited in the vagina during intercourse swim through the cervix into the _____. Sperm may meet an egg cell, or _____, in the uterus or uterine tubes, and fertilization may occur.
embryo endometrium	**14.27** If fertilization occurs, the resultant developing organism, called an _____ for the first 8 weeks, is implanted in the lining of the uterus, called the _____.
placenta	**14.28** The vascular (blood-rich) organ that develops in the uterine wall to nourish the embryo and fetus is called the _____.
amniotic sac fluid	**14.29** The membrane sac surrounding the embryo is the _____ _____. It is filled with a protective fluid called amniotic _____.
fetus	**14.30** After 8 weeks, the developing organism is no longer called an embryo; instead, it is called a _____.
meconium	**14.31** The first stools of a newborn develop from intestinal discharges of the fetus, called _____.
mamm/o mammary	**14.32** Recall that the two combining forms for breast are *mast/o* and _____. Using the adjective form of the latter, the term for the glands in the female breast that make milk is _____ glands.
nipple	**14.33** The mammary papilla is the _____ of the breast, through which milk flows to the infant.

Self-Instruction: Gynecologic Symptomatic Terms

Study this table to prepare for the programmed review that follows.

TERM	MEANING
amenorrhea ă-men-ō-rē′ă	absence of menstruation
dysmenorrhea dis-men-ō-rē′ă	painful menstruation
oligomenorrhea ol′i-gō-men-ō-rē′ă	infrequent menstruation
anovulation an-ov-yū-lā′shŭn	absence of ovulation
dyspareunia dis-pa-rū′nē-ă	painful intercourse (coitus) (*dys* = painful; *para* = alongside of; *eunia* = bed)
leukorrhea lū-kō-rē′ă	abnormal white or yellow vaginal discharge
menorrhagia men-ō-rā′jē-ă	excessive bleeding at the time of menstruation
metrorrhagia mē′trō-rā′jē-ă	bleeding from the uterus at any time other than normal menstruation
oligo-ovulation ol′i-gō-ov′yū-lā′shŭn	irregular ovulation

Programmed Review: Gynecologic Symptomatic Terms

ANSWERS	REVIEW
men/o discharge, without amenorrhea	**14.34** The combining form for menstruation is _____. A number of symptomatic terms for different menstrual conditions are made with this combining form. Recall that the suffix -*rrhea* means _____. The prefix *a*- means _____. Therefore, the term for being without menstrual discharge (the absence of menstruation) is _____.
painful dysmenorrhea	**14.35** The prefix *dys*- means faulty, difficult, or _____. The term for painful menstruation (menstrual discharge) is _____.
deficient oligomenorrhea	**14.36** The prefix *oligo*- means few or _____. The term for infrequent menstruation is _____.
oligo-ovulation	**14.37** The same prefix (-*oligo*) is used in the term for irregular (deficient) ovulation: _____-_____.

ANSWERS	REVIEW
without anovulation	**14.38** The prefix *an-* means _____. The absence of ovulation, therefore, is termed _____.
blood or bleeding menorrhagia	**14.39** The suffix *-rrhagia* means to burst forth, usually referring to _____. Excessive bleeding during menstruation is therefore called _____.
uterus metrorrhagia	**14.40** The combining form *metr/o* means _____. Using this combining form, excessive bleeding from the uterus, other than in normal menstruation, is called _____.
leukorrhea	**14.41** The combining form *leuk/o* means white. An abnormal white or yellow discharge (from the vagina) is termed _____.
painful, difficult, or faulty dyspareunia	**14.42** Using the prefix *dys-* (meaning _____), painful intercourse is called _____.

Self-Instruction: Gynecologic Diagnostic Terms: General

Study this table to prepare for the programmed review that follows.

TERM	MEANING
cervicitis ser-vi-sī′tis	inflammation of the cervix
congenital anomalies kon-jen′i-tăl ah-nom′ah-lēz	birth defects that cause abnormal development of an organ or a structure (e.g., double uterus or absent vagina); also called *congenital irregularities*
congenital irregularities kon-jen′i-tăl ir-reg′yū-lăr′i-tēz	birth defects that cause abnormal development of an organ or a structure (e.g., double uterus or absent vagina); also called *congenital anomalies*
dermoid cyst děr′moyd sist	congenital tumor composed of displaced embryonic tissue (teeth, bone, cartilage, and hair); typically found in an ovary and usually benign
displacement of uterus (see **Figure 14-6**) dis-plăs′ment of yū′tĕr-ŭs	displacement of the uterus from its normal position
anteflexion an-tē-flek′shŭn	abnormal forward bending of the uterus (*ante* = before; *flexus* = bend)
retroflexion re-trō-flek′shŭn	abnormal backward bending of the uterus
retroversion re-trō-věr′zhŭn	backward turn of the whole uterus; also called *tipped uterus*

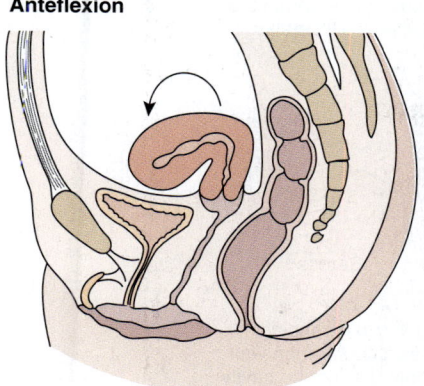
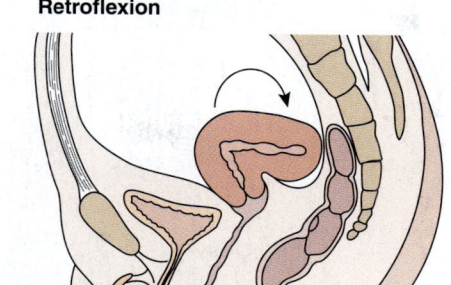
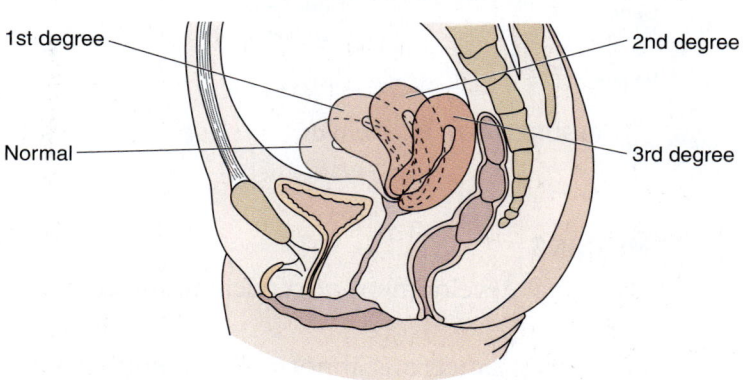

FIGURE 14-6 ■ Displacements of the uterus.

TERM	MEANING
endometriosis *en′dō-mē-trē-ō′sis*	condition characterized by migration of portions of endometrial tissue outside the uterine cavity
endometritis *en′dō-mē-trī′tis*	inflammation of the endometrium
fibroid (see Figure 14-7) *fī′broyd*	benign tumor in the uterus composed of smooth muscle and fibrous connective tissue; also called *fibromyoma* or *leiomyoma*
fibromyoma (see Figure 14-7) *fī′brō-mī-ō′mă*	benign tumor in the uterus composed of smooth muscle and fibrous connective tissue; also called *fibroid* or *leiomyoma*
leiomyoma (see Figure 14-7) *lī′ō-mī-ō′mă*	benign tumor in the uterus composed of smooth muscle and fibrous connective tissue; also called *fibroid* or *fibromyoma*
fistula *fis′tyū-lă*	abnormal passage, such as from one hollow organ to another (*fistula* = pipe)
rectovaginal fistula *rek-tō-vaj′i-năl fis′tyū-lă*	abnormal opening between the vagina and rectum
vesicovaginal fistula *ves-i-kō-vaj′i-năl fis′tyū-lă*	abnormal opening between the bladder and vagina

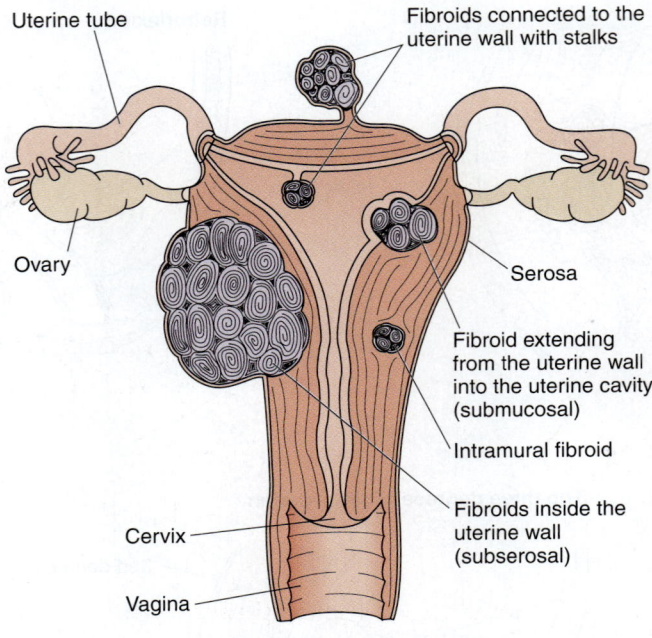

FIGURE 14-7 ■ Fibroids.

TERM	MEANING
cervical neoplasia sĕr′vi-kăl nē-ō-plā′zē-ă	abnormal development of cervical tissue cells
cervical intraepithelial neoplasia (CIN) sĕr′vi-kăl in′tră-ep-i-thē′lē-ăl nē-ō-plā′zē-ă	potentially cancerous abnormality of epithelial tissue of the cervix, graded according to the extent of abnormal cell formation: CIN-1: mild dysplasia CIN-2: moderate dysplasia CIN-3: severe dysplasia Also called *cervical dysplasia*
cervical dysplasia (see **Figure 14-11B**) sĕr′vi-kăl dis-plā′zē-ă	potentially cancerous abnormality of epithelial tissue of the cervix, graded according to the extent of abnormal cell formation: CIN-1: mild dysplasia CIN-2: moderate dysplasia CIN-3: severe dysplasia Also called *cervical intraepithelial neoplasia* (CIN)
carcinoma in situ (CIS) of the cervix kar-si-nō′mă in sī′tū of the sĕr′viks	malignant cell changes of the cervix that are localized, without any spread to adjacent structures
menopause men′ō-pawz	cessation of menstrual periods caused by lack of ovarian hormones
oophoritis ō′of-ōr-ī′tis	inflammation of one or both ovaries
parovarian cyst par-ō-var′ē-ăn sist	cyst of the uterine tube (fallopian tube)

TERM	MEANING
pelvic adhesions pel′vik ad-hē′zhŭnz	scarring of tissue within the pelvic cavity resulting from endometriosis, infection, or injury
pelvic inflammatory disease (PID) pel′vik in-flam′ă-tōr-ē di-zēz′	inflammation of organs in the pelvic cavity; usually includes the fallopian tubes, ovaries, and endometrium; most often caused by bacteria
pelvic floor relaxation (see Figure 14-8) pel′vik flōr rē-lak-sā′shŭn	relaxation of supportive ligaments of the pelvic organs
cystocele sis′tō-sēl	pouching of the bladder into the vagina
rectocele rek′tō-sēl	pouching of the rectum into the vagina
enterocele en′tĕr-ō-sēl	pouching sac of peritoneum between the vagina and the rectum
urethrocele yū-rē′thrō-sēl	pouching of the urethra into the vagina
prolapse prō-laps′	descent of the uterus down the vaginal canal
salpingitis sal-pin-jī′tis	inflammation of a fallopian tube

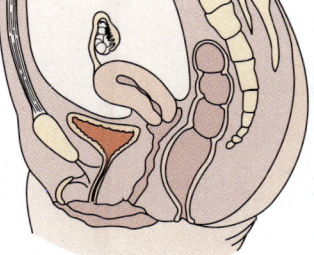
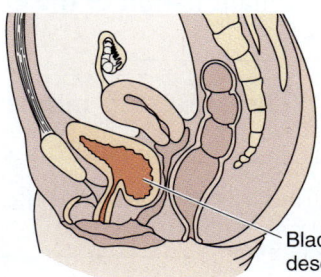
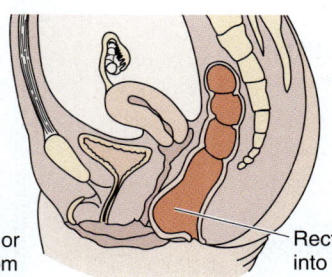
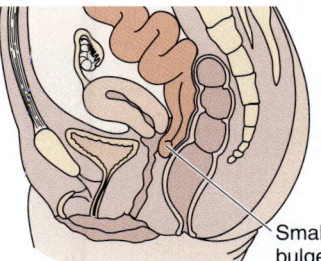
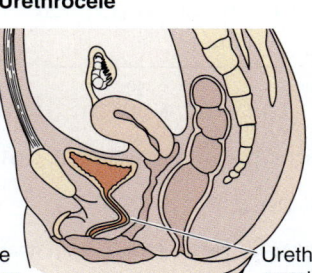
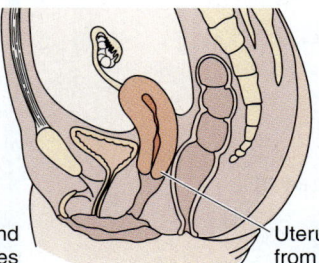

FIGURE 14-8 ■ Pelvic floor relaxation.

TERM	MEANING
vaginitis *vaj-i-nī'tis*	inflammation of the vagina with redness, swelling, and irritation; often caused by a specific organism, such as *Candida* (yeast) or *Trichomonas* (a sexually transmitted parasite)
atrophic vaginitis *ă-trof'ik vaj-i-nī'tis*	thinning of the vagina and loss of moisture because of depletion of estrogen, which causes inflammation of tissue
vaginosis *vaj-i-nō'sis*	infection of the vagina, with little or no inflammation, characterized by a milk-like discharge and an unpleasant odor; also known as nonspecific vaginitis

Programmed Review: Gynecologic Diagnostic Terms: General

ANSWERS	REVIEW
-itis cervicitis	14.43 The suffix for inflammation is _____. Inflammation of the cervix is called _____.
oophor/o oophoritis	14.44 The two combining forms for the ovaries are *ovari/o* and _____. Using the latter, inflammation of the ovaries is termed _____.
salping/o salpingitis	14.45 The combining form for fallopian tube (or Eustachian tube) is _____. Therefore, the term for inflammation of the fallopian tube is _____.
endometritis	14.46 Inflammation of the endometrium is _____.
condition endometriosis	14.47 The suffix *-osis* means increase or _____. Another condition of the endometrium, which involves endometrial tissue migrating outside the uterus, is called _____.
anomalies or irregularities dermoid	14.48 Birth defects involving abnormal development of a structure are called congenital _____. A congenital tumor composed of displaced embryonic tissue is called a _____ cyst.
displacement anteflexion backward version	14.49 In some women, the uterus is in a position in the abdomen that is somewhat different from normal. This atypical position is called a _____. If the uterus is bent (flexed) forward, the position is called _____. Retroflexion, however, is an abnormal _____ bending of the uterus. If the whole uterus is tipped or turned backward, it is called retro_____.

ANSWERS	REVIEW
-oma leiomyoma fiber or fibrous, fibromyoma fibroid	**14.50** Muscle and connective tissue in the uterus can give rise to tumors. The common suffix for a tumor is _____. Combined with *lei/o*, meaning smooth, and *my/o*, meaning muscle, the term _____ refers to a benign smooth muscle tumor, especially of the uterus. A synonymous term uses the combining forms for muscle and tumor, preceded by the combining form *fibr/o* to indicate the _____ consistency of the tissue: _____. An additional synonym simply refers to a uterine tumor that resembles fibers: _____.
fistula rectovaginal vesicovaginal	**14.51** An abnormal passage from one organ to another is called a _____, from the Latin word *fistula* (pipe). An abnormal opening between the rectum and vagina is a _____ fistula. An abnormal opening between the bladder (*vesic/o*) and the vagina is called a _____ fistula.
men/o menopause	**14.52** Again, the combining form for menstruation is _____. A cessation (pause) of menstruation, usually occurring in older women, is called _____.
uterine or fallopian	**14.53** A parovarian cyst is a cyst in the _____ tube.
pelvic adhesions	**14.54** Scarring of tissue in the pelvic cavity resulting from endometriosis, infection, or injury can cause pelvic tissues to adhere together; this is called _____ _____.
pelvic inflammatory	**14.55** Inflammation of the pelvic cavity, including the fallopian tubes, ovaries, and endometrium, is called _____ _____ disease (PID).
cervical neoplasia dysplasia	**14.56** Neoplasia is a general term describing a new formation of abnormal tissue, which may be benign or malignant. Any new formation of abnormal cervical tissue is called _____ _____. The term describing a condition of faulty formation of tissue with cancerous potential is _____. Cervical dysplasia is

ANSWERS	REVIEW
cervical intra	also known as _____ _____ epithelial neoplasia (CIN) and is classified according to the extent of abnormal cell formation. CIN-1 refers to _____ dysplasia, CIN-2
mild	
moderate	refers to _____ dysplasia, and CIN-3 refers to
severe dysplasia	_____ _____. Malignant neoplasia of the cervix that is localized without any spread to adjacent
in situ	structures is called carcinoma ____ _____ (CIS) of the cervix.
	14.57 Pelvic organs are supported with ligaments and other connective tissue. Relaxation of these supportive tissues, called
pelvic floor	_____ _____ relaxation, may allow anatomic changes or displacements. A descent of the uterus down the
prolapse	vaginal canal is called a _____.
	14.58 Recall that the suffix -*cele* means hernia or
pouching	_____. A pouching of the rectum (*rect/o*) into the
rectocele	vagina is called a _____.
	14.59 A pouching of the urethra (*urethr/o*), which is the tube that carries urine to outside of the body, into the vagina
urethrocele	is called a _____.
	14.60 *Cyst/o* is a combining form for bladder. A pouching of
cystocele	the bladder into the vagina is called a _____.
pouch	**14.61** An enterocele is a _____ing sac of peritoneum between the vagina and the rectum.
	14.62 Recall that the suffix meaning inflammation
-itis	is _____. Inflammation of the vagina is called
vaginitis	_____ and is often caused by a specific organism such as *Candida* (yeast) or *Trichomonas* (a sexually transmitted parasite). The specific kind of vaginitis involving thinning of the vagina and loss of moisture because of depletion of
atrophic	estrogen is called _____ vaginitis.
	14.63 The suffix -*osis* means increase or, simply, a
condition of	_____ ____. A vaginal condition involving infection but little or no inflammation is called
vaginosis	_____.

Self-Instruction: Gynecologic Diagnostic Terms: Sexually Transmitted Diseases

Note that sexually transmitted diseases are also referred to as *sexually transmitted infections* (STIs). Study this table to prepare for the programmed review that follows.

TERM	MEANING
MAJOR BACTERIAL SEXUALLY TRANSMITTED DISEASES (STDs)	
chlamydia *kla-mid′ē-ă*	most common sexually transmitted bacterial infection in North America; often occurs with no symptoms and is treated only after it has spread, such as after causing pelvic inflammatory disease (PID)
gonorrhea *gon-ō-rē′ă*	contagious inflammation of the genital mucous membranes caused by invasion of the gonococcus *Neisseria gonorrhoeae*; the term refers to the urethral discharge characteristic of the infection, which was first thought to be a leakage of semen (*gono* = seed; *rrhea* = discharge); the genus is named for the Polish dermatologist Albert Neisser
syphilis *sif′i-lis*	infectious disease caused by a spirochete transmitted via direct, intimate contact and that may involve any organ or tissue over time; usually manifests first on the skin, with the appearance of small, painless, red papules that erode and form bloodless ulcers called chancres
MAJOR VIRAL STDs	
hepatitis B virus (HBV) *hep-ă-tī′tis B vī′rŭs*	virus that causes an inflammation of the liver; transmitted through any body fluid, including vaginal secretions, semen, and blood
herpes simplex virus type 2 (HSV-2) (see Figure 14-9) *hĕr′pēz sim′pleks vī′rŭs tīp 2*	virus that causes ulcer-like lesions of the genital and anorectal skin and mucosa; after the initial infection, the virus lies dormant in the nerve cell root and may recur at times of stress
human immunodeficiency virus (HIV) *hyū′măn im′yū-nō-dē-fish′en-sē vī′rŭs*	virus that causes acquired immunodeficiency syndrome (AIDS), permitting various opportunistic infections, malignancies, and neurologic diseases; contracted through exposure to contaminated blood or body fluid (e.g., semen or vaginal secretions)

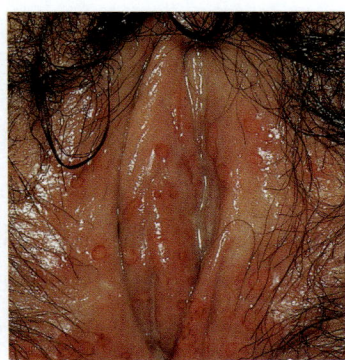

FIGURE 14-9 ■ Herpes simplex virus type 2.

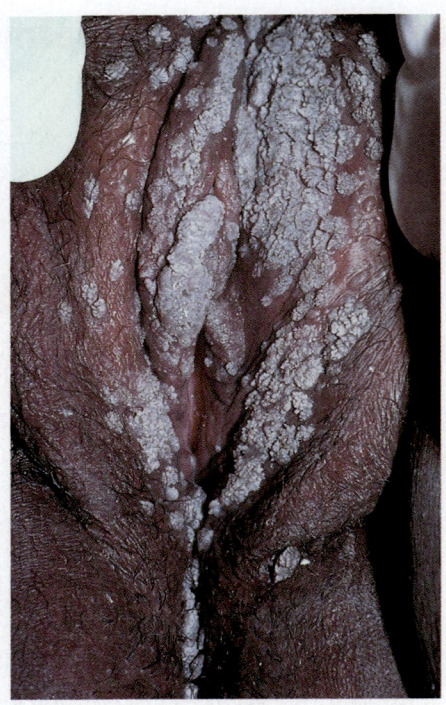

FIGURE 14-10 ■ Condylomata acuminata (genital warts) caused by human papillomavirus (HPV).

TERM	MEANING
human papillomavirus (HPV) (see Figure 14-10) hyū′măn pap-i-lō′mă vī′rŭs	virus transmitted by direct sexual contact; infection can manifest on the skin or mucous membranes of the genitals
condyloma acuminatum (pl. condylomata acuminata) kon-di-lō′mă ă-kyū′mi-nā′tŭm (kon-di-lō-mah′tă ă-kyū′mi-nā′tă)	lesion that appears as a result of human papilloma virus; on the skin, the lesions appear as cauliflower-like warts, and on mucous membranes, they have a flat appearance; also known as *venereal warts* or *genital warts*

Programmed Review: Gynecologic Diagnostic Terms: Sexually Transmitted Diseases

ANSWERS	REVIEW
chlamydia	**14.64** Most sexually transmitted diseases (STDs) are caused by bacteria or viruses. The most common bacterial STD in North America is _____. Like many bacterial diseases, chlamydia gets its name from the Latin genus name for the bacteria: *Chlamydia*. It may have no symptoms until it spreads, and it can cause pelvic inflammatory disease (PID).

ANSWERS	REVIEW
gonorrhea	**14.65** Another bacterial STD, the genus of which was named for the Polish dermatologist Albert Neisser, is called _____. It causes an inflammation of genital mucous membranes.
syphilis	**14.66** The bacterial STD caused by a spirochete that over time can involve any body tissue or organ is called _____.
hepatitis B	**14.67** Several viruses also cause STDs. The virus that causes inflammation of the liver, which can be spread through any body fluid, is _____ ____ virus (HBV).
herpes simplex virus	**14.68** HSV-2 is the abbreviation for the STD virus which typically lies dormant after the initial infection but recurs at times of stress: _____ _____ _____ type 2. It causes ulcer-like lesions on genital and anorectal skin.
human immunodeficiency virus	**14.69** The virus that causes acquired immunodeficiency syndrome (AIDS) is _____ _____ _____ (HIV).
papilloma	**14.70** HPV is the abbreviation for human _____ virus, which is characterized by lesions on the skin or mucous membranes. A condyloma is a warty growth; the plural of this term
condylomata, acuminata	is _____. Condylomata _____ are warty growths in the genital area caused by HPV.

Self-Instruction: Gynecologic Diagnostic Terms: Breasts

Study this table to prepare for the programmed review that follows.

TERM	MEANING
adenocarcinoma of the breast ad′ĕ-nō-kar-si-nō′mă of the brest	malignant tumor of glandular breast tissue
amastia ă-mas′tē-ă	absence of a breast
fibrocystic breasts fī-brō-sis′tik brests	benign condition of the breast consisting of fibrous and cystic changes that render the tissue more dense; patient feels painful lumps that fluctuate with menstrual periods
gynecomastia gī′nĕ-kō-mas′tē-ă	development of mammary glands in the male caused by altered hormone levels

TERM	MEANING
hypermastia *hī-pĕr-mas′tē-ă*	abnormally large breasts; also called *macromastia*
macromastia *mak-rō-mas′tē-ă*	abnormally large breasts; also called *hypermastia*
hypomastia *hī′po-mas′tē-ă*	unusually small breasts; also called *micromastia*
micromastia *mī′kro-mas′tē-ă*	unusually small breasts; also called *hypomastia*
mastitis *mas-tī′tis*	inflammation of the breast; most commonly occurs in women who are breastfeeding
polymastia *pol-ē-mas′tē-ă*	presence of more than two breasts
polythelia *pol-ē-thē′lē-ă*	presence of more than one nipple on a breast; also called *supernumerary nipples*
supernumerary nipples *sū-pĕr-nū′mĕr-ār-ē nip′ĕlz*	presence of more than one nipple on a breast; also called *polythelia*

Programmed Review: Gynecologic Diagnostic Terms: Breasts

ANSWERS	REVIEW
mast/o condition of without amastia	**14.71** There are two combining forms for breast: *mamm/o* and _____. The latter is used more frequently in gynecologic diagnostic terms. Recall that the suffix *-ia* means _____ _____. The prefix *a-* means _____. Thus, the condition of an absence of a breast is _____.
excessive hypermastia large macromastia	**14.72** The prefix *hyper-* means above or _____. The condition of abnormally large breasts is called _____. Recall that the prefix *macro-* means long or _____. It is used to form a synonym for hypermastia: _____.
hypo- micro- hypomastia, micromastia	**14.73** The prefix with a meaning opposite to that of *hyper-* is _____. The prefix with a meaning opposite to that of *macro-* is _____. Therefore, two terms for unusually small breasts are _____ and _____.
many polymastia condition of	**14.74** The prefix *poly-* means _____. The condition of having more than two (many) breasts is termed _____. The suffix *-ia* means _____ _____.
woman gynecomastia	**14.75** The combining form *gynec/o* means _____. The condition of a man developing mammary glands (i.e., developing like a woman) is called _____.

ANSWERS	REVIEW
-itis mastitis	**14.76** Again, the suffix denoting inflammation is _____. An inflammation of the breast is called _____.
fibrocystic	**14.77** A benign condition of the breasts in which fibrous and cystic changes occur is referred to as _____ breasts.
malignant	**14.78** An adenocarcinoma of the breast is a _____ tumor of glandular breast tissue.
many polythelia numerary	**14.79** The Greek word for nipple is thele. The prefix *poly-* means _____. The condition of having more than one nipple on a breast is called _____. These are also called super_____ nipples.

Self-Instruction: Gynecologic Diagnostic Tests and Procedures

Study this table to prepare for the programmed review that follows.

TEST OR PROCEDURE	EXPLANATION
biopsy (Bx) (see **Figure 14-11**) bī′op-sē	removal of tissue for microscopic pathologic examination
aspiration biopsy as-pi-rā′shŭn bī′op-sē	needle draw of tissue or fluid from a cavity for cytologic examination; also called *needle biopsy*
needle biopsy nēd′ĕl bī′op-sē	needle draw of tissue or fluid from a cavity for cytologic examination; also called *aspiration biopsy*
endoscopic biopsy en′dō-skop′ik bī′op-sē	removal of a specimen for biopsy during an endoscopic procedure (e.g., colposcopy)
excisional biopsy ek-sizh′ŭn-ăl bī′op-sē	removal of an entire lesion for microscopic examination
incisional biopsy in-si′zhŭn-năl bī′op-sē	removal of a piece of suspicious tissue for microscopic examination (e.g., cervical or endometrial biopsy)
stereotactic breast biopsy ster′ē-ō-tak′tik brest bī′op-sē	use of x-ray imaging, a specialized stereotactic frame, and a computer to calculate, precisely locate, and direct a needle into a breast lesion to remove a core specimen for biopsy
sentinel node breast biopsy sen′tĭ-nel nōd breast bī′op-sē	biopsy of the sentinel node (the first lymph node to receive lymphatic drainage from a tumor) in a breast with early cancer to determine metastases and, if no malignancy is found, to avoid the extensive removal of axillary nodes, which causes lymphedema (swelling under the arms); includes radionuclide imaging to locate the sentinel node (sentinel refers to guarding a point of entry)
colposcopy (see **Figure 14-12 A,B**) kol-pos′kŏ-pē	examination of the vagina and cervix using a colposcope, a specialized microscope which often has a camera attachment for photographs; used to document findings and for follow-up treatments

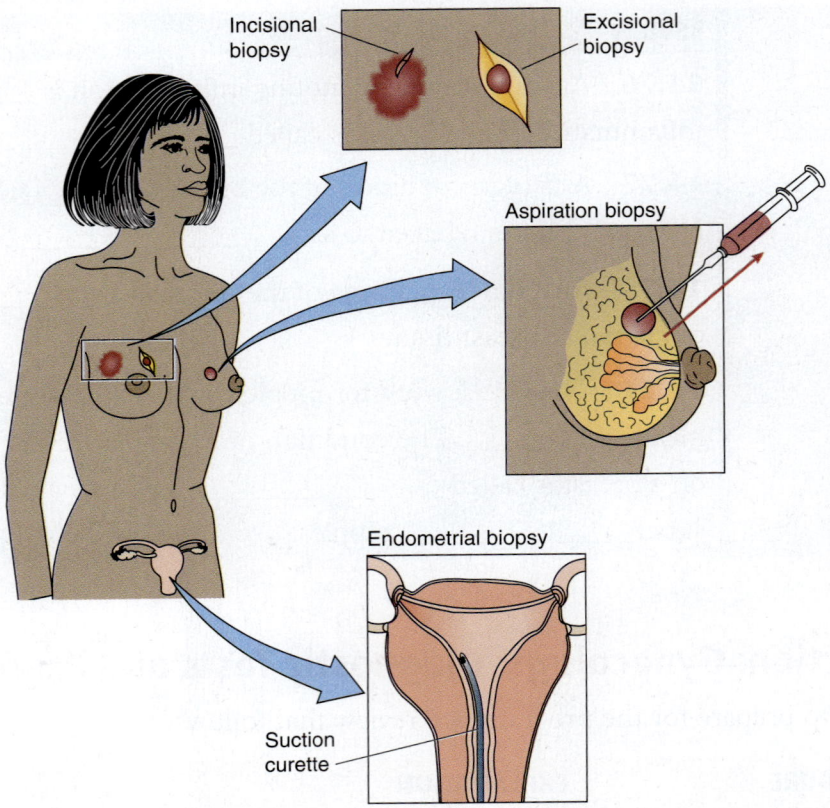

FIGURE 14-11 ■ Different types of biopsy.

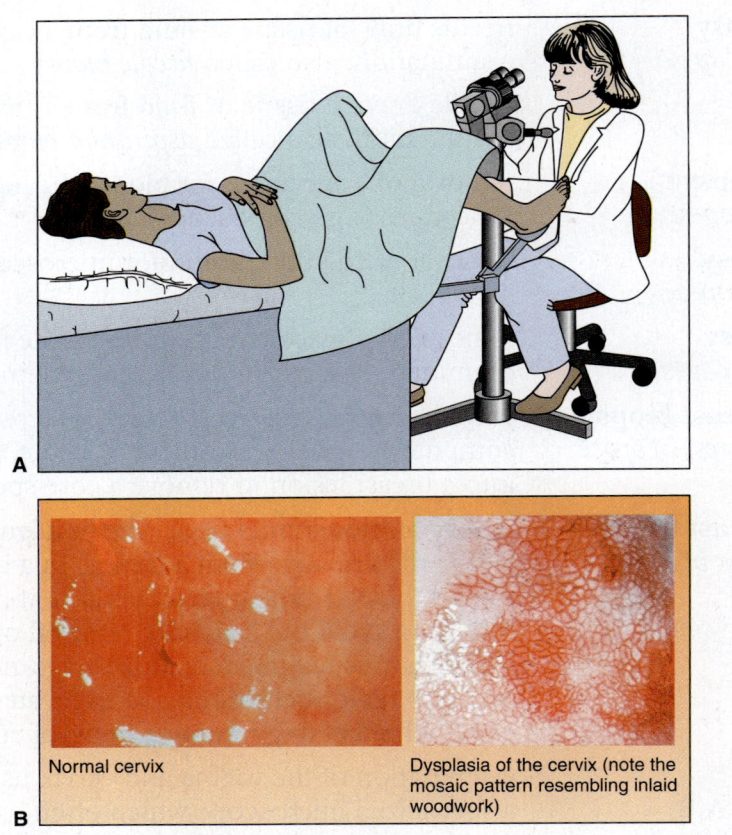

FIGURE 14-12 ■ **A.** Colposcopy. **B.** Photographs taken during cervical colposcopy.

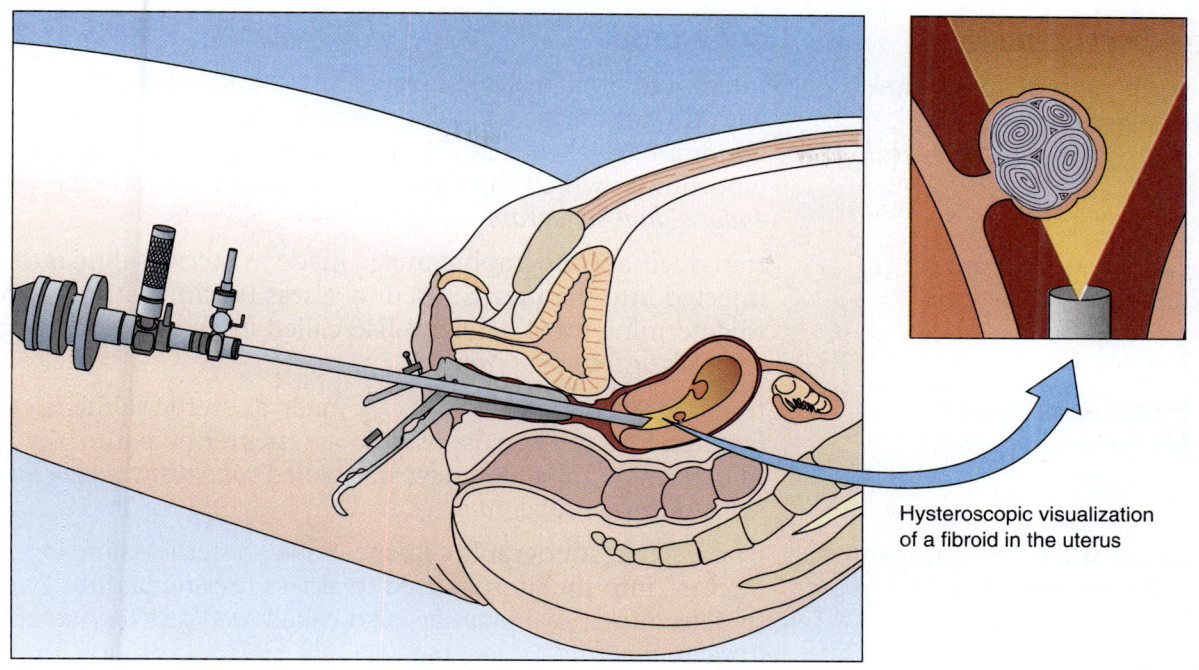

FIGURE 14-13 ■ Hysteroscopy.

TEST OR PROCEDURE	EXPLANATION
hysteroscopy (see Figure 14-13) *his′ter-os′kŏ-pē*	use of a hysteroscope to examine the intrauterine cavity for assessment of abnormalities (e.g., polyps, fibroids, or anomalies)
magnetic resonance imaging (MRI) *mag-net′ik rez′ō-nănts im′ă-jing*	use of nonionizing images to detect gynecologic conditions (e.g., anomalies of the pelvis or soft tissues of the breast) or to stage tumors arising from the endometrium or cervix
Papanicolaou (Pap) smear *pa-pă-ni′kō-lū (pap) smēr*	study of cells collected from the cervix to screen for cancer and other abnormalities
radiography *rā′dē-og′ră-fē*	x-ray imaging
hysterosalpingogram *his′tĕr-ō-sal-ping′gō-gram*	x-ray of the fallopian tubes after injection of a contrast medium through the cervix; used to determine tubal patency (openness)
mammogram *mam′ō-gram*	low-dose x-ray imaging of breast tissue to detect neoplasms
pelvic sonography (see Figure 14-14A) *pel′vik sŏ-nog′ră-fē*	ultrasound imaging of the female pelvis
endovaginal sonogram *en′dō-vaj′i-năl son′ō-gram*	ultrasound image of the uterus, tubes, and ovaries made with the ultrasonic transducer within the vagina to detect conditions such as ectopic pregnancy or missed abortion (abortion in which the fetus dies in utero); also called *transvaginal sonogram*

TEST OR PROCEDURE	EXPLANATION
transvaginal sonogram (see Figure 14-14B) *trans-vaj'i-năl son'ō-gram*	ultrasound image of the uterus, tubes, and ovaries made with the ultrasonic transducer within the vagina to detect conditions such as ectopic pregnancy or missed abortion (abortion in which the fetus dies in utero); also called *endovaginal sonogram*
sonohysterogram *son'ō-his-tĕr-ō-gram*	transvaginal sonographic image made as sterile saline is injected into the uterus; used to assess uterine pathology or to determine tubal patency; also called *hysterosonogram* and *saline infusion sonogram*
hysterosonogram *his-tēr-ō-son'ō-gram*	transvaginal sonographic image made as sterile saline is injected into the uterus; used to assess uterine pathology or to determine tubal patency; also called *sonohysterogram* and *saline infusion sonogram*
saline infusion sonogram *sā'lēn in-fyū'zhŭn son'ō-gram*	transvaginal sonographic image made as sterile saline is injected into the uterus; used to assess uterine pathology or to determine tubal patency; also called *sonohysterogram* and *hysterosonogram*
transabdominal sonogram *trans-ab-dom'i-năl son'ō-gram*	ultrasound image of the lower abdomen, including the bladder, uterus, tubes, and ovaries, to detect conditions such as cysts and tumors

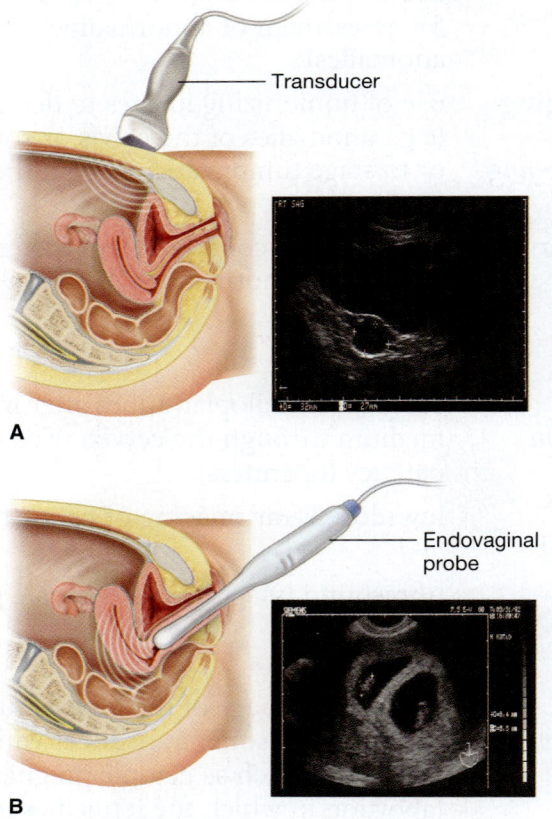

FIGURE 14-14 ■ Ultrasound. **A.** Pelvic ultrasound. **B.** Transvaginal ultrasound.

Programmed Review: Gynecologic Diagnostic Tests and Procedures

ANSWERS	REVIEW
biopsy needle excisional endoscopic incisional	**14.80** The removal of tissue from any part of the body for microscopic pathologic examination is called _____ (Bx). Several forms of biopsies can be performed in the female reproductive system. Use of a special, hollow needle to draw tissue or fluid from a cavity is called an aspiration biopsy or a _____ biopsy. If the entire lesion is removed (excised) for examination, this is called an _____ biopsy. Removal of the biopsy specimen during an endoscopic examination is called an _____ biopsy. Cutting out (incising) a small tissue sample for examination is called an _____ biopsy.
stereotactic breast	**14.81** Use of a computer, x-ray imaging, and a specialized stereotactic frame to direct a needle into a breast lesion to remove a core specimen for biopsy is called a _____ _____ biopsy.
sentinel node biopsy	**14.82** Sentinel refers to guarding a point of entry. The first lymph node to receive lymphatic drainage from a tumor therefore is referred to as the _____ node. Removal and microscopic pathologic examination of this node in a breast with early cancer is called a sentinel _____ _____.
process colp/o colposcopy	**14.83** Recall that the suffix *-scopy* means _____ of examination with an instrument. The two combining forms for vagina are *vagin/o* and _____. Using the latter form, the term for examination of the vagina using a specialized microscope is called _____.
hyster/o hysteroscopy	**14.84** Recall that the combining forms for uterus are *metr/o*, *uter/o*, and _____. Utilize the last form in the term for use of a special microscope to examine inside the uterus: _____.
magnetic resonance	**14.85** Gynecologic conditions are also diagnosed with nonionizing images made using _____ _____ imaging (MRI).
Pap	**14.86** The study of cells collected from the cervix to screen for abnormalities is called (in short) a _____ smear, named for Dr. Papanicolaou.

ANSWERS	REVIEW
radiography record mamm/o mammogram	**14.87** The medical term for x-ray imaging is _____. Recall that the suffix *-gram* means _____. The two combining forms for breast are *mast/o* and _____. Formed from the latter, the x-ray record of breast tissue made to detect neoplasms is called a _____.
salping/o uterus hysterosalpingogram	**14.88** The combining form for fallopian tube is _____. The medical term for an x-ray of the fallopian tubes after injection of a contrast medium uses this combining form as well as *hyster/o*, which means _____. This kind of x-ray image is called a _____.
pelvic within endovaginal through transvaginal transabdominal	**14.89** Sonography is the imaging modality using ultrasound. Ultrasound imaging of the female's pelvic area is called _____ sonography. Recall that the prefix *endo-* means _____. A sonogram made with the ultrasound transducer within the vagina is called an _____ sonogram. The prefix *trans-* means across or _____. An endovaginal sonogram is also called a _____ sonogram, because the sound waves pass through the vagina. An ultrasound image of the whole lower abdomen is called a _____ sonogram.
hyster/o sonohysterogram hysterosonogram	**14.90** Recall that the combining forms for uterus are *metr/o*, *uter/o*, and _____. Formed from the last of these combining forms, the term for a sonogram of the uterus made as sterile saline is injected into the uterus, is called a _____ or _____.

Self-Instruction: Gynecologic Operative Terms: General

Study this table to prepare for the programmed review that follows.

TERM	MEANING
adhesiolysis ad-hēz-ē-ol′ŏ-sis	breaking down or severing of pelvic adhesions; also called *adhesiotomy*
adhesiotomy ad-hē-zē-ot′ŏ-mē	breaking down or severing of pelvic adhesions; also called *adhesiolysis*
cervical conization sĕr′vi-kăl kō-nī-zā′shŭn	removal of a cone-shaped portion of the cervix

TERM	MEANING
colporrhaphy kol-pōr′ă-fē	suture to repair the vagina
colporrhaphy anterior repair kol-pōr′ă-fē an-tēr′ē-ōr rē-pār′	repair of a cystocele
colporrhaphy posterior repair kol-pōr′ă-fē pos-tēr′ē-ōr rē-pār′	repair of a rectocele
colporrhaphy A&P repair kol-pōr′ă-fē ā and pē rē-pār′	anterior and posterior repair of cystocele and rectocele
cryosurgery (see Figure 14-15 A–C) krī-ō-sŭr′jĕr-ē	method of destroying tissue by freezing; used for treating dysplasia and early cancers
dilation and curettage (D&C) (see Figure 14-16) dī-lā′shŭn and kū-rĕ-tahzh′	dilation of the cervix and scraping of the endometrium to control bleeding, to obtain tissue for biopsy, or to remove polyps or products of conception
hysterectomy his′ter-ek′tŏ-mē	removal of the uterus
abdominal hysterectomy ab-dom′i-năl his′ter-ek′tŏ-mē	removal of the uterus through an incision in the abdomen
vaginal hysterectomy vaj′i-năl his′ter-ek′tŏ-mē	removal of the uterus through the vagina
total hysterectomy tō′tăl his′ter-ek′tŏ-mē	removal of the uterus and the cervix

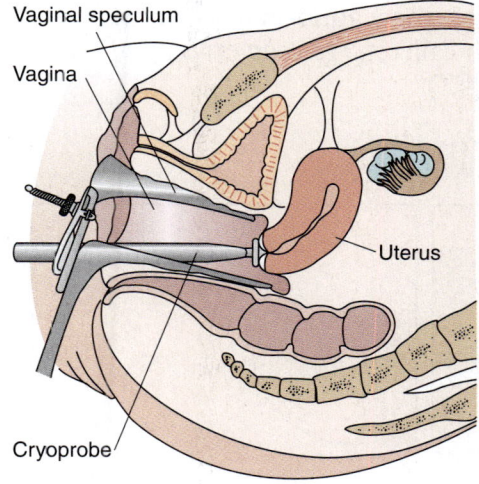

A

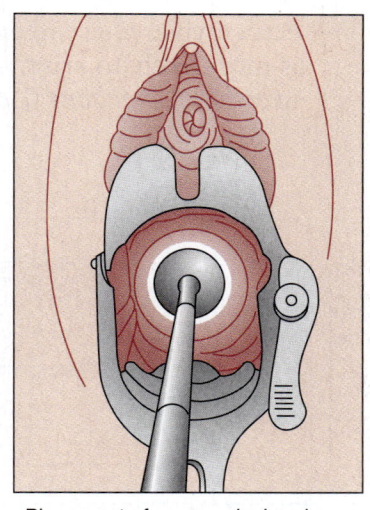

Placement of cryosurgical probe at treatment site

B

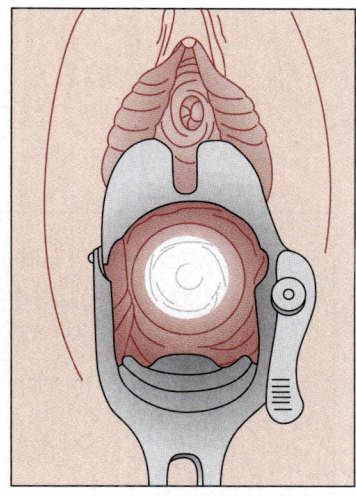

Ice crystals seen immediately after freezing treatment

C

FIGURE 14-15 ■ A–C. Cryosurgical procedure.

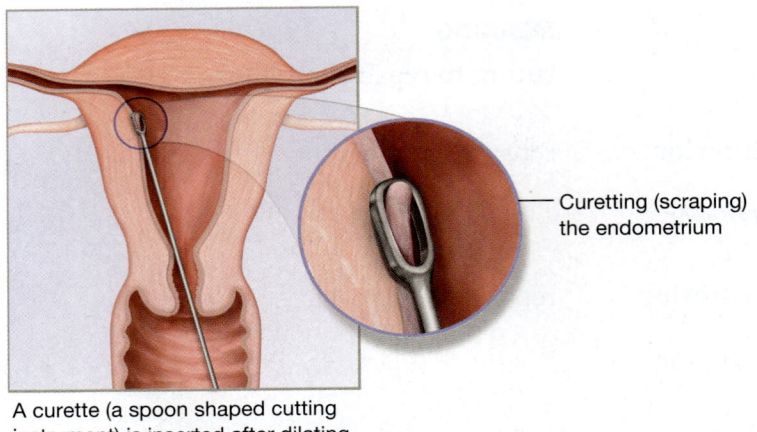

FIGURE 14-16 ■ Dilation and curettage (D&C).

TERM	MEANING
laparoscopy lap′ă-ros′kŏ-pē	inspection of the abdominal or pelvic cavity with a laparoscope, which is an endoscope used to examine the abdominal and pelvic regions
laparoscopic surgery lap-ă-ro-skop′ik sŭr′jĕr-ē	surgical procedures within the abdominal or pelvic region using a laparoscope
laser surgery lā′zer sŭr′jĕr-ē	use of a laser to destroy lesions or to dissect or cut tissue; used frequently in gynecology
loop electrosurgical excision procedure (LEEP) (see Figure 14-17 A–C) lūp ē-lek-trō-sŭr′ji-kăl ek-sizh′ŭn prō-sē′jŭr	use of electrosurgical or radio waves transformed through a loop-configured electrosurgical device to treat precancerous cervical lesions by simultaneous excisional biopsy and treatment of affected tissue (e.g., cervical dysplasia or human papilloma virus [HPV] lesions); note that the transformation zone is the area of the cervix (between the endocervix and ectocervix), where neoplasia (new abnormal cell formation) is most likely to arise; also called *large-loop excision of the transformation zone* (LLETZ)

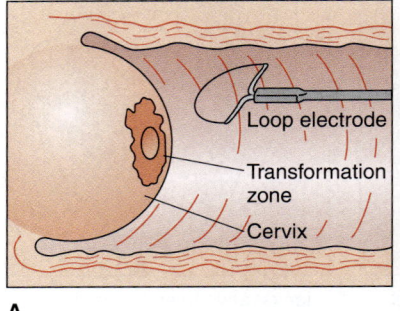
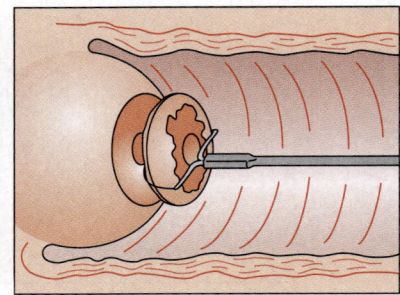
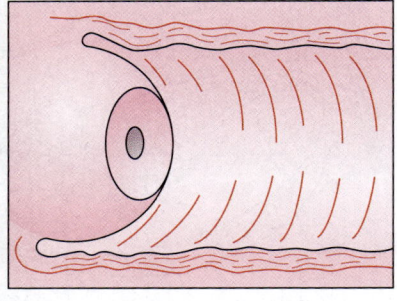

FIGURE 14-17 ■ Loop electrosurgical excision procedure (LEEP) or large-loop excision of the transformation zone (LLETZ). **A.** Electrode approach. **B.** Removal of transformation zone. **C.** Excision site (region between endocervix and ectocervix).

TERM	MEANING
large-loop excision of the transformation zone (LLETZ) (see Figure 14-17 A–C) larj-lūp ek-sizh'ŭn of the trans-fōr-mā'shŭn zōn	use of electrosurgical or radio waves transformed through a loop-configured electrosurgical device to treat precancerous cervical lesions by simultaneous excisional biopsy and treatment of affected tissue (e.g., cervical dysplasia or human papilloma virus [HPV] lesions); note that the transformation zone is the area of the cervix (between the endocervix and ectocervix), where neoplasia (new abnormal cell formation) is most likely to arise; also called *loop electrosurgical excision procedure* (LEEP)
myomectomy mī'ō-mek'tō-mē	excision of fibroid tumors
oophorectomy ō'of-ō-rek'tō-mē	excision of an ovary
ovarian cystectomy ō-var'ē-ăn sis-tek'tō-mē	excision of an ovarian cyst
salpingectomy sal'pin-jek'tŏ-mē	excision of a uterine tube
bilateral salpingo-oophorectomy bi-lat'ĕr-ăl sal-ping'gō-ō'of-ō-rek'tŏ-mē	excision of both uterine tubes and ovaries
salpingotomy sal-pin-jek'tō-mē	incision into a fallopian tube; often performed to remove an ectopic pregnancy
salpingostomy sal-ping-gos'tō-mē	creation of an opening in the fallopian tube to open a blockage
tubal ligation tū'băl lī-gā'shŭn	sterilization of a woman by cutting and tying (ligating) the uterine tubes

Programmed Review: Gynecologic Operative Terms: General

ANSWERS	REVIEW
excision hysterectomy abdominal vaginal total hysterectomy	14.91 Recall that the suffix *-ectomy* means _____ (or removal). Removal of the uterus is called _____. When performed through an incision in the abdomen, it is called an _____ hysterectomy. When removed through the vagina, it is called a _____ hysterectomy. The total removal of the uterus and cervix is called a _____.
myomectomy	14.92 A tumor of muscle tissue is called a myoma. Surgical removal of fibroid tumors from the muscle tissue of the uterus is called _____.
ovary oophorectomy	14.93 The combining form *oophor/o* means _____. Excision of an ovary is _____.

ANSWERS	REVIEW
ovarian cystectomy	14.94 Removal of an ovarian cyst is called an _____ _____.
salping/o salpingectomy	14.95 The combining form for uterine (fallopian) tube is _____. Excision of a fallopian tube is called _____.
both both bilateral salpingo-oophorectomy	14.96 The prefix *bi-* means two or _____. Thus, the term bilateral generally means on _____ sides. The term for excision of both uterine (fallopian) tubes and ovaries is _____ -_____.
incision salpingotomy	14.97 The operative suffix *-tomy* means _____. An incision into a fallopian tube is called a _____.
opening salpingostomy	14.98 The surgical suffix *-stomy* means the creation of an _____. The creation of an opening in the fallopian tube to open a blockage is called a _____.
tubal ligation	14.99 Ligation means tying off. The procedure for cutting and tying the uterine tubes to cause sterilization is _____ _____.
-tomy adhesiotomy breaking down	14.100 The surgical suffix for incision is _____. The breaking down or cutting of pelvic adhesions is called adhesiolysis or _____. The suffix *-lysis* means _____ _____ or dissolution.
cervical conization	14.101 The surgical removal of a cone-shaped portion of the cervix is called _____ _____.
suture colp/o colporrhaphy anterior posterior repair; pouching or hernia A&P	14.102 The surgical suffix *-rrhaphy* means _____. The two combining forms for vagina are *vagin/o* and _____. Formed from the latter form, a suture to repair the vagina is termed _____. A repair of a cystocele (in the front of the vagina) is an _____ repair. The repair of a rectocele (the back of the vagina) is called a _____ _____. Recall that *-cele* means a _____. When both the bladder and the rectum pouch into the vagina, creating both a cystocele and a rectocele, the repair of both is called an _____ repair (anterior and posterior repair).
cryosurgery	14.103 The combining form *cry/o* means cold. Surgery that destroys tissue by freezing it is called _____. This is used for treating dysplasia and early cancers.

ANSWERS	REVIEW
cervix dilation, curettage	**14.104** The D&C procedure is performed to control bleeding, to obtain tissue for biopsy, or to remove polyps or the products of conception. The _____ is dilated, and the endometrium is scraped (curettage). The abbreviation D&C stands for _____ and _____.
examination laparoscopy laparoscopic	**14.105** Recall that the suffix *-scopy* means process of _____ with a visualizing instrument. The combining form *lapar/o* refers to the abdomen generally. Thus, the examination of the abdominal and pelvic cavity with a special scope is called a _____. Surgery performed through the laparoscope is called _____ surgery.
laser	**14.106** A laser is often used in gynecologic procedures to destroy lesions or cut tissue. This is called _____ surgery.
loop electrosurgical excision transformation zone	**14.107** LEEP refers to a procedure using a loop-shaped device to make an electrosurgical excision of the transformation zone of the cervix; it is used to treat precancerous lesions, such as cervical dysplasia. LEEP is the abbreviation for _____ _____ _____ procedure. This procedure is also called LLETZ, or large-loop excision of the _____ _____.

Self-Instruction: Gynecologic Operative Terms: Breasts

Study this table to prepare for the programmed review that follows.

TERM	MEANING
lumpectomy lŭmp-ek′tŏ-mē	excision of a breast tumor without removing any other tissue or lymph nodes; usually followed by radiation or chemotherapy if the tumor is cancerous
mastectomy (see **Figure 14-18 A–C**) mas-tek′tŏ-mē	removal of a breast
simple mastectomy sim′pĕl mas-tek′tŏ-mē	removal of an entire breast but with the underlying muscle and axillary lymph nodes left intact
radical mastectomy rad′i-kăl mas-tek′tŏ-mē	removal of an entire breast along with the underlying chest muscles and axillary lymph nodes
modified radical mastectomy mod′i-fīd rad′i-kăl mas-tek′tŏ-mē	removal of an entire breast and lymph nodes of the axilla

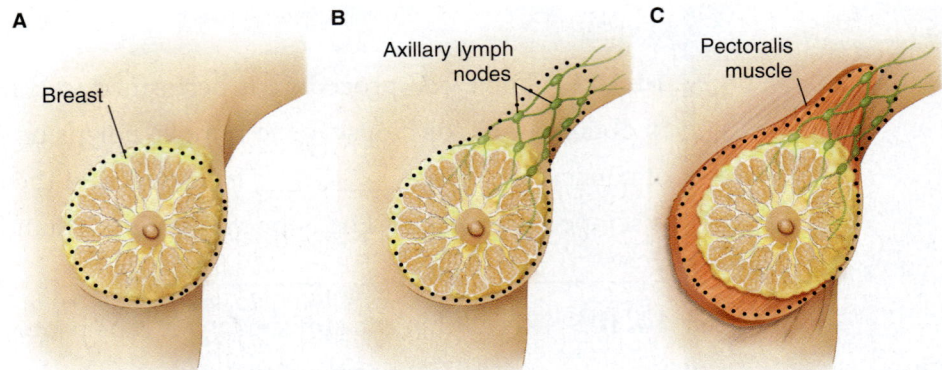

FIGURE 14-18 ■ Types of mastectomies. **A.** In a simple mastectomy, only the breast is removed. The underlying muscle and associated lymph nodes are not removed. **B.** In a modified radical mastectomy, the breast and lymph nodes of the axilla are removed. **C.** In a radical mastectomy, the breast, pectoralis muscle, and lymph nodes and fat tissue from the axillary region are removed.

TERM	MEANING
mammoplasty *mam′ō-plas-tē*	surgical reconstruction of a breast

augmentation mammoplasty
    (see Figure 14-19 A,B)
    awg-men-tā′shŭn mam′ō-plas-tē
	reconstruction to enlarge the breast, often by insertion of an implant

reduction mammoplasty *rē-dŭk′shŭn mam′ō-plas-tē*	reconstruction to remove excessive breast tissue
mastopexy *mas′tō-pek-sē*	elevation of pendulous breast tissue

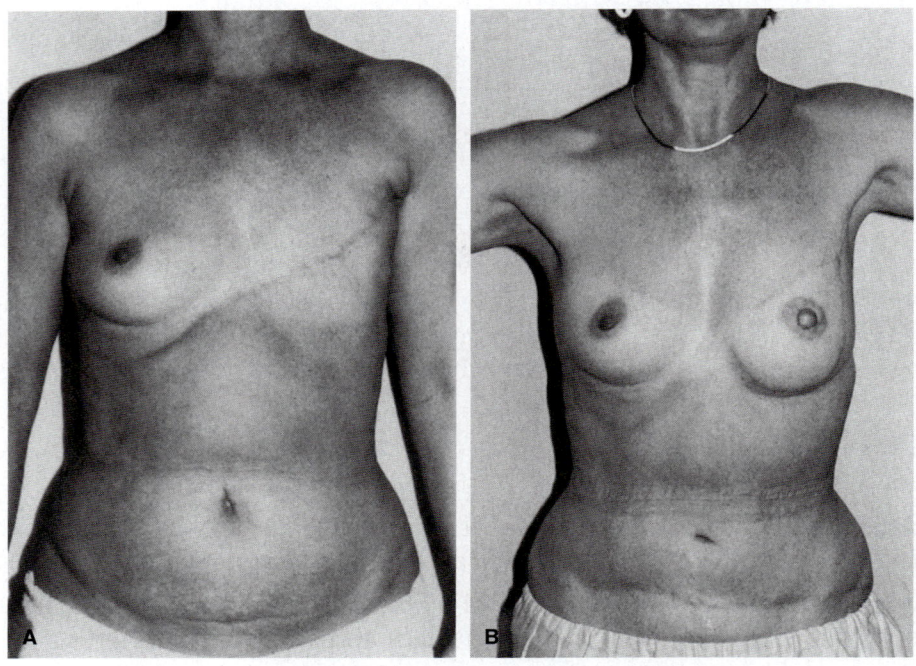

FIGURE 14-19 ■ Augmentation mammoplasty. **A.** Left modified radical mastectomy in a 53-year-old woman (3 months postoperation). **B.** Same patient 10 months after augmentation mammoplasty.

Programmed Review: Gynecologic Operative Terms: Breasts

ANSWERS	REVIEW
-ectomy lumpectomy	**14.108** The surgical suffix for excision (removal) is _____. The surgical removal of a breast tumor (lump) without removing other tissue or lymph nodes is called a _____.
mast/o mastectomy simple, radical mastectomy	**14.109** There are two combining forms meaning breast: *mamm/o* and _____. Formed from the latter, the term for surgical removal of a breast is _____. There are several different types of mastectomies, depending on how much tissue is removed to ensure the cancer is excised. Removal of just the breast, leaving the underlying muscle and axillary lymph nodes intact, is called a _____ mastectomy. A _____ mastectomy involves the removal of the breast as well as the underlying chest muscles and the axillary lymph nodes. A modified radical _____ removes the breast and lymph nodes only.
-plasty mamm/o mammoplasty	**14.110** Recall that the suffix for surgical reconstruction is _____. The two combining forms meaning breast are _____ and *mast/o*. Using the first of these, the term for surgical reconstruction of the breast is _____.
augmentation reduction mammoplasty	**14.111** A mammoplasty performed to enlarge the breast, usually by inserting an implant, is called _____ mammoplasty. A reconstruction performed to remove excessive breast tissue and, thereby, reduce the size of the breasts is called a _____ _____.
mast/o fixation mastopexy	**14.112** In addition to *mamm/o*, the other combining form for breast is _____. The surgical suffix *-pexy* means suspension or _____. The procedure to elevate pendulous breast tissue by fixing tissues higher is called a _____.

Self-Instruction: Gynecologic Therapeutic Terms

Study this table to prepare for the programmed review that follows.

TERM	MEANING
chemotherapy *kem-ō-thār′ă-pē*	treatment of malignancies, infections, and other diseases with chemical agents that destroy selected cells or impair their ability to reproduce
radiation therapy *rā-dē-ā′shŭn thār′ă-pē*	treatment of neoplastic disease using radiation to deter the proliferation of malignant cells

TERM	MEANING
hormone replacement therapy (HRT) hōr′mōn rē-plās′ment thār′ă-pē	use of a hormone (e.g., estrogen or progesterone) to replace a deficiency or to regulate production
hormonal contraceptives hōr-mō′năl kon-tră-sep′tivz	hormones used to prevent conception by suppressing ovulation
oral contraceptive pill (OCP) ōr′ăl kon-tră-sep′tiv pil	birth control pill
contraceptive injection kon-tră-sep′tiv in-jek′shŭn	injection of a contraceptive hormone (e.g., Depo-Provera) into the body
contraceptive implant kon-tră-sep′tiv im′plant	insertion of a contraceptive capsule under the skin to provide a continual infusion over an extended period
barrier contraceptives ba′rē-ĕr kon-tră-sep′tivz	products that provide a physical barrier to prevent conception (e.g., condoms or diaphragms)
intrauterine device (IUD) in′tră-yū′tĕr-in dē-vīs	contraceptive device inserted into the uterus that prevents implantation of a fertilized egg
spermicidals spĕr-mi-sī′dălz	creams, jellies, lotions, or foams containing agents that kill sperm (*cid/o* = to kill)

Programmed Review: Gynecologic Therapeutic Terms

ANSWERS	REVIEW
chemotherapy	**14.113** The combining form referring to chemical agents is *chem/o*. The treatment of malignancies, infections, and other diseases with chemical agents that destroy targeted cells is called _____.
radiation therapy	**14.114** Some kinds of cancer are treated with radiation, which deters the proliferation of malignant cells. This is called _____ _____.
hormone replacement	**14.115** If a woman is deficient in the production of a hormone, such as estrogen, treatment may involve administering a replacement hormone to the person. This is called _____ _____ therapy (HRT).
contraceptives against contraceptive contraceptive implant	**14.116** Hormones administered to prevent conception and pregnancy are called hormonal _____. The prefix *contra-* means _____ or opposed to. Oral _____ pills are generally called birth control pills. A hormonal contraceptive that is injected is called a _____ injection. Hormonal contraceptives also can be administered in a capsule that is placed under the skin to give a continual infusion; this is called a contraceptive _____.

ANSWERS	REVIEW
barrier	**14.117** Contraceptive methods that create a physical block to prevent sperm from reaching the ovum are called _____ contraceptives (e.g., a condom or a diaphragm).
intrauterine within	**14.118** IUD is the abbreviation for _____ device, which is inserted into the uterus to prevent implantation of a fertilized egg. The prefix *intra-* means _____.
spermicidals	**14.119** Contraceptive creams, jellies, lotions, and foams that contain an agent that kills (*cid/o* means to kill) sperm are called _____.

Self-Instruction: Obstetric Symptomatic Terms

Study this table to prepare for the programmed review that follows.

TERM	MEANING
gravida (see Figure 14-20) *grav′i-dă*	a pregnant woman; gravida followed by a number indicates the number of pregnancies
nulligravida *nŭl-i-grav′i-dă*	having never been pregnant
primigravida *prī-mi-grav′i-dă*	first pregnancy
para (see Figure 14-20) *par′ă*	to bear; a woman who has produced one or more viable (live outside the uterus) offspring; para followed by a number indicates the number of times a pregnancy has resulted in a single or multiple birth
nullipara *nŭ-lip′ă-ră*	a woman who has not borne a child (*nulli* = none; *para* = to bear)
primipara *prī-mip′ă-ră*	first delivery (*primi* = first; *para* = to bear)
multipara *mŭl-tip′ă-ră*	a woman who has given birth to two or more children (*multi* = many; *para* = to bear)
cervical effacement *sĕr′vi-kăl ē-făs′ment*	progressive obliteration of the endocervical canal during delivery
estimated date of confinement (EDC) *ĕs-ti-mā′ted dāt of kon-fīn′ment*	expected date for delivery of the baby; normally 280 days or 40 weeks from last menstrual period (LMP); also called *estimated date of delivery* (EDD)
estimated date of delivery (EDD) *ĕs-ti-mā′tĕd dāt of dē-liv′ĕr-ē*	expected date for delivery of the baby; normally 280 days or 40 weeks from last menstrual period (LMP); also called *estimated date of confinement* (EDC)

The following abbreviations are used in recording an obstetrical history.

GPA terms:
G   gravida   number of pregnancies
P   para   number of viable birth experiences (may include multiple births)
AB abortus   abortions
   SAB   spontaneous abortion
   TAB   therapeutic abortion

Arabic numerals are placed after each abbreviation to indicate the number of pregnancies, viable births, or abortions.

Example:

Obstetric history: G2, P1, AB1 or gravida 2, para 1, abortus 1.
[The patient has been pregnant twice, had one birth experience that resulted in the delivery of at least one viable offspring, and had one abortion.]

TPAL terms:
T   term infants
P   premature infants
A   abortions
L   living children

Example:

Obstetric history: 5 term infants, 0 premature infants, 0 abortions, 5 living children or Obstetric history: 5-0-0-5.
[The patient has delivered five term infants, no premature infants, no abortions and has five living children.]

Occasionally, combined GPA and TPAL abbreviations are used. For example:

Obstetrical history: gravida 3, 4-0-0-4
[The patient has been pregnant three times, had four term infants, no premature infants, no abortions, and has 4 living children. (Numbers indicate one twin birth.)]

FIGURE 14-20 ■ Obstetric history abbreviations.

TERM	MEANING
meconium staining mē-kō′nē-ŭm stān′ing	presence of meconium in amniotic fluid
ruptured membranes rŭp′chūrd mem′brānz	rupture of the amniotic sac, usually at onset of labor
macrosomia mak-rō-sō′mē-ă	large-bodied baby commonly seen in diabetic pregnancies (*macro* = large; *soma* = body)
polyhydramnios pol′ē-hī-dram′nē-os	excessive amniotic fluid

Programmed Review: Obstetric Symptomatic Terms

ANSWERS	REVIEW
pregnant nulli primigravida, first	**14.120** The obstetric term gravida refers to a _____ woman. The term for a woman who has never been pregnant is _____gravida, and the term for a woman in her first pregnancy is a _____. The prefix *primi-* means _____.
para no primipara multipara, multiple or many	**14.121** Similarly, there are several obstetric terms for women who have borne children, based on the term _____, which means to bear. A nullipara is a woman who has borne _____ children. A woman who has given birth once is _____. A woman who has borne multiple (two or more) children is _____. The prefix *multi-* means _____.
estimated date confinement, estimated date delivery last menstrual period	**14.122** A pregnant woman is given an expected due date by her obstetrician. In medical language, this date is referred to by two expressions: the _____ _____ of _____ (EDC), or the _____ _____ of _____ (EDD). This calculation is based on the date of the LMP, which stands for _____ _____ _____.
uterus many polyhydramnios	**14.123** Problems may occur with the amniotic fluid or sac. Recall that the amniotic sac surrounds the embryo and fetus in the woman's _____. The term for the condition of excessive amniotic fluid begins with the prefix *poly-*, which means _____ or much, and uses the combining form *hydr/o*, meaning water or fluid. This condition is called _____.
ruptured	**14.124** When the membranes of the amniotic sac break, usually during labor, this is called _____ membranes.
meconium staining	**14.125** Recall that the term for intestinal discharges of the fetus is _____. The presence of meconium in the amniotic fluid is called meconium _____.
effacement	**14.126** As labor progresses and approaches delivery, the endocervical canal is progressively obliterated in a process known as cervical _____.
large macrosomia	**14.127** Recall that the prefix *macro-* means _____ or long. The term for a large-bodied baby, often occurring in diabetic mothers, is _____.

Self-Instruction: Obstetric Diagnostic Terms

Study this table to prepare for the programmed review that follows.

TERM	MEANING
abortion (AB) ă-bōr′shŭn	expulsion of the products of conception before the fetus is viable (able to live outside the uterus)
spontaneous abortion (SAB) spon-tā′nē-ŭs ă-bōr′shŭn	miscarriage; naturally occurring expulsion of the products of conception
habitual abortion hă-bĭ′chū-ăl ă-bōr′shŭn	spontaneous abortion occurring in three or more consecutive pregnancies
incomplete abortion in-kom-plēt′ ă-bōr′shŭn	incomplete expulsion of the products of conception
missed abortion mist ă-bōr′shŭn	death of a fetus or embryo within the uterus that is not naturally expelled after death
threatened abortion thrĕ′tend ă-bōr′shŭn	bleeding with the threat of miscarriage
cephalopelvic disproportion (CPD) sef′ă-lō-pel′vik dis-prō-pōr′shŭn	condition preventing normal delivery through the birth canal; either the baby's head is too large or the birth canal is too small
eclampsia ek-lamp′sē-ă	true toxemia of pregnancy characterized by high blood pressure, albuminuria, edema of the legs and feet, severe headaches, dizziness, convulsions, and coma
preeclampsia prē-ē-klamp′sē-ă	toxemia of pregnancy characterized by high blood pressure, albuminuria, edema of the legs and feet, and puffiness of the face, without convulsion or coma; also called *pregnancy-induced hypertension* (PIH)
pregnancy-induced hypertension (PIH) preg-nan′sē-in-dūsd hī′per-ten′shŭn	toxemia of pregnancy characterized by high blood pressure, albuminuria, edema of the legs and feet, and puffiness of the face, without convulsion or coma; also called *preeclampsia*
ectopic pregnancy ek-top′ik preg′năn-sē	implantation of the fertilized egg outside the uterine cavity, often in the tube or ovary, or, rarely, in the abdominal cavity
erythroblastosis fetalis ĕ-rith′rō-blas-tō′sis fē-tā′lis	disorder that results from the incompatibility of a fetus with an Rh-positive blood factor and a mother with an Rh-negative blood factor, causing red blood cell destruction in the fetus; this condition necessitates a blood transfusion to save the fetus
Rh factor r-āch fak′tŏr	presence, or lack, of antigens on the surface of red blood cells that may cause a reaction between the blood of the mother and the fetus, resulting in fetal anemia, which causes erythroblastosis fetalis
Rh positive r-āch poz′i-tiv	presence of antigens
Rh negative r-āch neg′ă-tiv	absence of antigens

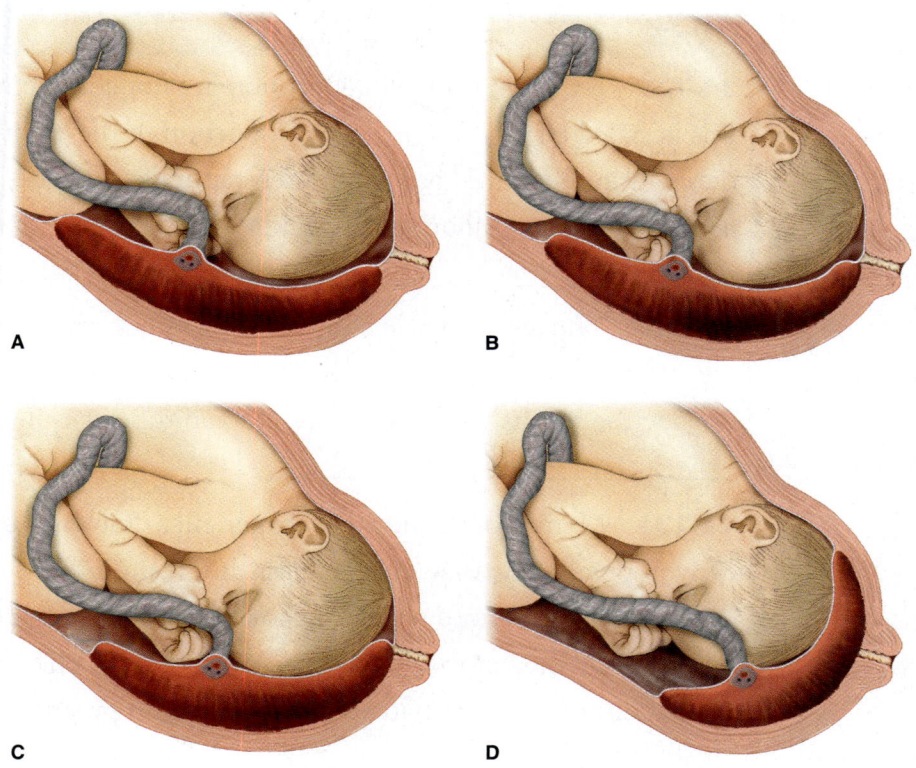

FIGURE 14-21 ■ Classification of placenta previa. **A.** Low-lying placenta. **B.** Marginal placenta previa. **C.** Partial placental previa. **D.** Complete central placental previa.

TERM	MEANING
hyperemesis gravidarum hī′pĕr-ē-mĕ′sis grah-vē-dar′ūm	severe nausea and vomiting in pregnancy that can cause severe dehydration in the mother and fetus (*emesis* = vomit)
meconium aspiration mē-kō′nē-ŭm as-pi-rā′shŭn	fetal aspiration of amniotic fluid containing meconium
placenta previa (see Figure 14-21 A–D) plă-sen′tă prē′vē-ă	displaced attachment of the placenta in the lower region of the uterine cavity
abruptio placentae ab-rŭp′shē-ō pla-sen′tē	premature detachment of a normally situated placenta

Programmed Review: Obstetric Diagnostic Terms

ANSWERS	REVIEW
abortion spontaneous habitual	**14.128** The expulsion of the products of conception before fetal viability is called _____. An abortion can occur naturally or therapeutically. A miscarriage, in which the expulsion occurs naturally, is called a _____ abortion (SAB). Spontaneous abortions occurring in three or more consecutive pregnancies are called _____ abortion.

ANSWERS	REVIEW
incomplete missed threatened	**14.129** If the products of conception are not completely expelled, this is called an _____ abortion. If the embryo or fetus dies within the uterus but is not then naturally expelled, this is called a _____ abortion. Bleeding with the threat of miscarriage is called a _____ abortion.
ectopic pregnancy	**14.130** The term ectopic comes from a Greek word meaning out of place. A pregnancy in which the fertilized egg is implanted outside the uterus, such as in the fallopian tube, is called an _____ _____.
excessive hyperemesis gravidarum	**14.131** Many women normally experience "morning sickness" early in pregnancy, but severe nausea and vomiting can cause dehydration. The word emesis means vomit. Recall that the prefix *hyper-* means above or _____. The term for the condition of severe nausea and vomiting in pregnancy is _____ _____.
high before preeclampsia pregnancy-induced excessive	**14.132** A serious condition that can occur in pregnancy, eclampsia is characterized by _____ blood pressure and other symptoms, leading to convulsions or coma. Recall that the prefix *pre-* means _____. A condition of high blood pressure similar to eclampsia, but occurring without convulsions or coma, may precede eclampsia. It is called _____, or _____-_____ hypertension (PIH). The prefix *hyper-* means _____ or above.
Rh positive Rh	**14.133** Certain antigens may or may not be present on the surface of red blood cells; this is called the _____ factor. The presence of antigens is designated as Rh _____, and the absence of these antigens is designated as _____ negative.
condition erythroblastosis fetalis	**14.134** If the blood of the mother is Rh negative and the blood of the fetus is Rh positive, a reaction will occur that causes fetal red blood cell destruction. Red blood cells are also called erythroblasts. Recall that the suffix *-osis* means increase or _____. The condition that results in the fetus from this incompatibility of Rh factors is called _____ _____. A blood transfusion is usually necessary to save the fetus.

ANSWERS	REVIEW
before placenta previa	**14.135** The term previa comes from a Latin word formed by the combination of *pre-*, meaning _____, and *-via*, meaning the way. If the placenta is attached in an abnormal position low in the uterus, it may obstruct the movement of the fetus out of the uterus at childbirth. This condition of a displaced placenta is called _____ _____.
abruptio placentae	**14.136** An abruption is a tearing away or detachment. The premature detachment of a normally situated placenta is called _____ _____.
amniotic meconium aspiration	**14.137** Recall that meconium staining refers to the presence of meconium in the _____ fluid. If this occurs, the fetus may suck this into its lungs, a condition called _____ _____.
head cephalopelvic	**14.138** Normally, the infant's head passes easily through the birth canal in the mother's pelvis. Recall that the combining form *cephal/o* means _____. If the infant's head is too large or the mother's pelvis is too small, a condition of _____ disproportion exists, complicating childbirth.

Self-Instruction: Obstetric Diagnostic Tests and Procedures

Study this table to prepare for the programmed review that follows.

TEST OR PROCEDURE	EXPLANATION
chorionic villus sampling (CVS) (see **Figure 14-22A**) kō-rē-on'ik vil'ŭs sam'pling	sampling of placental tissue for microscopic and chemical examination to detect fetal abnormalities
amniocentesis (see **Figure 14-22B**) am'nē-ō-sen-tē'sis	aspiration of a small amount of amniotic fluid for analysis of possible fetal abnormalities
fetal monitoring fē'tăl mon'i-tŏr-ing	use of an electronic device for simultaneous recording of fetal heart rate and uterine contractions
pelvimetry pel-vim'ĕ-trē	obstetric measurement of the pelvis to evaluate proper conditions for vaginal delivery
pregnancy test preg'nan-sē test	test performed on urine or blood to detect the presence of human chorionic gonadotropin hormone (secreted by the placenta), which indicates pregnancy

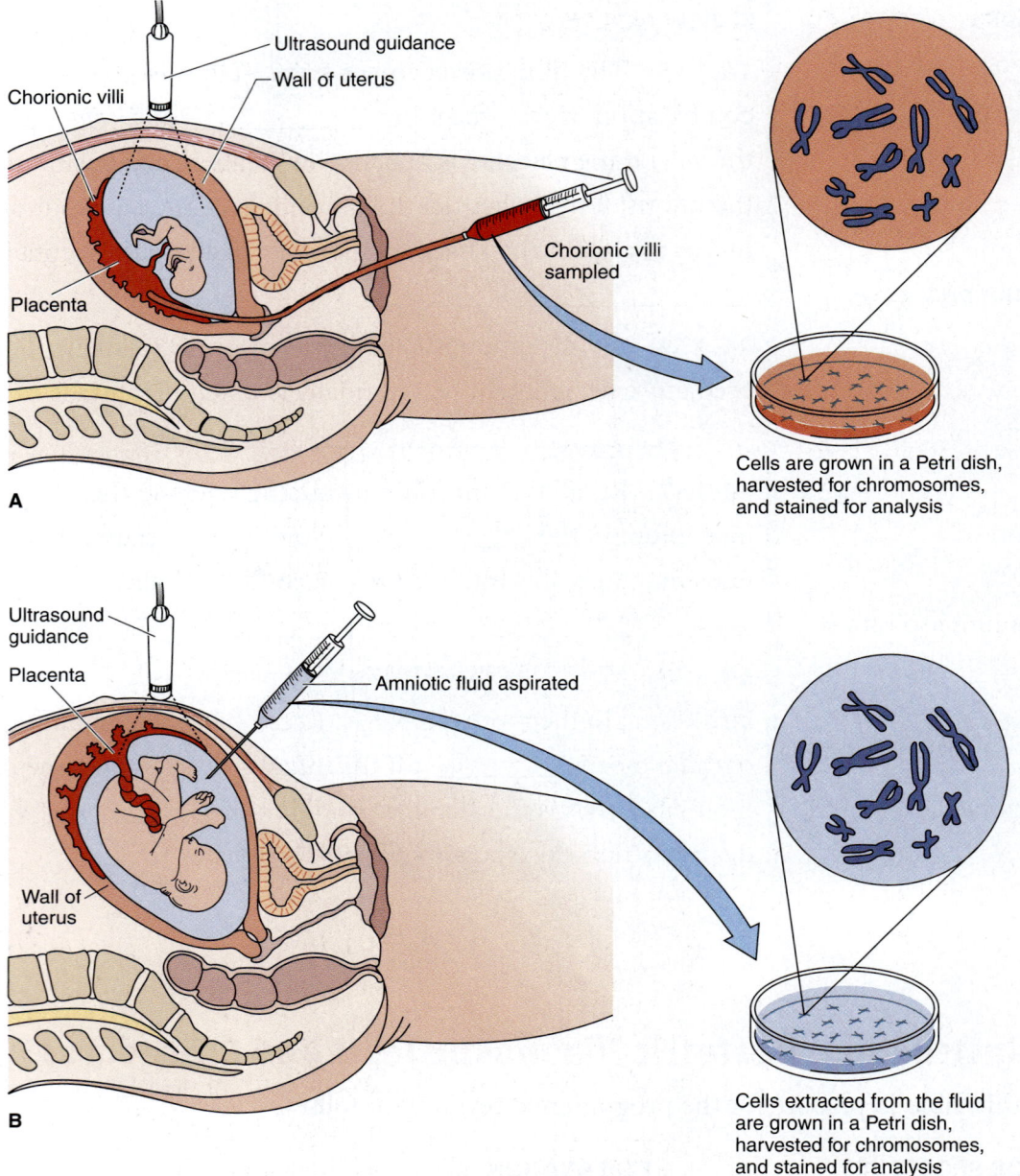

FIGURE 14-22 ■ Fetal cell sampling. **A.** Chorionic villus sampling (9 to 11 weeks). Chorionic villus sampling is a test performed by withdrawing cells from the villi of the chorion (the fetal portion of the placenta) through a needle inserted into the vagina. **B.** Amniocentesis (14 to 18 weeks). Amniocentesis collects cells from the amniotic fluid.

TEST OR PROCEDURE	EXPLANATION
pelvic sonography (see Figure 14-14) pel′vik sŏ-nog′ră-fē	ultrasound imaging of the female pelvis
endovaginal sonogram en′dō-vaj′i-năl son′ō-gram	ultrasound image of the uterus, tubes, and ovaries made after introduction of an ultrasonic transducer within the vagina; useful for detecting pathology (e.g., ectopic pregnancy or missed abortion); also called *transvaginal sonogram*

CHAPTER 14 • FEMALE REPRODUCTIVE SYSTEM AND OBSTETRICS

TEST OR PROCEDURE	EXPLANATION
transvaginal sonogram *trans-vaj′i-năl son′ō-gram*	ultrasound image of the uterus, tubes, and ovaries made after introduction of an ultrasonic transducer within the vagina; useful for detecting pathology (e.g., ectopic pregnancy or missed abortion); also called *endovaginal sonogram*
obstetric sonogram (see Figures 14-4 and 14-5) *ob-stet′rik son′ō-gram*	ultrasound image of the pregnant uterus to determine fetal development

Programmed Review: Obstetric Diagnostic Tests and Procedures

ANSWERS	REVIEW
aspiration amniocentesis	**14.139** Various diagnostic tests are often performed during pregnancy. Recall that the suffix *-centesis* refers to puncture for _____. Puncturing the amniotic sac and aspirating a small amount of amniotic fluid for analysis is called _____.
chorionic villus	**14.140** Another fetal sampling procedure is performed with placental tissue to detect fetal abnormalities. This is called _____ _____ sampling (CVS).
fetal monitoring	**14.141** The fetal heart rate and uterine contractions can be monitored with an electronic recording device; this process is called _____ _____.
-metry pelvimetry	**14.142** Recall that the suffix meaning process of measuring is _____. Obstetric measuring of the pelvis for conditions related to vaginal delivery is called _____.
pregnancy test	**14.143** A woman who suspects that she may be pregnant can have a _____ _____ performed with a blood or urine sample to detect whether she is pregnant.
obstetric within endovaginal transvaginal	**14.144** An ultrasound image of the pregnant uterus is called an _____ sonogram. Recall that the prefix *endo-* means _____. A sonogram made with the ultrasound transducer within the vagina is called an _____ sonogram, or a _____ sonogram (*trans* = through).

Self-Instruction: Obstetric Operative and Therapeutic Terms

Study this table to prepare for the programmed review that follows.

TERM	MEANING
OPERATIVE TERMS	
cesarean section (C-section) se-zā′rē-ăn sek′shŭn	surgical delivery of a baby via an incision through the abdomen and into the uterus
dilation and evacuation (D&E) dī-lā′shŭn and ē-vak-yū-ā′shŭn	dilation of the cervix and removal of the products of conception; most commonly performed in the second trimester of pregnancy, after a missed abortion
episiotomy e-piz-ē-ot′ō-mē	incision of the perineum to facilitate delivery of a baby
THERAPEUTIC TERMS	
amnioinfusion am′nē-ō-in-fyū′zhun	introduction of a solution into the amniotic sac; an isotonic solution is most commonly used to relieve fetal distress
therapeutic abortion (TAB) thār-ă-pyū′tik ă-bōr′shŭn	abortion induced by mechanical means or by drugs for medical reasons
version ver′zhŭn	manual method for reversing the position of the fetus, usually done to facilitate delivery
external version eks-těr′năl ver′zhŭn	abdominal manipulation
internal version in-těr′năl ver′zhŭn	intravaginal manipulation
COMMON THERAPEUTIC DRUG CLASSIFICATIONS	
abortifacient ă-bōr-ti-fā′shent	drug that causes abortion (e.g., mifepristone—formerly known as RU-486)
oxytocin ok′sē-tō′sin	hormone secreted by the pituitary gland that causes myometrial contraction; used to induce labor
Rh immune globulin r-āch i-myūn′ glob′yū-lin	immunizing agent given to an Rh-negative mother within 72 hours after delivering an Rh-positive baby to suppress the Rh immune response
tocolytic agent tō-kō-lit′ik ā′jent	drug used to stop labor contractions

Programmed Review: Obstetric Operative and Therapeutic Terms

ANSWERS	REVIEW
cesarean section	**14.145** The delivery of an infant through a surgical incision is named for a famous Roman emperor who was reputedly delivered in this manner: _____ _____ (C-section).

ANSWERS	REVIEW
episi/o, -tomy episiotomy	**14.146** There are two combining forms for vulva: *vulv/o* and _____. Recall that the suffix for incision is _____. Made with the latter combining form, the term for the surgical incision of the perineum to facilitate delivery is _____.
amnioinfusion	**14.147** To infuse means to introduce a fluid into a body area. The introduction of a solution into the amniotic sac is called _____.
abortion therapeutic abortion abortifacient	**14.148** Again, the expulsion of the products of conception is called an _____. When it is performed deliberately by mechanical or pharmacologic means, this is called a _____ _____ (TAB). A drug that causes abortion is called an _____.
dilation evacuation remove missed	**14.149** D&E is an abbreviation for _____ and _____, a surgical procedure performed in the second trimester of pregnancy to dilate the cervix and evacuate (or _____) the products of conception. This is typically done in cases of _____ abortion.
delivery external internal version	**14.150** Manual manipulation to change the position of the fetus to facilitate _____ is called version. This manipulation of the abdomen from the outside is called _____ version. When performed from within the vagina, it is called _____ _____.
oxytocin	**14.151** A hormone secreted by the pituitary gland causes uterine contractions. It is sometimes given to a pregnant woman to induce labor. This hormone is called _____.
birth tocolytic	**14.152** Recall that the combining form *toc/o* means _____. The suffix *-lytic* can mean to stop something. A type of drug given to stop labor contractions is called a _____.
immune globulin	**14.153** An Rh-negative mother who delivers an Rh-positive baby may have an immune response. The agent given to the mother to suppress that response is called Rh _____ _____.

Chapter 14 Abbreviations

ABBREVIATION	EXPANSION
AB	abortion
AIDS	acquired immunodeficiency syndrome
A&P	anterior and posterior
Bx	biopsy
CIN	cervical intraepithelial neoplasia
CIS	carcinoma in situ
CPD	cephalopelvic disproportion
C-section	cesarean section
CVS	chorionic villus sampling
D&C	dilation and curettage
D&E	dilation and evacuation
EDC	estimated date of confinement
EDD	estimated date of delivery
GYN	gynecology
HBV	hepatitis B virus
HIV	human immunodeficiency virus
HPV	human papillomavirus
HRT	hormone replacement therapy
HSV-2	herpes simplex virus type 2
IUD	intrauterine device
LEEP	loop electrosurgical excision procedure
LLETZ	large-loop excision of the transformation zone
LMP	last menstrual period
MRI	magnetic resonance imaging
OB	obstetrics
OCP	oral contraceptive pill
Pap	Papanicolaou (smear)
PID	pelvic inflammatory disease
PIH	pregnancy-induced hypertension
SAB	spontaneous abortion
STD	sexually transmitted disease
STI	sexually transmitted infection
TAB	therapeutic abortion

PRACTICE EXERCISES

For each of the following words, write out the term parts (prefixes [P], combining forms [CF], roots [R], and suffixes [S]) on the lines below the word. Then define the term according to the meaning of its parts.

EXAMPLE
ectocervical
ecto / cervic / al
P   R   S
DEFINITION: outside/cervix or neck/pertaining to

1. vulvitis
   _____ / _____
      R   S
   DEFINITION: _____

2. polymastia
   _____ / _____ / _____
      P   R   S
   DEFINITION: _____

3. ovoid
   _____ / _____
      R   S
   DEFINITION: _____

4. tocolysis
   _____ / _____
     CF   S
   DEFINITION: _____

5. salpingotomy
   _____ / _____
     CF   S
   DEFINITION: _____

Write out the expanded term for each abbreviation.

6. IUD _____

7. HPV _____

8. CVS _____

9. D&C _____

10. HBV _____

Write the letter of the matching term in the space provided.

11. removal of a uterine tube and an ovary _____ a. CPD
12. white vaginal discharge _____ b. leukorrhea
13. condition when baby's head is too big for birth canal _____ c. polythelia
14. presence of more than one nipple on a breast _____ d. ectopic
15. implantation of a fertilized egg outside the uterus _____ e. salpingo-oophorectomy

Write the correct medical term for each of the following definitions.

16. _____ condition of benign lumps in the breast that fluctuate with menstrual cycle
17. _____ abnormal opening between the bladder and vagina
18. _____ cutting and tying the uterine tubes
19. _____ having more than two breasts
20. _____ bacterial STD caused by a spirochete

Complete each medical term by writing the missing word or word part.

21. _____ pause = cessation of menstruation
22. _____ rrhea = painful menstruation
23. _____ rrhea = absence of menstruation
24. _____ rrhea = infrequent menstruation
25. _____ rrhagia = excessive bleeding at the time of menstruation

Identify the following terms related to abortion.

26. _____ a naturally occurring miscarriage
27. _____ a miscarriage occurring in three or more consecutive pregnancies
28. _____ fetal expulsion with parts of the placenta remaining, with bleeding
29. _____ fetal death within the uterus
30. _____ an abortion induced by mechanical means or by drugs

Write the letter of the matching term in the space provided.

31. retroflexion _____ a. genital warts
32. condylomata _____ b. pouching of the bladder into the vagina
33. para 2 _____ c. woman who has given birth twice
34. prolapse _____ d. backward bending of the uterus
35. cystocele _____ e. descent of uterus from normal position

Circle the combining form that corresponds to the meaning given.

36. birth or labor
    a. tox/o   b. toc/o   c. troph/o
37. vagina
    a. uter/o   b. metr/o   c. colp/o
38. uterine tube
    a. vagin/o   b. oophor/o   c. salping/o
39. menstruation
    a. men/o   b. mamm/o   c. mast/o
40. cervix
    a. colp/o   b. cervic/o   c. salping/o

Write the correct terms for the anatomic structures indicated.

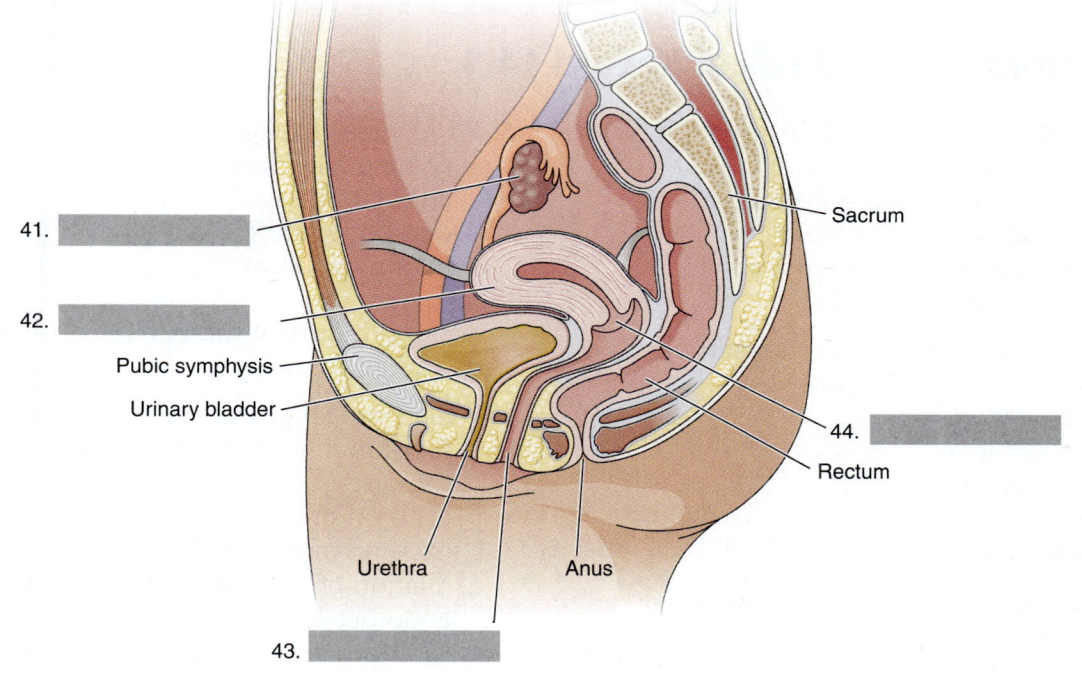

41. _____   43. _____
42. _____   44. _____

Circle the correct spelling in each set of words.

45. a. gonorrhea   b. gonorhea   c. ghonarhea
46. a. dispareunia   b. dyspareunia   c. dysparunia
47. a. tokolytic   b. toecolytic   c. tocolytic

Give the noun used to form each adjective.

48. chlamydial _____   49. areolar _____   50. syphilitic _____

MEDICAL RECORD ANALYSIS
Medical Record 14-1

GYN CHART NOTE

S: This 44 y/o female, gravida 2, para 2, c/o extremely heavy periods for the past several years that have been getting worse for the past 2 months and have been accompanied by moderately severe cramps. Pap smears have been normal. She has no bladder or bowel complaints.

O: On pelvic examination, the uterus is found to be retroverted and irregularly enlarged with several large fibroids palpable. There are no adnexal masses.

A: Leiomyomata uteri with secondary menorrhagia

P: Schedule vaginal hysterectomy; donate one pint of blood for autologous transfusion, if necessary

Questions About Medical Record 14-1

1. What is the patient's OB history?
   a. has never been pregnant
   b. has been pregnant only once
   c. has had two miscarriages
   d. has been pregnant four times
   e. has had two live births

2. Identify the patient's most significant symptom.
   a. amenorrhea
   b. dyspareunia
   c. leukorrhea
   d. menorrhagia
   e. metrorrhagia

3. Which of the following was one of the objective findings?
   a. tipped uterus
   b. forward bending uterus
   c. backward bending uterus
   d. presence of several ovarian tumors
   e. migration of portions of endometrial tissue

4. What was the condition of the patient's uterine tubes?
   a. not stated
   b. normal
   c. inflamed
   d. enlarged
   e. had been removed previously

5. What was the diagnosis?
   a. congenital tumor composed of displaced embryonic tissue
   b. cyst of the uterine tube
   c. inflammation of the organs of the pelvic cavity
   d. smooth muscle tumors in the uterus
   e. ovarian tumors

6. What surgical procedure is planned?
   a. incision into the uterine tube to remove the cyst
   b. excision of the uterus
   c. excision of the ovaries
   d. dilation of the cervix and scraping of the endometrium
   e. excision of the uterine tubes and both ovaries

ANSWERS TO PRACTICE EXERCISES

1. vulvitis
   R: vulv
   S: itis
   DEFINITION: vulva (covering)/inflammation
2. polymastia
   P: poly
   R: mast
   S: ia
   DEFINITION: many/breast/condition of
3. ovoid
   R: ov
   S: oid
   DEFINITION: egg/resembling
4. tocolysis
   CF: toco
   S: lysis
   DEFINITION: birth or labor/breaking down or dissolution
5. salpingotomy
   CF: salpingo
   S: tomy
   DEFINITION: uterine tube/incision
6. intrauterine device
7. human papilloma virus
8. chorionic villus sampling
9. dilation and curettage
10. hepatitis B virus
11. e
12. b
13. a
14. c
15. d
16. fibrocystic breasts
17. vesicovaginal fistula
18. tubal ligation
19. polymastia
20. syphilis
21. menopause
22. dysmenorrhea
23. amenorrhea
24. oligomenorrhea
25. menorrhagia
26. spontaneous abortion
27. habitual abortion
28. incomplete abortion
29. missed abortion
30. therapeutic abortion
31. d
32. a
33. c
34. e
35. b
36. toc/o
37. colp/o
38. salping/o
39. men/o
40. cervic/o
41. ovary
42. uterus
43. vagina
44. cervix
45. gonorrhea
46. dyspareunia
47. tocolytic
48. chlamydia
49. areola
50. syphilis

ANSWERS TO MEDICAL RECORD 14-1

1. e
2. d
3. a
4. b
5. d
6. b

APPENDIX A

GLOSSARY OF PREFIXES, SUFFIXES, AND COMBINING FORMS

TERM PART TO ENGLISH MEANING

TERM PART	MEANING
A	
a-	without
ab-	away from
abdomin/o	abdomen
-ac	pertaining to
acous/o	hearing
acr/o	extremity or topmost
-acusis	hearing condition
ad-	to, toward, or near
aden/o	gland
adip/o	fat
adren/o	adrenal gland
adrenal/o	adrenal gland
aer/o	air or gas
-al	pertaining to
albumin/o	protein
-algia	pain
alveol/o	alveolus (air sac)
ambi-	both
an-	without
an/o	anus
andr/o	male
angi/o	vessel
ankyl/o	crooked or stiff
ante-	before
anti-	against or opposed to
aort/o	aorta
appendic/o	appendix
aque/o	water
-ar	pertaining to
-arche	beginning
arteri/o	artery
arthr/o	joint

TERM PART	MEANING
articul/o	joint
-ary	pertaining to
-ase	an enzyme
-asthenia	weakness
ather/o	fatty paste
-ation	process
atri/o	atrium (chamber)
audi/o	hearing
aur/i	ear
B	
bacteri/o	bacteria
balan/o	glans penis (penis head)
bi-	two or both
bil/i	bile
-blast	germ or bud
blast/o	germ or bud
blephar/o	eyelid
brachi/o	arm
brady-	slow
bronch/o	bronchus (airway)
bronchi/o	bronchus (airway)
bronchiol/o	bronchiole (little airway)
bucc/o	cheek
C	
capn/o	carbon dioxide
carb/o	carbon dioxide
carcin/o	cancer
cardi/o	heart
cata-	down
-cele	pouching or hernia
celi/o	abdomen
-centesis	puncture for aspiration

TERM PART	MEANING
cephal/o	head
cerebell/o	cerebellum (little brain)
cerebr/o	cerebrum (largest part of brain)
cerumin/o	wax
cervic/o	neck or cervix
cheil/o	lip
chol/e	bile
chondr/o	cartilage (grainy)
chrom/o	color
chromat/o	color
chyl/o	juice
circum-	around
col/o	colon
colon/o	colon
colp/o	vagina (sheath)
con-	together or with
conjunctiv/o	conjunctiva (to bind together)
contra-	against or opposed to
corne/o	cornea
coron/o	circle or crown
cost/o	rib
crani/o	skull
crin/o	to secrete
cutane/o	skin
cyan/o	blue
cyst/o	bladder or sac
cyt/o	cell

D

TERM PART	MEANING
dacry/o	tear
dactyl/o	digit (finger or toe)
de-	from, down, or not
dent/i	teeth
derm/o	skin
dermat/o	skin
-desis	binding
dextr/o	right or on the right side
dia-	across or through
diaphor/o	profuse sweating
dips/o	thirst
dis-	separate from or apart
doch/o	duct
duoden/o	duodenum
-dynia	pain
dys-	painful, difficult, or faulty

E

TERM PART	MEANING
-e	noun marker
e-	out or away
-eal	pertaining to
ec-	out or away
-ectasis	expansion or dilation

TERM PART	MEANING
ecto-	outside
-ectomy	removal (excision)
-emesis	vomiting
-emia	blood condition
en-	within
encephal/o	entire brain
endo-	within
enter/o	small intestine
epi-	upon
epididym/o	epididymis (testes)
episi/o	vulva (covering)
erythr/o	red
esophag/o	esophagus
esthesi/o	sensation
eu-	good or normal
ex-	out or away
exo-	outside
extra-	outside

F

TERM PART	MEANING
fasci/o	fascia (a band)
femor/o	femur
fibr/o	fiber

G

TERM PART	MEANING
gangli/o	ganglion (swelling)
gastr/o	stomach
-gen	origin or production
gen/o	origin or production
-genesis	origin or production
gingiv/o	gum
gli/o	glue
glomerul/o	glomerulus (small ball)
gloss/o	tongue
glott/o	opening
gluc/o	sugar
glyc/o	sugar
gnos/o	knowing
-gram	record
-graph	instrument for recording
-graphy	process of recording
gynec/o	woman

H

TERM PART	MEANING
hem/o	blood
hemat/o	blood
hemi-	half
hepat/o	liver
hepatic/o	liver
herni/o	hernia
hidr/o	sweat
hist/o	tissue

APPENDIX A • GLOSSARY OF PREFIXES, SUFFIXES, AND COMBINING FORMS

TERM PART	MEANING
histi/o	tissue
hormon/o	hormone (set in motion)
hydr/o	water
hyper-	above or excessive
hypo-	below or deficient
hypn/o	sleep
hyster/o	uterus

I

TERM PART	MEANING
-ia	condition of
-iasis	formation of or presence of
-iatrics	treatment
-iatry	treatment
-ic	pertaining to
-icle	small
ile/o	ileum
immun/o	safe
infra-	below or under
inguin/o	groin
inter-	between
intra-	within
ir/o	iris (colored circle)
irid/o	iris (colored circle)
-ism	condition of
iso-	equal or like
-ist	one who specializes in
-itis	inflammation
-ium	structure or tissue

J

TERM PART	MEANING
jejun/o	jejunum (empty)

K

TERM PART	MEANING
kerat/o	hard or cornea
ket/o	ketone bodies
keton/o	ketone bodies
kinesi/o	movement
kyph/o	humped-back

L

TERM PART	MEANING
lacrim/o	tear
lact/o	milk
lapar/o	abdomen
laryng/o	larynx (voice box)
lei/o	smooth
-lepsy	seizure
leuc/o	white
leuk/o	white
lex/o	word or phrase
lingu/o	tongue
lip/o	fat
lith/o	stone
lob/o	lobe (a portion)

TERM PART	MEANING
-logist	one who specializes in the study or treatment of
-logy	study of
lord/o	bent
lumb/o	loin (lower back)
lymph/o	clear fluid
-lysis	breaking down or dissolution

M

TERM PART	MEANING
macro-	large or long
-malacia	softening
mamm/o	breast
-mania	abnormal impulse (attraction) toward
mast/o	breast
meat/o	opening
-megaly	enlargement
melan/o	black
men/o	menstruation
mening/o	meninges (membrane)
meningi/o	meninges (membrane)
meso-	middle
meta-	beyond, after, or change
-meter	instrument for measuring
metr/o	uterus
-metry	process of measuring
micro-	small
mono-	one
morph/o	form
multi-	many
muscul/o	muscle
my/o	muscle
myc/o	fungus
myel/o	bone marrow or spinal cord
myos/o	muscle
myring/o	eardrum

N

TERM PART	MEANING
narc/o	stupor or sleep
nas/o	nose
nat/i	birth
necr/o	death
neo-	new
nephr/o	kidney
neur/o	nerve

O

TERM PART	MEANING
ocul/o	eye
-oid	resembling
-ole	small
olig/o	few or deficient
-oma	tumor

TERM PART	MEANING
onc/o	tumor or mass
onych/o	nail
oophor/o	ovary
ophthalm/o	eye
-opia	condition of vision
opt/o	eye
orch/o	testis (testicle)
orchi/o	testis (testicle)
orchid/o	testis (testicle)
or/o	mouth
orth/o	straight, normal, or correct
-osis	condition or increase
oste/o	bone
ot/o	ear
-ous	pertaining to
ovari/o	ovary
ov/i	egg
ov/o	egg
ox/o	oxygen
P	
pachy-	thick
palat/o	palate
pan-	all
pancreat/o	pancreas
para-	alongside of or abnormal
-paresis	slight paralysis
patell/o	knee cap
path/o	disease
pector/o	chest
ped/o	child or foot
pelv/i	hip bone
-penia	abnormal reduction
per-	through or by
peri-	around
perine/o	perineum
peritone/o	peritoneum
-pexy	suspension or fixation
phac/o	lens (lentil)
phag/o	eat or swallow
phak/o	lens (lentil)
pharyng/o	pharynx (throat)
phas/o	speech
-phil	attraction for
-philia	attraction for
phleb/o	vein
phob/o	exaggerated fear or sensitivity
phon/o	voice or sound
phor/o	to carry or bear
phot/o	light
phren/o	diaphragm or mind
plas/o	formation

TERM PART	MEANING
-plasia	formation
-plasty	surgical repair or reconstruction
-plegia	paralysis
pleur/o	pleura
-pnea	breathing
pneum/o	air or lung
pneumon/o	air or lung
pod/o	foot
-poiesis	formation
poly-	many
post-	after or behind
pre-	before
presby/o	old age
pro-	before
proct/o	anus and rectum
prostat/o	prostate
psych/o	mind
-ptosis	falling or downward displacement
pulmon/o	lung
purpur/o	purple
py/o	pus
pyel/o	basin
pylor/o	pylorus (gatekeeper)
Q	
quadri-	four
R	
radi/o	radius or radiation (especially x-ray)
re-	again or back
rect/o	rectum
ren/o	kidney
reticul/o	a net
retin/o	retina
retro-	backward or behind
rhabd/o	rod shaped or striated (skeletal)
rhin/o	nose
-rrhage	to burst forth
-rrhagia	to burst forth
-rrhaphy	suture
-rrhea	discharge
-rrhexis	rupture
S	
salping/o	tube (uterine or auditory)
sarc/o	flesh
schiz/o	split or division
scler/o	hard or sclera

APPENDIX A • GLOSSARY OF PREFIXES, SUFFIXES, AND COMBINING FORMS

TERM PART	MEANING
scoli/o	twisted
-scope	instrument for examination
-scopy	process of examination
seb/o	sebum (oil)
semi-	half
sial/o	saliva
sigmoid/o	sigmoid colon
sinistr/o	left or on the left side
sinus/o	hollow (cavity)
somat/o	body
somn/o	sleep
somn/i	sleep
son/o	sound
-spasm	involuntary contraction
sperm/o	sperm (seed)
spermat/o	sperm (seed)
sphygm/o	pulse
spin/o	spine (thorn)
spir/o	breathing
splen/o	spleen
spondyl/o	vertebra
squam/o	scale
-stasis	stoppage, standing still
steat/o	fat
sten/o	narrow
stere/o	three-dimensional or solid
stern/o	sternum (breastbone; chest)
steth/o	chest
stomat/o	mouth
-stomy	creation of an opening
sub-	below or under
super-	above or excessive
supra-	above or excessive
sym-	together or with
syn-	together or with

T

TERM PART	MEANING
tachy-	fast
tax/o	order or coordination
ten/o	tendon (to stretch)
tend/o	tendon (to stretch)
tendin/o	tendon (to stretch)
test/o	testis (testicle)
thalam/o	thalamus (a room)
thorac/o	chest
thromb/o	clot
thym/o	thymus gland or mind
thyr/o	thyroid gland (shield)
thyroid/o	thyroid gland (shield)
-tic	pertaining to
toc/o	labor
tom/o	to cut
-tomy	incision
ton/o	tone or tension
tonsill/o	tonsil
top/o	place
tox/o	poison
toxic/o	poison
trache/o	trachea (windpipe)
trans-	across or through
tri-	three
trich/o	hair
-tripsy	crushing
troph/o	nourishment or development
tympan/o	eardrum

U

TERM PART	MEANING
-ula	small
-ule	small
uln/o	ulna
ultra-	beyond or excessive
uni-	one
ur/o	urine
ureter/o	ureter
urethr/o	urethra
urin/o	urine
uter/o	uterus
uvul/o	uvula

V

TERM PART	MEANING
vagin/o	vagina (sheath)
varic/o	swollen or twisted vein
vas/o	vessel
vascul/o	vessel
ven/o	vein
ventricul/o	ventricle (belly or pouch)
vertebr/o	vertebra
vesic/o	bladder or sac
vesicul/o	bladder or sac
vitre/o	glassy
vulv/o	vulva (covering)

X

TERM PART	MEANING
xanth/o	yellow
xer/o	dry

Y

TERM PART	MEANING
-y	condition or process of

ENGLISH MEANING TO TERM PART

MEANING	TERM PART
A	
abdomen	abdomin/o, celi/o, lapar/o
abnormal	para-
abnormal	-penia reduction
above	hyper-, super-, supra-
across	dia-, trans-
adrenal gland	adrenal/o
after	post-, meta-
again	re-
against	anti-, contra-
air	aer/o, pneum/o, pneumon/o
air sac	alveol/o
airway	bronch/o, bronchi/o
all	pan-
alongside of	para-
alveolus	alveol/o
anus	an/o
anus and rectum	proct/o
aorta	aort/o
apart	dis-
appendix	appendic/o
arm	brachi/o
around	circum-, peri-
artery	arteri/o
atrium (chamber)	atri/o
attraction for	-phil, -philia
away	e-, ec-, ex-
away from	ab-
B	
back	re-
backward	retro-
bacteria	bacteri/o
basin	pyel/o
before	ante-, pre-, pro-
beginning	-arche
behind	post-, retro-
below	hypo-, infra-, sub-
bent	lord/o
between	inter-
beyond	meta-, ultra-
bile	bil/i, chol/e
bile duct	choledoch/o
binding	-desis
birth	nat/i, toc/o
black	melan/o
bladder	cyst/o, vesic/o, vesicul/o
blood	hem/o, hemat/o
blood condition	-emia

MEANING	TERM PART
blue	cyan/o
body	somat/o
bone	oste/o
bone marrow	myel/o
both	ambi-, bi-
brain	cerebr/o (largest part of brain), encephal/o (entire brain)
breaking down	-lysis
breast	mamm/o, mast/o
breathing	-pnea, spir/o
bronchus	bronch/o, bronchi/o
bud	-blast, blast/o
burst forth	-rrhage, -rrhagia
C	
calculus	lith/o
cancer	carcin/o
carbon dioxide	capn/o, carb/o
carry	phor/o
cartilage (grainy)	chondr/o
cavity (sinus)	atri/o, sin/o
cell	cyt/o
cerebellum	cerebell/o
cervix	cervic/o
change	meta-
cheek	bucc/o
chest	pector/o, steth/o, thorac/o
child	ped/o
circle	coron/o
clear fluid	lymph/o
clot	thromb/o
colon	col/o, colon/o
colon, sigmoid	sigmoid/o
color	chrom/o, chromat/o
colored circle	irid/o, ir/o
condition	-osis
condition of	-ia, -ism, -ium, -y
contraction, involuntary	-spasm
coordination	tax/o
cornea	corne/o, kerat/o
correct	ortho-
creation of an opening	-stomy
crooked	ankyl/o
crown	coron/o
crushing	-tripsy
cut (to cut)	tom/o

MEANING	TERM PART
D	
death	necr/o
deficient	hypo-, olig/o
development	troph/o
diaphragm	phren/o
different	hetero-
difficult	dys-
digit (finger or toe)	dactyl/o
dilation or expansion	-ectasis
discharge	-rrhea
disease	path/o
dissolution	-lysis
division	schiz/o
down	de-
downward placement	-ptosis
dry	xer/o
duct	doch/o
duodenum	duoden/o
E	
ear	aur/i, ot/o
eardrum	myring/o, tympan/o
eat or swallow	phag/o
egg	ov/i, ov/o
enlargement	-megaly
enzyme	-ase
epididymis	epididym/o
equal	iso-
esophagus	esophag/o
examination	-scopy
excessive	hyper-, super-, supra-, ultra-
expansion or dilation	-ectasis
extremity	acr/o
eye	ocul/o, ophthalm/o, opt/o
eyelid	blephar/o
F	
falling	-ptosis
fascia	fasci/o
fast	tachy-
fat	adip/o, ather/o, lip/o, steat/o
faulty	dys-
fear, exaggerated	phob/o
femur	femor/o
few	olig/o
fiber	fibr/o
fixation	-pexy
flesh	sarc/o

MEANING	TERM PART
foot	pod/o, ped/o
form	morph/o
formation	-plasia, plas/o, -poiesis
formation of	-lasis
four	quadri-
from	de-
fungus	myc/o
G	
ganglion (swelling)	gangli/o
gas	aer/o
germ or bud	-blast, blast/o
gland	aden/o
glans penis (penis head)	balan/o
glassy	vitre/o
glomerulus	glomerul/o
glue	gli/o
good	eu-
groin	inguin/o
gums	gingiv/o
H	
hair	trich/o
half	hemi-, semi-
hard	kerat/o, scler/o
head	cephal/o
hearing	acous/o, audi/o
hearing condition	-acusis
heart	cardi/o
heat	therm/o
hernia	-cele, herni/o
hip bone	pelv/i
hormone (set in motion)	hormon/o
humped-back	kyph/o
I	
ileum	ile/o
incision	-tomy
increase	-osis
inflammation	-itis
instrument for examination	-scope
instrument for measuring	-meter
instrument for recording	-graph
J	
jejunum (empty)	jejun/o
joint	arthr/o, articul/o
juice	chyl/o

MEANING	TERM PART
K	
ketone bodies	ket/o, keton/o
kidney	nephr/o, ren/o
kneecap	patell/o
knowing	gnos/o
L	
labor	toc/o
large	macro-
larynx	laryng/o
left or on the left side	sinistr/o
lens	phac/o, phak/o
light	phot/o
like	iso-
lip	cheil/o
liver	hepat/o, hepatic/o
lobe	lob/o
loin (lower back)	lumb/o
long	macro-
lung	pneum/o, pneumon/o, pulmon/o
M	
male	andr/o
many	multi-, poly-
measuring, instrument for	-meter
measuring, process of	-metry
meninges	mening/o, meningi/o
menstruation	men/o
milk	lact/o
mind	psych/o, phren/o, thym/o
mouth	or/o, stomat/o
movement	kinesi/o
muscle	muscul/o, my/o, myos/o
N	
nail	onych/o
narrow	sten/o
near	ad-
neck	cervic/o
nerve	neur/o
net	reticul/o
new	neo-
normal	eu-, ortho-
nose	nas/o, rhin/o
not	de-
nourishment	troph/o

MEANING	TERM PART
O	
oil	seb/o
old age	presby-
one	mono-
one who specializes in	-ist
one who specializes in the study or treatment of	-logist
opening	glott/o, meat/o
opening, creation of	-stomy
opposed to	anti-, contra-
order	tax/o
origin	gen/o, -gen, -genesis
out	e-, ec-, ex-
outside	ecto-, exo-, extra-
ovary	oophor/o, ovari/o
oxygen	ox/o
P	
pain	-algia, -dynia
painful	dys-
palate	palat/o
pancreas	pancreat/o
paralysis	-plegia
paralysis, slight	-paresis
perineum	perine/o
peritoneum	peritone/o
pertaining to	-ac, -al, -ar, -ary, -eal, -ic, -ous, -tic
pharynx	pharyng/o
place	top/o
pleura	pleur/o
poison	tox/o, toxic/o
portion	lob/o
pouching	-cele
presence of	-iasis
process	-ation
process of	-y
production	gen/o, -gen, -genesis
prostate	prostat/o
protein	albumin/o
pulse	sphygm/o
puncture for aspiration	-centesis
purple	purpur/o
pus	py/o
pylorus	pylor/o

MEANING	TERM PART
R	
radius	radi/o
record	-gram
recording, process of	-graphy
rectum	proct/o, rect/o
red	erythr/o
removal (excision)	-ectomy
resembling	-oid
reticulum	reticul/o
retina	retin/o
rib	cost/o
right or on the right side	dextr/o
rod shaped	rhabd/o
rupture	-rrhexis
S	
sac	cyst/o, vesic/o, vesicul/o
safe	immun/o
saliva	sial/o
same	homo-
scale	squam/o
sclera	scler/o
sebum	seb/o
secrete	crin/o
seizure	-lepsy
self	auto-
sensation	esthesi/o
sensitivity, exaggerated	phob/o
separate from	dis-
sigmoid colon	sigmoid/o
sinus	sinus/o
skeletal	rhabd/o
skin	cutane/o, derm/o, dermat/o
skull	crani/o
sleep	hypn/o, somn/i, somn/o
slow	brady-
small	-icle, micro-, -ole, -ula, -ule
small intestine	enter/o
smooth	lei/o
softening	-malacia
sound	phon/o, son/o
sheath	vagin/o
specializes, one who	-ist
speech	phas/o
sperm	sperm/o, spermat/o

MEANING	TERM PART
spinal cord	myel/o
spine	spin/o
spleen	splen/o
split	schiz/o
sternum	stern/o
stiff	ankyl/o
stomach	gastr/o
stone	lith/o
stoppage, standing still	-stasis
straight	orth/o
striated	rhabd/o
structure	-ium
study of	-logy
study of, one who specializes in the	-logist
stupor	narc/o
sugar	gluc/o, glyc/o, glycos/o
surgical repair or reconstruction	-plasty
suspension	-pexy
suture	-rrhaphy
swallow	phag/o
sweat	hidr/o
sweat, profuse	diaphor/o
T	
tear	dacry/o, lacrim/o
teeth	dent/i
tendon	ten/o, tend/o, tendin/o
tension	ton/o
testis (testicle)	orch/o, orchi/o, orchid/o, test/o
thalamus	thalam/o
thick	pachy-
thirst	dips/o
three	tri-
three-dimensional	stere/o or solid
throat	pharyng/o
through	dia-, per-, trans-
thymus gland	thym/o
thyroid gland	thyr/o, thyroid/o
tissue	hist/o, -ium
to or toward	ad-
together	con-, sym-, syn-
tone	ton/o
tongue	gloss/o, lingu/o
tonsil	tonsill/o
topmost	acr/o
trachea	trache/o

MEANING	TERM PART
treatment	-iactrics, -iatry, -iatr/o
treatment of, one who specializes in the	-logist
tube (uterine or auditory)	salping/o
tumor	-oma, onc/o
twisted	scoli/o
two	bi-

U

MEANING	TERM PART
ulna	uln/o
under	infra-, sub-
upon	epi-
ureter	ureter/o
urethra	urethr/o
urine	ur/o, urin/o
uterus	hyster/o, metr/o, uter/o

V

MEANING	TERM PART
vagina	colp/o, vagin/o
vein	phleb/o, ven/o
vein, swollen or twisted	varic/o

MEANING	TERM PART
ventricle	ventricul/o
vertebra	vertebr/o, spondyl/o
vessel	angi/o, vas/o, vascul/o
vision, condition of	-opia
voice	phon/o
voice box	laryng/o
vomiting	-emesis
vulva	vulv/o, episi/o

W

MEANING	TERM PART
water	aque/o, hydr/o
wax	cerumin/o
weakness	-asthenia
white	leuc/o, leuk/o
windpipe	trache/o
with	con-, sym-, syn-
within	en-, endo-, intra-
without	a-, an-
woman	gynec/o
word, phrase	lex/o

Y

MEANING	TERM PART
yellow	xanth/o

APPENDIX B

ABBREVIATIONS AND SYMBOLS

Abbreviations and symbols that appear in red font are considered "Dangerous Abbreviations" and should not be used.

ABBREVIATION OR SYMBOL	MEANING
A	
ā	before
A	anterior; assessment
A&P	auscultation and percussion
A&W	alive and well
AB	abortion
ABG	arterial blood gas
a.c.	before meals
ACE	angiotensin-converting enzyme
ACS	acute coronary syndrome
ACTH	adrenocorticotropic hormone
AD	right ear
ad lib.	as desired
ADH	antidiuretic hormone
ADHD	attention-deficit/hyperactivity disorder
AIDS	acquired immunodeficiency syndrome
AKA	above-knee amputation
alb	albumin
ALS	amyotrophic lateral sclerosis
ALT	alanine aminotransferase (enzyme)
a.m.	morning
amt	amount
ANS	autonomic nervous system
AP	anterior-posterior
APKD	adult polycystic kidney disease
aq	water
AS	left ear
ASD	atrial septal defect

ABBREVIATION OR SYMBOL	MEANING
AST	aspartate aminotransferase (enzyme)
AU	both ears
AV	atrioventricular
B	
Ⓑ	bilateral
BAEP	brainstem auditory evoked potential
BAER	brainstem auditory evoked response
BCC	basal cell carcinoma
BD	bipolar disorder
b.i.d.	twice a day
BKA	below-knee amputation
BM	bowel movement
BMP	basic metabolic panel
BP	blood pressure
BPH	benign prostatic hypertrophy; benign prostatic hyperplasia
BRP	bathroom privileges
BS	blood sugar
BUN	blood urea nitrogen
Bx	biopsy
C	
c̄	with
C	Celsius; centigrade
C&S	culture and sensitivity
CABG	coronary artery bypass graft
CAD	coronary artery disease
cap	capsule
CAT	computed axial tomography
CBC	complete blood count

559

ABBREVIATION OR SYMBOL	MEANING
cc	cubic centimeter
CC	chief complaint
CCU	coronary (cardiac) care unit
CF	cystic fibrosis
CHF	congestive heart failure
CIN	cervical intraepithelial neoplasia
CIS	carcinoma in situ
cm	centimeter
CMP	comprehensive metabolic panel
CNS	central nervous system
c/o	complains of
CO	cardiac output
CO_2	carbon dioxide
COPD	chronic obstructive pulmonary disease
CP	cerebral palsy; chest pain
CPAP	continuous positive airway pressure
CPD	cephalopelvic disproportion
CPR	cardiopulmonary resuscitation
CSF	cerebrospinal fluid
CSII	continuous subcutaneous insulin infusion
CT	computed tomography
CTA	computed tomographic angiography
cu mm or mm^3	cubic millimeter
CVA	cerebrovascular accident
CVS	chorionic villus sampling
CXR	chest x-ray
D	
d	day
D&C	dilation and curettage
D&E	dilation and evacuation
DC	discharge; discontinue; doctor of chiropractic
DDS	doctor of dental surgery
DJD	degenerative joint disease
DKA	diabetic ketoacidosis
DO	doctor of osteopathy
DPM	doctor of podiatric medicine
dr	dram
DRE	digital rectal exam
DTR	deep tendon reflex
DVT	deep vein thrombosis
Dx	diagnosis

ABBREVIATION OR SYMBOL	MEANING
E	
ECG	electrocardiogram
echo	echocardiogram
ECT	electroconvulsive therapy
ECU	emergency care unit
ED	erectile dysfunction
EDC	estimated date of confinement
EDD	estimated date of delivery
EEG	electroencephalogram
EGD	esophagogastroduodenoscopy
EKG	electrocardiogram
EMG	electromyogram
ENT	ear, nose, and throat
EPS	electrophysiological study
ER	emergency room
ERCP	endoscopic retrograde cholangiopancreatography
ESR	erythrocyte sedimentation rate
ESWL	extracorporeal shock wave lithotripsy
ETOH	ethyl alcohol
EUS	endoscopic ultrasonography
F	
F	Fahrenheit
FBS	fasting blood sugar
Fe	iron
FH	family history
fl oz	fluid ounce
FS	frozen section
FSH	follicle-stimulating hormone
Fx	fracture
G	
g	gram
GAD	generalized anxiety disorder
GERD	gastroesophageal reflux disease
GH	growth hormone
GI	gastrointestinal
gm	gram
gr	grain
gt	drop
gtt	drops
GTT	glucose tolerance test
GYN	gynecology
H	
h	hour
H&H	hemoglobin and hematocrit

ABBREVIATION OR SYMBOL	MEANING
H&P	history and physical
HAV	hepatitis A virus
HBV	hepatitis B virus
HCT or Hct	hematocrit
HCV	hepatitis C virus
HD	Huntington disease
HEENT	head, eyes, ears, nose, and throat
HGB or Hgb	hemoglobin
HIV	human immunodeficiency virus
hpf	high-power field
HPI	history of present illness
HPV	human papilloma virus
HRT	hormone replacement therapy
h.s.	hour of sleep
HSV-1	herpes simplex virus type 1
HSV-2	herpes simplex virus type 2
Ht	height
HTN	hypertension
Hx	history

I

I&D	incision and drainage
ICD	implantable cardioverter defibrillator
ICU	intensive care unit
ID	intradermal
IM	intramuscular
IMP	impression
IOL	intraocular lens
IP	inpatient
IUD	intrauterine device
IV	intravenous
IVP	intravenous pyelogram
IVU	intravenous urogram

J

JCAHO	Joint Commission on Accreditation of Healthcare Organizations

K

kg	kilogram
KUB	kidneys, ureters, bladder

L

L	liter
Ⓛ	left
L&W	living and well
LASIK	laser-assisted in situ keratomileusis
lb	pound
LEEP	loop electrosurgical excision procedure
LH	luteinizing hormone
LLETZ	large-loop excision of transformation zone
LLQ	left lower quadrant
LP	lumbar puncture
lpf	low-power field
LTB	laryngotracheobronchitis
LUQ	left upper quadrant

M

m	meter
ⓜ	murmur
MCH	mean corpuscular (cell) hemoglobin
MCHC	mean corpuscular (cell) hemoglobin concentration
MCV	mean corpuscular (cell) volume
MD	medical doctor; muscular dystrophy
mg	milligram
MI	myocardial infarction
ml or mL	milliliter
mm	millimeter
mm³ or cu mm	cubic millimeter
MPI	myocardial perfusion image
MRA	magnetic resonance angiography
MRI	magnetic resonance imaging
MS	multiple sclerosis; musculoskeletal
MSH	melanocyte-stimulating hormone
MUGA	multiple-gated acquisition (scan)
MVP	mitral valve prolapse

N

NAD	no acute distress
NCV	nerve conduction velocity
NG	nasogastric
NK	natural killer (cell)
NKA	no known allergy
NKDA	no known drug allergy
noc.	night
NPO	nothing by mouth
NSAID	nonsteroidal anti-inflammatory drug
NSR	normal sinus rhythm

ABBREVIATION OR SYMBOL	MEANING
O	
O	objective
O_2	oxygen
OA	osteoarthritis
OB	obstetrics
OCD	obsessive-compulsive disorder
OCP	oral contraceptive pill
OD	right eye; doctor of optometry
OH	occupational history
OP	outpatient
OR	operating room
ORIF	open reduction, internal fixation
OS	left eye
OU	both eyes
oz	ounce
P	
p̄	after
P	plan; posterior; pulse
PA	posterior-anterior
PACU	postanesthetic care unit
$PaCO_2$	partial pressure of carbon dioxide
PaO_2	partial pressure of oxygen
Pap	Papanicolaou (smear)
PAR	postanesthetic recovery
p.c.	after meals
PCI	percutaneous coronary intervention
PD	panic disorder
PDA	patent ductus arteriosus
PE	physical examination; pulmonary embolism; polyethylene
PEFR	peak expiratory flow rate
per	by or through
PERRLA	pupils equal, round, and reactive to light and accommodation
PET	positron-emission tomography
PF	peak flow
PFT	pulmonary function testing
pH	potential of hydrogen
PH	past history
PI	present illness
PID	pelvic inflammatory disease

ABBREVIATION OR SYMBOL	MEANING
PIH	pregnancy-induced hypertension
p.m.	after noon
PLT	platelet
PMH	past medical history
PMN	polymorphonuclear (leukocyte)
PNS	peripheral nervous system
p.o.	by mouth
post-op or postop	postoperative
PPBS	postprandial blood sugar
PR	per rectum
pre-op or preop	preoperative
p.r.n.	as needed
PSA	prostate-specific antigen
PSG	polysomnography
pt	patient
PT	physical therapy; prothrombin time
PTCA	percutaneous transluminal coronary angioplasty
PTH	parathyroid hormone
PTSD	posttraumatic stress disorder
PTT	partial thromboplastin time
PUD	peptic ulcer disease
PV	per vagina
PVC	premature ventricular contraction
Px	physical examination
Q	
q	every
q.d. or QD	every day, daily
qh	every hour
q2h	every 2 hours
q.i.d.	four times a day
q.o.d.	every other day
qt	quart
R	
R	respiration
®	right
RA	rheumatoid arthritis
RBC	red blood cell; red blood count
RLQ	right lower quadrant
R/O	rule out
ROM	range of motion
ROS	review of symptoms
RP	retrograde pyelogram

ABBREVIATION OR SYMBOL	MEANING
RRR	regular rate and rhythm
RTC	return to clinic
RTO	return to office
RUQ	right upper quadrant
Rx	recipe; prescription
S	
s̄	without
S	subjective
SA	sinoatrial
SAB	spontaneous abortion
SAD	seasonal affective disorder
SC	subcutaneous
SCA	sudden cardiac arrest
SCC	squamous cell carcinoma
SH	social history
Sig:	instruction to patient
SLE	systemic lupus erythematosus
SOB	shortness of breath
SPECT	single-photon emission computed tomography
SpGr	specific gravity
SQ	subcutaneous
SR	systems review
s̄s̄	one-half
STAT	immediately
STD	sexually transmitted disease
SUI	stress urinary incontinence
suppos	suppository
SV	stroke volume
Sx	symptom
T	
T	temperature
T_3	triiodothyronine
T_4	thyroxine
T and A	tonsillectomy and adenoidectomy
tab	tablet
TAB	therapeutic abortion
TB	tuberculosis
TEDS	thromboembolic disease stockings
TEE	transesophageal echocardiogram
TIA	transient ischemic attack
t.i.d.	three times a day
TM	tympanic membrane
TMR	transmyocardial revascularization
tPA or TPA	tissue plasminogen activator
Tr	treatment
TSH	thyroid-stimulating hormone
TURP	transurethral resection of the prostate
TV	tidal volume
Tx	treatment; traction
U	
UA	urinalysis
UCHD	usual childhood diseases
URI	upper respiratory infection
US or U/S	ultrasound
UTI	urinary tract infection
V	
VC	vital capacity
VCU or VCUG	voiding cystourethrogram
V/Q	ventilation/perfusion
VS	vital signs
VSD	ventricular septal defect
V_T	tidal volume
W	
w.a.	while awake
WBC	white blood cell; white blood count
WDWN	well developed, well nourished
wk	week
WNL	within normal limits
Wt	weight
X	
x	times; for
x-ray	radiography
Y	
y.o. or y/o	year old
yr	year
♀	female
♂	male
#	number; pound
°	degree; hour
↑	increase; above
↓	decrease; below
✓	check
⊖	none; negative
⚢	standing
⚣	sitting
⚤	lying
×	times; for
>	greater than

ABBREVIATION OR SYMBOL	MEANING
<	less than
i	one
ii	two
iii	three

ABBREVIATION OR SYMBOL	MEANING
iv	four
I, II, III, IV, V, VI, VII, VIII, IX, and X	uppercase Roman numerals 1–10

APPENDIX C

TOP 100 COMMONLY PRESCRIBED DRUGS

This list has been selected to be representative of the most commonly prescribed drugs for the year 2016 (see references). The list is arranged starting with the most prescribed prescription medication. It includes the brand name, generic name, the drug's general class, and major therapeutic use. Combination products have their individual ingredients listed.

	BRAND NAME	GENERIC NAME	CLASS	USE
1	Norco	hydrocodone and acetaminophen	opioid analgesic	pain
2	Prinivil, Zestril	lisinopril	antihypertensive	hypertension
3	Synthroid	levothyroxine	thyroid hormone	hypothyroidism
4	Norvasc	amlodipine	antihypertensive	hypertension
5	Lipitor	atorvastatin	antihyperlipidemic	hyperlipidemia; hypercholesterolemia
6	Prilosec	omeprazole	proton pump inhibitor	peptic ulcer, gastroesophageal reflux
7	Zocor	simvastatin	antihyperlipidemic	hyperlipidemia; hypercholesterolemia
8	Glucophage	metformin	antidiabetic	type 2 diabetes mellitus
9	Amoxil	amoxicillin	antibiotic	bacterial infection
10	Zithromax	azithromycin	antibiotic	bacterial infection
11	Xanax	alprazolam	benzodiazepine	anxiety, muscle relaxant
12	Microzide	hydrochlorothiazide	antihypertensive	hypertension
13	Neurontin	gabapentin	anticonvulsant	neuralgia, epilepsy
14	Flonase	fluticasone propionate	nasal corticosteroid	allergic rhinitis
15	Ultram	tramadol	opioid analgesic	pain
16	Motrin	ibuprofen	nonsteroidal anti-inflammatory	pain, inflammation, fever
17	Zoloft	sertraline	antidepressant	depression
18	Deltasone	prednisone	steroid	inflammation; allergy
19	Lopressor	metoprolol tartrate	antihypertensive	hypertension
20	Toprol XL	metoprolol succinate	antihypertensive	hypertension
21	Cozaar	losartan	antihypertensive	hypertension

	BRAND NAME	GENERIC NAME	CLASS	USE
22	Lasix	furosemide	antihypertensive	hypertension
23	Ambien	zolpidem	hypnotic	insomnia
24	Celexa	citalopram	antidepressant	depression
25	Percocet	oxycodone and acetaminophen	opioid analgesic	pain
26	Pravachol	pravastatin	antihyperlipidemic	hyperlipidemia; hypercholesterolemia
27	Singulair	montelukast	leukotriene receptor antagonist	asthma
28	ProAir HFA, Ventolin HFA	albuterol	inhaled beta-2 agonist	asthma, bronchitis
29	Flexeril	cyclobenzaprine	skeletal muscle relaxant	muscle spasms, muscle spasticity
30	Klonopin	clonazepam	benzodiazepine	epilepsy, seizures, anxiety
31	Prozac	fluoxetine	antidepressant	depression
32	Prinzide, Zestoretic	lisinopril and hydrochlorothiazide	antihypertensive	hypertension
33	Tenormin	atenolol	antihypertensive	hypertension
34	Protonix	pantoprazole	proton pump inhibitor	peptic ulcer disease (PUD), gastroesophageal reflux disease (GERD)
35	Mobic	meloxicam	nonsteroidal anti-inflammatory	osteoarthritis
36	Lexapro	escitalopram	antidepressant	depression
37	Desyrel	trazodone	antidepressant	depression
38	Augmentin	amoxicillin and clavulanate	antibiotic	bacterial infection
39	Ativan	lorazepam	benzodiazepine	anxiety, preoperative sedation, epilepsy, seizures
40	Cipro	ciprofloxacin	antibiotic	bacterial infection
41	K-Dur, Klor-Con	potassium chloride	mineral supplement	hypokalemia
42	Coreg	carvedilol	antihypertensive	hypertension
43	Keflex	cephalexin	antibiotic	bacterial infection
44	Plavix	clopidogrel	anti-platelet	reduction in stroke or myocardial infarction risk by excessive clot prevention
45	Bactrim	sulfamethoxazole and trimethoprim	antibiotic	bacterial infection

APPENDIX C • TOP 100 COMMONLY PRESCRIBED DRUGS

	BRAND NAME	GENERIC NAME	CLASS	USE
46	Coumadin	warfarin	anticoagulant	thromboembolic disorders
47	Crestor	rosuvastatin	antihyperlipidemic	hyperlipidemia, hypercholesterolemia
48	Flomax	tamsulosin	alpha-1 blocker	benign prostatic hypertrophy (BPH)
49	Zantac	ranitidine	H_2 antagonist	peptic ulcer disease (PUD), gastroesophageal reflux disease (GERD)
50	Naprosyn	naproxen	nonsteroidal anti-inflammatory	pain, inflammation, fever
51	Diflucan	fluconazole	antifungal	fungal infections
52	Cymbalta	duloxetine	antidepressant	depression
53	Roxicodone	oxycodone	opioid analgesic	moderate to severe pain
54	Wellbutrin XL	bupropion XL	antidepressant	depression
55	Effexor XR	venlafaxine ER	antidepressant	depression
56	Zyloprim	allopurinol	antigout	gout
57	Medrol	methylprednisolone	corticosteroid	inflammation, immunological disorders, allergies
58	Adderall	amphetamine salts IR	stimulant	attention-deficit/hyperactivity disorder (ADHD)
59	Zofran	ondansetron	antiemetic	nausea, vomiting
60	Kenalog	triamcinolone	topical corticosteroid	allergy
61	Nexium	esomeprazole	proton pump inhibitor	peptic ulcer disease (PUD), gastroesophageal reflux disease (GERD)
62	Hyzaar	losartan and hydrochlorothiazide	antihypertensive	hypertension
63	Valium	diazepam	benzodiazepine	anxiety, skeletal muscle spasm, epilepsy, seizures
64	Ergocalciferol	vitamin D_2	vitamin	vitamin deficiency
65	Elavil	amitriptyline	antidepressant	depression
66	Paxil	paroxetine	antidepressant	depression
67	Catapres	clonidine	antihypertensive	hypertension
68	Tricor	fenofibrate	antihyperlipidemic	hyperlipidemia, hypertriglyceridemia, hypercholesterolemia
69	Glucophage XR	metformin XR	antidiabetic	type 2 diabetes mellitus

	BRAND NAME	GENERIC NAME	CLASS	USE
70	Advair Diskus	fluticasone/salmeterol	inhaled beta-2 agonist/ corticosteroid	asthma
71	Fluvirin, Afluria, Fluzone	influenza vaccine	vaccine	influenza
72	Vibramycin	doxycycline	antibiotic	bacterial infection
73	Amaryl	glimepiride	antidiabetic	type 2 diabetes mellitus
74	Aldactone	spironolactone	antihypertensive	hypertension
75	Maxzide, Dyazide	triamterene and hydrochlorothiazide	antihypertensive	hypertension
76	Levaquin	levofloxacin	antibiotic	bacterial infection
77	Valtrex	valacyclovir	antiviral	viral infection
78	Tylenol #2, #3, #4	acetaminophen and codeine	opioid analgesic	moderate to severe pain
79	Lamictal	lamotrigine	anticonvulsant	epilepsy, seizures
80	Topamax	topiramate	anticonvulsant	epilepsy (partial seizures); migraine prevention
81	Mevacor	lovastatin	antihyperlipidemic	hyperlipidemia, hypercholesterolemia
82	Seroquel	quetiapine	antipsychotic	psychoses (e.g. schizophrenia)
83	Flagyl	metronidazole	antibiotic	bacterial infection
84	Vyvanse	lisdexamfetamine	stimulant	attention-deficit/ hyperactivity disorder (ADHD); binge-eating disorder
85	Phenergan	promethazine	antihistamine, antiemetic	allergy, motion sickness, nausea
86	none	folic acid	vitamin	nutritional supplement
87	Fosamax	alendronate	bisphosphonate	osteoporosis, Paget disease
88	Glucotrol	glipizide	antidiabetic	type 2 diabetes mellitus
89	Lantus Solostar	insulin glargine	long acting insulin	type 1 diabetes mellitus type 2 diabetes mellitus
90	Cleocin	clindamycin	antibiotic	bacterial infection
91	Xalatan	latanoprost	ophthalmic antiglaucoma	glaucoma
92	Concerta	methylphenidate ER	stimulant	attention-deficit/ hyperactivity disorder (ADHD)
93	Vasotec	enalapril	antihypertensive	hypertension

	BRAND NAME	GENERIC NAME	CLASS	USE
94	Lyrica	pregabalin	anticonvulsant	nerve pain, muscle pain, fibromyalgia
95	Tessalon Perles	benzonatate	antitussive	cough
96	Inderal	propranolol	antihypertensive	hypertension
97	Omnicef	cefdinir	antibiotic	bacterial infection
98	MS Contin	morphine	opioid analgesic	pain
99	Adderall XR	amphetamine salts ER	stimulant	attention-deficit/hyperactivity disorder (ADHD)
100	Imitrex	sumatriptan	antimigraine	migraine

ER, extended release; IR, immediate release; XL, extended release; XR, extended release.

www.drugtopics.modernmedicine.com

www.online.lexi.com

Index

Page numbers followed by an f denote figures.

A

-a, 12
a-, 13
A. *See* Assessment
ab-, 13
AB. *See* Abortion
Abbreviations, 559–564
   blood, 292
   cardiovascular system, 342–343
   for digestive system, 428
   ear, 230
   endocrine system, 260
   eye, 204
   in history and physical examination and progress notes, 34–35
   integumentary system, 74
   lymphatic system, 292
   male reproductive system, 488
   musculoskeletal system, 119
   nervous system, 173
   respiratory system, 382
   urinary system, 462
Abdomen
   anatomic divisions for, 399f, 400–401
   clinical divisions of, 399f
   computed tomography of, 419
   distention of, 402f
   endoscopy of, 417, 417f
   pain, characteristic of, 400f
   sonography of, 419, 419f
Abdominal aorta, images of, 435f
Abdominal hysterectomy, 523
Abdominal paracentesis, 423
Abdominal sonogram, 419, 419f, 450
abdomin/o, 24, 390
Abdominocentesis, 423
ABG. *See* Arterial blood gas
Abortifacient, 540
Abortion (AB), 534
   TAB, 540
Above-the-knee prosthesis, 117f
Abruptio placentae, 535
Abscess, 61
Absence seizure, epilepsy, 145

Absorption, 389
-ac, 8, 19
Accessory organs
   endoscopy of, 417, 417f
   gastrointestinal system related, 410, 410f, 416f
Accommodation, 190
-aces, 12
Acne, 59, 59f
acous/o, 212
Acoustic neuroma, 219
Acquired immunodeficiency syndrome (AIDS), 62, 62f, 281
acr/o, 24
Acromegaly, 250, 250f
Acronyms, 559–564
   blood, 292
   cardiovascular system, 342–343
   for digestive system, 428
   ear, 230
   endocrine system, 260
   eye, 204
   in history and physical examination and progress notes, 34–35
   integumentary system, 74
   lymphatic system, 292
   male reproductive system, 488
   musculoskeletal system, 119
   nervous system, 173
   respiratory system, 382
   urinary system, 462
ACS. *See* Acute coronary syndrome
ACTH. *See* Adrenocorticotropic hormone
Actinic keratosis, 61, 61f
Active immunity, lymphatic system, 276
-acusis, 212
Acute coronary syndrome (ACS), 319
ad-, 13
aden/o, 24, 236
Adenocarcinoma of breasts, 515
Adenohypophysis, 238f, 242

Adenoid, 355
Adenoidectomy, 376
ADH. *See* Antidiuretic hormone
ADHD. *See* Attention-deficit/hyperactivity disorder
Adhesiolysis, 522
Adhesiotomy, 522
adip/o, 46
Adnexa, 498
Adrenalectomy, 257
Adrenal glands, 237f, 238f, 241
   diagnostic terms for, 249
Adrenaline, 241
adrenal/o, 236
Adrenal virilism, 249
adren/o, 236
Adrenocorticotropic hormone (ACTH), 242
Adult polycystic kidney disease (APKD), 445
-ae, 12
aer/o, 24, 212
Aerotitis media, 219
Affect, 163
Afferent nerves. *See* Sensory nerves
Agnosia, 143
Agranulocytes, 272, 272f
AIDS. *See* Acquired immunodeficiency syndrome
Airways, 350, 350f
-al, 5, 8, 19
Alb. *See* Albumin
Albinism, 59
Albumin (Alb), 450
albumin/o, 435
Albuminuria, 442
-algia, 18
Alive and well (A&W), 34
Allograft. *See* Homograft
Alopecia, 57
ALS. *See* Amyotrophic lateral sclerosis
Alveoli, 355
alveol/o, 350
Alzheimer disease, 143

571

Amastia, 515
Amblyopia, 190
Amenorrhea, 505
Amniocentesis, 537, 537f
Amnioinfusion, 540
Amnion, 502
Amniotic fluid, 502
Amniotic sac, 502
Amputation, 111
Amyotrophic lateral sclerosis (ALS), 144
an-, 13
Anal fistula, 406
Anal fistulectomy, 423
Anastomosis, 335, 423
Anatomical position, 93, 93f
Anatomic divisions, for digestive system, 399f, 400–401
Anatomic position, 93–98, 93f, 95f–96f
    with body planes, 93–94, 93f
Anatomic terms, 49–50
    for autonomic nervous system, 138
    in blood, 271–274, 271f
    bone related, 86–90, 87f–88f
    for cardiovascular system, 306–310
    for central nervous system, 135–137
    for digestive system, 394–398, 394f–395f
    for ear, 212f, 214–217
    for endocrine system, 241–245
    for female reproductive system, 498–504, 499f–502f
    for integumentary system, 49–50
    joints and muscles related, 90–92, 90f–91f
    in lymphatic system, 274–277, 275f
    for male reproductive system, 470–474, 471f
    for nervous system, 135–140
    for peripheral nervous system, 137
    for respiratory system, 350f, 354–358, 354f
    for urinary system, 438–441, 439f
andr/o, 239
Androgens, 241
Anemia, 281
Anencephaly, 147
Aneurysm, 315, 315f
Angina pectoris, 315
angi/o, 5, 24, 304
Angiogram, 329
Angiography, 329
Angioscopy, 335
Anisocytosis, 278
ankyl/o, 83
Ankyloglossia, 405
Ankylosis, 100

Annulus fibrosus, 91
an/o, 390
Anorchism, 475
Anorexia, 401
Anorexia nervosa, 167
Anovulation, 505
ante-, 14
Anteflexion, 506
Anterior chamber, 180, 181f, 184
Anterior pituitary, 238f, 242
anti-, 13
Antibiotic ophthalmic solution, 203
Antibody, lymphatic system, 276
Antidiuretic hormone (ADH), 243
Antigen, lymphatic system, 276
Anuria, 442
Anus, 396
Anvil, 214
Anxiety disorders, 166–167
Aorta, 307, 308f
Aortic valve, 307
aort/o, 304
Aortogram, 329
Apathy, 163
Aphagia, 401
Aphakia, 190
Aphasia, 140
APKD. See Adult polycystic kidney disease
Aplastic anemia, 281
Apnea, 358
Appendectomy, 423
Appendicitis, 406
appendic/o, 390
Appendicular skeleton, 86
Appendix, 396
aque/o, 181
Aqueous humor, 180, 181f, 184
-ar, 8, 19
-arche, 495
Areola, 501
Arrhythmia, 319, 320f
Arterial blood gas (ABG), 369
Arteries, 307, 308f
    diagnostic terms related to, 319, 320f, 321–322
arteri/o, 304
Arteriogram, 329
Arterioles, 308, 308f
Arteriosclerosis, 315
Arthralgia, 98
Arthritis, 100
arthr/o, 24, 83
Arthrocentesis, 111
Arthrodesis, 111
Arthrogram, 109
Arthroplasty, 111
Arthroscopy, 111, 112f
Articular cartilage, 88f, 89
Articulation, 90, 90f
articul/o, 83

-ary, 19
Ascending colon, 396
Ascites, 401, 402f
ASD. See Atrial septal defect
Aspermia, 474
Aspiration biopsy, 517
Assessment (A), 34
Astereognosis, 143
-asthenia, 130
Asthenopia, 188
Asthma, 363, 363f
Astigmatism, 190
Atelectasis, 363
Atherectomy, 335, 336f
ather/o, 304
Atheromatous plaque, 315, 316f
Atherosclerosis, 315
Athlete's foot. See Tinea
-ation, 19
Atopognosis, 143
Atrial flutter, 319
Atrial septal defect (ASD), 319
atri/o, 304
Atrioventricular (AV) bundle, 313
Atrioventricular (AV) node, 313
Atrium, 301, 303f, 306
Atrophic vaginitis, 510
Atrophy, 98
Attention-deficit/hyperactivity disorder (ADHD), 167
audi/o, 212
Audiogram, 222
Audiologist, 222
Audiometer, 222
Audiometry, 222, 222f
Auditory acuity testing, 222
Auditory prosthesis, 228
Auditory tube, 211, 215
Augmentation mammoplasty, 528, 528f
aur/i, 212
Auricle, 211, 214
Auscultation, 326, 326f, 371
Autism, 167
Autograft, 71
Autoimmune disease, 281
Autologous blood, 292
Autonomic nervous system, 128
    anatomic terms for, 138
A&W. See Alive and well
-ax, 12
Axial skeleton, 86, 87f
Axon, 127
Azoospermia, 474
Azotemia, 446

B

Babinski reflex, 156, 156f
Babinski sign, 156, 156f
Bacterial endocarditis, 317f, 319
Bacterial STDs, 478–479, 479f

bacteri/o, 435
Bacteriuria, 442
BAEP. See Brainstem auditory evoked potential
BAER. See Brainstem auditory evoked response
Balanitis, 475
balan/o, 469
Bariatric surgery, 423
Barium enema, 418
Barium swallow, 418, 419f
Barrier contraceptives, 530
Bartholin glands, 501
Basal cell carcinoma (BCC), 45f, 62
Basic metabolic panel (BMP), 284
Basophil, 272, 272f
BCC. See Basal cell carcinoma
BD. See Bipolar disorder
Behavioral therapy, 171
Benign prostatic hyperplasia (BPH), 477, 477f
Benign prostatic hypertrophy (BPH), 477, 477f
bi-, 14
Bicuspid valve, 307
Bilateral salpingooophorectomy, 525
bil/i, 390
Biliary ducts, 395f, 397
Bilirubin, 450
Biopsy (Bx), 67, 67f, 482, 517, 518f
    aspiration, 517
    bone marrow, 288
    for digestive system, 415, 415f
    endoscopic, 517
    excisional, 67, 67f, 415, 517
    incisional, 67, 67f, 415, 517
    kidney, 448
    lung, 371
    needle, 415, 415f, 517
    of prostate, 482, 482f
    renal, 449
    sentinel node breast, 517
    shave, 67, 67f
    stereotactic breast, 517
    testicular, 482
Bipolar disorder (BD), 166
-blast, 268
blast/o, 268
Blepharitis, 191
blephar/o, 181
Blepharochalasis, 191
Blepharoplasty, 199
Blepharoptosis, 191
Blepharospasm, 188
Blood
    abbreviations for, 292
    anatomic terms in, 271–274, 271f
    cellular components of, 271–273, 272f
    combining forms for, 268–270
    diagnostic terms for, 281–284
    diagnostic tests and procedures, 284–287, 289–291
    functions of, 267–268
    in iron deficiency anemia, 278f
    in pernicious anemia, 278f
    smear, 278f
    symptomatic terms for, 277–280
    therapeutic drug classifications for, 292
    therapeutic terms for, 292–294
Blood chemistry, 284
    panels, 284
Blood circulation, 303f, 304f
Blood component therapy, 292
Blood culture, 285
Blood glucose, 254
Blood indices, 287
Blood pressure (BP), 34, 310, 311f
Blood sugar (BS), 254
Blood transfusion, 292
Blood urea nitrogen (BUN), 452
BMP. See Basic metabolic panel
Body, organization of, 27–30, 27f
Body movements, 95, 96f
Body planes, anatomic position with, 93–94, 93f
Body positions, 94–95, 94f
Boil. See Furuncle
Bone grafting, 111
Bone marrow, 88f, 89
Bone marrow aspiration, 288, 288f
Bone marrow biopsy, 288
Bone marrow transplant, 291
Bones, 86
    classification of, 87–88
    flat, 87
    irregular, 88
    long, 87
    sesamoid, 88
    short, 87
    tissue, types of, 87
Bone scan, 109
Bony necrosis, 101
Bowman capsule, 440
BP. See Blood pressure
BPH. See Benign prostatic hyperplasia; Benign prostatic hypertrophy
brachi/o, 83
Brachytherapy, 487
brady-, 14
Bradycardia, 319
Bradypnea, 358
Brain, 135, 135f
    PET scans of, 155, 155f
Brainstem, 136
Brainstem auditory evoked potential (BAEP), 223, 223f
Brainstem auditory evoked response (BAER), 223
Breasts, 501, 501f
    adenocarcinoma of, 515
    diagnostic terms, 515–517
    fibrocystic, 515
    gynecologic operative terms for, 527–529, 528f
Breathing terms, 358
Bronchi, 350f
Bronchial tree, 355
Bronchiectasis, 363, 363f
bronchi/o, 350
Bronchioles, 350f, 355
bronchiol/o, 350
Bronchitis, 364
bronch/o, 350
Bronchogenic carcinoma, 364
Bronchoscopy, 369, 370f
Bronchospasm, 364
BS. See Blood sugar
Buccal, 401
bucc/o, 390
Bulbourethral glands, 472
Bulimia nervosa, 167
Bulla, 52f, 53
BUN. See Blood urea nitrogen
Bundle of His, 313
Bunion, 101
Burn, 60, 60f
Bursa, 90
Bursectomy, 111
Bursitis, 101
Bx. See Lung biopsy

C

CABG. See Coronary artery bypass graft
CAD. See Coronary artery disease
Calcitonin, 243
Calices, 438
Calyces, 438
Canal of Schlemm, 184
Cancellous bone tissue, 87
Capillaries, 308, 308f
capn/o, 350
Capsule endoscopy, 417
carb/o, 350
Carbuncle, 61
carcin/o, 25
Carcinoma in situ (CIS) of cervix, 508
Cardiac catheterization, 329–330, 330f
Cardiac conduction, 312–314, 313f
Cardiac muscle, 91
Cardiac output (CO), 330
Cardiac sphincter. See Lower esophageal sphincter (LES)
Cardiac tamponade, 319
cardi/o, 5, 8, 24, 304
Cardiomyopathy, 319
Cardiopulmonary resuscitation (CPR), 378

Cardiovascular system
   abbreviations related to, 342–343
   anatomic terms for, 306–310
   blood pressure terms for, 310–312
   cardiac conduction, 312–314, 313f
   combining forms for, 304–306
   diagnostic terms related to, 319, 320f, 321–322
   diagnostic tests and procedures for, 326–334
   operative terms for, 335–338
   overview of, 301–302, 302f–304f
   symptomatic terms for, 315–318
   therapeutic drug classifications for, 340
   therapeutic terms for, 339–342
Cardioversion, 339
Carina, 355
Carotid endarterectomy, 159
Caseous necrosis, 359
Casting, 114, 115f
CAT. See Computed axial tomography
cata, 130
Cataract, 191, 191f
Cataract extraction, 199
Catatonia, 164
Catecholamines, 241
CBC. See Complete blood count
CC. See Chief complaint
CD4 cell count, 285
Cecum, 396
-cele, 18
celi/o, 390
Cells, 27–30
-centesis, 19
Central nervous system (CNS), 128, 129f, 135
   anatomic terms for, 135–137
cephal/o, 24
Cephalopelvic disproportion (CPD), 534
cerebell/o, 128
Cerebellum, 135f, 136
Cerebral aneurysm, 144
Cerebral angiogram, 155
Cerebral arteriosclerosis, 144
Cerebral atherosclerosis, 144
Cerebral cortex, brain, 135, 135f
Cerebral embolism, 144, 144f
Cerebral hemispheres, brain, 135, 135f
Cerebral palsy (CP), 144
Cerebral thrombosis, 144, 144f
cerebr/o, 128
Cerebrospinal fluid (CSF), 136
Cerebrovascular accident (CVA), 144, 144f
Cerebrovascular disease, 144
Cerebrum, 135, 135f
Cerumen, 214

Cerumen impaction, 218
cerumin/o, 212
Cervical conization, 522
Cervical dysplasia, 508, 518f
Cervical effacement, 531
Cervical intraepithelial neoplasia (CIN), 508
Cervical neoplasia, 508
Cervical os, 500
Cervicitis, 506
cervic/o, 83, 495
Cervix, 500
   carcinoma in situ of, 508
Cesarean section (C-section), 540
Chalazion, 191, 191f
Cheeks, 395
Cheilitis, 405
cheil/o, 390
Cheiloplasty, 423
Chemical peel, 70
Chemosurgery, 70
Chemotherapy, 72, 292
   for female reproductive system, 529
   for male reproductive system, 487
   for nervous system, 161
Cherry angioma, 54, 54f
Chest pain (CP), 34
Chest x-ray (CXR), 372
Cheyne–Stokes respiration, 358
CHF. See Congestive heart failure
Chickenpox. See Varicella
Chief complaint (CC), 34
Childhood, disorders diagnosed in, 167
Chlamydia, 478, 513
Cholangiogram, 418
Cholangitis, 410
chol/e, 390
Cholecystectomy, 423
Cholecystitis, 410
Cholecystogram, 418
Choledocholithiasis, 410, 410f
Cholelithiasis, 410, 416f
chondr/o, 83
Chondromalacia, 101
Chorionic villus sampling (CVS), 537, 537f
Choroid, 184
chromat/o, 268
chrom/o, 268
Chronic obstructive pulmonary disease (COPD), 364
Chyle, lymph vessels, 274, 275f
chyl/o, 268
Cicatrix of skin, 54
Cilia, 356
Ciliary body, 184
Ciliary muscle, 184
Ciliary processes, 184
CIN. See Cervical intraepithelial neoplasia

circum-, 13
Circumcision, 484, 484f
Cirrhosis, 410
CIS. See Carcinoma in situ
Claudication, 315
Clinic records. See Medical records
Clitoris, 500
Closed comedos, 57, 57f
Closed fracture, 102, 103f
Closed reduction, external fixation of fracture, 114–115, 115f
Closed reduction, percutaneous fixation of fracture, 115
CMP. See Comprehensive metabolic panel
CNS. See Central nervous system
c/o. See Complains of
CO. See Cardiac output
Coarctation of aorta, 319
Cochlea, 215
Cochlear implant, 228, 228f
Cognitive therapy, 171
Colitis, 406
Collecting duct, 439
col/o, 24, 390
Colon, 396
colon/o, 24, 390
Colonoscopy, 415
Colorectal polyps, 406, 416f
Colors, 23
Colostomy, 423, 424f
colp/o, 495
Colporrhaphy, 523
Colporrhaphy anterior repair, 523
Colporrhaphy A&P repair, 523
Colporrhaphy posterior repair, 523
Colposcopy, 517, 518f
Coma, 140
Combining forms, 2, 3f
   for blood, 268–270
   for cardiovascular system, 304–306
   and combining vowels, 4
   common, 23–26
   for digestive system, 390–394
   for ear, 212–214
   for endocrine system, 236, 239–240
   for eye, 181–183
   for female reproductive system, 495–498
   general, 25
   for integumentary system, 46
   for lymphatic system, 268–270
   for male reproductive system, 469–470
   for musculoskeletal system, 83–86
   for nervous system, 128–130
   patterns of, 8
   for respiratory system, 350–353
   rules of, 5
   for urinary system, 435–438

Comedos, 57, 57f
Comminuted fracture, 102, 103f
Compact bone tissue, 87
Complains of (c/o), 34
Complete blood count (CBC), 286, 286f
Complex fracture, 102, 103f
Compound fracture. *See* Open fracture
Comprehensive metabolic panel (CMP), 284, 285f
Computed axial tomography (CAT), 110
Computed tomographic angiography (CTA), 330, 331f
Computed tomography (CT), 109
  of abdomen, 419
  for endocrine system, 254
  of head, 155
  for lymphatic system, 288
  for respiratory system, 373
con-, 15
Conductive hearing loss, 220
Condylomata acuminata, 479, 514
Cones, visual receptors, 181, 185
Congenital anomalies, 506
Congenital anomaly of heart, 319, 321
Congenital irregularities, 506
Congestive heart failure (CHF), 321
Conjunctiva, 180, 181f, 184
Conjunctivitis, 192
conjunctiv/o, 181
Consent forms, 34
Consonant, 10–11
Constipation, 401
Constriction, 315, 316f
Constructing terms, basic rules of, 5–7
Contact lens, 203
Continent urostomy, 457f, 458
Continuous positive airway pressure (CPAP) therapy, 378, 379f
Continuous subcutaneous insulin infusion (CSII), 258, 258f
contra-, 13
Contraceptive implant, 530
Contraceptive injection, 530
Convulsion, 141
COPD. *See* Chronic obstructive pulmonary disease
Cornea, 180, 181f, 184
corne/o, 46, 181
Coronal plane, 93
Coronary angiogram, 329, 329f
Coronary artery bypass graft (CABG), 335, 336f
Coronary artery disease (CAD), 321
Coronary circulation, 302, 303f, 308
coron/o, 304
Cor pulmonale, 321

Corpus callosum, brain, 135, 135f
cost/o, 83
Cowper glands, 472
CP. *See* Cerebral palsy; Chest pain
CPAP. *See* Continuous positive airway pressure
CPD. *See* Cephalopelvic disproportion
CPR. *See* Cardiopulmonary resuscitation
Crackles, 359
Cranial nerves, 137
Craniectomy, 159
crani/o, 83, 128
Craniotomy, 159
Creatinine, 440
  clearance testing, 452
  serum, 452
  urine, 452
Crepitation, 99
Crepitus, 99
crin/o, 25, 239
Cross-matching, blood, 292
Croup, 364
Crust, skin surface, 53f, 54
Cryopexy, 199
Cryoretinopexy, 199
Cryosurgery, 70, 523, 523f
Cryptorchidism, 475f, 476
Cryptorchism, 475, 475f
C&S. *See* Culture and sensitivity
C-section. *See* Cesarean section
CSF. *See* Cerebrospinal fluid
CSII. *See* Continuous subcutaneous insulin infusion
CT. *See* Computed tomography
CTA. *See* Computed tomographic angiography
Culture and sensitivity (C&S), 67
Curettage, 70
Cushing syndrome, 249, 249f
cutane/o, 24, 46
Cutaneous lupus erythematosus, 62
CVA. *See* Cerebrovascular accident
CVS. *See* Chorionic villus sampling
CXR. *See* Chest x-ray
cyan/o, 23
Cyanosis, 359
cycl/o, 181
Cycloplegic, 203
Cystic fibrosis, 364
Cystitis, 446
cyst/o, 390, 435
Cystocele, 509
Cystoscopy, 448, 448f
cyt/o, 24, 268

D

d. *See* Day
dacry/o, 181
Dacryoadenitis, 192

Dacryocystectomy, 200
Dacryocystitis, 192
dactyl/o, 83
Day (d), 34
D&C. *See* Dilation and curettage
de-, 13
D&E. *See* Dilation and evacuation
Deafness, 219
Debridement, 70
Deep tendon reflexes (DTR), 156
Deep vein thrombosis (DVT), 322
Defecation, 396
Defibrillation, 339, 339f
Defibrillator, 339
Degenerative arthritis, 100
Degenerative joint disease (DJD), 101
Delirium, 140
Delusion, 164
Dementia, 141
Dendrites, 127
dent/i, 390
Deoxygenated blood, 302
Depigmentation, skin, 58
Depolarization, 314
Dermabrasion, 70
Dermatitis, 60
dermat/o, 24, 46
Dermatosis, 60
Dermis, skin layer, 46
derm/o, 24, 46
Dermoid cyst, 506
Descending colon, 396
-desis, 19
dia-, 13
Diabetes mellitus (DM), 249
Diabetic ketoacidosis (DKA), 247
Diabetic retinopathy, 192, 192f, 198f
Diagnosis (Dx), 34
Diagnostic imaging
  for lymphatic system, 288
Diagnostic suffixes, 18–19
Diagnostic terms
  for adrenal glands, 249
  for blood, 281–284
  for cardiovascular system, 319, 320f, 321–322
  for ear, 218–221
  for endocrine system, 249–253
  for eye, 190–196
  for female reproductive system, 506–512, 507f–509f
  gynecologic, 506–512, 507f–509f
  for integumentary system, 59–67
  for male reproductive system, 475–482, 475f–479f
  for musculoskeletal system, 100–108
  for nervous system, 143–152
  obstetrics, 534–537, 535f
  pancreas for, 249–250

Diagnostic terms (Continued)
  for parathyroid glands, 250
  for pituitary gland, 250
  related to arteries, 319, 320f, 321–322
  related to heart, 319, 320f, 321–322
  related to veins, 322–323
  for respiratory system, 363–369
  for thyroid gland, 250–251
  for urinary system, 445–448, 445f–446f
Diagnostic tests and procedures
  for blood, 284–287, 289–291
  for cardiovascular system, 326–334
  for digestive system, 415–422, 415f–419f
  for ear, 222–226
  for endocrine system, 254–257
  for eye, 197–199
  for female reproductive system, 517, 518f, 519–522, 520f
  for gynecologic, 517, 518f, 519–522, 520f
  for integumentary system, 67–68
  for lymphatic system, 287–291
  for male reproductive system, 482–484, 482f
  for musculoskeletal system, 109–111, 109f
  for nervous system, 153–158, 153f–156f
  obstetrics, 537–539, 538f
  for respiratory system, 369–375, 370f–373f
  for urinary system, 448–455
Diaphoresis, 315
Diaphragm, 350f, 355, 356f
Diaphysis, 88, 88f
Diarrhea, 401
Diastole, 311
Die, 46
Diencephalon, 136
Differential count, 287
Digestion, 389
Digestive system
  abbreviations for, 428
  abdomen pain, characteristic of, 400f
  absorption in, 389
  accessory organs related to, 410, 410f, 416f
  anatomic divisions for, 399f, 400–401
  anatomic terms for, 394–398, 394f–395f
  biopsy for, 415, 415f
  clinical divisions of, 399f
  combining forms for, 390–394
  computed tomography of, 419
  diagnostic terms related to, 405–407, 406f–410f, 409–414

diagnostic tests and procedures for, 415–422, 415f–419f
digestion and, 389
endoscopy for, 415, 416f
excretion and, 389
functions of, 389
imaging studies of, 417–420
lower
  diagnostic terms, 406–407, 407f–409f, 409, 416f
  endoscopy, 415
  series, 418
magnetic resonance imaging of, 417
operative terms for, 423–426, 424f
overview of, 389
radiography of, 417, 418f
sonography of, 419–420, 419f
stool studies and, 420
symptomatic terms for, 401–404
therapeutic drug classifications for, 427
therapeutic terms for, 427–428
upper
  diagnostic terms, 405–406, 406f, 416f
  endoscopy, 417
  series, 417, 418f
Digital rectal examination (DRE), 483
Dilation and curettage (D&C), 523, 524f
Dilation and evacuation (D&E), 540
Diplopia, 189
dips/o, 239, 435
Direction, 13–14
Directional terms, 93f, 94
Discectomy/diskectomy, 159
Displacement of uterus, 506, 507f
Dissecting aneurysm, 315, 315f
Distance visual acuity, 197, 197f
Diverticulitis, 407
Diverticulosis, 407, 407f, 416f
Diverticulum, 407
DJD. See Degenerative joint disease
DKA. See Diabetic ketoacidosis
DM. See Diabetes mellitus
doch/o, 390
Doppler sonography, 331, 332f
DRE. See Digital rectal examination
Drop (Gt), 204
Drops (Gtt), 204
Drugs list, 565–569
DTR. See Deep tendon reflexes
Ductus deferens, 472
Duodenal ulcer, 405
duoden/o, 390
Duodenum, 396
DVT. See Deep vein thrombosis
Dx. See Diagnosis
-dynia, 8, 18
dys-, 15

Dysentery, 407
Dyslexia, 167
Dysmenorrhea, 505
Dyspareunia, 505
Dyspepsia, 402
Dysphagia, 402
Dysphasia, 140
Dysphonia, 359
Dysphoria, 164
Dysplastic nevus, 55
Dyspnea, 358
Dysrhythmia, 319, 320f
Dysthymia, 166
Dysuria, 442

E

e-, 13
-e, 19
-eal, 5, 19
Ear
  abbreviations for, 230
  anatomic terms for, 212f, 214–217
  anatomy of, 212f
  combining forms for, 212–214
  diagnostic terms for, 218–221
  diagnostic tests and procedures for, 222–226
  external, 211, 212f
  internal, 212, 212f
  middle, 211, 212f
  operative terms for, 226–227
  overview of, 211–212
  symptomatic terms for, 217–218
  therapeutic drug classifications for, 229
  therapeutic terms for, 228–230
Ear instillation, 228
Ear lavage, 228
Eating disorders, 167
EBV. See Epstein-Barr virus
ec-, 13
Ecchymosis, 54, 54f
ECG/EKG. See Electrocardiogram
Echocardiography (echo), 330, 331f
Eclampsia, 534
ECT. See Electroconvulsive therapy
-ectasis, 5, 18
ecto-, 13
-ectomy, 5, 19
Ectopic pregnancy, 534
ector/o, 351
Ectropion, 192, 192f
Eczema, 61
ED. See Erectile dysfunction
EDC. See Estimated date of confinement
EDD. See Estimated date of delivery
EEG. See Electroencephalogram
Efferent nerves. See Motor nerves
EGD. See Esophagogastroduodenoscopy

Ejaculatory duct, 472
Ejection fraction, 330
Electrocardiogram (ECG/EKG), 320f, 326, 327f
Electrocautery, 70, 71f
Electroconvulsive therapy (ECT), 171
Electrodesiccation, 70
Electrodiagnostic procedures, 153
Electroencephalogram (EEG), 153, 153f
Electrolyte panel, 254
Electromyogram (EMG), 109
Electrophysiologic study (EPS), 327
Electrosurgical procedures, 70
Embolus, 316, 316f
Embryo, 502, 502f
-emesis (suffix), 391
EMG. *See* Electromyogram
-emia, 2, 18
Emphysema, 360f, 364
Empyema, 364
en-, 13
Encephalitis, 145
encephal/o, 128
Endarterectomy, 335
endo-, 8, 13
Endocardium, 302, 303f, 307
Endocrine system
 abbreviations for, 260
 anatomic terms for, 241–245
 combining forms for, 236, 239–240
 computed tomography for, 254
 diagnostic terms for, 249–253
 diagnostic tests and procedures for, 254–257
 functions of, 238f
 imaging procedures for, 254–255
 laboratory testing for, 254
 magnetic resonance imaging for, 255
 operative terms for, 257–258
 overview of, 236, 237f, 238f
 sonography for, 255
 symptomatic terms for, 245–248
 therapeutic drug classifications for, 259
 therapeutic terms for, 258–260
Endolymph, 215
Endometriosis, 507
Endometritis, 507
Endometrium, 498
Endorectal sonogram, of prostate, 483
Endoscopic biopsy, 517
Endoscopic retrograde cholangiopancreatography (ERCP), 417
Endoscopic ultrasonography (EUS), 420

Endoscopy, 369
 of abdomen, 417, 417f
 of accessory organs, 417, 417f
 capsule, 417
 for digestive system, 415, 416f
 lower digestive system, 415
 for upper digestive system, 417
Endosteum, 88, 88f
Endotracheal intubation, 379
Endovaginal sonogram, 519, 538
Endovascular neurosurgery, 159
Enteritis, 407
enter/o, 5, 24, 390
Enterocele, 509
Entropion, 192, 192f
Enuresis, 442
Eosinophil, 272, 272f
epi-, 8, 13
Epicardium, 302, 303f, 307
Epidermal growths, 55, 55f
Epidermis, skin layers, 46
Epididymectomy, 484
Epididymis, 472
Epididymitis, 476
epididym/o, 469
Epigastric region, 399f, 400
Epiglottis, 350f, 355
Epilepsy, 145
Epinephrine, 241
Epiphora, 192
Epiphysis, 88, 88f
Epiphysitis, 102
episi/o, 495
Episiotomy, 540
Epistaxis, 359
EPS. *See* Electrophysiologic study
Epstein–Barr virus (EBV), 282
ERCP. *See* Endoscopic retrograde cholangiopancreatography
Erectile dysfunction (ED), 476
Erosion, skin surface, 53, 53f
Eructation, 402
Eruption, skin, 57
Erythema, 57
erythr/o, 23, 46
Erythroblastosis fetalis, 281, 534
Erythrocytes, 271, 272f
Erythrocyte sedimentation rate (ESR), 285
Erythropenia, 279
-es, 12
Esophageal varices, 405, 416f
Esophagitis, 405
esophag/o, 5, 24, 390
Esophagogastroduodenoscopy (EGD), 417
Esophagoplasty, 423
Esophagus, 395
Esotropia, 193
ESR. *See* Erythrocyte sedimentation rate

Essential hypertension, 321
esthesi/o, 25, 128
Estimated date of confinement (EDC), 531
Estimated date of delivery (EDD), 531
Estrogen, 241
ESWL. *See* Extracorporeal shock wave lithotripsy
Ethyl alcohol (beverage alcohol), 34
EtOH. *See* Ethyl alcohol (beverage alcohol)
eu-, 15
Euphoria, 164
Eupnea, 358
EUS. *See* Endoscopic ultrasonography
Eustachian obstruction, 219
Eustachian tube, 211, 215
Evoked potentials, 153
-ex, 12
ex-, 13
Examination methods, 371
Exanthematous viral disease, 60
Excisional biopsy, 67, 67f, 415, 517
Excoriation, skin, 53, 53f
Excretion, 389
exo-, 13
Exophthalmos, 189, 245, 246f
Exophthalmus, 189, 245, 246f
Exostosis, 99
Exotropia, 193
Expectoration, 359
External acoustic meatus, 212f, 214
External auditory meatus, 212f, 214
External ear, 211, 212f, 214, 218, 218f
External version, 540
extra-, 13
Extracorporeal shock wave lithotripsy (ESWL), 460
Extracranial magnetic resonance angiography, 154, 154f
Eye
 abbreviations for, 204
 anatomy of, 181f
 combining forms for, 181–183
 diagnostic terms for, 190–196
 diagnostic tests and procedures for, 197–199
 functions of, 181
 operative terms for, 199–202
 overview of, 180–181, 181f
 symptomatic terms for, 188–190
 therapeutic drug classifications for, 203
 therapeutic terms for, 203–204
Eye instillation, 203
Eye irrigation, 203
Eyelid, 184

F

Fallopian tubes, 498
Family history (FH), 34
Fascia, 92
fasci/o, 83
Fasting blood sugar (FBS), 254
FBS. See Fasting blood sugar
Feces, 396
Female reproductive system. See also Gynecology; Obstetrics
    abbreviation for, 542
    anatomic terms for, 498–504, 499f–502f
    biopsy for, 517, 518f
    breasts
        diagnostic terms, 515–517
    chemotherapy for, 529
    combining forms for, 495–498
    diagnostic terms for, 506–512, 507f–509f
    diagnostic tests and procedures for, 517, 518f, 519–522, 520f
    functions of, 494–495
    hormone replacement therapy for, 530
    hormones, 494
    images of, 499f
    magnetic resonance imaging for, 519
    operative terms for, 522–529, 523f–524f, 528f
    overview of, 494–495
    pelvic sonography for, 519, 520f
    radiation therapy for, 529
    radiography for, 519
    sexually transmitted diseases and
        bacterial, 513
        viral, 513–514
    symptomatic terms for, 505–506
    therapeutic terms for, 529–531
femor/o, 83
Fetal monitoring, 537
Fetus, 502, 502f
FH. See Family history
Fibrillation, 319
fibr/o, 25, 83
Fibrocystic breasts, 515
Fibroid, 507, 508f
Fibromyoma, 507, 508f
First-degree burn, 60, 60f
Fissures
    brain, 136
    skin, 53, 53f
Fistula, 507
Flaccid, 99
Flaccid paralysis, 141
Flat affect, 163
Flat bones, 87
Flatulence, 402
Fluorescein angiography, 197, 197f
Fluoroscopy, 418
Foley catheter, 460
Follicle-stimulating hormone (FSH), 242
Foreskin, 472
Forms. See also Combining forms
    plural, 11–12
    singular, 11–12
Fovea centralis, 184
Fracture
    closed reduction, external fixation of, 114–115, 115f
    closed reduction, percutaneous fixation of, 115
    ORIF, 111, 113f
Fracture (Fx), 102, 103f
Fracture line, 102
Frontal lobe, brain, 135, 135f
Frontal plane, 93
Frozen section (FS), 68
FS. See Frozen section
FSH. See Follicle-stimulating hormone
Fulguration, 70
Full-thickness burn. See Third-degree burn
Fundus, 184, 498
Furuncle, 61
Fusiform aneurysm, 315, 315f

G

GAD. See Generalized anxiety disorder
Gallbladder, 397
Gallop, 326
gangli/o, 128
Gangrene, 61
Gastrectomy, 423
Gastric lavage, 427
Gastric resection, 423
Gastric ulcer, 405, 406f
Gastritis, 405, 416f
gastr/o, 5, 24, 390
Gastroenterostomglossectomy, 423
Gastroesophageal reflux disease (GERD), 405
Gastrointestinal system. See Digestive system
GCS. See Glasgow coma scale
Generalized anxiety disorder (GAD), 166
-genesis, 18
gen/o, 25
GERD. See Gastroesophageal reflux disease
German measles. See Rubella
GH. See Growth hormone
Gigantism, 250, 251f
Gingivae. See Gums
Gingivitis, 405
gingiv/o, 390
Glans penis, 472
Glasgow coma scale (GCS), 140, 141f
Glaucoma, 191f, 192
gli/o, 128
Glioma, 145, 145f
Glomerular capsule, 440
glomerul/o, 435
Glomerulonephritis, 445
Glomerulus, 440
Glossitis, 405
gloss/o, 390
Glossorrhaphy, 423
Glottis, 350f, 355
Glucagon, 241
gluc/o, 239, 435
Glucocorticoids, 241
Glucose, 450
Glucose tolerance test (GTT), 254
glucos/o, 239, 435
Glucosuria, 246, 442
glyc/o, 239, 435
Glycohemoglobin (HbA1c), 254
Glycosuria, 246, 442
Glycosylated hemoglobin (HbA1c), 254
gnos/o, 129
Goiter, 250, 251f
Goniometer, 95, 96f
Gonorrhea, 513
Gonorrhoea, 478
Gouty arthritis, 101
-gram, 19
Grandiose delusion, 164
Grand mal (big bad) seizure. See Tonic-clonic seizure
Granulocytes, 272, 272f
-graph, 19
-graphy, 19
Graves disease, 250
Gravida, 531, 532f
Greater vestibular glands, 501
Greek origins, 1–2
Greenstick fracture, 102, 103f
Growth hormone (GH), 242
Gt. See Drop
Gtt. See Drops
GTT. See Glucose tolerance test
Gums, 395
gynec/o, 25, 495
Gynecology. See also Obstetrics
    abbreviation for, 542
    anatomic terms for, 498–504, 499f–502f
    combining forms for, 495
    diagnostic terms, 506–512, 507f–509f
    diagnostic tests and procedures for, 517, 518f, 519–522, 520f
    operative terms, 522–529, 523f–524f, 528f
    operative terms for breasts, 527–529, 528f

symptomatic terms, 505–506
therapeutic terms, 529–531
Gynecomastia, 515
Gyri, 136

H

Habitual abortion, 534
Halitosis, 402
Hallucination, 164
Hammer, 214
Hard palate, 354
HbA1c. *See* Glycohemoglobin; Glycosylated hemoglobin
HBV. *See* Hepatitis B virus
Hct. *See* Hematocrit
HD. *See* Huntington disease
Head, eyes, ears, nose and throat (HEENT), 35
Healthcare provider patient care notes, 34
Hearing aid, 228
Heart, 237f
   blood circulation, 303f–304f, 308
   blood vessels of, 302, 303f, 307–308, 308f
   congenital anomaly of, 319, 321
   diagnostic terms related to, 319, 320f, 321–322
   layers, anatomic terms of, 303f, 306–307
   positron-emission tomography of, 328
   septum, anatomic terms of, 303f, 306–307
   structures of, 301–302, 303f
   valves of, 303f, 307
Heart attack. *See* Myocardial infarction (MI)
Heart murmur, 316
HEENT. *See* Head, eyes, ears, nose and throat
Hematemesis, 402
hemat/o, 5, 24, 268
Hematochezia, 402
Hematocrit (Hct), 287
Hematuria, 442, 442f
hemi-, 14
Hemiparesis, 141
Hemiplegia, 148
hem/o, 5, 24, 268
Hemochromatosis, 281
Hemodialysis, 460
Hemoglobin (Hgb), 271, 287
Hemolysis, 279
Hemophilia, 281
Hemoptysis, 359
Hemorrhoid, 407, 407f
Hemorrhoidectomy, 424
Hemothorax, 364
Hepatic lobectomy, 424
hepatic/o, 390

Hepatitis, 410
Hepatitis A, 410
Hepatitis B, 410
Hepatitis B virus (HBV), 479, 513
Hepatitis C, 410
hepat/o, 5, 24, 390
Hepatomegaly, 402
Hernia, 408
Herniated disc (disk), 145, 146f
Herniated disk, 103
herni/o, 390
Hernioplasty, 424
Herniorrhaphy, 424
Herpes simplex virus type 1 (HSV-1), 61
Herpes simplex virus type 2 (HSV-2), 61, 479, 513, 513f
Herpes zoster, 61, 145, 146f
Heterograft, 71
Heterotropia, 193, 193f
Hgb. *See* Hemoglobin
Hiatal hernia, 408, 408f, 418f
hidr/o, 46
Hilum, 438
Hirsutism, 246
histi/, 46
hist/o, 24, 46
History and physical (H&P) examinations, 31, 32f
   abbreviations in, 34–35
History (Hx), 35
History of present illness (HPI), 35
HIV. *See* Human immunodeficiency virus
Holter monitor, 327
Homograft, 71
Homologous blood, 292
Hordeolum, 192, 193f
Horizontal plane. *See* Transverse plane
Hormonal contraceptives, 530
Hormone replacement therapy (HRT)
   for endocrine system, 259
   for female reproductive system, 530
   for male reproductive system, 487
Hormones
   female reproductive, 494
   male reproductive, functions of, 468
hormon/o, 239
Hospital records. *See* Medical records
H&P. *See* History and physical
HPI. *See* History of present illness
HPV. *See* Human papillomavirus
HRT. *See* Hormone replacement therapy
HSV-1. *See* Herpes simplex virus type 1
HSV-2. *See* Herpes simplex virus type 2

HTN. *See* Hypertension
Human immunodeficiency virus (HIV), 62, 281, 479, 513
Human papillomavirus (HPV), 479, 514, 514f
Huntington chorea, 146
Huntington disease (HD), 146
Hx. *See* History
hydr/o, 24
Hydrocele, 476, 476f
Hydrocephalus, 146, 146f
Hydronephrosis, 445, 445f
Hymen, 500
hyper-, 2, 14
Hyperbilirubinemia, 402
Hypercalcemia, 246
Hypercapnia, 359
Hypercarbia, 359
Hyperemesis gravidarum, 535
Hyperesthesia, 142
Hyperglycemia, 246
Hyperinsulinism, 250
Hyperkalemia, 246
Hypermastia, 516
Hyperopia, 190, 190f
Hyperparathyroidism, 250
Hyperpigmentation, skin, 58
Hyperpnea, 358
Hypersecretion, 246
Hypertension (HTN), 311, 321
Hyperthyroidism, 250
   vs. hypothyroidism, 251
Hypertrophy, 99
Hyperventilation, 359
hypn/o, 129
hypo-, 14
Hypocalcemia, 246
Hypocapnia, 359
Hypocarbia, 359
Hypochondriac regions, 399f, 400
Hypochondriasis, 167
Hypochromic, 277, 278f
Hypogastric region, 399f, 400
Hypoglossal, 403
Hypoglycemia, 246
Hypokalemia, 246
Hypomastia, 516
Hypoparathyroidism, 250
Hypophysectomy, 257
Hypophysis, 242
Hypopigmentation, skin, 58
Hypopnea, 358
Hyposecretion, 246
Hypospadias, 476, 476f
Hypotension, 311
Hypothalamus, 138, 237f
Hypothyroidism, 251
   vs. hyperthyroidism, 251
Hypotonia, 99
Hypoventilation, 359
Hypoxemia, 360

Hypoxia, 360
Hysterectomy, 523
hyster/o, 495
Hysterosalpingogram, 519
Hysteroscopy, 519, 519f
Hysterosonogram, 520

I

-i, 12
-ia, 5, 19
-iasis, 18
-iatrics, 20
-iatry, 20
-ic, 19
ICD. *See* Implantable cardioverter defibrillator
-ices, 12
-icle, 19
Icterus, 402, 402f
I&D. *See* Incision and drainage
Ideation, 164
-ies, 12
Ileitis, 409
ile/o, 390
Ileostomy, 424
Ileum, 396
Imaging procedures
    of digestive system, 417–420
    for endocrine system, 254–255
Immunity, lymphatic system, 276
immun/o, 268
Immunocompromised, 279
Immunosuppression, 279
Immunotherapy, 292
IMP. *See* Impression
Impetigo, 61
Implantable cardioverter defibrillator (ICD), 339
Impression (IMP), 35
Incarcerated hernia, 408
Incentive spirometry, 379, 379f
Incisional biopsy, 67, 67f, 415, 517
Incision and drainage (I&D), 70
Incomplete abortion, 534
Incontinence, 443
Incus, 214
Infantile hypothyroidism, 251
Infarct, 316, 316f
Inferior vena cava, 302, 303f
infra-, 14
Inguinal hernia, 408, 408f
Inguinal regions, 399f, 400
inguin/o, 390
Insulin, 241
Insulin pump therapy, 258, 258f
Integument, 44
Integumentary system
    abbreviations for, 74
    anatomic terms for, 49–50
    diagnostic terms for, 59–67

diagnostic tests and procedures for, 67–68
functions of, 46
operative terms for, 69–72
overview of, 44–46, 45f
symptomatic terms for, 51–59, 51f–55f, 57f
therapeutic terms for, 72–74
Intellectual disability, 167
inter-, 14
Interatrial septum, 301, 303f, 307
Internal ear, 212, 212f, 215, 219
Internal version, 540
Interventional neuroradiology, 159
Interventricular septum, 301, 303f, 307
Intervertebral disk, 91, 91f
intra-, 14
Intracardiac electrophysiologic study (EPS), 327
Intracorporeal lithotripsy, 455, 456f
Intracranial magnetic resonance angiography, 154, 154f
Intraocular lens (IOL) implant, 200, 200f
Intrauterine device (IUD), 530
Intravascular stent placement, 337, 337f
Intravenous pyelogram (IVP), 449, 449f
Intravenous urogram (IVU), 449, 449f
Introitus, 500
Intussusception, 409, 409f
IOL. *See* Intraocular lens
Iridectomy, 200
irid/o, 181
Iridotomy, 200
Iris, 180, 181f, 184
Iritis, 192
ir/o, 181
Iron deficiency anemia, 278f, 281
Irregular bones, 88
-is, 12
Ischemia, 316, 316f
Islets of Langerhans, 237f, 238f, 241
-ism, 19
-ist, 20
-itis, 5, 18
IUD. *See* Intrauterine device
-ium, 8, 19
IVP. *See* Intravenous pyelogram
IVU. *See* Intravenous urogram
-ix, 12

J

Jaundice, 402
jejun/o, 390
Jejunum, 396
Joint, 90, 90f
Joint capsule, 91

Joints, anatomic terms related to, 90–92, 90f–91f
Juvenile diabetes. *See* Type 1 diabetes mellitus

K

Kaposi sarcoma, 62, 62f
Keloid, 54, 55f
Keratin, 46
Keratitis, 192
kerat/o, 46, 181
Keratoplasty, 200
Keratosis, 61, 61f
ket/o, 239, 435
Ketoacidosis, 247
Ketones, 450
    bodies, 443
    compounds, 443
keton/o, 239, 435
Ketonuria, 443
Ketosis, 246
Kidneys, 237f, 435, 436f, 438, 439f
    biopsy, 448
    dialysis, 460
    transplantation, 456
Kidneys, ureters, bladder (KUB), 449, 449f
kinesi/o, 129
KUB. *See* Kidneys, ureters, bladder
kyph/o, 83
Kyphosis, 104, 105f

L

(L). *See* Left
Labia, 500
Laboratory and diagnostic test reports, 34
Laboratory testing
    for endocrine system, 254
    for urinary system, 450, 451f, 452
Labyrinth. *See* Internal ear
Labyrinthitis, 219
Lacrimal ducts, 185, 185f
Lacrimal gland, 185, 185f
Lacrimal sac, 185, 185f
Lacrimation, 189
lacrim/o, 181
Lacteals, lymph vessels, 274, 275f
lact/o, 495
Lactogenic hormone, 243
Laminectomy, 159
Languages, influencing medical terminology, 1
lapar/o, 24, 390
Laparoscopic, 423
Laparoscopic surgery, 424, 524
Laparoscopy, 417, 417f, 524
Laparotomy, 424
Large intestine, 396
Large-loop excision of transformation zone (LLETZ), 524f, 525

Laryngitis, 364
laryng/o, 351
Laryngopharynx, 354
Laryngospasm, 364
Laryngotracheobronchitis (LTB), 364
Larynx, 350f, 355
Laser, 70
Laser-assisted in situ keratomileusis (LASIK), 200
Laser surgery, 70, 200, 200f, 524
LASIK. See Laser-assisted in situ keratomileusis
Latin origins, 1
LEEP. See Loop electrosurgical excision procedure
Left bronchus, 355
Left heart catheterization, 329
Left (L), 35
Left uterine appendage, 498
Left ventricular failure, 321
lei/o, 83
Leiomyoma, 103, 507, 508f
Leiomyosarcoma, 103
Lens, 180, 181f, 185
Lens capsule, 185
-lepsy, 130
LES. See Lower esophageal sphincter
Lesions, 51
   primary, 52–53, 52f
   secondary, 53–54, 53f
   types of, 51f
   vascular, 54, 54f
Leukemia, 282
leuk/o, 23, 46
Leukocyte, 272, 272f
   normal range of, 287
   type of, 287
Leukorrhea, 505
lex/o, 129
LH. See Luteinizing hormone
Ligament, 91
Light therapy, 171
lingu/o, 390
lip, 2
lip/o, 2, 24, 46
Lips, 395
lith/o, 25, 390, 435
Liver, 397
Living and well (L&W), 35
LLETZ. See Large-loop excision of transformation zone
Lobectomy, 376
Lobes, 355
lob/o, 351
-logist, 20
-logy, 5, 8, 20
Long bones, 87
   parts of, 88–89, 88f
Loop electrosurgical excision procedure (LEEP), 524, 524f
lord/o, 83

Lordosis, 104, 105f
Lou Gehrig disease. See Amyotrophic lateral sclerosis (ALS)
Lower esophageal sphincter (LES), 395
Lower gastrointestinal (GI) series, 418
Lower respiratory tract, 350f
LP. See Lumbar puncture
LTB. See Laryngotracheobronchitis
Lumbar puncture (LP), 153
Lumbar regions, 399f, 400
lumb/o, 83
Lumpectomy, 527
Lung biopsy (Bx), 371
Lungs, 237f, 302, 350f, 355
   pleural membranes with, 356f
   scan, 371, 371f
   sounds, 359
Lupus, 62
Luteinizing hormone (LH), 242
L&W. See Living and well
Lymph, 274, 275f
Lymphadenectomy, 291
Lymphadenopathy, 279
Lymphadenotomy, 291
Lymphangiogram, 288
Lymphatic system
   abbreviations for, 292
   anatomic terms in, 274–277, 275f
   combining forms for, 268–270
   computed tomography for, 288
   diagnostic imaging for, 288
   diagnostic terms for, 281–284
   diagnostic tests and procedures, 287–291
   functions of, 267
   immunity, 276
   operative terms for, 291–292
   organs of, 274
   positron-emission tomography for, 288
   structures of, 274, 275f, 276
   symptomatic terms for, 279–280
   therapeutic drug classifications for, 292
   therapeutic terms for, 292–294
Lymph capillaries, 274, 275f
Lymph ducts, 275f, 276
Lymph nodes, 274, 275f
   dissection, 291
lymph/o, 268
Lymphocyte, 272f, 273
Lymphocytopenia, 279
Lymphoma, 282
Lymph vessels, 274, 275f
-lysis, 18

M

-ma, 12
macro-, 14

Macrocytosis, 277, 278f
Macromastia, 516
Macrosomia, 532
Macula, 52, 52f
Macula lutea, 185, 198f
Macular degeneration, 191f, 192
Macule, 52, 52f
Magnetic resonance angiography (MRA), 154, 154f, 328
Magnetic resonance imaging (MRI), 109, 153
   of digestive system, 417
   for endocrine system, 255
   for female reproductive system, 519
   for respiratory system, 371
Major depression, 166
-malacia, 18
Male reproductive system
   abbreviations for, 488
   anatomic terms for, 470–474, 471f
   chemotherapy for, 487
   combining forms for, 469–470
   diagnostic terms for, 475–482, 475f–479f
   diagnostic tests and procedures for, 482–484, 482f
   functions of, 468
   hormones, 468
   operative terms for, 484–486, 484f–485f
   overview of, 468
   radiation therapy for, 487
   sexually transmitted disease and
      bacterial, 478–479, 479f
      viral, 479
   symptomatic terms for, 474–475
   therapeutic terms for, 487–488
Malignant cutaneous neoplasm, 62
Malleus, 214
Mammary glands, 501
mamm/o, 495
Mammogram, 519
Mammoplasty, 528
-mania, 130
Mania, 164
Mastectomy, 527, 528f
Mastitis, 516
mast/o, 495
Mastopexy, 528
-mata, 12
MCH. See Mean corpuscular hemoglobin
MCHC. See Mean corpuscular hemoglobin concentration
MCV. See Mean corpuscular volume
Mean corpuscular hemoglobin concentration (MCHC), 287
Mean corpuscular hemoglobin (MCH), 287
Mean corpuscular volume (MCV), 287

Measles. *See* Rubeola
meat/o, 435
Mechanical ventilation, 380, 380f
Meconium, 502
Meconium aspiration, 535
Meconium staining, 532
Mediastinum, 350f, 355
Medical records, 30–37
　abbreviations, 34–35
Medical terminology
　basic components of, 2–5
　basic structure of, 1–2
　construction of, rules of, 5–7
　defining of, through word structure analysis, 7
　formation of, 8–9
　language influences on, 1
　origins of, 1, 2
　pronunciation, rules of, 10–11
　singular and plural forms of, 11–13
　spelling of, 10
　vocabulary building, 13–26
Medullary cavity, 88f, 89
-megaly, 5, 18
Meibomian glands, 184
melan/o, 23, 46
Melanocyte-stimulating hormone (MSH), 242
Melanoma, 45f, 62
Melatonin, 242
Melena, 402
Ménière disease, 219
Meninges, 137, 137f
meningi/o, 129
Meningioma, 146
Meningitis, 147
mening/o, 129
men/o, 495
Menopause, 508
Menorrhagia, 505
meso-, 14
meta-, 14
Metabolism, 247
Metaphysis, 88, 88f
Metastasis, 282
-meter, 20
metr/o, 495
Metrorrhagia, 505
-metry, 20
MI. *See* Myocardial infarction
micro-, 14
Microcytosis, 277, 278f
Micromastia, 516
Microscopic findings, 450
Microsurgery, 159, 226
Middle ear, 211, 212f, 214, 219, 219f
Migraine headache, 147
Mineralocorticoid, 241
Miotic, 203
Missed abortion, 534
Mitral valve, 307

Mitral valve prolapse (MVP), 322
Mixed hearing loss, 220
Modified radical mastectomy, 527
Mohs surgery, 71
Mole. *See* Nevus
mono-, 14
Monocyte, 272, 272f
Mononucleosis, 282
Mons pubis, 500
Mood disorders, 166
morph/o, 25, 268
Motor deficit, 141
Motor nerves, 137
Mouth, 395
MRA. *See* Magnetic resonance angiography
MRI. *See* Magnetic resonance imaging
MS. *See* Multiple sclerosis
MSH. *See* Melanocyte-stimulating hormone
Mucopurulent discharge, 474
Mucous membranes, 355
multi-, 14
Multipara, 531
Multiple-gated acquisition (MUGA) scan, 328
Multiple sclerosis (MS), 147
Mumps, 405
Muscles, 91
　anatomic terms related to, 90–92, 90f–91f
　cardiac, 91
　ciliary, 184
　insertion of, 92
　of iris, 180, 181f
　origin of, 92
　skeletal, 81, 82f, 91
　smooth, 91
　striated, 91
Muscular dystrophy, 103
muscul/o, 24, 83
Musculoskeletal system
　abbreviations, 119
　combining forms for, 83–86
　diagnostic terms for, 100–108
　diagnostic tests and procedures for, 109–111, 109f
　operative terms for, 111–114
　overview of, 80–81, 81f–82f
　symptomatic terms for, 98–100
　therapeutic drug classifications, 116, 118
　therapeutic terms for, 114–115, 117–118
MVP. *See* Mitral valve prolapse
Myalgia, 99
Myasthenia gravis, 147
myc/o, 46
Mycobacterium tuberculosis, 366
Mydriatic, 203

Myelin, 127, 128f
Myelitis, 147
myel/o, 83, 129, 268
Myelodysplasia, 282
Myelogram, 155
Myeloma, 103
my/o, 24, 83, 304
Myocardial infarction (MI), 322
Myocardial radionuclide, 328
Myocardial radionuclide perfusion stress scan, 328
Myocarditis, 322
Myocardium, 307
Myodynia, 99
Myoma, 103
Myomectomy, 525
Myometrium, 498
Myopia, 190, 190f
Myoplasty, 111
Myositis, 103
myos/o, 83
Myringitis, 219
myring/o, 212
Myringotomy, 226
Myxedema, 251

N

NAD. *See* No acute distress
narc/o, 129
Narcolepsy, 147
Nasal cavity, 350f
Nasal polypectomy, 376
Nasal polyposis, 364
nas/o, 24, 351
Nasogastric (NG) intubation, 427
Nasolacrimal duct, 185, 185f
Nasopharyngoscopy, 369
Nasopharynx, 354
Nausea, 403
necr/o, 25
Needle biopsy, 415, 415f, 517
Negation, 13
neo-, 15
Neobladder, 458
Neoplasm, 55
Nephrectomy, 456
Nephritis, 446
nephr/o, 24, 435
Nephrolithiasis, 446, 446f
Nephrolithotomy, 456
Nephron, 439–440, 439f
Nephrorrhaphy, 455
Nephrosis, 446
Nephrotomy, 455
Nerve impulses, 212
Nervous system
　abbreviations, 173
　anatomic terms for, 135–140
　central nervous system, 128, 129f
　chemotherapy for, 161
　combining forms for, 128–130

diagnostic terms for, 143–152
diagnostic tests/procedures for, 153–158, 153f–156f
operative terms for, 159–161
overview of, 127–128, 128f
peripheral nervous system, 128, 129f
prefixes for, 130
psychiatric diagnostic terms for, 166–170
psychiatric symptomatic terms for, 163–165
psychiatric therapeutic terms for, 171–172
radiation therapy for, 162, 162f
stereotaxic radiosurgery for, 162
suffixes for, 130
symptomatic terms for, 140–143
term parts, 128–134
therapeutic drug classifications for, 162, 171
therapeutic terms for, 161–163
Neuralgia, 141
Neural tube defects, 147
neur/o, 24, 129
Neurohypophysis, 238f, 243
Neurons, 127
 anatomy of, 128f
Neuroplasty, 159
Neurosis, 164
Neutropenia, 279
Neutrophil, 272, 272f
Nevus, 45f, 55
Nipple, 501
Nitrite, 450
NKA. See No known allergies
NKDA. See No known drug allergies
No acute distress (NAD), 35
Nocturia, 443
Nocturnal enuresis, 442
Nodule, 52, 52f
No known allergies (NKA), 35
No known drug allergies (NKDA), 35
Noncontinent ileal conduit, 457, 457f
Nonseminoma, 478
Norepinephrine, 241
Normal sinus rhythm (NSR), 314, 320f
Normotension, 311
Nose, 350f, 354
NSR. See Normal sinus rhythm
Nuclear medicine imaging
 for cardiovascular system, 328
 musculoskeletal, 109
 for nervous system, 155
Nucleus pulposus, 91
Nulligravida, 531
Nullipara, 531
Nystagmus, 189

O

O. See Objective information
OA. See Osteoarthritis
Objective information (O), 35
Obsessive-compulsive disorder (OCD), 167
Obstetrics
 abbreviation for, 542
 diagnostic terms, 534–537, 535f
 diagnostic tests and procedures, 537–539, 538f
 operative terms, 540–541
 symptomatic terms, 531–533, 532f
 therapeutic drug classifications, 540
 therapeutic terms, 540–541
Obstetric sonogram, 539
obstetr/o, 495
Obstructive lung disorder, 360, 360f
Occipital lobe, brain, 135, 135f
Occlusion, 316, 316f
Occupational history (OH), 35
OCD. See Obsessive-compulsive disorder
OCP. See Oral contraceptive pill
ocul/o, 181
OH. See Occupational history
-oid, 18
-ole, 19
oligo-, 6, 14
Oligomenorrhea, 505
Oligo-ovulation, 505
Oligospermia, 474
Oliguria, 443
-oma, 19
Omentum, 396
-on, 12
onc/o, 25
Onychia, 62
onych/o, 46
oo-, 495
Oocyte, 499
Oophorectomy, 525
Oophoritis, 508
oophor/o, 495
Open comedos, 57, 57f
Open fracture, 102, 103f
Open reduction, internal fixation (ORIF), 111, 113f
Operative terms
 for breasts, 527–529, 528f
 for cardiovascular system, 335–338
 for digestive system, 423–426, 424f
 for ear, 226–227
 for endocrine system, 257–258
 for eye, 199–202
 for female reproductive system, 522–529, 523f–524f, 528f
 gynecologic, 522–529, 523f–524f, 528f

for integumentary system, 69–72
for lymphatic system, 291–292
for male reproductive system, 484–486, 484f–485f
for musculoskeletal system, 111–114
for nervous system, 159–161
obstetrics, 540
for respiratory system, 376–378, 376f–377f
for urinary system, 455–459, 456f–457f
ophthalm/o, 181
Ophthalmoscopy, 197, 198f
-opia, 182
Optic disc, 185, 198f
Optic nerve, 180, 181f
opt/o, 181
Oral cavity, 394
Oral contraceptive pill (OCP), 530
Orchidectomy, 484
orchid/o, 469
Orchiectomy, 484
orchi/o, 469
Orchiopexy, 484
Orchioplasty, 484
orch/o, 469
Organ of Corti. See Spiral organ
Organs, 24–25, 27–30
 accessory
  endoscopy of, 417, 417f
  gastrointestinal system related, 410, 410f, 416f
 of lymphatic system, 274
 radionuclide organ imaging, 109
 of urinary system, 434, 435f
ORIF. See Open reduction, internal fixation
Origin of muscle, 92
or/o, 24, 351, 390
Oropharynx, 354
orth/o, 25
Orthopedics, 81
orthopnea, 358
Orthosis, 116, 116f
Orthotopic bladder, 458
-osis, 19
Ostealgia, 99
oste/o, 5, 24, 83
Osteoarthritis (OA), 100, 101f
Osteodynia, 99
Osteoma, 103
Osteomalacia, 103
Osteomyelitis, 104
Osteoplasty, 111
Osteoporosis, 104, 104f
Osteosarcoma, 103
Osteotomy, 112
Otalgia, 217
Other specialty reports, 34
Otitis externa, 218, 218f

Otitis media, 219, 219f
ot/o, 212
Otodynia, 217
Otoplasty, 226
Otorrhagia, 217
Otorrhea, 217
Otosclerosis, 219
Otoscopy, 224, 224f
-ous, 19
Oval window, 215
Ovarian cystectomy, 525
Ovaries, 237f, 238f, 241, 499, 499f
ovari/o, 495
ov/i, 495
ov/o, 495
Ovum, 499
ox/o, 351
OXT. See Oxytocin
Oxytocin, 540
Oxytocin (OXT), 243

P

P. See Plan; Pulse
Pacemaker, 339, 339f
PaCO$_2$, 369
Palate, 354, 395
Palatine tonsils. See Tonsils
palat/o, 351
Palpebra, 184
Palpitation, 316
pan-, 14
Pancreas, 237f, 238f, 241, 397
    diagnostic terms for, 249–250
Pancreatectomy, 257, 424
Pancreatitis, 250, 410
pancreat/o, 239, 390
Pancytopenia, 279
Panic disorder, 166
PaO$_2$, 369
Papanicolaou (Pap) smear, 519
Papule, 52, 52f
para-, 6, 14
Para, 531, 532f
Paralysis, 141
Paranasal sinuses, 350f, 354
Paraplegia, 148
Parasympathetic nervous system, 138
Parathyroidectomy, 257
Parathyroid glands, 237f, 238f, 242
    diagnostic terms for, 250
Parathyroid hormone (PTH), 242
Parenchyma, 356
-paresis, 130
Paresthesia, 142
Parietal lobe, brain, 135, 135f
Parietal pericardium, 307
Parietal pleura, 356f
Parkinson disease, 148
Paronychia, 63, 63f
Parotiditis, 405

Parotitis, 405
Parovarian cyst, 508
Partial seizure, epilepsy, 145
Partial-thickness burn. See Second-degree burn
Partial thromboplastin time (PTT), 285
Passive immunity, lymphatic system, 276
Past medical history (PMH), 35
Patch, 52, 52f
    test, 68
patell/o, 83
Patent ductus arteriosus (PDA), 321
path/o, 25
Patient (Pt), 35
PCI. See Percutaneous coronary intervention
PCP. See Pneumocystis jiroveci pneumonia
PDA. See Patent ductus arteriosus
PE. See Physical examination; Pulmonary embolism
Peak expiratory flow rate (PEFR), 372
Peak flow (PF), 372
pector/o, 304
Pediculated polyp, 406
Pediculosis, 63, 63f
ped/o, 25
PEFR. See Peak expiratory flow rate
pelv/i, 83, 495
Pelvic adhesions, 509
Pelvic floor relaxation, 509, 509f
Pelvic inflammatory disease (PID), 509
Pelvic sonography, 519, 520f, 538
Pelvimetry, 537
-penia, 18
Penile prosthesis, 487
Penile self-injection, 487
Penis, 472
Peptic ulcer disease (PUD), 405
Percussion, 371
Percutaneous coronary intervention (PCI), 335, 336f
Percutaneous transluminal coronary angioplasty (PTCA), 329, 329f, 337, 337f
Perfusion deficit, 316
peri-, 6, 14
Pericardial cavity, 307
Pericarditis, 322
Pericardium, 302, 303f, 307
Perilymph, 215
perine/o, 469
Perineum, 472, 501
Periosteum, 88f, 89
Peripheral nervous system (PNS), 128, 129f
    anatomic terms for, 137
Peritoneal cavity, 396

Peritoneal dialysis, 460
peritone/o, 390
Peritoneum, 396
Peritonitis, 409
Pernicious anemia, 278f, 281
PERRLA. See Pupils equal, round and reactive to light and accommodation
Persecutory delusion, 164
Petechia, 54, 54f
Petit mal (little bad) seizure. See Absence seizure
-pexy, 19
Peyronie disease, 476, 476f
PF. See Peak flow
PFT. See Pulmonary function testing
pH, 369, 450
PH. See Past medical history
phac/o, 181
Phacoemulsification, 201
phag/o, 25, 268, 390
phak/o, 181
Pharyngeal tonsil. See Adenoid
Pharyngitis, 364
pharyng/o, 351
Pharynx, 350f, 354, 395
phas/o, 25, 129
-phil, 19
-philia, 19
Phimosis, 477, 477f
Phlebitis, 322
phleb/o, 304
Phlebotomy, 284
Phobia, 166
phob/o, 25, 129
phor/o, 129
phot/o, 181
Photophobia, 189
phren/o, 129, 351
Physical examination, 35
Physical therapy (PT), 116
PI. See Present illness
PID. See Pelvic inflammatory disease
Pigmentation, skin, 58
PIH. See Pregnancy-induced hypertension
Pineal body, 237f, 238f
Pineal gland, 242
Pinkeye. See Conjunctivitis
Pinna, 211, 214
Pituitary gland, 237f, 242
    diagnostic terms for, 250
Placenta, 502, 502f
Placenta previa, 535, 535f
Plan, 35
Plaque, 52, 52f
Plasma, 271
Plasmapheresis, 292
plas/o, 25, 46, 268
-plasty, 19

Platelet count (PLT), 287
Platelets, 272f, 273
-plegia, 130
Plegia, 148
Pleura, 355, 356f
Pleural cavity, 355, 356f
Pleural effusion, 364, 365f
　treatments of, 376f
Pleurisy, 365
Pleuritis, 365
pleur/o, 351
PLT. See Platelet count
Plural forms, 11–12
PMH. See Past medical history
-pnea, 351
Pneumatic otoscopy, 224, 224f
pneum/o, 24, 351
Pneumoconiosis, 360f, 365
Pneumocystis jiroveci pneumonia (PCP), 365
Pneumohemothorax, 366
Pneumonectomy, 376
Pneumonia, 365, 365f
Pneumonitis, 366
pneumon/o, 24, 351
Pneumothorax, 366, 366f
PNS. See Peripheral nervous system
-poiesis, 20
Poikilocytosis, 278
Polarization, 314
Poliomyelitis, 148
poly-, 14
Polycythemia, 282
Polydipsia, 247
Polyhydramnios, 532
Polymastia, 516
Polymorphonuclear (PMN) leukocyte, 272, 272f
Polyneuritis, 148
Polypectomy, 416f, 424
Polysomnography (PSG), 153, 154f
　for respiratory system, 371
Polythelia, 516
Polyuria, 247, 443
Position, 13–14
Positron-emission tomography (PET), 155, 155f
　of heart, 328
　for lymphatic system, 288
post-, 14
Posterior chamber, 180, 181f, 185
Posterior pituitary, 238f, 243
Postprandial blood sugar (PPBS), 254
Posttraumatic stress disorder (PTSD), 166
PPBS. See Postprandial blood sugar
pre-, 14
Preeclampsia, 534
Prefixes, 2–3, 3f
　common, 13–17
　general, 15
　for nervous system, 130
　patterns of, 8
　rules of, 6
Pregnancy-induced hypertension (PIH), 534
Pregnancy test, 537
Premature ventricular contraction (PVC), 319
Prepuce, 472
Presbyacusis, 220
Presbycusis, 220
presby/o, 182
Presbyopia, 190
Present illness (PI), 35
Primary hypertension, 322
Primary lesions, skin, 52–53, 52f
Primigravida, 531
Primipara, 531
PRL. See Prolactin
pro-, 14
Proctitis, 409
proct/o, 390
Proctoplasty, 424
Proctoscopy, 415
Progesterone, 241
Programmed learning segments, 2
Progress notes, 33–34, 33f
　abbreviations in, 34–35
Prolactin (PRL), 242
Prolapse, 509
Pronunciation
　rules of, 10–11
　shortcuts to, 10–11
Prostate, 472, 473
　biopsy of, 482, 482f
　endorectal sonogram of, 483
　PSA test, 483
　transrectal sonogram of, 483
　TURP, 485, 485f
Prostate cancer, 477
Prostatectomy, 485
Prostate gland, 472
Prostate-specific antigen (PSA) test, 483
Prostatitis, 478
prostat/o, 469
Prosthesis, 116, 117f
Prostrate, 473
Protein, 2, 450
Proteinuria, 442
Prothrombin, 286
Prothrombin time (PT), 286
Pruritus, 58
PSA. See Prostate-specific antigen
Pseudophakia, 192
PSG. See Polysomnography
Psoriasis, 64, 64f
Psychiatric diagnostic terms, for nervous system, 166–170
Psychiatric symptomatic terms, for nervous system, 163–165
Psychiatric therapeutic terms, for nervous system, 171–172
psych/o, 25, 129
Psychosis, 164
Psychotherapy, 171
Psychotic disorders, 168
Pt. See Patient
PT. See Physical therapy; Prothrombin time
PTCA. See Percutaneous transluminal coronary angioplasty
Pterygium, 193, 193f
PTH. See Parathyroid hormone
-ptosis, 19
Ptosis, 191
PTSD. See Posttraumatic stress disorder
PTT. See Partial thromboplastin time
PUD. See Peptic ulcer disease
Pulmonary angiography
　for respiratory system, 373, 373f
Pulmonary artery, 302
Pulmonary circulation, 302, 303f, 308
Pulmonary edema, 360
Pulmonary embolism (PE), 366
Pulmonary function testing (PFT), 372
Pulmonary infiltrates, 360, 365f
Pulmonary tuberculosis (TB), 366
Pulmonary valve, 307
Pulmonary veins, 302
pulmon/o, 351
Pulse (P), 35
Pulse oximetry, 372
Pupil, 180, 181f, 185
Pupils equal, round and reactive to light and accommodation (PERRLA), 35
Purkinje fibers, 314
Purpuric lesions, 54, 54f
purpur/o, 46
Pustule, 52f, 53
PVC. See Premature ventricular contraction
Px. See Physical examination
pyel/o, 435
Pyelonephritis, 446
Pyeloplasty, 456
Pyloric sphincter, 396
Pyloric stenosis, 405
pylor/o, 390
py/o, 24, 435
Pyothorax, 364
Pyuria, 443

Q

Quadri-, 14
Quadriplegia, 148
Quantity/measurement, 14

R

Ⓡ. See Respiration
RA. See Rheumatoid arthritis
Radiation therapy, 72
    for female reproductive system, 529
    for male reproductive system, 487
    for nervous system, 162, 162f
Radical mastectomy, 527
radi/o, 83
Radiography, 109, 155
    of digestive system, 417, 418f
    for female reproductive system, 519
    for urinary system, 449–450
Radioiodine therapy, 258
Radiology, 329, 372
Radionuclide organ imaging, 109
Rales, 359
Range of motion (ROM), 95
Rash, 58
RBC. See Red blood cell
re-, 14
rect/o, 390
Rectocele, 509
Rectovaginal fistula, 507
Rectum, 396
Red blood cell (RBC), 271, 272f, 287
Red bone marrow, 88f, 89
Red cell morphology, 287
Reduction mammoplasty, 528
Reflex testing, 156
Refractive errors, 190
Renal angiogram, 449
Renal arteriogram, 449
Renal artery, 438
Renal biopsy, 449
Renal cortex, 438
Renal medulla, 438
Renal pelvis, 440
Renal transplantation, 456
Renal tubule, 440
Renal vein, 438
ren/o, 25, 435
Repolarization, 314
Resectoscope, 455
Respiration (R), 35
Respiratory system
    abbreviations for, 382
    anatomic terms for, 350f, 354–358, 354f
    combining forms for, 350–353
    computed tomography for, 373
    diagnostic terms for, 363–369
    diagnostic tests and procedures for, 369–375, 370f–373f
    functions of, 349–350, 350f
    magnetic resonance imaging for, 371
    operative terms for, 376–378, 376f–377f
    overview of, 349–350, 350f
    polysomnography for, 371
    pulmonary angiography for, 373, 373f
    structures of, 349–350, 350f
    symptomatic terms for, 358–363
    therapeutic drug classifications for, 380
    therapeutic terms for, 378–381
Respiratory tract, 350f, 354f
Restrictive lung disorder, 360, 360f
reticul/o, 268
Reticulocytosis, 278
Retina, 180, 181f, 185, 198f
Retinal detachment, 193
Retinitis, 193
retin/o, 182
retro-, 14
Retroflexion, 506
Retrograde pyelogram (RP), 450
Retrograde urogram, 450
Retroversion, 506
Return to clinic (RTC), 35
Reveal cards, 2
Review of symptoms (ROS), 35
rhabd/o, 83
Rhabdomyoma, 103
Rhabdomyosarcoma, 103
Rheumatic heart disease, 322
Rheumatoid arthritis (RA), 101, 102f
Rh factor, 534
    blood, 281
Rh immune globulin, 540
rhin/o, 25, 351
Rhinorrhea, 360
Rh negative (Rh⁻), 534
    blood, 281
Rhonchi, 359
Rh positive (Rh⁺), 534
    blood, 281
Rickets, 103
Right bronchus, 355
Right heart catheterization, 330
Right lymphatic duct, 275f, 276
Right Ⓡ, 35
Right uterine appendage, 498
Right ventricular failure, 321
Rigidity, 99
Rigor, 99
R/O. See Rule out
Rods, visual receptors, 181, 185
ROM. See Range of motion
Root, 2–4, 3f
ROS. See Review of symptoms
RP. See Retrograde pyelogram
-rrhage, 19, 20
-rrhagia, 19, 20
-rrhaphy, 8, 19, 20
-rrhea, 18, 20
-rrhexis, 8, 19, 20
RTC. See Return to clinic
Rubella, 60
Rubeola, 60
Rule out (R/O), 35
Ruptured membranes, 532

S

S. See Subjective information
SAB. See Spontaneous abortion
Saccular aneurysm, 315, 315f
Saccule, 215
SAD. See Seasonal affective disorder
Sagittal plane, 94
Saline infusion sonogram, 520
Salivary glands, 395
Salpingectomy, 525
Salpingitis, 509
salping/o, 212, 495
Salpingostomy, 525
Salpingotomy, 525
sarc/o, 83
SCA. See Sudden cardiac arrest
Scabies, 64
Scale, skin surface, 53f, 54
Scar formations, 54, 55f
SCC. See Squamous cell carcinoma
schiz/o, 130
Schizophrenia, 168
Sciatica, 141
Sclera, 180, 181f, 186
Scleral buckling, 201, 201f
Scleral venous sinus, 184
Scleritis, 193
scler/o, 25, 46, 182
Sclerotherapy, 72
scoli/o, 83
Scoliosis, 104, 105f
-scope, 20
-scopy, 20
Scotoma, 189
Scout film, 449
Scratch test, 68
Scrotum, 470
Seasonal affective disorder (SAD), 166
seb/o, 46
Seborrhea, 64
Seborrheic keratosis, 61, 61f
Secondary hypertension, 322
Secondary lesions, skin, 53–54, 53f
Second-degree burn, 60, 60f
Seizure, 141
Semen, 472
Semen analysis, 483
semi-, 14
Semicircular canals, 215
Seminal vesicle, 472
Seminoma, 478
Sensorineural hearing loss, 220
Sensory deficit, 141

Sensory nerves, 137
Sentinel node breast biopsy, 517
Septicemia, 282
Sequestrum, 101
Serotonin, 242
Serum, 271
Sesamoid bones, 88
Sessile polyp, 406
Sexually transmitted diseases (STDs)
 bacterial, 478–479, 479f, 513
 viral, 479, 513–514
Sexually transmitted infection (STI).
 See Sexually transmitted
 diseases (STDs)
SH. See Social history
Shave biopsy, 67, 67f
Shingles. See Herpes zoster
Short bones, 87
Shortness of breath (SOB), 35
sial/o, 390
Sialoadenitis, 405
Sibilant rhonchus, 359
Sigmoid colon, 396
sigmoid/o, 391
Sigmoidoscopy, 415
Signs, 33
Simple fracture. See Closed fracture
Simple mastectomy, 527
Single-photon emission computed
 tomography (SPECT) brain
 scan, 155
Singular forms, 11–12
Sinoatrial (SA) node, 313
Sinusitis, 366
sinus/o, 351
Skeletal muscles, 81, 82f, 91
Skeleton, 81, 81f
Skin
 anatomy of, 45f
 cicatrix of, 54
 eruption of, 57
 grafting, 71
 layers, 46
 pigmentation, 58
 primary lesions, 52–53, 52f
 purpuric lesions, 54, 54f
 secondary lesions, 53–54, 53f
 tests, 68
 vascular lesions, 54, 54f
SLE. See Systemic lupus
 erythematosus
Sleep apnea, 148, 366
Slit lamp biomicroscopy, 197, 198f
Small bowel series, 418
Small intestine, 396
Smooth muscle, 91
SOAP notes. See Progress notes
SOB. See Shortness of breath
Social history (SH), 34
Soft palate, 354
Solar keratosis. See Actinic keratosis

Somatic nervous system, 128
somat/o, 130
somn/i, 130
somn/o, 130
son/o, 25
Sonography, 110, 197, 330
 of digestive system, 419–420, 419f
 for endocrine system, 255
Sonohysterogram, 520
Sonorous rhonchus, 359
-spasm, 18
Spasm, 99
Spastic, 99
Spastic paralysis, 141
Specific gravity (SpGr), 450
SPECT. See Single-photon emission
 computed tomography
Spelling
 of medical terminology, 10
Sperm, 468, 470, 471f
spermat/o, 469
Spermatocele, 478, 478f
Spermatozoon, 471f, 472
Spermicidals, 530
sperm/o, 469
SpGr. See Specific gravity
sphygm/o, 304
Spider angioma, 54
Spina bifida, 147, 147f
Spinal cord, 137
Spinal curvatures, 104, 105f
Spinal fusion. See Spondylosyndesis
Spinal nerves, 137
Spinal tap. See Lumbar puncture
 (LP)
spin/o, 130
Spiral fracture, 102, 103f
Spiral organ, 212, 215
spir/o, 351
Spirometry, 372, 372f
Spleen, 274, 275f
Splenectomy, 291
splen/o, 268
Splenomegaly, 279
Splinting, 114, 115f
spondyl/o, 83, 130
Spondylolisthesis, 104, 106f
Spondylosis, 104
Spondylosyndesis, 112, 159, 160f
Spongy bone tissue, 87
Spontaneous abortion (SAB), 534
Sprain, 104
Sputum, 359
squam/o, 46
Squamous cell carcinoma (SCC),
 45f, 62
SR. See Systems review
Stapedectomy, 226
Stapes, 215
Staphylococcus aureus, 61
-stasis, 20

STDs. See Sexually transmitted
 diseases
steat/o, 46, 391
Steatorrhea, 403
sten/o, 25
Stenosis, 316
Stent placement, 456, 456f
stere/o, 130
Stereotactic breast biopsy, 517
Stereotactic frame, 162, 162f
Stereotaxic frame, 162, 162f
Stereotaxic radiosurgery, for nervous
 system, 162
stern/o, 83
Steroid hormones, 241
steth/o, 304, 351
Stethoscope, 326
Stirrup, 215
Stomach, 394f, 395
Stomatitis, 405
stomat/o, 391
-stomy, 5, 19
Stool
 culture and sensitivity (C&S), 420
 occult blood study, 420
Strabismus, 193, 193f
Straight catheter, 460
Strangulated hernia, 408
Strata, 46
Stress echocardiogram (stress echo),
 331
Stress electrocardiogram, 327, 328f
Stress urinary incontinence (SUI),
 443
Striated muscle, 91
Stridor, 359
Stroke, 144f, 145
Stroke volume (SV), 330
sub-, 8, 14
Subcutaneous layer, skin layer, 46
Subjective information (S), 35
Sublingual, 403
Subluxation, 104
Substance abuse disorders, 167
Substances, 24
Sudden cardiac arrest (SCA), 322
Suffixes, 2–3, 3f
 adjective endings, 19
 combining of, 4
 common, 18–23
 diagnostic, 18–19
 diminutive endings, 19
 general, 19–20
 for nervous system, 130
 patterns of, 8
 rules of, 5
 surgical (operative), 19
 symptomatic, 18
SUI. See Stress urinary incontinence
Sulci, 136
super-, 14

588 INDEX

Superficial burn. *See* First-degree burn
Superior vena cava, 302, 303f
Supernumerary nipples, 516
Supine, 95, 95f
Suppuration, 58
supra-, 14
Suprapubic catheter, 460
Suprarenal glands, 241
Surgical (operative) suffixes, 19
SV. *See* Stroke volume
Sx. *See* Symptoms
sym-, 15
Sympathetic nervous system, 138
Symptomatic suffixes, 18
Symptomatic terms
    for blood, 277–280
    for cardiovascular system, 315–318
    for digestive system, 401–404
    for ear, 217–218
    for endocrine system, 245–248
    for eye, 188–190
    for female reproductive system, 505–506
    gynecologic, 505–506
    for integumentary system, 51–59, 51f–55f, 57f
    for lymphatic system, 279–280
    for male reproductive system, 474–475
    for musculoskeletal system, 98–100
    for nervous system, 140–143
    obstetrics, 531–533, 532f
    for respiratory system, 358–363
    for urinary system, 442–445
Symptoms (Sx), 33, 35
syn-, 15
Syncope, 141
Synovial fluid, 91
Synovial joint, structure of, 90f
Synovial membrane, 91
Syphilis, 479, 479f, 513
Systemic circulation, 303f, 308
Systemic lupus erythematosus (SLE), 62
Systems, 27–30
Systems review (SR), 35
Systole, 311

T

T_3. *See* Triiodothyronine
T_4. *See* Thyroxine
TAB. *See* Therapeutic abortion
tachy-, 14
Tachycardia, 319
Tachypnea, 358
Tactile stimulation, 141
T and A. *See* Tonsillectomy and adenoidectomy
Tarsal glands, 184, 185f
tax/o, 130
TB. *See* Pulmonary tuberculosis
TEE. *See* Transesophageal echocardiogram
Teeth, 395
Telangiectasia, 54, 54f
Temporal lobe, brain, 135, 135f
Tendinitis, 104
tendin/o, 83
tend/o, 83
Tendon, 92
Tendonitis, 104
ten/o, 83
Tenotomy, 112
Term components
    introduction to, 1–2
    overview of, 4–5
    parts of, 2–5, 3f
    rules for constructing terms, 5–7
Term formation
    acceptable, 9
    exceptions of, 9
    patterns of, 8
Term part, 549–558
Testes, 237f, 238f, 243
Testicle, 470
Testicular biopsy, 482
Testicular cancer, 478
Testis, 470
test/o, 469
Testosterone, 243
Tetany, 99
thalam/o, 130
Thalamus, brain, 135, 135f
Therapeutic abortion (TAB), 540
Therapeutic drug classifications
    for blood, 292
    for cardiovascular system, 340
    for digestive system, 427
    for ear, 229
    for endocrine system, 259
    for eye, 203
    for lymphatic system, 292
    for musculoskeletal system, 115–116, 118
    for nervous system, 162, 171
    obstetrics, 540
    for respiratory system, 380
    for urinary system, 460
Therapeutic terms
    for blood, 292–294
    for cardiovascular system, 339–342
    for digestive system, 427–428
    for ear, 228–230
    for endocrine system, 258–260
    for eye, 203–204
    for female reproductive system, 529–531
    gynecologic, 529–531
    for integumentary system, 72–74
    for lymphatic system, 292–294
    for male reproductive system, 487–488
    for musculoskeletal system, 114–115, 117–118
    for nervous system, 161–163
    obstetrics, 540
    for respiratory system, 378–381
    for urinary system, 460–462
therm/o, 25
Third-degree burn, 60, 60f
Thoracentesis, 376, 376f
Thoracic duct, 275f, 276
thorac/o, 83, 351
Thoracoplasty, 376
Thoracoscopy, 376
Thoracostomy, 376, 376f
Thoracotomy, 376
Thought disorder, 164
Threatened abortion, 534
Three times a day (t.i.d.), 35, 74
thromb/o, 268, 305
Thrombocytopenia, 279
Thrombophlebitis, 323
Thromboplastin, 285
Thrombus, 316, 316f
Thymectomy, 257, 291
thym/o, 130, 239, 268
Thymosin, 243
Thymus, 274, 275f
Thymus gland, 237f, 238f, 243
thyr/o, 239
Thyroidectomy, 257
Thyroid function study, 254
Thyroid gland, 237f, 238f, 243
    diagnostic terms for, 250–251
thyroid/o, 239
Thyroid-stimulating hormone (TSH), 242
Thyroid uptake and image, 255, 255f
Thyroxine (T_4), 243
TIA. *See* Transient ischemic attack
-tic, 19
t.i.d. *See* Three times a day
Tidal volume (TV/V_T), 372
Time, 14
Tinea, 64
Tinnitus, 217
Tissues, 27–30
    bone, 87
TM. *See* Tympanic membrane
toc/o, 495
Tocolytic agent, 540
-tomy, 5, 19
Tongue, 395
Tonic–clonic seizure, 145
ton/o, 83, 130
Tonometry, 197, 198f
Tonsillectomy, 376
Tonsillectomy and adenoidectomy (T and A), 377
Tonsillitis, 366

INDEX

tonsill/o, 351
Tonsils, 350f, 355
top/o, 130
Total hysterectomy, 523
toxic/o, 25
tox/o, 25
Trabecular meshwork, 186
Trachea, 237f, 350f, 355
trache/o, 351
Tracheostomy, 377, 377f
Tracheotomy, 377, 377f
Traction (Tx), 115, 115f
trans-, 13
Transabdominal sonogram, 520
Transcranial Doppler sonogram, 156, 156f
Transesophageal echocardiogram (TEE), 331
Transient ischemic attack (TIA), 145
Transrectal sonogram of prostate, 483
Transurethral resection of prostate (TURP), 485, 485f
Transvaginal sonogram, 520, 520f, 539
Transverse colon, 396
Transverse fracture, 102, 103f
Transverse plane, 94
Tremor, 99
tri-, 14
Trichiasis, 193
trich/o, 46
Tricuspid valve, 307
Triiodothyronine (T_3), 243
troph/o, 25
TSH. See Thyroid-stimulating hormone
Tubal ligation, 525
Tumor, 52, 52f
Tuning fork, 222, 223f
TURP. See Transurethral resection of prostate
TV/V_T. See Tidal volume
Tx. See Traction
Tympanic membrane (TM), 212f, 214
Tympanitis, 219
tympan/o, 212
Tympanometry, 224
Tympanoplasty, 226
Tympanotomy, 226, 227f
Tympanum, 214
Type 1 diabetes mellitus, 249
Type 2 diabetes mellitus, 249

U

UA. See Urinalysis
UCHD. See Usual childhood diseases
-ula, 19
Ulcer, skin, 53, 53f
Ulcerative colitis, 406
-ule, 19
uln/o, 83
ultra-, 14
Ultraviolet therapy, 72
-um, 12
Umbilical hernia, 408
Umbilical region, 399f, 400
uni-, 14
Upper respiratory infection (URI), 366
Upper respiratory tract, 350f
Urea, 440
Uremia, 446
Ureter, 440
ureter/o, 435
Ureteropelvic junction, 440
Ureters, 435, 436f
Urethra, 435, 436f, 440
Urethral meatus, 440
Urethral stenosis, 446
Urethritis, 446
urethr/o, 435
Urethrocele, 509
Urethrocystitis, 446
Urethrogram, 483
URI. See Upper respiratory infection
Urinalysis (UA), 450, 451f
Urinary bladder, 435, 436f, 440
Urinary catheterization, 460
Urinary diversion, 457
Urinary retention, 443
Urinary system
   abbreviations for, 462
   anatomic terms for, 438–441, 439f
   combining forms for, 435–438
   diagnostic terms for, 445–448, 445f–446f
   diagnostic tests and procedures for, 448–455
   functions of, 434
   laboratory testing for, 450, 451f, 452
   operative terms for, 455–459, 456f–457f
   organs, 434, 435f
   overview of, 434, 435f
   radiography for, 449–450
   symptomatic terms for, 442–445
   therapeutic drug classifications for, 460
   therapeutic terms for, 460–462
Urinary tract infection (UTI), 446
Urine, 440
Urine culture and sensitivity, 452
Urine occult blood, 450
Urine sugar and ketone studies, 254
urin/o, 5, 24, 435
ur/o, 5, 24, 435
Urobilinogen, 450
Urologic endoscopic surgery, 455, 456f
Urticaria, 52f, 58
-us, 12
Usual childhood diseases (UCHD), 35

Uterine tubes, 498
uter/o, 495
Uterus, 237f, 498, 499f
   displacement of, 506, 507f
UTI. See Urinary tract infection
Utricle, 215
Uvula, 355, 395
uvul/o, 351

V

Vagina, 500
Vaginal hysterectomy, 523
Vaginal orifice, 500
Vaginitis, 510
vagin/o, 495
Vaginosis, 510
Valve replacement, 335
Valves of veins, 307
Valvuloplasty, 335
Varicella, 60
Varicella zoster, 60
varic/o, 305
Varicocele, 478, 478f
Varicose veins, 323, 323f
Vascular endoscopy, 335
Vascular lesions, skin, 54, 54f
vascul/o, 5, 8, 25, 305
Vas deferens, 472
Vasectomy, 485, 485f
vas/o, 5, 25, 305, 469
Vasopressin (VP), 243
Vasovasostomy, 485
VC. See Vital capacity
VCU/VCUG. See Voiding cystourethrogram
Vegetations, 316, 317f
Veins, 308, 308f
   diagnostic terms related to, 322–323
Venipuncture, 284
ven/o, 305
Venogram, 329
Ventilation–perfusion (V/Q) scan, 371, 371f
Ventricle, 301, 303f, 307
Ventricles, 136, 136f
Ventricular septal defect (VSD), 321
ventricul/o, 130, 305
Ventriculogram, 330
Venules, 308, 308f
Vermiform appendix, 396
Verruca, 55, 55f
Version, 540
Vertebral lamina, 141f, 159
vertebr/o, 83, 130
Vertigo, 217
Vesicle, 52f, 53
vesic/o, 435
Vesicovaginal fistula, 507
Vestibular schwannoma. See Acoustic neuroma

Vestibule, 215
Viral STDs, 479
Visceral pericardium, 307
Visceral pleura, 356f
Vital capacity (VC), 372
Vitiligo, 52f, 64
vitre/o, 182
Vitreous, 186
Vitreous humor, 180, 181f
Vocabulary, building blocks of, 13–26
Voiding cystourethrogram (VCU/VCUG), 450
Volvulus, 409, 409f
Vowels, combining of, 4
VP. *See* Vasopressin

V/Q scan. *See* Ventilation–perfusion (V/Q) scan
VSD. *See* Ventricular septal defect
Vulva, 500, 500f
vulv/o, 495

W

WBC. *See* White blood count
Wheal, 52f, 53
Wheezes, 359
White blood cell, 272, 272f
White blood count (WBC), 286
Within normal limits (WNL), 35
WNL. *See* Within normal limits
Word structure analysis, defining medical terms through, 7

X

xanth/o, 46
Xenograft. *See* Heterograft
xer/o, 46
Xeroderma, 58

Y

-y, 12, 19
Year old (y/o), 35
Year (yr), 35
Yellow bone marrow, 88f, 89
y/o. *See* Year old
yr. *See* Year

Z

Zeis glands, 184